Middle East Studies

History, Politics, and Law

Edited by

Shahrough Akhavi
University of South Carolina

A Routledge Series

MIDDLE EAST STUDIES: HISTORY, POLITICS, AND LAW
SHAROUGH AKHAVI, *General Editor*

NEW PYTHIAN VOICES
Women Building Political Capital in NGOs in the Middle East
Cathryn S. Magno

Islamic Law, Epistemology and Modernity

Legal Philosophy in Contemporary Iran

Ashk P. Dahlén

Routledge
Taylor & Francis Group
NEW YORK AND LONDON

Published in 2003 by
Routledge
711 Third Avenue,
New York, NY 10017

Published in Great Britain by
Routledge
2 Park Square,
Milton Park, Abingdon,
Oxfordshire OX14 4RN

First issued in paperback 2015

Routledge is an imprint of the Taylor and Francis Group, an informa business

Library of Congress Cataloging-in-Publication Data for this book is available from the Library of Congress

ISBN 13: 978-0-415-76240-3 (pbk)
ISBN 13: 978-0-415-94529-5 (hbk)

MIX
Paper from responsible sources
FSC www.fsc.org FSC® C013056

Printed and bound in Great Britain by
TJ International Ltd, Padstow, Cornwall

To my parents
in love and devotion
for opening my eyes to the splendour of words

Save love there was no companion for me,
not before, not after nor at the beginning.
The soul makes me sing from within:
'Let me play a part in the path of love'

جز عشق نبود هیچ دمساز مرا
نی اوّل و نی آخر و آغاز مرا
جان میدهد از درونه آواز مرا
کی کاهل راه عشق در باز مرا

Jalāl-dīn Rūmī, *Dīwān-i Shams-i Tabrīzī*, Quatrain 42.

Contents

Preface ix
List of transliteration xi

CHAPTER I: Introduction 3
A. Purpose and nature of the study 3
B. Theory and methodology 7
C. Previous research 14
D. Introductionary remarks on analytical concepts 19
E. Modernity, postmodernism and secularism 25

CHAPTER II: The Nature of Islamic law 39
A. An Islamic legal system? Law, jurisprudence and ethics 39
B. Law and spirituality: Shi'i esoterism 51

CHAPTER III: Categories of traditional Islamic epistemology 55
A. Knowledge and science 55
B. The 'historical-empirical' epistemic scheme 59
C. The 'theological', 'philosophical' and 'mystical' epistemic schemes 64
D. The 'juristic-rational' epistemic scheme 69

CHAPTER IV: Shi'i legal dogmatics 77
A. *Uṣūl al-fiqh* (legal theory) 77
B. The constant sources of law: The Qur'an, *sunnat* and *ijmāʿ* (consensus) 79
C. The non-constant source of law: *ʿaql* (reason) 82
D. *Ijtihād* (independent reasoning) and *taqlīd* (emulation) 87
E. *Ḥauzah-yi ʿilmīyah* ('precinct of knowledge') 90
F. Hermeneutical principles 92
G. Interpretative pluralism and *ikhtilāf* (divergence) 97

CHAPTER V: Islamic traditionalism and Islamic modernism 103
A. An Introduction to Islamic traditionalism 106
B. The Islamic traditionalist position of ʿAbdullāh Jawādī-Āmulī 126
C. An Introduction to Islamic modernism 143
D. The Islamic modernist position of Muḥammad Mujtahid-Shabistarī 163

CHAPTER VI: Surūsh on the nature of Islamic law 187
A. The Biography of ʿAbd al-Karīm Surūsh 187
B. Style of communication 194
C. Philosophical foundation: Critical realism 197
D. Modernity and the West 202
E. Religion 210
F. Jurisprudence 223
G. *Ijtihād* 241
H. *Ḥauzah* 246

CHAPTER VII: Surūsh's theory of contraction and expansion of religious knowledge 253
A. Its principal objectives 253
B. History: The Stage of natural man 255
C. Critical rationality: Self-determining and liberated 263
D. Science: Falsification and corroboration 267
E. Religious epistemology: Divine absolute or provisional conjecture? 287
F. Epistemological ambiguities: A priori and a posteriori 296
G. Epistemic relativism or epistemological relativism 309
H. Hermeneutics: There is nothing beyond the text 316
I. Divergent interpretations: The Problem of truth and probability 333

Conclusions 343

Bibliography 369

Index 387

Tables:
I. Contemporary positions on Islamic law 24
II. The textual corpus of ʿAbd al-Karīm Surūsh 193

Preface

"But our beginnings never know our ends!" T.S. Eliot's paranthetical remark about friendship in *Portrait of a lady* applies to ideas as well as individuals. My interest in Islamic law originates in the days before I took up academic philosophy, and the present study is in some respects a personal statement based on many years of 'inner dialogue'. My first encounter with ʿAbd al-Karīm Surūsh was in 1996 as a visiting-student at Tehran University. My newly awakened interest in Persian Sufi literature had brought me to the book market in the traditional *bāzār* to purchase a copy of *Maṯnawī-yi maʿnawī*, the *magnum opus* of Jalāl al-dīn Rūmī. Instead, the shopkeeper recommended another book to me, *Qiṣṣah-yi arbāb-i maʿrifat* (Story of wise-men), which was partly devoted to Rūmī's poetry and thought. The name of the author, ʿAbd al-Karīm Surūsh, was completely unknown to me. I immediately purchased that book as well as the *Maṯnawī* and returned to the university dormitory to discover that Surūsh was a hot name in Iran, especially among the students. His lectures at the university, discreetly organised by several Islamic student-organisations, were attended by thousands of predominantly young listeners and his books were printed in thousands of copies and distributed at the campus.

Some of my close friends during that time suggested to me that Surūsh was shaking the epistemological foundations of traditional Islamic thought in Iran; he was the man of the future. Working keenly to improve my meagre knowledge of Persian, I concentrated on his essays on mysticism and found them not only inspiring and appreciative but in some respects scholarly correct. When I had acquainted myself with Surūsh's books at large, it became clear to me, however, that Surūsh's major contribution to Shi'i thought is not in mysticism but in law, more properly legal epistemological theory. As I contemplated preparing a doctoral thesis on the subject of *ijtihād* in Islam, my interest in Surūsh's ideas made me simultaneously decide to focus on his legal epistemology. I have had the opportunity to meet Surūsh in person twice, in Istanbul in 1997 and in Tehran in 1999. He has been kind enough to answer all my curiosity and questions but I am sure that I still have not correctly grasped his architectonic work in all its aspects. It is my sincere hope that the results of my work, as presented in this study, will prove useful for further research, not only into the special contribution of Surūsh to Islamic thought, but also, within a larger discussion on the relationship between the Islamic intellectual tradition and modernity.

All research is supported by the work and goodwill of others. In recognition of this I would like to extend my special thanks to Professor Bo Utas, my supervisor, for guidance, constructive criticism, steadfast support and never-failing encouragement. I am also grateful to Professor Jan Hjärpe, Lund University, for providing invaluable help with critical comments and ideas. I also wish to express my sincere gratitude to Professor Seyyed Hossein Nasr of George Washington University, Professor Gudrun Krämer of Freie Universitaet Berlin as well as Professor Said Amir Arjomand of Stony Brook University, who all read my manuscript at an early stage and made helpful suggestions. It is also a pleasure to thank Professors Naṣrullāh Pūrjawādī, Ghulāmriḍā ʿAwānī and Sayyid Jaʿfar Shahīdī of Tehran University for initiating me into the intellectual environment of Tehran and Qum during my three visits to Iran. I have also received a great deal of help from a variety of individuals during the years. I would like to mention a few: Professor Yann Richard of Sorbonne nouvelle (Paris III), for his encouraging and pertinent suggestions regarding the final shape of this book, Shaikh Parvez Manzoor for sharing with me his critical perspective on Islamic matters, and my mentor Tage Lindbom for providing me with a theoretical and practical philosophical training grounded in perennial spiritual teachings.

The present book has previously been published in the *Acta Universitatis Upsaliensis*. I wish to thank the editorial committee of Uppsala University Press for approving the publication of a second, revised version. Two persons have also been involved in the task of making my English look acceptable. Abdulaziz Lohdi checked a large part of a preliminary version and Pamela Marston corrected the final version. All resemblance to proper English is to their credit. Finally, for her encouragement and forbearance during the three years it has taken me to get this far, I am deeply indebted to Mana, my wife.

There is no prospering except in God — و ما توفيق الا بالله

Vindö, Sweden, 24 August 2002.

List of transliteration

Persian characters

ء	ʾ
ب	b
پ	p
ت	t
ث	ṯ
ج	j
چ	ch
ح	ḥ
خ	kh
د	d
ذ	ḏ
ر	r
ز	z
ژ	zh
س	s
ش	sh
ص	ṣ
ض	ḍ
ط	ṭ
ظ	ẓ
ع	ʿ
غ	gh
ف	f
ق	q
ك	k
گ	g
ل	l
م	m
ن	n
و	w
ه	h
ى	y

Long vowels

ا	ā
و	ū
ى	ī

Short vowels

ُ	u
َ	a
ِ	i

Diphthongs

وَ	au
ىَ	ai

Islamic Law, Epistemology and Modernity

CHAPTER I

Introduction

A. The Purpose of the study

Like all great religions, Islam has experienced the impact of the manifold potencies of modern life and responded to this challenge in diverse forms and manners. In the sense that the exploratory elaboration of law for centuries has been the dominant mode of self-expression in Islam, one of the key themes of contemporary Islamic thought is the search for a legal identity. The aim of the present thesis is to analyse the major intellectual positions in the philosophical debate on the meaning of *sharīʿat* (the revealed law of Islam) that is occuring in contemporary Iran, and which involves subjects such as epistemology, methodology and hermeneutics. My study consists of two parts, framed by an Introduction and Conclusions. The first part (chapters 2, 3, 4) is made up of a purely descriptive account of the general aspects of Shi'i law and its methodological and hermeneutical sources and principles.[1] Since the characteristic features of the formative period of Islamic law have a direct bearing on the modern development of legal thought, the contemporary positions have to be set against the established background and normative repertory of Islamic tradition. It is within this broad examination of a living legacy of interpretation, *par excellence* the genres of *ʿilm al-tafsīr* (Qur'anic exegesis) and *uṣūl al-fiqh*, that the theological and juristic context for the concretisations of traditional as well as modern Islamic learning are enclosed.

The second part of my study (chapters 5, 6, 7) involves an explorative and comprehensive investigation of contemporary Islamic positions where in the main the legal-theological discourse of ʿAbd al-Karīm Surūsh is highlighted. This part is structured according to the main themes of the thesis and necessitates a semantic analysis of the key legal terms, featured in the authors' works, which in the Islamic context always have a religious meaning. Hence, so as to account for language variations and change, the tenacity of the established historical tradition as well as synchronic 'innovative' reinterpretations and explanation will be taken into consideration. From a theoretical point of view, the thesis is thus a study of the history of ideas and can be seen as an attempt to present some diverse

1 When the English forms 'Shi'i', 'Shi'ite' and 'Shi'ism' are referred to in the present thesis, they are used to denote Twelver Shi'ism, unless specifically noted otherwise.

ways of interpreting religion, located in the arena between the revealed text and the reading subject, within the contemporary world.

The modern debate on the nature, function and aim of Islamic law came to prominence within Shi'i Islam at the beginning of the constitutional revolution, in the early twentieth century, which represented the first direct encounter between traditional Islam and the modern West in Iran. Under the ideological challenge of secular forces, Iranian theologians and jurists were then compelled to explain the relation between the Islamic religion and the driving principles of European modernism. During the twentieth century, certain more or less genuine undertakings attempted to develop an Islamic modernism as opposed to rejecting the demand for radical change. After the 1979 revolution, the problem of the reform and renewal of the traditional Islamic law has again acquired great urgency, as the new theocratic order confronts a political reality that is not addressed by definite formulations in the traditional *fiqh* corpus. Since there is no clear or hard position under *sharīʿat* in many areas of law, such as substantive laws, the Shi'i *fuqahā* (jurists) are divided among themselves as to the best legal solutions to many problems facing contemporary society. This situation and the ensuing controversy have forced traditional as well as modern educated scholars into two different intellectual camps: one adheres to the methodology of *fiqh-i sunnatī* (traditional jurisprudence), also called *fiqh-i jawāhirī* while the other advocates a new and more radical approach, which while being far from uniform, is generally designated as *fiqh-i pūyā* (dynamic jurisprudence) or *fiqh-i maṣlaḥatī* (expedient jurisprudence).

As some observers have noticed, the intellectual debates and paradoxes that are taking place in contemporary Iran defy any monolithic characterisation of Shi'i Islam. Partly due to the attempts to apply traditional Islamic jurisprudence in the political sphere of the modern state, Islam, being an a priori source of religious normativity, is increasingly 'crystallised' into a contested myriad or body of competing intellectual discourses, where the access to interpretation of the revealed legal texts has become more plural and the Shi'i authority of *marjaʿ al-taqlīd* (source of emulation) no longer possesses a natural monopoly in spiritual matters. In contemporary Iran, a number of lay Muslim intellectuals participate in developing various discourses on religious epistemology and hermeneutics side by side with the *ʿulamā* and the key figure in the criticism against traditional jurisprudence is a lay intellectual: ʿAbd al-Karīm Surūsh. He published his first philosophical articles on legal epistemology and hermeneutics in 1988, in which he connects to Kantian notions of second-order cognitive theory. Surūsh's thought has developed partly as a refutation of Marxist concepts of science and society and partly as a critique of the 'ideologicalised' interpretation of religion as commonly presented by Islamic modernists.

Due to the relationship between global modernity and the religion of

Islam, the question of *sharīʿat* has indisputably come to occupy a wider perspective than its traditional formulations and this raises the question as to whether modernity is still categorically conceptualised as an external phenomenon among Iranian religious intellectuals, or if there is instead an effort on their part to develop indigenous forms and expressions of modernity. Whereas the early Islamic modernists discussed the adaptability of Islam to modernity, and from the middle of the twentieth century made attempts to 'islamise' modernity, I'll later argue that a new formation of Islamic intellectuals emerged after the 1979 revolution; Islamic postmodernism, which problematises modernity, but not in a conscious attempt to islamise it. In contemporary Iran, Islamic intellectuals are concerned with issues such as the existence of Muslim varieties of modernity, possible beneficial aspects of the postmodernist review of enlightenment modernism, whether modernity at all may be transcended, etc. In this respect, the Iranian intellectual panorama has undoubtedly witnessed a prospering not restricted to traditional Islamic theology, jurisprudence, mysticism, and art, but which also includes modern political philosophy, hermeneutics, gender studies and philosophy of law. As Mehrzad Boroujerdi (1996:157) elucidates, "Far from engaging in esoteric and trivial polemics, the discussions now taking place in Iran are philosophically sophisticated, intellectually sound, socially relevant and politically modern".

Hence, the objective of the present thesis is precisely to examine if it is possible or even correct to speak of internal Shi'i expressions of modernity as indicated by my very use of terms such as 'Islamic modernism' and 'Islamic postmodernism'. I shall indicate the extent to which this is so but also the very serious limit to which such an expectation must necessarily be confined. In the realm of epistemology, the growth of epistemological 'subjectivism' is considered to be the underlying ontological foundation of modernity, which has prioritised a moment of self-awareness in the adjunction of knowledge. The present thesis considers the turning away from things, the object of thinking, to the subject, having thoughts, to be the mark of modern Western philosophy (Kant is the one credited with articulating the problem of subjectivity as a problem in itself), which evolved originally because of the residue of theoretical doubt in cases which other religions and cultures, Islam included, were inclined to call certain knowledge. In contrast to Descartes, who interpreted truth as certainty, premodern philosophers in different religions were, for instance, inclined to interpret truth in terms of beauty and goodness (Judovitz 1988).[2]

[2] In the present thesis, the terms 'subjectivity' and 'subjectivism' are primarily used to designate an empirical subject, whose content is subjective, that is, personal, intentional and individual and it is consequently not restricted to the Cartesian foundation of its conditions of possibility from a transcendent perspective. As a matter of fact, the terms 'subjectivity' and 'subjectivism' did not figure prominently in Cartesian nomenclature, but are concepts that

As far as the primary cognitive and interpretative questions for contemporary Islamic intellectuals are essentially similar to those of the Western hermeneutical tradition, the concern of the present thesis is to what extent primarily ʿAbd al-Karīm Surūsh's understanding of Islamic epistemology and hermeneutics as well as conflicting interpretations, is engendered by the cognitive structures of modernity. I presuppose that a connection only may be assumed when explicit and clearly identical Western themes and terminology is present in the Persian texts. In this respect, it can further be questioned whether the hermeneutical approach of Islamic postmodernism should instead be considered as an attempt to 'postmodernise' Islam in order to disintegrate the Islamic tradition.

Besides Islamic postmodernism, the present thesis, focusing on paradigms rather than on actors, considers two different philosophical positions with regard to the contemporary theoretical discussion on *sharīʿat*; Islamic traditionalism and Islamic modernism, and their main representatives. These positions, which are delineated in the first chapter of the second part of my study in order to determine the central patterns and elements in the respective positions, are subsequently and consistently highlighted in comparison to Surūsh in the concluding analysis in order to substantiate my thesis that Surūsh's position constitutes a paradigm-shift in Shi'i speculation on divine law. Among the pivotal figures who are considered in this respect are primarily ʿAbdullāh Jawādī-Āmulī and Muḥammad Mujtahid-Shabistarī, but also included are other individuals who belong to the Islamic intellectual elite of Iran, and whose ideas exercise a deep influence on the Persian-speaking intelligentsia. These positions are in many ways intertwined, and often the arguments of one participant are articulated in response to the writings or views of another position. My intention is to highlight the variety of stances found in the debate, and hence establish some form of taxonomy and typology, as it from this reasoning it is clear why no position remains fixed but is rather constantly redefined in new contexts.

My choice of individual thinkers is directed by the fact that their ideas are widespread among intellectuals in Iran and have an ideological relevance as well as the fact that they, in consonance with my hypothesis, represent different positions. The focus on Surūsh is motivated by the fact that his post-1988 writings on the nature of Islamic law, legal epistemology and hermeneutics accommodate *fiqh* to modernity to an extent unsurpassed by other Shi'i positions, at least in the Iranian context.[3] In this respect, I shall

have emerged later and which are retrospectively used to define the ontological foundations of modernity.

[3] From Surūsh's extensive textual corpus that covers more than twenty years of intellectual output, the present study concentrates on his post-revolutionary writings (i.e. those published after 1981), in particular *Qabḍ wa basṭ-i tiʾūrīk-i sharīʿat* (The Contraction and expansion of legal theory), *Tafarruj-i sunʾ* (Excursion of creation), *Ṣirāṭhā-yi mustaqīm* (Straight paths) and *Basṭ-i tajrubah-yi nabawī* (Expansion of prophetic experience). His pre-revolutionary writings will only be referred to in brief to highlight a specific stage or transformation in his thought.

argue that Islamic postmodernism has paradigmatic relevance and reflects a thoroughly transitional phenomenon within contemporary Shi'i Islam. My choice of the specific texts from each of the authors is further based on the common *problematique* of the thesis. In the concluding part of the thesis, the characteristics of the various positions are analysed with specific reference to the phenomenon of modernity, in order to arrive at intrinsic similarities and differences in the positions. As far as the positions are participants in the modern age and that the choice of Islamic traditionalists to reject modernity is also something 'modern' in terms of being a response to the latter, my attempt is to define some of the contents of a supposed Islamic modernity.

B. Theory and methodology

No method is cognitively and morally neutral and, hence, ideologically innocent but to not discuss the methodology of one's choosing may leave the logic of the adopted procedure to chance. Methods are inevitably normative, and they will not on their own *explain*, for example, the nature or origin of religion. My intent is not so much to theorise about religion as to understand certain religious positions. For the determination of the religious and philosophical positions of the authors, I follow a philological and analytical method and base it on a textual analysis of Persian sources. By adopting a parochially Western point of departure, the thesis makes use of a methodological scheme that is the product of centuries of European hermeneutical thinking. This specific historical tradition has developed out of certain religious and philosophical conditions characteristic of later Western Christianity. Due to its significant relevance for the contemporary philosophical discussion on Shi'i law, I find the hermeneutical method as such useful, particularly in bridging existing cultural and intellectual gaps in the precluding of Orientalism, which constructs Islam as the ultimate *other*.

The study of religious tradition was until relatively recently exclusively the work of the bearers of that tradition. Only with the emergence of the modern West has the situation has been altered radically by the perspective of Orientalism. Scholarly attempts to explain religious expressions in alien, cultural traditions generally pale in comparison to the spiritual reality of what appears. In responding to the presence of the *other*, the academician must come forward himself. We are no longer attuned to the traditional forms of expressions, but immersed in a world that grants very little reality to the religious dimensions of existence. Thus, the modern sphere clearly challenges us with the task of renewed understanding. This amounts to saying that the hermeneutic dilemma of recovering the meaning of a text has surfaced in an exemplary way in theology and religious thought.[4] I further believe that the study of traditional as well as contemporary legal-theological trends in Islam is not simply necessary from a comparative cross-cultural point of view, or from the view of understanding the 'Islamic intellect', but that it is most urgently needed for increasing creativity and comprehensiveness in the philosophic endeavours of contemporary law and philosophy in general.

As the aim of the thesis is to examine the logical connections that exist between different philosophical positions among Shi'i intellectuals in Iran and their relationship to the Islamic revealed sources and the legal tradition in general, I shall elucidate the theoretical content and the logical structures of these texts. The problem of texts cannot be solved without considering the problem of interpretation, which is basically a hermeneutic art that tries to clarify the concept of *verstehen*, that is, deciphering the meaning of texts.[5] Whereas hermeneutics in earlier times was comprehended as the art of theological-exegetical understanding, after Hans-Georg Gadamer, the focus is on the hermeneutic phenomenon in ontological terms (hermeneutics of being) while still being concerned *a priori* with language. Gadamer argues that since understanding is not automatic, whenever it occurs it involves interpretation. Although I do not share Gadamer's notion that modern hermeneutics is concerned with gaining universal truth and insight in human experience, since it is not teleological, it may be applied to the examination and constructing of Persian texts that I am proposing here.

Hermeneutics, as a theory of interpretation or 'art of reading' (as distinct from practical philosophy or speculative ontology) and structural analysis may have a complementary function. Even if there is no meeting point between the two, there may be a superimposition of levels. Whereas the depth of a text belongs to hermeneutics, the surface belongs to structural analysis. Hermeneutics addresses itself to the intention in the pattern that the structure displays and works beyond the horizon of structural linguistics. This is very similar to what Paul Ricoeur, the best-known French representative of phenomenological hermeneutics, means by appropriation,

[4] This is the reason why Muslims generally responded negatively to Orientalist studies of Islam and have been repelled by the distortions introduced by externalist viewing and exteriorising comprehension (in spite of its many insightful observations and meritious accumulation of factual information). Nevertheless, the number of examples among the Orientalists that have been successfully dedicated to bridging existing cultural and intellectual gaps should be mentioned. Some of the most classical and outstanding examples are the theological compassion of Louis Massignon, the perennial philosophy of Henry Corbin and the Diltheean historical imagination of Marshall G. Hodgson.

[5] Hermeneutics– literally, 'interpretation'– is derived from *hermeneuein*, the Greek word for 'to interpret'. *Per se*, both words designate the same reality, the first coming to us from Greek and the second from Latin. In conventional theological usage, hermeneutics is the enterprise that identifies the principles and methods prerequisite to the interpretation of texts. Modern hermeneutics took its shape in the nineteenth century, a somewhat late arrival in terms of the usual periodisation of modern philosophy (seventeenth and eighteenth centuries).

namely second-order dialectic of structural *explanation* and hermeneutic *understanding*, i.e. a structural analysis of a text that does not exclude the very act of interpretation (Ricoeur 1974). Ricoeur's view goes against the psychological hermeneutics of Schleiermacher and Dilthey. He also goes against Gadamer to the extent that his primary concern is the study of linguistic structure rather than the development of a hermeneutic ontology. For Ricoeur, the text that comes down to us in tradition or from another culture is above all a structural object that possesses its own intrinsic sense and its own laws of formal intelligibility. Its meaning is its textuality. Understanding occurs in interpretation. The meaning of a text lies *in front of* it in the space of interpretation, that is, in the dynamic interaction between reader and text:

> The moment of 'understanding' corresponds dialectically to being in a situation: it is the projection of our ownmost possibilities, applying it to the theory of the text. For what must be interpreted in a text is a *proposed world* which I could inhabit and wherein I could project one of my ownmost possibilities. This is what I call the world of a text, the world proper to this unique text (Ricoeur 1981:142).

As a methodological pluralist I do not reject the structuralist linguistics of the oft-cited Swiss scholar Ferdinand de Saussure simply because it does not (according to hermeneutical theory) lead to a deeper understanding of authors. For some it may seem useless to determine the objective intentions of authors, but it is nevertheless not without academic relevance to search for a presumably original meaning of a text. No text is completely autonomous and the initial phase of the hermeneutic task should begin with a study of the historical circumstances and linguistic symbols of the author. The authors I examine do not exist in a closed or homogeneous milieu but rather are in contact with a continually changing religious tradition or even various traditions. The individual ideas and thoughts are therefore always part of the larger social context, even if they are not confined to sociological determinants. Hence, I have certain methodological reservations about Ricoeur's 'hermeneutics of suspicion' as well as his ontology. While it is a commonplace of historical analysis that ideas develop in response to actual events, my study is not concerned with gaining an understanding of the social interaction or behaviour of the authors, since legal or theological theories "once formulated have a life of their own and develop in response to purely formal exigencies of logic, structure and juristic elegance" (Calder 1982:4).

In Ricoeur's words, the text is after all the first reality that the interpreter is confronted with and also the last reality to which one can have recourse. The author and first 'receiver', as well as the situation of the original discourse, somehow disappear in the text. Writing makes the text autonomous with respect to the author's intention: what a written work means does not necessarily coincide with what the author has meant. This concentration of the text makes it possible to explore the possible meanings of the text *as text*. Henceforth, avoiding semiotics (the study of signs), my thesis is not concerned with establishing the structure of the texts in question, but rather with isolating the most credible meaning and extracting a signification. The thesis also examines the style of the authors and the role of the individual influence in the formation of texts, the very important principle of text composition.

It is widely acknowledged that contemporary Islamic thought is experiencing a transitional phase, as the languages of Muslim lands endure considerable semantic changes that affect their linguistic states. As far as a strict distinction of the diachronic and synchronic discounts language variations and change, the present thesis only applies the division with respect to periods relatively well separated in time. The retrospective diachronic part of my study is concerned with isolating the structure of the text from the tradition of which the text is a particular case. All too often in the past, linguists and historians have taken texts from separated periods and treated them as monolithic samples of the same language, hence opening the possibility of a kind of terminological anachronism. In the case of Saussure, his definition of synchrony cannot be absolutely opposed to the historical but it passes over the diachronic, as the latter only can be rendered comprehensible if viewed as a transition from one synchronic state to another.[6] The notion of *langue*, as an intellectual construction to be studied *only* as a complete and static relational system at a given point in time, is not sufficient. In itself, structuralism is reductionistic in its neglect of the 'speaking' subject, insofar as it abstracts from the *life* of a text– its history, cultural, social, or religious milieu.

But whether Saussure's relativism, in contrast to weaker or stronger versions of universalism (the Prague School, etc), is essential to structuralism or not, it is evident that it does not exhaust the meaning of symbolic words and in some respects disregards semantic richness by neglecting the relation between a sign and the signified. [7] All words are

[6] Saussure (1983:89) writes: "It is clear that the synchronic point of view takes precedence over the diachronic, since for the community of language users that is the one and only reality (cf. p. 117). The same is true for the linguist. If he takes a diachronic point of view, he is no longer examining the language, but a series of events which modify it". Structural analysis therefore constitutes a stage in the course pursued by the text against the irretrievable flight of time. We are always outside the texts that come down to us from the past or from alien cultural traditions. Texts always project before us a distance from the situation in which we find ourselves. They create a distance from the author, from the original situation of the discourse and from the original addressees.

[7] Although the terminology of *Cours de linguistique gênérale* is not consistent on this point, Saussure's 'Copernican' definition of meaning in *langue* suggests a delimited structure of meaning as far as it is determined by internal binary oppositions and lacks transcendent substance. It is largely concerned with an arbitrarian difference between signs, and to define a sign may appear more complicated than expected. But in the sense that language constitutes a system, it can never be entirely arbitrary since the system needs a certain rationality, and if I

polysemic, i.e. they possess within them a certain potential for opacity, which is also their richness. Further, the figurative discourse of poetry, as distinct from literal discourse, also exploits plurivocity in words and sentences to create new meanings. The present thesis is hence concerned with semantics and textual communication of meaning, with the primary focus on conceptual lexical meaning and not structural meaning of sentences.

It is, in other words, essential to avoid subjectivism in textual analysis by emphasising the historical situatedness of discursive understanding as well as the openness of language. There is always the danger of enlarging the meaning of a text being interpreted. It can prove difficult to retain the original message of a text in the midst of contextual changes– linguistic, cultural, ecclesiastical, etc., where the most elaborate structure spreads itself into time and finite interpretations endlessly follow one another without ever succeeding at penetration. In hermeneutics, repetition creates the original as much as the original permits the repetition or as Alain Blancy (1973:56) states in similar terms: "In fact the repetition of the reading constitutes the unfolding of a text in the process of being woven". For instance, Islamic law interprets the revealed texts of the Qur'an and the *ḥadīṯ* (prophetic saying) corpus as well as the statements of those who have formed the Islamic legal tradition, developed it and continue to do so– a process which has become crystallised into texts. As such, Islamic law possesses a signifying unity, an established and fixed structure, or *normative repertory*, which I shall argue cannot be projected into a 'system', as it is subject to hermeneutical necessity as a potential reading. It is, one could say, a tradition of readings without an interpretative finality within its own normative framework. To say that law is enmeshed in language is then not sufficient: texts are the manner in which legal thinking is accomplished. As law produces texts when it reflects on texts, the core of Islamic thought is essentially a linguistic and semantic topic.[8] Legal tradition, as far as Islam is concerned, is therefore understood as a paradigmatic phenomenon, perceived to be living and relevant: "*Fiqh* is (or, at its best, can be) precisely a dynamic reading of revelation, which effects the transformation of event into process, giving it ongoing significance" (Calder 1997:64).

The hermeneutical circle is furthermore never purely philological in the

---

understand Saussure (1983:67–68) correctly, the linguistic sign, as a dual entity of *signifié* and *signifiants*, is arbitrary in the sense that there is no internal connexion between a concept (*signifié*) and a sound pattern (*signifiants*).

[8] While Islamic tradition in some aspects distrusts the text and far from every Islamic discourse about God has texts as its basis, texts nevertheless constitute the sustaining sources of Islamic legal thought. In the contemporary Muslim world, the traditional *madāris* (institutions of learning) have for this very reason been forced to respond to the new developments in the sphere of information technology. For instance, at the *ḥauzahhā-yi ʿilmīyah* (precincts of learning) in Qum, several thousands of traditional legal and theological texts have been converted to electronic form.

manner of Heidegger's elaboration; that is, it is not simply an exegetical movement between the parts and the whole of a text that is present before us as an object. It is rather a movement between the text and our situation as interpreters of it and, hence, I am concerned with the place of self-understanding in the interpretative event. Since the pursuit of universal (intuitive) knowledge of things lies beyond the grip of discursive thought, with respect to a text, understanding involves knowing what the text means as well knowing how we stand in respect to it in the situation in which we find ourselves. Schleiermacher's particular contribution to hermeneutics is the very idea that understanding and interpretation are always what is singular and unique. Although I do not comprehend understanding as the fusion of the historical and linguistic *horizon* of the present hermeneutical situation with that of the text (where two things become indivisible), it is essential to maintain the *openness* to the text, which allows the interpreter to be enriched by it.

Textual understanding should, hence, be motivated by some degree of alienation and self-criticism, since every reader conditions her/his interpretation of a given text by a kind of linguistically mediated preunderstanding arising from her/his 'hermeneutic situation'. I define preunderstanding as a body of assumptions and attitudes which a person consciously and unconsciously brings to the perception and interpretation of reality or any aspect of it. We can never separate ourselves from the linguistic world in which we have been growing and have been educated. As a person living in the twenty-first century shaped by my historical situation, modernity, I interpret the meaning of a certain sacred or profane text differently from a medieval scholar like Naṣīr al-dīn Ṭūsī or Jalāl al-dīn Rūmī. For the traditional interpreter, to interpret was to meditatively find more to say than the literal meaning by discovering still deeper meanings and to apply them to oneself, whereas the modern interpreter stands outside the text and tests its truth as a collection of propositions about the world.[9]

[9] As Henry Corbin (1993:1) elucidates, for the traditional interpreter the mode of understanding is conditioned by the mode of being of the one who understands. "The lived situation is essentially *hermeneutic*, a situation, that is to say, in which the true meaning dawns on the believer and confers upon his existence. This true meaning, correlative to true being– truth which is real and reality which is true– is what is expressed in one of the key terms in the vocabulary of philosophy: the word *haqiqat*". It is at the time of the reformation that a decisive change first occurs within European traditional hermeneutics, when Luther delivered the Bible from the Latin of the priesthood to the vernacular of the common people. Both Luther and Calvin identified the literal meaning of the Bible with the text's subject matter, i.e. its doctrinal content and its meaningfulness as a life prescription in contrast to the earlier Christian tradition, championed by Augustine, for which the plain sense of the Biblical text was not so much the *sensus litteralis* as the *sensus spiritualis*. The reformation opened the way for the more fundamental change and break with traditional hermeneutics in the enlightenment period. This was a break that ruined the sacred power in symbol and resulted in the desacralisation of the world. As H. Smolinski (1988) elucidates, exegesis became in many cases philology without consequences for theology, inspired by the so-called reform programme of Biblical humanism.

However, the fact that the knower's own being comes into play in his knowledge never harms the limitation of objectivity and method, but, quite the opposite, makes the interpreter's universe of discourse apparent and conscious (Weinsheimer 1985:225).

Nevertheless I am of the opinion that the religion of Islam, just by its capacity of being a religion, has transcendent moorings that exist independent of individual interpretations. I assert this in the sense that revelation by definition comes from God, who is the only One not being a prisoner of His text. The text is only His creation. As a matter of fact, not all texts are for reading and the word *text* contradicts this idea! As far as the Qur'anic scripture is concerned, it is not enough to speak of it as a text, but rather as the earthly substrate, in the form of recitation, of a text that only God has seen, the *umm al-kitāb* (literally, 'mother of the book'). However, this does not contradict the idea that the Qur'an is for study and that exoteric as well as esoteric exegesis of revelation flourished in history. The medieval mystic Sahl al-Tustarī explicated in this respect that the *waḥy* (revelation) was sent down upon the Prophet's *qalb* (heart) through inner vision, and that the Prophet was given the task to *tafsīr* ('interpreting it') in the form of recitation and text (Böwering 1980:137). For the Muslim believer, the Qur'an is *par excellence* a living and dynamic personality through which she or he journeys her/his life and the person who completes a *tajwīd* (cantillation) and begins anew is hence called *al-ḥall al-murtaḥal* (the sojourning traveller).[10] And yet, my aim with this thesis is not so much to expose the genuine and true form or articulation of Shi'i Islam as it is to critically and empirically examine how adherents of a normative religious tradition encounter modernity's implacable demands for change and accommodation. In other words, the aim is to unravel how the Islamic repertory of *a priori* textual references are continuously selected, combined and interpreted for this purpose while never losing their status of normativity for the actors involved.[11] My presentation is thus in conformity with the demands of academic impartiality. It does not argue for any partisan position.

[10] As Michael J. Fischer (1990:103) elucidates, the *tajwīd* is aimed at "preserving the original celestial music of the Qur'an, that sound which encodes senses beyond human language".

[11] This is very similar to the central ideas of Gudrun Krämer's (1999:175) discussion of 'readings of Islam', even if she adopts a more reductionistic and historicist/sociological point of view.

C. Previous research and sources

During the last century, a number of Orientalist scholars have made important contributions to the study of the origin and development of Islamic law and Islamic legal theories. Although a number of seminal works exists on aspects of Islamic law generally, there is still no completely comprehensive guide to the history of Shi'i law that includes a penetrating description of the legal principles underlying it. Furthermore, Orientalist studies that once considered law as an integral part of religion and laid the emphasis on textual criticism have recently been scrutinised through the prism of social sciences. This transformed the notion of *sharī^cat* into a more reduced and arcane concept, the 'Islamic legal system', a kind of undefined Islamic positive 'essence'. The historian Joseph Schacht, who following the lead provided by Ignaz Goldziher, initiated a radical re-examination of the traditional Islamic law, is now recognised as an authority in the field of Sunni law.[12]

Schacht (1950 and 1964) demonstrated that the traditional theory of *sharīᶜat* was the outcome of a complex historical process spanning over a period of three centuries and that the process of 'canonisation' of the *ḥadīṯ* corpus was a purely human construct. More specifically, his concern was to break the hermeneutical nexus, and to separate history from theological construct by, for instance, breaking the historical link between *ḥadīṯ* and *fiqh*. He argued that the origin and 'raw material' of *sharīᶜat* was the practice of local schools. His work is, however, not without its critics and a number of Orientalists and Islamic scholars, such as H.A.R. Gibb, Wael B. Hallaq, Norman Calder, John Burton and Mohammad Hashim Kamali, have challenged the scope and extent of Schacht's conclusions.[13]

Norman Calder has suggested a redefined but preliminary definition of Islamic law as a hermeneutical discipline that explores and interprets revelation through tradition. He draws on the hermeneutical theories of Gadamer to demonstrate that Islam is "worthy of as much sustained effort of observation and analysis as can be managed within the structures of

[12] It is interesting that while Goldziher's hypothesis was substantially ignored, Schacht is considered the true author of the historic revision of Islamic law.

[13] Schacht surely neglects to see ideas as 'real things' (whether constructed or not) that also play part in history. As he comprehends the Qur'an and *ḥadīṯ* not as the product of the Prophet's lifetime, but rather as the result of hundreds of years of community history, he naturally has obstacles in explaining the historical richness of Islam. Yet, John Burton (1977) proves in his major work that the Quran was in fact collected together in its final form during the time of the Prophet and that the major source for the formation of *ḥadīṯ* was the early discussions on *tafsīr*. His research has recently been confirmed in a study by Estelle Whelan (1998), which presents new historical evidence for the early collection of the Qur'an. Hallaq's (1997) contribution consists of an excellent refutation of the research of Robert Brunschwig and Schacht on the closing of the gate of *ijtihād*. He shreds the myth of a monolithic Islamic legal theory and ascertains the existent notion of individuality and individual human experience in Islamic tradition.

contemporary modes of discourse" (Calder 1997:48).[14] In fact, the modern study of Islamic hermeneutics is in its infancy, something that partly depends on the vast and complicated structure of the hermeneutical field itself. Textual hermeneutics is very much the meeting-point of many different sciences and disciplines that were characteristic for traditional Islam, such as theology, law, exegesis, philosophy and mysticism. Each of these areas created particular conceptions of textual interpretation and each had its own distinct methodologies and epistemologies, developed over centuries, while at the same time tending to overlap each other. It should also be noticed that there is no general introduction to Islamic legal epistemology written in any of the European languages, which is also evidently a neglected area of Islamic studies. My presentation of the traditional Islamic legal epistemic standards is instead largely based on other related studies in the field, such as the scholarly work of Franz Rosenthal (1970).

Subsequent Orientalist scholarship has nevertheless been aimed at developing Joseph Schacht's thesis in its essentials and has demonstrated precisely how closely the growth of the law was linked to contemporary social, economical and political conditions. H.A.R. Gibb (1963) concedes that as Islam developed under new philosophical and social circumstances, legal hermeneutics was continually readjusted to the new ideas and ideals, preserving *sharīʿat* as the most far-reaching agent in moulding the social order of the Muslims. Norman J. Coulson (1997) is the author of an almost comprehensive introduction to the history of the traditional Islamic law, which includes one section on modern developments and modifications. While admitting that the thesis of Schacht is irrefutable in its broad essentials, in his critique on the denigration of the *sunnat*, he states that while the material in the *ḥadīṯ* could not be proven to be authentic, it should not be rejected as a fabrication of later periods merely for lack of definitive proof of authenticity. Even fabricated *ḥadīṯ* represent the developing usage of the Islamic community, and thus have some relevance for determining the content of Islamic law.[15]

A well-articulated motive of Coulson's (1997:7) is to make certain the supposition that Orientalist scholarship on Islamic law provides the basis of

[14] Bassam Tibi (1990:74) is another scholar who has discovered the immense centrality of hermeneutics to the traditional Islamic textual discourse. Requesting innovation in the process of contemporary law-making, he calls for an adoption of a modern hermeneutic cognitive method as an enormous enrichment of Islamic law.

[15] Coulson is a good example of the lawyer or legal scholar who has become Orientalist in order to study Islamic law as an exercise in comparative law. His study, however, has its problems, which are related to the examination of past law interchangeable with present law. To let past theoretical law explain present social reality, as long as both are 'Islamic', without even considering difference in the superstructure of the socio-economic formation, is to distort the principal historical relevance of certain concepts. Such as is the case with his liberalist interpretation of the term *ijtihād*.

historical fact to support the principles underlying Islamic legal modernism, "Once the classical theory is seen in its historical perspective, as simply a stage in the evolution of the Shari'a, modernist activities no longer appear as a total departure from the one legitimate position, but preserve the continuity of Islamic legal tradition…".[16] Whether such a connection exists or not, Western scholarship, as often is the case, here seems to fall short of its striving for neutral objectivity. Instead of describing the Islamic legal discussions, it participates in them, thereby transforming the subject of their study by their own attitudes towards things spiritual. Whether this "participation from the outside" is more desirable than the a priori outward examination, which takes apart Islamic thought into isolated and inert elements, or not, the fact remains that we are only in position to fully appreciate the original interdependence and intimate structure of the imagined categories in Islamic thought by transposing them into ourselves. The new conclusions achieved by Islamic studies in the field have, however, had very little impact on the study of Islamic law in the Shi'i world. A notable exception is Seyyed Hossein Nasr (1966), who has engaged in a discussion with N. J. Anderson in reference to the immutable character of Islamic law. Since Shi'i jurists perceive law as juristic and not historical or judicial, they find it difficult to appreciate the conclusions made by Orientalists, not least the idea that the so-called 'canonisation' of *fiqh* resulted in a profound intellectual inertia.

Coulson's work, which is still the foremost introduction to the history of Islamic law, is also characteristic of the general tenor of Islamic studies, in that the Shi'i variant of Islam is merely treated in passing. This shortcoming in Western scholarship has very recently begun to be remedied. The study of Shi'i Islam was hitherto largely neglected in Islamic studies or misleading, because the analyses were based on fragmentary and polemical Sunni sources.[17] The small number of important research that existed on Shi'i jurisprudence was limited to translations of traditional texts and manuscripts. No major European library regarded the purchase of Shi'i manuscripts as a priority, and the editing was largely dependent on individual initiatives. It was first in the late 1960's, on the initiative of Abdoldjavad Falaturi, that Die Schia-Bibliothek des Orientalischen Seminars at the Universität zu Köln was established as the first European library entirely devoted to traditional Shi'i literature (K.A. Arjomand 1996,

[16] Coulson draws conclusions with regard to the content of 'traditional' *sharīʿat* that reject the Islamic conception of law as it is reflected in the legal manuals. He claims that legal practice served as an equally important ingredient in the concept *sharīʿat*, and his object with linking *sharīʿat* with the jurisdiction of the *sharʿī* courts is to create a modern conception of an 'Islamic legal system' (Coulson 1977:1449–51).

[17] The attitude of dubbing Shi'ism as a heresy or heterodoxy is misleading because of the conceptual relativity of these terms in an Islamic context. But whereas the inclination to view early Shi'ism through the polemical prism of Sunni heresiographical works is distorting, it may nevertheless be valuable for an understanding of the problems involved.

K.A. Arjomand and Falaturi 1996). The first path breaking studies of Shi'ism were the contributions of Ignaz Goldziher (1981), who made the first serious analysis of Shi'i theology and law, respectively Dwight M. Donaldson (1933), who was credited with the first scientific account entirely devoted to Shi'i Islam. Their works have recently been superseded by two excellent introductions to the history and doctrine of the Shi'i religion from its beginnings to the present time (Momen 1985 and Halm 1991).

Of late, certain scholars, such as Hossein Modarresi, Etan Kohlberg, Wilfred Madelung, Harald Löschner and Devin J. Stewart have increased our knowledge of the formative phase of Shi'i legal thought. Modarressi (1984, 1991) has made significant analyses in his major works on Shi'i law, which also include an extensive bibliography on the subject, as well as in a number of articles. Norman Calder's doctoral thesis of 1980 is a very valuable secondary source, which is concerned with the problem of authority in Shi'i jurisprudence. Wilfred Madelung (1979 and 1998a) has made a significant contribution to the field of Shi'i law by refuting the argument made by Schacht that the so-called 'sectarian' schools of law adopted the Sunni legal theory with minor modifications by demonstrating that all the schools had a contemporary and similar starting-point. Concerning the periods immediately preceding modern times, such as the Ṣafawīd and Qājār Iran, we are indebted to the scholarly efforts of A.K.S Lambton, Hamid Algar, Mangol Bayat and Said Amir Arjomand, etc. The former, particularly, has made a valuable contribution to our knowledge of the implementation and role of *sharīʿat*, along with that of the *ʿurf* (customary law) in premodern Persia (Lambton 1981 and 1987).

Although the first international colloquium devoted exclusively to the Shi'i variant of Islam took place in Strasbourg in 1968 and illustrated a significant progress in the field, it was only after the Iranian revolution of 1979 that Shi'ism became a major subject of importance in Islamic studies. Since then, a vast amount of analyses and commentaries have been written on the function of religion in Iranian society. Some of these are aimed at expounding the intellectual background of the recent 'politicisation' of the Shi'i concept of religion. In these later types of works, it is customary to include analyses of the ideas of Ruḥullāh Khumainī, Muḥammad Ḥusain Ṭabaṭabāʾī, Murtaḍā Muṭahharī, and ʿAlī Sharīʿatī, etc (Richard 1980, Dabashi 1993, etc.). Yann Richard's study of 1990 on clerical-intellectual rivalities in the Islamic Republic of Iran was the first case of academic attention given to ʿAbd al-Karīm Surūsh, which has subsequently increased noticeably.

While there are a number of scholarly examples that highlight different aspects of Surūsh's thought from analytical as well as functional angles (Jalaeipour 1997, Mir-Hosseini 1999, Jahanbakhsh 2001, etc.), very few are explicitly concerned with the relationship between his religious thought and the phenomenon of modernity. In a recent doctoral thesis written by Farzin

Vahdat (1998) as well as in an article by John Cooper (1998), Surūsh's notions of epistemology are placed in the broader discussion on Iran, Islam and modernity. Vahdat's book is also of special importance for the present study, as far his definitions of modernity are concerned. Surūsh's criticism of Islamic modernist thought and the project of 'islamisation' has been examined by Behrooz Ghamari-Tabrizi in his recent doctoral dissertation of 1998 as well as in an article by Afshin Matin-asgari (1997) on the secularisation of post-revolutionary Islamic thought. The influence Surūsh received from Karl R. Popper has been briefly analysed by Mehrzad Boroujerdi (1996) in his book on the role of nativism in modern Iranian intellectual discourses. This work also includes a chapter on the intellectual responses of Seyyed Hossein Nasr and ʿAlī Sharīʿatī on the impact of Western thought in Iran. Muḥammad Mujtahid-Shabistarī and ʿAbdullāh Jawādī-Āmulī are almost unknown to Western scholarship on Islamic studies. However, the former is mentioned in Asghar Schirazi's (1997) major work in reference to the post-revolutionary constitutional developments in Iran, as well as briefly in Boroujerdi's book. Consequently one may assert, on the one hand, that no comprehensive presentation of the historical development (the modern period included) and foundations of Shi'i legal theory is available to assist this research, and, on the other, that the individuals I intend to discuss in the thesis (Surūsh in particular), have not been subjected to a proper philosophical analysis with respect to their position on Islamic law. Hence, I hope that my study will help in focusing public and academic attention to some neglected, but I believe relevant, dimensions of the living spiritual tradition that Shi'i Islam represents.

My sources consist of primary and secondary ones, in Persian and in other languages. The primary sources consist partly of the traditional Shi'i textual corpus of law and jurisprudence, and partly of the writings of individual thinkers. The thesis is principally based on the second kind of sources. The secondary sources consist mainly of sources of different kinds in European languages (English, French and Italian), but also of works on theology and religious law in Persian. Some of these sources are not directly related to the topic of my study, but relate to topics of wider interest. It needs to be indicated that some articles of ʿAbd al-Karīm Surūsh were originally written in English and then translated into Persian. Consequently, these titles are counted as English primary sources. [18]

[18] Cf. The Evolution and devolution of religious knowledge, *Liberal Islam. A Sourcebook*, ed. C. Kurzman, New York, 1998, which was translated into Persian by Aḥmad Narāqī the same year as *Tafsīr-i matīn-i matn* (Fixed textual interpretation) and published in *Kiyān*.

D. Introductionary remarks on analytical categories

The scientific study of any subject is necessarily the systematic study of that subject, involving the deployment of classificatory and analytical concepts. Since most words are not fully self-explanatory but rather lexically ambiguous, i.e. have more than one meaning, the clarity of academic study requires clarity in the meaning of the categories used. The key words must be rendered unambiguous through the use of functional or stipulative definitions. This is indispensable in the translation of object language as well as in the use of analytical language. It is thus a fundamental assignment to initially explain the primary categories, such as 'modernity', 'modernism', 'tradition', 'paradigm', etc. that occur in the present thesis. My definitions are stipulative; they define not the essence or nature of a thing but rather clarify word usage. To study an alien religious tradition involves becoming familiar with its specific terminology. Key concepts in religions are very complex notions that cannot be translated unequivocally into the terminology of another language. Different interpretations of the same concepts coexist and meaning is, in general terms, subject to change through the course of time. It is essential to distinguish between one's ability to understand a certain concept in terms of its own context and one's capacity to translate the concept.

Religious concepts are always part of a complex set of religious dogmas and ideas, i.e. a theological system. Furthermore, many concepts of the language of theology are abstract, referring to nothing in direct sensed experience. As an example, the concept expressed in all Muslim languages as *sharīʿat* is not present in English or any other European language.[19] In old English jurisprudence, for instance, 'law' is used to signify an oath, or the privilege of being sworn; as in the phrases 'to wage one's law', 'to lose one's law'. If *sharīʿat* is translated as 'law' or if a compound term (as may be advisable) is employed, such as 'revealed law', the non-initiated will nonetheless be misled unless she or he is given an extensive explanation. In my study, all object-language concepts of special importance are rendered according to their sound in the original Persian or Arabic context. The

[19] It is customary in European languages to speak of Islam in terms of the whole body of Muslim peoples, countries and states in their socio-political as well as religious and cultural sphere. Robert Brunschvig (1955:49) asserts that the impact of Islam (in terms of being an organic intellectual unity with many complex interrelationships) on many elements of human culture has been so powerful that it would be impossible "to refuse to recognize an autonomous civilization there which was marked not just by the Islamic *element* but by the Islamic *factor*". In the present thesis, the contested terms 'Islam' and 'Muslim' are used for what we may call religion *respectively* for the overall society and culture associated historically with this religion. As long as the concern is to establish a constructive and meaningful analysis, Islam ought not to become a label for any mundane, temporal or non-religious practice connected to this whole body, but should rather denote its immediate existential meaning as well as the intellectual and artistic expressions connected to this religion.

process of translation is therefore not the substitution of one concept for another, but the transformation of one way of thinking into another way of thinking, and while philological research certainly is essential for philosophical studies, it should not be treated as an end, but as a means to an end.

As regards analytical metalanguage, I have used the term 'position' to categorise the different Shi'i theological-legal viewpoints. A given position here should not be understood as a clear-cut typological demarcation in the rigid sense, but rather as denoting a common conceptual cohesion in philosophical perspective and in the use of language. Before the early educational reforms during the Qājār dynasty, almost all learning in Iran was confined to the *madrasah*, the Sufi *khāniqāh* (orders) and the apprenticeship education of the Persian *ashrāfī* (court) circles. Intellectuals were a loosely defined class of men, *ahl al-ʿamāʾim* ('those wearing the turban', –as a sign of their learned status), and the word *ʿilm* (knowledge) referred most notably to knowledge contained within the intellectual framework and modes of religion. The institutions of learning made no attempt to distinguish the sacred from profane knowledge: "The learned members of society, ulama, were by definition men schooled in religious sciences. Theology, jurisprudence, philosophy, mysticism, Arabic language and grammar, and astronomy, among other disciplines, were all considered components of ilm, knowledge of the divine" (Bayat 1982:xiii).[20]

In the study of the dissemination of modern thought in Iran, there nevertheless are difficulties when examining particular positions or trends, as in reality existing formations on the intellectual scene generally are characterised by institutional discontinuities, transmutation in the use of language and complex notions of loyalty in society and politics. This entanglement has also produced a multiplicity in the various intellectual patterns, where components of one position even are employed by other discourses in their experience of modernity. Since the essential differentiation that historically existed within Shi'i Islam between law and *ʿirfān* (theosophy) has remained unsolved and the spread of modern learning

[20] In this respect, the present thesis seeks to provide an accurate picture of the unity and diversity of Islamic tradition by regarding the dichotomies that have existed, and continue to exist. While the philosophers and mystics throughout the centuries cultivated their disciplines by confining it to a restricted circle of disciples, the uncomplex polarisation between the 'orthodox' jurists and the 'heretical' Sufis will be misleading since, at least before modern times, a certain balance between the outward and the inward was the general rule. In pre-modern Iran, both speculative and jurisprudential thought co-existed within the large and loosely defined association that bore the epithet *ʿulamā*. The original textual sources provide evidence that Islamic scholars laid different stresses upon the philosophical, legal, theological and mystical dimensions of Islam and that the spectrum of thought was very intricate: "A single author frequently appears to be a Sufi in some of his works, and a jurist or theologian in other works. Many figures combine the contrasted perspectives in varying degrees... For their part, the jurists are famed for their internal disputes as are the theologians" (Chittick 1992:203–204).

and establishment of new social institutions has not been accompanied by any reform of traditional Shi'i philosophy, belief and worship, the tenacity of Islamic tradition has so far been exemplary in the Iranian case. Since no reformation or renaissance has occurred in Islam equivalent to that in Western Christianity, the *ʿulamā*'s confidence in the modern discourse of the intellectuals and their engagement in developing a new model that both conceptually and terminologically would respond to their discourse have until recently been very restricted (Gheissary 1998:11).[21]

The present thesis adopts the approach largely embraced by the discipline of Islamic studies that considers contemporary Islamic thought as a 'paradigmatic' or transitional phenomenon, a paradigmatic field, which epitomises a discursive dialogue between revelation and reason, unity and diversity, idealism and realism and tradition and modernity (Calder 1997, Gheissary 1998, Vikør 1996, etc.). Among others, Shahrokh Akhavi (1983:195) argues in this respect that the exchange of European ideas has incited the development of a complex set of competing normative discourses to the extent that the varieties of religious thought and action exhibited requires the use of terms like 'polycentrism' to characterise modern Shi'i Islam. Here, I should add that the term 'discourse' is used in the present thesis to indicate a specific individual and philosophical approach to certain aspects of life. While there henceforth exist certain individual discourses within Shi'i Islam concerning the issue of law, I however restrain from connecting this term with its poststructural understanding and application.

The term 'paradigm' is borrowed from the differentiation made by Thomas S. Kuhn (1962) in his *The Structure of scientific revolutions* between scientific revolutions and normal science. While the use of the term is complicated by its multiple and inconsistent definitions in Kuhn's own exposition, signifying both philosophy, science, metaphysics, and concrete instrumentation, I find the term useful for describing religious thought.[22] In the present thesis, a paradigm consequently represents 'a philosophy', 'a whole tradition', 'a source of tools' or 'a set of beliefs', and it is concerned with a clearly metaphysical notion or entity rather than 'a universally recognised scientific achievement'. By considering paradigm as a

[21] Since the advent of modernity in Iran, the *ʿulamā* have been in a transitional status and they have, relatively speaking, lost much of their influence in the sphere of law and education. While they have tended to reject the intrusion of modern thought, as Vida Garoussian (1974:172) argues, their reaction to the government's modernisation strategies did not differ essentially from that of the secular elite, i.e. it greatly varied since their traditional societal function had been to legitimise the ruler (albeit one that adhered to the *sharīʿat*). Many *ʿulamā*, such as Sayyid Muḥsin Ṣadr al-Ashraf and Mirzā ʿAbd al-Raḥīm Rahnamā, were more or less absorbed into the institutions of the modern state, which also is true in the case of Ḥasan Mudarris and Sayyid Abū al-Qāsim Kāshānī, who nevertheless resisted professionalisation and transformation.

[22] Kuhn (1962:150 and 157) actually describes the personal process of repudiating an old paradigm and embracing a new one in religious terms, as a "conversion experience", adding that "a decision of that kind can only be made on faith".

philosophical and hence epistemological type, it is generally acknowledged that an entrenched paradigm normally contests, and even suppresses, "fundamental novelties because they are necessarily subversive to its basic commitments" (Kuhn 1962:5). In this respect, Kuhn's definition of 'instant-paradigm', which suggests that the switch to a new paradigm must be regarded as the very same thing as its invention, is dogmatic since it takes years or decades (rather than hours) to develop a potential new paradigm to the point where it can challenge an entrenched paradigm: "Heretical thinking must have been going on for a long time before paradigm-change can occur" (Watkins:1970:37).

In contrast to Kuhn, who supposes that it is the nature of a paradigm to enjoy a monopoly in its hold on individual thinking, I assume that the present overall situation in Islam is characterised by the dual phenomenon of tradition vis-à-vis modernity, which has generated the possibility of competing paradigms struggling for mastery. While there has occurred a change in the interpretation of religion, the majority of Shi'i discourses nevertheless resist the 'switch' to the new paradigm. In this respect, I believe that the advocates of the entrenched paradigm are no less justified than the more mobile advocates of the new paradigm. This does not amount to saying, however, that there are good reasons for every possible choice. A significant factor in the formation of a multiple paradigm phenomenon is the very existence of a paradigmatic field, in which, as Ali Gheissary (1998:9) elucidates, different paradigms coexist and "knowledge of different paradigms becomes possible and accessible to others, no matter how relative or limited such a knowledge may be".

In this respect, the objective of the present thesis is to provide a sketch of three paradigms of Islamic thought and experience by adopting three separate categories of typological classification, namely traditionalism ('precritical'), modernism ('critical') and postmodernism ('postcritical'). Since typological and taxonomic systems even when they are well-built never go beyond a level of pure classifier and preparatory and because the definition of prescriptive and descriptive notions of classification frequently has been at odds in the study of Islam, the present thesis makes no claims as to the final correctness of any of these positions. Furthermore, there naturally exist various nuances of these three categories, yet I have refrained from arranging them into further sub-classifications. The selection of these specific definitions is entirely my own and the terms are stipulative, but they are nevertheless not arbitrary, as they have a certain empirical foundation and correspond, with some modifications, to generally accepted classifications within the discipline of Islamic studies (Gibb 1975, Rahman 1975, etc). This is also the motive for why I have preferred the ambiguous term Islamic modernism rather than Islamic neo-traditionalism, which might have been more appropriate. Since intellectual debates with normative ideological bearing often are characterised by unclear definitions in language, my analytical classification is also challenged by the fact that most of the participants in the Iranian debate present their own interpretation of Islam 'as the position of Islam'. For the individual participant who wants to prove a preconditioned position, a vaguely defined term offers the advantage (on a level which is not made explicit) of sliding back and forth between different connotations of that term according to what his argumentation requires (at any particular moment).

In my terminology, the traditionalist position in general terms adheres to the paradigm of pre-modern Islamic tradition by identifying legal epistemology (woven into methodology) with Aristotelian syllogism.[23] In philosophical terms, it is precritical and considers cognitive matters in the light of a basic sacred cosmology. The traditionalist hermeneutic is therefore one of appropriation of divine mysteries, that is, to meditatively apply the revealed texts to oneself. It is premodern in the sense that it wants to preserve a position anterior to modernity (that is, anti-modern, philosophically speaking). In contrast, the genuine effort of Islamic modernism, in the sense of representing the appearance of an autonomous critical consciousness, is to break with the entrenched premodern paradigm in the realm of epistemology. It signifies a genuine effort to accommodate religion to the scientific (albeit not always ethical) structures of modernity, emancipated from the traditional theological and legal philosophy. While the result of the reflection of the critical consciousness is the desacralising of the world that makes the sacred power in symbol vanish, the recent hermeneutical turn of certain modernists' discourses do not accept the full implications of a retreat before critical thinking and instead rework interpretative methods in the light of the critical methods of modern science. Islamic modernism represents understanding as a dialogue that involves exchange, where the focus of hermenutics is located in between object (text, phenomenon) and subject (interpreter).

In this respect, Islamic postmodernism constitutes a further paradigm-shift in Shi'i speculation on revealed law, in the sense that it contests the modernist's belief in epistemic certainty by considering all human knowledge, religious as well as 'secular', as hypothetical and conjectural at best. In the realm of epistemology as well as methodology, Islamic postmodernism absorbs the paradigm of modernity to an extent unsurpassed by other Shi'i intellectual discourses, at least in the Iranian context. In contrast to the typical modernists' submission for rational criticism in the name of truth, postmodernism accepts no unshakable foundations on which to adjudicate claims of justified true knowledge and hence also meaning. It

[23] A precise definition of the word epistemology is liable to be contentious. The term is derived from the Greek *episteme* (knowledge) and *logos* (reason) denoting more or less systematic bodies of knowledge as well as what a person knows. In the present thesis, the term epistemology is defined in its general sense as an enquiry into the nature, origin and limits of knowledge concerned with theories of knowledge.

argues that the temporality of understanding that merges with its contextuality points out both the finitude and reflexivity of human understanding. Given that the postmodern is the continuation of the modern and to the extent this is so, my classification of Islamic postmodernism is contested. Its constituent characteristics will therefore be properly delineated in the concluding chapter on ʿAbd al-Karīm Surūsh. In my view, the crucial historical question for Shi'i Islam at the onset of the twenty-first century is, consequently, whether the challenge from the contemporary

Table 1. Contemporary positions on Islamic law

	Traditionalism:	Modernism:	Postmodernism:
Epistemology:	Objectivist epistemology.	Weak objectivist epistemology. Strong subjectivist elements.	Subjectivist epistemology. Strong relativist elements.
Methodology:	Aristotelian syllogism. *Ijtihād* is considered as *mustamarr* (continous) but limited to the *furūʿ* (branches) of jurisprudence.	*Ijtihād* is two-fold, covering legal (Aristotelian syllogism) and non-legal (phenomen-ological-hermeneut-ical method) spheres of human life.	Deconstructionism. *Ijtihād* is emancipated from the traditional categories of law and represents a universal effort of interpreting human existence.
Hermeneutics:	Maintains traditional meanings of legal concepts. Allows for limited projection of new concerns on revealed texts. Modern terminology is rarely employed in the theoretical discourse. Interpretative divergence is evaluated normatively.	Traditional terminology is given new meaning. History conceals the meaning of revealation. Emphasises pre-understanding in interpretation. Divergence is evaluated normatively or else empirically.	Human knowledge, subjected to laws of contraction and expansion, is hypothetical. Certainty is relative and there is no definite meaning of revelation: The texts are 'silent'. Divergence is evaluated empirically.
Dynamic jurisprudence:	Legal change is past-oriented. Accent on historical continuity of ideas. In favour of dynamic jurisprudence while preserving the integrity of Islamic legal philosophy. Reason means pure reason as a function of level in line with traditional cognitive and ontological principles.	For dynamic jurisprudence interpreted in line with modern science. Constructs a normative Islamic world-view, maybe a religious ideology. Accent on historical evolution of law. Reason is 'discursive' and dynamic, but governed by 'the inner logic' of the Qur'an.	Dynamism irrelevant. Critical to 'ideologisation' of religion. Legal change is contingent on contemporary theories of law. Jurisprudence is a consuming science that borrows its theoretical structure from producing sciences. Reason is conjectural. Religion is individual, limited to spiritual matters.

phenomenon of high modernity constitutes the beginning of new indigenous shifts in Shi'i legal thought that involve methodological positions beyond the traditional formulation of *ijtihād*, to the extent that it is relevant to speak of entirely 'modern' paradigm shifts.

E. Modernity, postmodernism and secularism

To find an unambiguously definition of the term 'modernity', which has so come to dominate the humans sciences, seems difficult. Modernity is at once philosophy, history and ideology. In the present thesis, modernity is not understood exclusively as a European intellectual phenomenon.[24] Even if it has its restrained roots and early history in a European context and unmistakably represents a European view of history, it cannot be considered as characteristically 'Western' since it is a reaction against, rather than a direct outcome of, the worldview of traditional Western Christianity, which is evident in the late scholastic condemnations of Descartes' philosophy (Ariew 1999). Since there is no one accepted European model or form of modernity, I will instead consider different *varieties* of modernity, where the term modernity itself refers to those features that allow us to speak of a modern age in the first place.

While the normative characteristics of modernity, such as hostility towards revelation and pure intellection, was initially limited to the post medieval Europe, at the turn of the eighteenth century almost coincident to Napoleon's intrusion in Egypt, modernity came to have global relevance. Modernity originates in Europe but it does not spread in terms of direct borrowing or adoption. It is rather a convergence, comprised of a series of transformations that may create new formations: "Modernity may thus be delineated in terms of a conjunction, with global implications, of a set of cultural, institutional, and cosmological shifts" (Wittrock 2000:53).[25] Since the transformation of traditional philosophies and theologies is more problematical than certain, I shall argue in favour of plural modernities that transcend the Western models and also attempt to define what this plurality exactly consists of in contrast to, for instance, Marshall Berman's (1988:13–36) convergent theory of modernity as a uniquely European phenomenon or S.N. Eisenstadt's (1983:23) definition of modernity as "a new type of civilisation".

Despite all its dilemmas, I hence find the term modernity useful as far as it

[24] The term 'modern' is derived from the fifth century Latin term *modernus* that was used to distinguish an officially Christian present from a Roman, pagan past. Thereafter, the term was employed to situate the present in relation to past antiquity. The emergence of modernity is frequently associated with the philosophical analyses of Descartes and Kant.

[25] For similar analyses of modernity, cf. Hodgson 1993:214, Mouzelis 1999:141–159, Taylor 1999 and Therborn 1995.

is related to certain normative characteristics that spring from the driving principles of European enlightenment, such as self-reflexivity, agency, historical consciousness and progress, rationalism and secularisation. Comprising a historical consciousness of evolution and change, more correctly differentiation, modernity in many respects constitutes an epoch that relates itself to the past as a result of the transition from the old (traditional) to the new (modern), and has consequently been described in terms of a new "mode of thinking" (Habermas 1987).[26] Heracleit's persuasion that everything we see is and always has been in flux is documented, yet modernity has one distinctive score: Differentiation has become qualitatively as well as quantitatively quickened and on a larger scale, self-conscious. Scott Lash (1987) describes modernity in the nineteenth century as precisely the effect of a process of cultural differentiation and social autonomisation that has resulted in the differentiation of the various spheres of life-world. Differentiation gave rise to a new aestheticism of 'art for art's sake' in the art world and new definitions of epistemology and ethics were formulated no longer as foundational or categorical in the Descartian or Kantian sense but as socially conditioned. As the normative structures of modern society is subjected to constant qualitative change, movement and diversification are permanent partners of the modern project.

In philosophical terms, modernity has as central to its reality the category of experience itself and might justifiably be thought of as the sovereignty of experience. Insofar as there is no higher authority for the modern world than experience, I believe that the universality of reason as well as the autonomy of the subject (notions rooted in the enlightenment thought of Descartes and Kant) equally serve as constitutive components of the philosophical but also social vision of modernity.[27] As Farzin Vahdat (1998:5) elucidates, subjectivity and universality have a peculiar relationship to each other in the modern period. While they are closely connected to each other, they can at the same time be polar opposites: "On the one hand, the subject in order to be a subject needs objects– i.e. the denial of the subjectivity of others. On the other hand, once humans acquire subjectivity, we all want to have it. This contradiction is probably one of the central aporias of our time…". In some respects, this dichotomy has also generated the emergence of two

[26] Enlightenment modernism conceptualised central terms such as progress to mean a kind of secularised salvation, taking place in the natural world. The consequence of this belief is that time ceases to be morally neutral, as the word *past* is connected with *negative* and the word *future* with *positive*. Furthermore, while a number of key-terms of modernity per definition are conceived of as positive, or more or less neutral (growth, mobility, objectivity, modernisation, geographical mobility, etc), many are explicitly negative (alienation, disintegration of society, philosophical nihilism, the Americanisation of the world, the cult of change and fashion, epistemological relativism, the culture of narcissism, the disenchantment of the world, the crisis of meaning, the hegemony of companies, etc.).
[27] For related analyses of modernity, cf. Wittrock 2000, Touraine 1995 and Seligman 1991.

clearly articulated poles to the modern scientific perspective, rationalism respectively empiricism.[28] While modern rationalism focuses on man's ability to think and reason and modern empiricism focuses on man's ability to experience, the interaction of the two may be said, in their complementarity, to constitute the very foundations of modern philosophy and science. The first pole is the faculty of reason that actually formulates the scientific theories and hypotheses and the second is the objective world of phenomena that supplies the raw materials of evidence and experiment by virtue of which scientific statements can be directly or indirectly verified. Modern rationalism as well as empiricism was influenced by the emergence of renaissance science and the disputes it produced led to certain scepticism about claims to knowledge and to the search for a method.

While subjectivity is not the central characteristic of the early modernity of the seventeenth century, the growth of subjectivity serves in any case as the underlying ontological foundation of modernity. Whereas for premodern epistemology human experience was always defined as subordinate to, and dependent, upon a greater extra empirical reality, which it symbolised, modernity reverses this relation and identifies the real with the experienced. In this respect, modernity might be characterised as the postulate of human autonomy linked to the categorical separation of subject and object, which after Descartes becomes logically prior to all others, accompanied by the emerging humanism with its anthropomorphic foundations. Humanism coincides with metaphysics and it represents the ultimate rationalistic reduction of everything to the measure of the human subject itself, thus forgetting the original ontological difference. In Descartes, Hobbes, Locke and Hume, the theory of human knowledge is largely 'subjectivist', possessed by some knowing subject, that is, the subjective pole of knowledge (as distinguished from premodern 'objectivist' epistemology). Despite Descartes' refutation of radical scepticism, his accent on the cognitive subject is exemplified by the fact that he initiated the constructive portion of his philosophy with the maxim '*Cogito ergo sum*' (I think, therefore I am). The existence of the thinker (the self) is necessarily implied by the fact of his thinking. In the present thesis, 'subjectivity' is hence used

[28] Empiricism is a frame of reference that permits man's mind to come to a scientific understanding of the nature of reality that is derived predominantly from sensory experience. As a philosophical doctrine, it acknowledges certain a priori truths such as the principles of mathematics and logic and holds that all knowledge is derived from experience, either through the mind or the senses. The English philosopher John Locke is considered to be the founder of modern empiricism. His most important work, *Essay concerning human understanding*, proposed that the human mind is born *tabula rasa* (a blank) upon which all knowledge is inscribed in the form of human experience. With its direct realism, empiricism seriously challenged Plato's joint ontological and epistemological idealism, which claimed that universal ideas are innate, more than any other philosophy. As a matter of fact, it was during the strong current of positivism that modern science was transferred to Muslim lands and carried with it the underlying empiricistic overtones, an outlook that separated the sciences from a theistic metaphysical framework.

to denote that the truth of some class of statements depends on the mental state or reactions of the individual making the statement, that is, knowledge is restricted to one's own perceptions. As the subject is accordingly itself involved in the object of perception, Descartes' ontology gave way to epistemology as we know it in the *strict* sense.

Modernity cannot, hence, be understood simply as a period or epoch, as it calls into existence new forms of knowledge and self-understanding to attest the uniqueness of that world and the subjective grounding of experience. While the notion of subjective knowledge is old (dating back to the sophist Protegra and his subjectivist maxim that 'man is the measure of everything'), the idea that it is the subjective self who knows becomes explicit with Descartes and his method of doubt. In Descartes' scheme, the distinction subject-object is itself wholly internal to the human *subject*– a division within *subjectivity* rather than a boundary between an immediately felt self-presence and an objective reality. Descartes' doctrine appears as a decisive separation by determining absolute presence by self-presence and subjectivity and by establishing the priority of self-relatedness (i.e. the human mind) over other-relatedness:

> To assume the Cartesian starting point is not only to make the subject-object dichotonomy decisive for thought and culture, but it is also to guarantee that the thinking self's relationship to *everything* else (beginning with its own body, or *res extensa*) will be mediated through this prior relationship to itself (understood as *res cogitans*). My capacity to be aware that I am aware– to 'think' that I am thinking– establishes both the intrinsic importance of self-relatedness and its priority to other-relatedness, in the sense that any possible 'other' must first pass through a moment of self-consciousness in order even to be apprehended *as* other (Michalson 1999:9).

By reducing science to mind and matter, extension (while innate to human intelligence like concepts such as God), becomes an essential attribute of matter, divorced from any ontological aspect other than quantity, which reduces and quantifies the physical world (Garber 1992). For a subjectivist notion of knowledge, the entire external world is, in other words, mediated to me through my own capacity for reflexivity. There is hence something deeply and profoundly privileged about my relationship to myself, as opposed to my relationship to anything 'outside' myself.

The prioritising of a moment of self-relatedness in the adjudication of knowledge was considerably strengthened in Kant's critical philosophy with his denial of existence as a real predicate. Instead of continuing in the attempt to discover universal and necessary truths through ordinary experience, Kant (1996:Bxvi) instead asked "whether we shall not make better progress in the problems of metaphysics if we assume that objects must conform to our cognition".[29] By demanding a critical evaluation of

[29] The thought of Kant was largely made possible through the premonitory nominalism of William of Ockham, which stressed that forms and language are only in the mind. Inspired by

pure reason, its boundaries and possibilities, his effort was to emancipate reason from what he took to be its dogmatic captivity and his most original contribution to philosophy was that it is representation that makes the object possible rather than the object that makes representation possible.[30] Kant introduced the human mind as an active and autonomic originator of experience, where the self in a sense creates the world, rather than perceives it as a passive recipient by reference to the a priori conditions of our empirical knowledge. In this respect, Kant draws a contrast between the epistemological claim that some rule is an inherently necessary condition of human thought, on the one hand, and the ontological claim that some rule is an inherently necessary feature of the object, and hence differentiates absolute necessity from conditional necessity, where the former categories of knowledge in his terminology are called "subjective conditions of thought" (Kant 1996:B 122). By arguing that legitimate assertions of necessity almost always are conditional rather than absolute, he asserts, "We cannot represent anything a priori, except for what we provide ourselves the reasons by means of our representational faculty, either by sensibility or reason…" (Kant 1997:R5935).

A critical activity, therefore, ceases to be viewed as an external differentiation between self and world, but becomes internalised (inner-subjective) and is hence reflexive without remainder. In this respect, although from a purely geometrical point of view the resulting image is more Ptolemaic than Copernican, the human subject of knowledge is placed at the centre of the realm of objects rather than vice versa. While later Western philosophy, following the terms for philosophy set by Descartes and Kant (i.e. the modern notion of autonomity), decided to begin with the referent of 'I', the dominant verdict of post-Nietzschean trends is negative to enlightenment by supposing that the human rational system lacks any absolute certainty and that all knowledge is conjectural.[31] For instance, according to analytical school of philosophy, natural laws are considered to be hypotheses and mathematical truths to be analytical. Nevertheless, philosophy is no less subject to the whims of fashion than other human

his discoveries in mechanism and dynamics, Ockham delivered a telling blow against the conception of creation as a total unity, a macrocosm, by proclaiming that existence is a multiversum where everything (even God) is individual. According to Ockham, we humans experience the world through our sensory and mental faculties and believe that the resulting concepts provide us with real knowledge. In this respect, medieval nominalism was distinguished from realism, which is rooted in the philosophy of Plato and Aristotle.

[30] Cf. Kant 1996:Aviii.

[31] In Nietzsche's criticism of the *cogito*, Descartes' conception of the self is refuted as a philosophical illusion or fiction suggested by an uncritical inference from the characteristics of a verbal expression to a supposed reality represented by it. Nietzsche is concerned with the problem known as the Cartesian circle, that is, the assertion that Descartes only interprets the 'I think' according to his own prejudices. In its recent deconstructionist forms, the Nietzchean attitude of scepticism about rationality, which rejects the idea of an absolute truth, is closely associated with relativism.

activities and since the early 1980s Kant's 'transcendent idealism' has come to seem a salubrious recommendation of epistemological modesty (Graham 1982).

Following Thomas Kuhn's (1977:336) definition of 'subjective' as opposed to 'objective', the concept 'subjectivist' epistemology is distinguished in the present thesis from 'objectivist' epistemology, which is independent of any human claim to know. As a form of philosophical realism, 'objectivist' epistemology suggests a correspondence theory of truth, according to which knowledge is true and justified only if it corresponds to reality, which is considered to be hierarchially constituted. Truth depends, in other words, upon the way the world is and not upon what we happen to believe.[32] Since objective truths are considered as independent of human wishes and beliefs, religion is not ultimately grounded in human understanding, but in the very nature of things. Following epistemic purports to have views on transparency and representation, the criterion of knowledge is conditioned by its correspondence to the ontological levels of reality and its capacity to bring forth certain knowledge. 'Objectivist' epistemology vindicates, in other words, a form of objective realism in the sense that knowledge and reality are not two things but identical and that questions about criterion of knowledge depend upon questions of reality. In epistemological terms, it is a rational inquiry in the premodern sense, a process of insuring that representations correspond to transcendent reality – so a fixed reality means a fixed method.

The primary concern of 'objectivist epistemology' is to identify the epistemic standards in accordance with the traditional concept of metaphysics, characterised by its belief in the innate human disposition to assent, belief, assert and act. Man is understood as pontifex, as a suspended bridge between the infinite and the finite, through his intellect. In contrast to 'subjectivist' epistemology, where the real is what our senses perceive, the

[32] Realism has had by far the longest tenure in the history of philosophy. As Henry Le Roy (1987:133) elucidates, realism "is the claim– deriving from Plato and Aristotle– that forms and universals are objectively real (whether *ante rem*, 'before things', as in Plato or *in re*, 'in things' as in Aristotle)". The premodern philosophical realism has a different meaning than the modern applications of realism (i.e. 'empirical' and 'critical' realism), which were born after Kant and holds the view that our knowledge is restricted to the phenomenal realm with no direct access to things in-themselves. Traditional philosophical realism is instead primarily concerned with the transparency of the cosmos, which consists of creation as a whole being viewed as symbolic in the sense of being a manifestation or reflection of the metacosmic Reality, which is realised through man's innermost reality. It is, in other words, not primarily concerned with the historical or time-bound but with the symbolism that originates in the transcendent. As Martin Heidegger (1997:6) elucidates concerning traditional metaphysics in the Christian tradition, realism represents a position taken on the problem of universals and holds that universals exist independently of both the human mind and particular things– a theory closely associated with the conceptual realism of Plato. He argues that in the thought of the scholastics, such as William of Champeaux, objective knowledge is non-discursive and purely rational. "It is rational in the highest sense and a priori because it is independent of chance experiences, i.e. it is pure science of reason".

reality of 'objectivist' epistemology is transcendent objectivity in its Platonic sense, perceptible through the world sensory experience. Natural things are lamps through which shines the light of their heavenly prototypes. In its mystical varieties, 'objectivist' epistemology ultimately considers knowledge as appropriation rather than considering knowledge as pure correspondence, since knowledge of the universe and its underlying reality must involve more than just the human mind as an agent of knowledge. Consequently, it is more or less indifferent to a posteriori empirical knowledge and considers all knowledge to be the unveiling of ontological knowledge, that is, an elucidation of the essence of pure reason and revelation, the twin sources of metaphysical knowledge as far as religion is concerned.[33] In the case of Islam, 'objectivist epistemology' prioritises necessary knowledge (*ʿilm ḍarūrī*), which is established in the mind through no effort on the subject's part and which the subject cannot doubt or deny, over knowledge that is acquired (*ʿilm muktasab*) by the subject's own reasoning.[34] While the Islamic jurists are primarily concerned with the latter form of knowledge, their point of departure is generally that the sources of law are directly imposed on the intellect, which also is of transcendent origin. The immediate nature of the knowledge that the revealed texts engenders eradicates any prospect of 'autonomous' rationalism.

While philosophers such as Descartes, Spinoza and Leibniz (and to a certain extent Kant), follow the metaphors of traditional (Greek) philosophy (with its belief in intuitive and conceptual representation), their approach represents only a weak form of epistemological 'objectivism' since they first of all include every kind of thought and every type of sensation or feeling in the mind where the mind is interpreted as mirroring the world rather than the universals. Looking out on the landscape of natural science, Descartes's

[33] While objectivist epistemology acknowledges a subject-object relation, in line with the traditional notion of metaphysics as a science comprising the first epistemological principles of beings as such and as a whole, it ultimately considers the knower and the known as identical, and, as in the case of Islam, grounds human subjectivity in the Deity. In its most esoteric expression, knowledge in the objectivist sense is not so much knowledge without a knower or a knowing subject as it is knowledge with an illusory knower. Plato claimed an objectivist existence of universals or ideas that we have access to through the intellect. Knowledge according to Plato is definitive and absolute. In contrast to philosophers of the modern period, who generally concede the reality of the objective realm as unattainable, Plato identified objectivity as pertaining to the world of forms. For Plato, the forms reside in a separate world, which is invisible to our sense, although obtainable through reason. Thus, Plato refers to real objects as the 'knowable forms' which include the objective truths of justice, beauty, truth and love. Cf. Plato 1997.

[34] In Islamic law, the term *ʿilm* is generally defined as the knowledge that can be discovered by means of legal reasoning through the highly complex methodology known as *ijtihād*. The Islamic jurists are primarily interested in the epistemic value of legal norms and the status of their *ratio legis*. In contrast to the enlightenment view of reason as an instrument to expand the known universe and to organise it through understanding, to the jurists reason is above all an instrument to accept and befriend a universe that God not only has created but of which He indicates the interpretation by revelation.

conception of reason has its fully developed profane philosophical demarcation, since it leads not to fideism but to the exact science (geometry). In this respect, the 'rationalist' position of Descartes is the model of modern so-called 'foundationalist' epistemology, which tore the link between pure intellection and revelation apart even further.[35]

In the present thesis, the term 'rationalism' has connotations to enlightenment thought. The term is, as will be seen, not completely satisfactory for describing pre-modern Islamic epistemic schemes. Although Islamic theologians and philosophers consider reason to be the principal device to reach the truth in religion, reason can, in a traditional Islamic context, never be the sole authority in contrast to the enlightenment conception of universal reason (which upholds the idea that truth exists but denies that anyone can possess it definitely). In the present study 'rationalism' is thus distinguished from 'rationality', which means treating any issue by using reason. Rationalism, so to say, turns to rationality when reason is prior to revelation. As Hamid Enayat (1991:8) elucidates, Islamic modernists have a range of features in common with the *muʿtazilah* school of theology in giving a rationalist and ethical interpretation of religion, but I'll make evident that the principle of rationality has rather come to receive the favourable welcome by many Iranian modernists without any commitment to particular *muʿtazilah* principles after the incursion of Western notions of rationality.

As a matter of fact, many contemporary religious and philosophical tendencies in Muslim lands are more appropriately analysed by reference to epistemological notions associated almost exclusively with modernity. By focusing on the openness of historical processes, the present thesis hence considers the generation of modernisation and globalisation not as a generic linear and homogenous process of change whose basic contours will be everywhere the same, but as a series of unilinear processes with a common core generating similar problems but non-uniform results. Modernity is defined as a dynamic process characterised by multiplicity rather than a state of equilibrium:

The existence of this common global condition does not mean that members of any single cultural community are about to relinquish their ontological and cosmological assumptions, much less their traditional institutions. It means, however, that the

[35] Foundationalism has taken many different forms with philosophers disagreeing over both the nature of the basic beliefs and their relationship to non-basic, derived ones and was originally a rebuttal of Descartes' notion of 'hyperbolic doubt'. Common to all classical versions, foundationalism is the internalist requirement that the justification for a belief must be cognitively accessible to the believer. Generally, one counts three major divisions of foundationalism: the rationalist (essayed by Descartes himself), the empiricist (Locke) and the commonsenseist (Russell and Reid). Descartes (1996) who in his *Meditations* put forth arguments tending to justify a radical form of sceptical doubt in fact was far from being a sceptic. While he put the problem of scepticism on the agenda of modern philosophy, his book was largely an effort to reply the very doubts it initially had raised.

continuous interpretation, reinterpretation, and transformation of those commitments and institutional structures cannot but take into account of the commonality of the global condition of modernity (Wittrock 2000:55–56).

While modernity developed in Europe as a consequence of specific internal conditions born of a break with Christianity, this was not the case in Muslim societies. During the recent century Islamic scholars have been in no position to dispute theological and philosophical questions among themselves without reference to ulterior standards, as they have had the more difficult task of finding their consciences in the midst of two contrasting normative standards of thought. Since the *ʿulamā* responded to the consequences of modernity rather than developing its complex philosophical presuppositions among themselves, the dogmas and congregational life of Islam has not been altered by the challenge of modernity, despite the tensions and instability which resulted from the temporal Westernisation. The response of different religions and cultures to the process of modernity has in fact its own unique characteristics that resist any sweeping generalisations:

In Iran's case this uniqueness seems to involve a preoccupation with the metaphysical foundations of modernity which has had the important ramification for the more 'superstructural' and institutional levels. Perhaps, the root of this peculiarity lies in Iran's deeply entrenched tradition of monotheism which goes back to its pre-Islamic religions, as well as the relatively long continuity of Iranian sense of cultural identity which again goes beyond the Islamic period (Vahdat 1998:412).

As I shall argue, one of the unique results of the in-depth encounter between Islam and modernity has been and still is the ability of Iranian Islamic intellectuals to examine the very foundations of modernity and thereby give internal synthetic answers within their own religious and cultural context. Yet, the dilemma of modernity is more momentous in this respect considering the fact that the universal reason of European enlightenment denies the equality of all cultural traditions. In the view of enlightenment modernism, all minds are endowed with the potential of attaining an objective truth, but only on the condition of employing the correct cognitive method. Due to the process of differentiation, enlightenment modernism as the final truth has, in a global context, increasingly been relativised to the status of one among many perspectives, useful for some purposes, but inadequate for others. It has become common within science as well as philosophy and the arts (yet significantly not in politics and governance) to speak of postmodernism. Unlike modernism, postmodernism appears to be no manifesto that one can consult so as to assure oneself that one has identified its ideas properly and the academic community is largely divided on the question of its precise nature. As suggested by the term itself, its perspective is not merely antimodernist sentiment, but the assessment "that humanity can and must go beyond the modern" (Griffin 1989:xii).

But beyond connoting this verdict, the term is used in a confusing variety of ways, some even contradictory to others. As David Ray Griffin argues, postmodernism refers essentially to two quite different positions in philosophical and theological circles, which both transcend the worldview that developed out of the Galilean-Cartesian-Baconian-Newtonian science. On the one hand, there is the *deconstructive* or *eliminative* postmodernism, closely related to the literary-artistic and variously inspired by pragmatism, physicalism, Wittgenstein, Derrida, Foucault and other French philosophers.[36] Their work draws upon Marxist, Freudian and Nietzschean insights concerning the dependence of consciousness upon its material conditions and is guided by Kant's search for the conditions of possibility underlying subjective experience. While this interpretation overcomes modernism through an anti-worldview that "deconstructs or eliminates the ingredients necessary for a worldview such as God, self, purpose, meaning, real world and truth as correspondence" and hence commonly issues in relativism and nihilism, the second form of postmodernism, called *constructive* or *revisionary*, on the other hand, seeks to overcome the modern worldview as such, yet by means of, "constructing a new worldview through a revisionary of modern premises and traditional concepts" (Griffin 1989:xii).[37]

The present thesis relates to the second definition of postmodernism and does not consider the concept as organically divorced from modernism, despite its specific characteristics such as the questioning and loss of faith in enlightenment modernism, a spirit of subjectivism, pluralism and scepticism and relativist rejection of final answers. In contrast to those who speak of the 'closure' of modernity (Vattimo 1988, etc), I rather signify postmodernism as a form of *high modernity* in the sense that it constitutes the flowering of the deepest impulse in it. If modernisation is differentiation, then postmodernity is cultural de-differentiation with the spread of mass-technology of communications accompanied by a growing simulation of reality, which at the same time seeks to dissolve the concepts of meaning, certainty and truth. As the transcendent and universal reason gives way to reason*s*, a plurality of immanent, subjective, historically contingent actualities, postmodernism is hostile to the idea of unique, objective and transcendent truth.

As far as epistemology is concerned, *deconstructive* postmodernism is

[36] To this list we can also add the philosophical pragmatism of Richard Rorty. The core of Rorty's (1986:6) philosophy or anthropology of the 'mind as a mirror' is the de-divinisation of all language and discourse which he believes ideally culminates in "the point where we treat nothing as a quasi-divinity" and only restrict meaning to what is finite and contingently existing.

[37] Walter Brueggemann is another scholar who has developed a definition of postmodernism which, inspired by Jean-Francois Lyotard's notion of 'metanarrative', is situated in opposition to concepts such as 'settled hegemony' and 'objective certitude'. Brueggemann's (1993) argument is that postmodern interpretation essentially is contextual, local and pluralistic.

sometimes credited with the 'destruction' of the epistemological subject and the objective world. In the case of thinkers such as Michel Foucault, Jacques Derrida, Jacques Lacan and Gilles Deleuze, this is true in the sense that they set themselves in opposition to the philosophical concept of constituent thinking subject and reject the notion of an objective external reality. Yet, while the sovereignty of enlightenment subjectivity is undermined, the epistemology of 'destructionism' is 'subjectivistic' as far as it reduces knowledge to "that field in which the questions of the human being, consciousness, origin, and the subject emerge, mingle, and separate off" (Foucault 1972:16). In fact, Foucault (ibid.:122) claims that the archaeology of specific discursive practices rejects a unified transcendental subject, as "the analysis of statements operates therefore without reference to a cogito because it focuses on specific discursive formations at the level of what is actually said in particular statements".[38]

Far from being an escape out of modernity, postmodernism is rather the current creed and philosophy of global modernity, in the sense that its epistemic pluralism and relativism are intended to apply as much within the Western world as other parts of the globe (Guerra 1994:22). The conditions set by postmodernism in terms of the changing categorisation of the universal and particular (where modernity's truth-claims are more modest) becomes paradoxically more favourable for a practitioner or jurist of Islamic law, since *sharīʿat* in principle tolerates social diversity and leaves the mechanism of institutionalisation in the community relatively vague. In fact, some scholars, such as Ninian Smart (1998:87) and Akbar Ahmed (1992), have interpreted postmodernism as the reinvention of premodern traditions rather than detraditionalisation *per se*, that is, a return to the premodern past and a recovery of traditions prior to modernity. By focusing on countervailing forces to the mega-trend of modernity and recognising the possibility that there might be several paths towards modernity, the aim of the present thesis is precisely to examine if it is possible or even correct to speak of internal Shi'i expressions of (high) modernity. I shall indicate the extent to which this is so but also the very serious limits to which such an expectation must necessarily be confined, since the tenacity of Islamic tradition, even when masked in modern terminology, has been exemplary in the field of Shi'i legal theory.

To conclude, the over-arching paradigm of the modern phenomenon is *par excellence* secularisation, the reduction of the spiritual and the sacred to the temporal and the profane, i.e. the will to no longer perceive things in the *mundus imaginalis* ('between heaven and earth'). As Arthur Koestler

[38] For Foucault's postmodernism, 'the end of man' is hence his claim that man neither is the transcendental foundation of knowledge nor the first object of empirical knowledge. While he is interested in the genealogy of the modern individual in terms of subjectivity and consciousness, the effort is rather to show that subjectivity is constituted on the basis of complex power-relations.

elucidates, the general characteristic of the modern paradigm in science as well as other spheres of human activity is its disinclination to interpret human existential experience as inevitably grounded in transcendent reality:

As a result man's destiny was no longer determined from 'above' by a super-human wisdom and will but from 'below' by the sub-human agencies of glands, genes, atoms, and waves of probability. This shift of the locus of destiny was decisive. So long as destiny had operated from a level of the hierarchy higher than man's own, it had not only shaped his fate, but also guided his conscience and imbued the world with meaning and value (Koestler 1959:539).[39]

According to the differentiation of life into separate domains in post-renaissance Europe, secularisation initially referred to a process whereby certain duties in society and the ownership of property is transferred from the Church to the temporal (secular) authorities, such as was the case in France and Russia at the time of their respective revolutions. As a consequence of secularisation, religion is no longer the predominant feature in public life and has very limited interaction in temporal affairs. But secularisation is much more than a simple dissociation of the spiritual and the temporal in social and political affairs, since such a distinction *de facto* exists in all societies even when concealed by a religious vocabulary. In fact, this restriction is not appropriate in describing Muslim societies (post revolutionary Iran being an exception) as far as they are characterised by a *de facto* separation between *ʿulamā* and state.[40] If we consent to the definition above, it will in H.A.R. Gibb's (1975:50) words, "be absurd to regard secularism as a purely Western importation to the Muslim world". Yet, whether secularisation is the expression of an unislamic world view or not, it is a fact that it has found its way to Muslim lands during the first part of the twentieth century and has irreversibly permeated their ordering. In almost every Muslim populated nation-state, positive law and state regulations have replaced rules drawn from or linked to *sharīʿat*. In particular the Islamic modernists have generally welcomed the specific aspect of criticism of religion, as a mechanism of theological purification

[39] With the fusion of Christian and ancient Greek elements in the construction of scholastic thought in medieval Europe, the concept 'secular' (Latin *saeculum*, 'epoch') became increasingly synonymous to *mundus*, which referred to the world as 'earth', to signify that which belongs to this world. In a sense these two terms illustrate the dichotomy between Hebrew and Greek perceptions of reality, represented by the aspect of time respectively space. While the traditional legal order of the Christian world was maintained, the law of *mundus*, as applicable to man, was increasingly isolated from the comprehensive divine and cosmic plane. *Saeculum* came to denote the world as defined by time and change, a *condition* at a particular time, in contrast to the Church, the domain where eternal life is granted. The modern use of the term secularisation as a historical process is connected with this polarisation and the process of secularisation is connected to modernity in the present thesis.

[40] Even if the setting up of the Iranian constitution of 1979 enforced a unity of religion and politics, the crisis of religious legitimacy has, as Oliver Roy (1996:202) argues, led to a growing supremacy of politics (as illustrated in the 1989 amendments) and a *de facto* secularisation.

and as beneficial to religion, while they keep rejecting secularism.

My study makes a distinction between the process of secularisation and the doctrine of secularism, as these terms carry various connotations that make it impossible to give them a precise definition. Whereas secularisation, as historical process, is *partial* and maintains openness to diverse religious worldviews, secularism, as a theory of truth, is *comprehensive* and operates on all levels of reality to privatise (and sometimes even oppose) religion. Secularism means a strict separation between religion and the public sphere and is a closed world view. It denotes the dogma of rationality with its fundamental assumptions: the material world as an amoral and immanent series of invariant relationships of cause and effect, the componentiality of objects, the reproducibility of actions, the insistence on innovation, and so on (Bruce 1996:51). Secularisation, in terms of being a product of secularism, implies the notion of the desacralisation of the world. Secularism only perceives *Vestigia hominis* (the footprint of men) in a world in which man once discerned the *Vestigia Dei* (the footprint of God):

> The process of secularisation is a more or less conscious effort to cut all the lines of communication, to close all ways, to deny and 'forget' all light that leads to the source of truth. But secularization is more than a negative or 'forgetting'; it is also an attempt to institute an independent human existence, without superior justice, without judgement, without mercy or pardon (Lindbom 1988:10).

Consequently, secularisation relates to a process where religion has become fragmented and individualised and essentially is a matter of personal choice. In the present condition of global high modernity, the fragmentation of the conception of religion can for instance be seen on the Internet, where the existence of virtual small communities and individuals has deterritorialised and subsequently individualised the relation of the self with religion. While the global spread of information-systems technology can be accounted as a part of the logic of high modernity, it remains to be seen to what extent the existence of and accessibility of traditional Islamic legal texts, which until very recently was an enclosed garden for initiates, on the Internet and CD-rom has affected the monopoly of the *fuqahā* (jurists) in term of the interpretative process of Islamic law. In this respect, I suppose that we are witnessing historical conditions, which, linked to the condition of "knowledge in computerised societies", are favourable to the emergence of a thoroughly new philosophical and interpretative position within Shi'i Islam: Islamic postmodernism (Lyotard 1999:3–6).

CHAPTER II

The Nature of Islamic law

A. The Islamic legal system? Law, jurisprudence and ethics

For well over a millennium, Islamic law has been the most dominant medium of Muslim self-realisation. While certain positions understood the religious instructions differently and *sharīʿat* since ancient times entered in competition with the legal patterns of *ʿurf* (custom), the majority of premodern Shi'i as well as Sunni scholars affirmed their basic loyalty to *sharīʿat*. In the sense that the nomocentric aspect of Islam was deemed to be the normative and generative of the Islamic understanding of existence, the *fuqahā* were regarded as the true guardians of the Islamic conscience.[1] It is first in the twentieth century that the interpretations of the *fuqahā* as a normative mode of appropriation were challenged, and then under the influence from alien forces. "The Muslims' sense of cosmic self-orientation and their ways of responding to divine challenge were deeply coloured by the Sharʿī spirit, however much they varied otherwise" (Hodgson 1977:358). To discuss law was therefore as essential to premodern Islam as the discussion of theology in medieval Christianity, even if this does not amount to saying that law constituted or constitutes the core of the Islamic spirit. It is theology that sets the terms of *fiqh* and is foundational to its body of knowledge. One should be careful to not overemphasise the legal aspect or define Islamic beliefs as 'nomothetic', that is, assuming that all aspects of Islamic tradition and Muslim lives can be explained by reference to law. In the following, I will specifically avoid the various corollaries that are rooted in the assumption of an essential equivalence between *sharīʿat* and law in its modern sense.

[1] Defining *sharīʿat* as the queen of Islamic sciences, Joseph Schacht (1964:1) asserts that "Islamic law is the epitome of Islamic thought, the most typical manifestation of the Islamic way of life, the core and kernel of Islam itself". Norman Calder (1982:3) agrees with Schacht's assertion that theology, philosophy and mysticism never were able to achieve a comparable importance to that of law in Islam. "The elaboration of divine law has been for centuries a dominant mode of Islamic self-expression". It should be noted that only the structures of mysticism were able to challenge the ascendancy of law, and in the end complemented it. In Shi'i Islam this reconciliation occurred in the late Ṣafawīd period when the cultivation of *ʿirfān* (theosophy) and the organisation of Shi'i Sufi orders for the first time provided a challenge for Shi'i self-realisation by presuming the norms of *fiqh* but proposing to go beyond its competence.

In the present thesis, the ambiguous term Islamic law is not understood as a compound 'system' signifying juristic and judicial as well as customary law, but is defined as equivalent to the Arabic word *sharī^cat*, which is derived from the root *sh-r-^c*. The term occurs in one instance in the Qur'an, referring to the way of God as He revealed it to the Prophets:

And now have We set thee (O Muhammad) on a clear road of (Our) commandment [*sharī^cah*]; so follow it, and follow not the whims of those who know not (*Qur.* 45:18).

In traditional Muslim literature, the noun *shar^cīat* had multiple connotations; 'water-spring', 'custom', 'way' and 'threshold', and so on (Mu^cīn and Shahīdī 1993:12568). In its juristic technical sense it was used equivalent to 'revealed law' and appeared in different genres, not exclusively in legal literature as is the case with the Jewish *halakha* of Rabbinic literature. The word had divine connotations, but referred in the narrower sense to the ahistorical ideal that the jurists strived to find through their explorations and analyses. Despite its centrality in modern Islamic thought, the traditional literature employed it less frequently in passing or used other forms of the root *sh-r-^c* (Smith 1965:585). According to an old definition by Abū Ja^cfar Muḥammad al-Ṭabarī, *sharī^cat* consisted of the legal content of the Qur'an, whereas the later literature understood it as the totality of God's guidance relating to the activity of man (Gibb and Kramers 1953:524). By extension, it embraced all orders of creation, corresponding to 'laws of nature', and was used by Islamic philosophers to be synonymous with *nāmūs* ('cosmic law', an Arabisation of the Greek *nomos*) (al-Farabi 1949).

The juristic expansion of the directives of *sharī^cat*, covering a field wide as the Qur'an, is *fiqh* (jurisprudence). In its most common applications, the term *fiqh* suggests origins in juristic reflection upon the *uṣūl al-sam^cī* ('revealed sources') of law and was in earliest times used almost equal to *^cilm* (knowledge). With the establishment of legal methodology, it passed from being a personal activity to mean a structured discipline and its resultant body of knowledge.[2] More specifically, *fiqh* is the human effort of giving a specific *ḥukm* (norm or ruling) on a particular human act by studying the relevant textual sources and investigating its proper context. As A.K. Reinhart (1983:193) observes, the taxonomy of the *ḥukm* is of three kinds: *ḥukm al-qāḍī* (determination of a judicial fact), *ḥukm al-waḍī*

[2] Concerning its etymology, the verb *faqaha* is usually translated as 'to comprehend' and its noun form, i.e. *fiqh*, means 'comprehension'. The fifth form of the verb *faqīha*, *tafaqqaha*, occurs in the Qur'an (9:122) and refers to the close study and understanding of a specific issue. *Fiqh* is related to knowing, and as A.J. Wensick (1932:110) elucidates, the word is best translated as 'insight' in its rudimentary form, since it did not occurr until the middle of the eight-century in its technical sense of jurisprudence. Schacht (1960a:888) agrees and underlines that the word was applied to any branch of knowledge, and refers to Abū al-Hanīfah's writings where it covers law as legal knowledge as well as theology. After the eighth century, law, theology and literature developed independent of each other.

(determination of validity) and *ḥukm al-taklīfī* (determination of moral status). While the two former are 'performative' and bring the determination into force, this is not the case with the third category, which is more of a legal assessment involving an ethical classification of human behaviour. In Reinhart's (ibid.:199) view, Islamic law is, hence, similar to the Platonic philosophy of law, organically related to ethics (in contrast to that of Hegel, which is related to history), something he believes is generally minimised in research undertaken by comparative lawyers in the field.

While normative religious ethics started in the revealed sources of Islam, the whole range of ethics was absorbed by law in a formal sense and at the same time *akhlāq* (morality) came to be treated separately from the law in the strict sense, since the Qur'an envisages no consistent distinction between a moral norm and a legal norm.[3] As George Hourani (1985:1) elucidates, the legal theorists viewed revelation as the basis for all legal and ethical knowledge and the strong ethical element has never been obliterated in legal literature:

> This is true in a formal sense that normative ethics was worked out in legal books and judgements. But we may equally observe that the purpose of this vast legal structure was ethical in the modern sense. The relation may be proved by the evidence of several legal principles, fictions and practices which broke out of the strict mould of classical theory in order to accommodate the demands of justice and public interest.

Since both law and ethics in the traditional Islamic context were concerned with establishing rules of human behaviour, *sharīʿat* was organically associated with ethical reasoning. The traditional literature recognised in fact a separation between religion and law by identifying and separating legal rights and duties from their ethical counterparts. From the point of view of the lawyer of comparative law, such as Noel J. Coulson, it is not justified to differentiate between religious and legal rights and obligations, but as far as the crucial issue of the *sharīʿat* involved the determination of the morality of individual acts, rather than the establishment of a set of rules that must be followed in every subsequent instance, it is important to differentiate ethical acts from strictly legal acts. In Islamic law the practicalities of conduct were evaluated on a scale of five ethical values ranging from the *wājib* (obligatory) to *mandūb* (recommendable), *mubāḥ* (permissible), *makrūḥ* (reprehensible) and *ḥarām* (forbidden) and not confined to mandatory

[3] The legal matter of the Qur'an is essentially the bare formulation of the Islamic religious ethic and therefore it may be said to be ethical in quality. As N.J. Coulson (1997:11–12) points out, "Most of the basic notions underlying civilised society find such a mode of expression in the Qur'an. Compassion for the weaker members of the society, fairness and good faith in commercial dealings, incorruptibility in the administration of justice are all enjoined as desirable norms of behaviour without being translated into any legal structure of rights and duties. The same applies to many precepts that are more particular, and more peculiarly Islamic, in their terms".

commands or commands enforceable by courts. Of the mentioned values only two, which generally constituted a minority of actions, were of a strictly legal nature and applied in the *forum externum* (Kamali 1993:351).[4] Since the intentions of human beings can only be judged by the observation of their acts and not from their beliefs or convictions, there was a strong insistence on ethical norms and a systematic distinction between these and legal ones. In the sense that *sharīʿat* assumed a trans-legal ethical dimension where the concept of law was not prior to the concept of ethics, Wilfred Cantwell Smith even argues that the concept *sharʿī* primarily meant 'moral' rather than 'legal' and that *taklīf* meant "moral responsibility" rather than "legal responsibility" (Smith 1965:593). But while the pre-legal dimension of Islam recognised a normative ethical *fiṭrat* (natural disposition), Islamic law was never synonymous with virtue, since it, unlike the Hindu/Buddhist concept of *dharma* or the Confucian *li*, historically distinguished legal duties from moral duties.[5]

The early theoretical discussions on Islamic law generated in fact not cold statute law, but a discursive body of opinions and rules laced with ethical and theological precepts. Hence, Islamic jurisprudence is not the 'end product' of legal learning or law itself, but rather an 'open texture' as the process of understanding and inference, open to rational argumentation and the historical process. "It always refers to the human, and more or less academic, activity of exploration, interpretation, analysis and presentation of the law, whether this takes place in books, in schools, in the mind or in formal response to a specific question" (Calder 1996:981). In the notion of law as a process rather than a 'system' in the modern sense, Islamic law cannot be reduced to abstract structures, such as certain punishments and the almost eschatological expectation of salvation. It has not only an inner logic and history, but also a philosophy and a tradition of hermeneutics combined intrinsically with it. Every philosophy of law is furthermore part of a particular general philosophy, for it offers philosophical reflections upon the

[4] In this respect, *fiqh* clearly differs from theology that seeks to provide rational proofs for religious truths. Against the claims of theology that the exercise of universal reason leads to the acknowledgement of God's existence, *fiqh* asserts that human beings have access to God through revelation. As Reinhart's classification highlights, Islamic law is, nevertheless, not only concerned with the fulfilment of the prescribed *qaḍāʾī* (judicial) rights and duties, that is the judiciary's judgement on observable acts, but the individual is required to act under conscious acceptance of the *taklīfī* (obligatory) nature of the judicial precept *qua* ethical and religious norms that concerned the *forum internum* of the individual. Both al-Mufīd and *ʿallāmah* al-Hillī were of the position that individual human freedom is not a necessary condition since the notion of *taklīf* (obligation), i.e. to follow the legal norms, including *ẓann* (conjecture), is the overall pre-condition of divine *luṭf* (favour) (Brunschwig 1976:218, McDermott 1978:69).

[5] The primary matter for traditional Hindu jurisprudence was to explain the existence of rules of *dharma* ultimately derived from the divinely inspired Veda scriptures and justify obedience to them. In general, it treats *dharma* as pre-ordained cosmic law with special rules applicable to four basic castes (Rocher 1978 and Lee and Lai 1978).

general foundations of law.[6] This is all the more true for Islamic law even if the elementary subject of the nature of law is resolved by religion itself in terms that allowed for no compromise.

In the legal tradition that grew out of the Qur'an, the jurists reasoned *par excellence* on textual material or on cases that could be subjected to texts. As far as the hermeneutical situation of Islam inevitably is connected to the question of textual interpretation, legal literature is to be regarded as a reading of the Qur'an. With this consideration, Islamic law can more appropriately be defined as a textual discipline that "ascertains and discovers and interprets the terms of the Divine Will", distinct from *tafsīr*, philology, theology and ethics by its legal stress (Coulson 1969:2). In the words of John Wansbrough, the Islamic revelation, once separated from the prophetical *logia*, became independent scripture. In his study on Islamic soteriology, Wansbrough (1978:137) maintains that the normative Sunni expression was close to the Rabbinic concept of *torah*, that is; 'event' rather than 'historical process', something that was in part related to the dogma of the uncreated Qur'an. He asserts that in salvation history, conforming to its own laws, the Qur'an was once an event nostalgically recalled, time past contained in time past:

> ...[I]t seemed not unreasonable to detect in the formation of Islam an inception of the concept 'process' to that of 'event': an original notion of development seems at some point to have been truncated and replaced by a retroflective interpretation of community origins (ibid.:x).

Calder argues against Wansbrough's perception of Islamic history as nostalgia and event, and holds that the history of Islamic jurisprudence rather must be seen as a process. Since revelation, once it took on a written form, assumed an iconic force of its own, the meaning of the Qur'an is not only the meanings it once had, but the meanings that have been and still are discovered in it. "*Fiqh* is (or, at its best, can be) precisely a dynamic reading of revelation which effects the transformation of event into process, giving it ongoing significance" (Calder 1997:64).[7] But it seems that Wansbrough

[6] The word 'philosophy' is here used in its more general meaning, as an activity, and not in the narrower sense in which philosophy concerns only the kind of philosophical argumentation associated with scepticism. Although the Qur'an contains no organised philosophic exposition, numerous Qur'anic passages recommend the contemplation of beings, and hence philosophy was regarded as at least recommended by Islamic law. While Islamic law was intrinsically connected to philosophy, some jurists were of course satisfied with studying the mass of legal norms in front of them and leaving to others any general philosophical exploration of this world.

[7] While Wansbrough's interest in the Qur'an is predominantly historical, attempting a systematic study of the formal properties and principles of scriptural authority through a method of source analysis, Calder (1997:48–49) is interested in the hermeneutics as such, i.e. how it is read. "By a constitutive act of prejudgement, Islam is assumed to be as worthy of as much sustained effort of observation and analysis as can be managed within the structures of contemporary modes of discourse. That Wansbrough struggles to be of his time and to see Islam with an access of understanding that is available only to his time may be obvious, but

(1978:150) to some extent allows for a historical view of Islamic law as a process in the sense that revealed law by definition is archetypical and symbolic:

The relation between Law and History is not so much antithetical as aetiological: in terms of the monotheistic (covenantal) dispensation neither can be justified, even explained, without reference to the other... The historization of theodicy might, in other words, be thought to include not merely a plausible *mise en scène* for revelation, but also a chronological dimension into which it could be projected and thus preserved. The concept is *traditio/paradosis*: the after-life of an event perpetuated by constant reinterpretation. It is of course in that way that 'event' may be reformulated as 'process'.

To use the terminology of Paul Ricoeur (1977:5–6), the Qur'an "founded an epoch" and so "engendered history". In other words, the event of the Qur'an simply did not just occurr and pass away. While the primary aim of the traditional interpreters of the Qur'an was to strengthen the text rather than understand it, they imaginatively appropriated the text to create new meanings and referents through the infinite process of textual interpretation. Hermeneutics was considered to be an instrument of accessibility to the divine word, the *ipsissima verba* of God. For Muslims, revelation is, as Cantwell Smith (1980:490) expresses, God speaking from all eternity to all humankind; it is "the eternal breaking through time; the knowable disclosed; the transcendent entering history and remaining here, available to mortals to handle and to appropriate; the divine becomes apparent". In the context of Shi'i Islam, the need for interpretation of revelation was based on the assumption that the text was a source of Shi'i belief and dogma, and while the process was transformed through its 'canonisation', this was not inevitably so in the sense of cessation:

The book had to be read. Like all books, it could be read nostalgically, but experienced liturgically, it had a potentially transforming quality in spite of any credal beliefs that acted in the opposite direction (Calder 1997:57).

The interpretative activity that underlined and supported the new evaluation of the past was evident in the way in which material known in earlier texts was and still is assimilated to the *fiqh*. The hermeneutical tradition in Islam, exegetical and theological as well as legal, consists of three successive layers that constitute responses to the Qur'anic rhetoric: The original Qur'anic text transmitted, the process of transmitting it to new audiences, and the interpretations that begin to accompany the text as it passed through its varied audiences. Wael B. Hallaq (1997:ix) portrays legal hermeneutics as a dual phenomenon of "discovering rulings for unprecedented cases" as well as "involving the justification and re-enactment of time-honoured and long

---

might not reconcile Muslims *qua* Muslims, or historians *qua* historians, to the merit of his approach".

established legal rules and of the processes of reasoning that produced and continued to sustain them". The theoretical legal discourse constitutes an avenue to put forth distinctly original ideas, since once a written text becomes enshrined in the Islamic tradition, it binds the past and the future together in a consciousness of a continuous common past-oriented tradition:

Once a treatise is identified as pedagogical, it cannot be judged in isolation from other, usually larger works by the same author/professor. For it was the norm that textbooks and manuals constituted abridgements of longer works that expressed *particular* doctrines of *individual* authors (Hallaq 1992:186).[8]

The earlier versions of the Islamic hermeneutical tradition structured hence the reception of earlier texts and replicated themselves in the production of new texts, which gradually linked the *sharīʿat* into an indistinguishable unity of Qur'anic legal tradition. The legal study was clearly not a study of the revealed sources independent of the interpretations and commentaries through which it was handed down from the past. "Thus, learning and law did not inculcate a specific body of factual material but was designed to develop a mastery of a sequence of texts and commentaries" (Brown 1997:364). Significantly, ancient differences between Shi'i and Sunni positions on the meaning of the Qur'an were revealed as the hermeneutical genres developed. Hermeneutics was a major arena of polemics concerning the meaning of the Qur'an, where the Sunni *ʿulamā* accused their Shi'i counterparts of alteration of the sacred text, and the latter in their turn complained that the former had distorted the original message of revelation. But as Hossein Modarressi elucidates, the criticism of both sides concerned not the question of the authencity of the ʿUṯmānic Qur'an, as the *textus receptus*, but rather certain prevalent readings of revelation (Modarressi 1993).

In order to reach a proper definition of Islamic law, one has to acknowledge the existence of multiple definitions of the concept law itself. The Austinian definition is not the same as the Platonic, and the Justinian is not the same as the Biblical, and so on. In traditional Islamic legal theory, law is not understood as positive law, actually created by people, or Common law, developed through a continuing flow of cases and statutes, or exclusively as moral law, a right, just, natural law corresponding to ethical norms. Nor is it identical to Canon law, which is interested only in the proper organisation and government of the religious community.[9] As

[8] In this respect, even the audience as the final destination of theoretical discourse partook in shaping the text as is evident in the genre system of writing *mukhtaṣar* (abridgement), *sharḥ* (description) and *ḥāshīyah* (glosses) by the *mudarris* (teacher) as well as in the *taʿlīqāt* (notes) taken down by the pupils.

[9] Islam differs from Christianity in that it developed as an organic rather than ecclesiastical religious structure and in that it originally gave priority to society over the individual and mainly developed the duties of the latter. On the other hand, Christianity, which initially emphasised individual piety, became very soon an ecclesiastical and hierarchical structure,

revealed law, *sharīʿat* is instead considered as divine norm, a fusion of law and theology, which carried the notion of law-as-object to its furthest limit. "The law is, for the Muslim jurist, 'out there' before human beings even exist. 'Out there' must of course be understood as a metaphor, for the real 'locus' of the law is within God" (Weiss 1990:53). As both law and theology worked with the same *samʿīyāt* ('revealed texts'), the Roman law could not be formally received into Islam despite the fact that the *Corpus juris civilis* of Justinian was available to Islamic jurists. In Roman law, law had acquired its own texts and was in a substantive way separate from theology, albeit symbiotically connected to it (Weiss 1991:245).

This is the very rationale of traditional Islamic law: that law always is connected to commandment and embodies the will of God and that jurisprudence is the process of intellectual activity, an act of piety, which discovers the terms of the Divine Will. As far as Islamic law, at least in theory, is considered to be all encompassing; the crucial matter is to discover the legal norms, by means of *istinbāṭ* (inference). To further use a distinction of the father of legal positivism, John Austin, Islamic law is normative jurisprudence as differentiated from analytical jurisprudence and represents claims about 'law as it ought to be'. Although traditional Islamic legal theory never strictly separated law from morals, as is the case with legal positivism, and a will in nature may be a will of God as the immanence of divine value in creation, Islamic law has an extra meaning by means of revelation. As a matter of fact, the immanence of God in the world is by no means peculiar to pantheism, and Islamic theology cannot avoid the assumption of God in the world. But revelation has a specific legal meaning, the linguistical expression of what is divinely 'ought'. In Austinian terms, *sharīʿat* endeavours to answer the question 'what law ought to be', rather than 'what law is'.

This fact has led a number of Orientalists to establish a highly idealised view of *fiqh* that suggests Islamic law to be simply a religious de-ontology, equal to external duties. For instance, Christiaan Snouck Hurgronje (1957:261) claims, "it deals only with 'external' duties– i.e. those which are susceptible to control by a human authority instituted by God". He further states (influenced by Max Weber's definition of 'sacred law') that legal principles and rational methods are not appropriate in a normative system that derives the obligations it imposes from the revealed text (ibid.:256). For this very reason, Hurgronje refuses to designate *sharīʿat* as the 'law' of Islam. Despite the fact that Joseph Schacht also uses the term "system of religious duties", he states that even if the legal subject matter was

---

treating the individual as a mere object. Although there was much controversy as to the basis and scope of the authority of the Church, the latter used the techniques of Roman law to create a very effective machinery. The non-ecclesiastical character of Islamic law made a separation between the state and religion, in contrast to Canon law of medieval Christianity, impossible in theory at least.

‘islamised’ and systemised, it was not transformed simply into religious duty.[10] Nevertheless, the approach of reducing the whole phenomenon of Islamic legal tradition to a system of duties has persisted in a number of recent studies (Khadduri 1953:9, Liebesny 1972, Tibi 1990:69, Vesey-FitzGerald 1955).

Since Islamic jurisprudence can be characterised both as scholastic, as it is primarily the work of private jurists, and as casuistic, as it is elaborated through an examination of all the possible cases that occur to the jurist when examining a given area, the balance between realism and idealism must be established from text to text, and case to case. The cases are also worked out through the application of a consistent and complex set of legal principles. While detailed knowledge of the first stage in Islamic legal developments is necessarily conjectural, the earliest scholars worked, according to Schacht, with a realism which inherited only the pre-Islamic practice of *justice privée*, *taḥkīm* (arbitration), which was adopted by the Prophet. While there is little reliable information about the views of individual scholars, the primary concern of the Umayyad judges was efficient juridical decisions. The judges were no specialists in jurisprudence, but like the earliest jurists they gave judgement according to their own discretion and *raʾy* (probable opinion), basing their decisions on customary practice and Qur’anic norms (Schacht 1955:69). As jurisprudence developed, its principles tended to be envisaged through particular examples, in contrast to the modern Western elaboration of concepts and laws. In Schacht’s (1964:5) view, the ‘casuistical’ method, closely connected to analogical rather than analytical thinking, is the distinctive feature of Islamic legal thought, where high-level constructs develops not so much through the analytical refinement of concepts as through the casuistic and reasoned specification of applicable phenomena. It is first in the encounter with modern Western concepts of legality (as envisaged in the French Civil Code), which emphasises abstract analytical thought, that the traditional method of ‘case’ reasoning, in which general principles are adapted to particular circumstances through analogical extension, has been challenged.

As a matter of fact, the bulk of modern Western scholarship examines Islamic law from the point of view of the historian or practical lawyer. It rarely presents it in such a way as to call attention to its nature and values, but instead favours the study of law as a body of rights, obligations and rules of procedure, i.e. practical rules (Coulson 1977, Fyzee 1993, Linant de Bellefonds 1956, Vesey-FitzGerald 1979). For a study of the legal practice in Islamic society, and the problems of distinguishing between questions of

[10] Schacht (1964:200) writes, “But though it was incorporated into the system of religious duties, the legal subject-matter was not completely assimilated, legal relationships were not completely reduced to and expressed in terms of religious and ethical duties, the sphere of law retained a technical character of its own, and juridical reasoning could develop along its own lines”.

fact and questions of law, legal positivism would provide an analytical tool where *sharīʿat* would be considered to be a theological positivist order, and where the lawgiver would be formal, not theological. As Malcolm H. Kerr (1966:6) elucidates, positivism in relation to this matter is less concerned with the sources of law as much as law as a human institution. But it can prove problematical to study *sharīʿat* in strictly positive terms, since the jurists in general applied positive methods incompletely and gave less recognition to the importance of positive judicial classifications.[11] Yet, as Calder (1993:200) elucidates, Islamic legal theory, as a hermeneutical and logical discipline, was never purely theoretical, but rather was located "in the dynamic interplay between schema and reality, academic patterning and social practice..."

Since Islamic law in its totality is not a code of law in the modern sense, preceded by a state, it further applies to believers as persons (*l'homme*) and communities rather than citizens (*citoyens*) or territories, and clearly lacks a theory of natural right (Schulze 1995). Hence, in contrast to medieval Europe, the traditional Muslim had the same legal status wherever he or she went in the Muslim world, there being no change in citizenship status (Makdisi 1970:257). In this respect, the modern transformation of nation-states has once again raised the question of legal identity of the Islamic community. In the sense that the most salient feature of the modern state is the acceptance of territory as its body, Islamic law would in the words of Schacht (1960b:108) have to renounce its claim to universality in order to be codified. "But traditional Islamic law, being a doctrine and a method rather than a code...is by its nature incompatible with being codified, and every codification must subtly distort it". While some Muslim states recently have adopted codified versions of *sharīʿat* in an official campaign to 'islamise' the national legal system, the idea of law in its modern Western sense must be considered as unknown in traditional Islam.

In fact, the juridical part of *sharīʿat* was codified for the first time in the Ottoman so-called *Majallah* Civil code of 1869 by employing the originally Greek word *qānūn* (law) to designate law. But even then it only followed *sharīʿat* in substance and departed from tradition as it was administered in the state courts. One of the main characteristics of the *Majallah* codification was also the independence from any interpretative clarification of any kind, which silenced the open-ended argumentation of *fiqh*. "Accessibility in codes required that they be built in an orderly and regular fashion, ideally of conceptual units that could stand alone, equivalent in their logical self-

[11] Even if Islamic legal theory began as a formulation of a scheme of law in opposition to the existing practice of the Umayyad courts, *sharīʿat* recognises no term *strictissimi juris* for positive law or municipal law dissociated from the ethical and the religious sense. It does not have the usual imprint of case law, it is not judicially created in the positivistic sense and permits no independent process of man-made law alongside the divine ordinances (Coulson 1969:19).

sufficiency and in their independence from any need of interpretative clarification" (Messick 1992:56). As far as traditional Islam lacked an authority, personal or intuitional, invested with the power to create a juridical norm, it was apparently very difficult to define the limits of its 'jurisdiction'. The 'legalness' of Islamic legal texts therefore concerned essentially formal questions of genres of legal composition and the 'canonisation' of certain kinds of binding texts.[12]

In fact, the concept 'law' is derived from the Greek *nomos*, which exhibits a more complex, but limited meaning than *sharīʿat*. In the thought of the Sophists, *nomos* was interpreted as convention and human invention, in contrast to *physis*. Plato and others adjusted their view and maintained in elitist terms that while law is aimed at the structuring of the *polis*, it has a transcendent and objective reality (Rosenthal 1962:117). The *nomos* cosmology was, however, bound to produce an abstract way of thinking and speculation about the laws of nature that further generated the potential for man-made law. Broadly speaking, it came to have the force in the sense of "a single statutory enactment or the legal corpus of a given community" (Dodd 1935:25). In early Christianity, the continuity of the legal thought of ancient Greece is striking in the Roman law codes, *Corpus juris civilis*, despite the fact that the same Justinian who promulgated these codes closed the Platonist academy. In the late medieval period Thomas of Aquinas distinguished nature from grace and made possible the emergence of a distinctively modern transcendental basis for the legitimacy of human laws.13

The mistranslation of the word *sharīʿat* as *nomos* and the tendency to consider it as an unchanging law codex have at least in part been responsible

[12] The premodern jurists could not rely on the ongoing process of legislation beside interpretation of the revealed sources since no transition to lawmaking was made to set a codified law. After a notable proposal by Ibn al-Muqaffā in the eight century to codify *sharīʿat* and incorporate it into the ʿAbbāsīd state, the state developed a basically secular jurisdiction of its own. In premodern Iran, the *ʿurf* law varied in different parts of the country and was unwritten because no law other than the *sharīʿat* could be written. The administration of the law was carried out in two types of courts; civil law was dealt with by the *sharʿī* courts and criminal cases and offences against the rulers in the *ʿurf* courts which were administered by any official of rank. The highest *ʿurf* court was the *dīvān-i shāh*, which was the last court of appeal. *Sharʿī* cases could be tried by an *ʿālim* and such trials were often informal in character and usually took place in the house of the *ʿālim* concerned. The *ʿālim* could only arbitrate between parties who consented to lay their case before him (Floor 1992).

[13] The deepest of these changes began soon after scholasticism, and involved the upheaval of Natural law. It was when the Franciscan William Ockham declared that Natural law was not identical with the *lex aeterna*, the will of God. As a consequence, Christian law, insofar as it applied to man, became much less certain than the laws of nonhuman nature, which were later reduced to mathematical foundations in the thought of Hugo Grotius, Spinoza and Leibniz. Spinoza put everything under doubt and Grotius formulated a theory of law according to which rights are valid in themselves *etsi Deus non daretur* (regardless of whether God exists). Once the idea of laws in nature had become generally accepted, it was possible to reject the original theological standpoint. The originally Thomistic differentiation between the *humanitas* and the *christianitas* of the individual was triumphant (Friedrich 1958).

for the common misapprehension of Islam as a 'formalistic' religion, since *sharīʿat* is not confined to laws. Any discussion on Islamic conceptions of law has therefore to begin with the basic observation that nowhere in the Islamic legal tradition is there a term to express the concept of law in its positive sense, although the parallel to the Justinian distinction between *jus* (transcendent law) and *lex* (enacted, man-made law) may seem striking. While the determination of legal norms in Roman as well as Islamic law took the form of law finding, as the transcendent law was eternal and unchanging, there is nothing in the Roman law to match the Islamic claim of divine *amr* (command) or prophetic revelation in the widest sense, appealing to the heart, mind and will of man. It is hence more appropriate to speak of concrete *fiqh* as a treasure of theoretical legal opinions, thrown up during long centuries of endless discussions, on the basis of which a variety of legal positions were formed, even though these opinions themselves did not constitute law in the strict sense. In this respect, legal variation was restricted only by the finite revelation, the authoritative source common to all positions. "All Islamic legal systems exhibit a common framework of juristic topics (purity, prayer, pilgrimage, *zakāt*, and so on) together with an elaborate and tortuous set of details, subject to variation and doubt within and between schools" (Calder 1989:60).

The notion that law is something universal and the tendency to identify symptoms in various societies that respond to the notions of law and characterise them as 'legal systems', a term introduced by comparative law, is actually very problematical. As Schacht (1965b:389) confirms, this complexity can, for instance, be seen in the anachronistic studies of the contemporary Middle Eastern legal 'systems', where comparative lawyers examine past-law more or less as inter-changeable with present law (as long as both are Muslim). This ahistorical anachronism is the case with scholars such as N. J. Coulson (1977), S.G. Vesey-Fitzgerald (1955) and J. N.D. Anderson (1976), who study Islamic law as an excercise in comparative law and let past law explain present social reality, where *fiqh* constitutes an independent source, a body of substantive rules rather than a process and methodology. Their research is primarily concerned with the influence *sharīʿat* exercises over the modern codes in the Muslim world where rules and provisions are isolated that can be traced back to an Islamic origin. As far as the aim of legal studies and comparative law is to teach the substantive content of law and the structures and operation of legal systems, it would be misleading to consider the modern Middle Eastern legal systems as prolongations of the *sharīʿat*, i.e. that the two are co-extensive. The denomination of *sharīʿat* by comparative legal scholars as the only law of the Middle East worthy of consideration is inaccurate. In fact, the modern legal system is an extensive mosaic that derives from various sources such as codes and judicial institutions of European origin, national statuary legislation, decisions of various courts and *ʿurf* legal patterns as well as *sharīʿat*. Modern legal systems exist not in a vacuum but are involved in a network of international juridical exchanges within areas, conventions and diplomatical agreements, which to a large extent have had no equivalents in the Islamic legal tradition.

While Islamic law possesses a normative and established structure, it nevertheless resists codification of any kind as a potential unfolding of the revealed sources. Due to this flexibility, it carried on as an open argumentative discourse even when enforced by a closed codification or enforcement, as was the case in late twentieth century Iran when European notions of law were adopted.[14] In post revolutionary Iran, the 'islamisation' of positive law has not meant a direct return to the rich Shi'i legal literature, but a large-scale codification of Islamic law according to modern textual forms, which was not essentially Western:

> Irrespective of the extent and method of reforms, the end result has been the creation of a hybrid family law, which is neither the Shari'a nor Western. Both the process of codification and the concept of a unified legal system which has the state as an enforcing authority behind it are alien to the Shari'a (Mir-Hosseini 1993:11).

B. Law and spirituality: Shi'i esoterism

As revealed law, *sharīʿat* is considered to be the indispensable means through which spirituality, that is holiness, is cultivated. Spirituality is an undeniable concern of Islamic traditional law, as demonstrated by the importance that the terms *qalb* (heart) and *rūḥ* (spirit) have in reference to adherence to the law. For the jurist, the mastery of the law is the highest expression of piety and 'to seek' (Arabic *ṭalaba*) knowledge of its details is holy in itself. The commandments are understood not only as norms of behaviour, but also as objects of contemplation, which lead toward the perception and the love of God. In fact, the very contribution of later *taṣawwuf* (Sufism) to the legal study in Sunni Islam was the idea of how to systematically "internalise the *shari'a* without losing its exoteric

[14] Although the reception of European law, and the acceptance of legal codification, represented an indigenous movement in the sense that it was driven by the Iranian state's drive for modernisation and state building, it was not in coherence with the premodern Islamic tradition. As the determined positivisation of *sharīʿat* has resulted in a closed and uniform system, the religious norms were left out and its integrative effects decreased. In Iran, the version of the Belgian law code remained in effect after the revolution of 1979, and the Iranian courts of today are more hierarchically and formally organised than the preexisting Islamic ones. The postrevolutionary Iranian state also kept the basic structures and characteristics of the system of education, while introducing some changes in style and content. In this respect, Sami Zubaida (1997:118) argues that the Iranian state and its institutions are only Islamic in its personnel, since the principles of traditional Islamic law that conflict with codification are abandoned in line with socioeconomic expediency in the attempt to codify the *sharīʿat*.

significance", that is, finding the inner meaning of legal rules and being able to experience the divine through their observances (Ayoub 1990:224).[15] Many mystics insisted that the mystical path only could be entered through *sharīʿat* and ʿAbd al-Raḥmān Jāmī (1958:117), a master of the Naqshbandī order, considered law as a medium to communicate spirituality. "The people who are nearest to God are those who struggle most for His commandments and follow closest the *sunnat* of His Prophet". In the sphere of legal norms pertaining to *ʿibādat* (worship), the mystics considered the exoteric prescriptions, such as the movements of the prayer, as a series of symbols serving as objects of contemplation aimed at leading man towards holiness and saintliness.

The generality of this practice allowed everybody to take part in spirituality, not only the elite. This was especially apparent in Shi'i Islam where the esoteric domain permeates the exoteric far more than in Sunni Islam, in the sense that the quintessence of its theological doctrine is the *imāmat*, interpreted as the Logos. In other words, by positing the doctrines of *ʿiṣmat* (immunity from sin) in the concrete person of the *imām*, Shi'i Islam increased the wellsprings of truth, in contrast to the Sunni consensus, which by its very nature is indefinite. In the religious structure of Shi'i Islam, knowledge has always been connected to the *imām* and since he in his cosmic and initiatic functions is considered a divinely designated individual, superiority in learning found an esoteric dimension and became knowledge *par excellence*. While the *harāmisah* (Hermetic) sciences, principally alchemy, were early integrated into Shi'i doctrines, it was first after the occultation of the twelfth *imām* that it came to make use of logic as an instrument for rational speculation on the religious tenets. Early Shi'i Islam was dominated by the esoteric and symbolical doctrines of the *ghulāt* and *bāṭinī* trends alongside the transmitted knowledge of the Prophet and the *imāms* (Hodgson 1965). As Bernard Weiss (1978:211) argues, Shi'i Islam placed a higher premium on knowledge than mainstream Sunni Islam by considering divine command and human intellection as complementary. "Because intuition is recognized as a valid source of ethical-legal values, legal knowledge is considered more to be in the reach of man in Shi'i tradition than it is in Sunni tradition".

The traditional Shi'i works on law and theology from the eighth century and onwards described the *imām* as the *quṭb* (esoteric pole) of creation, the *ḥujjatullāh* (proof of God) and the threshold through which God

[15] While there have existed vaguely different opinions within Sufism regarding the relationship between exoteric and esoteric knowledge, they generally overlap and interact. In the view of ʿAlī b. Uṯmān Hujwīrī (1926:383), they reinforce each other since the exoteric law is merely virtually separate from truth (*ḥaqīqat*). "The proof that the law and the faith is not fundamentally separate, but are one, lies in the fact that belief without profession is not faith, and conversely profession without belief is not faith... Therefore *sharīʿat* is man's act, while *ḥaqīqat* is God's keeping and preservation and protection, whence it follows that *ḥaqīqat* cannot possibly be maintained without the observance of *sharīʿat*".

communicates with creation. The *imām* is the guardian of *sharīʿat* and the only legitimate authority on the Qur'an after the Prophet (Madelung 1971, McDermott 1978:105–132). Similar to the Prophet, he is the source of *nūr al-muḥammadī* (prophetic light), which is the very cause and instrument of all the rest of creation. The authority of the *imāms* is intimately linked to their *ʿilm* and the views concerning its scope and nature ranges from the minimalist position, according to which it is largely confined to *al-ḥalāl wa al-ḥarām*, a superior knowledge of the law, to the theosophical conception of the *imām* as partaking of the knowledge of the *ghaib* (unseen). As elaborated and emphasised by the sixth *imām*, with reference to the meaning of *taʾwīl* (esoteric explanation), the *imām* is more than a *ʿalīm abrār* (pious man of learning). He is a divinely inspired possessor of a special sum of knowledge of religion that is passed on before his death to the following *imām* (Amir-Moezzi 1994:75).

Although the expansion of Shi'i legal theory was designed to fill the vacuum in religious authority brought about by *al-ghaibah al-kubrā* (the greater occultation), the seeds of Shi'i jurisprudence were sown during the lifetime of the first *imāms*. After the fourth *imām*, Zain al-ʿĀbidīn, whose life was spared during the tragic incident at Karbala, the succession of the *imāmat* was carried on automatically from father to son on the principle of nomination by *al-naṣṣ al-jalī* (explicit designation, literally 'clear text') of the living *imām*. The inception of Shi'i jurisprudence was marked by the fifth and seventh Shi'i *imāms*, Muḥammad al-Bāqir and Jaʿfar al-Ṣādiq, who adapted the esoteric and political character of early Shi'i religiosity to juristic argumentation. Extensive legal works are attributed to them, but the genuineness of their sayings cannot be substantiated in detail. Neither of them treated the subject of legal theory at an equivalent rank to that of al-Shāfiʿī (Halm 1991:30). While al-Shāfiʿī's works did not attract any commentaries or rebuttals until the advent of the tenth century, he had a great impact in the realm of legal reasoning by establishing the four Sunni sources of law and systemising the *sunnat*.[16] In contrast to al-Shāfiʿī, none of the *imāms* were methodologists *par excellence* although they enjoyed the respect of many *ʿulamā* during their lifetime and posthumously; Abū al-Hanīfah and Anas b. Malik, both founders of Sunni *maḏāhib* (schools of law) were, for instance, pupils of Jaʿfar al-Ṣādiq. It is not a coincidence that the first eight *imāms* occurred in many Sufi initiatic *silsilas* (transmission chains) as exemplars of spiritual virtues, which transcended the boundaries of Shi'i Islam (Algar 1990).

While al-Ṣādiq is regarded by posteriority as the founder of the Shi'i school of jurisprudence, also called *maḏhab al-jaʿfarī* because of the

[16] In this respect, Hallaq (1994) dates the real formation of the *uṣūl al-fiqh* to the tenth century and even argues that Shāfiʿī's work does not qualify in the field of *uṣūl al-fiqh* because of its rudimentary character.

primordial role he played in its formalisation, as Schacht (1950:262), Linant de Bellefonds (1970) and Calder (1996:984) argue, the literary evidence for the existence of a 'formalised' Shi'i legal 'system' is available first in the early part of the tenth century. They reject the alleged origins of Shi'i law in the Umayyad period and claim that it was distinguished from that of the Sunni schools in a later period. However, their view has been modified by Madelung (1979:70), Coulson (1997:104), Momen (1985:184) and Howard, who hold that the Shi'i and Sunni legal systems were not merely articulated at a similar date with a common starting-point in the late Umayyad practice, but that the Shi'i legal tradition, in contrast to Sunni law, represents a fundamental break from pre-Islamic *ʿurf* law. As I.K.A. Howard (1982:19) elucidates, a close reading of Muḥammad b. Yaʿqūb al-Kulainī's *al-Kāfi fī ʿilm al-dīn* (The one who is competent in religious sciences) demonstrates that the beginnings of the *maḏhab* were more strictly established by the fifth *imām*, which he regards as the true founder of Shi'i jurisprudence. While the early raw material of Shi'i and Sunni jurisprudence were almost similar, as Coulson (1997:105) argues, they only differed with regard to their channel of authority:

> ...[T]he raw material of their jurisprudence, the local popular and administrative practice, was the same; they shared the same general method of juristic speculation, were subject to the same influences, and evinced the same trend to ascribe their doctrines to their own representative authorities in previous generations.

CHAPTER III

Categories of traditional Islamic epistemology

A. Knowledge and science

While the question of epistemology as treated within the philosophy of science is something of a post-nineteenth century speciality, there have been earlier important discussions of knowledge. In modern as well as pre-modern times, Islamic philosophers, theologians, mystics and jurists have been engaged in answering the main epistemological questions, that is: What is the nature of knowledge? What kinds of knowledge are possible for the human mind? What are the sources of cognition and what are the limits of knowledge at all? Any discussion on the cognitive categories in traditional Islam has to be considered with reference to the Qur'an, traditionally considered as containing the roots of all knowledge in a general sense in terms of being revelation. In the Qur'an, the Arabic root *ʿ-l-m* occurs in all its derivations, the unrelated word *ʿālam* (world) excluded, and every single occurrence of the root is included to condition receptive minds to 'knowing' as a basic force in religion, something that confirms the great significance attributed to knowledge in Islam. The concept of *ʿilm* gave the Islamic civilisation its distinctive structure and complexion and there is probably no other concept that has been so operative as a determinant of Islamic civilisation in all its aspects to the same extent as *ʿilm*. Due to the Qur'anic stress on cognition, the Islamic quest for knowledge and its *bona fide* celebration of knowledge was not divorced from its sacred aspect.

As Franz Rosenthal elucidates in his study of the status of knowledge in Islam, the Qur'anic usage of the term *ʿilm* designates knowledge of certainty as equivalent to the Greek concept of *gnôsis*, and only later was the term differentiated from *maʿrifat* (cognition) and *ḥikmat* (wisdom).[17] Since all knowledge ultimately comes from God in Qur'anic terms, true human

[17] As a matter of fact, the differentiation in Arabic usage involving a distinct preference for employing the root *ʿ-r-f* for translating the Greek *gignôskô* and its derivatives (i.e. *gnôsis*) is traceable only in much later times. While the distinction between 'wisdom' and 'knowledge' is part of the Semitic heritage, in the Western Church it gained much more from the linguistic situation in Greek and Latin, both which possessed two distinct words rivalling for greater recognition (*sophia-epistêmê* and *sapientia-scientia*). Christian theology gave, hence, further impetus to putting 'wisdom' on a pedestal high above 'knowledge' in contrast to the Qur'an where the outstanding position accorded to knowledge led to the practical elimination of *ḥikmat* as something superior or indeed rival to *ʿilm* (Rosenthal 1970:24 and 36).

knowledge is equal to religious insight and *ʿilm* appears in fact once as equated with *īmān* (faith), paired in a set phrase, where 'believing' and 'being given knowledge' are parallel expressions. "Allah will exalt those who believe among you and those who have knowledge, to high ranks"(*Qur.* 58:11). Other Qur'anic verses even suggest that knowledge is a necessary consequence of faith (*Qur.* 2:26). In their philosophical conception of knowledge, the *muʿtazilah* and the Shi'i theological positions went further by explicitly considering knowledge as belief or *sukūn al-nafs* ('rest of the soul') (Rosenthal 1970:63).

But while all human knowledge of real value in Qur'anic terms is religious knowledge, the revelation refers to ordinary and empirical knowledge possessed by human beings. The vocabulary of the Qur'an reveals awareness of the manifold shades of human intellectual perception by its use of the other relevant Arabic roots (such as *ʿ-q-l*, *f-h-m*, *f-k-r*, *ʿ-r-f*). We also find the existence of graduations of conception in the ascending scale of certitude: (i) knowledge by inference that depends either on the truth of its presupposition as in deduction, or it is only probable as in induction: *ʿilm al-yaqīn* (knowledge of certainty), (ii) knowledge by perception or observation that is scientific or historical based on experience or reports: *ʿain al-yaqīn* (seeing with the eye of certainty), (iii) knowledge by intuition or personal experience which assumes identity of meaning for *ḥaqq* (truth) and certainty: *ḥaqq al-yaqīn* (truth with certainty).[18] Experience that comes from the last source gives the highest degree of certitude and includes revelation, divine inspiration, guidance or revelation, knowledge by the heart. In addition to human knowledge, mundane as well as religious, there also exists a divine knowledge which ultimately is identical with human knowledge while at the same time it is somehow of a higher order, both quantitatively and qualitatively. There can, so to say, be no human knowledge, mundane or religious, without the knowledge of the Divine:

> The worth of knowledge and indeed the mere fact that something can be considered knowledge depends on the existence of a relationship between such knowledge and what is thought of as God's knowledge or as being in harmony with it… Whenever one speaks of human knowledge, he has to keep in mind the connection that exists between such knowledge and the form of knowledge that is suitable only for the deity. Knowledge appears as something varied and immense, but it is in a sense finite and monolithic (Rosenthal 1970:31–32).

While the concept of *ʿilm* designates religious as well as mundane knowledge, the predominant trend in traditional Islam was to identify "the totality and specificity of knowledge" with religious knowledge, which was considered as superior to the mundane (ibid.:44). The term *ʿilm* was initially used to refer to the process of knowing or finding, but also came to include

[18] (i) *Qur.* 102:5, (ii) *Qur.* 102:7, 25:2, 3:137, 3:190, (iii) *Qur.* 69:51, 53:10, 41:30, 2:97, 56:95.

introspective intuition according to the different disciplines and methodologies of traditional Islam. As the word subsequently became one of the numerous sections of total *ʿilm*, which also admitted methodical systematizing in the form of *ʿulūm* (scientific disciplines), the separate disciplines were in no way essentially different from 'knowledge' as a whole. As Rosenthal (ibid.:44) highlights, by referring to a number of writings of different Muslim authors (al-Zamakhsharī, Ibn Ḥazm, Ibn Taimīyah, etc.), the various traditional sciences did not essentially differ from each other, and their apparent differences concerned only the details and fine points. "The attitude underlying this view may be turned into a plea for an intensive, non-discriminatory cultivation of all recognized branches of learning. All *ʿulūm* must be considered interdependent".

In this respect, the various sciences, as categories or standards of knowledge, may be said to represent different *epistemic schemes*, which were considered to complement each other in the sense that they bordered on each other. Sciences such as law and theology were not only considered to belong to totally different spheres but their methods and principles were also believed to be as different as their contents. While an individual traditional scholar might have rejected one specific epistemic scheme, the general tendency was to consider knowledge in hierarchial terms.[19] The typical Islamic philosophical mode of dealing with the structure of reality was to divide it into hierarchial levels of qualitative vertical, but also horizontal, relationships, where the sciences were perceived to be related to the sacred, extending in a hierarchy from an empirical and rational mode of knowing to the highest form of intuitive intellection. An ontological and cosmic *tartīb* (hierarchy), or even *tadrīj* (gradualness), was considered to lie at the root of all things, against which the particular was always deduced from the universal, the relative from the absolute or the concrete from the abstract. "Furthermore the arts and the sciences were made, first by the philosophers and then by various thinkers and writers, the object of a series of lists (*ihsāʾ al-ʿulūm*) and classifications of the sciences (*marātib al-ʿulūm*)" (Lewis, Menage and Pellat 1965:1133). In this respect, the philosophical picture of the human individual as microcosmic harmony was normative, since it

19 By claiming that the hierarchial status of being requires a hierarchial status of knowing, the philosophers and the mystics went beyond the cognitive standards of law, which integrated epistemology into methodology. In general terms, the epistemic schemes of philosophy (which was defined as an 'alien science') and Sufism proved to be the most contested ones to those jurists who considered all essential truth as contained in revelation, but there was no consensus on this point and while al-Mufīd, Muḥammad ʿAli al-Bihbahānī, Ibn Taimīyah and others were against the principles of *falsafah* (philosophy) and Sufism, Anas b. Malik, Fakhr al-dīn al-Rāzī, Muḥammad al-Ghazālī and many others were in favour of Sufism. Nasrollah Pourjavady (1999) elucidates that the Shi'i hostility to Sufism first arose in the tenth century and primarily had to do with the fact that the latter were Sunnis. He also argues that Shi'i thinkers became increasingly ambivalent towards Sufism after the fourteenth century when very much of the Sufi terminology had been integrated into Shi'i belief and dogma and the discipline of *ʿirfān* was established in the educational curriculum.

corresponded ideally to the macrocosmic order in equilibrium with the Divine. "Based as it is on the structure of the macrocosm, it is seen to pertain to the objective nature of things" (Murata 1992:249).[20]

While the idea of a hierarchial cosmic order was endorsed by many *ʿulamā* such as Muḥammad al-Ghazālī, who in his *al-Faiḍāl al-tafriqah* (The Grace of divergence) divided existence into several ontological degrees (and claimed these to be unanimously recognised by all Islamic schools), the ancestry of the idea of *tartīb* was highly debated in traditional Islam (Bello 1989:53–54). Due to the strength of the 'historical-empirical' methods of the transmitted sciences, such as *ʿilm al-ḥadīṯ* (the science of the reliability of *ḥadīṯ*) and the rejection of any notion of hierarchial structure of the world without causalistic reasons by *ashʿarī* theology, many modern scholars have underlined the alien nature of hierarchial notions in Islam. Fazlur Rahman (1982:3 and 23), for instance, argues that the term *tartīb* originally was adopted from outside sources, mainly Platonic and Neo-Platonic philosophy, since Muslims initially possessed "no detailed, intellectually worked-out system of thought". Rahman's assertion is correct, if he indicates that Muslims did not begin to cultivate science in the form of complete disciplines until they became familiar with the Greek, Persian and Indian civilisations that predated the Qur'anic revelation. But while Islamic philosophy and Sufism adopted much originally Greek terminology, such as the general classification of science into *kullī/juzʾī* (universal/particular) and *naẓarī/ʿamalī* (theoretical/practical), it remains to be stressed that the epistemic schemes of philosophy and mysticism were not necessarily antagonistic to the religious universe of the Qur'an, which itself recognises a specific cosmological order of things in line with the Qur'anic verse, "And everything with Him is measured" (*Qur.* 13:8).[21] The Islamic adoption of Greek philosophy and science was also selective and took primary interest in the doctrines of the Pythagorean-Platonic as well as Aristotelian teachings that endorsed the principle Divine Unity. In this respect, Islamic scholars integrated various types of science and modes of knowledge, which created a multifaceted structure in which the parts (the separate disciplines) were harmonised with each other. "Islamic intellectual tradition upholds the idea of the hierarchy and unity of knowledge and of the modes of knowing. There

[20]One of the earliest philosophical works which was clearly clearly influenced by Neo-Platonism (the idea of emanation) was *Rasāʾil ikhwān al-ṣafā* (Treatise of the brotherhood of purity). There, the relationships of the existent things to God is like the relationships of the numbers to one, in the manner of Pythagora: the intellect is like two, the soul like three, prime matter like four, nature like five, the body like six, the celestial sphere like seven, and so on. (Widengren 1979).

[21] While the Qur'an is essentially a religious book, it deals with all those problems that religion and philosophy have in common and throws light upon conceptions of appearance and reality. In Qur'anic terms, God is the ultimate reality, the Lord of the worlds, and is 'immanent' both in the *anfās* (souls) and the *āfāq* (horizons), that is the spatio-temporal order (*Qur.* 1:2 and *Qur.* 41:53).

are many sources and forms of knowledge, and there are many ways of knowing" (Bakar 1997:941).[22]

B. The 'historical-empirical' epistemic scheme

As far as Sunni Islam is concerned, the earliest interpreters of revelation were in the first case concerned with the domain of *naqlī* (transmitted) knowledge or more correctly, acquired 'historical-empirical' knowledge, that is, knowledge of the revealed sources as constructed from *ḥadīṯ* handed down from the Prophet. As the traditional Islamic sciences crystallised, the *muḥaddiṯūn* (scholars of *ḥadīṯ*) gave priority to the *ʿulūm naqlīyah* (transmitted sciences) over the *ʿulūm ʿaqlīyah* (rational sciences). Consequently, transmitted knowledge, such as grammar, prosody, biography and especially *ḥadīṯ* was considered superior to independent judgement in terms of *raʾy* (opinion), *ijtihād*, *qiyās* (analogical deduction) and *kalām* ('word', i.e. theology). The proper subject of early Islamic epistemological considerations, in fact, largely concerned *ḥadīṯ* and its transmission to the extent that the initial exclusive reliance on textual substantiation even shaped an ensuing fraction within Sunni Islam, the *aṣḥāb al-ḥadīṯ* (followers of *ḥadīṯ*) who objected to the rational arguments of *aṣḥāb al-raʾy* (followers of opinion) (Melchert 1997:1–7). In the primitive 'historical-empirical' epistemic scheme, man was considered bound by his or her built-in intellectual and existential limitations to make the leap from rational capabilities to faith in the pursuit of understanding the universe. Concerned with factual transmitted knowledge, the revealed texts assumed literal importance rather than understanding the whole or parts of these as metaphors in the sense that texts were supposed to be as they appear to be. As common sense is considered valid, the epistemic standard of early Sunni Islam might be characterised as a 'naive realism'.

The nature of the early religious intellectual development differed in Shi'i Islam, which, as Etan Kohlberg (1979) elucidates, possessed infallible guidance until the middle of the tenth century, when the twelfth *imām* disappeared in occultation, and also as it possessed an inherent predilection for esoteric explanation and considered the *imām*s as the *muḥaddiṯūn* and

[22] As a matter of fact, the various traditional Islamic epistemologies enumerate at least three so called *laṭīfah* (subtle organs) or three aspects of the human *nafs* (soul): *ʿaql* (comprising both the Latin *intellectus*, pure reason, and *ratio*, discursive reason), *qalb* (heart) and *rūḥ* (Spirit). Each of these perceives its own world and are intermediate in regard to the others. Taken by itself, the word *nafs* hence expands beyond the modern Western notion of the soul by designating the lower psyche as well as the higher levels of the heart and the spirit. While the pure reason (*intellectus*), which has the means of perceiving transcendent realities, and discursive reason (*ratio*) are part of the same intelligence, i.e. *ʿaql*, the latter, by capacity of being a prolongation of the former, has the means of cognitive analysis and discursive thought. Cf. chapter IV.c below.

transmitters of knowledge *par excellence*.[23] While the *naṣṣ* period, as far as Sunni Islam is concerned, stopped with the Prophet, Shi'i Islam extended it to the *imāms*, and as Mohammad Ali Amir-Moezzi (1994:12, 19) argues, the original Shi'i tradition can more accurately be described as 'esoteric supra- or nonrational', to further distinguish it from the later tradition of "theological-juridical rational Imamism", which was heavily influenced by the *muʿtazilah* school. In this respect, he confines the early Shi'i definition of *ʿaql* exclusively to a priori 'hiero-intelligence'. "The early *'aql* was defined as the axis of the religion of the imams, like an indispensable key for opening the mysteries of their teachings and for opening oneself to these teachings". As Hossein Modarressi (1984:32) elucidates, Shi'i legal positions completely neglected rational procedural reasoning until the latter part of the tenth century, but the differences between Shi'i and Sunni Islam tended to decrease after the occultation of the twelfth *imām* when Shi'i collectors of *ḥadīṯ* followed the example of Sunni *ʿilm al-ḥadīṯ* by including a chapter on *ʿilm* in the collections of *akhbār*, such as in the case of *al-Kāfī fī ʿilm al-dīn* of al-Kulainī. These developments were nevertheless restricted to *ḥadīṯ* and the Shi'i legal tradition continued to implicitly reject knowledge obtained from conjectural methods such as *qiyās* and *ijtihād*.[24] The term *ʿilm* was equated with certainty and it was regarded as the duty of the jurist to seek absolute truth in his legal reasoning.

While Shi'i jurisprudence until the thirteenth century remained largely confined to the 'historic-empirical' epistemic scheme, the development of various Shi'i legal readings of the Qur'an and the division between *uṣūlī*, *akhbārī* and *ghulāt* positions has a long precedent before the jurisprudential problems caused by the occultation of the twelfth *imām* as well as the later theological disputes during the Ṣafawīd period. In fact, the terms are first used as binary divergent factions by ʿAbd al-Jalīl al-Qazvīnī in the eleventh century (Madelung 1980a:56). As a process of understanding, jurisprudence allowed for a certain opposition between human reason and the revealed texts and in the sense of corresponding to two possible responses for the resolution of this conflict, the *akhbārī* and *uṣūlī* represented two original informal *ṭuruq* (ways) of Shi'i law. Since earliest times there existed one

[23] Unlike Sunni Islam, which at an early stage was confronted with the task of establishing a practical system of legal administration that ushered the systematisation of *uṣūl al-fiqh*, Shi'i Islam taught that legal authority was personified in the *imām* and the concept of *ẓann* (conjecture) in its epistemological sense and the equally authoritative *ikhtilāf* was considered diametrically opposed to the integrity of the *imām*. For as long as the *imām*, the vehicle of God's communication, was present and alive, he was the ultimate authority, who laid down the law and acted as an *ad hoc* arbiter in disputes in the same way as the Prophet.

[24] As the ninth century Shi'i jurist Abū Sahl Ismāʿīl argues in his treatise *Ibṭāl al-qiyās* (Refutation of analogy) *qiyās*, like *tamṯīl* in formal logic, does not necessitate knowledge and cannot be regarded as a proof in contrast to the later notion of *ijtihād al-sharʿī* (reasoning based on textual evidence provided by the revealed sources) (Brunschvig 1968:202).

tendency, which allowed a measure of speculative reasoning in the principles of law as well as another relying mostly on the transmission of *akhbār*:

The division of Imamites into partisans and adversaries of the use of dialectical reasoning in cases of sacred concepts does not date from the eleventh/seventeenth century, on the contrary, its first traces can already be felt in the proto-Shi'ites of the second-third/eight-ninth centuries (Amir-Moezzi 1994:14).[25]

Unlike the case of Sunni Islam, where the phenomenon of *maḏhab* came to regulate a compromise between the *aṣḥāb al-ḥadīṯ* and the *aṣḥāb al-ra'y*, the triumph of Shi'i rational legal theory was first secured in the middle of the nineteenth century, when the *akhbārī* school was almost entirely wiped off the religious map. Whereas some scholars confirm the fact that the *akhbārī* and the *uṣūlī* positions are tendencies inherent in Shi'ism that became stronger under the influence of the dominant *mu'tazilah* school during the ninth century, in common research the terms are used as a designation for two historical schools during the late Ṣafawīd period. A number of scholars have reduced these positions strictly to the Ṣafawīd disputes and maintain that the *akhbārī* school was founded by Muḥammad Amīn Astarābādī and the *uṣūlī* by Muḥammad Bāqir al-Bihbahānī, which largely is due to the fact that the term *ṭarīqat al-akhbārīyah* is the epithet the former used for his school (Bayat 1982:21, Cole 1983:39, Kohlberg 1985:717). Nevertheless, other scholars significantly distinguish the Ṣafawīd schools from the early developments of primitive *akhbārī* and *uṣūlī* positions (Kazemi-Moussavi 1996:32 and 77, Madelung 1968:21, Modarressi 1984:32–35, Scarcia 1968). For instance, Hamid Algar (1991:711) asserts that, "The origins of the Akhbari-Usuli divide go far back beyond the 18th century. Each side in fact identifies its own position as the perennially authentic doctrine of Shi'ism, and regards the other as an innovation".

In Shi'i Islam, the initial strength of the historic-empirical epistemic scheme was due to the well-established religious mentality that considered all kinds of rational argument as illegitimate, and precisely as their name suggests, the juristic methodology of the *akhbārī* position was that of collecting *ḥadīṯ* and *akhbār*. With its neglect for rational source-foundations, the *akhbārī* legal method was intensively factualist, allowing almost no leeway for private fancy, but relying on the readopting of *ḥadīṯ* and *akhbār*

[25] The common *problematique* the two tendencies debated was ancient, but since the very terms *akhbārī* and *uṣūlī* were used with different connotations, there is no clearcut distinction between them. In the works of the Shi'i theologians and jurists of the tenth to the twelfth centuries, *akhbārī* was used as synonymous to *muqallīdah*, *aṣḥāb al-ḥadīṯ*, *ahl al-ẓāhir* and *hashwīyah* since the key terms in Shi'i law had not yet acquired a standard technical mould for their expression. There existed a simultaneous use of the same terms in technical as well as non-technical use. Many terms, therefore, changed their connotation over the course of centuries before they acquired standard technical phraseology for their expression. It was first during the time of al-Mufīd in the tenth century that the legal terms acquired a noticeable increasingly technical connotation.

(Sourdel 1969:192). Since the revealed texts were considered to contain all of what one needs to know about God, the world and man, the representatives of *akhbārī* jurisprudence considered the narrative itself as the sole source of knowledge by the use of non-logical empirical textual arguments. The early Shi'i epistemic tendency to depend solely on revelation and *ḥadīṯ* was also a common denominator of Shi'i exegetical literature, that until the tenth century essentially was *tafsīr bi-maʾṯūr* (exegesis by means of *ḥadīṯ*). The Shi'i *ʿulamā* served initially as narrators of the *akhbār* of the *imāms*, had no separate training in jurisprudence and did not study jurisprudence separately from *ḥadīṯ*. As Brunschwig (1968:203) elucidates, the works of al-Kulainī, for instance, dealt nearly exclusively with *ḥadīṯ* and they clearly imply that he is an expert trained in the sayings of the *imāms* rather than someone trained in legal theory. "Pour Kulayni, tout cas peut être résolu par recours exclusif au Coran ou à la Sunna, à condition de les bien comprendre et savoir notamment remédier aux divergences dans l'interprétation des hadiths".

Muḥammad b. ʿAlī b. al-Babūyah was the first jurist who gave the Shi'i doctrine a structure. The fact that his work *Man lā yaḥḍuruʾ al-faqīh* (When no jurisprudent is present) included a chapter on *furūʿ* indicates that Shi'i jurists were gradually forced to explain new details of positive law. But in contrast to his contemporary, Abū ʿAlī Muḥammad b. al-Junaid, who was renowned for his reliance on the principle of analogy in legal matters, al-Babūyah maintained that *qiyās* was not even permissible in circumstances when the cause of an injunction was clearly mentioned in the Qur'anic text (Madelung 1998b:31). In the sense that al-Babūyah did not offer an analytical and systematic treatment of the law, while he drew rules from the *akhbār* and explained their meaning (that is not leaving them to speak for themselves), he was still a typical representative of the historical-empirical epistemic scheme, which is evident in his criticism of logic (Madelung 1968:13–20). But as the title of al-Babūyah's work indicates, the author produced the underpinnings for the inception of *uṣūl al-fiqh* by appearing as a *faqīh* rather than as an ordinary *muḥaddiṯ*.

While the 'historical-empirical' epistemic scheme continued to survive under the increasing challenges from the logocentricity that came to flourish after the ninth century, it was first in the seventeenth century that it regained its former vitality very much through the *akhbārī* school proper, which crystallised in the figure of Muḥammad Amīn Astarābādī. As Devin J. Stewart (1998:175–208) elucidates, Astarābādī's assault on the logocentric character of Shi'i jurisprudence was in large part a reaction to the work of scholars such as Zain al-dīn al-ʿĀmilī, who had called into question the reliability of many *akhbār* included in the canonical Shi'i collections by requiring strict complete *isnād* (chains of transmission). Astarābādī eschewed speculation and strictly rejected anything that had not been explicitly validated by the revealed sources. He saw all cognitive validity as within in the revealed text alone, that is, one is subject to the text, exposed to it, answerable to it for one's conduct and defined by its meanings. Since to understand the *akhbār* is to see oneself in its light, one's relation to the text is ontological rather than simply exegetical. Astarābādī rejected the semi-rationalisation of *uṣūl al-fiqh* by disallowing any major role whatsoever for reason in law, as he believed that rational reasoning could produce contradictory results. For this reason, he rejected contradictory *akhbār* and applied an attitude of *tawaqquf* (discontinuation) to not abide by two contradicting ones. The central idea underlying Astarābādī's view was that there is no essential difference between the legal state of Shi'i Muslims before and after the occultation, since the law has to conform with certainty to the transmitted utterances of the *imāms*. While Astarābādī considered syllogistic reasoning as the manipulation of tautologies, which not produced any results not pre-anticipated when the syllogism was set up, he nevertheless reintroduced *ẓāhirī* formulas of *al-yaqīn al-wāqʿī* (real certainty), *al-yaqīn al-ʿādī* (ordinary certainty) and *al-ʿaql al-hissī* (common sense), in order to interpret the *akhbār* more directly and provide more certitude in cognitive matters (Kazemi Moussavi 1996:33 and 93). As Kohlberg (1987a:848) asserts, he also more drastically excluded the Qur'an from the direct canonical sources of law, since its true meaning can only be obtained from *ḥadīṯ* and *akhbār*.

In the sense that Astarābādī asserted that not every truth is humanly attainable, the human intellect is limited and has to resort to faith. In this respect, it is not a coincidence that the *akhbārī* jurists tended to find inner-worldly salvation through the esoteric and hermeneutic comprehension of the revealed texts. In turning away from the logocentric basis of legal theory, many *akhbārī* jurists turned their attention to non-rational avenues of knowledge, primarily *ʿirfān*.[26] The most renowned *akhbārī* master of *ʿirfān* was Muḥsin Faiḍ al-Kāshānī, who integrated theosophical experience into legal thought by perceiving *al-ʿaql al-kull* (the universal Intellect) to be identical with *sharīʿat*. The work of Muḥammad Bāqir al-Majlisī, another great compiler of *ḥadīṯ*, was also the result of *akhbārī* prevalence, although he validated a number of principles of logic. al-Majlisī's legal position was very much of a synthesis between the 'historical-empirical' and 'juristic-rational' epistemic schemes (Modarressi 1984:54).[27] While *akhbārī*

[26] As Gerhard Böwering (1998:551) elucidates, the term *ʿirfān* (lit. 'knowledge') is a broad and somewhat amorphous concept adopted in post-Ṣafawīd times for intellectual developments "that combine Sufi thought and Twelver Shi'ite philosophy". While *ʿirfān* reached its climax in Ṣafawīd times with the school of Isfahan, it had modest beginnings in the vocabulary of Islamic thought and never constituted a key term in the writings of traditional Islamic thinkers, who instead tended to use *ʿilm* for describing their mystical experiences and esoteric doctrines.

[27] In contrast to earlier Shi'i *ʿulamā*, who for the most part wrote in Arabic, al-Majlisī also wrote a number of works in Persian, thereby making the Shi'i tradition more widely

conceptions of valid legal knowledge became dominant for a period after the downfall of the Ṣafawīd dynasty and the *akhbārī* position found support among many prominent jurists, such as Muḥammad Taqī al-Majlisī, al-Ḥurr al-ʿĀmilī, Ṣadr al-dīn Shīrāzī and Aḥmad Aḥsāʾī, there was no way for mainstream Shi'i jurisprudence to revert completely to the original *akhbārī* position. Despite its contribution to the development of *ḥadīṯ*, *ʿirfān*, *akhlāq*, *ʿilm al-adiyān* (science of religions), *tafsīr* and other disciplines, the *akhbārī* position lacked the provision of answers to the constantly new situations that Islam encountered in the nineteenth century. In contrast, the 'juristic-rational' epistemic scheme produced comprehensive legal analytical works and gave way to the emergence of new demonstrative Shi'i legal positions.

C. The 'theological', 'philosophical' and 'mystical' epistemic schemes

In contrast to the representatives of the 'historical-empirical' epistemic scheme, the Islamic speculative theologians, philosophers and mystics adopted a more liberated epistemic approach to the human intellect. The theologians shared with the transmitters of *ḥadīṯ* as well as the 'rationalistic' jurists their common view of the epistemic pursuit as situated along the transmitted sciences, in which the revealed texts accordingly define the frame of reference in the exercise of the intellect. Yet, the theologians went a step beyond the epistemic position of the latter by addressing questions that originate in an entirely different theological and philosophical reference. Whereas *ʿilm al-ḥadīṯ* and *fiqh* basically derived norms for human acts from texts, theology emphasised the authority of rational argument in defining religious dogma and belief. In the words of Montgomery Watt (1963:160), the logicians aroused a new epistemic conception, which in its essence as in favour of pure rational dialectic, that is, methodologically presenting a case and making judgement from reasoned argument, asserted that "the man who could give reasons for a doctrine he believed was superior to a man who merely held the doctrine, but could give no reason for it". In traditional Islam, the former subsequently came to be the *ʿālim* ('the learned', pl. *ʿulamā*) *par excellence* with an intellectual field of study comprising primarily of the realm of jurisprudence and speculative theology. Since the beginning of the tenth century, Islamic logicians identified the acquisition of knowledge as the task of *manṭiq* (logic). In theology, logic stood not merely as a set of tautologies in contrast to jurisprudence, but equally served as an epistemic system, possessing a unique universe of discourse with a specific terminology containing references not generally found in legal discourse.

---

accessible as well as *in extenso* preparing the ground for modern legal discourses that increasingly became articulated in Persian.

As far as Sunni Islam is concerned, the first steps towards rationalising faith were taken by jurisprudence, which established various methods for the inference of legal norms, while in Shi'i Islam the situation was the opposite: theology predated legal theory. In the Sunni development of the scholastic method, Islamic law was important in the sense that Greek philosophical concepts and methods had been studied and familiarised by jurisprudence (Makdisi 1974:648). As a matter of course, Aristotelian logic (through the works *Categoria* and *De interpretatione*) was among the earliest Greek materials made available in Arabic translation and Greek logic became the foundation of all Muslim epistemology, a position it has maintained by forming the major systematic scientific framework available for intellectual expression. In *Analytica posteriora*, Aristotle analysed scientific knowledge in terms of necessary propositions that express causal relations. Such knowledge takes the form of categorical syllogism and its formulation resides in *nous* (the intellect), which is part of the faculty of *psyche* (the soul). While acknowledging that knowledge is something that a person possesses, for Aristotle, actual knowledge was identical with its objects (Aristotle 1949). As Shams Inati (1997:803) elucidates, Aristotle's *Analytica priora* was not introduced into Arabic before the tenth century, which explains the rudimentary character of the early Sunni analogical deduction.[28] Islamic logicians, following Aristotle, studied all rational arguments, whether in the procedure of a syllogism, induction or analogy and argued in general terms that syllogism is the only reasoning process that leads to certainty. Since logic provides rules for determining the properly formed or valid from the improperly formed or invalid explanatory phrase and proof, the theologians as well as the philosophers deemed syllogism as the most reliable method capable of yielding apodictic knowledge and *burhān* (demonstration) as the most reliable form of the syllogism (Gutas 1988:178).

Logic provided the justification and system of classification not only for law, theology and philosophy, but also for transmitted sciences, such as *ʿilm al-ḥadīṯ* and *ʿilm al-tārīkh* (history), and the discussion of epistemology in the strict sense was not restricted to professional philosophers and logicians, but spread to form the foundations of mainstream Islamic thought. While there exists a great diversity between various theological schools and individual theologians, and no complete and consensus account of a theological theory of knowledge, all theological epistemologies set out knowledge in terms of a "dispositional attitude" according to which knowledge is generated by reason (Nuseibeh 1997:830).[29] The way to know

[28] In the Aristotelian *Organum*, analogy was actually used as syllogism and it is not irrelevant to recall that the term *qiyās* was chosen to translate the title of *Analytica priora*, while *burhān* was used as equivalent of *Analytica posteriora* (Brockelmann 1949:370, 376).

[29] Similar to the case of Aristotle in his logic, a central epistemological problem of Islamic thought was the question whether the *maʿlūm* (object known) prior to knowledge is an established fact or not. For the theologians, the human mind proceeds from some *badīhī*

something, the revealed sources included, was through *ḥujjat al-ʿaql* (rational proof). The theological formulation of Shi'i Islam appears to have been chiefly the work of the ninth-century theologian Abū Sahl Naubakhtī, who took a prominent part in formulating the doctrine of *ghaibat* and affirming the concept of *naṣṣ*. He was the first to interpret jurisprudential reflection as the basic function of the *imāmat* (Arjomand 1997:9).

In Sunni Islam, theology primarily manifested itself in the theological positions of the *muʿtazilah* and the *ashʿarī* schools. The *muʿtazilah* theologians, who were concerned with law, stressed the exclusive importance of analogical reasoning as an outgrowth of *naẓar* (rational speculation, 'pure reasoning').[30] Shi'i *uṣūlī* jurisprudence borrowed its epistemological standards from the *muʿtazilah* school and maintained that the human faculty of reason can know law and moral assessments. Since the quality of justice is considered as innate to the divine nature, there was also a greater emphasis on reason in Shi'i theology. The basis of a certain obligation may be nonrational, but the rules of conduct themselves have a rational substance. As the universe is conceived as a rationally integrated system, ethical values, such as justice and goodness, have an objective existence and can be known by independent human reason as well as revelation. Man is hence capable of knowing the *ḥikmat* (rationale) behind God's commands and God is obliged to command what is just for man (Schmidtke 1994).[31] In contrast, the *ashʿarī* school, the epistemological perspective that influenced Sunni legal theory, refused to accept any implied limit on the will of God and claimed that values are in their essence whatever God determines and commands. It subjected reason to will and to its kind of 'voluntarism':

> Like Spinoza, al-Ashʿari held that there is no purpose in the mind of God which would determine His activity. From this anti-teleological view it follows that as

(intuitive) a priori (or pre-existent axiomatic knowledge) to new concepts by means of definitions and knowledge is subdivided into *ḍarūrī* (necessary), *muktasab* (acquired) and *istidlālī* (demonstrative). They defined knowledge as the *iḍāfah* (relation) between the knowing subject and the object known, since knowledge must be either *badīhī* or *ḍarūrī*; if it were neither, circular reasoning would result since definition is possible only through knowledge itself (Rosenthal 1970:49).

[30] The *muʿtazilah* was founded by Wāsil b. ʿAṭā (d. 748), a disciple of Ḥasan al-Baṣrī, in Basra, and called itself *ahl al-ʿadl wa al-tauḥīd* (people of justice and Divine Unity). It took stock of the philosophic tools of Hellenistic antiquity, and applied reason in the solution of philosophical problems, leading thereby to the birth of *ʿilm al-kalām*. It was proclaimed official doctrine by the ʿAbbāsīd Caliph al-Maʾmūn and enforced by a *miḥnah* (a compulsory test of faith), a scrutiny of the beliefs held by the various religious authorities, among them Aḥmad b. Hanbal (Nyberg 1953).

[31] The immense impact of *muʿtazilah* teachings on Shi'i theology has inspired some scholars, such as Abu al-Fadl Ezzati (1976:11), to speak of a specific "Shi'i-Mu'tazili rationalistic school", which is incorrect because of the authority Shi'i Islam placed in the *imām*, which separated it from the outset from other streams of Islamic thought.

God's action is not teleological, He is not bound to do what is best for His creatures. He does whatever He wills (Hye 1963:236).

Abū Ḥasan al-Ashʿarī considered God's knowledge as eternal and hypostatic, and he subjected human rationality to *irjāʿ* (postponement) in matters not specifically referred to in the revealed texts. His famous terse reply to the question of rational explanation of the Divine was *bi-lā kaif* ('without why'). His theology formed the basis for later legal epistemology, where law is understood as the literal act of the will of God directed towards the conduct of man, and where the ultimate sanction of reasoning (whether discursive or not) is not reason but revelation. In contrast, Shi'i theology and law connected reason to the principle of *ḍarūrah* (necessity) to represent a priori intellectual certainty of premises and conclusions (Nettler 1983:118).[32]

Parallel to speculative theology, the Islamic *falsafah* (philosophy, from the Greek *philosophos*) also emerged out of the synthesis between Islam and the Greek intellectual tradition. While philosophy was part of the logocentric tendency, it adopted its own methods of *burhān* distinct from the dialectical form of theology. In contrast to the naive realism so characteristic of the 'historical-empirical' epistemic scheme, which also formed the epistemic schemes of law and theology, philosophical knowledge was primarily a matter of timeless concepts and essences. This does not, however, amount to saying that the philosophers disregarded the epistemic value of revelation or revealed law. An overwhelming number of philosophers were in fact jurists or had at least a rigorous education in law. Investigating which legal category the study of philosophy falls into in *fiqh*, Ibn Rushd, for instance, argued that philosophy is the teleological study of the world and hence it is obligatory by law for those capable of doing so to study philosophy (Bello 1989:153). Drawing partly on the Platonic imaginary of the cave, where different shades of reality are postulated, and partly on Qur'anic verses, which confirm the need to use imagination for communicating truth, the philosophers attempted to show that there are different grades of truth, not different or conflicting truths. In the view of the philosophers, theology was considered merely a part of the general science of *mā baʿd al-tabīʿah* (metaphysics), investigating such general concepts as being, unity, species, accidents and so on, since God is the principle of being in general (Genequand 1997:785).[33]

32 Contrary to the philosophers, a number of Sunni jurists, from al-Ghazālī to Ibn Taimīyah and al-Suyūṭī, doubted the existence of any inherently unchanging and universal essences and natural laws and argued for empirical verifiability of religious truths by asserting that the most important facts were very concrete and historical. As divine wisdom, similar to Divine Will, is above any condition or determination, faith becomes reduced to word and act by profession of belief and fulfilment of prescribed duties. For this reason, Sunni jurists wrote several refutations of Shi'i logicism. Among the most renowned is Ibn Taimīyah's *al-Minhāj al-sunnah* (The Path to the prophetic tradition).

33 The philosophers generally justified their activity not merely as an attempt to reconcile revelation and philosophy, but more importantly as a means to communicate faith. In this

The philosophers were not interested in transient and changing details, but rather described the world as terrestrial and extraterrestrial existence, where "the epistemic order reflects or corresponds to the ontic order" (Nuseibeh 1997:835). Philosophical knowledge was defined as *ʿilm irtisāmī* (science of representation) and constructed in terms of a mirror relationship between the knowing subject and the represented object, which is mirrored in the mental plane of existence.[34] As for Ibn Sīnā, he aspired to transcend Aristotelian philosophy and adopted a variety of cognitive categories, which are manifested in different epistemic states of the mind. Inspired by Neoplatonism, he also developed an emanist scheme, in which the heavenly motions are designed in accordance with the astronomical system of Ptolemy, to explain the emergence of multiplicity out of absolute unity. But in importing the mystical ideas and repertoire from Plotinus, he significantly selected the idea of *ittiṣāl* (contact) rather than *ittiḥād* (union) with God (Goodman 1997:298). While Ibn Sīnā's theory of emanation was rejected by Ibn Rushd who maintained a basically Aristotelian system, it was adopted and developed by Shihāb al-dīn Suhrawardī and the school of Isfahan in which philosophy merged with other currents of thought, such as Sufism and Shi'i Islam. In this respect, the Shi'i philosophers in general made more use of Neoplatonic teachings than their Sunni counterparts, who relied more on Aristotelianism.

While the traditional discourses, which held a special appeal to mysticism, similarly considered existence to be ontologically deployed in a certain order, the 'mystical' epistemic scheme developed moderately in opposition to the grain of Islamic logocentrism as well as nomocentrism. The 'mystical' epistemic scheme challenged the validity of these epistemologies in relative terms by proposing several alternative positions whose occupancy required an esoteric initiation, which barely could be incorporated *fiqh*. In contrast to the philosophers who were concerned with *kashf-i ʿaqlī* (unveiling to the intellect), the cognitive approach of the mystics and theosophers went beyond rational speculation and gave greater weight to the subtle organ called *qalb* (heart). As language is considered to obstruct rather than communicate understanding, the mystical cognition involved *mukāshafāt-i qalbī* (unveilings of the heart) and *mukāshafāt-i rūḥī* (unveilings of the

respect, it seems that they generally considered the meaning of philosophy only in the sense of its second derivative *sophia* (wisdom), that is, understood as divine wisdom in itself. "In reality, the term 'philosophy' is perhaps inappropriate: two words are used by Islamic tradition, *falsafa*, a simplified transription of the Greek term *philosophia*, and *hekmat-e elahi*, literally 'divine wisdom', which Corbin proposes to translate as 'theosophy'. This word at once indicates to us how philosophers are no longer mere speculators on metaphysical values: they undertake the spiritual adventure of the knowledge of God, and for that make use of other means than revelation and tradition" (Richard 1995:62).

[34] Abū Yūsuf al-Kīndī wrote, "Knowledge of the true nature of things includes knowledge of Divinity, unity and virtue, and a complete knowledge of everything useful, and of the way to it" (Ivry 1974:55). Cf. al-Farabi: 1981.

spirit), and in contrast to Islamic logocentrism, the mystical visionary knowledge involved no *taṣawwur/taṣdīq* (conception-judgement), but only conception. Since God is the only true reality, as nothing else in reality exists, mystics considered the whole epistemology in the unity of the knower, the known and knowledge itself, and presented no criterion for judging the validity of knowledge involved in the ordinary sense.[35] For the mystics, true cognition was the "immediate vision and knowledge of things unseen and unknown, when the veil of sense is suddenly lifted and the conscious self passes away in the overwhelming glory of the One True Light" (Nicholson 1922:18).

As far as Shi'i Islam is concerned, the dominating epistemological theme of later philosophy, *ʿilm al-ḥuḍūrī* (knowledge of presence), was influenced by the cognitive terminology of mysticism. Inspired by Suhrawardī's *ḥikmat al-ishrāq* (illuminative wisdom), the theosophers of the school of Isfahan considered genuine knowledge as presential illumination. While Suhrawardī specified the epistemic priority of a mode of immediate cognition and the non-predicative relation between subject and object with his notion of *iḍāfah al-ishrāqīyah* (illuminationist relation), Mīr Dāmād, Mīr Findiriskī, Ṣadr al-dīn Shīrāzī and the other intellectual voices of the school of Isfahan emphasised the intrinsic difficulties of both the theory of knowledge as representation and of that as relation. For them, knowledge was essentially based on the mystical *ittiḥād al-ʿāqil wa al-maʿqūl* (unity of the knower and the known). The theory of *ʿilm al-ḥuḍūrī* explicitly put the ordinary division of epistemology (that is, logic, physics and metaphysics) into the service of mysticism, and an important epistemic distinction differentiates the theory of knowledge by presence not only from peripatetic philosophy, but also from Suhrawardī's theory of illumination (Ziyai 1997:453).

D. The 'juristic-rational' epistemic scheme

In the development of jurisprudence, the traditional juristic positions in general attempted to reconcile the epistemological claims of the 'historical-empirical' scheme with various logocentric categories of knowledge and the core idea of the jurists was that science is useful insofar as it serves as a tool for understanding and implementing the revealed law. While the 'historical-empirical' epistemic scheme asserted that every humanly attainable truth could be found in the revealed text, the rationalistic jurists argued that these truths also could be logically extrapolated from truths that are found in that

[35] In this respect, the mystic Saʿīd al-dīn Faraghānī writes, "This is to say the first level–which is identical with this true Oneness-the knower, knowledge, and known, the agent, receptacle, and act, are all a single thing, without distinction or difference. Then on the second level the entity of the All-merciful Breath becomes entified and manifested from the Unseen of the Unseen" (Quoted in Murata 1992:105).

text. In other words, the domain of epistemic intellectual exercise was limited to the revealed texts not by way of direct and comprehensive acquaintance with it, but by way of developing the necessary skill to extrapolate from it. Similar to the theologians and the philosophers, the jurists developed the latter skill in the form of analogy or syllogism to make judgements over specific issues, which are covered, in the revealed texts. Legal literature adopted an epistemological prologue in the works on *uṣūl al-fiqh* and applied logical methodology to the legal sources, where the process was referred to as *istinbāṭ* (Rosenthal 1970:231).

In contrast to the theologians who adopted a distinctive dialectical methodology concerned with *ḍarūrī* knowledge, the jurists in general defined their deductive method as *muktasab* (acquired) knowledge, which by definition is attained through inference and reasoning. "Unlike necessary knowledge, it does not grip the mind. The fact that it is not immediate, and is obtained only by inferential operations of the mind, renders it subject to falsification and error" (Hallaq 1997:38). In this respect, the jurists followed the 'historic-empirical' epistemic scheme more closely by conceiving an ontological difference between the knowledge as revealed by God in Qur'anic texts, the Prophet's praxis or the community's consensus, and the knowledge which human beings acquire through their own reasoning. The discussion of knowledge as prevalent in jurisprudence furthermore stressed the essential relationship of knowledge with true Islamic faith, of which it considered knowledge to be a fundamental part as the key to the theory as well as to the practice of Islam.

The first major work in the field of Islamic legal methodology, al-Shāfiʿī's *al-Risālah fī uṣul al-fiqh* (Treatise on legal theory), was in fact genuinely occupied with subjects such as what constitutes legal knowledge and how legal knowledge is obtained, explained and justified in order to distinguish the scope of jurisprudence, but as a work on methodology, it was not concerned with questions of legal philosophy *per se*. While inference ultimately was deduced from reason in the elaborated hierarchy of knowledge, contradictions in terms of *raʾy* and *ẓann* (conjecture) was a regrettable practical necessity, since probability, not certainty, was a matter of degree. While the terms *raʾy*, *istiḥsān* (preference) and *qiyās* were initially used more or less synonymously, denoting individual reasoning in a general sense, al-Shāfiʿī rejected the two former, which lacked an agreed-upon conscious method, and replaced them with analogy (Schacht 1971a:1026–1027). As Goldziher (1981:51) elucidates, certainty was embodied not in reason but in *ijmāʿ* in the case of Sunni Islam, as the true possessor of *auctoritas interpretativa* whose relatively collective character safeguarded it from probability.

In Shi'i Islam, legal theory was gradually recognised as a distinctive sphere of learning others after the occultation of the twelfth *imām*, and as a living body of law it developed a distinct technical language in order to assert itself. Within the traditional legal corpus, it signified a body of tradition constituting the normative interpretative application of the revealed sources to the ongoing life of the Shi'i community and the point of departure of any discussion of Islamic law. While reason was projected from the level of the pure intellect to discursive thought and assigned a fundamental role in jurisprudence through the adoption of reasoned argumentation of theology already in the tenth century and logic no longer was peculiar to theology and philosophy, it was only treated in its general sense and not employed as a source of law and as a means of inferring new norms until the thirteenth century (Kazemi Moussavi 1996:1 and 96). The fact that the use of *ijtihād* was initially considered as a sort of *qiyās fāsid* (wrong analogy) was perhaps caused by some outward or terminological similarities, which suggests that the injunctions in Shi'i tradition "which forbade the practice of *qiyās* were also applicable to any other mode of rational analysis" (Modarressi 1984:29).

The first systematic exponent of the Shi'i 'juristic-rational' epistemic scheme, still in its rudimentary form, was Abū ʿAbdullāh al-Mufīd. He criticised the overemphasis on transmitted knowledge in his teacher Ibn Bābūyah's treatment on *ʿaql* and was the first to write an extensive work on legal theory, *al-Taḏkīrah bi-uṣūl al-fiqh* (Discourse in legal theory), something which gives him the credit of formulating the essential position on the subject. While the application of legal reasoning to inference from the revealed sources was known already during the *imāmat*, his teachings nevertheless marked the *sensu stricto* beginning of a determined logocentrism in Shi'i legal thought (Jaʿfariyān 1997:560). While al-Mufīd favoured methods of dialectic reasoning, rather than mere reproduction of *ḥadīṯ* material, he rejected inference by *qiyās* and the use of *ʿaql* was only permitted as an aid to handle contradictory *akhbār* that could not be replaced by rational considerations. His major achievements were in fact in the field of theology (by adopting the *muʿtazilah* doctrines of free will and temporal creation of the Qur'an in accordance with the concept of *ʿadl*, 'divine justice') and not in law, and later Shi'i legal theory owes much to theological epistemological considerations (Modarressi 1984:7).[36] al-Mufīd also formalised *ijmāʿ* as a source of law to imply only the consensus of the *imāms* and restricted the extent of the *imām*'s knowledge in order to promote a

[36] al-Mufīd was the first Shi'i jurist who regularly studied under Sunni as well Shi'i teachers. He is renowned for his discussions with the philosopher Abū Bakr al-Baqillānī and he also studied the rational sciences under *muʿtazilah* teachers in Basra, even if his theology was closer to the old Baghdad *muʿtazilah* school than to the later Basrian system of al-Qāḍī ʿAbd al-Jabbār. He appropriated certain fundamental elements as integral parts of his legal theory. In the field of *furūʿ al-fiqh*, al-Mufīd also set forth his teachings in response to those of al-Shāfiʿī, but less in the same manner as the later developments within Sunni law. As Shi'i law developed in opposition to its Sunni counterpart, it could make use of the latter's terminology and the evolution of Shi'i legal thought cannot be seen in isolation from Islamic law as it developed as a whole (Linant de Bellefonds 1968).

more demonstrative approach (McDermott 1978:125–127). As far as *ʿilm al-ḥadīṯ* is concerned, logic gained an upper hand over transmitted knowledge in the writings of Sayyid al-Murtaḍā ʿAlī b. Ṭāhir, who was a pupil of al-Mufīd and the *muʿtazilah* theologian ʿAbd al-Jabbār. While rational reasoning still had to move within the boundaries of transmitted knowledge, the obligatory standard was set by *ḥadīṯ* that correlated with reason and those *ḥadīṯ* that appeared absurd in the light of reason or were regarded as *al-khabar al-aḥad* (isolated *khabar*) because of their lack of sufficient ways of transmission were censured (Amir-Moezzi 1994:13).

More importantly, Sayyid al-Murtaḍā wrote the first systematic work in the field of legal theory, *Ḍārīʿah ilā uṣūl al-sharīʿah* (Acces to the sources of divine law), where a strict line of demarcation is drawn between *uṣūl al-dīn* and *uṣūl al-fiqh*. While the contribution of Sayyid al-Murtaḍā to the expansion of *furūʿ al-fiqh* has made some modern scholars, such as Abū al-Qāsīm Gurjī (1994:608), presume that *ijtihād al-muṭlaq* was recognised as valid at this stage, Brunschwig (1968:210), Madelung (1980b:26) and other scholars assert that al-Murtaḍā clearly acknowledged that sources and legal decisions had to be based on certainty and that the use of *ijtihād* was limited to questions left open by the revealed sources. In other words, the jurists could only undertake lawfinding and not derive any new legal norms. Due to the strength of the 'historical-empirical' epistemic scheme, the works of al-Mufīd and al-Murtaḍā would not have had definite bearing upon the Shi'i legal tradition unless they were corroborated by Abū Jaʿfar Muḥammad al-Ṭūsī, who is considered to be the founder of the Shi'i *fiqh al-istidlālī* (demonstrative jurisprudence) in the sense that he accommodated law to logical standards in a more independent manner. In seeking a synthesis between revelation and reason, he was decisive in changing the attitudes to *akhbār* by virtue of the application of reasoning to *ʿilm al-ḥadīṯ* (Kazemi Moussavi 1996:25). Significantly, he also enforced a new innovation by establishing the binding nature of *al-khabar al-aḥad*, which certainly was an influence from the *muʿtazilah* that, in contrast to other theological positions, expressed a subtle attitude towards *ḥadīṯ*.

Once the subject matter of the revealed sources stabilised, the competition between reason and revelation came to another prominence in jurisprudence, where also issues of methodology became central. While the legal method of the rudimentary 'juristic-rational' epistemic scheme combined the method of the 'historical-empirical' epistemic scheme with the logocentric categories of theology, reason was firmly established as a source of legal knowledge in the thirteenth century. Formal logic made its entry in legal theory but remained structurally external, in contrast to epistemology that was woven into methodology. In contrast to the earlier Shi'i works on legal theory, which never mentioned *ʿaql* as a source of law, Ibn Idrīs al-Hillī's work was the first instance, where the four sources of the Shi'i law were mentioned in the same order (Halm 1991:68). He was also the first to critically establish and rank, in order of priority, the sources and to determine the modalities of their usage. In this respect, *fiqh* was able to free *ʿilm al-uṣūl* from the clutches of *ʿilm al-kalām* (theology) and its independence was hence no longer relative. Through the composition of major works on legal theory, Shi'i law was substantiated as a well-developed discipline with an independent and systematic structure, which did not rely exclusively on *al-dalīl al-samʿī* (revelational proof).

The most notable Shi'i *ʿālim* of the thirteenth century was Nāṣir al-dīn al-Ṭūsī. While he is more associated with the integration of philosophy into theology and law, he also inspired his pupil *ʿallāmah* al-Ḥasan b. Yusūf b. ʿAlī al-Hillī, to strengthen the rational tendency in law. *ʿAllāmah*, who was the first to bear the name *āyatullāh* (sign of God), introduced new methods for *ḥadīṯ* criticism and incorporated rational elements into the fundamentals of Shi'i law (Halm 1991:68). Defining *ijtihād* as a *farḍ al-kifāyah* (duty to be fulfilled by a limited number of qualified persons), he substantiated and defined *ijtihād* in such a way that by making a distinction between *ẓann* and *raʾy*, *ijtihād* was legitimised on the basis of *ẓann*. As Wilfred Madelung (1982:169) elucidates, Shi'i acceptance of *ijtihād* lay in the general expansion of the legal meaning of that concept in general, which made it clearly discernable from that of *raʾy* and *qiyās* and therefore more receptive to "the traditional preoccupation of Imami thought with the notion of certitude in law".[37] By referring to *ʿilm* as presumptive knowledge derived from the revealed sources, he determined the flexibility and dynamism that was to characterise Shi'i law.

Nevertheless, it was first in the late eighteenth century that the 'juristic-rational' epistemic scheme came to dominate Shi'i legal thought, when the epistemic categories of the 'historical-empirical' epistemic scheme were refuted by Muḥammad Bāqir al-Bihbahānī, who declared that the followers of al-Astarābādī as well as the proponents of theosophy were heretics (i.e.by an act of *tafkīr*). The principles of jurisprudence as articulated by al-Bihbahānī and later modified by Murtaḍā al-Anṣārī has remained the normative Shi'i juristic position to the present time. As the category of *al-ḥukm al-ʿaqlī al-mustaqil* (independent rational norm) was recognised as

37 In fact, the need to limit the use of *raʾy* and *qiyās* in interpreting revelation owed much to the emergence of logocentricity in Shi'i and *muʿtazilah* circles. The individual aspect of legal inference could eliminate *raʾy* completely, but limited its arbitrariness. As far as Sunni Islam is concerned, practical considerations often necessitated a departure from strict analogical reasoning and *raʾy* was validated in the form of *istiḥsān* by Abū al-Hanīfah and *istiṣlāḥ* (consideration of the public interest) by Anas b. Malik. In fact, the two terms *istiḥsān* and *raʾy* were used synonymously at first. In constrast, the limiters of *istiṣlāḥ* (mainly the Shi'i, Shāfiʿīs, and *muʿtazilah*) took the position that law is source based and argued that the universal principles and purposes of *istiṣlāḥ* were given specific legal consideration by *sharīʿat*. Determining the *ratio legis* by means of *istiṣlāḥ* was not, strictly speaking, textual, but was inferred by rational proofs in accordance with the spirit of the law and this is the reason why the terms *istiṣlāḥ* or *maṣlaḥah* were absent in early Islam (Paret 1978).

fully valid, the element of flexibility in jurisprudence was strengthened remarkably. al-Anṣārī, who was regarded by posterity as the first effective *marjaʿ al-taqlīd*, contributed to the development of Shi'i legal theory by systematically revising and reconstructing the methodology of Shi'i law. His most important involvement was in deriving a set of principles to be used in formulating decisions in cases where there was doubt. al-Anṣārī divided legal decisions into four categories by distinguishing valid and non-valid conjecture by specific terms: *qaṭʿ* (certainty), *ẓann muʿtabar* (valid conjecture), *shakk* (doubt) and *wahm* (erroneous conjecture). Since the law could not always be discovered by resorting to the subject matter of the juristic sources, he laid down general principles for such circumstances, namely the *uṣūl ʿamalīyah* (procedural principles). The *uṣūl ʿamalīyah* covered all cases where the real obligation was not known and investigated the legal basis and the scope of validity according to four principles: *barāʾah* (exemption), *iḥtīyāṭ* (prudence), *takhyīr* (option) and *istiṣḥāb* (continuance) (Modarressi 1984:10). As Momen (1985:187) argues, al-Anṣārī adopted rational methodological mechanisms to create highly individual binding legal norms and hence ethical introversion, rather than legal formalisation, became the hallmark of Shi'i logocentricity:

> Whereas previously the mujtahids had restricted themselves to rulings on points where there was probability or certainty of being in accordance with the guidance of the Imams, the rules developed by Anṣārī allowed them to extend the area of their jurisdiction to any matter where there was even a possibility of being in accordance with the Imam's guidance. This effectively meant that they could issue edicts on virtually any subject.

By broadening the sections of *uṣūl al-fiqh* that dealt with the *uṣūl ʿamalīyah*, al-Anṣārī had a lasting impact on the methodology of Shi'i jurisprudence, and among the renowned followers of al-Anṣārīs school were, for instance, Muḥammad Kāẓim al-Khurāsānī, Muḥammad Ḥusain Nāʾinī, ʿAbd al-Karīm Ḥāʾirī Yazdī, Ḥusain Ṭabāṭabāʾī Burūjirdī, Abū al-Qāsīm al-Khuʾī and Rūḥullāh Khumainī. Muḥammad Kāẓim al-Khurāsānī, for instance, advanced legal theory and extended the sources to include any *kull* (general topic) that related to any of its individual problems, which strengthened the tendency to base derivation of legal prescriptions on *ʿaqlī* sources (Murata 1983:734). Other characteristics of the legal literature during the nineteenth century are, on the one hand, as envisaged in the genre of *tauḍīḥ al-masāʾil* (explanation of the problems), that the jurists expressed legal topics in a less technical way and thereby made their contributions more popular, and on the other hand, that they began to use Persian as an instrument in peripheral cases of the formulation of their legal discourse.

From this brief description of the historical expansion of the major traditional Islamic epistemic schemes, it is evident that the 'juristic-rational' epistemic scheme underwent continous differentiation and sought definition in premodern times. While it was continuously challenged by the 'historical-empirical' epistemic scheme, the development of Islamic jurisprudence from the ninth century and onwards can generally be characterised as that of a growing logocentricity through which epistemology, woven into methodology, in general terms was overshadowed by logic. If we, similar to Arent J. Wensinck (1932:248), emphasise the Hellenistic 'nature' of logic in essentialist terms, we would conclude, "Muhammad was overshadowed by Aristotle". Of course, the more solid acquaintance with logic, which came through the translations and offered Islamic theology and philosophy the opportunity to articulate sophisticated ideas of epistemology, was of Greek origin. And as the representative of mainstream Shi'i thought grew aware of the specificity of law, jurisprudence frequently engaged in strong polemics with cognitive rivals in the field of learning and education, with the exception of strict technical disciplines such as mathematics or astronomy. In some cases, versions of theology were even suspicious to the jurists and this is certainly more the case in Sunni law, which considered transmitted knowledge as a historical empirical instrument. This, in contrast to reason, was not considered to be based on unverifiable axiomatic propositions (i.e. the idea that logical arguments are a closed system). According to this view, the Prophet had brought to human beings supreme truth only through revelation, which is transmitted by the Islamic community from generation to generation: History has a beginning and an end in the course of which God gathers people to obedience through his prophets and promises reward for those who obey his law.

Consequently, it is not a coincidence that jurists such as Ibn Taimīyah refuted logic as *zandaqa* (heretical) and no doubt forbidden by the *sharīʿat* (Goldziher 1916:24). al-Ghazālī also subjected the cognitive claims of philosophy to penetrating criticism in his *Tahāfut al-falāsifah* (The Incoherence of the philosophers) and more so in his *al-Munqīḍ min al-dalāl* (Deliverance from error) in his capacity as a mystic. While he gave confidence to the scientific methodology of philosophy, he underlined its limitations when it comes to arriving at certainty of metaphysical truths. Although al-Ghazālī considered philosophy as a deviation from Islamic belief, he (as well as other Sunni jurists) accepted most of the basic principles of logic, since the problem of knowledge was not restricted to transmitted knowledge, but involved a number of epistemic categories elaborated in logic as well as mysticism:

> It is worth noting that some religious scholars, such as Ibn Ḥazm and al-Ghazālī, agree with philosophers that logic is of great value. While these religious scholars do not specifically advocate the idea that logic is necessary for the ultimate human happiness, they still find it useful not only for secular but also for religious studies (Inati 1997:809).

Even Ibn Taimīyah, who rejected the established form of traditional *uṣūl al-fiqh*, similar to Astarābādī, partly derived his epistemology from logic.[38] In this respect, the dichotomy between the intense factualism of the 'historical-empirical' epistemic scheme and the rational orientation of the 'philosophical' scheme remained the enduring tension in Islamic speculation on knowledge, truth and divine guidance in premodern times.

[38] In fact, Ibn Taimīyah's criticism of logic and his position that all universal propositions represent mental generalisations formed on the basis of empirical observation of external particulars (that is, nothing exists outside the realm of the external world and the human mind) was not only opposed to the position of Islamic philosophers, but also to that of the Sufis, the Shi'is and the Sunni theologians. As W.E. Hallaq (1993:xviii) elucidates, Ibn Taimīyah's arguments that the distinction between essential and accidential attributes is relative to the particular individual (i.e. subjected to categorisation according to a particular view) in some respects anticipates the more recent criticism voiced among others by John Locke.

CHAPTER IV

Shi'i legal dogmatics

A. *Uṣūl al-fiqh* (legal theory)

Legal dogmatics is one of the several subtypes of any legal 'system' and consists of the interpretation of canonical texts and the systematisation of legal norms. It is designed to serve as an aid to the correct understanding of the authoritative sources and legal interpretation. In traditional Islam, the *uṣūl al-fiqh*, also called *uṣūl al-sharᶜ*, as a science of source methodology, embodies the study and regulation of the sources of Islamic law, both revealed and auxiliary, by means of *ijtihād*. Since its beginnings it concerned itself with the establishment of principles and precepts that govern the procedure of *ijtihād*. Hence, Islamic law involves not only the written or oral tradition of fixed and established legal canon, but *a priori* certain settled methods to decide what is lawful in all legal and religious matters.[39] The structures of the law, in the form of topics, concepts and rules are, in their turn, set out in the second genre of juristic literature, the *furūᶜ al-fiqh* (applied branches of *fiqh*), a word that Schacht liberally translates as 'positive law' (Schacht 1964:59). As a matter of principle and methodology, *uṣūl al-fiqh* was never severed from *furūᶜ*, as jurisprudence constantly was reinterpreted in order to address the exigencies arising in the realm of positive law.[40]

In the view of Wael B. Hallaq (1997:125), *uṣūl al-fiqh* operates on two levels of discourse: The first level of discourse represents the constant substructure, which was thoroughly bound by the unalterable proposition of the divine command, while the second was the non-constant hermeneutical structure open to interpretation and intellectual manipulation. In Shi'i Islam, the three revealed sources of law comprise the first level of operation. These sources were the foundations of the law and the essentials of a hermeneutic without which no valid legal inference is considered to be possible. In other words, they are the basic data underlying and governing both levels of discourse and permit no amount of intellectual play on the first level.

[39] While George Makdisi (1984) argues that there is evidence that the Sunni *uṣūl al-fiqh*, at least into the tenth century, was also used to designate the principles of substantive legal rules, this use was too restricted to be regarded as a methodology that establishes the Islamic pedigrees of substantial legal rules. Hence, the term can generally be considered as designating a science of source methodology.

[40] The close link between *iftāʾ* ('giving a legal decision') and *ijtihād* is, for instance, evident in the fact that the *muftī* ('magistrate') first had to qualify as a *mujtahid* (Hallaq 1996).

According to Hallaq, what distinguishes constants from non-constants (the second level of discourse) is precisely what separates an *aṣl* from interpreting the *aṣl* (ibid.:126). As an integral methodology for legal development, *uṣūl al-fiqh* provided a set of criteria for the correct hermeneutical evaluation of the legal content of the sources and comprised the very normative repertory of the historical interpretations of the law:

One cannot overstress the multi-faceted nature of *uṣūl al-fiqh* which comprises what is equivalent in Western jurisprudence to legal theory, legal methodology, interpretation, and more importantly in this context, legal philosophy" (Hallaq 1992:184).

While legal theory, in contrast to the discipline of *tafsīr* (*tafsīr al-āyāt al-aḥkām* 'exegesis on the verses of injunctions', included), is primarily concerned with extending the rationale of a given text to cases that do not necessarily fall within the terms of its language, both of these strict hermeneutical disciplines are interested in the historical and biographical aspects and interplay with each other as well as with other disciplines, such as *ʿilm al-ḥadīṯ* and *ʿilm al-rijāl* (the study of transmitters of *ḥadīṯ*). As Hossein Modarressi (1984:7) argues, legal theory, as a theory of legal interpretation, never overlaps with other sciences, but rather borders on them and remains in some sense distant from Qur'anic exegesis, philosophy, theology and linguistics, which inform the latter of the principles of interpretation:

This discipline is a collection of general rules and regulations on how to deduce positive precepts from the sources. Some of these rules and principles have been borrowed from other disciplines such as logic, philosophy, theology and philology.[41]

Many Shi'i authorities on law and *ḥadīṯ*, such as Sayyid al-Murtaḍā, Abū Jaʿfar al-Ṭūsī and Muḥsin Fayḍ al-Kāshānī, were also renowned for their purely exegetical works and characteristically played across the substantive disciplines of Islam (prophetic history, theology, law, mysticism, and so on) and the linguistic ones (orthography, lexicography, syntax, rhetoric) to create highly complex and individual patterns as an intersection of the timeless and time bound. While the subject matter of legal theory was explicitly juristic, the adequate understanding of juristic works had a dualistic character, as it was dependent on other disciplines. In the view of Binyamin Abrahamov, this was so to the extent that an Islamic scholar was considered a *mufassir* ('exegete', 'interpreter') in the more general sense even though he did not

[41] Whether an individual jurist discussed methodological topics in his textual discourse or not, he never pretended that legal hermeneutics could posssibly function without recourse to some presuppositions and assimilated logical or theological elements. Sayyid al-Murtaḍā treated, for instance, legal theory in his *Ḍārīʿah ilā uṣūl al-sharīʿah* (Access to the sources of divine law), under two categories: *mabāḥīṯ al-alfāẓ* (semantics problems) and *adillah ʿaqlīyah* (rational evidences). Under the former category, the literal and metaphorical *mafāhim* (understandings) of some legal expressions in terms of injunctions were included.

write a *tafsīr* in the sense of commenting on the whole of the Qur'an.[42] Those *ʿulamā* who did not write a *tafsīr* in the strict sense were influenced by this genre and have themselves influenced it through the extensive interaction between the hermeneutical disciplines. "Therefore, it is possible to learn the ways of the Qur'an interpretation not only from mufassirun, but also from scholars who, naturally, have used the Qur'an in their writings" (Abrahamov 1996:30).

B. The constant *uṣūl* (sources) of law: The Qur'an, *sunnat* and *ijmāʿ*

In the view of the majority of jurists, the scope of Islamic jurisprudence essentially consists of the sources of *sharīʿat*. The classification of these sources is by no means a decisive or authoritative one. During the lifetime of the Prophet, only the two sources (the Qur'an and the *sunnat*) were recognised and the binding character of the latter was under dispute. In the tenth century, the first time a formalisation of Shi'i legal theory was attempted, only three sources were explicitly mentioned: the Qur'an, the *sunnat* and the *ijmāʿ*. The *ʿaql* and *lisān* (language) were seen as gates to the understanding of these sources (McDermott 1978:284). Islamic legal theory recognised no other categories of sources, such as *ʿurf* (interestingly, a noun from the verb *ʿarafa*, 'to know'), as legal sources *ipso facto*, even if the jurists (in particular of the *hanafī* and *malikī* schools) incorporated custom into *fiqh* by including certain practices in the category of *sunnat* or *ijmāʿ*. In this respect, Shi'i Islam underlined in particular the point that Islam instituted a new judicial normativity separated from the pre-Islamic by introducing the specific binding authority of the *imām* to indicate law and also by tacitly rejecting any *ʿurf* legal pattern that was not expressly ratified by revelation (Coulson 1969:32).

The one concrete image in Islam, the Qur'an, the *verbum Dei*, is the major source of Islamic law, but not *a priori* as a basis of legal speculation. It is the

[42] The *tafsīr* writing was disciplinary according to the classification of the major Islamic disciplines, but drew on conceptual structures of other sciences. There were various categories of Qur'anic exegesis but the two main categories were *tafsīr bi-maʾṯūr* (exegesis strictly based on texts) and *tafsīr bi-maʿqūl wa bi-dirāyah* (exegesis through intellectual reasoning). The latter category, for instance, includes *tafsīr al-lughawī* (linguistic exegesis), *tafsīr āyāt al-aḥkām*, *taʾwīl* (esoteric exegesis), *israʾīliyāt* (exegesis on Jewish subjects), *tafsīr bi-raʾy* (exegesis based on opinion) and *tafsīr al-riwāyah wa al-dirāyah* (exegesis through narration and proof). The early writing of *tafsīr* commented only on a selection of verses from the Qur'an, and a characteristic of the Shi'i exegetical works until al-Ṭūsī and al-Tabarsī was precisely the selective concern with the text of the Qur'an with the commentators paying attention mainly to verses with potential Shi'i allusions (Bar-Asher 1999:73). The pioneering work of Abū Jaʿfar Muḥammad al-Ṭabarī, *Jamīʿ al-bayān fī tafsīr al-qurʿān* (Comprehensive expositions of Qur'anic exegesis), was the first example of a *tafsīr* in its proper sense, which covers every aspect of exegetical investigation.

foundation of Islamic law and its basic norm, which initiates and delimits a new religious, ethical and legal tradition. While the Qur'an achieved pre-eminence as a source of the general principles of law from the earliest times, as Schacht (1950:224) rightly suggests, taken by itself, it can hardly "be called the first and foremost basis of early legal theory". Yet, the legal contents of the Qur'an constitutes the basis of what is called the *fiqh al-qur'ān* (The Qur'anic *juris corpus*), i.e. the close to 500 out of a total 6,219 verses that refer to legal subjects. Apart from these, other norms derived from the Qur'an were introduced into *fiqh* at a secondary stage. Needless to say, the Qur'an is not a law codex despite its absolute normativity since it contains many materials aside from legal. As the second source of Islamic law, the *sunnat* serves as the most important commentary on the Qur'an, which presupposes the Prophet not only as the deliverer of the Qur'an, but moreover as its interpreter. The main function of the *sunnat* is to reiterate and corroborate a norm which originates in the Qur'an, but also to explain and clarify norms on which revelation is silent. As the *sunnat* acquired its paramount role as a source of law at a relatively early stage, its exact wording and the circumstances of its origin became extremely important. The fabrication of *ḥadīṯ* is attested to have begun very early in Islam and the *muḥaddiṯūn* were in unanimous agreement on its extensive occurrence. As far as Shi'i Islam is concerned, the authenticity of a *ḥadīṯ* is guaranteed not by an *isnād* that begins with a *ṣāḥib* (companion) of the Prophet but by its relation to and transmission through the *ahl al-bait* (people of the house):

> Whereas the Sunnis received Tradition as transmitted by the Prophet's companions, Shi'is received it through his Family. In another respect, whereas Sunni legal schools follow the juridical opinions of some jurisconsults of Medina and Iraq, Shi'is follow the opinions of their Imam, who were descendants of the Prophet (Modarresssi 1984:2).

The most salient feature of the early period of Shi'i law was reliance upon oral tradition and its subsequent collection, but while the independent body of Shi'i *akhbār* emerged in the first half of the eight century, approximately at the same time as in Sunni Islam, its compilation in terms of books, was behind Sunni Islam by two centuries or more. The earliest Shi'i writings were in fact 'monographs' that substantiated theological and legal material acclaimed to be the oral sayings of the Prophet and the *imāms*. The number of *uṣūl* from the eighth century was estimated at 400, and was collectively referred to as *al-uṣūl al-arbaʿumīyah* (The four hundred monographs). It was generally claimed that each of these *uṣūl* were compiled by a different person, but as Etan Kohlberg (1987b:131) elucidates, Shi'i sources identify the mention of considerably less than this number. Concurrently, the sayings and sermons of ʿAlī b. Abī Ṭālib, *Nahj al-balāghah* (Mode of eloquence), were compiled nearly three hundred years after his death by Sharīf al-Raḍī. The earliest Shi'i systematic collection of *akhbār* was *al-Kāfī fī ʿilm al-dīn* by al-Kulainī, which was compiled immediately after the occultation of the twelfth *imām*. This work, which came to be acknowledged as the first book included in the Shi'i corpus of *ḥadīṯ*, the so-called *al-Kutub al-arbaʿīyah* (The four books), served as the most important source of Shi'i law after the Qur'an.[43] al-Kulainī arranged his collection, consisting of more than 15000 *akhbār*, by subject and the classification was made according to the levels of *fiqh* (i.e. *uṣūl, furūʿ* etc.). He also wrote several works in the field of *ʿilm al-ḥadīṯ* and *ʿilm al-rijāl*, sciences concerned with how to distinguish the reliability of genuine *akhbār* as well as their transmitters from dubious ones.[44]

While the *sunnat* was specified to be that of the Prophet alone, the living tradition of his family, companions and succeeding generations was relegated to the lower status of *ijmāʿ*. In Shāfiʿī's legal discourse, *ijmāʿ* was considered the fourth source of Sunni law, but not in the meaning of the agreement of a few jurists of a certain locality, as the retrospective majority opinion of all contemporary jurists. In Sunni Islam, the theory of *ijmāʿ*, while far from univalent, is interpreted as the agreement of the qualified jurists in a given generation and such consensus of opinion was deemed infallible. In the view of the majority of Sunni jurists, such a consensus could only be materialised with the agreement of the Shi'i jurists, and Abū al-Hanīfah even extended *ijmāʿ* to all believers. In a sense he thereby validated the Latin principle *vox populi vox Dei* by referring to the famous *ḥadīṯ* "My community will never agree upon an error". As far as consensus was grounds for validating legal propositions, the 'historical-empirical' as well as the 'juristic-rational' epistemic schemes were epistemologies that very much required *ijmāʿ* in various forms. But the idea of an assured *tawātur* (transmission by many authorities) was even present in the 'mystical' epistemic scheme in the form of *silsilah*, which served as a criterion of valid truth in the achievement of knowledge.

In contrast to Sunni Islam, the validity of *ijmāʿ* was a disputed subject among the Shi'i jurists, at least before the *ghaibat* of the twelfth *imām*. The ambiguity of Shi'i standpoints on *ijmāʿ* was due partly to the existence of infallible guidance, but also to the concurrent influence of *muʿtazilah* theology with its tendency to ethics as deontology, which was addressed to

[43] The other three books were b. Babūyah's *Man lā yaḥḍuruʾ al-faqīh* (When no jurist is present), and Abū Jaʿfar al-Ṭūsī's two compilations, *al-Istibṣār fī mā ukhtulīfa fīhī mīn al-akhbār* (The Perspicacious of disputed *akhbār*) and *Tahḏīb al-aḥkām* (Confirmation of decisions).

[44] The *akhbār* reports were classified according to their reliability into one of four major categories: *saḥīḥ* (correct), *ḥasan* (good), *muwaṯṯaq* (trustworthy) and *ḍaīf* (weak). The later *akhbārī* school accepted only the first and the fourth of these classifications. In addition, *ḥadīṯ* was classified as *al-khabar al-mutawātīr* ('sequenced' *khabar*), handed down in several reliable *isnād* or *al-khabar al-aḥad* transmitted through only one *sanad*. There were also two additional categories for a weak *akhbār*: *mursal* ('having no chain of transmission at all') and *muʿallaq* (missing a link in the chain) (Modarressi 1991:553).

individual convictions rather than those of the community. The fact that the subject of *ijmāʿ* was widely discussed by Shi'i jurists suggests that these scholarly views holding which hold it was refuted by Shi'i law clearly overstate the case. As Norman Calder (1980:188–190) elucidates, while the validity of *ijmāʿ* was for centuries rejected by Shi'i jurists *per se*, it was recognised as *ḥujjat* (proof) in order to establish the preservation of *samʿīyāt*. As the majority of Shi'i jurists supposed that only a *maʿṣūm* could be *ḥāfiẓ* (keeper) of the revealed law, the doctrinal justification rested on the presence of the *imām* and the notion that *sharīʿat* could not be preserved by the community. Consensus was limited to the *imāms*, but there are frequent references in Shi'i sources to the *ijmāʿ al-ʿiṣābah* (consensus of the learned body) or *ijmāʿ manqūl* (precedent consensus), that is, the consensus of the reporters themselves (ibid.:53). The jurists also established *ijmāʿ* on the ground of *tasharruf* (meeting the *imām* directly), which in their view was considered epistemologically certain, as the *imām* was in occultation. The notion of *ijmāʿ al-ʿiṣābah* was also substituted by *istiṣḥāb* (presumption of continuity) by Abū Jaʿfar al-Ṭūsī, who based his innovative argument on the *ʿamal al-ṭāʾifah* (the practice of the righteous sect).[45]

C. The non-constant *aṣl* (source) of law: *ʿaql* (reason)

It is a common human phenomenon that transmitted tradition and reason may oppose each other, as tradition, especially in the form of divine and revealed authority, causes continuity, while reason causes change. The problem of the relationship between reason and law has two different meanings, depending on whether the first or the second of the two terms is considered to be the most important one. In traditional Islamic law the accent is on the second term, as revealed in the concept *istinbāṭ al-fiqh* (juristic reasoning). Human reason is not considered to create law but functions only as the means by which the legal norms are discovered or constructed: "...[H]uman reasoning is a necessary tool for the interpretation of revelation, for the development of a methodology of norm construction and for the application of these norms to concrete cases" (Johansen 1998:39). In other words, Islamic legal theory considers reason to be a humanly fallible but necessary instrument for the implementation of the legal norms.

Reason is meant in a weak sense, as argumentation and calculation, but nevertheless involves the systematisation and expanding of irrational data by means of reasoning. The mere existence of the terms *ʿillah* (underlying reason) and *qiyās* is evidence for the belief in the basic 'rationalism' of law

[45] In particular the representatives of the 'historical-empirical' epistemic scheme relied on *istiṣḥāb* and determined rules on its basis in almost all instances where the 'juristic-rational' epistemic scheme applied *ijtihād* (ʿArablū 1983:35–38).

and the interest of the epistemological and ontological status of the *ratio legis* itself. While reason is used to discover law, the probative value of analogy is generally discarded as not supported by reason. In the sense that the methodology and procedures of law-finding is regulated by logic, without a belief in the existence of 'rational' law (founded on the command of the sovereign), the 'juristic-rational' epistemic scheme developed a "semi-rationalisation" of law. The fact that Islamic law is based on revelation and that casuistry did not lead to logical highly developed abstract propositions, made Schacht (1964:202–203), using the Weberian classification, reject *fiqh* as both substantially and procedurally irrational. But Schacht's classification of Islamic law seems to miss the point. Although *fiqh* has a certain formal irrationality by the fact that law was found beyond the control of reason as it by definition was of divine source, legal theory was generally characterised by the innovative substantive use of reason in the process of law-finding. In his study on the sphere of Sunni contract law, John Makdisi (1985a) argues that the Islamic jurists were seriously concerned with achieving a "structure" of internally consistent norms to govern new situations. Makdisi (1985b:89) also claims that legal syllogism is determined by a number of competing variables which were taken into account and therefore it does not strictly represent a case of absolute syllogism:

> If one accepts the notion that legal reasoning is the syllogistic interpretation of precedent and that premises must be shaped as much as the conclusion, the process may nevertheless be identified as rational.

Shi'i Islam adopted the rationalistic principle in the formulation of legal theory from the *muʿtazilah* theology. Reason was thereby recognised as a fundamental principle of Shi'i law, the fourth *aṣl* in place of *qiyās* of the Shāfiʿī system, after the Qur'an, *sunnat* and *ijmāʿ*. In contrast to Sunni law, which was concerned with law simply as the product of God's command, Shi'i legal theory tended to allow reason a wide field as it acknowledged reason to be in full harmony with divine commands. The formalisation of Shi'i legal theory was to a large extent the acclimatisation of logic, where the position of faith *in* reason, rather than the polarisation faith *and* reason came to triumph. While the relevance of the *muʿtazilah* tenet that the human mind is capable of distinguishing between good and evil went in diametrical opposition to Sunni jurisprudence, it was embraced in the Shi'i 'juristic-rational' epistemic scheme in which the unifying role of reason and law held the conviction that God supplies the model for man's mind. The Shi'i approach to knowledge, albeit not sceptical, never wholly restricted faith to ultimate matters, that is, to the fundamental principles beyond which one may only penetrate through contemplation. However, the legal subject matter was at the very outset disposed against any *Weltanschauung* that contravened the premise of law squarely grounded in divine deontology.

The word *ʿaql* is absent in the Qur'an, only occurring in the simple form *ʿaqala* ('to perceive'), but was used from earliest times as a capital aspect of the Shi'i teachings in connection to *ʿilm al-bāṭin* (esoteric science). The word had cosmogonic, ethical-epistemological, spiritual and soteriological dimensions denoting the innate faculty of transcendent knowledge (Amir-Moezzi 1994:6–13). In the view of Amir-Moezzi (ibid.:62), the *imāms* were in fact critical of the theological use of the word and considered the purely speculative theological dialectic as unable to grant knowledge of God. He maintains, for instance, that they used the term *ʿilm al-tauḥīd* (science of unity) rather than *ʿilm al-kalām* for the word theology.[46] Hossein Modarressi disagrees with his view and argues that the same material i.e. the early *ḥadīṯ* collections, verify that the *imāms* praised and encouraged the theologians of their times. Modarressi (1984:25) also asserts that some of the companions of the *imāms*, such as Hishām b. al-Ḥakam and Abū Ḥasan b. Aʿyān Zarūrah, were eminent theologians although the Shi'i rational trend was restricted due to the dominance of esoteric *ghulāt* doctrines and empirically transmitted knowledge. "On some occasions, the Imams themselves followed what they advised as the correct method of reasoning and thus instructed their followers on the proper procedure for inference of legal precepts".

While Shi'i jurists of the 'juristic-rational' epistemic scheme were *per se* against the Sunni character of *muʿtazilah* theology, they 'rationalised' *ʿaql* by projecting it from what Amir-Moezzi (1994:12) defines as 'hiero-intelligence' (lat. *intellectus*) to discursive human reasoning (lat. *ratio*). In the Shi'i legal definition, reason was distinctly *muktasab* (acquired) and equated to *naẓar* based on *dalīl* (proof), but as M.J. McDermott (1978:67) also asserts, it was never divorced from *badīhī* (intuitive) and *ḍarūrī* (necessary) knowledge or from revelation. Whereas early Shi'i Islam did not accept the idea that good and evil are discernible by human reason by postulating the *imām* as the source of *ʿilm yaqīn* (certain knowledge), the 'juristic-rational' epistemic scheme developed the principle of *qaʿidāt al-mulāzamah* (rules of correlation), which stated that *kull mā ḥakama bi-l-ʿaql ḥakama bi-l-sharʿ* ('whatever is ordered by reason, is also ordered by law') to signify the capacity of human reason in understanding the ethical quality of law (Modarressi 1984:4). As Abdulaziz Sachedina (1988:7) elucidates, Shi'i logocentricity endorsed *ijtihād* to establish the intrinsicality of a norm derived from the revealed sources "that derived from the authority of reasoning because the point is that rational ruling is intrinsic in revelation ruling (not additional to it)". As Modarressi and Bernard Weiss claim, the exact philosophical usage of *ʿaql* in Shi'i law is hence not to be confused with 'rationality' as such. Modarressi (1984:3–4) writes: "By 'reason' as a

[46] *ʿAql*, the faculty through which fundamental truths are intuitively apprehended, is different in its definition as well as its implications from its definition in Islamic theology and philosophy, where it denoted as a source of knowledge and as such being the antithesis of *naql* (written source) (Chittick 1987:195).

source for Shi'i law is meant categorical judgements drawn from both pure and practical reason. A clear instance is the judgement of practical reason that justice is good and injustice is evil".[47] Weiss (1987:212) also explains that there was not a question of real analogical deduction *from* the text, but rather a simple declaration of what was found *in* the text. While Shi'i law came to terms with scientific method and modes of thought, it is essential to stress that *ʿaql* as an abstract substance, unlike the other concrete sources of law, was never comprehensively defined by the jurists.

The jurists of the 'legal-rational' epistemic scheme were inclined to reject analogy in the process of *istinbāṭ*, but considered it as valid through the recourse of *ijtihād* and *ʿaql* rather than *qiyās per se*. They instead called *qiyās* by other various names, such as *mafhūm al-muwāfaqah* (obvious meaning), *faḥwaʿ al-khiṭāb* (implied meaning of a communication) or *manṭūq al-kalām* ('import of speech'), and so on. (Hasan 1986:416). As Shi'i Islam showed a corresponding complexity in the application of other types of rational arguments than *qiyās*, Modarressi (1991:549–50) argues that the mode of analysis adopted by the Shi'i jurists bore no connection with the Sunni definition of the latter. "The Shi'ites argue that *qiyas* discovers a probable rationale, not a definite one, and that mere human presumption cannot derive the law of God". Reason was, so to say, used at arriving at a *qaṭʿī* (decisive) judgement through Aristotelian syllogism ('thinking together') rather than deductive analogy, and denoted an *a fortiori* mediate argument.[48] The Shi'i standard of discursive thought was hence the syllogism, a model of thought, which catches the successive nature of thought, i.e. the fact that it is necessary to proceed through a series of premises in order to reach a conclusion.

Corresponding to the Aristotelian syllogism, the Shi'i logocentrism also rejected *sharṭī* (conditional) syllogism and induction as proofs, since these methods suggest that the conclusion was not *implied* in the premises from the beginning. As M. G. Carter argues, the very distinction between the

47 In his critical review of Sachedina's book on juristic authority in Shi'i Islam, Modarressi (1991) claims that the former confuses the exact philosophical usage in Shi'ite law with 'reasoning'.

48 A mediate argument is an argument of universal character in which an inference is drawn about the relation between two terms from two premises that state the relation of each of the two terms to the same third term. For instance, 'The morning star is Venus; the evening star is Venus; therefore the evening star is the morning star or *vice versa*.' It is also usual to say that syllogism is deductive reasoning and requires the application of a general premiss to relevant cases. For example, 'All planets move in elliptical orbits; Venus is a planet; therefore Venus moves in an elliptical orbit.' But as far as both syllogism and formal analogy (as distinct from functional and semantic) is confined to quantitative relationships and exclude the qualitative (similarities must be weighed and not merely counted) or those of particular character ('Some planets...), they seem very difficult to distinguish from each other. Nevertheless, both the Shi'i and Sunni legal reasoning were dependent on a precedent source, and reason was in that sense a *dalīl muqayyad* (relative proof). In the case of of Shāfiʿī, he limited the use of *ijtihād* to *qiyās manṣūṣ al-ʿillah* (analogy whose effective cause is indicated in the precedent *naṣṣ*), and he also explicitly rejected analogy not based on a precedent (Khadduri 1987:32).

obliging force of purely rational arguments and analogy is that the conclusion of the latter refrains from establishing any essential relations, in contrast to the former, which is not innovative of necessity but proved as universal and affirmative:

Briefly, analogy is a technique for infinitely extending a finite corpus of data to meet new circumstances, while syllogism authenticates the rationality of that technique without itself creating a new law or linguistic usage… (Carter 1997:104).

The 'semi-rationalisation' of Shi'i as well as Sunni legal theory was in all cases based on Aristotelian foundations, the same foundations as the intellectual life of Western Christianity, as distinct from the foundations of Indian or Chinese thought. In fact, by stressing the comparative and exclusive character of the Shi'i as well as Sunni definitions of legal reason, Mohammad Hashim Kamali (1991:220) rejects Modarresi's and Weiss' view and argues that differing opinions on *qiyās* transcended sectarian divisions:

But the Uṣūlī branch of the Shi'ah validate action upon certain varieties of *qiyās*, namely *qiyas* whose *ʿillah* is explicitly stated in the text (*qiyās manṣūṣ al-ʿillah*), analogy of the superior (*qiyās al-awlā*) and obvious analogy (*qiyās jālī*). The Shi'i varieties of *qiyās*, in the view of the Uṣūlīs, are not mere speculations; they either fall within the meaning of the text or else constitute a strong probability (*al-ẓann al-qawī*) which may be adopted as a guide for conduct.[49]

Although syllogism and analogy were clearly differentiated both historically and qualitatively, Kamali's position may very well be correct, since *qiyās*, as a relative term, referred both to the pure Aristotelian syllogism as well as to legal analogy. As Wael B. Hallaq (1997:105) illuminates, its definition and structure varied from one jurist to another, and deduction and categorical syllogism were almost epistemologically equivalent, used side by side by in one logical operation. "Even many of those who stood on the periphery of, or outside Sunnism, and who rejected *qiyās* on principle, admitted that perspicuous *qiyās* (*al-qiyās al-jālī*) and linguistic inferences (e.g., uttering 'fie' before parents) represents two forms of authoritative and valid *qiyās*". The Shi'i and Sunni jurists were in fact internally split on the matter. While Sayyid al-Murtaḍā considered *qiyās mansūs al-ʿillah* as *mardūd* (dubious), it was accepted as a valid proof by Najm al-dīn Muḥammad Qāsim al-Hillī, *ʿallāmah* al-Hillī and the *uṣūlī* tradition after them (ʿArablū 1983:145). The fact that the jurists of the 'juristic-rational' epistemic scheme definitely adopted the term *qiyās* as such is also evident in the writings of the nineteenth century jurist Mīrzā Muḥammad Ḥasan Nāʾinī, who in his

[49] Shi'i jurists gradually accepted these latter types of *qiyās* from the fourteenth century onwards, as evident in a short monograph by Nūr al-dīn ʿAlī al-Karakī (1985:47), *Ṭārīq istinbāṭ al-aḥkām* (Method of derivation of the norms), which validated the kind of analogy based on an expressly indicated *ʿillah*, such as is the case with *qiyās manṣūṣ al-ʿillah*.

discussion on *istinbāṭ* in relation to *istidlāl muyassar* (practicable demonstration) distinguishes between different levels of the process of *qiyās* (Yaʿqūbī 1997:92). All Shi'i jurists nevertheless rejected the kind of *qiyās* called *mustanbīt al-ʿillah*, which was accepted in some Sunni legal theories, since the *ratio decidendi* and common factor between two similar matters was not clear or it was difficult to distinguish.[50]

D. *Ijtihād* and *taqlīd*

During the first Islamic centuries, the word *ijtihād*, derived from the Arabic verb *ijtihada* (to exert oneself), was not yet elaborated into legal theory, but was closely associated with *raʾy* and *qiyās*. In general usage, it signified the utmost effort expended in a certain activity, and in its technical legal connotation it denoted "the thorough exertion of the *faqīh*'s mental faculty in finding a solution for a case" (Hallaq 1995:178). For reasons explained in the previous chapters, early Shi'i legal theory considered *ijtihād* as dubious, since it implied reaching a norm which is only probable. The first Shi'i jurist generally acclaimed to have adopted the *ijtihād* in its strict and absolute juristic sense was *ʿallāmah* al-Hillī (Kazemi-Moussavi 1990:21). Whereas his predecessors had contented themselves with making use of the semantic characteristics of the sources, for him *ijtihād* provided a theoretical corroboration for the notion that the jurist by use of *ʿaql* is capable of inferring valid norms from the revealed sources even in matters of belief. In his view, the more definitive meaning of *ijtihād* was hence "exerting oneself to the utmost of one's ability in order to accomplish a difficult action" (Cooper 1988:241). The *ʿallāmah* sketched the principles of *ijtihād* in a chapter in his major work *Mabādīʾ al-wuṣūl ilā ʿilm al-uṣūl* (Points of departure from which knowledge of the principles is attained), where accordingly, the *mujtahid* (literally 'he who exerts himself') as the spokesman of the hidden *imām* exerts *ijtihād* in an absolute sense, that is, directly from the sources of the law.

The fact that Juan R. Cole and others reject the relatively more receptive character of Shi'i jurisprudence in relation to its Sunni counterpart seems therefore to be based on a miscomprehension of the contribution of the *ʿallāmah*. Cole (1983:36) argues that the Shi'i notion of *ijtihād* was theoretically far more restricted than that of the Sunnis, since it disallowed for any kind of probability. "The door of ijtihad may not have been closed among the Shi'is, but the 'ijtihad' they were allowed to practice was a far more narrow procedure than even the relative ijtihad of the later Sunnis". As

[50] The Arabic term *ʿillah* is ultimately derived from the Syriac with the etymological meaning 'defect' or 'weak', a meaning still current in Arabic phonology, where it is not yet confused with *ʿillah* in the sense of 'cause' (Carter 1997:107).

Abu al-Fadl Ezzati (1976:89) elucidates, many Shi'i jurists (including the *ʿallāmah*) adopted the definition of *ijtihād* as the exertion of one's self to form a *ẓann* (probable) rule, even if many others interpreted it in far more limited terms as the capacity of inferring valid definite legal norms from the revealed sources. The general linguistic expansion of the term *ijtihād* nevertheless drew Shi'i jurisprudence closer to Sunni law, even if the latter may have closed the door of *ijtihād muṭlaq* (absolute *ijtihād*) in the tenth century by means of *ijmāʿ*, only permitting the *ijtihād al-muqayyad* (relative *ijtihād*) of the jurist *fī al-maḏhab* (within the legal school) and *fī al-masāʾil* (on specific issues).

The common view in Orientalist scholarship that Shi'i Islam accepts *ijtihād*, while Sunni Islam rejects it, has its roots in the conception that the latter closed the gate to *ijtihād* in the ninth century (Strothmann 1926). Recently, the established view of Schacht (1964:70–71) that the mention of the *ʿinsidād bāb al-ijtihād* (closure of the gate to *ijtihād*) in the Sunni juristic literature indicates that legal theory was confined to explanation of the founders of the Sunni *maḏāhib*, after the ninth century, has been challenged. Even if Schacht acknowledges that the legal activity of later jurists was no less creative, Montgomery Watt (1974) claims that no such agreement ever took place and that *ijtihād* was considered as legitimate throughout Islamic history. Hallaq (1986) also argues that a close reading of the traditional Sunni sources reveals that the *bāb al-ijtihād* was never closed either in theory or in practice, since *ijtihād* was considered to be an indispensable ingredient in law. He also demonstrates that some individual jurists, such as Muḥammad al-Juwainī, worked beyond the limits of *ijtihād fī al-maḏhab* as far as he set up an independent legal position that exceeded Shāfiʿī's legal theory. A number of scholars have come to the defence of Schacht, either explicitly or implicitly, by demonstrating that the Islamic tradition speaks about several grades of *ijtihād*, and that the highest grade indeed becomes extinct (Anderson 1976, Coulson 1997:81, Gibb 1963:104, Jackson 1996). As Schacht himself does not even recognise any grading of *ijtihād*, this is probably too generous a treatment of him. To summarise, the development of Sunni law after the tenth century was in short not a radical eradication of former explanations, but rather "the juxtaposition of different solutions to one and the same problem" (Johansen 1998:447).

As far as Shi'i Islam is concerned, the concept of *taqlīd* was an outgrowth of the application of legal theory and denoted the individual choice of juristic authority, unlike Sunni Islam, which after al-Shāfiʿī defined the *taqlīd* as that of all believers to the founder of a *maḏhab* (Calder 1998:138) The word appeared in its rudimentary form very early, but was introduced in its technical sense in the thirteenth century, while there was still no consensus on its meaning among the jurists. Whereas numerous *akhbār* required the *ʿammī* (individual believers) to refer to the *ʿulamā* in order to obtain guidance in *sharīʿat*, it is significant that the term *taqlīd* only appeared in one *ḥadīṯ mursal* (report lacking a chain of transmission). The procedure of *taqlīd* was validated by rational proofs and was first brought forward as an initial subject in a juristic manual by Sayyid Muḥammad Kāẓim Yazdī in the nineteenth century (Kazemi-Moussavi 1996:3). In contrast to the 'historical-empirical' epistemic scheme that forbade *taqlīd* of anyone not *maʿṣum*, the 'juristic-rational' epistemic scheme contended that a *mujtahid* was required to have recourse to *ijtihād* when the *sharīʿat* gave no unequivocal *dalīl qaṭʿī* (definite proof).

Whereas Islam recognises no strict clergy in the Christian sense of a body of persons specially ordained to perform sacraments, the Shi'i evolution of *ijtihād de facto* came very close to that, since it gave religious validity to the daily practices of the individual believers. But the terms priesthood and clergy are inappropriate since they imply the act of consecration to perform a 'sacerdotal' function. The main body of Shi'i *ʿulamā* provided a loosely non-formalised structure and consisted of regular *mujtahid*s who were recognised as such by virtue of the special *ijāzah* (licence) they received from their teachers. Below them were the lowest rank of the general religious class called *mullāh* or *rūḥānī*.[51] According to *ʿallāmah* al-Hillī, the *mujtahid* was primarily obliged to have knowledge of the Arabic language, rhetoric, lexicography and semantics, but also to know those *akhbār* and *ḥadīṯ* that indicate the rules of the law, at least by reference to revealed sources and the *aḥwāl al-rijāl* (biographies of the transmitters). More specifically, the *mujtahid* was expected to have a full grasp of the legal contents, the *ayāt al-aḥkām* (verses on injunctions) of the Qur'an, including knowledge of the related *tafsīr āyāt al-aḥkām*, and in addition also know where the *ijmāʿ* occurs and what material of the Qur'an is abrogated and recognise what is *muṭlaq* (absolute) and *muqayyad* (relative, i.e. contextually restricted) (Cole 1988:241).

During the nineteenth century there was a major shift within Shi'i law as the concept of the *marjaʿ al-taqlīd* came to be institutionalised in the position of the supreme jurist and a voluntary tax, the *sahm al-imām* (share of the *imām*), was introduced to strengthen the socio-economical autonomy of the *ʿulamā*. The concept of *taqlīd* and the idea of recourse to authority (from the Arabic *rajaʿa*, hence *marjaʿ*) was always a part of the theory of *ijtihād*, as the Shi'i jurists rejected *taqlīd al-mayit* (the imitation of a dead man) and advocated that each generation was in need of a *mujtahid* as a *farḍ kifāyah* (collective obligation). But the first jurist to be recognised as *marjaʿ al-taqlīd* was the nineteenth century jurist Muḥammad Ḥasan al-Najafī, who was also the first to contemplate the *niyābat al-ʿamm* as the collective

[51] As Cole (1983:46) argues, the key-notes in the non-formalised scale of Shi'i learning and prestige were charisma, compromise and negotiation, rather than formally derived power and strict hierarchy. "The Shi'i religious institution thus attained an ability to alternate between a Roman Catholic-type model wherein there was one supreme, recognized authority, and a more Eastern Orthodox model, wherein there were several almost coequal leaders".

function of the jurists. His successor, Murtaḍā al-Anṣārī, elaborated the juristic authority of the jurists on behalf of the hidden *imām* and argued explicitly for the necessity of following the opinion of a *mujtahid* in matters of law. He even regarded it as impermissible to transfer the loyalty from one *mujtahid* to another except on the grounds that the second was more *aʿlamīyat* (superior in learning). If two *mujtahids* were to be found equal in this respect, the individual believer could choose either one of them according to their *taqwā* (piety) and *iḥtiyāṭ* (prudence). With al-Anṣārī, the Shi'i *ʿulamā* established an informal structure of authority presided over by a single or multiple *marjaʿ al-taqlīd al-aʿlā* (supreme model of emulation), where in reality the jurist was in an intermediary position between God and the individual believer, something that created theoretical obstacles because of the inescapable presence of the hidden *imām* who alone personified all supreme authority (Arjomand 1981:52).

E. *Ḥauzah-yi ʿilmīyah* ('Precinct of knowledge')

For centuries Islamic law was taught in mosques, mosque-inn complexs and private homes. The first *madrasah* (school) with established curricula was al-Azhar in Cairo, which was set up by the *ismāʿīlī* Fāṭimīd dynasty in the ninth century. Large schools were established in different parts of the Muslim world and with time they multiplied. As travel in pursuit of *ḥadīṯ* material was crucial to the development of the *madrasah* as a separate institution, the Islamic schools came into being essentially as a centre for legal studies with the objective to strengthen individual *maḏāhib* (schools). As Makdisi (1981:10) elucidates, the term *madrasah* was related both etymologically and semantically to the word *darasa*, which has the technical meaning 'to study jurisprudence'. While the curriculum varied and there were ancillary disciplines and various means of secular and private education, most educated members of Islamic society had concepts of law as their primary currency of cultural exchange (Makdisi 1980). The Shi'i *madrasah* in Najaf was founded shortly after the establishment of the al-Azhar in Cairo, but it seems that no significant educational contacts were established between the *ismāʿīlī* and other Shi'i centres of learning.

With the establishment of the Ṣafawīd dynasty, a number of Shi'i schools were founded in major Iranian cities to rival those of the *ʿatabāt* (thresholds) in Najaf and Karbala. In Iran, the *madrasah* had the shape of autonomous private organisations, loosely associated with one another through the informal network of *ʿulamā* relations and was called *ḥauzah-yi ʿilmīyah*. The *ḥauzah* consisted of libraries, at least one hall for general lectures and a number of *ḥujrah*s (chamber) in which most of the *ṭullāb* (students) resided. Each *mudarris* (teacher) had his seminary, which was normally set up directly by the *mujtahid.* From its beginnings, the Islamic intellectual activity was based on fluctuation in the sense that the places of education varied as particular *ʿulamā* were present. In educational terms, the *ḥauzah* was an informal school and had no hierarchial and organised program of specialised degrees and a graded curriculum equivalent to that of a modern university. It was rather the preserve of the teacher and the relationship between him and the students was intensively personal, since the former not only was supposed to communicate learning but also religious insight. Since Islamic law developed due to the initiative of individual jurists, it resisted professionalisation of the legal process during the overwhelming part of its existence. The schools of Islamic law were not formal educational systems or officially sanctioned law-making bodies, but were rather groups of jurists each following a certain 'guild school of law'.

The *ḥauzah* was primarily expected to give a basic education in *sharīʿat,* something that rendered momentous epistemic strength to the nomocentricity of Islamic thought. The courses of study corresponded to the *trivium* of the liberal arts and included *fiqh, manṭiq, tafsīr, ʿilm al-balāghah* (rhetoric), *adab* (literature and 'belles-lettres'), *ʿilm al-tārikh, tajwīd* (cantillation), higher grammar and so forth. Among other subjects were *ʿirfān, akhlāq,* medicine and agronomy (Stanton 1990). Characteristic of the Shi'i *ḥauzah* was the persistence of a creative theosophical tradition that reached its culmination in the intellectual voices of the 'school of Isfahan' in the seventeenth century. The Shi'i *trivium* consisted of three levels: *al-muqaddamāt* (the preliminary), *al-sutūḥ* (the externals) and *dars al-khārij* (graduation classes). Characteristic of the last level was that there where no set texts, but that the student referred to whichever texts he needed to follow up lectures and write a *risālah* (treatise). The culmination of the education was the receipt of an *ijāzah* from a *mujtahid* to exercise *ijtihād,* and then to be recognised as a *mujtahid* to get a following. This procedure was very informal, and there were examples of *mujtahid muḥtaṭ* (*mujtahid* in abeyance), which were not recognised as such by others. Females educated in the legal disciplines were entitled the rank of *mujtahid* on very rare occasions, and disagreement existed on the attribution of the title *mujtahid* to female *ʿulamā* (Calmard 1993:223). The Shi'i jurist had hence the potential of becoming a very integrated and self-contained figure, educated in the *ʿulūm naqlīyah* as well as the *ʿulūm ʿaqlīyah.*

F. Hermeneutical principles

The *ʿulamā* approach and interpret the Qur'an from multiple angles; theological, legal, philosophical and mystical. They work linguistically and historically, pondering over the words of the Qur'an and their construction according to the requirements of the Arabic language and in the setting of specific contexts. The hermeneutical principles constitute the prerequisite for human reasoning, since inference of legal norms presupposes knowledge in textual interpretation, which always requires verification. In developing legal theory, the jurists initially borrowed various instruments necessary for the hermeneutical task from other disciplines, such as *tafsīr*, but also developed others on their own. As traditional Islamic legal dogmatics never attempted to create alternative hermeneutical possibilities, it remained true to its basic immutable tenets. Traditional hermeneutics knew nothing of modern textual linguistics and interpretative theory, but rather perceived the Qur'an as a given entity. Its immediate context was not essentially an externally critical hermeneutics, as it took for granted a certain sacred tradition of normative reading, where discourse was not concerned with its own historicity. To some extent this explains the jurists' lack of interest in questions of philosophical hermeneutics for the understanding of revelation *itself*:

> To any Westerner conversant with post-Hegelian theology, the most striking thing about Shi'ite theological debate surely must be the refusal to deal with theological discourse as itself a social and linguistic phenomenon in a wider sense than the rhetoric and hermeneutics internal to Islamic belief (Fischer 1980b:69).

The criticism of the jurists was by no means modern as far as their epistemological scheme is concerned. It did, however, include abstract rational criticism of each source in sequence and of the answers hazarded to several questions as well as a 'historical' criticism of sources and the 'philological' and 'literary' criticism of the meanings of words and phrases. The intellectual creativity and innovation of the jurist was, in other words, restricted to his given cognitive structure, since he could never stand completely outside the system in which he put forth his work. While some extra-revelational subjects were marked as questionable or *tawassulī* (things that should be explored) in order to be accurately understood in the traditional discourses of *fiqh*, the key principles remained *taʿabuddī* (things that should be done and not criticised) and explicable only through established procedures (ibid.:76).

Whereas Islamic scholars never worked purely descriptively or used a 'historical-critical' discussion of revealed texts, there was a discussion on the creation of revelation and its historical context from earliest times. Besides these theological issues, they specialised in the study of history and genealogy in the realm of *ʿilm al-ḥadīṯ* as a means of verifying authenticity of the *isnād*. In Qur'anic exegesis proper, the explanation of the literal aspects of revelation was connected to the decisive subject of *asbāb al-nuzūl* (occasions of revelation), which consisted of the clarification of the historical circumstances of "its coming to be". The word *nuzūl*, which is derived from the same Arabic root as *tanzīl* (to descend), does not appear in the Qur'an, but the concept of 'coming down' and 'sending down' was vital for the correct understanding of the hermeneutics of God's speaking to man (Wild 1996). Textual meaning was, in other words, established by facts of the occasions of revelation, without which the text was considered unintelligible to the human mind. Interestingly enough, the specific cases of *asbāb al-nuzūl* were never arranged in light of the general socio-historical background, despite the vast records in the books of *ḥadīṯ*, *sīrah* (biographies of the Prophet) and *maghāzī* (raids), but rather assessed in "gratuitous chronology" (Wansbrough 1978:11). In the sense that the historical approach of the *ʿulamā* was an internal one, it also excluded outside influences on the Islamic tradition and for the historian, their approach is clearly an ahistorical one. The traditional notion of Islamic law clearly lacked the dimension of historical depth in the sense that Islamic legal philosophy essentially was the theoretical elaboration of *sharīʿat*. While Canon lawyers of medieval Christianity engaged in the study of *utriusque ius*, of Roman as well as their own law, the Islamic jurists mostly acted in the ivory tower of their own tradition. The absence of comparative methods is often felt in their reasoning and gives it a theoretical, scholastic direction. In constrast to the Church, which was influenced by Roman law and Germanic custom, the Islamic jurists were rarely drawn away by new ideas, alien to their own tradition.

However, the subject of *asbāb al-nuzūl* presupposed a thorough knowledge of the linguistic conventions prevalent among the Arabs during the time of revelation. Hermeneutics involved the field of *ʿilm al-lughah* (semantics) where the text, the *lafẓ* (uttered word), rather than rational arguments was the instrument of manifestation of meaning. "The comprehensive textual basis of law demanded the articulation of a linguistic typology, a science of legal language proper" (Hallaq 1997:37). The divine meaning was considered transferred from the *ab initio* hidden in the manifest through the *lafẓ*. The domain of language was important for the jurists in attempting to find the solution to a hitherto unsolved legal case, since textual material constituted the ultimate frame of reference:

> His task begins with a search for a text that appears to be most relevant for the case at hand. Such relevance is determined by a multi-layered process in which the text is subjected to linguistic analysis. On the most general level, this analysis is of two types, one that relates to the identification of words, the other to the meaning or the semantic force of these words once they have been identified. While the latter belongs to legal reasoning associated with *qiyās*– a later stage in legal construction– the former appertains to linguistic interpretation *par excellence* (ibid.:42).

Knowledge of the semantic rules of hermeneutics was essential to a proper understanding of legal texts and in acquiring more than a superficial knowledge of the revealed sources, since the aim of semantics was to reduce the margins of individual arbitrariness (Weiss 1990:63). The Islamic interpreters were accustomed to the idea that the Qur'an has several meanings and these meanings overlap. They considered the task of interpretation to be the extraction of true meaning, since the surface meaning was not necessarily identical to the deeper, 'true' meaning. Revelation itself makes clear that its contents are divided into two kinds of verses:

He it is Who hath revealed to thee (Muhammad) the Scripture wherein are clear revelations [*muḥkamāt*]– They are the substance of the book– and others (which are) allegorical [*mutashābihat*]. But those in whose hearts is doubt pursue, foorsooth, that which is allegorical seeking (to cause) dissension by seeking to explain it. None knoweth its explanation save Allah. And those who are of sound instruction [*waw al-rāsikhūn fī al-ʿilm*] say: We believe therein; the whole is from our Lord; but only men of understanding really heed (*Qur.* 3:7).[52]

From the Qur'an itself, the jurists learned that some verses stand in want of interpretation and should be regarded as similes and interpreted figuratively. In Shi'i Islam, the inner meaning of the Qur'an could only be obtained through an interpretation derived from the *imām*, and a distinction was made, for instance, in al-Kulainī's collection of *ḥadīṯ*, between revelation itself as *al-qur'ān al-ṣāmiṭ* (the silent Qur'an), which is in need of an interpreter, and the *imām*, *al-qur'ān al-nāṭiq* (the speaking Qur'an): its true interpreter (Poonawala 1988:200). But the Shi'i scholars were split on the question of the definition of the terms *muḥkam* and *mutashābih*. While b. Babūyah and others considered the *muḥkam* verses to be accessible to the *ʿulamā* and the *mutashābih* to be comprehended only by God, Abū Jaʿfar al-Ṭūsī defined the *muḥkam* in his *Kitāb jāmʿī al-bayān fī tafsīr al-qur'ān* (The Book of the complete exegesis on the Qur'an) as what may be understood with sufficient knowledge of the revelation, leaving no room for contradiction. This is in contrast to *mutashābih*, which are symbolic verses that deal with realities beyond the ken of human perception and require a figurative language of explanation (Fyzee 1943:79, Akhtar 1987:144). As the Qur'an itself declares, the whole of revelation is symbolic in this sense, "God hath (now) revealed the fairest of statements [*mutashābih*]" (*Qur.* 39:23), but the question of tropology should not be overemphasised as far as jurisprudence is concerned, since the majority of the jurists presumed that technical legal terms normally indicate the meanings for which they were coined. While

[52] Philologically, the word *muḥkam* is a cognate of *ḥukm* and *ḥikmat* in contrast to *mutashābih* that is a cognate of *shibh* (likeness) and *shubhah* (obscurity). In other words, *muḥkam* is that which reveals its hidden meaning. The most controversial part of exegesis regards the *waw* in verse 3:7, whether it is a connective or disjunctive. While the majority of Shi'i exegeses interpret *al-rāsikhūn fī al-ʿilm* as the twelve *imāms*, the Sunni exegetes tended to regard the *waw* as disjunctive.

there was a constant discussion whether texts containing ambiguous or homonymous words are to be legally binding, legal language always deposited *maʿnā* (meaning) and *mafhūm* (understanding) as linguistic entities.

Legal theory consequently covered numerous issues, such as the problem of etymology and semiotics, which were drawn from literature and linguistics, which did not constitute its essentials. The question of connotative versus denotative meaning of a text continually challenged the exegetes and each relevant word was analysed in one or more of these categories. In the case of allegorical meanings, the text was supposed to have deeper multitudes of meanings not accessible to every reader, due to the possibility of polysemy. A common method of the Shi'i commentators of the Qur'anic text regarding the problem of the absence of references to Shi'ism in the text was to point at symbolic and allegorical aspects even if they rarely used a purely allegorical-symbolic interpretation. In Shi'i textual interpretation, the fundamental distinction between the two aspects of *ẓahir* (exoteric) and *bāṭin* (esoteric) was developed very early and, for instance, applied in the *tafsīr* attributed to Jaʿfar al-Sādiq. Yet, it can be questioned whether these were considered as a dual two-point pattern comprising its literal respectively allegorical expression (Nwiya 1962). Abū Jaʿfar al-Ṭūsī classified six exegetical principles, each consisting of two elements, relevant to the understanding of revelation: *ḥaqīqī* (true) and *majāzī* (allegorical), *awāmīr* (permission) and *nawāhī* (prohibition), *ʿumūm* (general) and *khuṣūṣ* (specific), *muṭlaq* (absolute) and *muqayyad* (relative), *mujmal* (brief) and *mubayin* (explanatory), *nāsikh* (abrogating) and *mansūkh* (abrogated). It is significant that these antithetical headings were precisely those that were elaborated in the *muʿtazilah* tradition (Calder 1980:Chapter 7).

Perhaps no less important in the repulsion of legal anomalies was the controversy over the concept of repeal, called *naskh* (abrogation), and the related question of God's eternal knowledge.[53] Disagreement ensued not only on which were the abrogating and abrogated verses, but also on the effect of abrogation, whether it should permanently invalidate the abrogated rule or not. Since the *naskh* doctrine, through the concept of *badāʾ* (God's revision of His knowledge), infringed on the perfection of the Qur'an and the idea of God's immutable and eternal knowledge, it was transformed by the Shi'i jurists that interpreted *naskh* as a change through explanation rather than of knowledge. As David S. Powers (1988:119) highlights, the fact that the majority of pairs of abrogated and abrogating verses were not identified as such in the text further explains why the genre of *naskh* developed hand in hand with the *asbāb al-nuzūl* on the one hand and *usūl al-fiqh* on the other. In other words, the range of theories that are represented in the term *naskh*

[53] The term *naskh* itself occurs once in the Qur'an when referring to the text itself. "Whatever verse We replace or cause to be forgotten, We bring a better or the like to it" (*Qur*. 2:106).

and the vast field that it covers (*tafsīr*, *ḥadīṯ*, *fiqh*, etc.) makes evident the all-inclusive character of the subjects of the traditional Islamic legal discourse.

As the symbolic expression in human language of spiritual realities, the Qur'an was considered to contain profounder spiritual meaning than surface meaning. Traditional Islamic hermeneutics extracted the esoteric meanings of revelation by means of *taʾwīl*. The word itself is deduced from the numeral *awwal*, has the meaning 'reducing to its beginning' and was used more or less synonymous to *tafsīr* in its early stage (Arberry 1957:16). In Sunni legal hermeneutics, a verse with a *ẓāhir* (manifest) meaning was considered to be open to *taʾwīl*, but in theory it was only correct and relevant if it could be accepted "without recourse to forced and far-fetched arguments" (Kamali 1991:90). Therefore, *tafsīr* was used more comprehensively than *taʾwīl* for Qur'anic words and expressions, but as the Sufis took the precaution of avoiding the terminology of exoteric exegesis, *taʾwīl* became an epithet of the esoteric interpretation of the Qur'an, where even *muḥkam* verses were interpreted according to a systematic metaphysical point of view.

Due to its early predilection to gnosis, Shi'i Islam tended to emphasise *taʾwīl*, not in the meaning of literal or allegorical interpretation, but as a penetration into the symbolic meaning, that is, an ontological reality, by reaching a divinely predisposed sense placed within the revealed text through which man himself becomes transformed. In Shi'i theosophy it signified a specific disposition or approach to interpretation, *par excellence* performed by the *imāms* themselves:

> *Tafsīr* could be accomplished by anyone who had the proper qualifications, and concerned the outward meaning (*zāhir*) of the Book, but *taʿwīl* involved knowledge of a special kind possessed only by the Imams from the family of the Prophet (*ahl al-bait*), which enabled them to interpret the inward meaning (*bātin*) (Cooper 1989:27).[54]

It went beyond the literal meaning of words and sentences and read into them a hidden meaning that was often based on speculative reasoning. The spiritual meaning was 'transferred' from the historical or literal meaning because of the latter's surplus of meanings. The theosophers hence never restricted *taʾwīl* to the appropriation of the revealed text, but their exegesis also included that of the archive of meditative interpretation that surrounds it. In other words, the esoteric understandings were not merely mediated by tradition, but by the mystical experience of the text in a direct sense. "They

[54] The symbolic interpretation of revelation was inherent in Shi'i Islam that emphasised inner reality as the source of the outward through the recognition of the *imām* as the Logos. "That the Qor'an has a spiritual meaning, or rather several spiritual meanings, that everything exoteric has an esoteric aspect, and that the mode of the true believer depends on his knowledge of these spirtual meanings, was already affirmed from the earliest days of Islam; it expresses an essential aspect of Shi'ism, from which Imamology is inseparable" (Corbin 1994:122).

are attempts to express in the language of man the effects of the spiritual, human-Qur'anic-Divine experience, as it appears narrowly limited and fragmented when transferred to the plane of writing and interpretation of individual verses" (Habil 1987:26).

G. Interpretative pluralism and *ikhtilāf* (divergence)

What mattered in Islamic theological and legal hermeneutics was not only what lay behind the text in the form of an originating intention, but also what was in front of it when the text was put to play. While the 'juristic-rational' epistemic scheme considered legal theory to provide criteria for demarcating justified from unjustified opinion and the search for epistemological foundations to be aimed at revealing such criteria, a certain epistemological scepticism was nevertheless fundamental for legal theory, which acknowledged the difference between absolute truth on the one hand and fallibility of human interpretation on the other. The validity of divergence on the same issues was a basic principle of jurisprudence, since no part could deny the other to reach different conclusions concerning the same material and methods. Orientalist scholarship on Islamic law has until recently tended to downplay the significance of *ikhtilāf* when examining legal disputes by arguing that differences did not concern matters of principles, but rather were aimed at demarcating 'orthodoxy' (Hurgronje 1957:235 and Schacht 1964:28, 1965a:1061). While Ignaz Goldziher (1981) made many more complex and differentiated verdicts on the subject, the views of Hurgronje and Schacht remained commonplace in Orientalist scholarship.

As Coulson (1997:86–102) reveals, there were, however, many issues in traditional Islamic law, such as divorce and succession, which provided a clear-cut distinction between the various positions and hardly can be classified as *trivia*, subsidiary points of detail, but nevertheless were tolerated. Baber Johansen, as well as Calder, Hallaq, Madelung and others with them, also argues that Islamic legal hermeneutics undoubtedly allowed for a wide spectrum of interpretative possibilities within the limitations of the revealed sources and legal tradition despite the existence of given methodological premises that restricted the range of possible interpretations:

> The respect of normative pluralism (ikhtilāf) is possible only because the fiqh scholars conceive an ontological difference between the knowledge as revealed by God in Koranic texts, the prophet's praxis or the community's consensus on the one hand, and the knowledge which human beings acquire through their own reasoning (Johansen 1998:65–66).

The concept *ikhtilāf* was first validated in the legal theory of al-Shāfiʿī, but it was perhaps implicit in the earlier legal literature, as the beginnings of Islamic law were characterised by freedom of legal reasoning within the boundaries of revelation. While hermeneutics largely was a method for resolving hermeneutical *ikhtilāf*, it nevertheless granted a kind of flexibility and tolerance within the umbrella of transcendent unity in accordance with the principle of *ibāḥah* (giving liberty). As Coulson (1969:29) elucidates, "It refers to the tolerance of the lawgiver, Allah, who allows his creatures on earth freedom of action and behaviour outside the area covered by his specific commands and prohibitions". In this respect, the jurists also found interpretative disagreements, since they believed it to be a theoretical impossibility for the text to reveal conflicting doctrines:

> The multiplicity of rulings thrown up by the tradition, or devised by the individual jurist, becomes a means to discover the facets through which a legal concept is revealed. Where the tradition offers dispute (*ikhtilāf*), it too becomes a device to achieve a finer and more qualified perception of what a concept implies (Calder 1996:991).

As far as Sunni Islam is concerned, the doctrine of *ikhtilāf* came, over time, to represent the mutual tolerance that each of the legal schools showed to one another as well as the tolerated disagreement within every *maḏhab*. Numerous schools of *fiqh* developed during the earliest centuries of Islam yet decreased from the tenth century and onwards, reducing the inherent pluralism of Islamic law as new doctrines limited legal pluralism by means of the process of *ijmāʿ* (Johansen 1997:3). While the Shi'i theological doctrine disallowed for a plurality of legal schools, the comparative jurisprudential literature, such as Abū Jaʿfar al-Ṭūsī's *al-Khilāf fī al-aḥkām* (Differences in legal norms) considered different legal schools, Sunni and Shi'i alike, as various juristic denominations of Islam (Weiss 1978:212).[55] In its acknowledgement of normative pluralism, jurisprudence differed from theology, which never accepted the formula of *ikhtilāf*. In the realm of theology, which included subjects such as *uṣūl al-dīn* (principles of belief), no divergence was permitted, since the very *raison d'être* of theology was to demonstrate truth and to uphold the articles of religious creed, as manifested in the theological concept of *barāʿah* (exemption) (Kohlberg 1986).

While the different legal positions within Islam acknowledged each other in theory, they expressed themselves in different and even contradictory ways in concrete matters. While each Muslim was free to follow the juristic position of his or her personal choice, legal disputes were undeniably polemical in content. The disputes underlined the distinction between schools and caused outbreaks of bitter enmity between them, as was the case

[55] Many Shi'i jurists, such as al-Mufīd and al-Ṭūsī, studied under Sunni teachers and even participated as teachers in Sunni *madāris*. The fact that some of the standard text-books in the Shi'i legal curriculum in the formative period were written by Sunni authors influenced in particular the science of *furūʿ al-fiqh* (branches of jurisprudence), which with a few exceptions was identical to those in Sunni law (Stewart 1998:100–102). The substantive differences between Shi'i and Sunni Islam do not pertain to *furūʿ* but rather cover the *uṣūl* (principles) of religion.

with the *uṣūlī* and *akhbārī* positions within Shi'i Islam or with various Sunni attitudes to the *ẓāhirī* doctrine that discarded human reasoning. As Johansen (1998:475) rightly claims, the traditional normative legal pluralism was also by and large abandoned in modern times when a particular school was assimilated by the modern state, as in the case of post-revolutionary Iran, where the *ḥauzah-yi ʿilmīyah* lost its former autonomous character.

Since Islamic legal theory, unlike Christian Canon law, provided no stringent hierarchal structure to ecclesiastical society with the authority of canonising a certain creed equivalent to the Christian councils, synods and sees, legal debates often ended with the words: *waʾllāhu aʿlam* ('and God alone really knows'). Consequently, it does not make sense to use the concepts 'orthodox' and 'heretical', as, for instance, Schacht (1971b:14) does, to denote different legal currents within Islam, since these terms in themselves are polemical and conceal a web of intricate doctrinal relationships. The concept of *ikhtilāf* was also validated by the Prophetic *ḥadīṯ* that states, "Difference of opinion among my community is a sign of the bounty of God", and it is reiterated in the seventh article in Abū al-Hanīfah's book *al-Fiqh al-akbar* (*Magnum opus* of jurisprudence) as well as in *ʿallāmah* al-Hillī's comprehensive work *Mukhtalaf al-shīʿah fī aḥkām al-sharīʿah* (The divergences among the Shi'is on the norms of law).[56]

Legal divergence penetrated the veil of traditional legal theory and can to some extent be regarded as a clue to the historical growth of *sharīʿat*. Jean-Paul Charnay (1967:223) claims that the purpose was in any case conservative, since interpretations that fell outside the theoretical principles of the legal framework were liable to the charge of *raʾy* and *bidʿah* (innovation). "L'*ikhtilāf* a pour mission de limiter les écarts d'interprétation contendus dans le *Sunna*, en opposition à leur dépassement par l'innovation dangereuse: la *bidʿa*". But since the possibilities of Islam were never exhausted or made entirely explicit in any epoch, some jurists allowed for the concepts of *raʾy al-ṣawāb* (rewarded opinion) and *bidʿah al-ḥasanah* (good innovation). The modern scholar Jaʿfar Shahīdī (1983:13) even argues that there were examples of *tafsīr bi-raʾy* (opinioned interpretation) that were considered to be *mamdūḥ* (praiseworthy). While Islamic hermeneutics predicated the possibility of multiple interpretations through the different senses they find in the Qur'an as a condition of exegesis, it suggested a unified or univocal hierarchy of meanings rather than a polysemous range of interpretations. Where polysemy existed, it was to be understood as a claim to textual stability rather than the opposite, an intermediate state of endlessly deferred meanings and unresolved conflicts.

[56] Cf. *Qur*. 30:22. The latter covered the question of legal divergence among Shi'i jurists in minute detail and included a number of issues, such as *salāh al-jamʿah* (Friday prayer) and *jihād* (religious war). Cf. Sachedina 1988:173–204.

While the question whether it is possible to establish an authentic proof by means of evidence derived through *ẓann* or not was under dispute. In Shi'i as well as Sunni legal theory, *ẓann* was part of an epistemological ranking from *yaqīn* (certainty) to *ghalabah al-ẓann* (likelihood), to *shakk* (uncertainty) to *shubhah* (suspicion) where it, in contrast to the latter two, was not considered as a sub-species of ignorance.[57] In this respect, *ẓann* differed from *ʿilm*, that is, certain knowledge as opposed to *jahl* (ignorance), but neither it nor *shakk* was equal to the vernacular English sense of 'presumptive' or 'dubious', since there were no attempts in traditional Islam of a hypothetical destruction of or universal doubt in the surrounding world of religious tradition, comparable to that of, for instance, the modern Western philosopher Descartes (Reinhart 1997). In this respect, *ẓann* is still a matter of strict deduction, since the term designates a more probable but true belief, in line with the idea that evey *mujtahid* is correct. Aron Zysow (1997:282) also asserts that as *ẓann* became prevalent, the doctrine of *infiṭāh* (openness) was elaborated to establish valid avenues of knowledge and valid types of probability.

As the individual's submission to the law in Shi'i Islam developed to imply the result of a individual relationship towards a *mujtahid* rather than the the local custom or jurisdiction, the elaboration of the notion of *marjaʿ al-taqlīd* can also be characterised as pluralistic, in the sense that the *muqallid* ('follower') was directed to personal conscience in the selection of *mujtahid*. From a theoretical point of view, the pluralism was due to the significance of the notion of *nīyah* ('mental attitude') and *ikhtiyār* (choice–from the same root as *khair* 'good'; 'choice of what is good') for an individual abiding by a certain norm. As Wilfred Madelung (1982:169) elucidates, even the Shi'i development of the concept of *ijtihād* considered a multitude of simultaneous interpretations as constituting a logical system of internally consistent teachings to be held true for all time. "[A] consensus of the Shi'ite ulamā, in contrast to the Sunnite situation, is of no legal consequence. No question open to ijtihād itself can thus ever be settled conclusively through a consensus of the Shiite ulamā…". Since infallibility was an essential character of *ijtihād*, neither the prophets nor the *imāms* exerted it. During the occultation of the twelfth *imām* all legal inferences by the *mujtahids* were also considered provisional and thereby accepting of the possibility of two contradictory norms. "Differences of opinion and opposing standpoints among the mujtahids are not only allowed for by the system, but the whole system is actually based on the fact that binding authority must itself necessarily be fallible" (Halm 1991:102). In case two conflicting norms were of a different nature, they were reconciled through a

[57] In the late nineteenth century, the concept of *ẓann* was a major dispute between Muḥammad Kāẓim al-Khurāsānī, who accepted it where knowledge or proof is absent, and Muḥammad Taqī Shīrāzī, who considered it invalid (Amanat 1988:100).

procedure known as *tashkhīṣ al-ʿamm* (specifying a part from the general), but the general position was enshrined in the principle *kull mujtahid musīb* ('every *mujtahid* is right'), a legal maxim originally developed by al-Shāfiʿī (Calder 1989:71).

Since the process of *ijtihād* was dialectically related to the major sources of law, the legal norms could never be final or immutable. The continuous hermeneutical discussions such as the question of *ḥujjīyat-i ẓawāhir-i kitāb* (the literal proof of the book) epitomised major *maʿrakah-yi ārāʾ* (arena of opinions), where discussion was meant to go on and on, and where there was always room for more dialogue. While holiness for the jurist consisted in the analysis of the trivial and commonplace *qīl wa qāl* (specific matters) through penetrating logic and criticism, his chief rites were, in other words, *dalīl* (proof) and *baḥṯ* (debate).[58] The effort of *ijtihād* had to be constantly renewed in the hope of coming closer to objective truth and remaining an open process until the return of the hidden *imām*, who alone could offer perfect certainty and truth. As he is supposedly hidden and alive, legal doctrines were not frozen in immutable positions. "If he does not manifest himself, the truth must lie in both parties and, indeed, as long as the Hidden Imam remains in occultation, the Shi'i community can be sure it has produced no ruling that is in error" (Momen 1985:186).

[58] Roy Mottahedeh has written an excellent description of the internal atmosphere of argument that was prevalent in the traditional Shi'i *madrasah* in Iran. The jurists generally tended to make use of a dialectical involvement of the audience through different methods of teaching such as the characteristic *masʾalah-sāzī* (constructing examples). The *masʾalah-sāzī* consisted of posing a hypothetical legal problem and then exploring all the possible ramifications and resolutions of the problem. In the view of Mottahedeh (1985:108), such dialectics were intended to develop pragmatism and an informed moral presence. "These highly developed techniques tended to homogenise learning and to encourage arguments (and technical vocabulary) to cross over from one field into another– for example, from philosophy to rhetoric to grammar to law and back to philosophy. In this way even the various disciplines were brought into disputations with each other". Cf. Fischer 1980a.

CHAPTER V

Islamic traditionalism and Islamic modernism

Islamic law has never been static. Since unprecedented rapidity of innovative change is one of the most evident facts of modernity, the tenacity of traditions are equally important in the sense that religious change and variation have always been present. While a great deal of uniformity exists at the present time, none of the uncongenial legal and philosophical systems that Islamic law was faced with in premodern times can be compared to the encounter with the more or less secularised West of the nineteenth and twentieth centuries. The situation of Islam could no longer be settled by a few legal adjustments or reconciliary theories since *in religiosis* it did not deal with fairly analogous metaphysics, but with directly disruptive non-religious scientific and philosophic trends. European notions of the modern national state and its concepts of law infected the Muslim lands, not to be 'islamised' on the first occasion, but to displace much of the *sharʿī* institutional structure. Since the tension between adherence to the traditional theory of sources and modern legal practice are not unique in any way to Islam, but are found in other legal systems as well, Alan Watson (1984) argues that the tension must be seen as indicative of a transitional stage in the development of a legal tradition rather than as deficiencies peculiar to the Islamic legal tradition.

During the second part of the nineteenth century, the 'juristic-rational' epistemic scheme of Shi'i law emerged successful in combining *ʿaqlī* and *naqlī* proofs for the *istinbāṭ* of legal norms. The 'historical-empirical' epistemic scheme remained concerned with maintaining the legal methodology within the boundaries of explicit recorded *akhbār* of the *imāms*.[1] The 'juristic-rational' epistemic scheme used reason to extend the law to new territories and to serve as a vehicle for 'rationalising' existing jurisprudence. The infiltration of logic into an important strand of Shi'i jurisprudence heralded a significant change in the attitudes of the jurists towards the epistemological status of legal theory. Logic was seen as instrumental in grounding legal theory within a larger system of knowledge,

[1] The last prominent representative of the *akhbārī* school was Muḥammad b. al-Nishāpūrī al-Akhbārī, and after him the school rapidly declined. The only *akhbārī* community known to have survived in the twentieth century existed in the region of Khurramshahr and Abadan (Kohlberg 1985:718).

a system that was already recognized in the discipline of theology. But still, knowledge meant knowledge of the law and the methods and the procedures that lead to this end. Due to the eminent position of reason in Shi'i jurisprudence, which had proved to be a major instrument of change, Shi'i Islam was compliant to produce various legal solutions and trends regarding the question of the role of religion in the modern world. The redefinition and expansion of *fiqh* began to gradually take place as Islamic law transcended and expanded beyond its traditional formulations.

At the turn of the twentieth century, Iran was increasingly infiltrated by European legal thought and its constitutional revolution formed a part of a process of exchange with European culture and philosophy that began as early as in the middle of the nineteenth century. Although the difficulties facing Islamic law in the conflict between the traditional and modern thought had become visible earlier, it was during the constitutional revolution that the issue came to the fore on a public level. While Shi'i jurisprudence possessed the inevitable tools to permit adjustments within *fiqh* to innovation, the introduction of modernity in Iran was largely the achievement of intellectuals who frequently were more familiar with the rational philosophy of enlightenment than the traditional Islamic scholastic tradition. The intellectual supremacy of the traditional *ʿulamā* became hence increasingly questioned as modern notions of constitutionalism, democracy and science were familiarised. The pressures exerted by modern ideas, together with forces of change and quasi-colonial interregnum, led to a polarisation within Iranian Islamic thought between the wholesale rejection of various forms of modernity to the resolute defence of its major forms. While the religious constitutionalists shared certain distinctively modern concerns, the secular reformers, such as Fatḥ ʿAlī Ākhūndzādah, ʿAbd al-Raḥīm Ṭālibūf and Mīrzā Āqā Khān Kirmānī, ruled out any reconciliation between Islamic law and the modern state. For the religious-minded reformers, such as Mīrzā Malkam Khān, Jamāl al-dīn Asadābādī (Afghānī) and Muḥammad Khān Sinakī, the law of a centralised state created by the people's representatives in a legislative assembly was thought to be compatible with traditional Islamic law. Mīrzā Malkam Khān was the first Persian reformist writer to have an adequate knowledge of French and English philosophical thought, and it was he who introduced such key terms as *qānūn* (codified law), *majlis* (consultative assembly) and *iṣlāḥāt* (reforms) in Iran. He favoured the equality of *sharīʿat* and *ʿurf* by arguing that modern conceptions of law are inherent in Islam:

> We have discovered that ideas which were in no way acceptable when they came from our agents in Europe, were immediately accepted with the greatest joy, when it was demonstrated that they were already latent in Islam (Abrahamian 1983:68).

While the *ʿulamā* had an edge over other participants in the constitutional debate in terms of argumentative skills, they did not initiate the constitutional movement and were not proponents of constitutionalism *per se*. Their basic motive was conservative: to limit the privileges of the Qājār monarch and put an end to foreign political and cultural encroachment (Hairi 1976). The reforms brought uncertainties as to the place of Islamic law in the modern state and hence they were followed by a series of Shi'i theoretical justifications of modern state building. As Kazemi Moussavi (1996:42) argues, the jurists leaned towards a kind of philosophical intricacy and, as in the case of Mīrzā Muḥammad Ḥasan Nā'īnī, incorporated parts of *ʿilm al-kalām* and *falsafah* into their *uṣūl al-fiqh* works. The first voices were also heard in favour of reforming the *ḥauzah-yi ʿilmīyah* and instituting religious seminars with a curriculum that included the traditional subjects alongside with modern science. An example of this kind is a relatively unknown tract called *Maslak al-imām fī salāmat al-islām* (The Doctrine of the *imām* for the well-being of Islam) written by a theology student, Asadullāh Mamaqānī (Qeissary 1998:32–34).

In contrast to the Sunni modernists that struggled to secure the approval of *ijmāʿ* for theoretical reformulations of *ijtihād* under the impact of a purist strand originating in the writings of Ibn Taimīyah, the flexible and open use of *ijtihād* remained a particular characteristic of the Shi'i legal tradition. According to William G. Millward (1973:113), the emotional and esoteric character of Shi'i Islam as well as its predilection for Islamic theosophy were also major factors underlying the fact that Shi'i modernism in Iran, as distinguished from any reformism, emerged later than Sunni modernism in the Arab world and India. But one should also indicate that Iran was not directly colonised and hence was more intellectually isolated from the modern West. Although it had a fragmentary existence since the 1930s, Shi'i modernism transpired as a solid systematic intellectual position or line in the late 1960s. In this respect, the rudimentary modernism was basically naive and in strict terms unmodern, since it failed to grasp the real challenges of modernity. While a striking methodological feature of early modernist discourse was its display of awareness of modern systems of thought, its idealism, in the sense of romanticism, tended to ignore or de-emphasise the major obstacles of modern concepts such as constitutionalism, democracy, liberalism, and the like, to Islam. Hence, its view of Islamic law as such remained essentially traditional in outlook, despite government modernisation, secularisation and the growing influence of communism among the secular intelligentsia. In fact, the first Islamic modernists, such as Mahdī Bāzargān and Maḥmud Ṭaliqānī, presented Islam in general terms as a way of cultural self-realisation and a cure for the moral decay caused by modernisation.

The essential epistemological and ontological question for Shi'i jurists and intellectuals in the encounter with modernity was consequently one of authenticity, namely, what are the legitimate considerations that can be taken into account when inferring or even constructing new legal norms? Unlike modern Western law, where the legislator enjoys a flexibility in decisions and may change the basic legal norm, traditional *fiqh* is not easily adjustable to change, since there is no recognised competence in producing its laws. It provides no simple unified legal system for society, such as codified law and rules to be enforced by the state. In general terms, Islam was challenged to question the nature and basis of its traditional conceptions of law in order to accommodate *fiqh* to modern conditions without dethroning the link with the historic community. In practical terms, the traditional *sharʿī* courts remained the dominant element in the Iranian state until the 1920s, when the division between religious and customary law was obliterated and law became codified for the first time. This development of differentiation and separation of religion and politics was further made triumphant in the new legislation of 1960s as the religious institutions became independent of the state. In post-revolutionary Iran, this trend was reversed, as an 'islamisation' of the modern state was accomplished in order to transform traditional Shi'i law into state law. The most striking and paradoxical element of continuity during the whole twentieth century was actually the continuing growth of the state in Iran, which largely effected traditionalist as well as modernist orientations within Shi'i thought, and made legislation as well as codification major concerns of the jurists (Arjomand 1988:173).

A. An Introduction to Islamic traditionalism

In the present thesis, Islamic traditionalism is to be not confused with 'traditional Islam', which is equivalent to Islamic tradition, the one mainstream tendency of theological and legal thought that, despite some inconsistency, remained very much the same in Muslim lands until the twentieth century. Islamic traditionalism, rather, constitutes a response to modernity in the sense that it presents a critique of modernity. In this respect, it frequently focuses on the quintessentially separate epistemologies of the premodern concept of reality and that of modernity. While traditionalism is modern (in the sense of contemporary), it is not 'modernist', since it maintains that the traditional conception of reality is not to be changed, but that modernity rather must adjust to the truths of religion. As Said Amir Arjomand suggests, traditionalism must be distinguished from 'traditional' in order to make an adequate definition:

> Whereas traditional man is at best only dimly conscious of the sources of the tradition and of the rationale for certain concrete traditional patterns of action, the traditionalist idealises tradition and constructs a fairly rationalised set of norms which are linked to the sources of tradition and are sharply contrasted to the alien norms of the rival belief system (Arjomand 1984:195).

While Islamic traditionalism in many respects is a continuation of pre-modern reformism, it is characterised by an aspiration of answering the challenges of contemporary transitions in reference to traditional definitions of *istinbāṭ*. The core idea of Islamic traditionalism is the viewpoint that Islamic law, as a transcendent reality that embodies the divine Will, is eternal and immutable, but more specifically it underlines that criticism of contemporary issues must conform to former expositions within the Islamic legal tradition. For Islamic traditionalism, *sharīʿat* is connected to our terrestrial existence on the basis that reality is comprised of multiple *marātib al-wujūd* (states of existence) of which the physical world is the lowest and furthest removed from divine origin. Since religion belongs to a higher order of existence, the traditionalists argue that *sharīʿat* is by no means abrogated if it does not conform to the dominating ideas of a certain location and time. Traditionalism places the accent on the historical continuity of ideas and generally do not consider recent history as a major rupture with the past that has decisively interrupted the pertinence of the authority of the accumulated legal tradition. Rather than being concerned with maintaining *status quo*, legal change is, as Seyyed Hossein Nasr (1988:117) argues, in other words, past-oriented and justified, in coherence with traditional philosophical and cosmological principles:

> Those who are conquered by such a mentality want to make the *Sharīʿah* 'conform to the times' which means to the whims and fancies of men and the ever changing human nature which has made 'the times'. They do not realize that it is the *Sharīʿah* according to which society should be modelled not vice versa. They do not realize that those who practiced *ijtihād* before were devout Muslims who put their interest in Islam before the world and never surrendered its principles to expediency.

Nasr (1980 and 1992), who is commonly recognised as the leading interpreter of Islamic traditionalism in the contemporary world, directs a major critique of the epistemological foundations of modernity in his main writings. Both in terms of philosophy and science, he believes that modernism is based on a denial of the relevance of the Divine and argues that the conflict between the *sharīʿat* and the secular Western laws is embedded in the discrepancy between the Islamic view of knowledge as embued with the sense of the sacred and secular learning in the form of modern science. In this respect, he underlines that the elevation of reason in traditional Islamic legal theory by no means permits any kind of discursive rationalism or *ad hoc* treatment of the divine commandment:

> ...[B]ecause man can reach *tawhīd* through his own *ʿaql* only under the condition that this *ʿaql* is in a wholesome state (*sālim*). And it is precisely the *Sharīʿah* whose practice removes the obstacles in the soul which prevents the correct functioning of the intellect and obscures its vision (Nasr 1981:26).

More importantly, Islamic traditionalists assert that the *istinbāṭ* from the revealed sources must furthermore conform to the traditional methodology and employ modern elements of law only as subjects (such as state-building, banking and insurance etc.) in the legal discourse. The traditional methodological principles are preserved and the *istinbāṭ* of legal norms is considered invalid as long as it does not include knowledge of the *muqaddamāt* (preliminaries) of *ijtihād*, which are specified in the traditional *uṣūl al-fiqh* literature. While traditionalism defends the immutability of Islamic law, it also admits the need for change and seeks new interpretations. It attempts to introduce balance into traditional interpretations while opposing any radical rethinking of jurisprudence in the manner of Islamic modernism. The dilemma that faces the modernists as well as the traditionalists is to achieve a fresh synthesis from the handling of new material. As Michael J. Fischer and Mehdi Abedi point out, the pivotal difference between them is that while the aim of traditionalism (Muṭahharī) is to purify religion by means of criticising the categories of modern thinking, modernism (Sharīʿatī and Ṭāliqānī) goes further and proposes an extensive reconstruction of traditional Shi'ism with reference to modern conceptions of man and society (Fischer and Abedi 1990:186).

In Iran, Islamic traditionalism was born in the prelude to the constitutional revolution of 1906–1909, when Shi'i jurists were forced to explain the relationship between Islam and various aspects of modern life for the first time. The *ʿulamā* were divided into two main tendencies: those who tried to reconcile constitutionalism with *sharīʿat* and were advocating *mashrūṭah* (constitutionalism) and those who basically were totally against constitutionalism but put forward the idea of *mashrūṭah al-mashrūʿah* (religious constitutionalism), such as Faḍlullāh Nūrī and Ṯiqat al-islām Tabrīzī. The main theoretical justification of constitutionalism was put forth by Muḥammad Ḥusain Nāʾinī, who justified the constitutional system in conformity with the *uṣūlī* legal tradition by referring to the principle of *muqaddamah-yi wājib* (obligatory prerequisite), that is, that the adoption of constitution is obligatory as a precondition for Muslim welfare and security (Enayat 1991:170). He posited the rule of law as the surest guarantee against arbitrary government, but neglected to explore the possible conflict between *sharīʿat* and *qānūn*, because of his vague understanding of the underlying principles of liberal European democracy, even if he separated the *umūr-i sharʿī* (matters covered by Islamic law) from the *umūr-ī ʿurfī* (customary matters) (Hairi 1977). In this respect, the early traditionalism remained, in general, an unsystematic defence of the Islamic legal tradition at the theoretical level against European influences and Christian assaults that responded to certain practical socio-political problems that the semi-colonial situation of Iran had caused. While it dealt with matters of social and political relevance, these matters were highlighted issue-by-issue rather than as a social or political philosophy.[2] The juristic discourses never addressed their problems in and with modernity, but remained principally traditional in terms of disposition and engagement.

While early traditionalism included new subjects connected to the modern world in legal reasoning, its representatives lacked in-depth knowledge of European languages, which affected their comprehension of Western thought. Their attempt was essentially one of identifying original Islamic concepts with modern principles, since it was first in the mid-1930s that access to European thought was gradually made possible, mainly from the channel of translation from French and English.[3] While the traditionalists were differentiated from one another on the issue of practical concerns and priorities, they were united in their view of constitutional law as essentially being the enforcement of *sharīʿat*, as envisioned in the constitution. They were above all concerned with establishing the rule of Islamic law rather than harmonising religion and modernity. "The divergent attitudes within the clerical estate are best looked at as relatively superficial differentia resting on a common outlook" (Arjomand 1981b:184). The potential incompatibility between parliamentary law and *sharīʿat* was not entirely clear to the jurists and even Faḍlullāh Nūrī, who argued that there can be no legislation in Islam, but only *istinbāṭ* by means of Aristotelian syllogism, defined the term *majlis* as "the great Islamic house of consultation established through the

[2] As Vanessa Martin (1989:7) elucidates, the secularising tendency of Western thought and the radical institutional changes it engendered were not necessarily apparent to those of the Shi'i jurists who gave it their attention. "Virtually none of them had any experience of Western-style government. Furthermore, the reformers couched their proposals in strictly orthodox terms in the hope of not offending the 'ulama and involving them in the protest movement. The penetration of Western ideas was still slight, which probably explains why the body of 'ulama made little effort to support or refute them before the revolution".

[3] As Ali Gheissary (1998:5) argues, the translation of European literature, prominently prose literature, began already in the nineteenth century, either directly from the original or through their earlier Arabic translations. During the time of Nāṣir al-dīn Shāh, a royal department of publications was founded under the direction of Iʿtimād al-Salṭanah with the purpose of transferring European works in mainly history, geography and literature into Persian. Among its achievements was the first translation of a work of Western philosophy that happened to be a piece of Descartes (*Discours de la méthod*) that was rendered the title *Muntaẓam-i nāṣirī* (Nāṣirī's instruction), presumably to allude to Nāṣir al-dīn al-Ṭūsī's *Akhlāq-i nāṣirī* (Nāṣir's ethics). The translation, which was published in 1862, was made by Mullāh Lālihzār and commissioned by Arthur Comte de Gobineau. But it was not until after the constitutional revolution that Iranian writers began to turn out translations with some degree of professional competence, as more serious attempts were made to ground Iranian thought in modern Western philosophical tenets. The first introduction to Western philosophy, Muḥammad ʿAlī Furūghī's *Sair-i ḥikmat dar urūpā*, which was published in the 1930s, was, for instance, considered a standard work on Western philosophy even after 1960s when the major works of Western philosophy (Hegel, Kant, Marx, Spinoza) were rendered into Persian. In addition to the translation factor, the inception of modern Western ideas were also made possible as a growing number of Iranian intellectuals began to make contact with Western academic and intellectual centres. The return of these intellectuals to Iran was a major source of discrepancy between modern ideas of law and the Iranian legal reality and tradition.

efforts of *ḥujjat al-islāms* (the proofs of Islam)" (Dabashi 1984).[4]

Among the traditionalist jurists of the first part of the twentieth century, Ḥusain Ṭabāṭabāʾī Burūjirdī was probably the most distinguished, in the sense that he is considered to be a champion of Shi'i *uṣūlī* thought by later Islamic traditionalists. He was outstanding in the field of *ʿilm al-ḥadīṯ* and instigated a critical revision of traditional Shi'i *ḥadīṯ* collections. He also composed a new type of collection, *Jamāʿah aḥādīṯ al-shīʿah* (Collection of Shi'i *ḥadīṯs*) with a comparative rendering of transmitted material from Sunni sources. Due to Burūjirdī's admiration of the transmitted sciences, Leonard Binder (1965:125) and others have questioned the extent to which *ijtihād* and even legal theory itself was allowed by him. But Burūjirdī's interest in the modern world is evident in the fact that he, in his capacity of being the sole *marjaʿ al-taqlīd*, encouraged some jurists (among them ʿAlī Ḥujjatī-Kirmānī, Mahdī Muḥaqqiq and Murtaḍā Muṭahharī) to enter university and also sent the first Shi'i *ʿulamā* to Western universities and established a number mosques abroad.[5] The presence of this new generation of traditionalist *ʿulamā*, with a dual educational background, had a deep impact on the intellectual discourse in Iran with its prolific writings.

During the latter part of the twentieth century, Islamic traditionalism in Iran was championed by a number of intellectual personalities, such as Ruḥullāh Khumainī, Muḥammad Ḥusain Ṭabāṭabāʾī, Jalāl al-dīn Ashtiyanī, Murtaḍā Muṭahharī, Seyyed Hossein Nasr, Jalāl al-din Humāʾī, Muḥammad Taqī-Jaʿfarī, Muṣṭafā Muḥaqqiq-Dāmād, Nāṣīr Makārim-Shīrazī and others. It is characteristic of jurists such as Khumainī, Muṭahharī, Taqī-Jaʿfarī and Muḥaqqiq-Dāmād that their work touches not only upon the traditional theoretical as well as the practical sciences not restricted exclusively to their subjects, but also comprises matters of modern intellectual discourse.[6] As Yann Richard (1995:67) argues, several of the above company of thinkers also have their preference for Islamic esoterism in common. In this respect, Ṭabāṭabāʾī, a philosopher in the tradition of Ibn Sīnā and Ṣadr al-dīn Shīrāzī, was perhaps the most erudite of all of them.[7] In his book *Shīʿah dar islām*

[4] As far as the constitution is concerned, the description of law as the *sharīʿat* was dominating and believed literally. A rescript at the moment of the establishment of *ʿadālat-khānah* (state house of justice) reads, "The establishment of a state house of justice to execute the laws of the *sharīʿat* and ensure the security of the subjects is our foremost objective. To carry out this sacred objective, the law of Islam, which consists of the boundaries and the execution of the precepts of the *sharīʿat*, must be enforced immediately throughout the land" (Kirmānī 1979:366).

[5] A part of these achievements was that Muḥammad Kāẓim-ʿAṣṣār, ʿAbd al-Jawād Falātūrī and Mahdī Hāʾirī-Yazdī (the son of ʿAbd al-Karīm Hāʾirī-Yazdī) were the first Iranian *ʿulamā* to take doctoral exams from European universities.

[6] Cf. Khumainī, n.y., Muhaqqiq-Dāmād 1998–1999, Taqī-Jaʿfarī 1998. In his book *Āshināʾī bā ʿulūm-i islāmī. Uṣūl-i fiqh wa fiqh*, Muṭahharī (1999) provided perhaps the first general introduction to the subject of legal theory in modern Persian.

[7] Ṭabātabāʾī was born in 1903 in Tabriz. He completed his preliminary religious education in

(Shi'ism in Islam), he classified three traditional *ṭuruq* (methods) of valid religious knowledge; the *ẓawāhir* (exoteric) method of the law, the *ʿaqlī* (rational) method of theology and *falsafah*, and the *kashf* (unveiling) method of mysticism (Ṭabāṭabāʾī 1984:45–70). This is in fact the general way to present epistemology among the traditionalists. Aside from transmitted knowledge derived from revelation, there is also logic and mystical intuition. In his book *Shinākht az dīdgāh-i qurʾān* (Comprehension from the viewpoint of Islam), ʿAbd al-Karīm Biyāzār-Shīrāzī (1984), for instance, treats epistemology from the point of view of revelation, various forms of Aristotelian logic (syllogism, induction, deduction, etc) and mystical intuition, which all are considered legitimate, but separate, avenues of knowledge parallel to the knowledge obtained from revealed texts.[8]

Ṭabāṭabāʾī's theosophical orientation was deeply reflected in his extensive Arabic Qur'an commentary, *Tafsīr al-mīzān* (The Equilibrium), and also his general philosophical treatise *Uṣūl-i falsafah wa rawish-i riʾālīsm*, where he defended philosophical realism (in the medieval sense of the word) against modern dialectical philosophies such as Marxist materialism. He identified 'realism' with Islamic philosophy as situated between Berkeleyian idealism and positivist materialism, which gives primacy of empirical perception to the human intellect (Ṭabāṭabāʾī 1999:53). According to Ṭabāṭabāʾī, the recovery of epistemological sophistry in philosophy was marked by Descartes' break with Aristotelian logic and Kant's division between

his hometown and then moved to Najaf, where he studied *uṣūl-i fiqh* with Mīrzā Muḥammad Ḥusain Nāʾinī. Ṭabāṭabāʾī became a master of law, but abandoned the task of teaching jurisprudence (which would have gradually secured him the status of *marjaʿ*) and instead moved to Qum to teach Islamic philosophy. His influence was lasting in the field of philosophy, where he was very much a link between lay traditionalist intellectuals and the *ʿulamā*. He is renowned for his discussions in the 1960s and 1970s with the French Islamicist Henry Corbin, which were attended by a number of influential Iranian intellectuals, such as S.H. Nasr, Dāriyūsh Shāyigān, ʿĪsā Sipahbudī and others (Ṭabāṭabāʾī 1992). Ṭabāṭabāʾī died in 1981 and left behind him a generation of immediate and remote students.

[8] In Biyāzār-Shīrāzī's chapter on *shinākht-i qawānin-i ilāhī az rāh-i ijtihād* (knowledge of divine laws through *ijtihād*), he mentions all the necessary preliminary conditions that are obligatory for the *mujtahid*. His list is almost identical to that of *ʿallāmah* al-Hillī. For a similar classification of valid religious knowledge, cf. Muṭahharī 1992:83–110. There also exists a number of contemporary traditionalist expositions of knowledge from the point of view of Islamic philosophy, mostly Ṣadr al-dīn Shīrāzī's definition of *ʿilm al-ḥuḍūrī*. In his major work on epistemology, Humāyūn Himmatī, a pupil of the prominent Shi'i philosopher Faṭhullāh Mujtabāʾī, for instance, grounds knowledge in ontology (i.e. divine Being) and asserts that Islamic definitions of cognition are different from 'scientific epistemology' that focuses on the sociological, psychological or biological nature of human knowledge. In the view of Himmatī (1983:21), the Islamic view of knowledge is therefore not strictly concerned with epistemology in its modern sense but religious ontology. "Some Western philosophers believe that the subject matter of philosophical knowledge is not existence but knowledge. This opinion is incorrect from the point of view of Islamic metaphysics since it has been demonstrated in this philosophy that knowledge also constitutes a part of existence and therefore must be treated from the angle of philosophy, or more precisely ontology, and discussed as a category of existence within that science of ontology which metaphysics is".

noumenon and phenomenon, which no longer identified philosophy with the unveiling of truth and gave way to the historicism of Hegel and Marx (ibid.:161, 169). While Ṭabāṭabāʾī's works recognised the centrality of the Qur'an to a much larger extent than contemporary modernist approaches to philosophy, his work nevertheless marked the beginning of a new Persian genre of 'defensive' literature, which is aware of the philosophical and epistemological consequences generated by modernity, but critical to the intrusion of modern science and values.

While the traditionalists in general avoid the use of modern words and concepts, such as *jahānbīnī* (worldview) or *hirminūtīk* (hermeneutics), which are neologisms for Western terms, they adopt these concepts in order to confirm their traditionalist arguments.[9] For instance, the term *jahānbīnī*, corresponding to the German *Weltanschauung*, was coined by ʿAlī Sharīʿatī and was rapidly and generally adopted by Iranian intellectuals. That the term occurs in traditionalist writings is not a coincidence, but a sign of the general influence of the modernist position on the religious paradigmatic field. The fact that Murtaḍā Muṭahharī, a pupil of Ṭabāṭabāʾī, occasionally adopted certain key terms of Islamic modernism, such as the concept of *tauḥīd* (unity) and *jahānbīnī*, can hence largely be explained by the fact that these terms gained common accuracy at the time. But in contrast to the modernists, Muṭahharī (1998b:36–37) treated these subjects from the point of view of a theologian, where *tauḥīd* refers *a priori* to the Essence of God in His unity and where the Attributes are considered as a means to perceive and know the Essence of God.

Murtaḍā Muṭahharī wrote an extensive commentary on Ṭabāṭabāʾī's *Uṣūl-i falsafah wa rawish-i riʾālīsm*, which is much less technical and more comprehensible for the average reader than Ṭabāṭabāʾī's text.[10] In this

[9] As far as hermeneutics is concerned, traditionalist essays on the subject, such as those of Yaḥyā Yaṯribī (1998), Sayyid Ṣadr al-dīn Ṭāhirī (1998) and Riḍā Ḥaqqpanāh (1999) adopt the loan-word *hirminūtīk* (German 'hermeneutik') in their criticism of Mujtahid-Shabistarī's book *Hirminūtīk, kitāb wa sunnat* (Hermeneutics, revelation and *sunnat*), but disapprove of the latter's redundant use of Latin concepts and words, which they consider alien to the Islamic tradition, and, for instance, identify the interpreter's presuppositions with the traditional hermeneutical disciplines and their subjects (*ʿilm al-lughah*, *asbāb al-nuzūl* and *akhbār* connected to *tafsīr* and *sīrat*, etc). Muḥammad Ḥusain Ṭabāṭabāʾī, who is the most renowned Shi'i exegete of modern times, introduced some new notions of *tafsīr* writing, such as the view that the Qur'anic chapters are unities, but argued in traditionalist terms that the Qur'anic text is not immediately accessible to the ordinary believers and that textual interpretation must follow certain rules in order to distinguish the *muḥkam* from the *mutashābih*, the *nāsikh* from the *mansūkh*, and so on. By also arguing that certain parts of revelation are defined by other parts of revelation, he guaranteed that no other external factor would enter the *tafsīr* (Ṭabāṭabāʾī, n.y.:21–88). Ṭabāṭabāʾī's work was highly influential in traditionalist' circles, which is evident, for instance, in Muṭahharī's (1998a and 1999:40–47) elaboration on the subject.

[10] Murtaḍā Muṭahharī was born in 1919 in Fariman (Khurasan). He received his elementary religious education in Mashhad, but moved to Qum in 1928 where he studied *fiqh* under the

respect, he was more a simplifier of traditional Shi'i learning who presented traditional subjects in modern idiom than a first-rate scholastic mind equivalent to Jalāl al-dīn Āshtīyanī or Mahdī Hā'irī-Yazdī. But for Ṭabāṭabā'ī, as well as for Muṭahharī, the corrupting effects of modernity lie in the various doctrines originating from materialistic philosophy that neglect to consider truth as the correspondence of concepts, as mental contents, with external realities that are permanent:

There is within the immense world of existence a permanent and abiding reality that pervades it (and which reveals itself to intelligence). Yet, each of the phenomena of this world that possesses the reality that we discover as conscious and perceiving human beings loses their reality sooner or later to become non-existent. It is evident from this fact itself that the visible world and its parts are not the essence of reality, which can never be obliterated, but they rather rely upon a permanent reality through which they gain reality and by means of which they enter into existence (Ṭabāṭabā'ī 1984:68).

For Muṭahharī (1997:127), jurisprudence is considered as a certain science that provides a certain model of religious conduct by means of *istinbāṭ* from the revealed sources, that is, by obtaining a legal ruling from the revealed sources through theoretical and syllogical arguments.[11] While he was acquainted with the theory of natural law, his idea of natural rights was also grounded in traditional Islamic philosophy and theology (mainly the *muʿtazilah* view of reason as prior to revelation), by asserting that "God has revealed the laws of religion in compliance with the laws of nature" (Muṭahharī 1979:47). Muṭahharī (1998c:14) argued that the laws of nature and Islamic law are universally congruent to each other and the latter is immutable and unchangeable in principle since the method of lawfinding through syllogism is "a definite principle and the necessities of Islam". His surveys on *uṣūl-i fiqh* and *ijtihād* also demonstrated a traditionalist outlook in that legal interpretation requires *ahlīyat* (legal competence) and *takhaṣṣuṣ-i fannī* (specialised knowledge), even if he elaborated on the subject from an analytic and partly diachronic perspective with the object of popularising

auspices of Sayyid Muḥammad Taqī-Khānsārī and Sayyid Muḥammad Riḍā Gulpaigānī along with *falsafah* and *ʿirfān* for Ruḥullāh Khumainī and Muḥammad Ḥusain Ṭabātabā'ī. In 1957, Muṭahharī went to Tehran where he started teaching Islamic philosophy at the University and the Madrasah-yi Marwī (Marwī school), the most prominent *ḥauzah* in the capital. From the middle of the 1970s, he was professor at the university and was also a member of the board of Anjuman-i shāhanshāhī-yi falsafah (The Imperial academy of philosophy) that was under the presidency of Seyyed Hossein Nasr at that time. On the eve of the revolution, Muṭahharī was made chairman of the *shūrā-yi inqilāb* (revolutionary council) set up by Ruḥullāh Khumainī, but was assassinated a few months later. The Imperial academy of philosophy, which until the revolution was under the royal patronage of empress Faraḥ Dībā, changed its name in 1980. It is led today by Ghulām-Riḍā ʿAwānī, a former pupil of Nasr, and serves as a gathering place for many traditionalist intellectuals.

[11] For a similar view by Ṭabātabā'ī, cf. Ṭabātabā'ī 1976:43.

knowledge of these subjects. In reference to the revealed sources of law and demonstrative arguments, he classified *qiyās, istiḥsān, istiṣlāh* as impermissible and referred to al-Hillī's definition of the *muqaddamāt* of valid inference (1979:102–103).[12] He vehemently opposed *ijtihād bih raʿy* by asserting that a jurist is not allowed to initiate new laws in the sense of *taqnīn* (legislation) and *tashrīʿ* (legislation), but only to infer 'existing' legal norms from the revealed sources (1979:97).

Nevertheless, Muṭahharī asserted that the jurist must have knowledge of the modern world and attend the historical exigencies of modernity. He mentions that Burūjirdī on one occasion compared the *akhbārī* jurisprudence to Western scientific empiricism, which surfaced successfully in Iran respectively England at a similar date even if he did not draw any further conclusions from this suggestion in terms of possible connections of the exchange of ideas. By also referring to Burūjirdī's view against mere hypothetical invention in *fiqh*, he asserted that *ijtihād* operates *mustamarr* (continuously) in connection to particular historical conditions.[13] Yet, the inference of legal norms is still relative only to the subjects of *fiqh*, not its principles or methods. While Muṭahharī (1982:14, 81) acknowledged the impact of a jurist's *jahānbīnī* on his inferred legal norms, he did not refer to the compatibility of the subjects of modern law (for instance insurance) with the Iranian constitution or civil law, but rather compared their technical aspects and its compatibility with the principles of Shi'i legal theory. This is the very logic of Muṭahharī's philosophy, namely that what is *essential* in the Aristotelian meaning of the word (i.e. the principles of intellection) is what really matters, not the accidentals:

> The secret of *ijtihād* is to correspond to new problems and the changing events by reference to general principles. The true *mujtahid* is one, who having known this secret is attentive to the changing (nature of the) subjects, which naturally calls for a corresponding change in the (legal) norms (Muṭahharī 1997:120).[14]

The most renowned Shi'i traditionalist of the twentieth century was probably Khumainī, the founder of the Islamic republic.[15] By according philosophy

[12] Among the most important preliminaries for studying *fiqh*, Muṭahharī (1999:16) mentioned knowledge of *adabīyāt-i ʿarab* (Arabic learning), *tafsīr-i qurʿān, ʿilm-i ḥadīṯ, ʿilm-i rijāl* and *ʿilm-i uṣūl-i fiqh*. For an explanation of these sciences, cf. chapter III.

[13] In his attempt to revive the rationalist tendency in Shi'i philosophy and in giving his approval to the *uṣūlī* school of Shi'i jurisprudence against the *akhbārī* school, Muṭahharī was in particular critical of his contemporary colleagues within the *ʿulamā* who paid no attention either to modern philosophy or modern social forms of life.

[14] In his book *Islām wa iḥtīyājāt-i wāqiʿī-yi har ʿasr* (Islam and the exigencies of every age), Muḥammad Ḥusain Ṭabāṭabāʾī (1990:41) argued similarly that there are legal norms in Islam that are *ṯābit* (constant) and others that are *mutaghayir* (changing) and that the latter have "a historical and local aspect".

[15] Khumainī was born in 1902 in Khumain. He received his education in Arak and Qum under the eminent teacher ʿAbd al-Karīm Hāʾirī-Yazdī. In the 1930s, Khumainī completed his *dars-i*

full equality with jurisprudence among the traditional sciences, where the two are considered as different manifestations of the same truth, emanating from the same source, Khumainī's (1981:395, 412) objective was essentially to integrate social norms with higher mystical values. While he disapproved of the reduction of religion to its legal or social dimension and therefore discarded modernist interpretations of religion as *iltiqātī* (eclectic) thought, his post-revolutionary legal discourse reveals a pragmatic aspect in the use of modern concepts such as *inqilāb* (revolution) and *jumhūrī* (republic) (Khumainī 1982:229). Khumainī (1997:6–11) remained strictly within the borders of the traditional methodology and his attempt was essentially to 'maximalise' the practical realms of *fiqh* and implement *sharīʿat* in the modern state by stressing the use of reason as a proof in law-finding and obliterating the theoretical division religious/customary law (as is evident in his inter-changeable use of *qānūn* and *sharīʿat*).[16] By considering the intellectual as well as practical question of modernity as essentially political, he accepted many modern notions (i.e. institutions), while rejecting the values and ideas of modernity. He viewed modernity as an *external* phenomenon and hence avoided a direct philosophical and theoretical involvement that reifies the meaning and dynamics of modernity. In contrast to the modernists, who accept modern science and interpret Islam according to it, Khumainī's attempt was essentially one of appropriating the notion of the modern state to Islam.[17]

khārij level of Islamic law and was also a well-known teacher of *ʿirfān*. Khumainī's teachers in *ʿirfān* were Jawād Malikī Darjazīnī, Sayyid Abū Ḥasan Qazwīnī, Muḥammad ʿAlī Shāhābādī and also Mīrzā ʿAlī Akbar Ḥakīm-Yazdī, who was a pupil of Hādī Sabziwārī (Knysh 1992). In the early 1960s, Khumainī was made *āyatullāh al-ʿuzmā* ('higher sign of God'), but was soon expelled from the country to Najaf, Iraq, due to his criticism of the monarchy. In 1971, he wrote his well-known treatise on Islamic government, *Wilāyat-i faqīh* (The Authority of the jurist), which also included a practical program for the creation of an Islamic state in Iran. Due to his principal role in the revolutionary movement, Khumainī came to be recognised as the founder of the Islamic republic in 1980 and remained its leader until his death in 1989.

16 While Khumainī kept strictly to the traditional juristic terminology in his book *Wilāyat-i faqīh*, his notion of government was, as Norman Calder (1992) argues, a clear departure from the traditional post-Ṣafawīd dualism of religious-political power and an innovation in its identification of rule or political order with the modern state.

17 In practical terms, Khumainī united the institution of *marjaʿīyat* with that of *rahbarī* (leadership) in the person of the *walī-yi faqīh* by referring to the traditional principles of *istiṣlāh* and *ḍarūrat* (necessity) rather than *shūrā*. While *istiṣlāḥ* had no recognised status as an *aṣl* of law in Shi'i Islam, Khumainī made it a source of law in its own right as long as it did not conflict with *sharīʿat*. In this respect, Khumainī met with criticism from other traditionalist *ʿulamā* who opposed any appropriation of or dialogue with modernity whatsoever and wanted to preserve the traditional dualism of religious and political power. As a matter of fact, the doctrine of *wilāyat-i faqīh* has been subject to controversy among the Shi'i jurists in post-revolutionary Iran. Besides its number of rebuttals from several *marjaʿ al-taqlīd*, such as the late Abū al-Qāsim al-Khuʾī, the related subject *al-fiqh al-siyāsah* (political jurisprudence) is, for instance, debated with specific reference to *wilāyat-i faqīh* in a book by *ḥujjat al-islām* Muḥsin Kadīwar (1998).

As Vanessa Martin (1996) elucidates, Khumainī's concept of *wilāyat-i faqīh*, which uses the term *faqīh* in singular, was highly influenced by concepts of governance found in traditional Islamic philosophy, mainly the post-Suhrawardīan tradition and Ibn Rushd's concept of *sharīʿat* as the law of an ideal state. Since the philosopher through his absorption of knowledge by presence possesses understanding beyond the ordinary jurist, it is the philosopher who should govern yet by virtue of his familiarity with Islamic law. The traditional philosopher consequently emerges as a jurist in Khumainī's book *Wilāyat-i faqīh*. Considering the discussion on *wilāyat-i faqīh* as a juristic topic discussed in the *ḥauzah* and Islamic law not only as ethics but worship as well as governance, he maintained that Islamic government is the rule of the *qānūn-i ilāhī* (divine law) upon people:

> [I]n Islam the legislative power and competence to establish laws belongs exclusively to God Almighty. The sacred Legislator of Islam is the sole legislative power. No one has the right to legislate and no law may be executed except the law of the ruling of the [divine] Legislator (Khumainī 1997:33).[18]

Hence, there exists no legislative body since only God has the right to create new laws. With the purpose of establishing a just society "in order to nourish an *insān-i mahḏab* (spiritually refined human being)", Khumainī (ibid.:62) made the application of *sharīʿat* the centre of Shi'i speculation on revealed law. While distinguising the ontological status of the *faqīh* from the *imām*, in asserting that the former enjoys the *iʿtibārī* (extrinsic), and not the *takwinī* (intrinsic) authority of the latter, he maintained that the jurist rules in the place of the ruler. "Since Islamic government is a government of *qānūn*, those acquainted with the law, or more precisely, with religion, that is the *fuqahā*, must supervise its functioning" (ibid.:61).[19] While the pragmatic nature of Khumainī's legal doctrine, characterised by the implementation of *sharīʿat* within the boundaries of the modern state, was a catalyst in the contemporary rise of the legal trend called *fiqh-i pūyā*, he remained himself an advocate of traditional methodology. He underlined in fact the importance of keeping the religious education within the limits of *fiqh-i sunnatī*, where *ijtihād* is confined to the syllogistic method:

---

[18] Khumainī (1997:3) actually emphasised that while *wilāyat-i faqīh* is an object for study at the *ḥauzah*, it has not received attention due to "the social circumstances prevailing among Muslims in general, and in the *ḥauzahhā-yi ʿilmīyah* in particular".

[19] Khumainī (1997:85) admitted that textual demonstration from the revealed sources was not conclusive for the concept of *wilāyat-i faqīh*, and later he brought into his ruling the Sunni (*malikī*) concept of *istiṣlāh*. By allowing *istiṣlāh* to be a legitimate basis for legal rulings, Khumainī expanded his theory to make it a principal component of legal theory and methodology, where the legal proofs do not have to be source-based but content-based. In 1988, he replaced *wilāyat-i faqīh* by *wilāyat-i muṭlaqah-yi faqīh* (absolute authority of the jurist) in the official terminology and asserted that the rulings of the ruling *faqīh* have priority over all derivative religious commandments, including the *namāz* (prayer) and *ḥajj* (obligatory pilgrimage).

But with reference to the education and research programs at the *ḥauzahs*, we advocate the *fiqh-i sunnatī* and *ijtihād-i jawāhirī* (elemental *ijtihād*) and consider divergence from it as impermissible. In these terms, *ijtihād* is correct, but this does not exclude the fact that *fiqh* is dynamic and that *zamān wa makān* (time and place) are two decisive elements in *ijtihād* (Khumainī 1988:73).[20]

While the contextual element of *zamān wa makān* plays a role in the change of the subjects of jurisprudence as well as the branches of law, such as in the recognition of new subjects, the principles, so to say, remain immutable, except in rare cases of "public and logical interest" (Mihrpūr 1992:73). As a matter of fact, the notion of *zamān wa makān* is a key word in post-revolutionary traditionalist juristic rhetoric where it signifies the *mustamarr* performance of *ijtihād*. In light of the effort of implementing Islamic law within the structure of the modern state, *fiqh-i pūyā* is essentially interpreted by Islamic traditionalists to be the practical implementation of the eternal *sharīʿat* into changing human conditions (Mugāhī 1997). In the middle of the 1990s several conferences were held to highlight the function of *zamān wa makān* in Islamic law. The papers from these conferences were published in 1996 in over twenty volumes. In many of these articles, the subject of *fiqh-i sunnatī* and *fiqh-i pūyā* were highly debated (Jaʿfarī 1996).

Khumainī's traditionalism preserved the integrity of traditional legal methodology and epistemology and only justified an acquisition of modern knowledge, which was limited to the practical technological and administrative sphere. It represented an attitude of coming to terms with the demands of the contemporary world by implementing *sharīʿat* in the sphere of lawmaking within the structures of the modern state while rejecting modernity in the realm of ideas. In this respect, he did not pay enough attention to the philosophical difficulties that stem from a fundamental conflict between the theology underlying the nation-state (i.e. its ontology and mythology) and that of traditional *fiqh*, since the modern perception of reality is largely articulated through the prism of the modern state. The legacy of Khumainī's doctrine is, for instance, apparent in Sayyid Muḥammad Khātamī's book *Bīm-i mauj* (Fear of the wave), where the subject of *zamān wa makān* is touched upon on. This book is essentially an intellectual appraisal of Ruḥullāh Khumainī and Murtaḍā Muṭahharī in terms of a critique against Islamic modernism, such as that of the Egyptian thinker Muṣṭafā al-Sabaʾī, which he argues "consciously or unconsciously justifies the modern manner of thought and culture and attempt to examine Islam with criteria and rules borrowed from the West" (Khātamī 1994:77).[21] In this

[20] According to Asghar Schirazi (1997:275), the term *fiqh-i jawāhirī* has its etymology from the nineteenth century jurist Muḥammad Ḥasan Jawāhirī, who was the author of a collection of legal questions entitled *Jawāhir al-kalām* (Elements of revelation), which is still used in teaching at the seminaries in Iran.

[21] Khātamī was born in Ardakan in 1943. He attended the religious seminars of the *ḥauzahs* of

respect, Khātamī (ibid.:107) believes that modernism, by adapting Western cognitive standards, violates Islamic principles "so that the fundamentals and bases of thought and ethics of modern culture in no way are harmed". While he suggests that modernity cannot be neglected, he asserts that Muslims must consider the dynamics of their own civilisation. Khātamī (1997a:283 and 288) is hence critical of many features of Western modernity, such as the uninhibited capitalism of the presently triumphant "liberal-democratic" system as well as its epistemological relativism that "by relativising the Absolute is the cholera of thinking and prevents the journey to the Truth". In contrast to Khumainī, he advocates a more selective and non-essentialist approach to the West, which takes into account what contribution Muslims can make to modernity (Khātamī 1997b:9).

As far as several Islamic traditionalists are concerned, the traditional affirmative Shi'i viewpoint on *ijtihād* is a matter of proud assessment. In his introduction to the subject of legal theory, Muṣṭafā Muḥaqqiq-Dāmād (1998a:15), for instance, argues in polemical terms that the Sunni viewpoint closed the door to *ijtihād*, disallowed originality and only permitted *taqlīd* to the four founders of the major Sunni *maḏāhib*.[22] In this respect, he also goes into polemics with the *ashʿarī* theological viewpoint, adopts the *muʿtazilah* attitude to ethics and argues that man is able to distinguish between good and bad by means of pure and practical reason. He divides rational legal proofs into two categories: independent rational proofs and dependent rational proofs. In accordance with traditional principles of law, he asserts that the first category of proofs relies on the revealed sources and therefore may be established also by *ẓannī* rational proof in contrast to the latter, which essentially is *qaṭʿī*:

> *Mustaqallāt-i ʿaqlīyah* (independent rational proofs) signify that sequence of rational norms that reason infers in an independent manner, that is without the *dakhālat-i sharʿ* (invention of the divine law), such as justice is good and oppression is evil. In this respect, a logical analogy and demonstration is formed for discovering and arriving at the *sharʿī* norm in such a way that the produced norm is established by reason in the *ṣughrā* (premise). By afterwards extending the general *kubrā*

Qum in 1961 and also studied philosophy at the universities of Isfahan and Tehran. After receiving his M.A. in philosophy, he later resumed his studies at a *ḥauzah* in Qum to receive an *ijāzah* in *ijtihād*. In 1979, he was made director of the Markaz-i islāmī (Islamic center) in Hamburg, West Germany, but returned to Iran at the time of the revolution to be elected as a member of the first parliament. Khātamī has held a number of significant official positions in the Islamic republic and in 1997 was elected president.

[22] Muḥaqqiq-Dāmād was born in Qum in 1945. As the son of the respected scholar Sayyid Muḥammad Dāmād, he began his studies at a *ḥauzah* in Qum very early and also studied law and philosophy at the University of Tehran. After having received a doctorate in law at the University of Brussels, Belgium, he returned to Iran and was made professor of law at the University of Tehran and also elected for a number of semi-official posts. Muḥaqqiq-Dāmād is fluent in Arabic and English and has also a working knowledge of French. He is most renowned for his numerous writings on *fiqh* and modern legal issues.

(conclusion, i.e. of the analogy) by reference to [the principle] that "everything that is ordered by reason is ordered by the divine law", we may assume that the matter also embraces a *sharʿī* norm (Muḥaqqiq-Dāmād 1998b:116–117).[23]

In contemporary Iran, Islamic traditionalism is also advanced to a lesser degree by the traditional Shi'i *marājʿ al-taqlīd*, who have continued to teach in the *ḥauzahs* and edit and comment upon the traditional texts of Shi'i literature. They are seldom interested in the challenges of the modern world and essentially ignore modern scientific methods and theories. Nevertheless, they have not been reluctant to present rigorous criticism against the modernising policies of the Iranian state as well as the tendency to integrate modern knowledge into the *ḥauzah-yi ʿilmīyah* (Chehabi 1990:218). Out of these, Muḥammad Riḍā Gulpāigānī, Abū al-Qāsim al-Khūʾī, Shihāb al-dīn Maʿrashī-Najafī, Sayyid ʿAbdullāh Mūsāwī-Shīrāzī, Sayyid Muḥammad Rūḥānī and Muḥammad ʿAlī Arākī recently passed away.[24] At the present, there are a number of senior *ayātullāhs* among whom Sayyid ʿAlī Ḥusainī Sīstānī, ʿAbdullāh Jawādī-Āmulī, Sayyid Mūsā Shābirī-Zanjānī, Mīrzā Jawād Tabrīzī and Sayyid Muḥammad Ḥusainī-Shāhrūdī have succeeded as the most esteemed ones.

Following the publication of ʿAbd al-Karīm Surūsh's articles on the contraction and expansion of religious knowledge in 1988, a number of Islamic traditionalist writers went into strong polemics with the former on questions such as modern hermeneutics, epistemology and neo-positivistic definitions of science. These topics had not been highlighted seriously by earlier traditionalists except for Muḥammad Ḥusain Ṭabāṭabāʾī's (1999) and Murtaḍā Muṭahharī's (1998d and 1998e) writings on materialist philosophy and historicism. The traditionalists were forced to refine their arguments and confront topics that had no previous equivalents in the Islamic tradition. The major critics of Surūsh's theories on science and the evolution of religious knowledge were, for instance, *āyatullāh* Jaʿfar Subḥānī, *ḥujjat al-islām* Ṣadiq Lārījānī, ʿAṭāʾullāh Karīmī, Ḥusain Ghaffārī, Muḥammad Taqī-Faʿʿālī and others.[25] The major objection of Lārījānī and Subḥānī as well as Ghaffārī

[23] In his discussion on *uṣūl ʿamalīyah*, Muḥaqqiq-Dāmād (1999:168–169) also sticks closely to the *uṣūlī* tradition after Murtaḍā al-Anṣārī and applies them to spheres of law covered neither by the revealed sources nor by reason. In his discussion on *qiyās*, he confirms furthermore the traditional Shi'i viewpoint by rejecting all kinds of analogical deduction where the *ratio decideni* is ambiguous or difficult to discover, such as in the case of *qiyās mustanbīt al-ʿillah* and therefore approves *qiyās manṣūṣ al-ʿillah* as well as *qiyās aulāwīyat*.

[24] As Saskia Gieling highlights, after the demise of these senior *marājʿ al-taqlīd*, the Iranian state juridical authorities and media encouraged the emergence of one sole *marjaʿ* in the person Sayyid ʿAlī Khāminaʾī. But as Khāminaʾī announced his withdrawal since he merely regarded himself as the sole political *marjaʿ* for Shi'i outside Iran, the *marjaʿ* selection instead came to follow the traditionally sanctioned process of consensus and adherence. Nevertheless, the Iranian government is still in doubt about the explicit boundaries of political and religious authority (Gieling 1997). Cf. Khāminaʾī 1995.

[25] Cf. Karīmī (1990), Lārījānī (1993) and below.

concerns Surūsh's use of Popper's idea of falsification and Hempel's principle of the paradox of confirmation that they believe are inappropriate in the context of Islamic law. In their view, the positivistic definition of knowledge is irreconcilable with a religion that is governed by the sincere objective to discover divine norms in the context of particular examples and cases as an act of devotion:

We know that the Islamic scholar or researcher as far as religious science is concerned has to search for knowledge that is valid from the point of view of the divine law. Now if the scholar is indifferent in the search for the will of the divine law and gives us to understand that his research is of no value from the perspective of the divine law and religion, then will his research be coherent? Now we are sure that this is not so, since the proofs (that have been presented in their contexts) indicate that the meaning of religious knowledge in theology, the origin (of the world), resurrection, the knowledge of the prophets and their intermediates (i.e. the *ʿulamā*) is certain knowledge and not *iḥtimālī* (probable) (Lārījānī 1988:10).

In contrast to Surūsh's own methodological account that recognises a deductive methodological element, Lārījānī argues that Surūsh's theory without circumspection follows an inductive methodology that cannot surpass the validity of logical demonstration, whether it be in theology or jurisprudence.[26] While Lārījānī accepts that the notion that human knowledge develops is commonsense (i.e. it has no need of rational demonstration), he argues that the content of the traditional religious sciences are not determined by the new discoveries in the modern sciences since the hypotheses constructed from an inductive method by definition are unfinished:

In other words there is a great difference between the claim that there is a *wāṯiq* (regular) relationship between various realms of human learning and that every hypothesis, which is confirmed or falsified in the natural sciences actually influences the understanding of Islamic law on the other (ibid.:11).

In this respect, Lārījānī suggests that as soon as the direct relationship between juristic *istinbāṭ* and non-religious philosophical foundations is accepted as a general rule, there is no reason to claim that *ijtihād* can be conducted in an independent and correct manner. His criticism is also directed against Surūsh's vindication of scientific 'objectivity', which he regards as methodological vulgarity since Surūsh as a true Popperian should not be concerned with verifying and making judgments on the legal opinions

[26] *Ḥujjat al-islām* Ṣādiq Lārījānī is a pupil of Muḥammad Miṣbāḥ-Yazdī and he received his religious education at a *ḥauzah-yi ʿilmīyah* in Qum. In 2001, he was elected into the the *shūrā-yi nigahbān* (Guardian council) by ʿAlī Khāminaʾī. At present, he teaches at the *ḥauzahs* in that city and is in particular renowned for his works in *kalām-i jadīd* and *falsafah-yi dīn* (religious philosophy). As a matter of fact, Lārījānī's views on the nature of religious knowledge are almost identical with those of his teacher. Cf. Miṣbāḥ-Yazdī 1998.

of others, such as in the case of his comments on Muḥammad Ḥusain Ṭabāṭabāʾī's exegetical opinions:

It is strange that the respected writer [i.e. Surūsh] considers Karl Popper's principle of falsification as the criterion of science, since someone who accepts falsification as the criterion of science should not search for verification or confirmation in science, but look for the emergence of theories from falsified and contradictory propositions, and Popper himself gave categorical emphasis to this point (ibid.:12).

Taking into account that Popper is a philosopher with non-religious credentials, Lārījānī (ibid.:13) continues to accuse Surūsh of some form of epistemological *shakkākīyat* (scepticism):

To my belief, the rationale of the author's work [i.e. Surūsh's] is nothing but full-fledged scepticism concerning all knowledge, including the religious sciences. ... In this respect, the author of the article is fully reliant on the views of Karl Popper, which is not concealed for those well-informed of his work.

In contrast to Surūsh's empirical and inductive method of science, Jaʿfar Subḥānī asserts that the acknowledgement of the existence of a hierarchy of *buṭūn* (inner levels) that corresponds to the ontological levels of reality is a precondition of Islamic hermeneutics.[27] He argues that these inner levels of meaning give reasons for the multiple existences of divergent but correct interpretations of revelation that never exhaust the meaning of the divine word:

Indeed, all this requires that the exegete adopts the correct rules of interpretation and refers to the (relevant) verses where the scientific discoveries and conclusions are presented in the light of constant rational rules. In this case, the exegete's viewpoint becomes [a form of] instrument that neither exhausts the meaning nor the intention of the Qur'an (Subḥānī 1988:13).[28]

Subḥānī (ibid.:11) argues that Surūsh altogether neglects the fact that Islamic law has not only constant revealed and transmitted sources, but also a number of rational elements which are constant throughout the process of

[27] *Āyatullāh* Jaʿfar Subḥānī was born in Tabriz in 1930. He finished his preliminary religious education at the Maktab-khānah-yi Mīrzā Maḥmūd Fāḍil in his hometown. In 1946, Subḥānī went to Qum to study *fiqh*, *falsafah* and *tafsīr* under Burūjirdī, Gulpāigānī, Khumainī and Ṭabāṭabāʾī. He also participated in the Ṭabāṭabāʾī's private classes and translated his *Uṣūl-i falsafah wa rawish-i riʾālīsm* into Arabic. After the revolution, he was elected as a member of *Majlis-i khubragān-i qānūn-i asāsī* (The Assembly of experts of constitutional law) which was responsible for the drafting of the new constitution. In 1980, Subḥānī began to publish a theological magazine called *Kalām-i islāmī* (Islamic theology) and he is at large the author of over 140 books. At present, he teaches the *khārij* courses in *fiqh* and *uṣūl al-fiqh* at the *ḥauzahs* in Qum.

[28] As far as Islamic law is concerned, Subḥānī argues that the *āyāt al-aḥkām al-qurʾān* as a category of *muḥkam* verses are subjected to very limited hermeneutical variation and that *ikhtilāf* is restricted to the sphere of *furūʿ al-fiqh* since all jurists follow a common method for the inference of legal norms (Subḥānī 1988:14).

inference of rational proofs in law. "In the sphere of rational rulings (practical reason) there exists a sequence of constant and stable perceptions that are not adjusted or changed by the process of time or the development of the sciences". More importantly, Subḥānī asserts that far from all Muslims have the *ṣalāḥiyat* (competence) to interpret the revealed sources and infer legal norms, since *ijtihād* requires knowledge in the *muqaddamāt* of *ijtihād* that are mentioned in the traditional legal sources.[29] As the preliminaries are considered as a pre-conditional and principal aspect of Islamic jurisprudence, Lārījānī turns to Surūsh's departure from the traditional legal discourse in matters of methodology as a major object of his own critique. He argues that Surūsh distorts truth when he claims that the traditional hermeneutical discourse acknowledges no presuppositions, when in reality these presuppositions are identical with the *muqaddamāt* of *ijtihād*. He takes *ʿilm al-lughah* (linguistics) as an example and argues that it is a necessary precondition "for textual understanding, its grammatical rules and the application of rational rules to attribute meaning to the author, etc." and that all jurists are "in agreement with this kind of *tawaqqufhā'ī* (interruptions, i.e. in the act of *istinbāṭ*)" (Lārījāni 1995:49). Lārījāni (ibid.:53) also claims that neither Surūsh nor Muḥammad Mujtahid-Shabistarī present any demonstrative and rational proofs for their viewpoint that non-religious presuppositions determine the juristic *istinbāṭ* or for the latter's justification of the hermeneutical circle. In fact, he argues that Surūsh's hermeneutical principle of *intiẓār-i mā az dīn* (our expectation of religion) cannot be considered as a preliminary of legal inference, since every correct legal norm is concealed in the sources themselves from the very outset (ibid.:55). In the view of the traditionalists, the question of *ikhtilāf* is hence a normative one that depends on the degree of knowledge of the preliminaries of *ijtihād* among the jurists themselves (Ghaffārī 1990:165).

Similar to Lārījāni, Subḥānī argues that the relationship between the different sciences is not an *aṣl-i kullī* (general principle), but that all scientific disciplines rather operate with different methodologies by recognising different criteria and theories of science itself. In this respect, he considers the demonstrative approach of logic as superior to induction, since syllogism constitutes a guarantee for maintaining the principle of correspondence in epistemology. By rejecting modern Western philosophies as non-realist forms of epistemology that reduce science to relative dialectical standards, Subḥānī (1988:12) defines philosophy as first philosophy or metaphysics and argues that natural science does not influence philosophy that operates on a higher cognitive level:

[29] Among these *muqaddamāt*, Subḥānī (1988:13), similar to Muṭahharī, mentions knowledge of the Arabic language, *uṣūl al-fiqh* and *ʿilm al-rijāl* as the most important ones, but also refers to *tafsīr al-āyāt al-aḥkām* as well as knowledge of earlier *fatwās* on specific cases as obligatory preconditions for the inference of legal norms.

Natural science only operates with hypotheses and theories and cannot, similar to mathematics and philosophy, rely on certain demonstration in accordance with its own category of subjects... Indeed, one cannot submit the destiny of philosophy, which is a completely rational and demonstrative science in the context of expansion and development, to the service of natural science, which is only concerned with experience, experiment and hypotheses.[30]

To conclude, Subḥānī (ibid.:13) restricts the influence of non-religious sciences on the subjects of Islamic law to the process of *ijrā'* (implementation) and excludes hence the act of inference itself. He also points to the fact that the majority of Islamic jurists never let their position on philosophy or mysticism influence their elaboration on jurisprudence (ibid.:14). In Subḥānī's view, Surūsh neglects altogether the epistemological difference between Islamic philosophy and modern Western philosophy, which he considers as a new form of the ancient Greek school of scepticism. He contends, in fact, that ancient Greek philosophy was very primitive in character and that it was only completed through the harmonising effort of Islamic philosophers who combined reason with faith (ibid.:12). In the sense that Surūsh's major inspiration is modern Western philosophy, Subḥānī believes that it is not coincidental that Surūsh's conclusions are very similar to those of Hegel even if they adopt very different methods.

Ḥusain Ghaffārī, a former pupil of Muṭahharī and director of the philosophical group of the faculty of Humanities at Tehran University, focuses his critique of Surūsh's work on the epistemological aspects of the latter's ideas. He charges Surūsh with "paving the way for Islamic Protestantism", that is, for espousing cognitive standards taken from modern epistemology and thereby becoming a tool for "Western cultural intrusion" (Ghaffārī 1990:21, 311). In essentialist terms, he argues that "the cognitive principles and cultural foundations of every people and culture" constitutes "the very air particles of the atmosphere of that culture" (ibid.:190). Ghaffārī's claim is that the sources and methodological principles of Islamic law are immutable and eternal characteristics of Islam as such and his refutation of Surūsh's arguments is similar to those of Lārījānī and Subḥānī directed against Surūsh's employment of inductive reasoning and its lack of scientific validity. For instance, Ghaffārī (ibid.:169) believes that the observable interaction of the sciences does not suggest that religious science, such as *fiqh*, is dependent on the modern sciences for its accomplishment. In this respect, he traces Surūsh's epistemology to Popper's notion of 'third world knowledge', i.e. the autonomous and collective 'objective' world of scientific knowledge where knowledge also decisively changes with time:

Besides the fact that Popper's views have influenced the general framework of the writer's [i.e. Surūsh's] discussion, it has inspired his opinions and expressions, in

[30] Cf. Subḥānī 1988:10.

particular, as far as the recent issue is concerned, that is: the development of religious knowledge and the relative nature of the truths of every period. The views of the writer can be considered as excerpted from Popper's specific concept labelled 'third world' as well as some of the fundamental principles of his philosophy such as the principle of evolution that includes (evolution of) beliefs (ibid.:187).

While Ghaffārī acknowledges that Surūsh's epistemology differs from Popper in that Surūsh acknowledges the existence of God and religion, he believes that Surūsh's position comes very close to the latter in the sense that the conception of *sharīʿat-i ṣāmit* as Islamic law in itself, impossible to grasp in its essentials, is very close to the view that religion is socially constructed (ibid.:187–188). He suggests that Surūsh's theory in fact results in a form of epistemological relativism "where everyone infers the legal norms from the view of his own understanding in a way that is compatible with modern science" (ibid.:160). More importantly, Ghaffārī (ibid.:166) asserts that Surūsh's epistemological categories are alien to Islam and therefore incorrect. "The distinction between *sharīʿat-i ṣāmit* and 'our understanding of *sharīʿat*' is an incorrect and distorting division that is influenced by the opinions of Western philosophers". Ghaffārī's view is shared by many other Islamic traditionalists, such as Muḥammad Madadpūr (1998:146), who in an article on the crisis of modern civilisation identifies Surūsh's distinction between religion and religious knowledge as the most comprehensive expression of secularising Islamic thought in Iran:

To separate religion from religious knowledge is the most wide-ranging form of secularism in modern religious thought that also makes the correlation and unification of Islam and Western culture possible in general terms. Here, 'religion' is considered as *intiẓāʿī* (non-contingent) (constant and silent) whereas 'religious knowledge' is historical, human and *inḍimāmī* (contingent). Because of this differentiation the kernel of religion becomes invalid, illusory and unintelligible, viewed through the prisms of human science. Since a constructed human religious science has no sacred character, it remains non-sacred and transient.

Similar to Lārījānī, Ghaffārī (1990:163) furthermore argues that *sharīʿat* is divine and aims to "provide a complete plan for the practical life of human beings" in their quest for spiritual perfection. Another aspect of Ghaffārī's discourse is that acquired definite proofs, whether transmitted or rational, essentially and eternally are identical to *sharīʿat-i ṣāmit*:

The principle of *ijtihād* has been stipulated by the divine Legislator Himself as a means to extract divine norms. The *halāl wa harām*, which are produced from the process of *ijtihād*, are themselves identical to the *halāl wa harām* of the divine Legislator and not an addition or reduction in regard to that (ibid.:162).

In his general introduction to the subject of epistemology, Muḥammad Taqī-Faʿʿālī, a prominent pupil of ʿAbdullāh Jawādī-Āmūlī, also presents a thoroughly traditionalist discourse on the subject of knowledge. His departure is that *maʿrifat-shīnāsī* (epistemology) is not something which is essentially new, even if modern philosophers constantly approach its central topics from new angles. Taqī-Fa‘‘ālī is in particular disapproving of empiricism which in the shape of logical positivism reduces science, philosophy and hence epistemology to *dādah-yi ḥissī* (sense data). He argues that empirical facts can only be one of many possible sources of knowledge as far as Islam is concerned and among those other sources he mentions revelation and reason, but also transmitted knowledge, which is distinguished from strict empirical facts. Hence, the Qur'an, the *sunnat*, *ijmā‘* and *‘aql* serve as sources of religious knowledge, which is produced from *dalīl-i ‘aqlī* (rational proof) (Taqī-Fa‘‘ālī 1999:329). In this respect, Taqī-Fa‘‘ālī's viewpoint is essentially that knowledge is identical to justified (true) belief, whether this form of belief derives from revelation, reason, transmission or empirical proof. Religious knowledge, in other words, cannot be *iḥtimāl* (probable) but only *mumkīn* (possible):

> *Shinākht-i dīnī* (religious comprehension) is either correct or incorrect. This principle signifies that comprehension either corresponds to religion or not. In both cases comprehension is different from the principle of religion. Religion is independent of the individual, but religious comprehension rests on the human individuals… But while it is *mumkin* (possible) for religious comprehension to be in error, such a comprehension does not count as knowledge (ibid.:329).

In his essay on the concept of meaning in linguistic philosophy, Taqī-Fa‘‘ālī (1998:135) furthermore conceptualises the identity of knowledge in deductive and propositional terms and asserts that "knowledge never expands or contracts according to a descriptive theory of meaning". Therefore, he concludes that epistemological changes in reality occur only in the realm of *guzārahhā* (propositions) and *bāwarhā* (beliefs), which are added or deleted in the process of knowing, and that "anything, such as *farbahī-yi ma‘ārif* ('expansion' of knowledge) is impossible to identify" (ibid.:134).

B. The Islamic traditionalist position of ʿAbdullāh Jawādī-Āmūlī

One of the most prominent traditionalists in contemporary Iran is ʿAbdullāh Jawādī-Āmulī. He has emerged as one of the most distinguished *āyatullāhs* during the last decade, partly due to the deaths of a number of senior high-ranking Shi'i scholars.[31] For Jawādī-Āmulī (1998a:198–200) epistemology is never divorced from the religious ontology. His point of departure is that metaphysical science or philosophy of Being is the first element of Islamic hermeneutics since man himself is the possessor of *fiṭrat-i ilāhī* (divine nature) and *rūḥ* (divine Spirit). Since the traditional Islamic cosmology is considered superior to the values and philosophies of contemporary modernity, the principles of Islamic philosophy, or more correctly theosophy, is considered the foundation in Jawādī-Āmulī's discourse. True knowledge, in the strictest sense is, in other words, not jurisprudence, philology, grammar, or medicine but theosophy, and science is nothing but the external garb of Qur'anic science. Referring to the *ḥadīṯ* depicting ʿAlī b. Abī Ṭālib as the door of knowledge, Jawādī-Āmulī asserts that true knowledge is the esoteric knowledge of the teachings of the Prophet and the *imāms*. It is above discursive thought and only accessible to the initiated Shi'i believers (Jawādī-Āmulī 1998b:15). By defining science as the objective knowledge of the cosmic and natural order, Jawādī-Āmulī's point of departure is that the true relationships of science are qualitative and intuitive, not quantitative. Hence, he is more interested in philosophy, theology and mathematics, which he believes explain the objective and *takwīnī* (intrinsic) relationships in the cosmos in contrast to the empirical

[31] *Āyatullāh* ʿAbdullāh Jawādī-Āmulī was born in Amul, Iran, in 1933, into a family of eminent religious scholars. At the age of fourteen, he entered a *ḥauzah* in his hometown and after finishing the *muqaddamāt* (primary level) of religious education, he went to Tehran in 1952 to study *fiqh*, *ʿilm-i kalām*, *manṭiq*, and *ʿulūm-i adabī* (literature) under the auspices of Muḥammad Taqī-Āmulī at Madrasah-yi Marwī (Marwī school). His teachers during these years included Abū al-Ḥasan Shaʿrānī, Mīrzā Mahdī Muhī al-dīn Ilāhī-Qumshaʾī, a renowned Qur'anic exegete, and Ḥusain Fāḍil-Tūnī, an authority on Ibn al-ʿArabī who initiated Jawādī-Āmulī into the discipline of *ʿirfān*. Jawādī-Āmulī completed the highest level of pre-*khārij* lessons in Tehran and then went to Qum to study *fiqh* for Sayyid Muḥammad Ḥusain Burūjirdī, Sayyid Muḥammad Dāmād and Rūḥullāh Khumainī, who were among the most renowned Shi'i scholars at that time. He participated in the *falsafah* classes of Muḥammad Ḥusain Ṭabāṭabāʾī as well, and his 25 years of study under the latter also included the *khārij* level of *ḥikmat-i mutaʿālīyah* (transcendental wisdom), a subject on which he is recognised as the second highest authority in contemporary Iran (Jawādī-Āmulī 1999a). He has written on a number of topics generally related to the traditional Islamic sciences, but also criticism of modern epistemology, materialistic philosophy, human rights, and the like. He has published more than a hundred articles in various newspapers and magazines, such as *Pāsdār-i islām* (Guardian of Islam) and *Khiradnāmah-yi ṣadrā* (Ṣadrā journal of wisdom), and has also made a contribution to the commemoration volume of Muḥammad Ḥusain Ṭabāṭabāʾī (Jawādī-Āmulī 1983).

sciences that have a thoroughly *iʿtibārī* (estimative) dimension (Jawādī-Āmulī n.y.:124).

For Jawādī-Āmulī, to speak of spirituality is *ipso facto* to raise the question of the sources of knowledge, since divine truth and philosophical truth are identical but not interdependent. Religion is considered to be *hastī-shināsī-yi ilāhī* (divine ontology), which guides human reason towards specific philosophical principles and the method is one of truth-reaching, that is, seeking the truth methodologically. While God can be known through discursive reasoning, He is only known in His totality through Himself (Jawādī-Āmulī 1998a:361).[32] Jawādī-Āmulī is not opposed to the exercise of reason, but only to its modern secular employment. He believes that modern science constitutes a direct challenge to the Islamic worldview, which claims a knowledge of reality based not solely on reason, but also on revelation and intuition. The proper use of the mind in the quest for truth is, so to say, within the bounds of Islamic faith and revelation as 'divine capacity', since the scientific enterprise emphasises the spiritual receptivity of the scientist rather than his mere conceptual comprehension (ibid.:390). Reason is hence the perceiver of that which exists and even if man considers reason as his own, he is not himself its source or fountainhead since reason is rooted in the Divine Being. In the view of Jawādī-Āmulī, knowledge that does not take into account God's reality can never grasp the true and intrinsic nature of phenomena since it neglects to comprehend the world as a cosmological totality. In this respect, real intelligence is contemplative intelligence, the immanent divine spark called *ʿaql*. As a divine endowment, reason is conditioned by the "clear spring of revelation, which cleanses and purifies all its dust", and there is ultimately no difference between faith and science. Even if reason is positioned in opposition to *naql*, science is considered the 'purification of the heart' and reason and revelation, the two major sources of valid knowledge, are used complementarily:

> Just as God reveals His message through the transmission of the *maʿṣūmīn* (Peace be upon them), He also conveys His command by means of demonstrable reason since both [reason and transmission] are explorers of divine guidance in terms that one of them, i.e. revelation, is superior to the other. Yet, both of them are divine proofs and complement each other (ibid.:211).[33]

By adopting the traditional hierarchy of knowledge, Jawādī-Āmulī's (1998b:12) account of scientific knowledge is founded on a position that regards science as related and subordinated to a higher order. He maintains

[32] In this respect, Jawādī-Āmulī (n.y.:85) acknowledges that love for God is the necessary foundation of all understanding. "The most excellent way to approach the contents of the divine word is to proceed on the way of divine love. Only attachment to the world intrudes on divine love. The levels of understanding of the word of God's revelation are compatible to the level of love for God and also to the levels of veils".

[33] Cf. Jawādī-Āmulī 1998a:157.

that science is comprised of *darajāt* (levels) and that the Islamic worldview is "constant throughout the realm of existence". By interpreting cognitive matters in these terms, he considers the function of science within the boundaries of Islam, which involves seeing knowledge as basically spiritual and speculative, as opposed to the positivism and secularism of modern science. Metaphysics and philosophy precede their applications, i.e. the sciences, and all sciences comprise a hierarchy of levels not only in the three-fold division of knowledge (i.e. empirical, rational, intuitive), but also within each of these three domains in the sense that "each one of them is certain and solid within its own category, but quivering and inefficient outside that category" (Jawādī-Āmulī 1998a:189). In this respect, rational and intuitive methods are the only fully reliable methods for certain and valid knowledge since these, in contrast to empirical or inductive methods, are believed to decipher the constant and intrinsic nature of things:

> Empirical knowledge is obtained through the senses and achieved with experiment and induction. It is connected to the natural world and like nature it is shifting and changing. [...] Rational knowledge is a conceptual skill that is connected to the constant realities and which also conceals the moving and changing matters of the natural world. It is higher and more expanded than the empirical sciences and similar to its *maʿlūm* (known), it is solid and reliably established (ibid.:188).

Differentiating reason from various forms of illusion, Jawādī-Āmulī (1986:4) in fact underlines that the Islamic sciences "are essentially not science but religion as such" or even more explicitly "science is religion itself".[34] As far as Islamic jurisprudence as well as ethics is concerned, these sciences are intimately connected with spirituality and meticulous theological questions such as the nature of the *asmāʾ-i ḥusnā* (most beautiful Divine Names). Since the whole purpose of the creation of man is to be guided towards his utmost potentiality and approximate his ontological realities to the most beautiful Names, God has created *ʿaql* as the means of divining the law (Jawādī-Āmulī 1998c:6). In fact, Jawādī-Āmulī argues that the same primary sources, revelation and reason, are used in jurisprudence, theology and theosophy and that only the methodology differs (i.e. the latter, for instance, makes use of the language of logic to explain mystic experience). In all cases, logic leads to the transcendent itself, when it is used correctly and by an intellect that is not corrupted by the lower passions of the soul:

[34] In an interview with the author, Jawādī-Āmulī (1999) stated that reason as it attempts to operate apart from religious commitment is doomed to become fantastic and issue in despair. He maintained that while reason very well might be dynamic and discursive, it should never be mixed with fantasy or *wahm* (illusion), which is the lowest level in the hierarchy of knowledge.

Science is among the perfections of Being and the necessary means for every spiritual traveller. But as he reaches Divine Unity, all sciences are annihilated in comparison to infinite knowledge of Truth that accepts no share for anything else (Jawādī-Āmulī 1998b:26).

Consequently, Jawādī-Āmulī connects to the Islamic philosophical tradition for contemplative purposes, that is, as a means for spiritual progress to Divine Unity rather than for only having a rational picture of the realm of existence. For Jawādī-Āmulī (1998a:219) human subjectivity is divinely mediated in a total and immediate sense. It is symbolic, and similar to the theoretical sciences such as theosophy, Islamic law serves as an instrument for human perfection in terms of "turning the space of nature into focus for human vicegerency" so that "when man observes it in its entirety, he becomes the *khalīfatullāh* (vicegerent of God)". By reference to the Qur'anic verse where God revealed His portents or signs within human beings (*Qur.* 41:53), Jawādī-Āmulī claims that human nature is a theomorphic being in the sense of constituting a *tajallī* (theophany) of the Divine Names. Since God explained the reality of the Names to man and not to the angels, man has a high spiritual potential that is reflected in that all essential knowledge is ultimately based on the identity of the knower and the known. In the view of Jawādī-Āmulī (1997a:136) the knower and the known is ultimately one:

If the *ʿālim* (knower) and the *maʿlūm* (known) and the *shāhid* (observer) and the *mashhūd* (observed) are one, then we are identical with the Names or as expressed by the seventh *imām*. "By God! We are the most beautiful Names".

In other words, the unity of subject and object means that man's most immediate experience is that of his own intuitive awareness, which can achieve a direct apprehension of ultimate reality that reveals it to be spiritual. Epistemologically, truth and reality are rolled into one. Reality embodied in the form of divine creation calls for nothing but respectful contemplation and the fulfilment of man's supra-human potential. Valid knowledge consists in the infallible possession of an inner searchlight which man can train upon his conscious state. In the sense that Jawādī-Āmulī (1998b:9) in esoteric terms considers the objective of science to be to "light up the world" and that science must correspond directly to the *maʿlūm* (known) whether this be the world (in the sense of a theophany) or God, he principally takes an 'objectivist' (and realist) approach to the subject of epistemology where realism is not interpreted as in Western positivism, but rather connected to the tradition after Muḥammad Ḥusain Ṭabāṭabāʾī.

Since modernity is intimately related to the history and philosophy of the modern West from Jawadī-Āmulī's point of view, he connects modern epistemology to Western forms of philosophical materialism, which he suggests have no natural function in the pursuit of knowledge since they "reject (cognitive) reliability and the sacred character of the principles and branches of religion". Since modern epistemology is not concerned with the reality taken as a whole or as an authentic order in the spiritual sense, it only has legitimacy to give *guzārish* (report) on the arrangement of the a priori views on specific objects, but never to judge these views. In the view of Jawādī-Āmulī (1998a:256, 262, 341), only the proficient *ʿulamā* have the competence to decide the nature of religious epistemology since the judgements of modern scientists and philosophers are nothing but a *bāzī-gīrī* (play) for the modern mind. In this respect, Jawādī-Āmulī asserts that the major disintegration of Christian as well as Jewish religious thought occurred during the enlightenment, when ontology was divorced from religion and the demonstrative method of the scholastics was replaced by empirical methods in science that refuted religion as 'non-verifiable data'. In fact, he considers empiricism and scienticism or what he calls "materialistic philosophy" as the very anti-thesis of religious ontology in its reduction of all existents to matter. In its essentials, Jawādī-Āmulī's (ibid.:168,185, 253) epistemology employs a *mabāḥiṯ-i hastī-shināsānah-yi maʿrifat* (ontological discussion on knowledge) that prioritises the nature of science before the historical development of science and repudiates the claim of the positivists and materialists to engage in metaphysical matters.

The Qur'an is the first source of knowledge in Jawādī-Āmulī's epistemology and it emerges as the most frequent reference in his works. He considers it the "book of life" that contains the answers to the hidden and manifest aspects of human existence, and matters concerning spirituality and worship as well as the efficient administration and planning of society. The Qur'an is the first source of the bulk of human learning, in particular the human sciences, but also for a major part of natural science:

> Indeed, the Qur'an is the first source of all human sciences and some natural sciences. The Qur'an is the foundation for *jahānbīnī*, philosophical themes and theological argument. It is the foundation for the topics of creation and resurrection and all that is between creation and resurrection (Jawādī-Āmulī 1998c:276).

In the view of Jawādī-Āmulī (n.y.:302), the central role of the Qur'an is justified precisely by the fact that revelation concerns the goal of creation and embraces all individual things of existence in contrast to modern science that "merely deals with and examines the specific limited internal structure of (individual) things".[35] In this respect, Jawādī-Āmulī supposes that the tradition of Islamic philosophy is not merely deeply rooted in the Qur'anic worldview, but operates within a cosmos in which revelation is accepted as the major binding reality and source of knowledge. He argues that revealed law commands the study of philosophy for those who have had the native

[35] In his criticism of Darwinism, Jawādī-Āmulī (1998:173) for instance argues that the revealed texts include descriptions of creation that "cannot be altered" and hence must be prioritised before the philosophical conclusions drawn from the discoveries in modern natural science.

ability to pursue it and the actual philosophical training. Since Islamic philosophy is an integrated part of religion, he develops a meta-theory according to which philosophical truths and religion are identical and therefore cannot contradict each other. Ontologically, he suggests that the existence of Islamic philosophy is contingent on the being of a religious agency and that Islam includes a theory of knowledge from which philosophy can be derived. The epithet Islamic gives an identity to knowledge and there are certain beliefs that derive their justification not because their truth is rationally deducible or empirically verifiable but because they correspond to a criteria that establishes their identity as Islamic:

Islamic philosophy appeared with Islam. Islam is the divine religion that all prophets instructed mankind... As a matter of course, Islam brought the world philosophy. Since Islam is a *dīn-i burhānī* (demonstrable religion) it also instructed other religions in rational learning by means of logical demonstration (Jawādī-Āmulī 1986:7).

In this respect, the Shi'i *imāms* were heirs to the mantle of esoteric prophetic knowledge, but also to its exoteric aspect in the sense that they substantiated the principles and methods of Islamic philosophy, jurisprudence, and the like. By reference to numerous *akhbār*, Jawādī-Āmulī (1986:7) suggests that the Islamic *jahānbīnī* is a rational one which "by means of reason has fixed the necessary and fundamental principles of revelation". Consequently, the religious sciences are considered to have pure divine descent and not to have their roots in historical or cultural environments on the terrestrial level of existence. "The religious sciences are a constant collection of knowledge, which is protected from the hold of and adaptation to any imagination and fancying. They are immune from the harm of contemporary trends" (Jawādī-Āmulī 1998a:145). In the case of Islamic law, he believes that it cannot become an object of *bāz-sāzī* (reconstruction) or transformation" even if he acknowledges that *bāz-fahmī* (re-understanding) is possible to a certain extent, something that also is characteristic of his hermeneutics (ibid.:146).

But what seems to remain unnoticed by Jawādī-Āmulī is the role the movement of translation from Greek into Arabic had in the shaping of Islamic philosophy and logic, which took shape in the late Umayyad period. While he acknowledges that the Islamic adoption of Greek philosophy was selective, taking no interest in the impious Greek pantheon, he also neglects to account for the fact that the majority of leading logicians up to the end of the tenth century (al-Kindī excluded) were Christians and that logic only afterwards became a tool for Islamic philosophy and theology.[36] Jawādī-

[36] Cf. Watt 1985:38. It is interesting to note that the influence of the movement of translation was recognised by Jawādī-Āmulī's teacher, Muḥammad Ḥusain Ṭabāṭabā'ī (1984:59), who acknowledged that Muslims "were not familiar with philosophical thought until they saw examples of it in the beginning of the second century in the translation of certain

Āmulī (ibid.:357) hints at the issue as a philosopher rather than as a historian and he views logic as the key to philosophy, the pursuit of which (knowledge) is the key to human happiness. Secular philosophy cannot apprehend the truth of existence, because of the priority it assigns to reason over faith. It is faith that begins with existence and reasons from it, not the opposite. Secular reason cannot therefore apprehend the truth of the self, of the world, or of God but only construct various possible views of it. Faith, as Jawadi-Amuli speaks of it, is, so to say, not in the category of mere opinion, and insofar as it is directed to God, it is lifted out of the realm of private judgement to constitute the objective factor that saves the believer from falling into subjectivism. True metaphysical belief counts, in other words, as knowledge.

Evidently, Jawādī-Āmulī is concerned with *falsafah ūlā* (first philosophy), which means that an investigation into the nature and classification of science must be preceded by a similar kind of inquiry into the nature of philosophic knowledge. He reaffirms the Aristotelian division of philosophy into its theoretical and practical parts according to an ontological criterion, that is, the former are *muṭlaq* (absolute) while the latter are *mutaʿayīn* (determined) (Jawādī-Āmulī n.y.:85, 1998b:274). But in contrast to Aristotle and the Islamic Peripatetic philosophers, he employs the Ṣadrāian distinction *ʿirfān-i naẓarī* (theoretical theosophy) for *ʿulūm-i kullī* (general sciences) and *ʿirfān-i ʿamalī* (practical theosophy) for *ʿulūm-i juzʾī* (partial sciences). His view that theosophy, interpreted as Qur'anic guidance in its most general sense, is situated on a level higher than philosophy also suggests that his classification of science ultimately is inspired by the definition of the epistemological status of intuitive knowledge found in Suhrawardī's theory of *ʿilm al-ḥuḍūrī*.[37] In this respect, the ideal man for Jawādī-Āmulī (1998a:55–67, 157) is a sage philosopher, a man who fully lives up to the demands of the tradition of theoretical as well as practical knowledge. While he does not view every concern with the time-bound and the accidental as irrelevant or unworthy, the whole realm of the historical is, however, merely relevant to self-cultivation in connection to revealed sayings and texts.

Following the tradition after Ṣadr al-dīn Shīrāzī, Jawādī-Āmulī (1998b:10, 17) exemplifies that the terms *ʿirfān-i naẓari* and *ʿirfān-i ʿamalī* signify the sciences, which possess a separate worldview and the sciences that borrow their worldview from philosophy respectively. While he avoids dividing

philosophical works into Arabic". In this respect, Jawādī-Āmulī withholds that Islamic philosophy is not only different from ancient and modern Western philosophies, but also distinct from the philosophical output of Islamic intellectuals.

[37] In other words, the subject of theosophy proper is interpreted in the tradition from Suhrawardī through Ṣadr al-dīn Shīrāzī as compatible to illuminative knowledge, which is not representational in the ordinary sense, but is instead an immediate presence of the known, in the way that he who knows Himself is present to himself.

these categories into further sub-classifications, it seems that philosophy includes the former sciences, such as metaphysics, theology and logic, while jurisprudence and ethics form part of the second category of science in addition to a third category of science, which includes those sciences that use empirical methods (and where natural sciences are included). He takes the relation between philosophy and ethics as an example how the practical sciences make use of the subjects that philosophy offers:

Ethics is essentially a partial science in the garb of philosophy. Similar to other partial sciences, it obtains its subject from philosophy. But *ʿirfān-i naẓarī* is above philosophy, since the subject of philosophy as well as the existence and truth of being is unconditional (Jawādī-Āmulī 1986:8).[38]

Jawādī-Āmulī's position does not differ very much from the estimation of the Peripatetics that the theoretical sciences seek knowledge of the truth and the practical knowledge of the good. His scheme, however, diverges from the traditional classification of the Islamic sciences, as first developed by al-Fārābī, where natural science and mathematics are included in the category of theoretical philosophy (Bakar 1997:931). While philosophy is not easily distinguished from theology, or even from law or grammar, since many of the questions within these contexts have direct philosophical relevance, Jawādī-Āmulī (1986:8) argues that the case of natural science is different. Natural science has no worldview of its own and its discussion is restricted to physical matters. "Neither of these (i.e. religious) topics are part of natural science since one cannot confirm or falsify them empirically. Nor is it possible to confirm or disconfirm the existence of the spirit since natural science does not discuss the source of existence but specific characteristics of particular (physical) phenomena." For Jawādī-Āmulī (ibid.:8) philosophy is consequently identical to worldview and he argues that only philosophical arguments (not the methods of empirical science) are legitimate for the validation or refutation of religious subjects:

In conclusion, if someone seeks to refute the higher principle, or the existence of the soul, angels and supernatural things, he has to refer to philosophical materialism and the like, which is philosophy. Physics and the like cannot discuss the source of the world and the comprehensiveness of the world.

In his tribute to logical methods, Jawādī-Āmulī refers to the Qur'anic description of faith as the source of certainty in knowledge and argues that any contradiction between reason and revelation is illusory. Since logic is not a separate knowledge, but a scientific method that transcends all sciences

[38] In this respect, the proper discipline *ʿirfān* has ascendancy not merely over theoretical sciences such as philosophy and theology but also over practical sciences such as *fiqh*. Practical science, ethics and jurisprudence furthermore derive their principles from Islamic law and are disposed towards "the refinement of the soul" (Jawādī-Āmulī 1986:8).

with the task of distinguishing true scientific statements from false ones (that is, those which correspond with reality from those which do not), the Islamic criterion of knowledge is, as he puts it, not its status at the *ḥauzah-yi ʿilmīyah*, but it is rather conditioned by its correspondence to the ontological levels of reality and its capacity to bring forth certain knowledge. Knowledge and reality are, in other words, not two things, but identical, and questions about criterion of knowledge depend upon questions of reality:

> Since *uṣūl-i fiqh* is an Islamic science, many other human sciences and even natural sciences can hence be counted as Islamic sciences. In this respect, the reliance (of the sciences) on Islam is definite, if their scientific validity is certain and the extent of their reliance on Islam is *muẓannah* (conjectural), if their measurement of verification is conjectural (Jawādī-Āmulī 1998a:99).[39]

As far as jurisprudence is concerned, the task of logic is, in the view of Jawādī-Āmulī, essentially to justify questions such as certainty and conjecture by means of the fundamentals and principles of syllogistic corroboration. By endorsing an ontological hierarchical classification of knowledge, which, as mentioned, extends from the empirical to the rational and the intuitive modes of knowing, he claims that no contradiction is possible between *ʿaql-i qaṭʿī* (definite reason) and revelation, but only between defect reason (i.e. wrong inference, false analogues, etc) and revealed texts that are apocryphal and *ẓannī*. In case a contradiction occurs, definite rational proof is superior to probable or conjectural revealed proof:

> When definite reason contradicts conjectural revelation, as has been said, definite reason is superior. The definite is superior to the probable in all cases, whether (the conflict concerns) a contradiction between definite revelation and probable revelation or between definite reason and probable reason (Jawādī-Āmulī n.y.:112).[40]

If one knows anything to be true, it can, in other words, not be probable or conjectural and therefore mistaken. If a conflict occurs between religion and

[39] Cf. Jawādī-Āmulī 1998a:158 and 312.

[40] In this respect, Jawādī-Āmulī (n.y.:281, 1998a:284) believes furthermore that "empirical scientific hypotheses do not influence the *qawānīn-i sharʿī* (religious laws) at all" since in the case where contradiction occurs between Islamic law and natural science, the legal proof is superior to the empirical proof if it is justified by definite proof, but otherwise definite empirical proof is superior. The empirical scientific method is, hence, not taken as the ultimate source of knowledge and is only related to observable facts, such as physics and inanimate objects. "Hence, if there occurs a contradiction in questions of *ḥikmat-i ʿamalī*, such as jurisprudence, ethics, and law, between empirical conjectural proof (which is based on a hypothesis and does not rest on the evident) and conjectural *fiqhī* proof, then one cannot neglect the *fiqhī* proof and make the experimental conjectural proof superior to that *fiqhī* proof, which is identical to revelation. Similarly, one cannot disrespect and neglect an empirical conjectural proof if a contradiction occurs in matters pertaining to empirical science, such as natural science and medicine and the like, between empirical conjectural proof and transmitted verbal proof…". Cf. Jawādī-Āmulī 1998a:163 and 1998b:10.

science it is commonly due to misinterpretation of the revealed sources or philosophical reasons (such as scienticism, empiricism and atheism). Due to the ontological foundation of all knowledge, the changes that occur in natural science never affect philosophy nor hermeneutics, except in cases validated by definite empirical proof against probable revealed proof:

> Human intellectual activity is not a pool where all knowledge is mixed. While philosophical materialism is the logical conclusion of a purely rational mind and empiricism focuses on the senses as the sole measure of reality, philosophy as well as hermeneutics is *wujūd-shināsānah* (ontological) from the perspective of Islam. Philosophy and hermeneutics are grounded in revelation and reason, independent of empirical science (Jawādī-Āmulī 1999a).

Jawādī-Āmulī (1998a:269) highlights the specific issue of Islamic legal epistemology and its relation to modern philosophy for the first time in his book *Sharīʿat dar āʾīnah-yi maʿrifat* (Islamic law in the light of knowledge), where he connects to the Shi'i designation of philosophical realism as it has been elaborated in the works of Muḥammad Ḥusain Ṭabāṭabāʾī and interpreted on the basis of the epistemological principle of correspondence.[41] Jawādī-Āmulī (ibid.:269) considers the principles of knowledge, matters concerning the nature of cognition and the existence of reality as intuitive and a priori and argues that "the rejection of each one of these (principles) results in sophistry". By assuming that the status of a scientific proposition is "determined by its subject and method" and that "the question of subject is a divine matter related to (a specific) principle of reality and existence", Jawādī-Āmulī considers Surūsh's theory of contraction and expansion a contradiction in terms, since it proceeds from the hypothesis that religion, revealed law and God are materialised in a mixture of truth and false at the level of 'is':

> One cannot consequently argue that religion itself is constant and absolute, but that human understanding is situated in the possibility of development and periodical change, since even the assertion that religion is constant and absolute is a part of human understanding (ibid.:69).

Jawādī-Āmulī (ibid.:269) argues that Surūsh by his adherence to Neo-Kantian philosophy and its claim that human knowledge is contingent on the constitution of the human mind, interpreted as fluid data, relativises truth:

> In contrast to what some thinkers, such as Kant, asserted, the justification of [Surūsh's notion of] the periodical character of human knowledge requires the

[41] The book was originally a series of weekly lectures delivered in 1989 and 1990 at a *ḥauzah-yi ʿilmīyah* in Qum to refute the theory of contraction and expansion of knowledge as articulated by ʿAbd al-Karīm Surūsh. While Jawādī-Āmulī fiercely criticises Surūsh's ideas, he at the same time recognises his importance in terms of drawing attention to his discourse (even if Surūsh is not mentioned by name throughout the 464 page work, but by the title of his book, which is the customary way of addressing other writers at the *ḥauzahs*).

acceptance of the presupposition that the human mind is not constituted of firm mental forms identical for all people in all ages, but that these forms are rather formed under the influence of temptations and different psychical, social, economical, political factors, etc.

In other words, Jawādī-Āmulī suggests that Surūsh's rejection of the capability of the human mind to know reality in absolute terms results in the relativisation of truth. In contrast to the ancient scepticism that "denied the existence of objective reality", and the direct realism of empiricism that "considered sense cognition as the only means to know external reality", he believes that the post-Kantian critical realism "complicated doubt and sophistry" not by explicitly rejecting the existence of an external reality, but by interpreting "the source of reality in terms of the periodical or relative quality of human understanding" (ibid.:270).

For the escape out of Surūsh's trap of relativism, Jawādī-Āmulī (ibid.:88, 90) establishes his norm of valid religious knowledge where "religion is identical to revealed texts" and where "the sacred character of spiritual religion is an integral aspect of religious knowledge in line with the notion of the unity of the knower and the known". The constant character of religious sciences is established on an esoteric philosophical criterion and the existence of *jahān-i ghaib* (the hidden world). Jawādī-Āmulī's (1998a:72) epistemology hence emerges with his ontology where, accordingly, religious knowledge that "corresponds to reality is constant and absolute". In contrast to the empirical sciences, which are established by means of induction, contingent on non-confirmed presuppositions and exposed to change and transformation, he claims that the religious sciences "transcend the boundaries of induction" and are established on *sunnat-i ṯābit-i ilāhī* (the divine constant tradition) (ibid.:161). Jawādī-Āmulī acknowledges that the jurists are continuously in contact with new legal subjects and cases, but he argues that this encounter does not affect the science of jurisprudence as such. Inspired by Ṣadr al-dīn Shīrāzī's notion of *ḥarakat-i jauharī*, he maintains that in reality it is the mind of the jurists that is transformed spiritually through the levels of existence, which are mirrored in the religious sciences:

The levels and degrees of science are consequently always constant and never shift. What is shifting and acquiring expansion is in reality nothing but the scholar himself. The scholar progresses at the horizon [i.e. the horizon of the Divine Names] in terms that he is a *maujūd-i jismānīyat al-ḥudūṯ* (corporeal being of divine manifestation)... The expansion and development of science transpire in relation to constant truths that are arranged in the hidden world and therefore essentially constitute the expansion and development of the *nafs-i ʿālam* (world soul) itself (ibid.:162).

In his book *Sharīʿat dar āʾīnah-yi maʿrifat*, Jawādī-Āmulī refers to the etymological meaning of *sharīʿat* as "the way that leads to water" to demonstrate that the law primarily is an instrument that "connects man to heaven". He also employs the concept *sharīʿat* diametrically to *ʿurf*, but interchangeably to *qānūn* as "the only law which is acceptable in an Islamic context" (ibid.:117, 212). While the purpose of reason as well as revelation is to divinely guide human beings, the role of reason in the inference of legal norms as the fourth source of divine law is essentially "to approve the necessity of Islamic law and revelation" and "to clarify and distinguish (legal) rulings" (ibid.:211). For Jawādī-Āmulī (ibid.:222), Muḥammad Bāqir al-Bihbahānī is the model for the contemporary revival of Islamic law and he interprets *ijtihād* in the modern *uṣūlī* tradition as dynamic and *mustamarr* (continuous):

Continuous *ijtihād* clarifies all rulings of *sharīʿat* in relation to all subjects, such as new subjects without precedence, and establishes the need of continuation of *wilāyat* for the social (situation) of Muslims.[42]

Inspired by the writings of Khumainī and Muṭahharī, Jawādī-Āmulī (ibid.:225–227) underlines that the jurist must be "conscious of the time and its needs" and implement *ijtihād* in the realm of private life as well as public life through a number of legal principles, among them *maṣlahat*. Nevertheless, *ijtihād* covers only the *furūʿ-i fiqh* and must be conducted by a qualified *mujtahid* learned in the religious sciences. By reference to a *khabar* stating that "It is for us (i.e. the *imāms*) to expound the *uṣūl* and for you to deduce the *furūʿ*", Jawādī-Āmulī (ibid.:170) suggests that any revival of Islamic law must be restricted to the *istinbāṭ* of the *mujtahid* in the realm of *furūʿ*:

Those who conduct *ijtihād* from the *uṣūl* and principles, which are established by the direction of revelation, are in the position to infer the full amount of *furūʿ* through them. An important part of the science of *uṣūl-i fiqh* concerns *uṣūl ʿamalīyah*, that is, the principles *barāʾah* (exemption), *ishtighāl* ('occupation') and *istiṣḥāb* which are based on a certain standard. For instance in the case of *ijtihād*, by reference to *istiṣḥāb* it may only be conducted after five years of continuous scientific work on the level of *suṭūḥ* and *khārij* and is based on a principle and norm from the *maʿṣūmīn* [i.e. the *imāms*] that states "Certainty is never to contradict or to doubt".[43]

By reference to the *khabar* of Ibn Hanzalah, Jawādī-Āmulī (ibid.:134, 370)

[42] Jawādī-Āmulī develops his ideas on the social and political nature of the *wilāyat* doctrine in his book *Bunyān-i marṣūṣ-i imām Khumainī* (The Stable structure of Khumainī), where he explicitly underlines the socio-political duty of "the true Islamic scholars" in the struggle against "every kind of cultural invasion" from the West. Selecting the nineteenth-century jurist Aḥmad Narāqī as an exemplary model in the formulation of *wilāyat-i faqīh*, he asserts that the foundation of society is theological rather than juristic. In the view of Jawādī-Āmulī (1997b8:180, 242), Khumainī released the doctrine of *wilāyat-i faqīh* from its juristic clutches and "put it back in its original place, that is, theology", since the question of leadership is "a theological question in Shi'i culture" while "it is a juristic *furūʿ* question in Sunni Islam".
[43] Cf. Jawādī-Āmulī 1998a:103.

asserts that while the *mujtahid*, in contrast to the *imām*, also infers legal norms from *ẓannī* proofs, these norms are nevertheless "the law and legal ruling of God" and "the command of the *imāms*".[44] In other words, the inferred legal norms are considered "divine constant truths that are revealed to the *mujtahid*" and the conjectural character of some legal proofs "does not obstruct their essentially religious character" since the probable proofs are only used when "their reliance has been confirmed through certainty or is established on certainty (by other proofs)" (ibid.:171). In this respect, Jawādī-Āmulī (ibid.:172) argues that the methodological employment of logic in a number of Islamic sciences is not a unified one and that the lack of *ẓannī* proofs in other sciences than *fiqh* is an excellent example of this case:

Since specific methods are indispensable for (the execution of) the different objectives of each science in their own contexts, there exists no unified method in the inference of subjects from principles in the sciences... Indeed, one never relies on *ẓann-āvar* (presumptive) methods for [extracting] the principles of belief, which have the acquisition of certainty in relation to intrinsic truths as their objective.

In his book *Falsafah-yi ḥuqūq-i bashar* (Philosophy of human rights), Jawādī-Āmulī (1997c:40) argues that since man in his capacity as *maujūd-i takwīnī* (intrinsic being) only has a relative right to freedom in comparison to God, the Islamic conception of natural rights must be extracted by means of *ijtihād* from the revealed sources and reason. He criticises the U.N. proclamation of human rights for relying on *adab wa rusūm wa sunnathā-yi millī* (national customs and traditions) and suggests that the universal declaration of human rights must be grounded in something more unanimous and authentic, i.e. man's *fiṭrat-i ilāhī* (divine nature) in the sense of *rūḥ*, which is "accepted as a common source of all human beings" (ibid.:105). By suggesting that modernist interpretations of Islamic law cannot form the basis of Islamic law, as the reasons of modernity vary from place to place and from man to man, he believes that modernity serves to deform *sharīʿat* and disrupt the uniformity of Islamic society. In this respect, he, similar to most traditionalists, considers democracy to be incompatible with Islam, because the divine nature itself does not interpret existence or clarify laws, but constitutes the *manbaʿ* (source) or spring of Islamic law:

No one has the right to *qānūn-guzārī* (legislation) except God. The prophets and the *imāms* only communicate the divine norms and invite people to (follow these) commandments. [...] Consequently, one must not be deceived and believe that the logic of *tauḥīd* is compatible with the democratic system or the theory of *ḥuqūq-i fiṭrī* (natural rights) (ibid.:116).

[44] According to the famous report known as the *maqbūlah* of Ibn Hanzalah, Jaʿfar al-Ṣadiq transfers judicial *wilāyat* to those among his followers who know and understand *ḥadīṯ* (Momen 1985:197).

By considering hermeneutics as a genuine and profoundly theological determination of existence, Jawādī-Āmulī (1997a:59) approaches the question of hermeneutics from a transcendental perspective, making use of Islamic terminology and references. He is concerned with *tafsīr* in the sense of exegesis proper, and distinguishes two kinds of exegesis, *tafsīr-i mauḍūʿī* (subject exegesis) and *tafsīr-i tartībī* (compositional exegesis) and asserts that the latter precedes the former. In his book *Zan dar āʾīnah-yi jalāl wa jamāl* (Women in the mirror of Majesty and Beauty), he embarks on subject exegesis with reference to the status of women in Islam and adopts a holistic perspective on interpretation, where different aspects of the subject are evaluated on the basis of inference from the revealed sources. He asserts that the subject *tafsīr* has six levels: the collecting of relevant Qur'anic verses, the differentiation of these verses according to the traditional principles (*muṭlaq/muqayyad, muḥkam/mutashābih, ʿāmm/khāṣṣ, mujmal/mubīn*, etc), the collection of relevant *ḥadīṯ* and *akhbār*, the differentiation of these according to the same principles, and finally the assortment of the results from the above levels and the presentation of materials as an *aṣl-i jāmʿi* (comprehensive principle) (ibid.:61–62).[45]

In referring to the theosophical teachings of Ṣadr al-dīn Shīrāzī, Jawādī-Āmulī underlines that all interpretation is contingent on love for God since in order to benefit from revelation one must reach the esoteric level of divine love. In this respect, he asserts that the pivotal concern of Qur'anic interpretation is the consideration of God as manifested in the revealed text itself in the same sense that the natural world contains the divine *āyāt* (signs). "The Qur'an is the word of God and He is the author of this word. Similar to every other author, God is manifested in His word" (Jawādī-Āmulī 1998c:262). For this reason, Jawādī-Āmulī (ibid.:262) argues that the correct meaning of His communication is embedded in the cloth of language and reaches the *mustamaʿ-i rāstīn* (the sincere listener) who "sees through his heart" as well as the exoteric listener who "hears by means of *naql*".

[45] As far as the status of women in Islam is concerned, Jawādī-Āmulī (1997a:352) recognises that women may conduct *ijtihād* with *ʿidālat* (equity) and *muʿtabar* (unfailing), and even become *marjaʿ* by reference to *ijmāʿ-yi qaṭʿī* (the definite consensus), not of the community but of the *imāms*. Due to the implementation of Islamic law in contemporary Iran, many Islamic traditionalists are more receptive to the consideration of women issues. There are several women *mujtahids* in contemporary Iran and they have increased after the establishment of a number of major *ḥauzahs* for women, such as Madrasah-yi Faṭimah al-Zahrā in Tehran, which is directed by Faṭimah Amīnī. The most renowned women *mujtahid* in modern times was Sayyidah Nuṣrat Baigūm Amīn who passed away in 1983. She wrote several works on mainly Qur'anic exegesis, jurisprudence and theosophy. As far as the question of women and *ijtihād* is concerned, *āyatullāh* Muḥammad Ibrāhīm Jannātī (1994:15) for instance argues that Shi'i Islam in contrast to Catholic Christianity not only allows women to obtain independent rational norms from the revealed text, but it "declares that an *ijtihād* conducted by a woman is independent in its judgement even if its reasoning and decision diverge from that of a male *ijtihād*".

Hence, esoteric hermeneutics is essentially a form of listening or appropriation of the text, which in its exoteric and esoteric aspect corresponds to the nature of the Divine Names:

Since the highest Divine Essence possesses multiple Names, which are exoteric and esoteric, the Qur'an also has in effect exoteric and esoteric aspects. The exoteric Qur'an is the theophany of the exoteric names of Truth and the esoteric dimension of the Qur'an is the theophany of the divine esoteric Names (ibid.:262).

In other words, interpretation establishes a kind of dependency with respect to the text interpreted or a need to possess all meaning in an exclusive way. The interpreter participates in the text rather than operating on it from an analytical distance. For this understanding, the Qur'anic text is not the concrete unique ink-and-paper, but an ideal spiritual substance, a Platonic form of which the material thing is merely a 'copy'. The physical object is simply a medium, a channel in and through which the spiritual reality has become incarnate. By also imagining oneself as a *part* of the whole, any formal sense of textual wholeness is also undermined.[46] But while interpretation as appropriation never is shared (since no comprehension of the Qur'an contains all the Divine Names), all dimensions of revelation are known to and attained by the *insān-i kāmil* (perfect man). Jawādī-Āmulī's (1998a:190) hermeneutics is, in other words, the theoretical and practical interest in the way we interpret God's breaking into the structure of understanding. But since the conditions that would enable the human intellect to become active only are present in a small number of men, knowledge only exists in a potential state in the case of the majority of men.

For Jawādī-Āmulī (ibid.:143), the task of hermeneutics is essentially to extract the meaning that is embedded within the text itself. He believes that no content of revelation "in its essence is ambiguous, indefinite or false and offcast", since the Prophet and the *imāms* have explained all ambiguities of the text in their capacity of collectively being *sharīʿat-i nāṭiq* (the speaking *sharīʿat*). By differentiating the act of interpretation from *sharḥ* (explanation), he argues that interpretation involves the removal of the text's external layers, but that these in all cases must be preserved since the veil of language is essential to understanding:

To thoughtlessly look after the esoteric and 'veil-tearing' is something else than to remove veils. The exegete must remove the veils, not tear them apart. The exoteric and literal must be preserved in the same sense that the law of conversation must be maintained and protected... By respecting such a principle the exoteric dimension and the Islamic law are never neglected (Jawādī-Āmulī 1998c:267).

[46] This is consistent with the fact that the traditionalist *ʿulamā* do not possess any analytical or technical interpretative vocabulary, but apply to the text the words of the text itself, using one verse as commentary upon another (i.e. *tafsīr-i qurʾān bā qurʾān*). Cf. Ṭabātabāʾī n.y.

Jawādī-Āmulī's interpretation of hermeneutics is consequently an intellectual activity which can be better described as esoterism in contrast to the ecstatic mysticism of Sufism. Inspired by the theosophical tradition that dates back to Suhrawardī through the school of Isfahan, he believes that the distinction between *tafsīr* and *ta'wīl* concerns two different modes of approaching the revealed text. While *tafsīr* concerns both the exoteric and esoteric textual dimensions of the Qur'an, *ta'wīl* rather involves a kind of ultimately mystical appropriation of the text:

While there exists no important differences between the two concepts, *tafsīr* is defined as the removal of veils. No matter how far man advances, he is confronted with a diluted layer and veil that covers the knowledge of the Qur'anic sciences, but no matter how deep he advances it is still *tafsīr* (ibid.:268).

By referring to such diverse thinkers such as Muḥammad b. ᶜAlī b. Babūyah, Ibn al-ᶜArabī, Ṣadr al-dīn Qunawī, ᶜAbd al-Razzāq Kāshānī and Muḥammad Ḥusain Ṭabāṭabā'ī, Jawādī-Āmulī (ibid.:269) argues that *ta'wīl* is not concerned with linguistic structure, semantics, syntax, and the like, but involves an occupation with external existence. "*Tafsīr* is sometimes concerned with exoteric and sometimes with the esoteric, but *ta'wīl* is not concerned with any linguistic category. It is not a kind of *mafhūm* (understanding), but involves a sort of external reality". He also describes *ta'wīl* as "an encounter of the eye of the heart with God inside His word" and his mysticism has an unreservedly Shi'i character as it describes *ta'wīl* as "the appropriation of the truth [state] of *ahl al-bait*" (ibid.:271). In other words, the relation between revelation and the mystic, text and interpreter is one of appropriation; the claim of the one is answered by the other in the form of an appropriation of what is written. Hermeneutics develops therefore a comprehensive recipe of truth-reaching based on the belief of obtaining by human means a God's eye view from which the one and only meaning of phenomenon is contemplated.

For Jawādī-Āmulī (ibid.:281–283), the internal dimension of revelation is altogether known to the hidden *imām*, but also to the Shi'i *ᶜulamā*– whom he, in contrast to his teacher, Muḥammad Ḥusain Ṭabāṭabā'ī, includes in the Qur'anic notion *rāsikhūn fī al-ᶜilm* (the experts in knowledge)– and hence argues can appropriate the revealed message in its pure form by means of *ta'wīl*. As divine knowledge and the nature and the structure of that knowledge are revealed in descending gradation, so does knowledge of the possessors of knowledge ascend along the same line, beginning with the merely rational and proceeding to the intellectual and inward from the esoteric to the exoteric. In other words, the interpretative cognitive senses, rather than being distinct hermeneutical categories, are more like *marāhil-i buṭūn* (inner levels) and there is hence strictly speaking, no meaning in speaking of revelation as historically situated within time and space. "The word of God is not an hypothesis in reality and it is not historical. Since the level of God's revelation is beyond time and space, there is no room for history there, such as in the case where we would claim that it is related to 1400 years ago" (ibid.:272). In this respect, he seems to suggest that a historical-critical reading of the Qur'an reduces the sacred aspect of language by questioning its genuinely symbolic character, which in turn transforms the interpretative relation.

On the question of *ikhtilāf* in questions of law, Jawādī-Āmulī adopts a normative perspective in terms of defining the correct criterion of valid interpretation. He asserts that differences in interpretation concern the *juz'iyāt* (details) of Islamic law and not its *uṣūl* and methodology, which are constant. The inference of legal norms is comprehended as a source of plurality of ideas, but not discord, because "hermeneutics is sacred and sanctified" and since "diverse *mujtahids* are united by their belief in the superior validity of the *uṣūl-i ṯābit* (constant principles)" (Jawādī-Āmulī 1999a). Presumably influenced by Surūsh's categories of a priori and a posteriori epistemology, Jawadi-Amuli (1998a:346) nevertheless argues that *ikhtilāf* is not a question for epistemology, but for the science of jurisprudence. "The discussion about who has acquired a [corresponding] comprehension of reality and who is caught up in error is a juristic subject, which is external to the boundaries of epistemological scholarship". In other words, he essentially associates epistemology with its modern variants rather than linking the concept to his own elaboration on all those cognitive matters that belongs to this branch of learning. On the question of the revival of the learning of the *ḥauzah*, Jawādī-Āmulī (ibid.:95) stresses that religion is "eternally living" and needs no revival whatsoever, but that the religious sciences must be revived. Striking a strict line between the realm of the *ḥauzah* and that of the university, he suggests that only the religious sciences are in question as far as the *ḥauzah* is concerned, since the mathematical and natural sciences belongs to the field of responsibility of the university:

> From this perspective, the religious institutions of learning are in charge of the category of theoretical learning; philosophy, theology and the like, but also practical learning such as jurisprudence, ethics, and their preliminary sciences (i.e. logic, etc). In contrast, the field of responsibility of the universities includes the category of mathematical and empirical sciences and some practical sciences (Jawādī-Āmulī 1998b:17).

As a matter of fact, Jawādī-Āmulī (1986:8) considers the revival of rational sciences and rational methods as "the most proficient way to counter the exigencies of the contemporary situation". Aware of the fact that one of the originalities of Shi'i Islam is the recognition that metaphysical speculation and philosophical discourse have a place in religious knowledge, he indicates especially those sciences which were neglected in the curriculum before the revolution into consideration:

Following the revolution, the *ḥauzah* must be revived and strengthened. By and large, the matters which were abandoned and outmoded, such as *tafsīr-i ḥadīṯ* (exegesis through *ḥadīṯ*), rational proofs, rational sciences and philosophy and the like, must be made accessible and revitalised (ibid.:7).

Jawādī-Āmulī's suggestion is a legitimate one, since the Iranian law of 1934 had thinned down the curriculum of Islamic education so much that the substance of instruction in terms of material to be studied was considerably less than the matriculation standard and the syllabus totally removed the philosophical disciplines.[47] While the Shi'i *ḥauzah-yi ʿilmīyah* is the only seat of traditional Islamic learning in the world where the post-Platonic philosophical tradition remains alive, Jawādī-Āmulī's emphasis on the need for philosophy and rational methods is nevertheless interesting, when one bears in mind the suspicion with which philosophy was regarded by Islamic scholars from the beginning, despite the fact that large sections of philosophy were harmonically absorbed into the mainstream of Islamic thought.

C. An Introduction to Islamic modernism

Following the categories established by H.A.R. Gibb, Fazlur Rahman (1970) and others in their studies on modern revival and reform in Islam, the present thesis distinguishes Islamic modernism from European 'enlightenment modernism' as well as premodern Islamic reformism. In the view of Gibb (1975:63–64), Islamic modernism is "largely a product of European influences, and sometimes, as we have seen, they may go very deep indeed". He argues that the European element in modernism "involves a revolution in the very concept of knowledge itself" and hence has far-reaching implications for Islamic epistemological considerations. In more precise terms, Islamic modernism makes use of distinct modern Western methods of explanation and interpretation in order to change the traditional definition of *ijtihād* and *isṭinbāṭ* into new, more broad and contemporary ones. In contrast to traditional formulations of these concepts, Islamic modernists' viewpoints on legal change are not primarily concerned with the *furūʿ* of law, but its *uṣūl* and principles where the act of *ijtihād* is juxtaposed from jurisprudence to involve other disciplines, mainly theology or ethics that traditionally followed distinct and separate methodologies. In this respect, Schacht (1971a:1026) maintains that some modernists make "extravagant claims to a new, free *idjtihād* which goes far beyond any that was practised in the formative period of Islamic law". As a matter of fact, Islamic modernism frequently attempts to make conscious the ethical structure of Islam by

[47] Cf. Akhavi (1980:51) and Mohagheqh (1971).

providing a practical guide distinct from the traditional, more abstract, notions of ethics as a part of theology. Many modernists view Islam as a social justice ethics, or even as a socially-committed ideology interpreted in normative terms.

In the sense that the modernity with which the Islamic modernists want to reconcile their religion is modernity as interpreted by them, through the filters of their religious beliefs, modernism might best be characterised as an 'eclectic' incorporation of thought (Chehabi 1990:43). It borrows heavily from secular philosophy and science (its language, logic and rhetoric) to construct its own religious claims that also differ frequently from each other as far as their specific subject matter is concerned due to the transient nature of modernity itself. By reformulating the principal teachings of religion in the face of modern thought, for instance through a rearrangement of the traditional Islamic sciences, Islamic modernism represents a theoretical break from conventional legal wisdom. The modernists particularly criticise the hierarchical character of the traditional concept of knowledge and, as Hamid Enayat (1991:23) argues, "play down, if not totally reject, all the elitist, and esoteric accounts of their religion". The fundamental questions of Islamic modernism are conceptional and take place in the realm of ideas, where the traditional classification of *fiqh* is redefined, generally limited to the religious discourse at the expense of the modern sciences, primarily natural science or sociology. While modernist writings have made way for innovative interpretation of the revealed sources of law, they have nevertheless little bearing on the traditional discourse of Islamic law. Another common feature of Islamic modernism is the view of history as a constitutive element of meaning, according to which the genuine meaning of the revealed sources is considered concealed by its historical interpretations. Post-prophetic history is, so to say, considered as a fall and reduction. By seeking a renewed historical pertinence, the accumulated legal tradition is approached in critical terms as a human construct and the traditional notions of *taqlīd* are commonly rejected. In its essentials, Islamic modernism believes that human reason must take possession of itself and not accept what it inherits from the past.

While differentiated from one another in their concepts of religious reform, the Islamic modernists are related in their criticism of the exclusiveness of religion in traditional Islamic scientific inquiry and in their hailing of human reason as qualified to deduce and enact laws that complement or even supersede *fiqh*. While partly rooted in the Islamic tradition, their epistemological standards are given a broader (natural law) or more modern scientific conception (codified law) than that of traditional Islam, laying the ground for the unequivocal secularisation of knowledge. For instance, in the case of ʿAlī Sharīʿatī, the aim of his concept of *islām-shināsī* (Islamic studies) was precisely to apply religion to the needs of contemporary society rather than to contribute to the development and perfection of the traditional sciences. While he rejected emulation of so called *mitudhā-yi ʿilmī-yi urūpāʾī* (European scientific methods) and considered the traditional Islamic set of disciplines accurate in attending the dogmatic validation of faith, he dismissed the latter as irrelevant in the modern world (Sharīʿatī 1996:8).[48] For Shari'ati, the comprehension of Islam was contingent on modern philosophy, where the methods of contemporary human science are used to create a synthesis between faith and modern science:

Today, the scientific methods have changed and found a new direction in all fields (of knowledge) and religious research is also bound to adopt and select new methods. In this respect, everyone has the right to elaborate (the method) he believes is correct. In my capacity as an individual, I have the right to set out my own new *shinākht-i islām* (comprehension of Islam)... For this purpose we have to select a philosophical method, since the relation between man and God is examined in philosophy. Then, the earthly life of man must be considered, for which we have to use methods that are applicable in contemporary *ʿulūm-i insānī* (human science) (Sharīʿatī 1998a:56).

In Iran as elsewhere in the Muslim world, the early Islamic modernism was characterised by the effort to adjust Islam to the process of modernisation and the belief that Muslims would overcome their scientific and political shortcomings simply by acquiring the instrumentalities of modern European society. In its rudimentary form, Islamic modernism resulted in many cases in the increased understanding of *sharīʿat* as a symbol of judicial legality, i.e. denoting law in the narrower sense. In Iran, the first signs of modernism in the realm of Islamic law was seen in the works of the constitutionalists of the early twentieth century, such as Muḥammad Khān Sinakī's *Risālah-yi majdīyah* (Majdīyah's treatise), Yusūf Khān Mustashar al-Daulah's *Yak kalamah* (One word), but also Malkam Khān's newspaper *Qānūn* (Law). These reform thinkers defined Islamic law in terms of codification and identified reform with religion. Their work featured an apologetic defence of Islam that was thoroughly modern and they exposed Islamic views in terms of modernity. As far as Mustashar al-Daulah's *Yak kalamah* was concerned, the 'one word' he had in mind was law and he envisaged an adoption of the French consititution that was justified by applications of Islamic legal norms and conceptions of justice.[49]

[48] Sharīʿatī's *Islām-shināsī* was criticised by Islamic traditionalists in a number of books. Among the most notable refutals were Ibrāhīm Anṣārī-Zanjānī's *Islām-shināsī dar tarāzū-yi ʿilm wa ʿaql* (Islamic studies in the scale of science and reason) in 1973 and Nāṣir Makārim-Shīrāzī's *Āyā hukūmat-i islāmī bar pāyah-yi shūrā-ast?* (Is *shūrā* the foundation of Islamic governance?) printed in *Maktab-i islām* (Islamic discipline) in 1972. Makārim-Shīrāzī accused Sharīʿatī for having misunderstood the notion of *ijmāʿ* and for basing his ideas on unreliable Sunni *ḥadīṯ* material.

[49] Khān as well as al-Daulah expressed their concept of subjectivity as rooted in God's subjectivity where humans are depicted as God's *khalīfah* (Khān here adopted the word *adamīyat*). They vindicated a form of mediated subjectivity by asserting that man's rights are

Another thinker who frequently is associated with early Islamic modernism is Jamāl al-dīn Asadābādī (Afghānī). While Asadābādī wrote little on Islamic law and theology (despite his knowledge on these subjects), he used his rhetoric to argue that the modern notion of law can be found in Islam. For him, the objectives of Islamic law were more important than its specific rulings and linked to the assumption that *sharīʿat* is as capable as European law of "establishing laws and enforcing civilization" (Keddie 1983:107). While Asadābādī accused the traditional Islamic *fuqahā* of being "deprived of understanding of the benefits of law, the rules of civilisation and the reform of the world", he considered religion compatible with modernisation (Keddie 1983:107). He hailed modern science (Galileo, Newton, Kepler, etc) and belittled Islamic theosophy as outdated and even irrelevant. While he attempted to reconcile science and religion, defining the Qur'an as the Muslims' first teacher of philosophy and philosophy as the mother of all sciences, he similarly criticised the work of traditional Muslim philosophers as being too faithful to their Greek predecessors "as if Aristotle were one of the pillars of Islam" (ibid.:107).[50] In the view of Asadābādī, Islamic philosophy was no longer able to meet the challenges of the modern world. By also turning the foundation of epistemology from revelation and philosophy to science, he hailed modern science as the only true science and argued that the Qur'an is all-encompassing from a scientific point of view.

With the emergence of modernist tendencies within Islamic thought at large, Shi'i legal philosophy became a disputed subject and as hermeneutics was liberated from its traditional interpretations, religion also became amendable to new contexts. The first systematic modernist elaboration on Shi'i law *per se* was Muḥammad Muṣaddiq's doctoral thesis, published in France in 1914.[51] In the main part of the thesis, where the relationship

grounded in God's rights and by identifying law with the positive order. "Similarly, even though his [i.e. Khān's] conceptualisation of law, as we saw above, was marred by strong positivistic elements, nevertheless it was law with universal application" (Vahdat 1998:120).

[50] Cf. Mitra 1987:220–225. Asadābādī's scientific position is little known to Muslim intellectuals in Iran, since his essay in response to Ernest Renan's polemics on Islam in *Journal des debats* (May 18, 1883), where he praised the superiority of science over revelation, has never been rendered into Persian. Nevertheless, he is of special interest precisely because he is considered by contemporary Shi'i thinkers as the founder of modern Islamic movements (Yūsufī-Ishkiwarī 1998a:9–13, Muḥahharī n.y.:14–39, etc). In the view of Nikki Keddie, Asadābādī has been praised by modern Islamic activists largely because of his political pan-Islamism and she argues that his use of Islamic terminology was tactic, employed only more effectively mobilise Muslims against the European colonialists (for instance in persuading *shaikh* Mīrzā Ḥasan Shīrāzī to protest against the government concession-granting policies).

[51] Muṣaddiq was born in Aḥmad-Ābād in 1882 into a privileged family. He was active in the constitutional revolution and was elected deputy in the first parliament. In 1911, he went to Switzerland to study law and after obtaining his doctoral degree, he became the first European-educated doctor in law in Iran. During the Pahlawī dynasty, Muṣaddiq was elected governor and also deputy in the parliament on a number of occasions. Active in the formation

between Islamic law and reason is elaborated upon, Muṣaddiq (1914) argued that the existing contradictions in *fiqh* can only be disentangled by the free use of reason and through the creation of solid positive law. By asserting the superiority of *ʿaql* to the other sources of the *sharīʿat*, Muṣaddiq dwelled not upon the question of the nature of reason, but contended that since the foundation of Islamic law (i.e. God's existence) is a rational argument, the whole law must be based on human reasoning, whereby positive laws that are in conformity with reason also are in conformity with *sharīʿat* and *ʿurf*.

In his attempts to rationalise the major contents of Shi'i law, Muṣaddiq was followed by two thinkers of different intellectual visions, Aḥmad Kasrawī and Riḍā Qulī Sangalajī, who were particularly critical of popular forms of traditional religion. Kasrawī was eductated at a *ḥauzah* and worked as a secular judge. In numerous books and pamphlets, he condemned the modern Shi'i religion as a 'historical sect' and promoted what he called *pāk-dīnī* (pure religion). Speaking the language of enlightenment modernity, he advocated a utilitarian conception of religion and also considered a return to any "original Islamic teachings" as impossible (Kasrawī n.y.:53). More importantly, he identified knowledge with the Persian word *dānish* rather than the Arabic concept *ʿilm* in order to distinguish the sacred knowledge from the profane (Kasrawī 1957:27). Consequently, it is not an accident that Kasrawī's influence was largely restricted to secular intellectuals, such as Jalāl Āl-i Aḥmad, ʿAlī Dashtī and Sayyid Ḥasan Taqīzādah, while the Islamic traditionalists, among them Khumainī, disagreed severely with him.[52]

Similar to Kasrawī, Riḍā Qulī Sangalajī was also an *ʿālim* by education and considered Islamic legal tradition to be a distortion of true Islam. He argued for the eradication of the Shi'i concept *taqlīd* and promoted a new interpretation of religion compatible with modern science and social justice.[53] In his *Kilīd-i fahm-i qurʾān* (The key to the understanding of the Qur'an), Sangalajī emphasised the central and universal message of the Qur'an and called for a historical and contextual reading of it by also claiming the right of the individual believer to conduct *ijtihād* from the revealed sources without any intermediate interpreter. By reaccounting for

of Jabhah-yi millī (National front) and the anti-imperialist nationalisation campaign of Iranian oil, he became prime minister in the early 1950s. His government was yet soon overthrown in an U.S.-sponsored military coup, which forced him into exile. Muṣaddiq died in 1967.

[52] Khumainī wrote his *Kashf al-asrār* (The Unveiling of the secrets) as a critique of ʿAlī Akbar Ḥakamīzādah's book *Asrār-i hazār sālah* (Secrets of a thousand years) that was published at Kasrawī's press. In his book, Khumainī explicitly criticised the ideas of Sangalajī as well.

[53] While Sangalajī kept aloof from the public scene, he was, as Yann Richard (1998) asserts, associated with ʿAlī Akbar Dāwar, who was charged with drafting the first Iranian civil code. By declining any official positions, Sangalajī instead focused his attention on the establishment of his Dār al-tablīgh-i islāmī (Centre for Islamic propaganda) in Tehran, which was a major centre for the dissemination of Islamic reformist ideas in the 1930s.

the distinction between *ẓāhir* and *bāṭin* aspects of revelation, Sangalajī argued that the esoteric aspect of the Qur'an is identical to the intention of the text, which is accessible to everyone who reads it correctly. Influenced by Sunni jurists, such as Ibn Taimīyah, he emphasised a return to the pristine purity of Islamic teachings and questioned the Shi'i principle of the *rajʿah* (return) of the twelfth *imām*. His 'sunnification' of Shi'i dogma was later developed by ʿAlī Sharīʿatī, who openly relied on Sunni sources and discouraged many Shi'i ritual practices (Richard 1988).

During the latter part of twentieth century, Islamic modernism was championed by a number of Islamic intellectuals such as Mahdī Bāzargān, ʿAlī Sharīʿatī, Abū al-Ḥasan Banī-Ṣadr and Maḥmūd Ṭāliqānī.[54] In contrast to the traditionalist' predilection for theosophy, the modernists were in general motivated by their socio-political concerns, not in an attempt to rely on the traditional juristic discourse, but rather to replace the central importance of *fiqh* with innovative approaches to *akhlāq* and *uṣūl al-dīn*. For this purpose they frequently adopted a liberating interpretation of the traditional discourse directed, for instance, by the concepts *rūḥ-i ijtihād* (spirit of *ijtihād*) and *falsafah-yi wujūdī-yi ijtihād* (existential philosophy of *ijtihād*).[55] Along with the dissemination of Western philosophy and science, which increased in Iran during the whole twentieth century, modernism, nationalism and democratic ideas, together with criticism of traditional Islam, became prevalent themes in Islamic modernist' writings. This trend was also accompanied by a profound criticism towards the West that no longer was considered a potential symbol of Islamic ideals. Modernity (or what it was perceived to be) was conceptualised as an *external* phenomenon. In contrast to Islamic traditionalism, which in strict terms rejected modern terminology by remaining within the borders of traditional Islamic

[54] Many of these intellectuals were essential in the creation of various institutional organisations that worked for a more contemporary approach to religious method and practice, such as Anjuman-i guftār-i māh (Society of monthly talks) and Ḥusainīyah-yi irshād. These institutions further had their organisational background in the Kānūn-i nashr-i ḥaqā'iq-i islāmī (Centre for the propagation of Islamic truth) established by Muḥammad Taqī Mazīnanī Sharīʿatī, the late Sharīʿatī's father, in Mashhad in 1941 as well as Kānūn-i islāmī (The Islamic center), founded the same year in Tehran by Mahdī Bāzargān and Maḥmūd Ṭaliqānī. Muḥammad Taqī Mazīnanī was a pioneer in his attempt to present a progressive and liberating interpretation of Shi'i Islam. He argued that Islam is compatible with modern science, that modern civilisation is good and that the success of modern science is a proof that Islam is a great civilisation since Islam was the whole basis for the scientific revolution of the European renaissance. Influenced by Sharīʿatī, Muḥammad Nakhshab established an organisation called Nihḍat-i khudā-parastān-i sūsiyālīst (Movement of God-worshipping socialists) in Tehran in 1945 that was a major inspiration for leftish Islamic modernists, such as Abū al-Qāsim Shākib Niyā, ʿAlī Sharīʿatī and Ḥabībullāh Paimān. In the 1950s, the modernists cooperated with many traditionalists, mainly Murtaḍā Mutahharī, Muḥammad Taqī-Jaʿfarī and Seyyed Hossein Nasr, who one after the other left these institutions during the next decade (Rahnema 1998:226–279).

[55] Cf. Mūsāwīfarr 1997:23

principles, the Islamic modernists adhered to some distinctively modern philosophical and scientific principles. While the West was the source of their thought on the one hand, its political, cultural, and social intrusion into the Muslim world was, on the other hand, rejected. Their ambivalent attitude to the West in fact produced a monolithic, essentialist and undifferentiated conception of the West that is exemplified in the general use of the concepts *gharbzadigī* (dysisplexia) and *bāzgasht bih khīshtan* (return to the self) by Islamic modernists.[56] For Sharīʿatī, who coined the latter term, the underlying assumption in the necessity of the return to the self was an ontological bifurcation between Islam and the West, which consequently were considered as two quintessentially separate polarities.

By recognising the process of transforming initial contents and functions of the revealed texts into new ones, Islamic modernism has elements in favour of constructing contemporary ideologies that include the conception of Islam as a total socio-political system. These were syncretic ideologies, although termed Islamic, and in which Islamic tradition plays a subsidiary and sometimes only a decorative role because 'ideology' by definition is a post-religious proposition. The ideologisation of religion, as Ali Merad (1981:37) argues, refers to the attempt "to formulate the 'content' of Islam in terms of norms and values of socio-political order" and as Said Amir Arjomand (1988:97) explains, the construction of an Islamic ideology means "the arrangement of the readily accessible maxims constituting the sources of the Islamic tradition, the Koran and the sayings of the prophets and the Imams, in accordance with a pattern suggested by the Western total ideologies such as communism and fascism". Islamic modernism considers in general religion as an all-encompassing and integrist ideology by reference to the tradititional theological concept *tauḥīd* or ritual practices such as *amr bi-l-maʿrūf* (enjoining the good). Bāzargān (1998:282), who was the first Muslim intellectual to use the concept ideology, even adopted the word 'totalitarist' to describe the all-inclusive character of Islam. As Hamid Enayat (1991:155) mentions, ʿAlī Sharīʿati also turned the theological principle of oneness of God into a monolithic sociology of religion with socio-political implications:

> All facets of Islamic culture (mythology, history, theology, and even some elements of jurisprudence) are subordinated in his teachings to the compelling necessity of this fusion between 'theory' and 'praxis' which is but one manifestation of the principle of *tawhīd* (oneness of God).

While the traditional theological formulation of *tauḥīd* had its root in the

[56] Cf. Bāzargān 1999:19–42, Banī-Ṣadr 1979:78–82, Sharīʿatī 1998b:3–33, Ṭāliqānī 1965:127. As a matter of fact, the term *gharbzadigī* was coined by Aḥmad Fardīd and became so deeply entrenched in the Iranian political vocabulary of the 1960s and beyond that even Islamic traditionalists such as Khumainī (1997:15) used it in his *Wilāyat-i faqīh*.

Qur'an and was centred on the definition of the relationship between the Divine Attributes and Divine Essence (that is, whether the former had an hypostatic or independent existence apart from the latter or not), the modernist concept of *tauḥīd* disentangled it from the traditional symbolic understanding and interpreted it literally with preferentially 'secular' concerns, often equating as regards matters transcendent and immanent, God and the people.[57] In other words, *tauḥīd* was not merely one principle among other principles of religion, but rather the foundation of all other principles. By transferring this concept to contemporary socio-economical issues in an attempt to establish an Islamic form of economy, sociology, science, or government, Islamic modernists assert that the Islamic ideological system covers every aspect of human life:

According to the world-view of *tauḥīd*, there is therefore no contradiction in all existence: no contradiction between man and nature, spirit and body, this world and the hereafter, matter and meaning. Since *tauḥīd* implies a mode of looking upon all beings as a unity, it cannot accept legal, class, social, political, racial, national, territorial, genetic or even economic contradictions (Sharīᶜatī 1996:39–40).

While the modernists refer to the Qur'anic verse 2:31 that depicts man as the *khalīfatullāh* in a general sense to describe the *insān-i idi'hāl* (ideal man), there is a vast and documentable difference between the epistemological and hermeneutic approaches of Islamic modernism and traditional Shi'i law and theology. While the modernists consider human subjectivity as contingent on divine subjectivity in their objectification of subjectivity, they interpret divine vicegerency not as the contemplative projection of human subjectivity onto the attributes of the Deity, but as the responsibility for the creation of a just and temporary social order. In the words of Shariᶜatī (1996:39, 73), who considered consciousness as tantamount to ideology, this order was a *niẓām-i tauḥīdī* (unitarian order).[58] While the ontological cornerstone of the religious discourse of Islamic traditionalism is based on a movement away from nature to beyond nature, Islamic modernism, in other words, lays the emphasis more explicitly on an opposite relocation from metaphysics to social and political concerns.

The first Shi'i attempt in Iran to produce scientific justifications of Islam based on the assumption that modern scientific reasoning has universal validity was made by Mahdī Bāzargān. In his capacity as professor of thermodynamics at Tehran University, he published as early as 1943 a book on the scientific basis of the Islamic juristic prescription for *muṭahharāt* (personal cleanliness), in order to demonstrate that the Islamic rules concerning hygiene conformed to biochemical and mathematical formulae

[57] Cf. McDermott 1978:223–340.
[58] Cf. Ṭāliqānī 1979:118 and 1965:143–145.

(Bāzargān 1943).[59] Influenced by the prominent biologist Alexis Carrel and Pierre Lecomte de Noüy's theory of telefinalism, Bāzargān set out to prove that Islamic concepts are grounded in modern science. Instead of deploring the essential differences between modern science and Islam in their epistemological foundations, Bāzargān asserted that the theories and ideas of modern science correspond to Islam. In his attempt to prove the compatibility of religion and scientific modernity, he denied that the Western scientific advancement was largely the product of a secularisation of philosophy. While he criticised the phenomenon of secularism as such, he argued that modern science is neutral to religion by underlining that Darwin was a devout Christian (Bāzargān 1999:19–42).[60] Inspired by modern 'general systems theory', Bāzargān (1981:36) also claimed to have scientific evidence for the reconciliation of evolution and religion by reading *sīstīm-i hadaf-jū* (purposive system) into nature and history.[61]

In his essay *Baʿṯat wa īdiʾūlūzhī* (Prophetic mission and ideology), Bāzargān (1998:236) reconstructed the distinctive features of his *īdiʾūlūzhī-yi ilāhī* (divine ideology) by considering ideology to be "a collection of beliefs or a school of philosophy or theory that is considered as a foundation by the individual or collective for determining social means and method". In contrast to ancient and modern secular forms of Western ideology, such as Marxism, Bāzargān (1998:291) asserted that the Islamic ideology is superior in its *kāmilīyat* (completeness) since "it emanates from the highest presence of the Creator of the worlds". In more specific terms, he considered the divine ideology to be grounded in three distinct terms: *taslīm bih ikhtiyār* (submission by choice), *inshāʾ-i qānūn* (constituting of law) and *nigārandah-yi tārīkh* (the observer of history).[62] With emphasis on the third aspect, it is

---

[59] Bāzargān was born in in Tehran in 1907 into a family of pious merchants. In 1928, he was among the first Iranian students whom Riḍā Shāh sent to France to study engineering. He stayed in France for seven years and after his return to Iran began to teach at Tehran University, where he later became professor. He served as a minister to Muḥammad Muṣaddiq's government in the early fifties and in 1961 founded the Nihḍat-i āzādī-yi īrān (Freedom movement of Iran), which since its creation has worked for political freedoms and human rights in Iran. Due to his religious credentials, Bāzargān was made the first president of the interim government elected directly by Ruḥullāh Khumainī after the revolution in 1980. Bāzargān died in 1995.

[60] In an interview with Ibrāhīm Yazdī (1998), a former pupil of Bāzargān, he confirmed that modern science in its essentials is identical to religion and does not differ from the alien Greek, Iranian and Indian scientific traditions that Islam encountered in premodern times. Consequently, he argued that modern science could be 'islamised' in the same manner as in premodern times.

[61] In his *Sair-i taḥawwul-i tadrījī-yi qurʾān* (Discourse on gradual development in the Qur'an) and *Bād wa bārān dar qurʾān* (Wind and rain in the Qur'an), Bāzargān (1999b, 1974) also attempted to prove the validity of revelation by analysing its contents with the help of analogies drawn from mathematics and natural science and scientifically prove that Islamic descriptions of the relation between wind and rain correspond with modern meteorological discoveries.

[62] While Bāzargān identified religion with ideology to construct an Islamic ideology in his

not coincidental that Bāzargān approached the question of Islamic law in light of the modern concept of natural legal rights to prove that the contents of the revealed sources in fact correspond to the French civil law point by point (such as in the case of the workers' rights). As Hamid Dabashi (1993:350) argues, Bāzargān's major contribution to Islamic modernism was his "constitutional identification of the Islamic ideology with Shi'i law", which also included his concern for Islamic law, the question of rule of law and a new interpretation of the four sources of *fiqh*.

While Bāzargān gave enthusiastic approval to the traditional Shi'i theoretical stance of openness towards legal reasoning, he maintained that *ijtihād* nevertheless had been heavily restricted in practical terms. By, for instance, referring to the writing of *risālah-yi ʿamalī*, he argued that the Shi'i discourse on jurisprudence largely had been occupied with emulating the works of its earlier predecessors (Bāzargān 1999:392). His point of departure was that in order to change with the world, Islamic law must follow the trend in the modern accumulation at large towards specialisation and be divided into sub-specialities like physics (ibid.:394). By advocating a more dynamic interpretation of *ijtihād*, Bāzargān (ibid.:256) was highly critical of the prominence of *fiqh* in the traditional Islamic discourse on knowledge and blamed the *fuqahā* for the general decadence of Muslim societies:

> Indeed, jurisprudence is not superfluous and incompatible with Islam and the function of the *faqīh* is like that of the jurist in modern society. But sometimes when an external microbe penetrates into the human body, one organ grows over its propositions and captures the position and supplies of the adjoining organs and it creates a cancer.

For Bāzargān, law was hence not the most genuine or true expression of religion, and inspired by the tradition that dates back to the Stoics through Cicero and Thomas Aquinas, he instead made the idea of natural law the cornerstone of his religious worldview. Similar to Aquinas, Bāzargān's concept of natural law was normative, considering something as just if it is right according to the rules of reason and offering guidance as to how these rules are to govern human relationships.[63] But for Bāzargān, the 'nature' in

essay *Baʿṯat wa īdiʾūlūzhī*, he changed his view on the relationship between ideology and religion in his last works written in the early 1990s. In an article written originally for the French newspaper *Le Monde*, Bāzargān (1995:108) asserted (perhaps influenced by Surūsh) that religion and ideology are separate entities and that religion has no clearcut answers to many questions concerning the practicalities of human life. "We cannot hence expect Islam (or Christianity or Judaism) to give us definite and complete constitutions, law statutes, laws, concerning ideology, governance, economics, science, medicine and health".

[63] Cf. Milton 1981. Although the term natural law is not used in traditional Islamic legal writings, Bāzargān was of the opinion that true law is right reason in agreement with nature and hence natural law is of universal application, unchanging and everlasting. While he embarked on the central question mark of natural law, namely why the designation of the rational faculties of some people are more equal to the task of deriving natural law than others

natural law was of an essentially divine nature and the question of natural law was hence not a purely philosophical one, but rather a 'theological' doctrine, devised to understand basic notions of revelation. In other words, he presented the subject matter of ethics as natural command, but did not derive the content of its ethics or law, or seek to justify that content, by reference to inference solely (yet largely) drawn from the inductive observation of nature. In the view of Bāzargān (1998:295), the true meaning of Islamic ideology was nevertheless considered to be the idea that nature follows a particular set of laws that are established by God:

In divine ideology, the first and eternal legislator is God... What we mean here by law is the basic principles of ideology and the *qawānīn-i asāsī* (fundamental laws) that determine the general schemes, and not the branches and detailed secondary and executive laws that in general are approved in executive assemblies.[64]

Similar to Bāzargān, Maḥmūd Ṭāliqānī, an *ʿālim* educated at a *ḥauzah*, formulated a philosophy of history where Darwinist postulates were veiled in Islamic terminology extended from the Qur'an. Yet, in contrast to the former, Ṭāliqānī (1979:113) was in the first place inspired by modern dialectical philosophy as articulated in Marxist thought.[65] In his book *Islām wa mālikīyat* (Islam and ownership), he criticised centralised as well as free-market economies, but nevertheless adopted Marxist discourse and language ('capital', 'class', 'means of production', etc) in order to address religious themes in a way compatible with the prevailing exigencies of the times. While he acknowledged that Islamic jurisprudence "provides specific

---

and referred to the ultimate divine source of the law, his view posed a logical problem to legal theory as far as the main source of the law is thought to be identical with human reason.

[64] Aside from Bāzargān's natural law theory, there are very few commitments among Shi'i modernists to appropriate Islam to Western legal theories such as legal positivism or legal sociology, whereby Islamic law would be studied as a positive order. Despite the strong effort in Iran to implement *sharīʿat* within the positive order of the modern state, the modernist legal discourses instead tend to adopt certain variants of Husserl's phenomenology that struggled against both naturalism and positivism. As far as the constitution of the Islamic republic is concerned, God serves as the first principle in that text, but insofar as a number of metaphysical assumptions regarding His nature and the Shi'i cosmological universe are included, it proves difficult for Shi'i legal positions to appreciate a theological positivism that reduces the revealed law to practice. In this respect, it should also be stressed that the constitutive element of the Kantian epistemological notion of the science of law as cognition of law (where legal norms are created) is of a purely epistemological character and is fundamentally different from the creation of law by the positive legal authority that differentiates law from theology.

[65] Ṭāliqānī was born in Tehran in 1910 into a family of religious scholars and merchants. Following the footsteps of his father, Abū al-Qāsim Ṭāliqānī, he went in the early 1930s to Qum to study the Islamic sciences under ʿAbd al-Karīm Ḥāʾirī Yazdī and Muḥammad Taqī Khānsārī. After having received an *ijāzah* from Ḥāʾirī Yazdī in 1939, Ṭāliqānī began teaching in Madrasah-yi Sipahsālār in Tehran. In the 1950s and beyond, he became involved in politics as the founder of Nihḍat-i muqāwimat-i millī (National resistance movement) and contributed, together with ʿAlī Sharīʿatī, radicalising the religious discourse in Iran. Ṭāliqānī died in 1979.

definitions and conditions for formalising ownership and the acticivities leading to it", his attempt was essentially to 'islamise' patently Marxist terminologies (Ṭāliqānī 1965:146, 162). In the view of Ṭāliqānī (ibid.:116–117), the ideal economical system was one that "in the light of faith and belief" and "through strengthened belief in *tauḥīd*" would eradicate *tuyūl-dārī* ('feudalism') and social oppression. In this respect, he acknowledged the socio-historical basis of historical change:

Islam attests to the fact that the source of social and economic phenomena is human beings [...] Based on this view, whether the constant human principles dominate the environment or whether man becomes subject to the environment and economic means and conditions, the roots of societal structure and historical change lies in man himself. Indeed, the dynamic force in history comes from conflict between the constant principles and the rebellious human soul influenced by social conditions, pleasures, animal appetites, needs, and the environment.

Ṭāliqānī also wrote a four volume commentary on the Qur'an, *Partau'ī az qur'ān* (A Ray from the Qur'an), which is a rationalist and scientific commentary on revelation, in the sense that he made use of the discoveries of modern science to explain the message of the Qur'an. In the view of Rahmat Tavakol (1998:183), Ṭāliqānī's hermeneutic explanations were clearly a departure from the established tradition of *tafsīr* writing, such as his belief that all Muslims can interpret the Qur'an by finding the essential unalterable message of revelation on the basis of *muḥkamāt* principles and transcend the allegorical form of *mutashāhibāt*. The fact that Ṭāliqānī himself did not consider the book a traditional *tafsīr* is even evident from the title itself. It stands out as the most socially radical and politically conscious exegesis on the Qur'an of modern times, in that he rendered the revelation contemporary by connecting Qur'anic terms to socio-political concerns of his time (for instance invoking curses in Arabic against the Pahlawī monarchy) (Ṭāliqānī 1979:283). In this respect, Ṭāliqānī certainly contributed to the secularisation of traditional Islamic terminology.[66]

In his attempt to construct a system of Islamic economics, Ṭāliqānī was followed by Abū al-Ḥasan Banī-Ṣadr, a leading theoretician of Islamic modernism. In his explicit theo-centric vision, Banī-Ṣadr's interest in economy was more concerned with matters of ideological articulation than with the theoretical elements of a political economy and he actually constructed an entire 'theology', the so-called *iqtiṣād-i tauḥīdī* (monotheistic

[66] Ṭāliqānī (1979:11–16) criticised in particular the tradition of Shi'i theosophy and asserted that the traditional rules of *tafsīr* in fact made the revealed text irrelevant to "human consciousness by concealing the text for the modern reader". As Abdollah Vakily (1998) elucidates, the commentary was highly influential in the formulation of the ideology of the *mujāhidīn-i khalq* (The People's holy strugglers) in that a number of its publications applied dialectical materialism to the Qur'an and to the *sīrah* of the Prophet and the *imāms* by, for instance, using the concept *sunnatullāh* as interchangeable with 'law of evolution'.

economy), around economic factors such as labour, capital, means of production and ownership. While he acknowledged that human labour constitutes a relative claim to ownership in terms of man's function as God's *nimāyandah-yi ijrāʾī* (executive representative), his concept of religion was, needless to say, influenced by Marxist discourses on economy and its centrality for human existence (Banī-Ṣadr 1978:221).

Probably the most distinguished proponent of Islamic modernism in twentieth-century Iran was ʿAlī Sharīʿatī. The immediate background of his thought was the attempt to justify Western standards of philosophy and political ideology in Islamic terms.[67] By transforming religion into the primary agency of political socialisation, he contributed more than any other modernist to desacralise and contest traditional Islamic terminology. Similar to Bāzargān, he used the word 'ideology' in the sense of a body of doctrines inspired by religion and directed socio-political action that included Islam as a total, unified socio-political system based on the full unity of doctrine and practice. He affirmed that "Islam is in one word the ideology of my school" and distinguished between two separate understandings of Islam:

> Islam has two separate Islams. The first can be considered a revolutionary 'ideology'. By this I mean beliefs, critical programmes and aspirations, the goal of which is human development. This is true development. The second can be considered scholastic knowledge... This is why sometimes true believers can understand Islam better than the *faqīh*, the *ʿālim*, and the philosophers (Sharīʿatī 1996a:70).[68]

As an avant-garde intellectual with a partially French formation, Sharīʿatī was influenced by a number of prominent Western thinkers: the Jewish sociologist George Gurvitch, the Marxist intellectual Roger Garaudy, the Islamicists Louis Massignon and Jaques Berque, the political thinker Frantz

[67] Sharīʿatī was born in Mazinan (Khurasan) in 1933. He studied Arabic literature and French at Mashhad University. In 1960, he went to Paris, where he received a doctoral degree in Iranian studies. Five years later, he began to teach at Mashhad University, but soon afterwards moved to Tehran to establish the Ḥusainīyah-yi irshād, where he lectured until its closing in 1972. As the main ideologue behind the revolution of 1979, he was assassinated in London two years before its triumph.

[68] In the terminology of Sharīʿatī, the two understandings of Islam are also called *tashayyʿu-i alawī* and *tashayyʿu-i ṣafawī*. The first understanding of Islam is the revolutionary Shi'i Islam of the first *imām* ʿAlī b. Abī Ṭālib contrasts the second understanding, which is the institutionalised religion of the Ṣafawīd dynasty that in the seventeenth century established Shi'i Islam as the official creed in Iran. In the view of Sharīʿatī (1999:231–234), the former understanding of Islam was one that represented dynamic and radical *ijtihād* and rejected *taqlīd* and *taqīyah* (dissimulation). By arguing that atheism in the sense of a lack of metaphysical belief is a modern concept, Sharīʿatī (1998b:9, 22–26) insisted that the dialectic struggle in history was not comprised of a conflict between religion and non-religion, but rather between *tauḥīd* and *shirk* (multitheism). In this respect, the latter was not interpreted as multitheism in a metaphysical sense, but as "the religion of ignorance and fear" that functions as official legitimacy for oppressive social and political systems.

Fanon, the philosophical existentialist Jean-Paul Sartre, etc. While Sharīʿatī (1996a:50) denounced Marxism in general terms, he adopted an implicit Marxist view of history as governed by dialectical determinism, or what he called *jabr-i ʿilmī* (scientific determinism), where "history unfolds through dialectical contradictions" as well as the Marxist view that society must be governed by a total ideology. In this respect, he went so far as to claim that Marx himself did not believe in dialectical materialism but in 'dialectical determinism', which he maintained was approved by the Qur'an and hence more Islamic than Aristotelian logic (Sharīʿatī 1996c:103, 137, 205).

In his radical criticism of the historical development of Shi'i Islam, Sharīʿatī made heavy use of modern socio-historical principles borrowed from sociology and the history of science in constructing his dynamic and revolutionary Islamic ideology. Influenced by George Gurvitch's idea on social constructs, Sharīʿatī's (1996a:50–63) social thought and theories were highly reductionist in interpreting human history from creation and Cain and Abel to the modern period in terms of class struggle and in examining environment, occupation and class of human beings. He identified the traditional concepts *maktab* (school) and *ʿaqāʾid* (creed) with concepts such as "ideology", "social leadership" and "class foundation", *intiẓār* with "historical determinism" and "futurism", *ummat* with "a dynamic, committed and ideological vision" and *shirk* (multitheism) with "feudal system" (Sharīʿatī 1968:35, 1996a:70, 82, 1999b:218). As Yann Richard (1981:218–220) claims, he also reinterpreted the core Shi'i doctrine *imāmat* not as "belief in twelve pure, saintly, extraordinary names", but as "pure, honest, revolutionary conduct of the people and the correct foundation of society in terms of science, the expansion and independence of people's judgement".

Despite the socially radical nature of Sharīʿatī's reconstruction of Shi'i Islam, his epistemological underpinnings were not strictly sociological in the sense that his attention was directed to social theory. As Shahrough Akhavi (1983b:130) points out, Sharīʿatī instead followed "the direction of phenomenology" by emphasising experience of appearance and understanding of parts against the background of appropriate wholes.[69] By

[69] The term 'phenomenology' is a compund term of the Greek words *phainomenon* and *logos*. Phenomenology signifies the activity of giving an account, giving a logos, of various phenomena, of the various ways in which things can appear. By recognising the reality and truth of phenomena and denying any dichotomy between phenomenon and noumenon, the phenomena is not considered only as 'a picture' in the mind. The work that is generally considered to be the first work of modern phenomenology is Edmund Husserl's *Logische üntersuchungen* (Logical investigations) that was published in 1901. Husserl's phenomenology was developed by Heidegger and others and also to some extent influenced Gadamer's hermeneutics. By overcoming certain weaknesses of neo-Kantianism in initiating and employing phenomenology, Husserl's thought was driven by the ambition to turn philosophy back to the Absolute. "On the other hand, Husserl might with some justifications be viewed as one of the last strongholds of the nineteenth century, a reactionary who was

considering the external world of nature as composed of a series of *āyāt* (signs) and *sunan* (norms), i.e. phenomena, Sharīʿatī's (1996a:38) *tauḥīdī* worldview explicitly referred to the view of Husserl and the modern school of phenomenology in that we cannot know the absolute reality of phenomenon:

Phenomenology is in its most general sense based on the recognition that absolute truth, the ground and essence of the world, of nature, and of matter, lies beyond our grasp. What is knowable and accessible to our experience, knowledge and sense-perception, is *padīdah* (phenomenon) and not what is.[70]

While Sharīʿatī (1996a:38) distinguished his own definition of phenomenology from that of *waḥdat al-wujūd* (unity of existence) prevalent in Islamic theosophy in its "scientific and analytical character", his notion of subjectivity nevertheless attempted to guarantee the certainty of subjective experience by providing an objective basis for knowledge in the sense that the signs, indications and manifestations that science deals with nevertheless "are manifestations of being". In this respect, he underlined the necessity of *fahmīdan-i durust* (correct understanding) that requires considering *tauḥīd* as identical to *jahānbīnī*, *tārīkh-i ʿilm* (history of philosophy) and *zīrbanā-yi akhlāqī wa iʿtiqādī* (ethical and doctrinal foundation) (ibid.:93). Consequently, the phenomenological foundation of Sharīʿatī's position (which according to S.A. Arjomand was inspired by Durkheim's model of social reform) leads not to philosophical scepticism or epistemological relativism, but rather to faith and social struggle, where religious belief must be accepted a priori.[71] While Sharīʿatī (ibid.:93–94) adopted Marx's notion of praxis, he maintained that the system of scientific socialism always must be grounded in monotheism and have a value-judgemental character, since a purely experimental approach absolves the social scientists of social responsibility. In his use of practical reason instead of pure reason or revelation, Sharīʿatī's (ibid.:14) view of religion was essentially instrumentalist, especially in politics, even if the base of material forces of production and their corresponding relations are subjected to the *zīrbanā-yi*

dismayed by the historicist and relativist direction of Nietzsche and Dilthey, and longed to turn philosophy back to the Absolute. The Absolute, for Husserl had to be found in consciousness. He is thus the heir of Kant, Fichte, and Hegel, but also looks back to Descartes as his ultimate philosophical predecessor" (Solomon 1988:129).

[70] In this respect, Sharīʿatī (1996a:113) criticised the Anglo-Irish philosopher George Berkeley for divorcing science from ontology, but followed Husserl's view that the task of phenomenology is to study the physically observable facts as phenomena. "According to contemporary phenomenology, i.e. the school of Husserl, which is dominant in physics and psychology as well as sociology, the principal foundation of the sciences is that physics should not seek the essence of material objects, which is not possible, but rather consider material objects as phenomena, that is, different exoteric appearances of reality, which in its essence is non-perceptible".

[71] Cf. Arjomand 1982.

iʿtiqādī that emanates from the Islamic ideology. Due to the explicit social dimension of Sharīʿatī's interpretation of Islam, Hamid Dabashi (1993:25) considers it "the supreme ideological construct of Islamic modernity".

In Sharīʿatī's general reconceptualisation of Islam, jurisprudence was not a priority and by acknowledging the right of free examination of the revealed texts, he took *ijtihād* to have a more general meaning beyond its legal technical sense. In the view of Sharīʿatī (1996a:71, 1999a:232), *ijtihād* signified the rational ability of socio-politically progressive *raushānfikrān-i mujāhid* (struggling intellectuals) to exert, in a general manner, independent judgement in religious matters.[72] Defining *ijtihād* as the principle of *inqilāb-i dāʾimī* (permanent revolution) in Islamic ideology in the sense that its application makes it possible to constantly renew Islamic ideals, Sharīʿatī (1996b:66) maintained that the *fuqahā* were to be held responsible for the intellectual and social decay of Islamic culture:

> From the point of view of ideology, *ijtihād* renews thinking. In all times, it constitutes a revolution of thought that is never brought to a standstill. I do not know why *ijtihād* is only restricted to the *istinbāṭ* of *furūʿ* norms today, but I am convinced that we always have to be (in a condition of) *ijtihād* for understanding the Qur'an and for analysing, comprehending, scrutinising it and for (various) *nauʿ-i bardāsht* (types of interpretation), even for analysing religious beliefs.

For Sharīʿatī (1999a:232), the *mujtahid* was consequently the "free struggler and researcher" who extracts and infers new religious answers on the basis of "the spirit and orientation of religion, scientific logic and the four sources of Islam".[73] He maintained that all Muslims "personally have to conduct *ijtihād* in the realm of belief" in order to continuously reach a "better understanding" and more a "complete interpretation" of religion (Sharīʿatī 1996b:66). In criticising those who restrict the essence of religious science to the highly specialised field of *fiqh* far away from the scene of society and politics, he furthermore remarked that *ijtihād* must be renewed continuously with a *bīnish-i mutaḥawwil* (changing outlook) directed by *taḥqīq-i ʿilmī-yi āzād* (free scientific analysis) in order to ceaselessly reach a *fahm-i mutaraqqī-yi madhab* (progressive understanding of religion) (Sharīʿatī 1999a:232). In his appeal for free *ijtihād*, Sharīʿatī (1999c:393) attempted to liberate the Islamic legal discourse from its traditional boundaries and make

[72] Sharīʿatī's (1978:8) radical notion of *islām minhā-yi rūḥānīyūn* (Islam without clerics) has been widely discussed in contemporary Iran. Sayyid Ḥamīd Rūḥānī directed a critique against Sharīʿatī's religious credentials in the third volume of his book *Nihḍat-i imām Khumainī* (The Movement of Khumainī), which was published by Markaz-i isnād-i inqilāb-i islāmī (Centre of documentation on Islamic revolution) in 1993. Rūḥānī denounced Sharīʿatī as an *ilṭiqātī* (eclectic), Marxist and anti-Islamic thinker. Among those who have come to Sharīʿatī's defence is Ḥusain Razmjū in his book *Pūstīn-i wārūnah* (To turn the shroud inside out) that was published as a rebuttal of Rūḥānī's views in 1994.

[73] In another passage, Sharīʿatī (1998d:14) even claimed that a degree of *ijtihād* does not require the study of the Qur'an.

it radically applicable to the total domain (legal, economical, social, political, etc.) of human existence and thereby guarantee the modernisation of religion itself.

In contemporary Iran, Sharīʿatī's historiography as well as the sociological component of his ideas has been adopted by a number of Shi'i intellectuals, among whom the most important are Ḥabībullāh Paimān and *ḥujjat al-islām* Ḥasan Yūsufī-Ishkiwarī. Paimān considers himself one of the main guardians of Sharīʿatī's ideas and his writings in general deal with different aspects of his own version of Islamic socialism.[74] In his critique of the underpinnings of secular modernity, Paimān (1999b:24) asserts that Muslims must become aware of "the current blind alleys of modern Western civilisation" and find a solution to the present crisis of religion "with the help of scientific methods and historical examination". In the view of Paimān (ibid.:25, 1997:55), the true function of religion (*kārkard-i ḥaqīqī-yi dīn*) is its social expression, where the Prophet serves as the ideal model for "social struggle" and "all-encompassing political and intellectual revolutionary movement" in the struggle against oppressive and tyrannical political systems. As far as Islamic law is concerned, Paimān (1999b:58) considers *sharīʿat* as a pure human construction. By separating *sharīʿat* organically from the theological category *uṣūl-i dīn* that has a *takwīnī* (intrinsic) divine element, he reduces *sharīʿat* to practical rulings and verdicts that are "enacted and compiled by human beings":

> But *sharīʿat* in its present sense, that is *qawānīn-i mauḍūʿah* (subject rules) comprised of economical, political, social and scientific norms and rulings, are varied and diverse. The unity of religion on the one hand and the variable and mutable character of *sharīʿat* on the other indicate that religion is thoroughly influenced by the exigencies and limited context of time, space and culture in the process of its functioning and transformation into practical rulings and implementable norms (planning). Indeed, *sharīʿat* establishes the practical design of religion in space and time.

In his book *Kilīd-i fahm-i qurʾān* (Key to the understanding of the Qur'an), Paimān enters on the subject of Qur'anic hermeneutics with the precondition that the universal message of revelation is accessible to the people and not only to a group of experts. He claims that intermediaries create distance between man and God and generates favourable conditions for *shirk*. The esoteric explanations of the mystics are hence rejected, since the hierarchal exoteric-esoteric division of Qur'anic meaning "would suggest that the

[74] Paimān was born in Shiraz in 1935. He has a doctoral degree in dentistry, a bachelor's degree in sociology and was until 1995 a member of the Academy of medical science at Tehran University. Since the university years, he has been closely associated with diverse groups of Islamic socialists, such as Khudā-parastān-i sūsīyālīst and Junbish-i musalmān-i mubāriz (Militant Muslim movement). Among his most renowned political writings are his lectures on Islamic revolutionary thought (Paimān 1998a and 1999).

Qur'an is not a book of guidance for the people" (Paimān 1997:7). In both style and content, Paimān's hermeneutic account seems to have been worked out in response to ʿAbd al-Karīm Surūsh's discussion on the subject, but Paimān disapproves of the latter's distinction between *sharīʿat-i ṣāmit* and *sharīʿat-i nāṭiq* from another angle than the Islamic traditionalists. His argument is that the religious textual sources have a particular universal and original message to mankind:

According to the above theory [i.e. Surūsh's], the Qur'an has in its essence nothing to tell. It has no specific message and no guidance. The message of the Qur'an in the way it was articulated and understood during the time of the Prophet cannot be discovered and every new interpretation is nothing but the mental construction and judgment of the interpreter (ibid.:91).

In the view of Paimān (ibid.:91), the Qur'an is not "a silent or dead book", which is "empty of meaning and significance", but is "living and illuminating" and instructs the reader through guidance. Whereas his point of departure, similar to that of Sharīʿatī, is phenomenological, he elaborates on the subject of textual hermeneutics (its context, process and outcome) in a more systematic manner. For Paimān, the phenomenon of revelation possesses an objective and universal message that is the focus of hermeneutics and that is identical to the intention of God. Inspired by Martin Heidegger and Hans-Georg Gadamer, he believes that the task of hermeneutics is to essentially objectify the intention by means of the theory of the *dawār-i tafsīrī* (hermeneutical circle) whereby the perspective of the interpreter and perspective of the text emerges as one entity.[75] The first stage of interpretation is to find the common human condition of the author and the interpreter and then to extract the original message by means of interpretation. The objectification of textual meaning is hence largely "the compatibility of true meaning with the intention of revelation" in contrast to "false meaning where the acquired meaning is different from the original message" (ibid.:10). Despite his egalitarian viewpoint, Paimān's (ibid.:23) hermeneutics nevertheless incorporates an elitist element in the sense that the purpose of textual hermeneutics essentially is to "make the text meaningful for the people".[76]

Similarly to Paimān, Ḥasan Yūsufī-Ishkiwarī (2001:318) has contributed

[75] While the notion of 'hermeneutical circle' in its modern sense gained currency through Heidegger's writings, it had originally been developed in the old German theological hermeneutic tradition, namely in the notion that the whole can be understood only in the context of its parts and that the parts only can be understood in the context of their whole. Heidegger adapted the hermeneutical circle to shift the focus of attention from the object of interpretation to its subject. He maintained that everything could be understood only in the context of the subject since no subject can jump out of its historical context.

[76] Paimān (1997:61) also argues that since religious consciousness is the foundation of Qur'anic epistemology, only Muslim believers are competent to discover the original message of revelation.

extensively to the dissemination of Sharīʿatī's ideas in contemporary Iran, whom he considers "the greatest Islamic thinker and revivalist on the global level".[77] His intellectual debt to Sharīʿatī is visible in his emphasis on the all-encompassing ingredient of *tauḥīd* in the structure of the Islamic worldview and in his accent on the social aspect of religion. Yūsufī-Ishkiwarī (2000:232) embraces Sharīʿatī's view that permanent and revolutionary *ijtihād* is necessary in the whole body of religious belief and dogma and that *taqlīd* is *harām* (forbidden). In fact, he explicitly stresses the need for a free and independent *ijtihād* that releases subject matter of religious change from the trivialities of *aḥkām-i farʿīyah* (applicable legal norms):

The contemporary meaning of *ijtihād* differs from that which the jurists discussed in premodern times. In the view of Iqbāl Lāhūrī, the contemporary *ijtihād* transcends beyond the *ijtihād* of the premodern jurists that in general was limited to applicable legal norms. Indeed, the majority of contemporary Islamic intellectual currents and trends consider *ijtihād* beyond legal matters (Yūsufī-Ishkiwarī 2000:227).

But due to the experience of implementing Islamic law in the postrevolutionary Iranian state, Yūsufī-Ishkiwarī is inclined to modify Sharīʿatī's unified understanding of religion and state. In the view of Yūsufī-Ishkiwarī (1999a:6, 1999c:6), the expanded modern state has emerged as the most powerful contestant of the autonomy of Islamic thought, in that its civil and secular institutions "operate external to the realm of Islamic legal decrees". Therefore, he suggests that the religious authority, i.e. the *marjaʿ al-taqlīd*, must be divorced from the Iranian state in order for religious scholars "to state their opinion" (Yūsufī-Ishkiwarī 1999b:7).[78]

As far as religious epistemology is concerned, Yūsufī-Ishkiwarī, similar to Paimān, believes that Surūsh's theory of *sharīʿat-i ṣāmit* indicates that the Qur'an, the *ḥadīṯ* and the *akhbār* of the *imāms* have no message to communicate on their own. While he accepts the general distinction between religion-in-itself and religious knowledge, he asserts that religion is predisposed with a particular message before it crosses the threshold into the realm of human knowledge and understanding:

I believe that religion from its beginning and before it enters the realm of knowledge, understanding and interpretation of the religious believer possesses a specific message and expression (yet not one single expression). In other cases, it

[77] Ḥasan Yūsufī-Ishkiwarī was born in Rudsar in 1948. He entered a *ḥauzah-yi ʿilmīyah* in Qum in 1965 and for fourteen years mainly studied *fiqh*, *ʿilm-i kalām*, *ʿilm al-tārīkh* and *adabīyāt*. He was active in the Islamic movement before the revolution and became a member of the first parliament in the Islamic republic. He is currently a working member of the Daftar-i pazhūhish-gāh-i farhangī-yi duktur ʿAlī Sharīʿatī (Cultural research bureau of ʿAlī Sharīʿatī), which is responsible for the cultivation of Sharīʿatī's thought in Iran. He is also involved in research at the Muʿassasah-yi dāʾirāt al-maʿārif-i buzurg-i islāmī (Institute of the great Islamic encyclopaedia) in Tehran.

[78] Cf. Yūsufī-Ishkiwarī (2001) for his views on Sharīʿatī.

would be meaningless to speak of religion at all. Indeed, if we believe that everyone's interpretion of religion is his or her religion and that no one has access to the truth of religion, then religion has no external reality in order for us to speak of religious knowledge in the first place! (Yūsufī-Ishkiwarī 1998b:17)

While Yūsufī-Ishkiwarī shows consideration for Surūsh's criticism of the traditional *ʿulamā* and the standards of their epistemological discourse, he maintains that his refutation of the Islamic ideology fails to notice the innermost *raison d'être* of that concept, namely that ideology renders religion dynamic and socially relevant. Yūsufī-Ishkiwarī believes that ideology is necessary for revolutionary practice and for realising the ideal religious state of worldly justice. In his view, the contribution of Sharīʿatī to modern Islamic thought was precisely that he provided Muslim society with the means to dispose itself of social and cultural backwardness after centuries of intellectual and spiritual stagnation:

A society where poverty and social repression exist has no possibility to maintain a decent level of *akhlāq-i maʿnawīyat* (spiritual ethic). Indeed, Dr. Surūsh and Dr. Nasr must answer whether it is possible for spirituality and theosophy to prosper in an oppressive society where injustice, class struggle, gender inequality and race discrimination exist. In his favouring of socialism, Sharīʿatī basically argued that this is not the case and that social justice is the foundation of sound religiosity (Yūsufī-Ishkiwarī 1997b).

Since there are historical and anthropological reasons for the fact that Islam is the principal component in Iranian culture and society, Yūsufī-Ishkiwarī argues that the Iranian adoption of modernity will continue to be Islamic in orientation. While modernity is read as almost identical to modern Western philosophy and humanism, he acknowledges that it has "spread to all other cultures on a global level" and that Muslims have no other alternative but to develop their own form of modernity:

The only possible and rational approach is to encounter Western modernity with a refinement of our own cultural sources and with reliance on these notable and reconstructed resources in a way that the outcome of this encounter, endeavour and experience is a kind of *mudarnītah-yi sharqī-islāmī* (Eastern-Islamic modernity) (Yūsufī-Ishkiwarī 1997a:9).

In his book *Khirad dar ḍiyāfat-i dīn* (Wisdom at the reception of religion), Yūsufī-Ishkiwarī (2000:6) develops his idea of Eastern-Islamic modernity in more precise terms as a critique of tradition as well as aimed at creating "a modern and functional instruments of ideology and thought". While he recognises the different epistemological foundations of Islam and modern humanistic philosophy, he believes that the starting point of Islamic *insān-shināsānah-yi falsafah* (philosophical anthropology) must be redefined on the basis of the concept *tauḥīd*. In the sense that traditional Islamic thought elevated the mind but suppressed the body, he maintains that the contemporary definition of man in Islam must have *insāniyat* (humanity) as its criterion and orientation and replace the old monist view of the soul with one that guarantees the value of the body as well as the mind. In the sphere of Islamic law, he believes that the discussion on natural rights cannot be based on *fiqh*, but must rather be preconditioned on the equality of all human beings in a secular sense (Yūsufī-Ishkiwarī 1997a:344).

D. The Islamic modernist position of Muḥammad Mujtahid-Shabistarī

One of the most renowned Islamic modernist thinkers in contemporary Iran is *ḥujjat al-islām* Muḥammad Mujtahid-Shabistarī. With his deep acquaintance with the German language and continental philosophy, he has in particular contributed in introducing modern Protestant hermeneutical and theological thought to Iran.[79] While Mujtahid-Shabistarī follows the broad essentials of earlier Islamic modernist' thought, such as the view of Islam as an all-inclusive world-view and the critique of traditional Islam, he is critical to the dogmatic attempts of ideologising religion. He maintains that the notion of Islamic ideology is influenced by alien Western leftist conceptions of man and society and that its purpose is "to transform religion into a political ideology". As far as the religious character of Islamic ideology is concerned, Mujtahid-Shabistarī (1999a:7) maintains that it "has no concern for the religious tradition and merely attempts to benefit from religion as an instrument for struggle". In fact, he underlines that Muslims must redefine their religious position in a more genuine manner in order to compete with contemporary secular philosophies that claim the guidance of mankind in this world. But while the essentially Western globalisation process that transforms traditional cultures into "a unified cultural village" should be analysed critically, he believes that contemporary Muslims must maintain and develop their own characteristic strand of modernity distinct from the Western forms (Mujtahid-Shabistarī 1997a:174). Even if he rejects the philosophical dogma of secularism and is critical to the *māshīnīzism*

[79] Born in Shabistar in 1936, Muḥammad Mujtahid-Shabistarī started his higher education at a *ḥauzah-yi ʿilmīyah* in Qum at the age of fourteen. After several years of study (including eight years of *dars-i khārij* in *fiqh*), he received *ijāzah* of conducting *ijtihād* in Islamic law. In 1969, he was appointed director of the Markaz-i islāmī (Islamic center) in Hamburg, West Germany. He returned to Iran at the time of the revolution and was elected a member of the new parliament. Since Mujtahid-Shabistarī has no formal academic education in the modern sense, he received an honorary doctorate from *shūrā-yi ʿālī-yi inqilāb-i farhangī* in order to have permission to teach at the university. He is fluent in German, Turkish and Arabic and has reading knowledge of English and French. He is currently professor of theology at Tehran University, where he teaches *kalām-i jadīd* (modern theology). He is also a member of the Iranian academy of sciences.

(mechanisation, a transliteration form the French) element in modern life that springs from the development of modern technology, he does not reject all modernity. His critique seems instead to be closely parallel to the humanist critiques of the exploitive features of the modern project.[80] While he differs from the majority of Islamic modernists who consider technology merely as a set of means rather than a way of thinking, his concept of modernity is in general terms affirmative, by approving the positive aspects of its practical achievements such as democracy and human rights:

> If we accept that modernity is a global phenomenon today that is not exclusive to the West and that the West differs from other parts of the world only in the spread or limitations of modernity, then we must accept that the composition of human relations today requires new construction and planning on a global level. In this sense, human rights have become a global issue (Mujtahid-Shabistarī 2000:229).[81]

Mujtahid-Shabistarī rejects the myth of Muslims as capable of absorbing the technological systems of modernity and remaining immune from its underlying meaning system. He also believes that the Islamic world-view and its value system are compatible with modern natural science, even if the epistemological foundations of the humanities must be seriously examined by Muslim scientists, since they contain issues that the scientific method is unable to answer. Science is, in other words, not taken as the ultimate source of knowledge. He also maintains that the traditional Islamic sciences never developed on a firm Qur'anic basis independent of non-religious sciences but rather became heavily influenced in their theoretical structure by alien philosophical and scientific traditions such as Christian theology, Greek philosophy and Neo-platonic mysticism:

> This permeation and intermingling had the effect that an autonomous intellectual system of God, the world and man, purely Qur'anic in all its amalgamating units and components, has not developed sufficiently among Muslims (Mujtahid-Shabistarī 1986:6).

---

[80] Mujtahid-Shabistarī (1985:18) writes, "If man becomes the servant of the machine and suffers the loss of creativity and choice, he will not be a real human being and consequently not an Islamic human being. There exist forms of technology that put the humanity of man in danger. These forms of technology must be called to a halt".

[81] Mujtahid-Shabistarī (2000:241–242, 253) argues that the revealed sources do not contain all necessary facts and knowledge for political and social development, but that Islam must be interpreted by means of free use of *ijtihād* to accommodate religion to the exigencies of modernity, such as democracy and human rights. He is in particular critical of the Islamic traditionalists' rejection of democracy and human rights and asserts that the writings of ʿAbdullāh Jawādī-Āmulī and Muḥammad Ḥusain Ṭabātabāʾī on these subjects lack practical solutions and instead indulge in abstract and inadequate metaphysical argumentation. On the topic of democracy and Islam, Mujtahid-Shabistarī (1999a:10) underlines that the Iranian experience is not comparable to that of the West, where democracy turned against the Church, but nevertheless adopts an instrumentalist view of democracy as "a form and mechanism of government in opposition to the forms and mechanisms of dictatorship government".

In this respect, early Islam did not participate in the dialogue with Greek rational tradition and religious *tafaqquh* (understanding) was predominantly concerned with unsystemised faith rather than systemised theology or jurisprudence. While the Qur'an in the view of Mujtahid-Shabistarī contains all religious and moral truth in its essentials, he argues in his account on the Greek influence on Islamic logocentricity that Islam must constantly be accommodated to human rationality. In fact, he suggests that the whole history of Islamic philosophy and science represents an unceasing attempt to accommodate Islam to rationality and that the fundamental effort always must be to carry out such reconciliation.[82] By referring to the high value and importance of reason in the Qur'an, he characterises Islamic theology and jurisprudence as highly rational and exact in structure, in contrast to Christian theology, which is reduced to mystical contemplation (Mujtahid-Shabistarī 1999b:6). By claiming that religion embodies a form of reason, he has faith in Islam as a rational enterprise and argues that religion is as rational as philosophy.

Even if Mujtahid-Shabistarī rejects the Western philosophical dogma of secularism, he acknowledges that faith must be subjected to historical criticism and that religious freedom is a necessary feature of a vigorous and dynamic modern society. In fact, he devotes a whole book, *Naqdī bar qarā'at-i rasmī az dīn* (Critique of the official reading of religion), to criticising the official so-called *fiqāhatī* (legalistic) version of Islam that is propagated by the Iranian state authorities. This interpretation of Islam, with its stress on positive legality, marks in his view a break with the ethical and personal considerations that governed the traditional interpretation of Islamic law (Mujtahid-Shabistarī 2000:12, 24, 30). Since the Iranian state, by considering law in its modern sense as positive organisation and constitution, in reality departs from the traditional juristic method of legal inference, he asserts that its tendency to discover the concept of social change in traditional jurisprudence is inaccurate:

> All the programs for development are extracted from the modern sciences. The science of *fiqh* is a kind of legal interpretation that is engaged with the Qur'an and *sunnat*. *Fiqh* cannot explain the reality that exists in society and does not determine the mechanism of change (of programs). Besides rendering values, the legal dos and don'ts can only guide a part of the 'hows' of structural development towards a specific formation (Mujtahid-Shabistarī 1997a:89).[83]

[82] Mujtahid-Shabistarī's argument is accurate in the sense that the 'historical-empirical' epistemic scheme was constantly forced to make some concessions to rationality. It is significant that those who did not make any concessions, such as the *ḥashwīyah* and the *akhbārīyah*, were ultimately doomed to extinction.

[83] By adopting the traditional definition of Islamic jurisprudence as connected to a casuistic method of inference of divine norms, Mujtahid-Shabistarī is evidently not attracted to legal positivism or its major trend, critical legal hermeneutics, which considers law as a social

Similar to other Islamic modernists, Mujtahid-Shabistarī's study of religion is confessional, guided by the modernist interpretation of the theological principle of *tauḥīd* and directed by an attitude of faith. He considers *tauḥīd* as a type of relation between God and man, where man experiences the Divine and where "neither God nor man is neglected". Reconciling the two angles of the theomorphic subjectivity of man, he suggests that in a relation based on pure *tauḥīd*, "God's sovereignity is not competing with man but gives him meaning and solidifies him" (Mujtahid-Shabistarī 1997b:182). In his elaboration on *kalām-i jadīd*, he is heavily influenced by Protestant theologians such as Paul Tillich, Karl Barth and Emil Brunner, but also by Catholic modernists such as Karl Rahner, Hans Küng and others. Mujtahid-Shabistarī (1997a:43–63, 107–116) is also inspired by the American philosopher Ian Barbour's idea of science as an endeavour separate from and independent of religion. While *kalām-i jadīd*, similar to *ʿilm al-kalām*, aims to present the eternal truths of religion as a matter of faith, he argues that its objective is not to confirm a specific philosophical foundation. In contrast to *ʿilm al-kalām*, which is concerned with 'first philosophy' and considers temporary exigencies as of secondary importance, modern theology "approaches religion from a certain distance" with an emphasis on faith and is in its use of historic-critic method interested in "the role of religion as a living historical phenomenon" (ibid.:95). By identifying *kalām-i jadīd* as the evaluation of religious beliefs, principles, customs and institutions, Mujtahid-Shabistarī (ibid.:99) argues that "to remain in the settlings of historical tradition and be occupied in the whirlpool of *taqlīd* of earlier personalities is the cholera of faith". His negative view of the accumulated Islamic historical tradition also includes the realm of law, where his argument that the *bāb-i ijtihād* (gate to *itjihād*) must remain open seems a bit odd compared to the established Shi'i view of legal reasoning that very rarely relied on *taqlīd al-māyit* (the imitation of a dead man) (Mujtahid-Shabistarī 1997b:47).

Similar to his account of modern theology, Mujtahid-Shabistarī argues that the scientific field and methodology of modern legal philosophy is separate from the science of *fiqh* itself. Without acknowledging that epistemology in the strict sense only constitutes a branch of philosophy, he ultimately maintains, by reference to Kant's idea that all philosophy is epistemology, that legal philosophy is identical to Islamic epistemology of jurisprudence.[84]

phenomenon embodied in substantial rules enacted by courts. Rather, he looks for inspiration in the German tradition of philosophical hermeneutics championed by Gadamer and others. In fact, Mujtahid-Shabistarī recognises that the juridical instructions pertaining to social and political spheres of human life are limited in the traditional *fiqh* sources and argues that as far as the only religious duty of the Islamic government is to protect the faith of the believers, the specific model is secondary.

[84] In fact, epistemology stands in a close and special relationship to each of the different branches of philosophy (metaphysics, ethics, aesthetics, logic, etc), each of them which has its

By furthermore recognising that philosophy as well as science involves independent sources of knowledge, he argues that philosophy of law as well as history of law is something else than what is addressed at the *ḥauzahs*. While *fiqh*, similar to *ʿilm al-kalām* and *ʿirfān* and other religious sciences, searches for cognitive certainty, he asserts that legal philosophy is instead interested in the historical evolution of *fiqh*, that is; "law as equipped with a social and historical identity" (Mujtahid-Shabistarī 1999c:57). In the view of Mujtahid-Shabistarī (ibid.:58–59), philosophy of law further elucidates to what extent the *muqaddamāt-i ijtihād*, such as *uṣūl-i fiqh*, are influenced by non-religious science prior to the act of inference:

Philosophy of law explains which methodology a certain *faqīh* uses in his *istinbāṭ*, since the science of *uṣūl* is not capable of elucidating this matter alone. It informs us of the method of inference, that is, from where the inference begins and how it is practiced in order to determine a *fatwā*. At the *ḥauzah*, it is not discussed what foundation the jurist proceeds from, how he determines a *fatwā*, which preliminary sources he takes for granted, whether these sources are based on other sources or not and if the first sources are philosophical or theological.

Since the sources of jurisprudence must continuously be accommodated to various dimensions of modern life, Mujtahid-Shabistarī considers the question of *ijtihād* as the most critical issue for philosophy of law. In this respect, he suggests that while philosophy of law influences the philosophical foundations of *fiqh*, it never "affects legal methodology in a direct way" (ibid.:99). In contrast to Surūsh's theory of 'contraction and expansion' of religious knowledge, Mujtahid-Shabistarī (1994:18) does not consider human learning as a unified entity, but rather restricts his argument to the fact that religious teachings must be presented as compatible to modern science:

I do not say that all human learning constitutes a unified collection and develops in an unified manner, but rather that when man attempts to make his religious experience comprehensible and rational, it is necessary that this effort is carried out in a manner that does not contradict science and philosophy.

While Mujtahid-Shabistarī is critical of the traditional, or what he also calls *urtudūks* (orthodox), methodology of Shi'i jurisprudence, given his scholastic background it is not clear whether he advocates a change in the methodological principles of *fiqh* or not, at least not in his early writings. In an essay on the issue of the West in 1985, he affirms that the Aristotelian methodology of Islamic jurisprudence is an integral part of Islam, while there at the same time exists no explicit intellectual borders between the East

own subject matter. Each of these disciplines attempts to arrive at a systematic understanding of the issues that arise in its particular domain. In this sense, epistemology is at once a branch of philosophy that relates to each of its other branches.

and the West due to conceptual and methodological borrowings.[85] As Islamic law developed a methodological capability of its own in the tenth century and onwards, he argues that it was emancipated from the methodological system of *ʿilm al-kalām* to form its own distinct theoretical system:

The discipline *uṣūl-i fiqh* is a piece of equipment with full capability for inferring legal norms. Since the use of this method is also the all-encompassing standard in the Islamic world it is not necessary to embrace Western philosophy (Mujtahid-Shabistarī 1985:18).

But by recognising that philosophy of law coordinates the relationship between *fiqh* and other sciences and assists the jurists in the task of solving contradictions between the traditional groundwork of *fiqh* and modern life, his opinion on the traditional methodology is nevertheless ambivalent:

From this perspective, philosophy of law is beneficial to *fiqh*. When you examine the relation between *fiqh* and other sciences, it becomes clear that everyone who engages in *tafaqquh* bases his or her work on a certain groundwork. Then, if there is a weakness in the groundwork, *fiqh* has no capacity to give a *fatwā* on that foundation (Mujtahid-Shabistarī 1999c:60–61).

While *fiqh* has objectives and values it never clarifies approaches or mechanisms. It is science that elucidates the approaches and the mechanisms. In other words, there is a function for *fiqh* where (the jurist) discovers a *ḥukm* or a *ḥaqq* (right) and there is no place for *fiqh* where a norm or right is not discovered (ibid.:84).

In a number of articles, published in *Rūznāmah-yi īrān* (Iran newspaper) and *Kiyān* in 1998 to 2001, Mujtahid-Shabistarī proposes in fact a new methodological framework for Shi'i theological and legal reasoning by suggesting that the interpretation of religious texts must be aided by the use of philosophical categories adopted from modern phenomenology. His method is hermeneutico-phenomenological and is concerned with constructing a normative system of prophetic experience by implanting hermeneutics in phenomenology. As will be noted, his attention to methodology is not primarily to refer to the method employed, but to an analysis of the assumptions and logical limitations that characterises all methodology. It is largely influenced by some of the giants of the modern European hermeneutic tradition, such as Hans Georg Gadamer, and further enriched by Husserlian phenomenology in the sense that an emphasis is placed on human experience descriptions, as the human experience was

[85] Cf. Mujtahid-Shabistarī 2001a. On the question of methodological crossing points, Mujtahid-Shabistarī points at the theoretical correspondence between the Western philosophers Kant and Locke and the anti-logician Muslim jurist Ibn Taimīyah on the limits of human knowledge as well as that between Hume and Muḥammad al-Ghazālī on the subject of causality.

directed towards objects.[86] In his attempt to ground hermeneutics in phenomenology, Mujtahid-Shabistarī follows Heidegger's position of an ontology of understanding, where ultimately the aim is to produce a hermeneutic of human existence. Understanding is both a mode of knowledge and a mode of being. By emphasising the significance of faith as well as the ineluctable relation between phenomena and noumena, his metaphysics no longer considers reality as a myriads of permanent symbols reflecting higher realities, but rather as experience. Since phenomena are not symbols reflecting the divine or direct gateway to noumenal realities through the light of the pure intellect, Mujtahid-Shabistarī transforms the transparency of the traditional Islamic 'objectivist' epistemology into opacity, where phenomenon is subject to interpretation and conditioned experience.

By considering the logic of method as a necessary part of validating the knowledge that method purports to acquire through its given procedures, Mujtahid-Shabistarī (1994b:23–24) argues that there are essentially two different approaches to Islamic jurisprudence among the contemporary jurists; on the one hand, the traditional theory that seeks "to establish a legal norm from the Qur'an and the *sunnat* according to the traditional juristic five-fold scale" and on the other hand, a more dynamic approach that adopts a free and contemporary use of human reason with the objective "of achieving socio-economical progress". He asserts that the two approaches are grounded in two distinct philosophical and theological foundations and in fact criticises the advocates of the former method for defending *qarāʾat-i waḥīd az dīn* (one single reading of religion) and for being too faithful to the "metaphysical underpinnings of Platonic and Aristotelian metaphysics", since "Islam as such is not a philosophical ontology":

There is no *qaṭʿī al-inṭibāq* (certain conformity) in the world of man. All readings are *ẓannī* and *ijtihādī* and the coming into existence of new readings is always probable. [...] Discerning the definite aspects of every religion is a

[86] Already in 1997, Mujtahid-Shabistarī adopts the idea that religious experience is the pivotal question of modern theology, which is very characteristic of (Husserlian-inspired) modern Christian theology. Influenced by Barth's notion of the 'conjectural experience of God' and Emil Brunner's concept of truth as an encounter with God, he argues that the word 'experience' has no certain or definite meaning. As a form of Neo-Kantianism, Mujtahid-Shabistarī's use of Husselian phenomenology is fundamentally more Kantian than Kant by presupposing a pre-reflective or pre-predicative world, which is there prior to the transcendental assumptions of a priori thought, since Husserl's thought continued the Cartesian undertaking in the manner of transcendental phenomenology and represented a turn to subjectivity with the intention of arriving at objective truth, that is, reason's self-discovery in the presence of intelligible objects. Consequently, it is not strange that Mujtahid-Shabistarī (2000:58) traces the decisive break with traditional epistemology back to Descartes rational philosophy rather than Husserl, in the sense that it was "Descartes that separated thinking from existence".

phenomenological question that one can form an opinion about with a glance from the outside of religion (Mujtahid-Shabistarī 2000:246–247).

Consequently, Mujtahid-Shabistarī's method is not merely a method as he claims, but his phenomenological approach involves a substantial theoretical metaphysical position, including a set of doctrines about the world, the self and where truth is to be found. Attempting to find an objective basis for knowledge that would guarantee the certainty of subjective experience, he therefore follows Husserl more than Kant, who criticised the latter for not living up to the absolute claims of philosophy and for not conducting science as a *noematic* phenomenon, that is, as an intentional object.[87] While Mujtahid-Shabistarī distinguishes religious experience from law and rituals, his definitions of theology have a fundamental impact on his position on Islamic law and seem to be articulated somehow in response to ʿAbd al-Karīm Surūsh's epistemological writings as well as Sharīʿatī's phenomenology. In fact, Mujtahid-Shabistarī considers his renewal of phenomenology *through* hermeneutics and draws a distinction between his hermeneutico-phenomenological position, also called *hirminūtīk-i wujūdī* (existential hermeneutics), on the one hand and Surūsh's empirical and historical methodology as well as Sharīʿatī's adoption of phenomenology for ideological purposes, on the other:

The approach of one group (of reformists) to religion is positivistic, or more correctly neo-positivistic. Their religious perspective is, so to say, historical. [...] The other group has a hermeneutical perspective in the understanding of religion. While it approves of Islam's social dimension, it rejects that religion constitutes a political, economical and social system (Mujtahid-Shabistarī 1998:10).[88]

In this respect, Mujtahid-Shabistarī maintains that since the phenomenological approach is based on a specific philosophy, it differs from Surūsh's neo-positivistic method, which is primarily concerned with methodology. In contrast, his methodology is a theory of analogous meaning in terms of recovering the intentionalities of symbolic expressions. But while Mujtahid-Shabistarī's reason is ordered towards the truth of things, that is, the disclosure of and the confirmation of what things are, his phenomenology nevertheless lacks a criterion of truth, since it does not work from an absolutely transcendental viewpoint or shares in the teleology of thinking:

My approach is enriched by hermeneutical methology. This means that religious science is concerned with isolating a 'message' rather than knowing a *wāqiʿīyat-i khārijī* (an external object) as in natural science. In my approach, religious science is

[87] Cf. Rider 1998:25.
[88] Cf. Mujtahid-Shabistarī 2001a. Mujtahid-Shabistarī (2001b) suggests in fact that Sharīʿatī made use of phenomenology in an inconsistent and incomplete way by transforming its philosophical underpinnings into radical sociology.

to comprehend the message of religion. This message rests on understanding, not methodology (ibid.:10).

By considering the Prophet Muḥammad the prototype of *tajrubah-yi dīnī* (religious experience), Mujtahid-Shabistarī argues that the Prophet's religious experience was unique in the sense that it emerged from the Prophet himself to the external and not the opposite, as in the case of Sufi descriptions of religious experience. In this respect, the *imāms* have a similar status to the Prophet as models of religious conduct and channels of divine grace. But as Mujtahid-Shabistarī (1999a:17) argues in the context of the first *imām* ʿAlī b. Abī Ṭālib, the meaning of prototype is conditioned by human knowledge in each historical period, since "no meta-historical model of justice exists". While Mujtahid-Shabistarī's phenomenology hence acknowledges the supremacy of the Prophet and the *imāms* as prototype paradigms of Islamic ideals, he claims that the believers are responsible for interpreting and selecting the various associations these ideals connote in the historical context of modernity:

In the contemporary world, we have in my opinion to ask ourselves what the original message of this distinguished man [i.e. the Prophet] was and what colours his message has adopted during the course of history. This question is a scientific question that can be answered by phenomenological method. If we consider such a question, we know that the essence of his message is spiritual (ibid.:14).

As a matter of fact, Mujtahid-Shabistarī suggests that modern Western hermeneutics enables Muslim interpreters to go beyond examining the *asbāb* (occasions) of isolated texts towards a model of interpretation that examines the Qur'an as a unified entity. While he considers the comprehension of a religious message from the revealed sources as a theological activity, he defines it more properly as "a kind of *ijtihād* in the principles that changes the method of *ijtihād* in the *furūʿ*" (ibid.:14). Since the questions that face modern man are not restricted to a limited number of legal rulings, but extend to the realm of philosophy, his phenomenological method applies to the realm of theological thought as well as to the realm of jurisprudence. In fact, he argues that 'historical phenomenology' in the first instance discovers "the original law of the phenomenon of prophecy" and in the second case gives a norm for *sulūk-i tauḥīdī* (unitarian behaviour), which is "the valid criterion of every *ḥukm-i sharʿī* in that historical situation" (Mujtahid-Shabistarī 2000:270–271). Since all the details of *sulūk-i tauḥīdī* must be evaluated on the basis of revelation in the light of the contemporary historical situation, he asserts that to deal with matters deduced from modern philosophy, such as human rights, in the highly technical manner of *fiqh* is very awkward:

This kind of perspective [i.e. the *fiqhī* one] on human rights is essentially different from the modern perspective on human rights. The modern perspective on human rights is philosophical and prioritises the humanness of man over his beliefs. How is it possible to deduce a philosophical outlook from a religious text? ... This matter is not different from, say, that we build an aeroplane and refer to the Qur'an and *sunnat* to confirm that constructing an aeroplane has no prohibition. Is this really the nature of the question at hand? (Mujtahid-Shabistarī 1999a:19)[89]

By acknowledging that modern knowledge has no clear boundaries and that modern rationality is situated in a dialectal relationship to modern life forms, Mujtahid-Shabistarī considers contemporary *ijtihād* a more urgent task than ever before in Islamic history. He refers to Abū Jaʿfar al-Ṭūsī's jurisprudential realism as a model, but underlines that *fiqh* must respond to modern science in order to be capable of answering contemporary questions. "Legal reasoning is not possible without applying *uṣūl-i fiqh* and since this science comprises the human sciences and learning, we have to say that legal reasoning is only possible by using human sciences and learning" (Mujtahid-Shabistarī 1997b:37, 60). Nevertheless, he acknowledges that the revealed texts of Islamic tradition cannot be evaluated solely on the basis of modern rationality but must be considered in the light of what he calls *ʿaql-i dīnī* (religious reason).

While modern philosophy and science influence religious rationality, the Islamic use of reason remains, so to say, governed by what Mujtahid-Shabistarī (1999e:10) calls *manṭiq-i darūnī-yi payām-i qurʾān* (the inner logic of the Qur'anic message) that always is open to human interpretation and manipulation, i.e. it constitutes a *tafsīr-i pāyān-nāpazīr* (unending interpretation). To close down the dialogue by means of a final intepretation, a last word or final appeal to a rule of faith would be to close interpretation off from human life. While the inner logic of the Qur'an represents a category of pure meaning that is accessible from the phenomenological viewpoint, the text must always be situated in a culture of hermeneutics to have a force as a text. Inspired by Rahner's transcendental theology, which seeks to obliterate the distinction between the concealed and nature and Tillich's concept of revelation, as it is described in his *Systematische teologie* (Systematic theology), Mujtahid-Shabistarī asserts that the act of interpretation becomes constantly transformed into a form of revelation. But while the essential foundations of experience are identified within consciousness, the notion of 'continuous' revelation is not categorically metaphysical. "Some consider revelation an unusual and metaphysical phenomenon which is connected to metaphysics. Personally, I do not agree with this definition of revelation" (ibid.:10). Consequently, the question of subjectivity as well as transcendental pretence achieves a peculiar but

[89] While Mujtahid-Shabistarī refutes the attempts to deduce human rights from the revealed sources, he nevertheless argues that none of these sources conflict with even one paragraph of the U.N. Declaration of human rights.

significantly novel status in Mujtahid-Shabistarī's thought. In contrast to Husserl's transcendental subject, which never is affected by historical contingencies, he turns to Gadamer's philosophical hermeneutics by emphasising the historical situatedness of being and the openness of language in making thought a transcendental subject bound to the accidents of history. The core matrix for the normative content of his hermeneutics is hence the principle that subjectivity is grounded in consciousness but at the same time mediated circuitously through language and history, never at the expense of the universality of reason. By emphasising human experience he upholds the metaphysical assumptions of the theomorphic view of subjectivity, which is not of a totally immediate character, as it is mediated by and caught up by its contextual existential constituents and conditions:

Islam is a total reorientation and when there is a reorientation, there is an emerging from the 'self', a migration from the self, a travel from the self to the Other. It is our self from whom we must migrate, the self that constitutes the dimensions of human identity: the historical self, the social self, the civic self and the linguistic self. These four dimensions, in which human beings normally live, limit human existence: history, society, body and language. The role of divine revelation is to open another horizon and without negating the four dimensions, make them transparent, traversing the human toward God. To be certain, this *shaffāfīyat* (transparency) is always accompanied by dust and is hence never absolute or complete (Mujtahid-Shabistari 1997a:120).

While Mujtahid-Shabistarī claims that the influence of modern philosophy and science on *fiqh* is limited to the *mauḍūʿāt* of jurisprudence, he departs in practical terms from the traditional Islamic view that restricts *ijtihād* to the *furūʿ* of jurisprudence and limits its epistemological foundation to the Aristotelian methodology.[90] The close affinity between Islam and modern ideas in Mujtahid-Shabistari's legal thought is in fact not solely exposed in his belief that religious hermeneutics must correspond to the criterions of Husserlian phenomenology, but more importantly that *ijtihād* is a two-fold enterprise covering the sphere of law as well as strictly non-legal realms of human existence. Inspired by the modern Sunni thinker Muḥammad Iqbāl, he argues that *ijtihād* is a two-fold, all-inclusive and universal enterprise:

The continuous *ijtihād* of Islamic law is not possible without continuous *ijtihād* in *khudā-shināsī* (theology) and *insān-shināsī* (anthropology). Continuous *ijtihād* in these two fundamental disciplines is not possible without continuous enhancement from the human sciences and learning of every period (Mujtahid-Shabistarī 1997b:86).

Commenting upon the traditional Shi'i classifications of the sources and methodological principles of *fiqh*, Mujtahid-Shabistarī suggests that Shi'i

[90] Cf. Mujtahid-Shabistarī, 1997b:47.

law esteems reason. He values reason not only supplementary to the legal sources of law, but considers it a source in itself and a potential instrument for the general interpretation of Islamic jurisprudence in line with his reformulation of the concept of *ijtihād*. By emphasising the rational character of *fiqh*, he argues that legal reasoning always must be grounded in the prevailing rationality of the age. In referring to Sunni legal writings, such as al-Ghazālī and al-Shāṭibī, he suggests that contemporary *ijtihād* becomes meaningful only when the *maqāṣid al-sharīʿat* (objectives of Islamic law) are framed by reason (Mujtahid-Shabistarī 1999b:7). In addition to the Aristotelian method of legal inference, Mujtahid-Shabistarī advocates a dynamic use of the instrument of *amr bi-l-maʿrūf wa nahy az munkar* (enjoining the lawful and prohibiting the unlawful) in the realm of law in order to further integrate law into ethics. While the principle of *amr bi-l-maʿrūf wa nahy az munkar* was also the fifth tenet within the comprehensive theological system of Abū Huḏail (the first great systematic thinker among the *muʿtazilah*), Mujtahid-Shabistarī (ibid.:11) does not refer to any distinct *muʿtazilah* doctrines in his interpretation of this Qur'anic principle. He instead follows the line of Muḥammad Iqbāl and ʿAlī Sharīʿatī to interpret it liberally as a comprehensive change in the 'religious apparatus':

> The instrument of *awāmir wa nawāhī* takes different shapes in different historical periods. Indeed, it is always grounded in a *dastgāh-i iʿtiqādī wa akhlāqī* (creedal and ethical apparatus), to which it corresponds. In this respect, there is an Islamic apparatus in all times that possesses these two instruments in its bosom. My expression 'comprehensive change in the apparatus of Muslims' is actually borrowed from the late *ʿallāmah* Iqbāl's concept of *dastgāh-i dīnī-yi islāmī* (religious apparatus of Islam).[91]

Despite his frequent references to Sunni sources, Mujtahid-Shabistarī (1997b:223) argues that the Shi'i jurisprudence is more accommodating to social change than its Sunni counterpart. He claims that Shi'i law was never misused for worldly purposes, such as is the case with the Sunni Caliphate, and that *ijmāʿ* on many occasions was used by Sunni jurists "to silence opponents and to prevent the expression of innovative opinions and thought". But in his recognition of the free use of reason in non-legally binding areas of jurisprudence, Mujtahid-Shabistarī (ibid.:222) divorces in strict terms *fiqh* from *ʿaql*, which becomes equal to *ʿurf*, since *sharʿī* norms have no role to play in areas not covered by *ʿaql-i qaṭʿī*:

[91] Similar to Muḥammad Iqbāl, Mujtahid-Shabistarī (2000:50) defines the essential contents of the message of religion as ethical in orientation. "To make *fiqh* dominate religion is identical to taking away the spirit of religion and draining the roots of religious feelings, experience and message. The essential function of religion is to nourish religious feeling and to reinforce ethical and meaningful values in human life. This function of religion must be genuinely considered in our contemporary progressive society".

The Shi'i conviction is that one can only say that this law and ruling is from religion in the case that it is founded on the book of God, reliable *sunnat* and definite reason... *Sharʿī* norms have no function to play wherever the Qur'an and the *sunnat* lack a text on praxis or actuality or where reason also lacks a definite norm. In those cases, practice must follow a rational theory that determines all necessary decisions.

By acknowledging a form of secular autonomy for rational human thought, Mujtahid-Shabistarī evidently suggests that the responsibility of deciding non-legally binding norms rests with us. But since the accommodation of the Islamic legal tradition cannot be justified merely on the basis of social necessity, he is unmistakenly faced up with discovering new juristic foundations in genuinely Islamic principles. Consequently, he develops a definition of reason that is religiously oriented in contrast to modern secular reason, which "puts God in parenthesis" and tends to become 'atheistic':

Modern reason establishes itself with its own kind of foundations and does not pay attention to or accept any other (fundamentals). It has its own normativity and takes no notice of any (other) granted sources. The case of revealed rationality is different. Religious accounts must be understood in the same context that religious claims are considered. In contrast to the *ʿaql-i muʾassis-i mudirn* (modern self-determining reason), one must, in other words, make use of the 'context of message' and 'the spirit of the message-hearing' (Mujtahid-Shabistarī 1999d:10).[92]

In his book *Hirminūtīk, kitāb wa sunnat* (Hermeneutics, revelation and *sunnat*), Mujtahid-Shabistarī enters into the subject of hermeneutics proper by initially acknowledging the cross-disciplinary range of hermeneutics itself and identifying *tafsīr-i qurʾān* (Qur'anic exegesis) and *ijtihād-i fiqhi* (legal reasoning) as the two main interpretative traditions in Islam.[93] His point of departure is that modern hermeneutics is restricted to descriptive discourse and that the question of "judging between accurate and inaccurate interpretations and *fatwās* is a matter for *ʿilm-i tafsīr* and *ʿilm-i fiqh*" (Mujtahid-Shabistarī 1997b:7). Nevertheless, he suggests that hermeneutics enables Muslim interpreters to consider the revealed sources as unified entities, since legal discourse in his view is determined by other factors than the *muqaddamāt-i ijtihād*. Therefore, he criticises those Islamic traditionalists who believe the opposite of epistemological naiveté:

The idea that one can and even should embark on interpretation of the Qur'an and *sunnat* with a mind liberated of every kind of pre-understanding still prevails at our religious scientific centres. The advocates of this view not only consider this article

[92] Cf. Mujtahid-Shabistarī 1995:19.

[93] This book is the first introduction to the topic of modern hermeneutics in Persian and has been followed by a number of seminal introductions on the subject. Among the notable ones are Rīkhtagarī (1999) and Hadawī Tihrānī (1999). The subject of hermeneutics is also covered and enthusiastically discussed in the fifth and seventh volume of the journal *Kitāb-i naqd* (Critique review), published in Qum in 1998.

as possible, but as a condition for retaining the transparency of the meaning and the connotation of the revealed sources... This judgment is erroneous (ibid.:7).

Even if Mujtahid-Shabistarī does not develop any systematic view on the disclosure of truth by adopting the classical terms of European phenomenology ('evidence', 'noesis', 'noema', 'reduction', 'life world', 'transcendental ego', etc.), he maintains that the identity of meaning makes truth possible. In contrast to Husserl, Heidegger and others who turned understanding from methodological principle into an ontological category and who indulge in the hermeneutics of being, he approaches the question of hermeneutics as the knowledge of "textual interpretation and understanding of the interpreter's presuppositions, preferences and expectations" (Mujtahid-Shabistarī 1997b:8, 1999d:10). By defining hermeneutics as "a science of interpreting texts and utterances", he distinguishes hermeneutics from the traditional subject *maʿrifat al-nafs* (knowledge of the soul) of *falsafah* and *ʿirfān-i ʿamalī* which he believes does not pay enough attention to the constant changes that occur in science:

These sciences take no notice of the fact that philosophy, which is constantly influenced by the changes and development in [other] sciences, is forced to consider new questions and subjects or that many philosophical opinions adjust due to these changes and developments (Mujtahid-Shabistarī 1997b:48).[94]

Inspired by the German tradition of modern hermeneutics, Mujtahid-Shabistarī defines understanding as distinct from explanation, since understanding is not automatic but rather a form of *shinākhtan* (comprehending). Epistemology, in other words, becomes a necessary item on his agenda of theories of interpretation, where understanding is taken as a mode of knowing. Obviously this means that the justification of the proposed hermeneutical method is epistemological and accounts for the possibility and limitations of understanding objective meanings. Since someone, in his view, may read a text or hear a speech without understanding its message, the encounter with a text or speech presents two

[94] Mujtahid-Shabistarī (2001b) is knowledgeable about the fact that modern hermeneutics does not correspond to the Arabic concepts *tafsīr* or *taʾwīl* or to the Persian term *fahmīdan*, since these words do not take into account the multifarious *mabāḥiṯ* (discourses) that go into the word hermeneutics. He asserts that hermeneutics similar to other modern disciplines such as sociology, economy or psychology has its own distinct theoretical framework and methodology separate from the traditional Islamic hermeneutical sciences. He hence considers the efforts of constructing Islamic economics, sociology and psychology as very limited and even inadequate. With his explicit negative attitude towards Islamic mysticism, Mujtahid-Shabistarī (1992:11, 1995b:59) asserts that general hermeneutics is "connected to a rational and methodological understanding of texts" and distinct from the esoteric confessions of the mystics. In his view, there are no Islamic hermeneutics distinct from the general philosophical hermeneutics. He considers the wish of reviving hermeneutics on the basis of its traditional formulation as mere nostalgia, since going back in time is only possible as a methodological exercise in order to understand the origins of the present interpretative situation.

possibilities in coherence with Wilhelm Dilthey's *erklären-verstehen* dichotomy (that is, a shift from explaining to understanding), which also takes account of a dichotomy between truth and method.[95] Interpretation is, so to say, what understanding is all about:

One kind of encounter is to explain the text or speech as a phenomenon. In the process of explanation, the relationships of a phenomenon and the connected rules clarify and elucidate the consistency of the reality of the phenomena. The other encounter is interpretation of the text or speech and understanding it. In the act of interpretation, the text or speech becomes transparent and manifests its 'meaning' (ibid.:13).

Mujtahid-Shabistarī argues that as the discipline *tafsīr* was born out of the need to understand revelation in new contexts, it thus became concerned with the *sākhtār-i zabānī* (linguistic structure) of the Qur'an and the differentiation between the external structure and the inner meaning. Since all interpretation is aimed at eliminating textual structural contradictions, he argues that the most imperative aspect of understanding is to maintain an openness towards the given textual material that allows the interpreter to be enriched by it. He describes the hermeneutical act as a *dād ū sitad* (transaction) or dialogue where the interpreter must clarify his own hermeneutical situation. As far as jurisprudence is concerned, he maintains that the jurist must spell out the philosophical and theological basis of his inference and what kind of information he expects to extract from the revealed sources. By adopting the terminology of Heidegger, Mujtahid-Shabistarī argues that a hermeneutical circle exists in textual understanding:

The act of interpreting the Qur'an and *sunnat*, whether *fiqhī* or not, is a give and take phenomenon that continuously occurs between the interpreter and the text. It is a circular give and take. It is a movement from the interpreter to the text and then from the text to the interpreter and these two are continuously complementing each other. In the science of textual interpretation or hermeneutics, the word *dawār* (circle) is used in this context (Mujtahid-Shabistarī 1994b:21).[96]

[95] Wilhelm Dilthey is generally considered the primary creator of modern hermeneutics, together with his predecessor Friedrich Schleiermacher. In the age of positivistic philosophy, the main problem of Dilthey was to give philosophy and theology a validity comparable to that of the natural sciences (hence his distinction *erklären-verstehen*). His approach was similar to that of Schleiermacher, which was animated by the confidence of historical objectivism, namely the conviction that any historical contexts could be reconstructed and that the original meanings of any texts could be recovered.

[96] In this respect, Mujtahid-Shabistarī acknowledges that a separate ontology is beyond our grasp: it is only within the movement of interpretation that we perceive the being we interpret. The ontology of understanding is implied in the methodology of interpretation, following the ineluctable 'hermeneutical circle'. The hermeneutical circle has a self-fulfilling character, since only the assumed unity and completeness of the text makes interpretative choices possible, where the original projection of certain characteristics onto the text determines and validates interpretation. Mujtahid-Shabistarī, in other words, posits the completeness and

Ultimately following Schleiermacher's notion of capturing the 'spirit' of the author and his preoccupation with what is behind the text, Mujtahid-Shabistarī (1997b:128) believes that texts should be interpreted according to their intrinsic meanings that are disclosed in the act of interpretation.[97] He argues that the data of the Qur'anic revelation constitute a noumenal ground as the *waḥy fī nafsih* (revelation in-itself) from which the interpreter can derive phenomenal understandings. Inspired by Gadamer's belief that the hermeneutical task should go beyond scientific investigation, he also attempts to articulate the very question of truth as it emerges in experience and maintains that "the meaning of every text is a hidden reality that is revealed and made manifest by means of interpretation" and that "no text voluntarily manifests its meaning" (ibid.:15). While the task of hermeneutics is to understand revelation as noumenal reality, one must, in his view, consider five preludes and measurements of textual interpretation: 1) the interpreter's presuppositions and preunderstandings (i.e. the hermeneutical circle), 2) the interpreter's guiding preferences and expectations, 3) the interpreter's questioning of history, 4) extracting the centre of textual meaning as forming a 'unity' and 5) transcending the context or horizon of the interpreter that is determined by tradition or history by means of translation (ibid.:16–28). As far as the theology of the text is concerned, the goal of the translator is to repossess the authentic message of the original ideal text and re-embody that message in exegesis. While Mujtahid-Shabistarī sets out to disclose valid and certain knowledge, his approach is, in other words, a questioning of the traditional view of the possibility of valid understanding. Even if the objective of hermeneutics is to restrict the distance between the autonomy of the text *versus* the author's intention, its socio-cultural context and its original addressees, he conceptualises understanding as a creative *reformulation* and *reconstruction*.

In contrast to the traditionalist accounts of hermeneutics, Mujtahid-Shabistarī's ontological perspective is not primarily a matter of existential-spiritual realisation but conceptual grasping. As an exercise of discursive thought, he considers understanding a historical question since the historical and linguistic distance complicates the transparency of texts such as the Qur'an or *ḥadīṯ*. Adopting the terminology of Gadamer, he argues that textual communication and understanding can only be considered by acknowledging the existence of a set of historical horizons that signify "the

---

unity of the text as a rule, since the methodological 'objectivity' requires that hermeneutics moves in a series of concentric circles from objectivism to subjectivism and back.

[97] In the view of Schleiermacher, the hermeneutical task begins with an initial study of the historical circumstances of the author followed by an effort of 'divination', which he assumes can be realised when the interpreter identifies himself with the author in such a way as to grasp the author's purpose. The often-quoted statement of Schleiermacher (1959:87) bears this out, "The task can also be expressed in this way: to understand the text just as well as and then better than the author himself understood it".

human experience at a certain period of man and the world". Similar to Gadamer's notion of 'fusion of horizons', Mujtahid-Shabistarī argues that understanding is horizontal rather than vertical, that is, it is only possible by recognising the interpretative horizon by which one gains presuppositions of a given text. Since all interpretation is conditioned by its prior history and stands in a tradition of interpretation, the interpreter, similar to a translator, must serve the text through a dialogue during which the horizons of text and reader are fused:

> The idea that is embedded in the text must be translated into (the language) of the contemporary horizon (through an act) that assumes the character of translation. Interpretation becomes necessary when the horizon of the interpreter and (that of) the author of the text diverge and ambiguity appears. As long as ambiguity does not appear there is no need for interpretation.... If we want to understand correctly what the text says then we have to settle our language as a language for textual understanding, where our experience becomes situated to understand the text. Indeed, the text is correctly understood only when the *maṭlab-i markazī* (central subject) of that text is settled against the contexts and questions of the horizon that the interpreter experiences (Mujtahid-Shabistarī 1995c:134).

Understanding, in other words, involves all the paradoxes of historicity, that is, how can a historical being understand history historically? How can life objectify itself, and in objectifying itself, how does it bring to light meanings capable of being taken up and understood by another historical being, who then overcomes his own historical horizon? Or, in other words, if we receive texts only as mediated in historical tradition, does this allow for the distortion that tradition itself can introduce into the text?[98] While Mujtahid-Shabistarī is not capable of answering these questions of philosophical hermeneutics in definite terms, he, similar to Gadamer, turns to the question of historicality in terms of the interpreter's prejudices or accumulated interpretative *sunnat* (in the sense of tradition).[99] Since general hermeneutics does not allow the use of a specific methodology for a supposedly privileged text, such as the Qur'an, the prejudices or interpretative *sunnat* applies as an equal category, whether the text is religious or profane. The only allowance made for specific content consists in the variegated use made of methods approved by the science of hermeneutics:

[98] To those questions that Mujtahid-Shabistarī leaves largely unnoticed we could also add the fact that he is unable to distinguish between those prestructures and preunderstandings that are a necessary foundation of all understanding and the unnecessary and self-deceiving prejudices of any particular interpretative tradition.

[99] As far as the question of prejudice is concerned, it is interesting to note that Mujtahid-Shabistarī (1997b:95–122) classifies the collectors of *ḥadīṯ* and *akhbār* as interpreters of revelations, as they not merely retold existent material but also selected and prioritised certain texts in order to confirm certain presupposed beliefs.

Religious texts can be understood from within the tradition of religion (internal religious understanding) as well as from the outside of religious tradition (external religious understanding). The unfeasibility of producing understanding without presuppositions, prejudices, interests, expectations and questions applies equally to both of them. In case a person, who interprets the religious texts as immutable with faith and commitment to (a sum of interpretations) that people have gathered, he acquires his presuppositions, interests and expectations from that tradition. Indeed, his understanding is a re-understanding of his predecessors' understanding (Mujtahid-Shabistarī 1995b:58).[100]

Consequently, going beyond the structural aspects of a text, the original intention of the author that is supposed to be imbedded within the historical horizon, together with the question of textual communication, becomes important for Mujtahid-Shabistarī's hermeneutics. Hermeneutics is not only a general body of methodological rules that underlies interpretation but the philosophical exploration of the character and the requisite conditions for understanding. While the act or process of understanding contains a subjective element, the act must, so to say, be distinguished from its objective outcome, the message. Since the truth of a text can only be formulated in our encounter with the text, Mujtahid-Shabistarī argues that no understanding whatsoever is possible without an encounter with the author in one way or the other. Hence, the phenomenological aspect of Mujtahid-Shabistarī's (1994c:13) thought is closely associated with his belief in 'intentionality'. Every experience is intentional: it is essentially an experience of something where the point is not just to interpret the text, but rather to experience it and become transformed by it. In other words, the achievement reached in the fusion of horizons is not just a repetition of some pre-existing identity (as the traditionalists would seem to believe) but a

[100] While Mujtahid-Shabistarī's hermeneutical theory cannot be formulated without assuming a transcendental perspective (i.e. it is meant to be true and universal), he denies the very possibility of a transcendental perspective by ruling out the possibility of context-free subjects. On the one hand, he considers the breakdown of prejudices that occurs through hermeneutical understanding as the criterion of valid understanding, but on the other, he never considers whether the interpreter moves beyond tradition to the original meaning of a text or only moves within tradition toward a dialogical hermeneutical discourse. The latter position is represented by Gadamer, who speaks of 'historically effected consciousness', the awareness that one's own understanding of a text is achieved not despite one's historical placement, but precisely in and through it (Gadamer 1989:341). It is still not clear whether Gadamer's historical relativism is meant to be reflexive, since the context-independent knowledge is possible in the case that Gadamer alone has the privilege of being exempt from the constraints of his own contextual relativism. While Gadamer's notion of tradition functions against the claims of enlightenment rationalism to have replaced the authority of tradition with the allegedly eternal protocols of reason, Mujtahid-Shabistarī's use of the term seems to be directed against the traditional Shi'i interpretative conventions that are transmitted in the disciplines of *tafsīr* and *uṣūl al-fiqh* and promulgated by the traditional institution *marjaʿ al-taqlīd*. Cf. Gadamer 1976:6 and 1989:277.

moulding together in which the two horizons are transformed.[101]

Since the objective of interpretative explication is to render the hidden, but embedded, original meaning or intention transparent, Mujtahid-Shabistarī's expositions of the rules of interpretation lead ideally not only to the most probable or successful interpretation, but also safeguard the general validity of its results from the intrusion of subjective elements. The key concept in his hermeneutics is 'to listen to history' and he argues in this respect that the correct criterion for understanding the original intention or *markaz-i maʿnā-yi matn* (the centre of textual meaning) is to consider the text as a whole, as a unity, which appears as the horizon that guides the anticipation of perfection:

> The centre of meaning cannot be discovered unenlightened and without a test or criterion. The method of discovering is precisely 'to question history' or to place one's ear to history. The text can only be interpreted when considered as a unity, that is, by considering the text in terms of a *waḥīd* (unity) and *maʿnā-yi tamām* (complete meaning) beyond the meaning of word and sentence. Complete meaning can, in other words, only be grasped (through interpretation) (Mujtahid-Shabistarī 1997b:27).

In turning his back on traditional hermeneutics, Mujtahid-Shabistarī's approach to the Qur'an has some major similarities with fundamental assumptions of the Lutherian reformation, such as the claim that revelation alone is the hermeneutical norm, as well as the consideration of particular text passages in light of the intent and form of the whole. While Mujtahid-Shabistarī's hermeneutics is distinguished by its Islamic character (for instance, it is not aimed as a testimony of Christ), his emphasis on faith and religious experience as well as his treatment of the Qur'an as a whole corresponds well to Luther's stress on the right of private judgement and freedom of faith as well as to Calvin's and Matthias Flacius' instistence on the possibility of universally valid interpretation through a cohesive and

[101] While Mujtahid-Shabistarī (1995d) is interested in the historical mechanisms and factors that produced the traditional legal texts and argues that language is not the basis for absolute knowledge of the world and does not therefore exhaust the meaning of revelation, he nevertheless adopts no historic-critical reading of the Qur'an as compared to the modern Biblical criticism. He does not touch upon the question as to whether the interpeter, by considering the text as a whole or entity, in reality enlarges the meaning of the text being interpreted, instead of objectively appropriating the horizon of the text to his own hermeneutical situation. Mujtahid-Shabistarī's estimation that it is not enough to grasp the meaning of a religious phenomenon phenomenologically and decipher its message, but that it is also necessary to study and understand its history in order to unravel its historical changes and modifications, corresponds closely to Mircea Eliade's perspective on history of religions, where phenomenology and history are applied together and complement each other. In the view of Eliade, history cannot do without phenomenology since it is not able to grasp any sense of the religious. Similar to Eliade's view of history, Mujtahid-Shabistarī (1997a:105) also rejects the Hegelian a priori construction of teleological history and insists on a restriction to historical research in opposition to speculation by arguing that Islam knows of no 'salvation history'. Cf. Eliade 1969:8–9.

holistic hermeneutic of the Bible.[102] Similar to Luther, Mujtahid-Shabistarī also takes his stand on the non-mystical and literal truth of the revealed text by pointing towards the inner and spiritual that is mediated by its own logic even if he, in contrast to Luther, does not define theology as philology dealing with the Holy Spirit's language (*grammatica in Spiritus sancti verbis occupata*).[103] But more importantly, Mujtahid-Shabistarī's hermeneutical discussion demonstrates his interest in the three pillars of modern literary criticism, i.e. the analytic aspect, the subjective and the historical factor of understanding, where Qur'anic eternal truth is never separated from historical facts.

Since the traditional Islamic legal discourse makes use of a number of non-explicit non-religious philosophical presuppositions, Mujtahid-Shabistarī argues that no revival of Islamic law is possible without changing the presuppositions of traditional legal philosophy. In fact, he argues that "to achieve new comprehension is always grounded on presupposition and preunderstanding" (ibid.:16–17, 88). Islamic law is, in other words, itself modern when interpreted properly, that is, by projecting the demands and needs of contemporary society on the revealed texts. Similar to philosophy, anthropology, social philosophy and theology, the science of hermeneutics also assists the jurists in the act of the inference of legal norms:

> The *ḥauzahs* of Islamic sciences must receive the science of hermeneutics with full capability and pleasure, since the subjects of this science highlight the necessity of *tanqīḥ* (restricting) the preliminaries and capacities of interpretation of Islamic texts. Hermeneutics demonstrates in particular the necessity of juristic *ijtihād* and makes the realizisation of a methodologically approvable interpretation of Islam possible (ibid.:31–32).

On the question of interpretative divergence, Mujtahid-Shabistarī (1999b:6) adopts a semi-empirical point of view by supposing that the basic element of esoteric symbolism and representation in traditional Islamic hermeneutics cannot be the reason behind the *ikhtilāf* (divergence) of legal opinions. Since the hermeneutical openness to the text and the conflict of interpretations is not accommodated within traditional transcendental hermeneutics, he, like Gadamer, considers understanding to be determined by the inescapability of history and the concrete situations in which we find ourselves. While traditional Islamic hermeneutics presupposes that interpretation cannot mean

[102] While Islam knows of no ecclesiastial system comparable to that of the Catholic Church, Mujtahid-Shabistarī's view of hermeneutics as involving the general problem of comprehension rather than only a technique for specialists, evidently stands in conflict with the interpretative authority of the *marjaʿ al-taqlīd*, which does not consider the spirit of the law but the letter of the law in the first place.

[103] In Luther's view, the Bible was too simple for the preacher to expound its meaning and therefore he turned his interpretative considerations to its single fundamental meaning: *simplicissimae Scripturae simplicissimus sensus*. Cf. Luther 1970:178.

simply giving uniform representations of a text that is sealed off from the heterogeneity of human situations, Mujtahid-Shabistarī's view is, more accurately, that *ikhtilāf* depends on the existence of divergent presuppositions or prejudices among the jurists themselves and that inaccurate legal opinions are due to an adherence to inconsistent presuppositions and preunderstandings. His concern is not primarily with the production of interpretations but with the question of what it is to inhabit a given hermeneutical situation. In this respect, he takes *Tafsīr al-jawāhir* (Elemental exegesis) of Rifāʿah Rafī al-Taḥtawī that looked for exact scientific answers to natural science in religious texts as an example and seems to partake of the same epistemological positions as Galileo (maintained in his letter dated 21 December 1613 to Benedetto Castelli), that the Holy Scriptures are not suitable in addressing scientific questions, since religious claims cannot confront science directly in the scientific arena without becoming something else (Mujtahid-Shabistarī 1997b:23).[104]

While Mujtahid-Shabistarī clearly articulates the criterion of when interpretation is in order, he has more difficulties in answering the question of when interpretation is complete. While he seems inclined to think that interpretation is *pāyān-nāpazīr*, he calls upon a logic of probability by suggesting that divergence essentially concerns the probable existence of divine norms in specific circumstances, since the inference of norms follows from the casuistic method that always must be connected to particular examples and not merely hypothetical invention. By reference to the traditional principle of *ibāḥah* ('giving liberty'), he maintains that the jurists must be more appreciative of the divergence of opinions, since if consensus dominates legal and theological discourse it is only due to coincidence:

> When the interpretation of a text does not produce *ikhtilāf* it is not due to the text's voluntarily self-determining of meaning and its independency of interpretation, but rather is due to the fact that everyone interprets it in a homogeneous manner (Mujtahid-Shabistarī 1997b:15).

All claims to transcendental truth must therefore be mediated by rational argument. This allows, in Mujtahid-Shabistarī 's view, for a plurality of truth claims without doing away with the possibility of pursuing high Truth and without stifling the meaningful dialogue among the various interpretations. In this respect, he asserts that the pluralism of interpretations in the realm of Shi'i law has become a more urgent question after the 1979 revolution when different Muslim answers to questions such as political parties, nationality, public voting and social equity were raised to meet the new political reality.

104 The Egyptian jurist and exegete al-Taḥtawī translated the French civil code into Arabic and made the first attempt by any Muslim to a modern scientific exegesis of the Qur'an with reference to the *muʿtazilah* notion of *taḥsīn wa taqbīḥ* (rational approbation and disapprobation) and the *ashaʿrī* theory of God's *afʿāl* (creative acts).

In this respect, he argues that hermeneutics solves the outward divergence between opposing Muslim factions by highlighting the function of presuppositions in the act of interpretation:

For instance, if a jurist is influenced by the philosophy of 'freedom and human egalitarianism', he will automatically look for (Qur'anic) verses and *riwāyat* in the first place, from which this philosophy can be understood better. If he on the other hand believes in autocracy and righteous tyranny, he will look for verses and *riwāyat* that outwardly legitimate autocracy (Mujtahid-Shabistarī 1997b:38).

On the subject of the position and status of the traditional Shi'i institutions of learning, Mujtahid-Shabistarī (ibid.:217) argues that the *ḥauzah* seminaries in Iran cannot intervene in the theoretical-scientific realm of the modern university, but should rather complement it. He regrets that *ḥauzah*s have not gained much influence in the recent intellectual discourses in Iran despite their strong physical presence and supposes that its scientific backwardness is due to the technical character of its language of instruction, which is not compatible with modern scientific research, although it continues to communicate well with ordinary people. He further urges the *ḥauzah*s to distinguish traditional Islamic philosophy from Islam as such, and believes that the unity between the *ḥauzah* and the university will only materialise when the jurists make themselves understood at the university:

The discourse of the *ḥauzah* will be understood at scientific, academic and industrial gatherings the moment they converse with a recognition of realities and actualities. When the discourse of the *ḥauzah*s is understood, they have accomplished their message and the unity of the *ḥauzah* and the university will be realised (ibid.:220).

Since the revival of Islamic learning can only take place in light of the more comprehensive *ijtihād* in the realm of theology and philosophy, he argues that the intellectual efforts of the *ʿulamā* should not be directed towards *fiqh* but rather towards theology:

We must conduct philosophical and theological *ijtihād* in contemporary *zamān wa makān* before we consider the question 'juristic *ijtihād* in contemporary *zamān wa makān*', which is on the agenda today. I know that it is generally claimed that the theological and philosophical foundations have been established and developed sufficiently in history and that no renewal is necessary. Indeed, this is only a theory. Don't we have to analyse and examine this theory and its considerable claims at the *ḥauzah-yi ʿilmīyah*s in a completely free and scientific way, without fervour, in order to establish its validity or fallacy? (Mujtahid-Shabistarī 1994b:26)

In this respect, Mujtahid-Shabistarī believes that the contemporary generation of *ʿulamā* must transcend the contributions made by Muṭahharī and Ṭabātabāʾī on philosophical materialism and present critiques on moral philosophy, cultural relativism, the epistemic difference between *adrākāt-i ḥaqīqī* (real faculties) and *adrākāt-i iʿtibārī* (extrinsic faculties) from an Islamic perspective. While he believes that their treatment of modern theology was unsystematic and inconsistent, he is not convinced as to precisely what way Islamic jurists and theologians should adopt phenomenology or hermeneutics to achieve a general reformation of religious thought in functional terms. He seems to suggest that Islamic modernity is experiencing its genesis and that future Muslims will determine the position of hermeneutics in the structure of religious thought (2001b). In contrast to many other Muslim modernists who generally have received a modern education and identify themselves with the kind of knowledge that is the product of modern institutions, Mujtahid-Shabistarī values the merits of the traditional institution of religious learning and encourages the cultivation of an indigenous Islamic intellectual tradition enriched by modern science. Earlier Shi'i modernists such as ʿAlī Sharīʿatī or Mahdī Bāzargān did much to reorient the modern educated Muslim emotionally and socially toward religion but neglected any deeper acquaintance with traditional Islamic scholarship. Mujtahid-Shabistarī's approach, however, is more balanced and rooted in the juristic foundations of Shi'i Islam.

CHAPTER VI

Surūsh on the nature of Islamic law and legal theory

A. The Biography of ʿAbd al-Karīm Surūsh

Ḥusain Ḥāj Farajullāh Dabbāgh, more well-known by his pen name ʿAbd al-Karīm Surūsh, was born in southern Tehran in 1945.[1] His parents had a pious lower middle class background. Surūsh received his secondary education at the ʿAlawī private high school, a pioneering private institution in Tehran founded by *bāzārī* merchants with the objective of educating its students in modern natural sciences as well as traditional Islamic disciplines.[2] The principal of ʿAlawī school, Riḍā Rūzbih, had an exam in physics from Tehran University and had also studied *fiqh* at a *ḥauzah-yi ʿilmīyah* of Qum. At an early date, Surūsh visited the desert town of Gunabad in Khurasan where he met with Muḥammad Ḥasan Ṣāliḥ ʿAlī Shāh, the Sufi *pīr* (master) of the Niʿmatullāhī-Saʿādat ʿAlī-Shāhī order. This spiritual guide made an everlasting impression on Surūsh.

After initiating his higher education at the faculty of pharmaceutical sciences of Tehran University, Surūsh studied the traditional Islamic sciences, mainly *falsafah*, *fiqh* and *ʿilm al-kalām*, at the Masjid-i Sipahsālār under the private tuition of *ʿulamā* to whom he had been recommended by Murtaḍā Muṭahharī. He regularly attended lectures at the Ḥusainīyah-yi irshād during the height of ʿAlī Sharīʿatī's activities at that institution. Surūsh was especially influenced by Ṭabāṭabāʾī's work *Uṣūl-i falsafah wa rawish-i riʾālīsm* (The Principles of philosophy and the method of realism), which he took at the time as sole evidence of the indisputable superiority of traditional Islamic philosophy. In his own words, it made him believe that "the whole world is under my wings" (Soroush 2000:6).

[1] The present biography of Surūsh is largely based on an interview conducted by the author in Tehran, 26 Oct 1999.

[2] A number of *ʿulamā*, such as Muḥammad Ḥusainī-Bihishtī and Muḥammad Jawād Bāhunar were involved in the establishment of the ʿAlawī schools and taught extra-curricular courses in *fiqh* and *ʿilm al-kalām* there. The school followed the official Ministry of Education's program and its teachers consequently joined Iran Teacher's association, then dominated by secular policies (Boroujerdi 1996:92).

After completing his degree in pharmaceuticals from Tehran University, Surūsh went to England in 1973 to study chemistry at the University of London. After receiving his master's degree in chemistry, he changed to Chelsea College to study history and the philosophy of science, and prepared a dissertation on the topic of the history of monomolecular reactions. Surūsh's stay in Europe became a period of constant reflection and also one of intellectual transition. While he had no formal training in the traditional Islamic sciences, his deep acquaintance with the subject matter of these disciplines as well as modern science made him aware of the rift in modern science from Aristotelian scientific presuppositions and incited him to review his understanding of metaphysics. In the late 1970s, Surūsh's speeches and lectures were gradually transcribed and produced in book form, which resulted in the publishing of the following works in Iran: *ʿIlm chī-st? Falsafah chī-st?* (What is science? What is philosophy?), *Naqdī wa muqaddimahʾī bar taḍādd-i diyʾāliktīkī* (Critique and introduction to dialectical contradiction) and *Nahād-i nā-ārām-i jahān* (The restless nature of the universe). The first two books were aimed at presenting the ideas of Karl Popper on the boundaries of philosophy and science in order to intellectually challenge Marxist concepts of science and society that were widely disseminated in Iran at this date. The second book directly follows Popper's arguments against 'historical determinism' and 'scientific ethics' and argues that all scientific propositions must be 'falsifiable'.[3] The latter book, where the author aligns himself with the Shi'i theosophy of Ṣadr al-dīn Shīrāzī, received the approval and admiration of Ruḥullāh Khumainī.

Influenced by the growing political 'radicalisation' of the religious discourse among Muslim intellectuals in Iran and abroad, Surūsh participated in the activities of the Iranian mosque in West London, which

[3] After the revolution, the publishing of a number of translations of Western works in post-positivist philosophy into Persian contributed to the dissemination of positivist concepts of science among intellectuals in Iran. As Mehrzad Boroujerdi (1996:163) elucidates, the translation of Popper's *Conjectures and refutations* in 1984 and *The Open Society and its Enemies* in 1985 trigged a major debate in Muslim intellectual circles, which "was not over Popper (1902–1994) *per se* but over epistemological principles and political orientations as well". Two years before that publication, Kant's *Kritik der reinen Vernunft* had also been translated into Persian by Mīr Shams al-dīn Adīb-Sulṭānī and published in Tehran by Amīr Kabīr publishing house. The first book on the history of science in Persian was George Sarton's *A History of science*, which was translated by Aḥmad Ārām and published in 1957 by Khwārizmī publishing house. As Boroujerdi (1997:4) states, the more genuine contemplation of Western philosophy among Iranian intellectuals dates back to the 1934 Persian publication of René Descartes' *Discours de la méthode* after which philosophy in Iran increasingly immersed itself in Western schools of thought. "This immersion has expanded to such an extent that presently in the bookstores of most major cities in Iran one encounters the translated works of such thinkers as Arendt, Aron, Carnap, Dewey, Diderot, Habermas, Heidegger, Hume, Jaspers, Kant, Levi-Strauss, Locke, Marcuse, Nietzsche, Pascal, Popper, Rousseaux, Bertrand Russell, Sartre, Spinoza, Weber, Wittgenstein, and many others. As the above list indicates, some of the seminal figures of analytical philosophy (logical positivism, linguistic philosophy) and continental philosophy (phenomenology, existensialism, structuralism) have been introduced to Iranian readers".

held gatherings for Muslim students in England. On several occasions, he met with Murtaḍā Muṭahharī, Muḥammad Ḥusain Ṭabāṭabā'ī and Sayyid Muḥammad Ḥusainī-Bihishtī who visited that country before the revolution. He was also the first person to pay his respect to the next-of-kin of ʿAlī Sharīʿatī after his death (Rahnema 1998:368). His support for the Islamic revolutionary movement and its leader, Rūḥullāh Khumainī, as well as his contempt for the Pahlawī monarchy is evident in his early works where the late *shāh* Muḥammad Riḍā Pahlawī is referred to as the *shaiṭān-i siyāh* (black devil) and the formal sponsorship of the Pahlawī state towards culture and science is denounced as anti-Islamic, pseudo-scientific political propaganda that produced uncompromising and powerful secular advocates such as Aḥmad Kasrawī and Ṣādiq Hidāyat (Surūsh 1999c:157).

In 1979, the revolutionary events draw Surūsh back to Iran after he had finished his dissertation on philosophy of science.[4] While he remained a marginal figure during the revolution, Ruḥullāh Khumainī elected him directly into the Sitād-i inqilāb-i farhangī (Advisory committee of cultural revolution), later renamed Shūrā-yi ʿālī-i inqilāb-i farhangī (High council of cultural revolution) that was responsible for revising the curriculum of the country's new education system.[5] Surūsh was also active in the establishment of the Markaz-i nashr-i dānishgāhī (Central University press) and became at the same time a familiar name to the public through his lectures on Jalāl al-dīn Rūmī's poetry, which were broadcast on national television.[6] For a period of two years he also taught *kalām-i jadīd* at a *ḥauzah-yi ʿilmīyah* in Qum. While these factors contributed to introducing Surūsh publicly as one of the high-ranking ideologues of the Islamic republic, he still kept a low profile in politics. Rather than propagating for the ideological foundations of the new political system, he focused his intellectual efforts on teaching and lecturing during the first revolutionary decade. In late 1983, Surūsh left the High council, and has since then been teaching off and on at the faculty of Humanities of Tehran University. He has not occupied any governmental posts since his resignation, but held until recently the position of Dean at the Muʿassasah-yi taḥqīqāt-i ʿulūm-i insānī (Research institute for human sciences) in Tehran.

Since the primary responsibility of the High council of cultural revolution

[4] Cf. Vahdat 1998:388.

[5] The six other original members of the High council were Shams Āl-i Aḥmad, Muḥammad Jawād Bāhunar, Ḥasan Ḥabībī, Rabbānī Amlāshī, ʿAlī Sharīʿat-Madārī and Jalāl al-dīn Fārsī.

[6] These lectures, which later were discontinued on the advice of Khumainī, resulted in a number of articles on Rūmī published in various contexts as well as the edition of *Maṯnawī-yi maʿnawī* (Spiritual couplet poem) based on the oldest Kunya manuscript (Rūmī 1996). But Surūsh's edition is unlikely to become the scholarly standard since this manuscript was earlier made available in a facsimile by Naṣrullāh Pūrjawādī and was also used as a basis for Muḥammad Istiʿlāmī's edition. Surūsh (2001:5) also plans to publish a critical edition of Nicholson's classical translation of the *Maṯnawī*, with the original Persian text appearing alongside the English translation.

was to re-open the universities rather than close them down, Surūsh argues that his engagement in the formation of that institution was motivated by the effort to secure the future of humanities in the country's education system. As a matter of fact, he was in disagreement with the major Islamic intellectual discourse at that time, regarding his defence of the non-contingent nature of social sciences against traditional Islamic metaphysics. Surūsh's defence of modern analytic method and the independent validity of the social sciences resulted in a book, *Tafarruj-i ṣunʿ: Guftārhāʾī dar akhlāq wa ṣanʿat wa ʿilm-i insānī* (Excursion of creation. Lectures on moral, technology and humanities) published in 1987. The main thesis in this book is that the traditional Islamic sciences do not intrinsically differ from the modern sciences insofar as their definite human character is concerned. Furthermore, Surūsh (1999c:39-40) acknowledges that the other reasons for his resignation were his non-satisfaction with the course of the revolution, the emergence of disagreements between the Higher education ministry and the High council as well as the "cultural fascism" that became prevalent among the other members of the latter.[7]

Surūsh's articles on legal hermeneutics and epistemology, collected in *Qabḍ wa basṭ-i tiʾūrīk-i sharīʿat: Naẓarīyah-yi takāmūl-i maʿrifat-i dīnī* (Contraction and expansion of legal theory: The concept of evolution of religious knowledge), was first published in the journal *Kaihān-i farhangī* (Cultural world) between the years 1988-1991. Surūsh's argument that religious knowledge, devoid of sacredness, is one branch of knowledge among others, rather than divine by virtue of its subject-matter, evoked criticism from a number of *ʿulamā* and intellectuals. Surūsh was accused of disbelief and *gharbzadigī* and was forced to leave the journal that eventually closed down for a period. A number of its editors followed Surūsh and with personal investments founded a new bimonthly journal, *Kiyān* (Source), published by Muʿassasah-yi ṣirāt (Foundation of the path) in Tehran.[8] Surūsh contributes articles regularly to *Kiyān*. It has emerged as one of the most eminent critical journals in contemporary Iran. The continual existence of the journal has been threatened on several occasions. In 1996, its editorial director was convicted in court on charges of forgery and in January 2001 it was finally forced to close down for an undetermined period of time.

[7] After his return to Iran, Surūsh (1999k) gradually lost his belief in the possibility of 'islamising' the modern scientific disciplines. Modern epistemological thought and the idea of the historical growth of knowledge began to influence his world-view already during his stay in England. This made him undertake scientific research on religion during the following years, influenced by Popperian criterions of scientific theory and method. Surūsh (1999c:79) has expressed retrospectively that the recent decade has been the darkest as far as Iranian intellectual culture is concerned. He laments that a fascist interpretation of religion, which reduces religion to the legitimacy of totalitarianism and perceives the modern state as a goal in itself, has become more dominant after the revolution.

[8] The original editorial board of *Kiyān* included Sayyid Muṣṭafā Rukhṣifat, Riḍā Tihrānī and Maḥmūd Shams al-Wāʾizain.

In 1988, Surūsh began a series of lectures on the Shi'i concept of piety and governance at Masjid-i Ṣādiq (Ṣādiq mosque) in northern Tehran that was initially attended by many influential personalities of the political and religious establishment. These lectures were later published in three books.[9] Surūsh's essays on *rūḥānīyat* (the religious class) in particular provoked the anger and acrimony of a number of critics, and in 1994 he was forced to discontinue his lectures. The year after, Surūsh was physically attacked on two occasions and the dispute, which was due to the continuous raids carried out by a faction called Anṣār-i ḥizbullāh (Helpers of the party of God), made him abandon his regular classes at the university (which already had been reduced to a minimum).[10] Due to these events as well as to the shift in his writings from scientific considerations, such as epistemology, to a more overtly political discourse on subjects, such as religious democracy, liberalism and human rights, foreign media and academia came to pay attention to him. In 1996, the U.S. Council on foreign relations in New York, for instance, issued a study devoted to his political thought (Vakili 1996).

After the publication of the first edition of *Qabḍ wa basṭ-i tiʾūrīk-i sharīʿat: Naẓarīyah-yi takāmūl-i maʿrifat-i dīnī* in 1991, which by 1996 had gone through five editions, selling over 30000 copies, the debate on religious epistemology continued in the daily Iranian newspaper *Salām* (Greeting), where Surūsh was engaged in a debate with Muḥsin Kadīwar on the issue of religious pluralism. In 1998, these articles were published in the book *Ṣirāṭhā-yi mustaqīm* (Straight paths) and reprinted in a booklet in 1999 under the title *Munāẓarah darbārah-yi plūralīsm-i dīnī* (Debate on religious pluralism). Besides these specific writings on epistemology and comparative religion, Surūsh also published a number of works during the recent decade that focus more directly on social and political subjects such as positive law, political ideology, religious intellectualism, and so on.[11] In his latest book, *Qumār-i ʿāshiqān. Shams wa maulānā* (Gambling of Lovers. Shams and Rūmī), he reconnects to his deep and genuine interest in the poetry of the greatest of all Persian mystics, Jalāl al-dīn Rūmī, who is ubiquitous in Surūsh's voluminous production. Surūsh has also translated at least three English works into Persian, the most important of which is the neo-classical *Metaphysical foundations of modern physical sciences* by Edwin Arthur

[9] Cf. Surūsh 1992, 1994d, 1996a, 1997c.

[10] Ansār-i ḥizbullāh was founded in 1995 by its spokesman, Ḥusain Allāh-Karam, and is supported by Iranian political conservatives such as *āyatullāh* Aḥmad Jannatī, temporary *imām-i jumʿah* (Friday prayer leader) at Tehran University and a member of Shūrā-yi nigahbān (Guardian council) and *āyatullāh* Muḥammad Taqī Misbāḥ-Yazdī, a prominent lecturer at Madrasah-yi Ḥaqqānī in Qum and member of Shūrā-yi khubragān (Council of experts). The group is also supported by the former minister of international affairs, ʿAlī Akbar Wilāyatī, who has identified Surūsh as a "threat to the Iranian national security" and compared him to Aḥmad Kasrawī.

[11] Cf. Surūsh 1997a, 1996a and 1999c.

Burtt, which was published in 1991 in Iran.[12]

In addition to the shutting down of Surūsh's classes at the university, the accusations and criticism levelled against him also succeeded in banning him completely from the holy city of Qum, closing his lectures at several mosques, such as Masjid-i Ṣādiq and Masjid-i ʿIsā Wazīr (Jesus Vezir mosque) in Tehran and terminating him from the Research institute for human sciences in 1997.[13] Nevertheless, Surūsh continues to be one of the most "central figures in Iran's current intellectual and political contentions" (Matin-asgari 1997:96). His influence on the current discourse on Islamic theology and political philosophy in Iran and abroad has also contributed in characterising him as "the Luther of Shi'i Islam" (Amirpur 1996). The election of Muḥammad Khātamī for president in 1997, which promised a strengthening of civil society and rule of law, became a turning point for Surūsh, who was requested to resume his classes at the university and was also allowed to travel abroad after a period of travel restriction.[14] Since the government admits that they are not in the position to guarantee his security, Surūsh has for the time being refrained from resuming his teaching. Nevertheless, his thought continues to influence many strata of contemporary Iranian society, not least through his former students, of whom Aḥmad Narāqī is one of the most distinguished. He even has admirers among the members of the political elite, including the former minister of cultural affairs, ʿAṭāʾullāh Muhajirānī.[15]

Consequently, Surūsh's intellectual enterprise is not confined to the theoretical level of discourse, but engenders socio-political effects. His definition of democracy as a method for the transformation from revolution to reform and the subsequent incorporation of modern democratical ideas into the religious a priori discourse are significant for the social impact of his ideas (Surūsh 1996a:269). By referring to Surūsh's thought in the case of Iran, the French scholar Oliver Roy even argues that the moment of political Islam has passed and that the era of post-Islamism has begun. He speaks of post-Islamism as a new form of secularism that has grown out of the 'failure' of political islam. As Roy suggests, Surūsh's ideas may very well provide political reformists in Iran with a religio-political philosophy which combine religion with modern liberal notions of democracy:

[12] Two other works, Alan Ryan's *The Philosophy of the social sciences* and Daniel Little's *Varieties of social explanation: An Introduction to the philosophy of social science*, were published in Iran in 1988 and 1994.

[13] The official explanation behind the sacking of Surūsh from the Research institute for human sciences was that he, in his capacity of being a trained physicist, not was supposed to have any connection to a centre of humanities.

[14] In an interview with the British daily *The Times* (3 November 1997), Surūsh acknowledges that Muḥammad Khātamī is a personal friend of his and that he recently had a hand in securing the return of his passport. He also stated that Khātamī belongs to the genuine and progressive *rūḥānīyat*.

[15] Cf. *Iṭṭilāʿāt*, London, 17 October, 1995.

Table 2. The textual corpus of ʿAbd al-Karīm Surūsh

Title:	Year:	Main contents:
Dānish wa arzish (Knowledge and value)	1978	Scientific ethics, historical determinism, science/value, neo-positivism, Marxism.
Falsafah-yi tārīkh (Philosophy of history)	1978*	General introduction to the history of philosophy and science.
ʿIlm chī-st? Falsafah chī-st? (What is science? What is philosophy?)	1978 (abridged version 1982)	Science, philosophy, metaphysics, translations of K.R. Popper, A. Whitehead and P. Duhem.
Nahād-i nā-ārām-i jahān (The Restless nature of the universe)	1978	Theosophy, history, evolution, discourse on Ṣadr al-dīn Shīrāzī.
Naqdī wa muqaddimahʾī bar taḍadd-i diyāliktīkī (Critique and introduction to dialectics)	1978*	Science, neo-positivism, Hegelian dialectics, Marxism.
Īdiʾūlūzhī-yi shaiṭānī (Satanic ideology)	1980 (abridged version 1994)	Islamic cosmology, science, evolution, Marxism.
Taffaruj-i sunʾ (Excursion of creation)	1987 (abridged version 1991	Humanities, history, the West, ethics, discourses on Ṭabāṭabāʾī, Muṭahharī and Musā Ṣadr.
Rāzdānī wa raushanfikrī wa dīndārī (Secret-knowing, intellectualism and religious conviction)	1988 (abridged versions 1991, 1999)	Religious intellectualism, religious fascism, civil society, liberalism and Iranian identity.
Qabḍ wa basṭ-i tiʾūrīk-i sharīʿat (The Contraction and expansion of legal theory)	1991 (abridged versions 1992 and 1994)	Religious epistemology, hermeneutics, Islamic law, modern theology, science, religious revivalism.
Auṣāf-i pārsāyān (Attributes of the pious)	1992	Imamology, worship, discourse on *Nahj al-balāghah.*
Farbihtar az īdiʾūlūzhī (Loftier than ideology)	1994	Ideological science, political ideologies, *ḥauzah*, technology, modernism, mysticism.
Qiṣṣah-yi arbāb-i maʿrifat (Story of masters of wisdom)	1994	Discourses on Rūmī, Ḥāfiẓ, al-Ghazālī, Faiḍ al-Kāshānī, Islamic revivalism.
Ḥikmat wa maʿishat (Wisdom and subsistence)	1994 and 1997 (2 vols.)	Imamology, worship and prayer, theosophy, ethics and aesthetics.
Darshāʾī dar falsafah-yi ʿilm al-ijtimāʿ (Lectures in philosophy of social sciences)	1995*	Social sciences, philosophy and hermeneutics in the study of the functioning of human society.
Ḥadiṯ-i bandigī wa dilburdagī (Story of love and piety)	1996	Descriptions of prayer, wisdom of prayer, essays on spiritual subjects.
Mudārā wa mudīriyat (Tolerance and governance)	1997	Religious democracy, governance, secularism, clergy, nature of religion, Islamic revivalism.
Ṣirāṭhā-yi mustaqīm (Straight paths)	1998	Religious pluralism, hermeneutics, translations of Hick, Platinga, Basinger.
Basṭ-i tajrubah-yi nabawī (Expansion of prophetic experience)	1999	Religious experience, epistemology, nature of religion, hermeneutics, prophet-hood.
Siyāsat-nāmah (Book of governance)	1999 and 2000 (2 vols.)*	Essays, memoirs and letters on political subjects.
Qumār-i ʿāshiqān (Gambling of lovers)	2000	Islamic mysticism, discourses on Rūmī and Shams al-dīn Tabrīzī.

* These works have not been available to the author.

Although Soroush does not go so far as to reformulate the main concepts of the Constitution according to his views, it is clear that he provides the 'political philosophy' of the Khatamists: how to secularize politics in a society which cannot afford to reject its heritage and origin: an Islamic Revolution (Roy 1996:215).[16]

Surūsh is today a member of the Iranian Academy of Sciences. He is related to the Anjuman-i falsafah (Academy of Philosophy) and also conducts research at the Muʿassasah-yi dāʾirāt al-maʿārif-i buzurg-i islāmī (Institute of the great Islamic encyclopaedia) in Tehran. He spent the academic year 2001–2002 as a visiting professor at Harvard Divinity School, and was in this case also affiliated with the Center for Middle Eastern studies. Surūsh participates frequently at academic gatherings abroad, especially in the USA, England, Turkey and Malaysia, and several of his books and articles has been translated into different languages, such as English, Turkish, Arabic, Indonesian and Malay.[17]

B. Style of communication

Surūsh's writings give evidence of his vast learning. In contrast to the majority of modern intellectuals in Iran, who either had a modern academic training or a solid grounding in the traditional Islamic disciplines, Surūsh is at home in both contexts. He is well acquainted with contemporary scientific trends, the philosophical ideas of modern Western thinkers from René Descartes and Immanuel Kant to Karl Popper and Michel Foucault, and he manages the languages of European primary sources. As Surūsh is able to speak the same language and refer to the same metaphysical background as his Western intellectual counterparts, he truly partakes in the epistemological framework of the philosophical paradigm and world vision of modernity. Besides his acquaintance with Western philosophy, Surūsh is also familiar with the normative texts of Shi'i tradition, that is the Qur'an, the *Nahj al-balāghah* (Mode of eloquence), the *Ṣahīfah al-sajjādīyah* (Book of worship), the authoritative *akhbār* collections such as *Biḥār al-anwār* (Seas of lights), as well as the treasuries of Persian classical literature and the theological and mystical writings of Islamic thinkers from Muḥammad al-Ghazālī to Faiḍ al-

[16] It is interesting to note that Khātamī (1997a:282) in his book *Az dunyā-yi shahr tā shahr-i dunyā* (From the world of the city to the city of the world) considers the idea of regulated political power and rule of law as the most valuable achievements of modernity, which can be harmonised with Islamic government, although they originally were developed systematically in Western political philosophy.

[17] For instance, the most important translations of Surūsh's works into Turkish are *Ileriçi geriçilik* (Progressing backwardness), trans. Abdullah Kutlu, Ankara, 1990; *Ilim ve felsefeye giriş* (Introduction to science and philosophy), trans. Baris Güler, Ankara, 1990, and *Evrenin yatişmaz yapisi* (The Structure of unhindered development), trans. Hüseyin Hatemi, Istanbul, 1979. At present, an Arabic translation of *Qabḍ wa basṭ-i tiʾūrīk-i sharīʿat* is awaiting publication in Lebanon.

Kāshānī. Surūsh frequently expresses his ideas in an original and poetical manner with plenty of allegories, and throughout his writings exposes his wide knowledge of the classical poetry of particularly Jalāl al-dīn Rūmī, Shams al-dīn Ḥāfiẓ and Saʿdī Shīrāzī. It is not coincidental that the *Maṯnawī-yi maʿnawī* (Spiritual couplet poem) of Rūmī, and not the Qur'an, is the most frequently and approvingly cited reference in his work. Whether he uses metaphors such as the *ṣaḥrā-yi dānish* (desert of knowledge) or the *daryā-yi ʿilm* (sea of science), his aim is to explain specific questions in a more erudite manner that connects to the thought of the traditional Persian gnostics.

For Surūsh, poetical image serves as tool for legitimacy of ideas but also for reaching literary self-confidence, where he is able to make use of his own extraordinary command of Persian. His sentences are often sonorous and full of allusions, implicit references and weighty words of poetical derivation, which are sufficiently overt to be recognised by competent readers. Surūsh (1997a:321) frequently uses the rhythmic mode of Rūmī's poetry for rhetoric purposes to stress a certain aspect of his argument such as in the following where he refers to the etymological meaning of *fiqh* (comprehension) and *sharīʿat* (the way to the water-source):

You contemplate on the law of religion, I bid you to comprehend the law of the law: You have seen the water. Now, look through the water to the water! You speak of bodies forcefully subdued. I bid you to think of hearts that submit freely. You respect uniformity, emulation, and sanctity of *fiqh* and *faqīh*, I implore you to appreciate the complexity and colourfulness of belief, liberty, subtlety and the agility of faiths and volition. How inferior is body to soul, dirt to heart!

John Cooper (1998:54) has remarked that Surūsh's style might be considered as laborious and uninspiring, since it does not combine the love of both novelty and tradition, but nevertheless he creates a new rhetoric to convey his ideas, because "it would be difficult to deny that the rhetoric and the ideas do complement each other". The rhetoric style of Surūsh's writing is partly due to the fact that the bulk of his writings are edited texts of public lectures delivered in a variety of contexts and fora. Similar to modern Islamic 'defensive' literature in Persian, his writings are characterised by marked repetitions, a feature that becomes not only often unavoidable as an accompanying consequence of digression and innovation, but also indispensable in a discourse the aim of which is to convince and persuade. While not all of Surūsh's writings are apologetic in their contents, they have nevertheless a harsh apologetic, or more properly, polemical, character in their rhetoric structures and stylistic devices.

The tendentious nature of his work, aimed at different audiences, rather than being meant to be cumulative, comprehensive treatises with clear topical divisions for scholarly presentation, makes it difficult to establish the character and setting of the original audience. The difficulty to set definite boundaries of meaning of texts steeped in metaphorical language is even more constrained by the existence of multiple potential social contexts of audience, whether original or retrospective. While the adoption of literary style may make the content ambiguous or less scholarly than the use of the language of analytic philosophy, Surūsh (1999c:76-77) argues that his attachment to classical Iranian literature and the intention to address a wider general public have governed his choice of literary style. In a sense, he 'persianises' modern critical scientific research by generating and employing concepts and illustrations that take into consideration Iranian and Islamic intellectual tradition, worldviews and socio-historical contexts. This is further seen in his frequent use of the instructive language of the *ḥauzah* in order to appeal to *ʿulamā* and *ṭullāb* (theological students) at the seminaries in Qum and Mashhad.

In fact, Surūsh's effort can be said to be the attempt of illustrating the sort of points modern Western philosophers and scientists have made in terms of a language that strikes a resonance in a modern Muslim Persian-speaking audience. While he highlights the usefulness of other philosophers and theorists, particularly Kant and Popper, for thinking about modernity, he nevertheless rarely supplies a thorough, detailed reading of their texts, usually limiting himself to a reference to a single passage, sentence or aphorism. In this manner, he attempts not only to convey specific arguments, but rather also to naturalise them and demonstrate that they are both relevant and interesting to his Iranian contemporaries, that is: he believes that the philosophical issues that have arisen in the Western world have interesting and important implications for contemporary problems in Iran and other Muslim lands.

By using the colloquial idiom of the Iranian Muslim community mixed with a mystical literary bent and keeping neologisms to a minimum in several passages, Surūsh attempts in fact to liberate the modern speculation on *sharīʿat* and *ʿilm al-kalām* from the theoretical clutches of the traditional technical terminology. While largely indebted to former expositions of modern Shi'i 'defensive' literature, he revolutionises, in other words, the literary style of Islamic discourse on law in Iran by accommodating it to a modern Persian idiom no longer constrained to the boundaries of the highly technical language of *fiqh*. As Afshin Matin-asgari (1997:96) elucidates, ambiguities in Surūsh's intellectual mode of expression very much depend on this factor as well on the enormous range of his developing body of work and the political constrictions that he must observe. The socio-political context of contemporary Iran does not always readily lend itself to a free and open declaration of one's opinions in religious matters, and society certainly affords circumstances where it is safer to state one's beliefs more than one really does, notwithstanding that the reverse rule applies for secularist societies.

C. Philosophical foundation: Critical realism

A general characteristic of Surūsh's discussion on Islam and epistemology, or religious knowledge in general, is his attempt to withhold a critical realist foundation that strikes a mediate position between traditional religious metaphysics and recent postmodernist epistemic relativism. In his definition of the Arabic word *ʿilm*, Surūsh (1996b:11-12) distinguishes between two meanings of the concept: knowledge (Fr. connaissance) equivalent to Qur'anic definitions of *ʿilm* on the one hand and Western 'post-renaissance empirical science' on the other. Aware of the profound challenges that idealism (which stresses the role of the ideal or the spiritual in interpretation) poses against the independence of objects, Surūsh aligns himself with post-renaissance realist definitions of existence that distinguish between appearance and reality. He follows Kant and the positivists in his belief that phenomena are objects or events in time and space. While he shares the core positivist idea that the purpose of science is to describe the world of empirical phenomena as it is, and not add anything to it or reduce anything, he rejects nevertheless many characteristics of Western logical positivism, which he similar to philosophical pragmatists (such as Richard Rorty) considers as a replacement of metaphysics rather than a form of metaphysics. Similar to the non-realism of Rorty and others, which is directed against the idea of accurate representation itself, Surūsh (1999a:302) rejects the holistic belief of John Stuart Mill, Francis Bacon and the logical positivists in absolute empirical certainty and pure understanding (that he believes is impossible to verify):

> The positivism of Mill and Bacon based itself on the idea that brute facts were available and only needed an open eye to be captured by observation. But the later evolution and development of the philosophy of science demonstrated clearly, to their utter disappointment, that these brute facts existed nowhere except in the barren lands of wild hallucinations of the spectators. Even in simple inductive research, where the regular association of successive events is under scrutiny, one cannot be sure of the complete list of the relevant factors nor of the right aspects of the events subject to generalization.[18]

In the view of Surūsh (ibid.:303), the fundamental difference between the

[18] The expression 'positivism' was introduced by Auguste Comte and originally denoted the epistemological question of the existence of positive non-hypothetical knowledge. Its basic affirmation is that all knowledge regarding matters of fact is based on the positive data of experience. The development of logical positivism was a product of the Vienna circle under the leadership of the German logical empiricist philosopher Moritz Schlick. Logical positivism holds that all significant propositions are either those of logic or mathematics on the one hand or those of science on the other. Since utterances of metaphysics fall into neither of these categories, they are unverifiable in principle and can accordingly be rejected as nonsense. It is significant that Surūsh aligns himself with positivism, which in its basic ideological posture has proximate roots in the French enlightenment (that stressed the clear light of reason) and is hence wordly, antitheological and antimetaphysical.

philosophy of logical positivism and that of neo-positivism lies precisely in that the latter suggests that no brute facts exist in experience and that all experience is contingent on specific theoretical propositions. By acknowledging that the complex and illuminating conflict between realism and anti-realism in philosophy should be sustained, Surūsh follows the later postpositivism of the Austro-English philosopher of science, Karl R. Popper, who disavowed the early positivist empiricist insistence upon verifiability and induction.[19] In his general epistemology, Popper criticises rationalism as well as empiricism for looking for certain foundations for knowledge and (still being a realist) defines knowledge as hypotheses that have passed critical test and correspond to reality, a process that he calls falsification. In fact, according to Popper as well as to Surūsh, the whole question of the truth and falsity of our opinions and theories becomes pointless if there is no reality but only dreams and illusions:

If we accept that science has been successful in the task of manipulating nature, then how could we possibly interpret this success in rational terms except by admitting that it reflects reality? Is not every step of success with nature indicative of a step in the establishment of realism of science? Can a totally subjective and instrumental pseudo-epistemology (as some of the followers of the Frankfurt school accuse science of harbouring) be so successful in practice? Even an instrument, in order to be effective, must be appropriate to the medium in which it operates (Surūsh 1995a:9).[20]

Ibṭāl-pazīrī (falsifiability) does not mean that these laws (such as Einstein's law of relativity) must be falsified in absolute terms, but rather that a scientific law even if its warrant is determined, is open to falsification. In other words, an empirical discovery can make its proposition false. Falsification corresponds to *tajrubah-pazīrī* (empirical testability). A law is therefore scientific if it is empirically testable and vice versa, and if it is empirically testable it corresponds to the external world of phenomena (Surūsh 1996b:32).

In this respect, Surūsh's realist approach to epistemology and science consists in providing arguments to show that a theory that passes the said tests could be reasonable to be held true or at least correct. His realism is hence a critical realism that recognises that the only aim of science is to depict reality, which allows for gradations of the validity of scientific theories. The most salient aspect of his critical realism is in fact the view that reality to a large extent has lost its traditional symbolic and mythological

[19] Surūsh criticises these two tenets of logical positivism for the first time in his book *Naqdī wa muqaddimah'ī bar taḍādd-i diyālaktīkī* (Critique and introduction to dialectics).
[20] In his *The Logic of scientific discovery*, Popper (1992) insists that the meaning criterion should be abandoned and replaced by a criterion of demarcation between empirical and transempirical questions and answers, that is falsifiability (i.e. refutability). According to Popper such pseudo-sciences as astrology, metaphysics, Marxist history and Freudian psychoanalysis are not empirical sciences because they fail to adhere to the principle of falsifiability.

dimensions for modern man and, in other words, is *rāz-zidā'i* (cleansed of mystery), whereas the world of phenomenon still has a somewhat tangible existence that is made known to science.[21] Reality is, so to say, independent of knowledge and it is not constituted by it, even if knowledge by definition is associated with reality. Initially, Surūsh (1996c:164) refers to so diverse thinkers as the medieval nominalist philosopher William of Ockham and Jalāl al-dīn Rūmī (not Kant) to assert that certain basic features of the objects of our knowledge are due to the nature of our human faculties, that is: we can only know the world as it appears to us and not as it is in itself.[22] He distinguishes realism from idealism for which reality is the reflection of human a priori knowledge as well as from materialist positivism for which the reality is the tangible and comprehensible by the human senses since neither of the latter recognise the distinction between human representations of reality and brute phenomena:

[T]he theory of contraction and expansion of Islamic law is a realist theory, which means that it differentiates the thing from the conception of the thing. While idealism never separates between mind and external reality by considering mind and reality as identical, the minimum condition for a realist epistemology is the distinction between the object and the knowledge of it (ibid.:341).

In contrast to direct realism that supposes the possibility to inspect an object without inference to determine its properties, Surūsh asserts hence that original understanding is not immune to criticism and that the theses implicit in it are logically incoherent. In this respect, his critical realist position with its foundationalist elements is very much a middle position between logical positivism and pragmatism.[23]

The view that material objects exist outside the human consciousness and independently of what we take to be our perceptions of them (i.e. an object is distinguished from its representations regardless of their falsifiability or

[21] In his book *Basṭ-i tajrubah-yi nabawī* (Expansion of prophetic experience), Surūsh (1999a:321–374) elucidates the term *rāz-zidā'i* in detail. He explains that the modern rationalisation of existence has its theoretical background in the Newtonian theory of movement, stemming from the discoveries in natural science, which has created a speeding administration and organisation of human affairs. Cf. Surūsh 1994b:135.

[22] Yet, the reference to Rūmī is not very adequate, since Rūmī *in toto* comprehends the world as a veil over reality with a unified understanding of form and meaning. In Rūmī's terminology, *ṣūrat* (form) is a thing's outward appearance, while *ma'nā* (meaning) is its inward and unseen reality. As meaning ultimately is that thing as known to God Himself, Surūsh's reference to Rūmī's (1996:II 1020–22, IV 2994–95, etc) distinction between form and meaning must be considered as inaccurate. Cf. chapter IIIf.

[23] It seems however that the contested nature of the scientific classifications themselves is largely unnoticed by Surūsh, since philosophers such as Kant and Schopenhauer are customarily classified as idealists. Kant characterises his own system as transcendental idealism (or empirical realism), since he supposes that the human self constructs knowledge out of sense impressions upon which are imposed certain universal concepts called categories. Transcendental idealism differs from the subjective idealism of Berkeley as well as the objective idealism of Hegel which both offer speculative certainties about the ultimate nature of things. Cf. Landesman 1997:55.

validity), moreover exemplifies that Surūsh derives his understanding of 'realism' mainly from Kant rather than from its use in the medieval Christian debates (where it was opposed to nominalism) or the metaphysical theosophy of Muḥammad Ḥusain Ṭabāṭabā'ī. In his notion of falsifiability as the cornerstone of modern science, Surūsh's scientific approach differs remarkably from the epistemic standards of traditional theosophy, such as that of Ṣadr al-dīn Shīrāzī, who adhered to an objectivist conception of human knowledge, where man is the idealised reflection of divine nature and knowledge is identical with the Knower and the known.[24] Since we necessarily perceive the world as it appears to beings with our own particular kind of perceptual machinery, Surūsh (1996c:343) criticises what he calls *pūzītīvīsm-i fiqhī* (legal positivism) as well as "common idealism" for putting aside the boundaries between object and its representation, making subjectivity and existence inseparable:

We see again a case of idealist thought where the thing in itself is confused with the perception of the thing. In this sense, legal positivism and common idealism are two epistemological veils, since religious knowledge, similar to all other knowledge, unmistakably represents knowledge of religion.

Corresponding to a basic lesson of Kant that all human awareness involves the use of interpretative concepts, Surūsh asserts that interpretation is contingent on specific theories, i.e. it is theory-impregnated. For in the sense that interpretation is the most fundamental and defining feature of human cognition, all knowledge is theory-laden. He argues that even if we adhere to a nominalist position, which denies universal essences of meaning by reducing and changing former semantic senses, meaning is still dispositional, 'expectational' and theory-impregnated:

When an Aristotelian philosopher reads the word 'water' in the Qur'an, he involuntarily and unconsciously presumes an essence or quality that is called 'water'. A Ṣadrāian theosopher can neither accept that God could have created the quiddity of water for similar reasons that a modern chemist cannot imagine that God's intention of water is anything else than H2O. The same rule applies to the words 'knowledge', 'power', 'love', 'enmity', 'pride', 'envy', and the like... Since the meaning of all words is theory-laden, it is adequate for us to take the nominalist position (i.e. denial of universals) to see how the universal substances of the Qur'an change their meaning. The reason behind the fact that we commonly have uniform theories is that we are not as compliant to philosophical and scientific theories as we in earnest should be (ibid.:302).[25]

[24] In Shīrāzī's epistemology, reality is not perceived as consisting of objects but as a single *wujūd* (existence) whose deliminations by various *māhīyat* (quiddities) bestow the illusory appearance of a multiplicity of existents that possess no reality in themselves. Knowledge cannot hence have physical reality as its object but rather transcends the information provided by the senses in order to discover *maujūd*, that is, ultimately divine Being and the Absolute.
[25] Cf. Surūsh 1999a:157 and 1999d:2.

Since religion itself does not offer any methods or values, and understanding is not automatic, Surūsh believes that we are in need of certain tools and instruments for the deciphering of deeper meanings. These tools can, in his view, on a basic level be concentration and learning. By increasing our knowledge about a certain subject and its related matters, for instance by way of analogy or comparative analysis, we attain a deeper knowledge, while this knowledge is not equal to better learning.[26] He asserts that logic does not answer the crucial epistemological questions, such as what the correct criteria and methods of knowledge are, what the sources and mechanisms of cognition are, how our expectations of phenomena such as religion influence our observation, and so on. In order to answer these questions, Surūsh argues that we are in need of a *rawish-i stratizhīk* (strategic method), that is scientific theories, such as those of modern epistemology and hermeneutics, in order to elucidate the existing relationships or lack of relationships in observation and experience. He considers theories as instruments arranged and objectified to allow a better comprehension of the world of phenomena:

> We are in need of a theory in order to clarify what is related to a specific matter and what is not... All matters that are considered in a relationship are essentially contingent on a preceding theory for their clarification, since their relationship is not an observable dictum, but has to be discovered rationally. The discovery of a lack of relationship must also be considered in the light of theories (ibid.:121).[27]

> Our view is precisely that man, equipped with comprehensive and reliable theories, selects and sifts his or her other data in order to correlate and situate these (data) within them. [...] Theories limit the scope of research and pose specific questions. They tell us what we shall look for and that we cannot begin without searchlight (ibid.:256-257).

In Surūsh's view, the aim of science as well as philosophy is hence to construct theories that are consistent, synoptic, true to the facts and that possess explanatory power. Since we are dependent on theories for the clarification of scientific problems, he argues that these theories must at the same time correspond to the issue at hand and not be of old model. By claiming that "modern theories notify the solving of modern problems", theories related to the traditional scientific world-view become of little use in the present world (ibid.:122 and 166). According to Surūsh, this explains why Johannes Kepler's theories on social revolutions are outdated and unuseful for explaining the socio-political dynamics of the constitutional revolution in Iran and why new theories in chemistry must be discovered for the explanation of manifestation of colours and their relationship with the molecular constitution of things. Since the complex structure of modernity suggests that epistemic matters are not as simple as they were originally

[26] Cf. Surūsh 1996c:123, 129, 363 and 390.
[27] Cf. Surūsh 1996c:221.

thought to be, he asserts that the necessity of theoretical explanation and understanding is particularly essential in the contemporary situation. Closer attention to contemporary theories of science and religion reveals, in his view, important discontinuities in conceptual scheme, where the ontological relationships have been turned upsidedown, as for instance illustrated in the phenomenon of ideological interpretations of religion, which consider this world as more precious than the hereafter (Surūsh 1997a:198). As a matter of fact, Surūsh 's conviction that all knowledge is theory-laden puts him into conflict with 'ideological science' that makes dictums based on speculation about truth as well as with the effort to 'ideologise' religion. He maintains that ideology by definition is based on reductionism in the form of "unscientific beliefs" rather than rational argumentation:

To enter the temple of ideology, humans need to take off their shoes of reason, since ideology already has determined the duty of man by rigidly commanding him in what to think and what to say about humanity, history, society, ethics, and so on... Therefore, we say that opening the door of ideology inevitably results in shutting the door of freethinking (Surūsh 1996a:141).

By suggesting that metaphysics played a role in Marx's notion of ideology (in the form of non-provable propositions), Surūsh (ibid.:82) argues that the circle of ideology is connected to specific political interests which consider certain postulates about man, society and history, scientific as well as non-scientific, as closed to falsification:

Ideology is a non-cognitive command veiled in the garb of knowledge. It makes profit, power, faith, theology and ethics, and the like, which all have external sources, ideologised in the garb of knowledge. From what has been said, the endoplasm of ideology is therefore a collection of rules which are not subjected to logical investigation, empirical verification or falsification.

D. Modernity and the West

By referring to Thomas Kuhn's theories on paradigmatic change in science, Surūsh argues that modern man, after Copernicus, has acquired new scientific as well as non-scientific conceptions of reality. Increasingly, modern man has come to comprehend the earth as a location of play and competition where our epistemic standards constantly adjust to new emerging scientific discoveries and theories. Alluding to the Copernican revolution, Surūsh points out that the sun, which according to the ancients circled around earth, is now looked upon scientifically and critically as a constant star that earth revolves around. By suggesting that our changed perception of reality has brought forth a semantic change of religious and philosophical concepts, he argues that religious language has no constant meaning, but instead is continuously adjusting to the discoveries made by science.[28] Similar to Habermas, Surūsh therefore considers modernity as a unique historical possibility that begins with Kant's attempt to make reason critical. Characterised by its man-centred view of the world and its interest in critical rationality, modernity, or more correctly *mudarnīsm* (modernism), is principally a state of constant transition from equilibrium to non-symmetry which self-consciously detaches itself from its own prehistory (ibid.:351).[29] Nevertheless, he believes modernity to be a historical outgrowth of earlier human existential experience, a new phase that does not necessarily proceed beyond traditional assumptions except when change corresponds to the basic normative features of modernity.[30] The emergence of modernity is hence more precisely linked to the emergence of certain new knowledge systems that did not exist before. This has created a gap between modern man on the one hand and the traditional understanding of the cosmos on the other hand. In this respect, he assumes that there is no way to recover tradition and that everything we produce becomes a part of modernity, although our criticism of the latter suggests that we are coming out of modernity and are entering postmodernity. He agrees, so to say, with Habermas' view that modernity can and will no longer borrow the criteria by which it takes its orientation from the models supplied by another epoch. Modernity creates its own normativity out of itself and is in this sense self-defining.[31] In Surūsh's view, the very paradox of modernity is precisely the fact that every one of us partakes of it and at the same time formulates its definitions in a subject-object relation to both tradition and modernism:

It is possible to speak of modernism and observe it from a certain distance. The reason why the ancients never spoke of *sunnat* (tradition) is that they were enmeshed in it. To be enmeshed in tradition is something else than to discuss it. In order to discuss a certain subject it is essential to distance oneself from it. It is worthy to note that today we argue about modernism, which indicates that we gradually are coming out of it. Since modernism has become a questionable subject

[28] By comparing several poems of Ḥāfiẓ and Saʿdī concerning natural phenomena with formulas of modern chemistry and physics, Surūsh (1996c:130–133) argues that the traditional cosmology and its comprehension of Qur'anic desciptions of nature cannot be reconciled with modern science. But what he neglects to recognise is that the proposal that the sun is at the centre of the solar system was not in itself new; for it was known by certain Greek, Islamic and Indian philosophers and astronomers. He also ignores to that the renaissance consisted of proposing a non-spiritual vision of reality that dislocated man in cosmos.

[29] While the term *mudarnīsm* is used interchangeably with *mudarnītih* (modernity) in *Qabḍ wa basṭ-i tiʾūrīk-i sharīʿat* as well as *Farbihtar az īdiʾūlūzhī* Surūsh tends to use the concept *mudarnītih* in a more general sense in his later works. Cf. 1999f:34 and 1999c:27.

[30] For instance, Surūsh maintains that the values that preceded, caused and sustained the development of the modern West were not the result of a conscious world-historical project of their authors. He argues instead that the empirical science of Bacon, the secular religion of Luther and the amoral politics of Machiavelli, combined with other relevant ideas and events, created the edifice of the modern world.

[31] Cf. Habermas 1990:7.

for us, a paradox appears: We are experiencing a subject-object relationship to both tradition and modernism, which suggests that we are actually coming out of both of them (ibid.:351).

While Surūsh suggests that it is possible for modern man to take a reflective stand against tradition and modernism, and to disclose different dimensions of these phenomena, his position on the contemporary trend of postmodernism, as well as the entire issue of modernity *per se*, is much more ambivalent. As a major challenge to modernism, Surūsh associates postmodernism with philosophical relativism and the denial of any constructive role for reason. He considers, for instance, Foucault's study of madness as typically representating postmodernism, where no strict line between madness and reason is drawn. In his book *Farbihtar az īdīʾūlūzhī*, he believes that in the strictest sense that the age of postmodernism will begin when relativism becomes the official creed:

> The epoch of postmodernism is the official recognition of contempt of reason. It is the belief that no [place of] asylum exists for destitute reason. In the epoch of modernism, relativism torments like a thorn in the eye of reason, but in the present age this thorn is becoming publicly acknowledged by convincing reason to act as a go-between and to coexist with this thorn (Surūsh 1996a:362).

While Samuel P. Huntington's theory of the alleged clash between the Western and Islamic civilisations is considered by Surūsh (1999e:11) to be an ill-founded myth, he acknowledges that the advent of modernity has certainly challenged and put the internal Muslim balance between revealed text and human reason under serious question. Whereas Surūsh refutes the Derridean rejection of the a priori nature of the sacred on a religious and ethical basis, he accepts that no coherent concept or theory of truth exists outside of faith itself. In other words, he does not deny the value of meaning, but only suggests that the present situation has made the discernment of falsehood and truth, and even more so certainty, much more demanding than earlier (Surūsh 1994a:97). As new attempts to define and describe various aspects of reality continuously replace previous ones, Surūsh argues that modernity has made the boundaries of traditional civilisations more uncertain. He even insists that the geographical, and hence social, composition of traditional religious communities has been altered to the extent that being an apostate has no meaning today:

> We experience an epoch where there is no meaning of distinguishing Muslims from other human beings. There is no longer any point of saying that someone who leaves Islam brings harm to Islam. The epoch when the Truth shone like a clear sun, and therefore to turn one's back on Islam also meant to turn one's back on manifest truth, has elapsed (Surūsh 1999e:35).

Surūsh also suggests that the capital of modern Islamic civilisation, as far as Islamic intellectual life is concerned, is no longer Mecca, Qum, Fès or

Lahore, but London, located in the cradle of the Western world. In intellectual terms, Islam, so to say, has its centres and peripheries and the Middle East is no longer its only centre:

To enter or leave the *dār al-islām* (abode of Islam) was of significance as long as the spheres (of civilisations) had unmistakable geographical borders. These borders no longer exist. A colleague at an Islamic conference in London once said to me that London is the present capital of Islam. Yes, most Muslim scholars either reside in London or frequently visit that city. London houses a number of international conferences on Islam and there are hundreds of mosques in that city and a lot of notable books on Islam that are published there as well. For these reasons, the concept of citizenship has radically changed (ibid.:35).

The modern world has hence acquired far more complexity than the traditional world with its situation of ancient and medieval man. Particularly in the fields of economics, politics, communication and education, modernity develops thought and structures which are incomparably more complex, turbulent and sophisticated than before, hence generating highly complex and secular conceptions of reality. In Surūsh's view, the world we inhabit is, in its totality, not the same world as that of our forebears. While change traditionally was explained as partial, today it is considered as absolute and comprehensive. Many aspects of traditional life, such as monarchies or slavery, survive in the modern world, but are in his view mere formalities that lack a natural function and status (Surūsh 1997a:420). Using the metaphorical language of Rūmī, Surūsh explains that whereas traditional man was a traveller that looked at the world as an transient place, modern man is a non-content and critical inhabitant of this world. Modern man opposes and criticises everything in an attempt to create constant movement, change and revolution, secure rights and liberties and put the axioms of life under doubt. While *l'homme total* of modernity is involved in complicated relationships that force him to constantly re-evaluate the norms of identity as well as value, traditional man inhabited, in his view, a world in which the sun of religion shone clear:

The contrast between modernity and tradition does not end here: a modern person is critical and demanding (not merely understanding), in favour of revolution (not just reform), active (not passive), at home with scepticism and anxiety (not certitude), interested in clarity and causality (not bewilderment and enchantment), prone to pride and joy (not sorrow of separation), mindful of life (not death), in pursuit of rights (not only duties), sponsor of creative (not imitative) art, oriented to the external (not just the internal) world, a lover (not a despiser) of life, an intervener in (not merely a user of) the world, a user of reason in the service of criticism (not just of understanding). Modern humanity is, in a word, oblivious to its limits and proud of its creative possibilities (ibid.:422-423).

In his book *Tafarruj-i sun'*, Surūsh discusses the issue of the consequences of technology for religion and ethics. He seems to desire technological progress without a concomitant profanation of Islamic and Iranian culture. By referring to Jacques Ellul's criticism of science and technology, Surūsh (1994b:292-295) argues that technology is not value-based and that technological development has no blind alley since it is impossible to step out of modern society. He subjects man to the law-bound progressivism of history although he subscribes to the negative causes of technology as well as to the correctness of Ellul's conclusion that modern man no longer governs technological development, but himself is governed by it. While the secularisation of ethics, the rationalisation of happiness, the centrality of humanity, and the transposition of vices and virtues constitute the serving values that preceded the birth of socio-economic development, Surūsh (1995a:5) believes that such intimidating terms as "egocentrism" and "individualism" fail to express the central ideas of the modern era. He rather describes modernity as "a lowering and rearrangement of the system of values". In this respect he asserts that modernity, here equal to development, provides the opportunity for cultivating higher and more spiritual needs. In other words, it is socio-economic development that fulfils the primary needs, not the higher values, and the general development of values and spiritual needs can only follow material and technological development:

> The profound scientific, humanist and philosophical critiques of development that are current in the West are all the by-products of material development. Technology and development have run their course, revealing their own nature and assuming higher forms. This has also allowed human beings to experience and advance beyond technological and socio-economic limitations, where they can behold the higher horizons and learn new lessons. The advent of postmodernism is a case in point (ibid.:6).

Remarking that the term 'the West' gained currency in England primarily through the translation of Oswald Spengler's *Untergang des abendlandes* (The Decline of the West), Surūsh criticises his and others' notion of human civilisations as separate cultures with separate religio-cultural notions of science. He unconditionally rejects the theory of cultural relativism in science by asserting that scientific knowledge is "objective and universal" and "never relies on its particular origin or birth-place…" (Surūsh 1994b:98, 113). The date and place of birth is, in other words, no criteria for measuring the accuracy of ideas. But while Surūsh (ibid.:115) argues that science, natural science in particular, has a specific universal content, he rejects the reductionist restriction of science to empirical observation and experimentation as pure positivism and indeed a sign of disrespect for the humanities:

> Those who today believe that science does not become science unless it is disconnected from and detached from the culture, philosophy or world-view of a particular scholar are pure bearers of positivist thought, even if they in full confusion

and ignorance think that rejecting the *ʿilmīyat* (scientific character) of the human sciences is to the benefit of Islamic thought.

Surūsh follows Popper's proposition that the criterion of demarcation between science and philosophy is not empirically verifiable as suggested by the logical positivists and that philosophy is no less scientific than natural science. Similar to Popper, he believes that natural science is independent of philosophy and ideology at the level of justification, but not at the level of discovery where the scientist relies on a number of non-empirical factors (ibid.:116). At the level of justification, science is *bī-waṭan* (universal) and *wahshī* (wild) and only Islamic or Western as regards the cultural context of the scientists themselves:

Science is different from customs, morality, art and the habits of Westerners and disbelievers. Customs and mores are noncognitive phenomena (although some argue that they inform epistemology). Science however is a cognitive phenomenon. Customs are themselves realities that may become subject to scientific inquiry (Surūsh 1995a:10).

He therefore rejects the idea of a specific 'Islamic' philosophy for the same reason as he refutes all attempts to create an 'Islamic' economy or administration, or government. For Surūsh, these concepts are to all intents and purposes pre-religious attributes, which are not essential to the constant structure of the religious organism itself.[32] In his critic of Murtaḍā Muṭahharī's exposition of Islamic philosophy, he asserts in fact that the overall structure and characteristics of Islamic philosophy are rooted in Greek philosophy and by and large are a continuation and development of it. By refuting the proposed divine source of Islamic philosophy as an ill-grounded myth and neglecting the fact that much of Greek philosophy as a doctrine fits rather neatly into religion (for instance, the Neoplatonic insistence on the existence of one supreme Being out of which everything else emerges), he claims that the present as well as the historical character of Islamic philosophy is coincidental:

I here claim that what is called Islamic philosophy at the *ḥauzah-yi ʿilmīyah*s, irrespective of its Islamic and holy attribute, is nothing else but Greek philosophy, that is one philosophy among tens of philosophies. It is not the only possible philosophy and not the best possible one. As science, it is human and respectable and indeed profane. It was the first philosophy that the Muslims encountered and later on developed. Besides, one could ask which philosophy truly embodies Islamic philosophy? The philosophy of al-Fārābī or Fakhr al-dīn Rāzī or that of Suhrawardī or Rajab ʿAlī Tabrīzī? In the same sense as there is no unified Western philosophy, the views of all these philosophers diverge from each other (Surūsh 1996a:33).

For this reason, Surūsh similarly rejects the notion of a Western essence with definite boundaries, a Hegelian *Geist*, in terms with Hegel's deterministic

[32] Cf. Surūsh 1997a:205.

philosophy of history, since that would only leave modern Muslims with two alternatives: to either consent to everything Western or to reject it. Denouncing his opponents as Hegelians for their use of archetypical entities as a disguise for cultural relativism, Surūsh argues that contemporary Muslims are encountering a plurality of Western philosophers, artists and theologians rather than one unified Western philosophy, art, culture and religion. "We are not encountering a unified Western philosophy, but a number of individual Western philosophers who speak to us" (Surūsh 1994b:233). However, he does not refer to philosophical nominalism, but to Ṣadr al-dīn Shīrāzī's theosophical distinction between *māhīyat* (quiddity) and *wujūd* (existence) in order to prove that the notion of the West does not represent the unity of essence which issues from *waḥdat-i haqīqī* (true unity), i.e. of *maujūd* (being), of the Divine Principle itself:

Everyone who is familiar with theosophy knows that *maujūd* requires unity (there being no existence without unity). In many cases where unity is perceived, there is in reality no unity since essence and existence are bound to being. From this perspective, the dispute of the essence of the West depends on the confirmation of the true unity of the West rather than a deliberate unity. As long as this question remains unsolved, all the talk about the essence of the West is inadequate (ibid.:244-245).

While there are reasons to doubt the adequacy of Surūsh's reference to Ṣadr al-dīn's theosophical conceptions in this respect, his intention is to state that the West should not be considered a distant, abstract and vague *Other* or a set of ontological doctrines or a way of life, but rather that the West is concretely and immediately manifested in a plurality of individual personalities. In the sense that the scientific and cultural domination of the West in science and technology as well as its secularism is believed to be a gradual phenomenon, subject to the laws of expansion and contraction, he suggests that Muslims are no longer excluded from the shaping of the West. In reality, many actors, including Muslims themselves, construct the West, as is evident in the rhetorical slogans of *gharbzadigī* and *bazgasht bih khīshtan*.[33] Surūsh (1999c:153-165) further explains that all Iranians in fact are inheritors and bearers of three cultures: Pre-Islamic Iranian culture, which has mainly remained in the form of language and literature, Islamic culture, which is mainly represented by its spiritual and artistic expressions (which as far as the classical Islamic civilisation is concerned was completed

[33] Cf. Surūsh 1994b:233, 237 and 1999c:161–162. The concept of *gharbzadigī* was originally formulated by Aḥmad Fardīd and developed by Jalāl Āl-i Aḥmad, where the concept is used more flexibly to indicate the approach of Western customs, manners, and technology, causing the eviction of Iranians from their native land and the imitation of everything Western, even at the expense of immolating the most eminent Iranian cultural assets and legacies. The term has in some cases been interpreted to denote more a historical destiny in Hegelian terms, the conviction that Iranian culture is long past its prime, is exhausted and depleted and has to share the historical destiny of the West.

by the Iranians) and Western culture, which for the last two centuries has bestowed new life on Iranian culture. In contrast to earlier Iranian intellectuals such as Iḥsān Narāqī or Aḥmad Fardīd, who tended to neglect or wholesomely reject the Western component of modern Iranian culture, Surūsh asserts that the Western element in our day is as indispensable to Iranian culture as Islam.[34]

Surūsh's view that the West can neither be rejected nor embraced projects it nevertheless as a most formidable challenge to the modern historical dilemma of Islam. Philosophy and science appear to be only an internal aspect of the general process of cultural contamination, Westernisation and homologation of human cultures. He does not consider the global condition of modernity, which cannot be transcended as the tragic loss of archaic authenticity, since traditional civilisations are no closer to the original essence of humanity than contemporary modern society. While Surūsh's position makes no suggestions as to any counter-discursive strategies for Muslims to adopt that could reconstruct the Western historical experience and prevent the uninhibited immersion of Islam into the Western cognitive systems, his position's significance lies in the horizon it opens for the introduction of a new normative dimension. It contributes to replacing the subject-object relation that hitherto governed much of Western-Islamic mutual perceptions during the second part of the twentieth century.

Aware of the fact that Western influences ushered the Islamic world into the modern era, Surūsh (1999c:160) asserts that the modern challenge of the West (in contrast to the encounter between the Islamic world and the West during the Middle Ages) has not allowed Iranians to shape their own cultural identity in contemplative seclusion, which would be impossible in any case, since human cultures and identities are subjected to constant variation and modification. In this respect, the modern impact of the West has been much more than intellectual, which he believes, for instance, can be observed in the sphere of law, where the traditional notion of *sharīʿat* since the end of the nineteenth century has been challenged by Western philosophy of law. In contrast to the early centuries of Islam, when Muslim jurists borrowed ideas from the Roman and Iranian legal systems, the modern Islamic world has so far not been in a position of strength vis-à-vis its Western counterparts.

While Surūsh in the early 1980s considered ʿAlī Sharīʿatī's notion of *bāzgasht bih khīshtan* (return to selfhood) as synonymous to *ijtihād* and religious interpretation, he rejects the possibility of any pure Islamic or Iranian self-hood in an essay on Iranian culture written some years later. He argues that to determine an authentic Islamic-Iranian conception of self is an ambiguous and contradictory enterprise, since complex and varied notions of

[34] Here, Surūsh sharply distinguishes himself from earlier Islamic intellectuals such as Iḥsān Narāqī (1976), who restricted Iranian culture to religion, Persian language and literature and the pre-Islamic past by placing Iranian culture as diametrically opposed to Western civilisation.

cultural exchange and appropriation govern self-knowledge (Surūsh 1999c:166-167). Surūsh opens a plethora of possibilities as to alternative symbolic representations of 'self' and 'other'. He invites modern Muslims to "establish a new treaty" with science in the light of modern scientific developments by proposing more intensive scientific and intellectual exchange between human cultures. This would facilitate a totally fresh way of looking at science in Islam (Surūsh 1994b:237).[35] As he believes that contemporary Muslims must critically pass judgment on Western conceptions of science and philosophy and integrate them into Islam in the same manner as they did with Greek, Indian and Iranian learning in premodern times, Surūsh remains suspicious of the general tendency of contemporary Westerners to forsake the internal spiritual battle against passions and desires in favor of the external worldly battle, such as illustrated in the slogans of the French revolution 'Liberty, equality, fraternity'.

E. Religion

While Surūsh reconciles the one-sided views of his Descartian and Ṣadrāian rationalist predecessors in his early reinterpretation of Islamic theosophy in *Nahād-i nā-ārām-i jahān* (The Restless nature of the universe), he makes a decisive break with the tradition of rationalist philosophy as well as natural theology, which offers proofs of the existence of God and the soul, in his later writings, such as *Qabḍ wa basṭ-i tiʾūrīk-i sharīʿat*, which are more in line with neopositivistic empiricism.[36] Separating knowledge and being, he accepts that no coherent notion of truth ultimately exists outside faith itself, even if religion is not a theory in the scientific sense, since its basic tenets cannot be proved rationally. Following the dominant Western tradition of thought on the nature of faith from the time of St. Thomas Aquinas in the thirteenth century, Surūsh considers faith a propositional attitude that comes very close to the notion of faith as unevidenced or inadequately evidenced belief. While he still objects to the Derridean rejection of the a priori nature of the sacred, his position has affinities with Derrida's (1998:10-11 and 63-65) contribution on religion, which starts out with reference to Kant's doctrine of the *parerga*, considering religion as beyond our rational comprehension (even if he believes that religion is incompatible with the concept of freedom that forms the basis of Kant's practical philosophy).[37] In an article in *Kiyān* in 1999, polemically entitled *Rahāʾī az yaqīn wa yaqīn bih rahāʾī* (Deliverance from certainty and certainty of deliverance) as

[35] Cf. Surūsh 1994b:284 and 296–297.
[36] Cf. Surūsh 1999b.
[37] As for Aquinas, he discusses faith in all its aspects in his *Summa Theologica*, the second part of the second part, Questions 1–7.

against al-Ghazālī's renowned treatise *al-Munqiḏ mīn al-ḍalāl* (Deliverance from error), Surūsh reacts to the notion of independent religious reason and argues that religious knowledge is not essentially different from other domains of knowledge. In contrast to Aquinas' division between faith vis-à-vis reason, or more correctly *scientia* (knowledge), Surūsh (1999g:8) believes that the propositions that are believed by faith do not essentially differ from other domains of human thought even if the object of faith requires no acquiescence:

The answer of religion to the questions of the believer is within the boundaries of hypotheses, which can be verified and rejected, and interpreted within the expansion and contraction [of religious thought]. In short, the believer should keep his or her faith alive and awake and never give up the investigation [of new alternatives]. The believer should also avoid the topics and norms of jurisprudence which belong to the communal and external sphere of religion and which never cross the threshold to the inner sphere of the individual. The norms of an individual and *muḥaqqiqānah* (scientific) approach to religion differ, so to say, from those of a communal and *muqallidānah* (emulating) approach to religion.[38]

In contrast to the methodological attempt of Islamic modernists, such as Mahdī Bāzargān and Maḥmūd Ṭāliqānī, Surūsh is not interested in reconciling religion and science. His concern transcends their type of approach, in that he primarily is involved in observing the emergence of scientific theories from falsifiable propositions. While he considers the development of their ideas as worthy of note, he asserts that their thought is flawed in that it takes the present state of natural science as final. By considering science to be a matter of ongoing development (where the explanatory theories we presently accept may well be refuted in the future), Surūsh is as much in debate with Islamic modernism as with Islamic traditionalism and traditional religious thought. For Surūsh, religious knowledge is tentative, and the differences between reality as seen in science and faith ultimately reveal that the two sources are unequal in the magnitude and ultimate significance of their content. Religion has a far more limited rational content, that is: it has no right to claim objective truth in the scientific sense (Surūsh 1999g:8). As science is regarded as the epitome of human rationality, religion retreats into its own ghetto and, afraid of making claims that are subject to rational assessment, it can no longer claim to be of any universal significance.

In religious thought, there has long been a 'fideist' or 'existentialist' tradition exemplified, for instance, in the Persian Sufi tradition of personalities, such as Jalāl al-dīn Rūmī and Maḥmūd Shabistarī, and in the Christian theology of St. Augustine and Blaise Pascal, which epitomizes that faith goes beyond reason. In accordance with this tradition, Surūsh is impressed by the diversity of beliefs, convictions and modes of reasoning

[38] Cf. Surūsh 1999a:319–320.

found in different cultures to the extent of despairing of the possibility of rationally proving these. At first sight, he would seem to fit into this tradition, but his interest is not metaphysics or ontology, questions that he leaves open as a matter for faith rather than knowledge. While Surūsh rejects the idea of Auguste Comte that modern metaphysics and science have similar functions and goals, he believes that ontology must conform to science, since religious knowledge is subjected to the epistemic norms implied by the theory of falsification. Referring to Ludwig Feuerbach's (d. 1872) famous remark that "the secret of theology is anthropology", he comes very close to the latter's non-realist remark that the objects of religious faith are human projections, as mankind unconsciously creates God in its own image:

> Religion is a cloth for the shape of man and a nourishment and medicine suitable for human digestion. Someone who has a low view of man consequently has a low conception of religion and someone who has a high view of man, his religion also reaches highness and sublimity… Our concern is, in other words, not what ought to be, but what is, and thus involves description, not command (Surūsh 1996c:170).[39]

While Surūsh, in contrast to the anthropologists, is not ready to start off by believing that all religious claims are false, he believes that the content of religion very much is a projection of some feature of the human condition. Not quite suggesting that religious belief is not a reflection of some transcendent reality but rather a projection of human needs and aspirations, he argues "that the authentic reality of every human being is equivalent and identical to his or her knowledge of the world" (ibid.:286). But while science always is *guzīnishī* (selective) and particular and hence cannot solve or falsify holistic metaphysical matters, it presents, in his view, new questions and frame-works for new answers.[40] Surūsh nevertheless does not discuss the topic of the nature of religious faith as a central problem in the epistemology of religion, including the subject of religious faith and its relation to his definition of falsifiability. He neither defines any criterion of verifiability (where the theological statements of religious mode of experience are either verifiable or illusory) nor explains the nature of the relation between verification and falsification in the manner of, for instance, the Christian theologian John Hick, which would address some ambiguities regarding his concept of the religious claim of truth. [41]

---

[39] Cf. Surūsh 1996c:295 and 1996f:48. In Feuerbach's (1957) theology, if it can legitimately be called such, it is man himself who creates the concept of God and man is his own God– *homo homini Deo* (man who is is own God).

[40] As will be properly elucidated below, Surūsh considers science to consist of subjects and hypotheses in terms of theoretical presuppositions which represent the point of departure of all *kāwish-i tajrubī* (empirical investigation).

[41] Hick (1988:175–176) constructs a definition of theological verification where he argues that one can fail to verify without this failure constituting falsification. He speaks of verifying propositions concerning matters of fact and not of logically necessary truths, and hence

Surūsh's comprehension of religion essentially connects religion to belief, worship and spirituality. Inspired by the British philosopher Alfred North Whitehead (1926:37-47), he comprehends religion as reaching the deepest level of man's solitude, that is, as an attitude of the individual towards the universe rather than as as a social phenomenon. Surūsh is almost certainly influenced by Whitehead's notion of historical religious consciousness, as religion principally is interpreted as aiming at the transformation of man and as an answer to the eternal questions of existence rather than the temporal issues of specific historical situations.[42] To begin with, Surūsh's definition of Islam distinguishes between two types of religion, the normative *islām-i ḥaqīqat* (Islam of truth) and the historical *islām-i huwwīyat* (Islam of identity). He argues that while the latter refers to religion as a guise for cultural identity that, for instance, is a response to the contemporary *buhrān-i huwwīyat* (crisis of identity), the former denotes religion as a repository of transcendent truths revealed to the Prophet (Surūsh 1998b). Referring to Wittgenstein's theory of familial affinity, he also asserts that the nature of the relationship between different historical formulations of Islamic belief can be regarded as registers of Muslims. This assumption also includes the fundamental Shi'i notion of *uṣūl-i panjgānah* (five principles of belief) as a historical formulation subjected to flux and change (Surūsh 1998a:7). For his empirical view it stands to reason that there could be no unified and articulated Shi'i position during the lifetime of the *imāms*, since there was no single set of theological doctrines or legal principles that was generally accepted. As no religion has any orthodox or standardised principles of belief, Islam is similar to every other religion contingent on what Surūsh calls its essential *ḏātiyāt* (substances) rather than its exoteric *ʿaraḍiyāt* (accidentals) for its articulation and sustenance:

> A theory that constantly discovers new accidentals in the light of new constitutional propositions acquires a new character. This perspective points to the specific fact that no accidental norm can intervene in any substantial norm. The substances of Islam are *islām-i ʿaqīdatī* (belief Islam) and the accidentals of Islam are *islām-i tārīkhī* (historical Islam). In the context of belief, Muslims are therefore submitted to the substances (of religion). While *dīn-shināsī* (religious studies) is the undertaking of distinguishing the substances from the accidentals, juristic *ijtihād* is the *tarjumah-yi farhangī* (cultural translation) of the accidentals (of religion) (Surūsh 1999a:81-82).

While the 'substances' are constant and remain the same, the 'accidentals' are, in other words, subjected to constant alteration. But since there is no

verification is not to be identified with the concept of logical certification or proof. "What we rightly seek, when we desire the verification of a factual proposition, is not a demonstration of the logical impossibility of the proposition being false (for this would be a self-contradictory demand), but such kind and degree of evidence as suffices, in the type of case in question, to exclude rational doubt".

[42] Cf. Surūsh 1997a:159 and 1999g:8.

consensus as to where the line is to be drawn between the two entities, Surūsh argues that the criterion must be scientific. It must follow Surūsh's definition of falsification.[43] In his view, prophet-hood is the principal substance of Islam followed by the *maqāṣid-i sharīʿat* (objectives of Islamic law), and among the main objectives of *sharīʿat* he mentions religious belief and ethics, maintenance of religion, reason, life, descent and property (ibid.:80). Surūsh does not discuss the original intention of God in revealing the law in order to protect the interests of man but instead refers to traditional Sunni sources on the subject, such as Abū Isḥāq al-Shāṭibī and al-Ghazālī.[44] In contrast, Arabic language, Arabic culture, *asbāb al-nuzūl*, traditional legal theory, positive *sharʿī* law, and the like, which are contingent on specific historical, geographical or social contexts, form part of the category of accidentals:

> The first accidental characteristic of the Islamic religion is the Arabic language in the sense that any other language can acquire its position. The second accidental is Arabic culture. The third accidental is those propositions, corroborations, theories and understandings that are made used of by the *shāriʿ* (Lawgiver). The fourth accidental is the historical events that have made their way into revelation and *sunnat*. The fifth accidental is comprised of the questions and answers of the believers and disbelievers. The sixth accidental is the norms of *fiqh* and religious laws. The seventh accidental is the forgeries, attitudes and alterations that the disbelievers have formulated regarding religion. The eighth accidental is the capability and ability of religious preachers. To conclude, Islam (similar to any other religion) is after all Islam due to its substances, not its accidentals. A Muslim is someone who is responsible for and believes in the substances (ibid.:29-30).[45]

Surūsh is especially critical of the tendency at the *ḥauzahs* in Iran to only consider scientific works in Arabic as serious scholarship. He asserts that in the same manner that Persian tests its strength for carrying the load of modern sciences, it must also be retooled to expand the disciplines of the

[43] But Surūsh's position on the theory of falsification is ambigious, since he argues in favour of deconstruction as a superior model for presenting the distinctive characteristics of religion in the context of our historical situation, i.e. postmodernity. Cf. chapter VII.

[44] In contrast to Surūsh's (1996c:188) epistemological studies, in particular *Qabḍ wa basṭ-i tiʾūrīk-i sharīʿat*, where the term *sharīʿat* is employed to denote the divine commandment in its most general sense and to connote a number of disciplines exemplified by their religious content (*fiqh*, *ʿilm-i kalām*, *akhlāq* and *ʿirfān*), this term is used in its more strict context, signifying the body of Islamic law in his writings on overtly legal topics. It should be noted that Surūsh (1999i:18) furthermore considers the right to life and honour as a natural right independent of religion.

[45] While Surūsh (1999a:71) does not separate the different Qur'anic rulings into accidentals and substances, he argues that not all legal rulings are contingent on historical and geographical circumstances, but considers, for instance, the question of inequality between the sexes as well as the penal legal injunctions of the Qur'an as accidental features of Islam. But his position seems to to be ambivalent, since he argues in another discussion on the discrimination of non-Muslims and women and slaves in Islamic law that the complete structure of *fiqh* and not only certain details are accidental to Islam. "In general terms, the entire Islamic legal system is part of the accidentals of religion" (Surūsh 1999g:6).

ḥauzah (Surūsh 1996a:35). Arguing that 99 percent of Muslim positive law (including many Qur'anic rulings) is indebted to precedent in pre-Islamic *ʿurfī* legal patterns, he also believes that the Prophet would accept the major contents of the contemporary modern legal systems if he had been alive today (Surūsh 1999g:6). Surūsh's view on the non-integral character of Arabic language in Islam and his assertion that *asbāb al-nuzūl*, in terms of historical circumstances and events, is a coincidental and even perverting characteristic that has made its way into revelation and *ḥadīṯ* are unsurprisingly highly sensitive matters.[46]

Surūsh's purpose with in distinguishing between substances and accidentals of the religious phenomenon is to facilitate a radical transformation of traditional jurisprudence and theology which remains faithful to the religious spirit. When all the accidental features of Islam connected to Arabic culture and language are eventually abandoned, it will be possible to transform the cultural comprehension of Islam while still maintaining the spirit of the 'substances' of religion. He believes that the distinction between 'substances' and 'accidentals' solves a number of problems related to Islamic unity, of which the most important is related to the question of *ikhtilāf* in Islamic law or to the topic of customary features of Islamic culture (Surūsh 1997a:4-5). On the question of Muslim sectarianism, Surūsh (1999d:67) considers the two mainstream positions, Shi'i and Sunni Islam, as historical accidents that have reached their mature status. Sectarian distinctions are therefore no longer relevant and Islam is beyond this age-old conflict:

> We must accept that Shi'i and Sunni Islam constituted two possible responses to the preaching of the Prophet of Islam. They are two necessary historical expansions of Islam and not the product of a conspiration of the one or the other side. They are, so to say, two theological schools that have reached their finality, and have become frozen in their respectively ideological and historical forms.

Inspired by two Sufi masters of the Persian language, Rūmī and Shabistarī, Surūsh approaches religion from the angle of theosophy. He acknowledges that every religion has three categories or sources of cognition that represent three levels of truth which correspond to the Sufi distinction of *sharīʿat*, *ṭarīqat* and *ḥaqīqat*.[47] Referring to the *Maṯnawī-yi maʿnawī* of Rūmī, he concludes that the basic form of religiosity is *taqlīd* (emulation), which contrasts the higher forms of religious comprehension, which he believes are *ʿirfān*, the most supreme form of religious devotion, followed by theological-

[46] Cf. 1999a:29. The American Muslim scholar Hamid Algar is among those who have criticised Surūsh's idea that the Arabic language is accidental to Islam. The conflict between Algar, who is a well-known exponent of Khumainī's doctrine *wilāyat-i faqīh* (The Authority of the jurist), and Surūsh was one of the motives behind the trial against the editorial director of *Kiyān* journal in November 1996.

[47] As Surūsh (1998a:5) elucidates, this distinction is based on a *ḥadīṯ* report saying that "*al-sharīʿah* is my word, *al-ṭarīqah* is my action, and *al-ḥaqīqah* is my state".

philosophical thought (Surūsh 1999a:32, 171).[48] But despite his affection for Rūmī and the Persian Sufi literary tradition, he is, similar to Islamic modernists such as Bāzargān and Sharīʿatī, highly critical of the social structure of the Sufi orders, as exemplified in the relationship between master and disciple, which he believes promotes anti-intellectualism, homosexuality, immoral passivism, and so on. He suggests that *fiqh* with its more dynamic and worldly character, is better situated than *taṣawwuf* (Sufism) to help Islam adjust to the modern situation (Surūsh 1996a:347-348). Yet in another essay, he concludes that neither *fiqh* nor Sufism are major relevant issues of importance in modern Islam compared to questions of contemporary philosophy and anthropology concerning, for instance, the status of universal reason or the necessity of an Islamic identity in the era of postmodernity (Surūsh 1999e:11).

Claiming the unity of the soul-body relation, Surūsh proceeds to consider the purpose of religion as pertaining both to this world and the hereafter. Although Islam sets life towards an otherwordly goal, he believes that religion should avoid what he refers to as "Sufi other-worldliness". In this respect, he criticises the modern phenomenon of Islamic ideology by arguing that ideology secularises religion in the sense that it transforms it into a substitute for pure worldly interests:

> *Dīn-i dunyawī* (worldy religion) is, in exact words, the kind of religion that in reality considers the world as its master and sovereign, and becomes a servant of the world. This is the kind of religion that we refer to as 'secular religion' and it is world-struck and immanentist. In its own view, secular religion is true because it goes well with the world and since it goes well with the world, it is true. When we claim that religion cannot become ideology, it is precisely this kind of religion we have in mind. Ideology is a worldy manifestation and religion is not a worldy manifestation (even if it is not the enemy of the world) (Surūsh 1997a:168).[49]

For Surūsh, the world is, in other words, of worth only if it is for the benefit of the hereafter, and he keeps a careful eye on the kind of idealisms that he believes could create disharmony between the *dunyā* (temporal world) and the *ākhirat* (hereafter). Among these idealisms, he mentions the utopia of the modern nation-state, which only recognises itself as the sole legal authority,

[48] Surūsh (1999p) also refers to the Sufi classification of the religious phenomena into *maghz wa qashr* (brain and shell) in order to demonstrate that the inner dimension of religion is more precious than the external, and that the individual must pass from *fiqh* to truth. "*Fiqh* is the shell and exterior dimension of religion. It is only occupied with *taqlīdī* and exterior manners. The God of *fiqh* is someone who is asking the payment of what is due to human beings and nothing else. He is only concerned with terms such as vengeance, reward, prohibition and permission. There is hence no sign of love, sociableness or even ethics in *fiqh*. I do not suggest that *fiqh* is something evil but believe that it is disadvantageous to become absorbed by it and restrict oneself to its discourse. *Fiqh* must be transcended". Cf. Surūsh 1997a:6–12.

[49] Surūsh (1997a:190, 1996e:5, 11 and 1999a:168) also refers to the phenomenon of secular religion as 'protestantism', which he believes estimates religious salvation in terms of worldly success.

in contrast to *fiqh*, which does not acknowledge the law of the state as the supreme legally binding authority. In light of the strong impact of the idea of an Islamic state in post-revolutionary Iran and the attempt to spell out the interpretative process of Islamic law in positive terms as if *fiqh* constituted positive law, he suggests that the normative trend in Iran to maximalise *fiqh* very well may result in the true secularisation of religion. He argues that since secularisation is one of the major constraints of our historical condition, the traditional conceptions of *fiqh*, which conflict with secularisation, must reasonably be questioned at their very foundation as law becomes subject to substantial rationalisation:

> Firstly, we must acknowledge that *fiqh* basically remains a 'science of legal norms' in the sense that it cannot produce management. Secondly, such a maximalistic *fiqh* becomes in reality a substitute of rational, human and customary *maṣlaḥat-shināsī* ('skill of interest'). In this respect, it is not at variance with any of the current non-religious legal systems, since the solving of social issues and the rationalisation of existence is universal and in no need of being titled *fiqh*. So as to become 'maximalised', *fiqh* is deprived of its *fiqhī* and religious character... This is indeed one among the particular necessities of secularisation of religion in the modern period (Surūsh 1999a:92).

While this view of the term secularisation suggests that the relationship between religion and politics is much more complicated than merely separating or unifying them, Surūsh's definition of secularism is unmistakably more decisive in his essay on the sense and essence of secularism. There, he argues that the increasing *differentiation* of religion from other dimensions of human life in the modern world as a result of secularisation is a forgone conclusion.[50] While he makes an attempt to distinguish secularism as doctrine from secularisation as a process, the two are combined and moreover described as "'scientification" and "rationalisation of social and political thought and deliberation" (Surūsh 1997a:424).[51] In this sense, secularism has affinities with philosophical nominalism in its rejection of the existence of universals and constitutes a break from the 'presecular age', which is "marked by the hegemony of metaphysical thought in the political, economic and social realms" (ibid.:427). By asserting that modern scientific thought and rational management mean subjecting everything to critical and rational questioning, he argues that the meaning of secularism also signifies a political system in

[50] Influenced by Arthur Koestler's view of the most recent historical progress as differentiation of structure and integration of function, Surūsh (1994b:244) asserts that the contemporary situation of more differentiated parts demands the elaboration of co-ordination to create a well-balanced whole. In his discussion of the integration of traditional civilisations (which he stresses is a modern concept), he believes that modern Iranian culture is comprised of a pattern of relations between its different parts (i.e. the Iranian, Islamic and Western parts) and not by the sum of its parts.
[51] Cf. Surūsh 1999a:161–162.

the polity of which no values and rules are beyond human appraisal and verification. Secularism is hence *par excellence* the restriction of religious, in particular clerical, authority in the social and political sphere:

Naturally, when politics is desacralised (that is, when it becomes rational and scientific) while religion remains sacred, the two are separated. This is the meaning of and the reason for the separation of religion and state in secular societies. Like the separation of religion and science, this need not be an antagonistic breach. Religion is not identical to science, nor is it an offspring, an arbiter or a guide for it. Still less does it follow the objectives of science. At the same time, religion need not deny or oppose science. Everything that puts on the garb of science (be it government or management) enters a similar relationship with religion. Religious management or religious science is as inconceivable as religious thermodynamics or religious geometry. The truth is that politics can be mixed with religion only if a profane understanding of religion is juxtaposed with a profane method of administration. Otherwise, blending sacred religion with secular politics would be absurd (ibid.:429).

As religion has already lost its monopoly on the public conscience and morality in the modern world, Surūsh seems forced to believe that secularism is not opposed to religion but rather compatible with it. The separation between religion and science is, so to say, not necessarily an antagonistic breech. Human beings can remain spiritual and religious while enjoying the benefits of rational administration of their affairs. In his own words, secularism is not equal to the rejection of religion, but is, rather, 'non-religion' since it "pays no attention to religion in worldly matters and establishes social institutions and organisations without concern for religious values" (ibid.:407). But insofar as the processes of secularisation are not so explicit and identifiable and secularism posits a modern *Weltanshchauung* distinguished by its rational and scientific epistemology, which is averse to metaphysics, his idea that the private sphere of human existence can be hermetically sealed off from these procedures is problematical. This is particularly the case in our postmodern condition, where the communicative instruments of the modern nation-state and the multi-national corporations and pleasure industries penetrate deep into the farthest spots of the private sphere of human existence in order to control and shape personal self-images. In this respect, it may be discussed whether private life really is left free from the processes of secularisation.

Surūsh acknowledges, however, that non-religion is the embryo of secularisation and he believes that man, as an existential being, is dependent on religion for his spiritual nourishment and growth. Religion has, in other words, a contructive role to play in human life as far as it is concerned with the individual sphere and directed towards the hereafter. As Islam, therefore, is no appropriate instrument for science, governance or management, he asserts that his own intellectual objective essentially is to 'humanise' religion in order to save Islam from the misbehaviour of man:

To begin with, it is appropriate to let you know of a recent dialogue I had with one of my friends. With unsmiling contempt, he asked me, 'What is your view of the islamisation of science?' And then he went on ridiculing, 'In my opinion, you stress the scientification of Islam'. I answered him, 'I stress the humanisation of religion'. Indeed, to humanise religion is the precise and original underpinning that the whole structure of the theory of contraction and expansion of Islamic law rests on (Surūsh 1999a:318).

Surūsh's definition of religion in the more strict sense therefore presupposes an epistemological 'subjectivisation of religion' in the sense that theology no longer is aimed at providing rational proofs for religious truths and that faith is a matter of the individual. It is obvious that herein lies the seeds of a type of 'interiorising' of religion that breaks with the ethical-legal and theological ideal of traditional Islam. It instead has affinities with *ʿirfān* in its reliance on the contemplative and intuitive knowledge of the self. While Surūsh's (ibid.:319) definition of faith does not consider faith as a category of knowledge, he argues, similar to the gnostic teaching of inner experience and self-realisation, that "faith is the exclusive experience and private property of the individual" and that "while there may be collective rituals, there are no collective faiths".

In his defence of secularism and confidence in the separation of science and religion as well as politics and religion, Surūsh seems to be primarily concerned with saving religion from politics in contrast to the process of secularisation as it developed in Europe, where secularism was launched to save politics from religion. As far as secularism in his view is also a movement away from otherworldliness to life on earth, it also exhibits a form of humanism in terms of its interest in the possibilities of a fulfilment of human cultural achievements in this world. Claiming the hegemony of modern scientific knowledge in a way that allows for no exceptions or compromises, it is not a coincidence that his major opponents are not to be found amongst the secular intelligentsia, but among the proponents of Islamic ideology and the advocates of an Islamic state in Iran. By considering ideology primarily as a systematic cognitive and epistemological question rather than a question of social and historical pertinence, Surūsh uses in fact the falsification method in rejecting the pseudo-religious claims of Islamic ideology (i.e. religious ideas, not faith). In addition, similar to Popper, he negates the pseudo-scientific claims of Marxism as a distorted and falsified representation of a presupposed reality. Essentially, Surūsh (1996a:82) identifies ideology as the 'systematic error of reason' or *dugmātīsm-i niqābdār* (veiled dogmatism) in the sense that it suppresses reason by mixing proofs and causes in scientific knowledge when deriving its so-called 'truths' from non-provable propositions about man, science and history:

From what has been said, we may therefore determine the circle or the contents of ideology. The circle or contents of ideology consist of unproven false ideas or non-provable ideas. Non-provable ideas are of two sorts: Values or non-values. The former is made of antinomy norms and propositions or non-falsifiable propositions. (From this we understand why Marx considered theology and metaphysics as parts of ideology. Certainly, he observed that their contents are non-provable).[52]

Surūsh's disapproving criticism of Islamic ideology, as it is articulated in *Farbihtar az īdiʾūlūzhī* (Loftier than ideology), is more focused on other aspects of the relationship between religion and ideology, namely those pertaining to the nature of religion itself rather than the religious ideas. While religious ideas, similar to all other human thought, are subjected to the process of falsification, he asserts that the attempt to transform religion into ideology is bound to fall short because religion lacks a definite method of interpretation of the revealed sources and because the religious interpretations themselves never can be enclosed within the ideological system. In Surūsh's (ibid.:122) words, to ideologise religion is "to reduce the eternal, the ocean of attributes, the mystery, the radiance and ability of religion by transforming it into a shallow and low-grounded basin of no use while at the same time making universal claims".[53]

By stressing the spiritual and ethical character of religion, it is not unsurprising that Surūsh's exposition on the topic of *iḥyā* (revival) of Islamic law does not combine the love of tradition as well as innovation, which is characteristic of other Islamic revivalist writings, but rather generally defines the question of *fiqh* and jurisprudence in purely negative terms. In this respect, he asserts that the present revival of Islam differs from previous historical attempts to revive religion, which essentially were aimed at purifying religious teachings from philosophy and therefore failed to confront modernity's challenge to *fiqh*, which dominates Islamic thought. By requesting a methodologically more contemporary and constructive model of religious interpretation which is also epistemologically up-to-date, Surūsh (1994b:372) also disapproves of the connotation of returning to the first principles of Islam. In his view, this theme, in its idealist purism and in its opposition to Greek thought, was omnipresent in the works of early Islamic modernists, such as Muḥammad ʿAbduh and Rashīd Riḍā and their attempt to return to "the golden age of early Islam".

While Surūsh recognises the pioneering contribution of Bāzargān to Islamic revivalism in Iran and considers him the first modern Shi'i thinker, who also considered the discord of traditional *fiqh* with modern interpretations of Islam, he regrets that Bāzargān did not draw any further conclusions from his abundant use of modern science. Surūsh (1996c:50, 1994b:371, 389) argues that the same is also true of Sharīʿatī, "the champion

[52] Cf. Surūsh 1994a:27.
[53] Cf. Surūsh 1996:125–134.

of Protestant Islam" and "the founder of religious sociology in Iran", even if he went a little bit further by asserting that *fiqh* discusses the problems at hand but has no answer to them. While Surūsh in particular discusses Sharīʿatī's thought extensively, he never identifies himself with him or any other Islamic modernist, but rather presents a critique of their ideas by acclaiming the necessity of a purely scientific philosophical foundation.[54] Criticising the general juxtaposition of contemporary issues on religious texts, Surūsh (1996c:49) argues that the mistake commited by the revivalists of the twentieth century was to expect to find answers to specific scientific and technological issues in them. More responsive to practical social needs than to the intrinsic logic and cardinal pillars of modern philosophy, they expected Islam to have the answer to all human situations and problems, economic, moral, governmental or legal. Furthermore, they blamed the scientific and cultural stagnation on the Muslims' lack of faith, while in Surūsh's view, the relation was the opposite: Stagnation produced static interpretations of religion among Muslims that displayed a trend in Islamic scholarship away from openness and pluralism towards greater theological rigidity and defensive apologetics. Referring to the ideas of the British historian Arnold Toynbee, he maintains that stagnation occurs when a civilisation is not capable of answering the new challenges that it encounters, as he believes has been remarkably well illustrated in the context of Islam's encounter with modernity and the Muslims' lack of discernment of its contest to Islam:

> The efforts of our contemporary revivalists are devoted to the safe conduct of religion through the perilous path of the temporal world and to bestowing proper meaning and relevance upon it in an increasingly turbulent secular world. While utter submission to change and revival leaves no permanance and no religion worthy of the name, insistence on permanence and dogmatic resistance to change render religious life in the modern world impossible… Among Muslims, some superficial observers, incapable as they are of understanding the rhyme and reason of the modern world, ignorant of the nature, the geography and the geometry of religion, the history of religious culture and the interchanges and struggles of religious thought with other ideas, assumed that religion could be rejuvenated through cosmetic changes. They incorrectly attempt to extricate modern scientific insights from the bowels of ancient texts, boasting of the predictions of religion with respect to such phenomena as microbes, airplanes, electricity, vitamins, and the like. (ibid.:49).[55]

Since modern Islam as a whole has been subjugated to the historical

[54] In this respect, Surūsh (1994b:384) is most of all appreciative of Muḥammad Iqbāl, whom he regards as the first modern Muslim that took a serious step out of tradition in his effort to revive *ijtihād* within the fabric of the modern state. In order to rebuild the law of *sharīʿat* in light of modern thought and experience, Iqbāl (1984:46) supported the innovative use of *ijtihād al-muṭlaq* that he described as "the principle of movement in the structure of Islam".
[55] Cf. Surūsh 1997a:112.

situation of modernity without having any conclusive answer to offer, Surūsh believes that Shi'i Muslims in particular have been deceived by their "self-preening pride" of possessing a treasure such as *ijtihād*, which they believed the Sunnis did not possess. As far from all intellectual and socio-economical transformations in modernity are summoned up in legal transformations, he claims that Shi'i as well as Sunni Muslims have been and still are equally incapable of solving their own predicaments by means of *fiqh* or traditional definitions of *ijtihād*: "Why are the Shi'i and non-Shi'i communities grappling with identical problems, equally incapable of solving their own problems? Who says furthermore that all problems are juristic, so to that some form of *ijtihād* can resolve them?" (ibid.:49). He also maintains that the previous attempts to revive Islamic law were unsuccesful because of a subtle, but crucial, epistemological blunder, that is, modern Islam requires a new scientific theory so as to account for matters of epistemology and to reconcile permanance and change and to revive *ijtihād*. In this respect, he believes that Islamic revivalists did and still do not as much pose the wrong questions as they lack an adequate and functional theory of analysis for arriving at ample answers:

Reconciling eternity and temporality, the sacred and the profane; separating constant and variant, form and substance; reviving innovative *ijtihād*; finding courageous jurists; reinvigorating *fiqh*; changing the appearance while preserving the spirit of religion; acquainting Islam with the modern world; establishing modern Islamic theology: these have been goals of the religious revivalists, but they require a *naẓarīyah-yi maʿrifat-shinākhtī* (epistemological theory) that is absent in revivalist literature. The theory of contraction and expansion of religious knowledge humbly proposes such a theory. The missing link in the endeavors of the revivalists and the reformers of the past is the distinction between religion and religious knowledge (ibid.:51-52).[56]

In the view of Surūsh (ibid.:260), the lack of reliable scientific theories from an early date created obstacles to the emergence of an Islamic intellectual renaissance and also assured a general stagnation of Islamic scholarship in a number of scientific disciplines, such as history writing. He presumes in fact that it is only after the experience of the Islamic revolution in Iran that the study of Islam acquired a scientific character among Muslims as "religion entered the societal scene, came out of its potential and theoretical dimension, proceeded to execute supervisory plans of economical and social affairs, created expectations, agreed to the area of negotiation and acquired a practical form…" (Surūsh 1999a:85). In contrast to the philosophical idealism and utopian thought that dominated Islamic discourse before the revolution, he argues that contemporary Islamic thought to a much larger extent has been scrutinised and tested through the prisms of modern science. This made a practical materialisation of Islam possible in pragmatic terms.

[56] Cf. Surūsh 1996c:278–279.

He believes therefore that the Iranian Muslim conscience at the present is prepared to accept innovative inquiries into the matrix of religious faith and knowledge:

Before the Islamic revolution in Iran, the religious intellectuals and the *ʿulamā* were in opposition to a secular and un-Islamic state. Not until Islam became a dominating and powerful force in politics and society were they forced to tackle practical issues and ponder a whole range of issues related to modernity, such as historicity, hermeneutics, positivism, liberalism, structuralism and religious pluralism. Everybody, not least of all the *ʿulamā* themselves, is familiar with these concepts today. The rise of an Islamic state and twenty years of experience of an Islamic government has therefore opened new possibilities for serious intellectual exchange and dialogue. I am optimistic about the future (Surūsh 1999k).

F. Jurisprudence

By suggesting that far from all of society's problems are jurisprudential and that far from all intellectual concerns are legal, the core idea of Surūsh's standpoint on Islamic law is that the conception of *fiqh* as an all-encompassing system or way of life is incorrect and therefore must be amended. In general terms, his effort is essentially to stake out a scientific model for the study of Islamic law according to which jurisprudence, similar to religion, is complete only in the *ḥadd-i aqallī* (minimalist) sense. He argues that jurisprudence must be transcended and that the function of human reason is to improve the human comprehension of religion rather than to assist religion in order to make it complete:

The incorrect conception that religion and *fiqh* are all-encompassing must be amended. This conception is beneficial neither to religion nor to *fiqh*. One must not imagine that the all-embracing nature of religion means that religion has raised and solved every problem. Religion is *kāmil* (complete), but it is not *jāmiʿ* (comprehensive) and there is a difference between completeness and comprehensiveness (Surūsh 1997a:256).

Surūsh (1996c:191) suggests that new theoretical as well as methodological foundations are available for a transformed Islamic law that will be appropriate for modern times. But these new frame-works and sources are not within *sharīʿat* itself, since *fiqh* in its traditional form is considered to be a *mutawarrim* ('swollen') science, characterised by a normative theoretical closure. By distinguishing jurisprudence from philosophy, ethics, anthropology and theosophy, all of which are supposed to have a rational and analytical character, Surūsh's (1996a:6) point of departure is in essence negative to the subject of law. He characterises jurisprudence as an irrational science in the sense that it is based on *taqlīd* rather than rational reasoning and also discourages the free inspection of human reason:

The Islam of philosophy, theosophy and anthropology accept questioning, since they operate at the level of *taḥqīq* (research). By approving inquiry, these sciences do not force *taqlīd* upon the individual. The Islam of *fiqh* takes no account of questioning, since it works at the level of *taqlīd*. Indeed, it accepts no function whatsoever for rational inspection and irrespective of the current theory of *ijtihād* and *taqlīd*, it insists that the duty of the individual lay-man is to conduct *taqlīd* and to regard the word of the jurist as *ḥujjat-i taʿabbudī* (unquestionable proof).

By suggesting that the traditional formulation of *fiqh* is irrelevant in the historical condition of modernity, Surūsh is not genuinely interested in the attempt to revive the traditional legal theory by means of referring to its assumed novel and neglected aspects (such as those regarding the status of women or non-Muslim minorities) in the traditional legal texts. He asserts in fact that all talk about "unadulterated legal texts and sources" is meaningless, since no one asks why these data were not used of before or which philosophical world-view that is embodied in these texts (Surūsh 1996c:389). He is at variance with the efforts of Islamic modernists to modify the traditional legal theory as long as it accepts the traditional prepostulations about faith, knowledge and certainty. He raises objections against the method envisaged by Islamic modernists of, for instance, identifying European definitions of democracy in traditional Islamic concepts such as *shūrā* or *bayʿat* (allegiance), since these concepts mystify the elemental meaning of rational thought and management, which is the very lifeblood of the democratic social system. He considers this method to be a disguised form of 'ideologisation' of religion in the sense that the traditional terminology acquires a political function, which is opposed to the democratic concept of man as endowed with natural rights:

The combination of religion and democracy is a meta-religious artifice that has at least some extra-religious epistemological dimensions. The exclusive reliance on the religious laws and myopic focus on intra-religious *ijtihād* of the jurist in order to confirm or reject democratic religiosity is hence illconsidered and unsound (Surūsh 1997a:301).[57]

In this respect, Surūsh (1999a:364) moreover believes that traditional principles of *fiqh*, such as *istiṣlāḥ* or *maṣlaḥat*, have an accurate function in their own methodological context, but cannot contribute to anything but artificial legal change. In other words, *istiṣlāḥ* cannot serve as a new basis for modern *fiqh*, since its role is restricted to the theoretical and incalculable arguments of traditional *fiqh* that are inappropriate for a modern judiciary

[57] Cf. Surūsh 1996c:33, 268 and 1999c:74–75. With the staying influence of traditional jurisprudence in contemporary Iran in mind, Surūsh (1995a:6) believes that even if democracy is not available to all in practice, since it requires a certain level of socio-political development, it is desirable for all. "It requires a certain level of normative, political, and governmental development that is contingent upon economic development. Only those who have forged new human relationships among themselves will take democracy seriously and demand it earnestly".

system, which demands efficient and calculable management. While Surūsh (1999i:18) considers Khumainī's reliance on *istiṣlāḥ* as commendable, he finds it exceptionally out of date in the context of present-day Iranian society:

The modern world is not the place for new *furūᶜ*, but the place for new *uṣūl*. The jurists will be unable to give useful solutions (to issues of contemporary society) as long as they only consider matters of *furūᶜ*. It is correct and acceptable that some authors acknowledge the approval of the concept of *maṣlaḥat*, in particular as formulated by *imām* Khumainī, as an integral part of Shi'i *fiqh* and a great achievement, but there is a difference between accepting that *fiqh* is contingent on interest, discovering a new interest, establishing a modern *fiqh* or jurisprudence, considering *fiqh* as dependent on the (traditional) *uṣūl* on the one hand and to discover new presuppositions and foundations in order to construct a modern jurisprudence on the other. To neglect interest results in dry legalism and to overemphasise it ends up in disorderly pragmatism. The solution to the problem is to consider the sources and foundations, in particular the theological, anthropological and sociological ones. Don't we have to try to find out what comes after 'the period of interest', since modern society demands more than practical needs and requirements?

In his criticism of traditional *fiqh*, Surūsh argues that an elementary criterion of contemporary scientific epistemology is that there are no legal norms that are sacred, eternal or beyond human error. In contrast to the traditional classification of *furūᶜ-i fiqh* into the categories of *ᶜibādat* (worship) and *muᶜāmalāt* (social transactions) norms, according to which only non-Qur'anic rulings of the latter category are considered to be subjected to probability, he argues that all legal norms are speculative and contextual, since the scientific method itself is always context-dependent and connected to a specific historical and geographical context. While he acknowledges that legal norms connected to the *ᶜibādat* category in general are governed by their exclusive benefit in the hereafter and that the *muᶜāmalāt* norms are intended for defining social human relations in strict positive terms, he argues that this division is no longer relevant. In contrast to the traditional legal theory that considers this typology in the light of a deontology obliging the Muslim to act in conformity with the divine command, Surūsh (1999f:31-32) suggests that these categories, and in particular the latter, are limited to the historical circumstances that prevailed in seventh century Arabia:

Some jurists have always been inclined to give methodology a static and eternal attribute and to reject methodological variation as objectionable. They consider the *muᶜāmalāt* norms, similar to the *ᶜibādī* norms, as unalterable and possessors of a concealed [divine] rationale... Indeed, there exists no method that is absolute or most correct. Method is always context-dependent, that is contingent on the locality of human beings and the environment, situation and condition of where it is carried out. [...] Another aspect of social and religious norms is that these laws (as Shāh

Walīullāh Dihlawī highlights) are essentially connected to the period of the Prophet and his followers [in Arabia], since the propagation [of Islam] in other epochs and to other locations prompts in favour of new proofs. Of course, the jurists' [epistemological] foundation disagrees with this viewpoint since it has as its starting point that these laws eternally apply to any epoch.

By considering the traditional content-based distinction of the applicable branches of *fiqh* as out of place today, Surūsh prefers dividing Islamic law into chronological periods as regards the socio-political nature of the norms themselves. In this respect, he distinguishes the *ta'sīs* (formative) and founding period of law, restricted to the lifetime of the Prophet and "characterised by revolution and ground-breaking management", from the post-prophetic *istiqrār* (settlement) period that is typified by the interpretative effort to discover practical answers to legal problems. In contrast to the majority of Islamic traditionalists as well as modernists, who construct a diachronic perspective on Islam with the Medinian society as its model, Surūsh argues that the norms related to the later periods of Islamic law rather than those attributed to the Prophet and the Qur'anic revelation are of benefit to modern Muslim legal occupation, since contemporary man, as an historical being, is a product of some historical hermeneutical attempts of interpreting revelation rather than the particular religious idealism of early Islam. In his view, contemporary *ijtihād* has, in other words, nothing to benefit from appreciating legal norms associated with or contained in the Qur'anic revelation:

During its history, Islam has experienced two periods of significance: The period of *ta'sīs* and the period of *istiqrār*. Don't we have to distinguish those legal norms that belong to the period of *ta'sīs*, which were appropriate for that period from the norms connected to the period of *istiqrār*? May we not in this case suggest that all the norms that speak about unbelievers and apostates (such as the inequality of their rights as compared to those of Muslims and the permissibility to kill an apostate etc.), belong to the period of *ta'sīs* (i.e. the ground-breaking period of new management and turbulent conditions) and that *ijtihād* actually search for an alternative judgment in the period of *istiqrār*? Won't our *fiqhī* norms simply go through considerable transformations when we reconsider the *shar'ī* norms from this direction? (Surūsh 1999i:20)

By suggesting that the traditional definition of *fiqh* as a science of inferring legal norms through syllogism has reached a theoretical closure, Surūsh argues that Islamic law, similar to any other premodern legal system, is obliged to adjust itself to a modern philosophy of law if it is going to generate any effective force and positive practicability in the contemporary world. Similar to Muḥammad Iqbāl, who proposed the integration of *ijtihād* into the legislative power of the modern state, Surūsh asserts that *fiqh* at the outset has to be considered as a code of law, that is, codified regulation in line with positivist claims. While *fiqh* differs from secular legal systems by its religious content, it should, so to say, acquire the same function and coordination as that of any other modern legal system and be considered as the enforcement of a body of rules through a controlling human authority. In this respect, Surūsh's pragmatic conception of Islamic law as made by the society comes very close to the key ideas of legal positivism (whether in its modern Hartian or Kelsenian variations) that laws are laws by virtue of their form rather than of their religious or moral content and that legal systems are sets of rules (interpreted in a broad sense) applied by the judiciary as part of societal regulation by states:

I do not think that anyone familiar with the nature of law and religious jurisprudence will need to think very long before confirming what is being said here. Religious jurisprudence is a religious version of *ḥuqūq* ('a legal code'); in exactly the same way that, outside the religious sphere and in non-religious societies, too, there is *niẓām-i ḥuqūqī* ('legal system') for dealing with material questions and for settling of disputes. In religious societies and within the framework of the religious system in our country, we have religious jurisprudence instead of human and secular codes–and it has exactly the same principal function. Both law and religious jurisprudence are there to solve legal problems (Surūsh 1997a:253-254).[58]

The comprehension of religious law as a legal system in the modern sense also certainly explains why Surūsh (1999a:36) by and large downgrades the overall sacred character of religious law and, for instance, suggests that some religions, such as Buddhism, Hinduism and Christianity, lack any sort of legal dimension at all. Having defined *fiqh* as a code of law in the modern sense of the word, he at the same time proceeds to claim that the term *fiqh* from an etymological point of view is connected to *tafaqquh* (understanding) and therefore, at least in ideal terms, exhibits an unexpected hermeneutical openness. "As long as there is understanding, there is *fiqh* and as long as there is continuous understanding of *sharīʿat*, there is religious belief" (Surūsh 1996c:186). By considering the hermeneutical aspect of *fiqh*, he asserts that the application of the term in the early history of Islam was related to this general meaning rather than to its strict legal meaning of

[58] Similar to Surūsh, Muḥammad Iqbāl (1984:159–160) more or less considered *sharīʿat* as a set of identifiable rules independent of traditional methodology and institutions. "I know the Ulema of Islam claim finality for the popular schools of Mohammedan Law... but since things have changed and the world of Islam is to-day confronted and affected by new forces set free by the extraordinary development of human thought in its all directions, I see no reason why this attitude should be maintained any longer... The claim of the present generation of Muslim liberals to reinterpret the foundational legal principles, in the light of their own experience and the altered conditions of modern life is, in my opinion, perfectly justified". Iqbal's deliberate use of *ijtihād* was aimed at justifying results, regardless of whether the norms were based on traditional *fiqhī* criteria or not. He claimed that Islam espouses formal democracy by means of *ijmāʾ* in order to transfer the authority of interpretation from the *ʿulamā* to the Muslim legislative assembly. While Surūsh (1997a:305) basically has a instrumentalist notion of democracy, defined as a method of accountability for "rationalising politics", he refutes Iqbāl's identification of democracy in traditional Islamic concepts since they conflict with the unique value-system of democracy.

inferring norms regarding what is *ḥarām* (forbidden) and what is *ḥalāl* (lawful) (Surūsh 1996d:403).[59] In its essentials, he characterises *fiqh* as the sum or collection of all human hermeneutical judgments on Islamic law which are embodied in various legal schools and developments:

> For instance, the rise of the *akhbārī* sect and the disputes between the *uṣūlī* and *akhbārī* and the *arāyish-i adillah* (refinement of corroboration) of both sides as well as the subsequent *uṣūlī* victory over the *akhbārī*, and so on, are altogether the one and same science of *fiqh*. Comparable to theology, exegesis and any other human science, *fiqh* is a science of gradual accomplishment. There is therefore no such thing as the potential final opinion and last judgement in this science (Surūsh 1996c:203).[60]

Evidently, Surūsh's definitions of the concept of *fiqh* as a code of law as well as a science of jurisprudence subjected to the theories and processes of hermeneutics have its dilemmas. How is, for instance, a legal system narrowly structured in a legal code to be projected into a constant process of interpretation? In contrast to the traditional jurists who considered science, whether it be *fiqh* or any other discipline, as essentially consisting of subjects and topics, Surūsh views the scientific endeavour as an epistemological one, based on the theories of modern science and a modern theory of knowledge. By considering science as an entirely independent area of knowledge that is separate from any broader spiritual context, he also creates a strict dichotomy between science and religion that elevates secular values of science to a superior standing over religion. As will be noted, this perspective is problematical, since science surely is a series of normative truths and theories that operates in accordance with its own rules and because it divorces God from creation, the very creation that in Surūsh's view was brought into existence by God.

In Surūsh's view, the study of Islamic law is not *faqīhānah* (juristic) in terms of involving justification, but rather *maʿrifat-shināsānah* (epistemological) and descriptive in character. Aiming at depicting certain features of Islamic law and whether these should count as instances of knowledge (based on the falsification theory), he therefore considers *fiqh* as a hermeneutical process of understanding that is *bilā mauḍūʿ* ('having no subject') and is contingent on the frameworks and questions posed by the modern sciences (anthropology, sociology, natural science, etc.) (ibid.:261).

[59] Surūsh (1996b:5) argues that despite the fact that philosophy and theology largely were looked at with suspicion in traditional Islam, one should not draw the erroneous conclusion that *fiqh* was the crown of traditional Islamic science, since the importance given to jurisprudence was not secured in the curriculum of the *ḥauzah* until two hundred years ago. As the influence of *fiqh* increased in modern times at the expense of the rational sciences, individual scholars also largely neglected philosophy. He suggests that Muḥammad Ḥusain Ṭabāṭabāʾī and Murtaḍā Muṭahharī were extra-ordinary exceptions to this rule and that their interest in philosophy moreover prevented in particular the former from being recognised as *marjaʿ*.

[60] Cf. Surūsh 1996c:242.

By comparing *fiqh* to a modern secular legal system and also by asserting that Islamic law is contingent on the scientific theories, subjects and questions that are generated within the profane modern sciences, he leaves behind what comprises the most important characteristic of traditional *sharīʿat* as distinct from modern Western law, namely the idea that the determination as well as the result of law is the expression of the divine commandment. Surūsh's discourse and its major postulate that knowledge evolves from experience of the mind, abandons and renders meaningless the traditional belief that Islamic law not only regulates man's relationship with his neighbours or the state but also his relationship with God.

Surūsh's comprehension of *sharīʿat* as a code of law can primarily be explained by the increased identification of Islamic law as positive legality after the emergence of a strong centralised state structure during the Pahlawī dynasty and its sustenance in the Islamic republic. While the formally independent *ʿulamā* objected to the political reforms that stripped the determination of law from their hands and placed it with state authorities, the insistence of the modernising process on the value of the concrete cases, as opposed to the abstract thinking of law, resulted in the increased comprehension of *sharīʿat* as meaning law in the narrow sense that has generated its use as a symbol of legality.[61] In the constitution of the Islamic republic, the degree to which the *sharīʿat* is seen as prevailing is less connected to the traditional legal theories and institutions as it is to the degree to which the law of the modern state conforms to its norms. Islamic law is enforced as the first source of Iranian law (the other two being constitutional law and secular legislation), but there has been no distinction to separate *sharʿī* law from the *ʿurfī* legal tradition in practice even if all former laws contrary to *sharīʿat* were 'repealed' by the legal authorities. From traditionally having been a theoretical law elaborated by the *fuqahā*, *sharīʿat* became, in other words, transformed into *aḥkām-i ḥukūmatī* (governmental rulings) of the state and as indicated by Articles 2 and 163 of the Constitution. At the present, the Shi'i jurists are consequently more properly involved in lawmaking.[62]

[61] During the Pahlawī dynasty, from 1926 to 1939, the *mujtahids* gradually lost their influence in the legal sphere when the *sharʿī* courts ceased to exist, as opposed to the duality of the earlier legal system as endorsed in the Supplementary law of 1907 and the first civil code of 1911. Despite its modern form and organisation, the persistence of the traditional idea of the judiciary decelerated the speed of the implementation of the new civil code even when the *sharʿī* courts were formally subordinate to the state. More crucially, a law of 1936 required all judges to hold a degree from the Tehran faculty of law that created an alternative to the traditional education. For the first time since pre-Ṣafawid times, the division between the *sharʿī* and *ʿurfī* law was obliterated and law became codified. Cf. Akhavi 1980:38.

[62] In post-revolutionary Iran, the constant 'islamisation' of the Iranian legal system is problematical precisely because *sharīʿat* resists codification. The complex projection of the traditional Shi'i legal tradition into state law is to be seen in the limited room which exists for the discretion of the judge in determining the facts of a case (traditional law only accepts testimony, oath and confession as the formal means for establishing proof). Another

Equating religious law with a modern secular system of positive law, it can be questioned whether Surūsh's assumption of the divine origin of *sharīʿat* makes sense or not. That is: what is left of the sacred conception of Islamic law, when there is no understandable technique to take into account the expression of the divine command or the religious consciousness of the individual. Unlike the modern legal systems, *fiqh* does not confine itself to relations between man and man, but in addition defines in legal categories, applies legal terms and perceives through legal concepts the very relationship between man and God– as though God were a type of legal entity. This ambiguity in Surūsh's legal thought is, for instance, evident in his discussion on Islam and human rights, where he asserts that the concept of human rights as a pre-religious term must be considered in the extra-religious area of discourse:

> The first issue concerning human rights is that it is not a solely juristic intrareligious question. Discussion of human rights belongs to the domain of philosophical theology and philosophy in general. It is, so to say, an extra-religious area of discourse. Like other debates on matters that are prior to but influential in religious understanding and acceptance, such as the objectivity of ethical values, the problem of free will, the existence of God and the question of prophethood, human rights lies outside of the domain of religion. Whether one agrees or disagrees with this argument, the discussion takes place in an extra-religious area of discourse (Surūsh 1996a:281).

Since the formulation of human rights prefigures religious beliefs, the concept of natural right is perceived to be compatible to Islam in the abstract sense of God as the ultimate and transcendent Lawgiver. As far as natural rights involve principles whose observance promotes a more humane and rational life, Surūsh believes that human rights could be based on humanity's ultimate ends as revealed by the Lawgiver as well as determined by people's autonomous judgment:

> The discourse of Western political philosophers about natural and innate rights is to a certain extent the answer to the issue at hand. In the sphere of Islamic and religious thought we must also activate this debate and pay proper respect to it... Indeed, people have other rights (than their civil rights) and these are the natural and innate rights of people. These rights can in a sense be considered as being of divine nature since they are *khudā-pasandānah* (sanctioned by God) and have ultimately been approved by the Lawgiver (ibid.:50-51).[63]

---

implication is that the codification of the *qānūn-i ḥudūd wa qiṣāṣ* (the law of punishment and retaliation) resulted in the implementation of the penal provisions by the *sharʿī* courts rather than the *ʿurfī* courts that earlier had been the general practice (Arjomand 1988:186–188).

[63] Surūsh (1999g:5) argues that Islamic law never sets law, nature and religion apart, in contrast to the liberal natural notion of right and the Marxist historical notion of right on the one hand, but claims, on the other hand, that Islam is compatible with liberal notions of natural right in the case that the theological *fauq-i barrisī* (categorical) topics are put aside. In his view, religion is compatible with natural right, because Islam recognises no incontestable

Despite the fact that human rights in its modern form originally was formulated by enlightenment thinkers with no explicit allegiance to religion or concern with God's approval, Surūsh does not consequently consider religion as the antithesis of human rights nor liberalism as the supreme fount of human rights' notions. He believes, however, that the question of human rights might be problematical from an Islamic point of view, since revelation principally is concerned with the rights of God, or more specifically the *ḥudūd Allāh* (limits of God), where the rights of man stems from his own obligations. He argues that on those occasions where the rights of man are emphasised in the tradional legal texts, that besides being rare, these passages often "derive rights from duties" to the extent that the word right even can be used as "a synonym for duty" (Surūsh 1997a:432). Surūsh (ibid.:432) claims that the Islamic definition of rights is not therefore compatible with the conception of natural right in modern Western law, which more correctly is an *ʿilm-i ḥuqūq* (science of rights) rather than an *ʿilm-i takālif* (science of obligations).[64] In his criticism of God's subjecting of man to law, he is inspired by the affirmative position of *muʿtazilah* to the notion of right and their conception of obligation as directed by reason in terms of an ethical deontology. Surūsh (1999m:6) believes that the ultimate triumph of *ashʿarī* theology in Sunni Islam, which considered the revealed law as the only foundation of good and evil, over the *muʿtazilah* left a negative mark on the whole religious as well as cultural structure of Islam.

There are many factors that contributed to the lack of rights in traditional Islamic jurisprudence, primarily the mere fact that there was no social order equal to that of the modern state in premodern Muslim society. But since Surūsh's interest is to affirm the fundamental correspondence between *fiqh* and modern law, he does not attempt to explain relevant issues such as the fact that the sociology of modern positive law, in contrast to *fiqh*, proceeds from a condition of conflict between the interests of the individual and those of the state since the former in concrete terms is subjugated to the codified law of the latter. While neglecting the fact that Islamic law emphasises mediation among individuals rather than the regulation of their conflict of interests, Surūsh instead gives an account of human rights in strict polemics to traditional *fiqh*. Besides the fact that human rights is considered an extra-

---

or fixed human interpretative authority. "The important question concerns the authority that is invested with the right to oblige religion on human beings. The mere fact that someone makes religion incumbent upon himself in a rational way is compatible to liberalism, since liberalism believes in freedom, conscience and individual choice. The difficulty first appears when this obligation is issued from a social or political institution in conflict to liberalism".

[64] In the traditional Islamic legal literature the concept of *ḥaqq* (right) had a multiple of meanings but corresponded more or less to the English word right in the meaning of something established by *sharīʿat*. In the regulation of human relationships, the notion of *ḥaqq* (right), whether *ḥuqūq Allāh* or *ḥuqūq ʿibād* (servants' rights), were never detached from the natural order, and the value of the individual, as a person, was not a product of humanistic speculations of the nature of existence. Cf. Kamali 1993.

religious issue, he argues that these rights theoretically must exceed the rights of God since God is capable of assigning his own rights and since tyranny against the Divine is a contradiction in terms. While modern secular law and *fiqh* inevitably differ as regards philosophy of law, he suggests that modern Muslims have no pretext for neglecting to embrace the U.N. Declaration of human rights, since the traditional legal theory pertains to the *araḍiyāt* (accidentals) of religion. In the sense that Islam is compatible with human rights, he argues that the legislative body of the Iranian legal system must acknowledge freedom of religion and integrity of religious conscience as a fundamental principle:

Jurisprudence determines how the individual believer shall act in practice. But one important (and sometimes neglected) aspect is that *fiqh* and *sharīʿat* of religion always are consistent with the *ḥaqīqat* (truth) of religion. We must not imagine that our juristic norms and praxis are structured in such a way that our society is a religious society where religion, religious law and practice according to legal norms come about naturally and individuals are not capable of making conscious and sincere justifications for themselves. Law and truth should never contradict each other, since religion has not only the *manṭiqah-yi dil* (*forum internum*, 'realm of the heart') in mind when it teaches, 'There is no compulsion in religion'. Even if this was the case, the heart must always be coordinated with the other organs (of the body). Every legislative body that issues judgment in conflict with individual freedom shuts the doors to freedom and makes the realisation of freedom difficult. It is therefore no legislative body worthy of its name (Surūsh 1996f:47).

In his criticism of the increasing tendency in post-revolutionary Iran towards a nomocentric or *fiqāhatī* (legalistic) understanding of Islam, Surūsh (1996c:537) expresses his concern that religion should not be reduced to jurisprudence, since the depth of human existence is never penetrated simply by recourse to law. By arguing that *sharīʿat* is not identical with *fiqh*, he suggests that jurisprudence only constitutes a small part of human knowledge on religion. He also presumes that modern rationality in terms of socio-political and economical development is not within the range of jurisprudence and that 'islamisation' is not an alternative for acquiring progress in modern society:

Something has occurred in our country that I became aware of about 15 years ago. A particular interpretation of religion and Islam has become dominant: *islām-i fiqāhatī* (legalistic Islam). The religious classes in our society have gained power, and since *fiqh* is the major expertise of the religious scholars, their interpretation of religion is by and large confined to law. Jurisprudence is not the most lofty or significant message of religion but is made up of practical, individual and social norms and edicts. The modern world is also a serious contestant of *fiqh* in the realm of law in the sense that one cannot verify that the social jurisdiction of the modern world is inferior or superior to the jurisdiction of *fiqh* by means of rational argument. One cannot verify that the non-religious laws on, for instance, lease and rent in secular societies are inferior or superior to those of Islamic jurisprudence. In this context, religion has no message to contemporary man, since logic is the most superior form of corroboration. In my view, the Islamic republic has to a great extent detached itself from the modern world by its stress on *fiqh* and legalism (Surūsh 2001:5).[65]

Referring to Muḥammad al-Ghazālī's notion that *fiqh* is a *dunyawī* (this-worldly) science in the sense that it involves matters of practicability, Surūsh takes a *ḥadd-i aqallī* (minimalist) viewpoint on jurisprudence according to which *fiqh* only works out issues of an overtly legal character. As a minimalist science of derivative norms related to specific human acts, he asserts that it gives minimum answers, if any answers at all, to abstract legal issues and never explains or provides solutions to every human problem in modern society in its depth. He argues that the so-called *ḥadd-i akṯarī* (maximalist) notion of *fiqh* as having the capacity to lay out comprehensive programs for all aspects of human life is not essential to jurisprudence as such, but rather involves the projection of extra-religious postulations into specific legal norms. While neglecting the fact that *fiqh* since its beginning has had to deal with the problem of interpreting the revealed law *ʿalā al-ijmāl* (conjointly) in detailed cases (Arnaldez 1996:451), Surūsh (1997a:138-139) claims that the contemporary task of inferring legal norms, even when restricted to the domain of law itself, encounters insuperable dilemmas, since *fiqh* was originally formulated to respond to issues originating in a primitive nomad society:

The legal part of religion functions in a minimalist sense. This means that the purification norms of *fiqh* are not stipulated for a comprehensive hygiene and that *qiṣāṣ* (*quid pro quid*) and *diyāt* (mulct) do not prevent criminal acts in a maximalist sense. *Khums* ('the fifth', a Shi'i category of alms) and *zakāt* (obligatory Muslim alms) are not sufficient taxes for the running of governmental affairs either. Even if we acknowledge that these norms are of this-worldly concern (similar to Ghazālī's claim that *fiqh* basically is a this-worldly science), we still have to recognise the minimalist character of these norms for the sake of this world. In other words, rational management is indispensable for the maximalisation of *fiqh* as well as being essential in realising the minimalist meaning of *fiqh*.[66]

As the majority of problems in modern society, such as the destruction of the

[65] Cf. 1996c:549, 1997a:149 and 1999j. In this respect, Surūsh (1996c:248) compares *fiqh* to grammar in the sense that jurisprudence is concerned with norms, subjected to hermeneutical variation to the same extent as any secular legal system. "To make a comparison, *fiqh* is similar to grammar. What does grammar do? Does it teach people science and philosophy? Grammar does not give anyone the contents of thought, it does not make someone a philosopher, scholar, intellectual or economist. It gives only norms for those persons whose philosophical and scientific language takes these norms into consideration".

[66] Surūsh (19996d:56) believes that the fact that only a limited number of issues in modern society are solved by legal explanations is evident in the dilemma of considering gender issues accurately in contemporary Iran. He insists that the question of women's status ought not to be reduced to law or the technical language of *fiqh* since the meaning of gender is much broader and related to scientific data provided by modern disciplines such as anthropology, psychology and biology. Cf. Mir-Hosseini 1999.

world's forest cover, inflation, criminality, birth-control, taxes for economical development, growth of divorce, and so on, is not confined to legal problems, Surūsh (1999a:91) argues that religion ought to be more concerned with its essential purpose, i.e. the hereafter, and leave worldly planning and organisation to competent professional personnel. But in contrast to al-Ghazālī, who first of all was concerned with his contemporary colleagues' mistreatment of Islamic law and their negation of the preparation of man for the life of the world-to-come, Surūsh's request is not to revive *fiqh* by requesting a more dynamic and practical function, but to plead for its overall closure in terms of an appropriation to the modern conception of law. For him, the question of legal methodology is essentially a universal and non-religious issue, since religion by nature lacks particular methods or values for the deciphering of revelation and interpretation of the divine commandment.[67] He argues that while jurisprudence in legal terms may be *ghanā-yi ḥukm* (supplied with rulings), it is not *ghanā-yi rawish wa barnāmah* (supplied with method and management) (Surūsh 1999j:6). Since the hermeneutical responsibility of the jurists is to translate a transcendent norm into a temporal opinion, he suggests that all interpretations must conform to and acknowledge the epistemological difference between the absolute truth and the fallibility of human interpretations and expectations (Surūsh 1996c:390). Following Popper's argument (who adopted Hume's critique of inductive generalisation) that scientific theories cannot be verified by any accumulation of the observational evidence, Surūsh (1994b:467) similarly argues that neither deductive nor inductive methods alone can solve the problem of epistemic conjecture and that the purpose of method is instead to test the refutability of theories. In his critique of inductive method, he also makes some parallels to the traditional concept of *ijmāʾ* which he believes does not provide any definite, complete or final answer to the questions at hand but rather evolves endlessly in a non-verifiable manner (Surūsh 1999l:6).

In his criticism of the dominance of Greek philosophy in the methodology of the traditional Islamic disciplines, Surūsh argues that the use of Aristotelian logic or Neo-platonic theosophy are ulterior standards (and therefore no final instruments) for the deciphering of Qur'anic meaning, as compared to the methods provided by the modern social and human sciences. He questions, for instance, why the reliance upon the Aristotelian logic should be final and why the Peripatetic concept of *iṣālat-i māhīyat* (purity of quiddity) was refuted by some Islamic philosophers, such as Ṣadr al-dīn Shīrāzī, while Aristotelian logic is still considered immutable and

[67] In this respect, Surūsh is more receptive and amenable to religious interpretation and accomodation than other Muslim intellectuals, such as the Pakistani scholar Fazlur Rahman (1982:3), who considers Islamic philosophy and Sufism as intellectual constructs that are 'alien' to the Qur'anic revelation in contrast to *fiqh*, which is an integrative aspect of Islam.

eternal (Surūsh 1994b:235).[68] Surūsh maintains that the theory of contraction and expansion of religious knowledge elucidates the mechanism behind the adoption of Greek thought by traditional Islamic scientists and why it has dominated the traditional Muslim intellectual discourse until now. Moreover, he believes that it also exemplifies why the efforts to reconcile Hellenistic reason and revelation is a failed project, since Greek philosophy and religion, by and large, are mutually exclusive:

> Firstly, we can grasp the depth of animosity expressed by religious thinkers, such as *imām* Muḥammad Ghazālī [...] and Shihāb al-dīn Suhrawardī [...] toward Greek philosophy and that the enigma transcends such marginal issues as the difficulty of imagining a physical hereafter. The philosophical intrusion aspires in fact to secularise the entire edifice of religion and to replace essentially divine knowledge with essentially secular thinking. Secondly, we become aware of the subject matter of the bitter divergence between the *muʿtazilah* and the *ashʿārah* over whether (philosophical-Greek) rationalisation of religion leads to an unconditional surrender of religion to philosophy. Thirdly, we comprehend why Greek philosophy and religion essentially are unsociable and why the efforts to reconcile (philosophical) reason and Islamic law have failed. Fourthly, we distinguish the subtle and cunning methods by which *sikūlārītih* (secularity) penetrates human thought. This is the reason why we could compare some Islamic philosophers, nothwithstanding their critique of irreligion, to a Trojan horse within the fortress of religion. To the astonishment of many students of philosophy, we finally observe that modern philosophies are considerable closer to religious views and more flexible than the old 'islamised' essentialist philosophies in making the integration of philosophy into religion possible. Hereby, we discover the futility of the neo-Aristotelian attempts to 'islamise' sociology, economics and law (Surūsh 1997a:439).[69]

In considering Islamic jurisprudence as a *dunyawī* (this-worldly) science in contrast to, for instance, theosophy that is aimed at the hereafter, the

[68] In his criticism of Aristotelianism, Surūsh (1996c:402) also points to the incompatibility of the Aristotelian concept of nature with modern science as it developed after Galileo. "The Peripatetic philosophers contemporary to Galileo considered the telescope as deceitful and did not accept to look at the moon through the telescope, since they were afraid that the appearance of the heights and valleys on the moon would nullify one of the principles of Aristotelian natural laws, since (as you know) the moon is a celestial body that in contrast to Aristotle's view has no perfect geometrical shape".

[69] In his complaint of the dominance of Greek thought over Islamic culture, as well as in his methodology, Surūsh (1999k) follows the lead of Muḥammad Iqbāl, whom he considers the most prominent representative of Islamic revivalism in modern history due to his attempt to reconstruct Islam by means of a second-order (a posteriori) epistemology. With Surūsh's appreciation of the mystical tradition in mind, his choice of Iqbāl as the most prominent Muslim reformist is not coincidental, since the latter (in contrast to several other Islamic modernists) largely derived his philosophy of religion from the Sufi tradition. But Surūsh's view of the relationship between religion and philosophy differs from that of Iqbāl (1984:154), who believed that the truths of revelation cannot be submitted to any authority except their own. "Philosophy no doubt has jurisdiction to judge religion but what is to be judged is of such a nature that it will not submit to the jurisdiction of philosophy except on its own terms. While sitting in judgement of religion, philosophy cannot give religion an inferior position among its data".

conclusive question of Surūsh's legal discussion is very much whether *fiqh* is possible in modernity or not when the professional lay expertise rather than the *ʿulama* will control society. His suspicion that legal reinterpretation does not render religion its proper place in the modern world in the sense that reinterpretation tends to cause more conflict and affliction, makes his position about the credentials of *fiqh* in the contemporary world pessimistic. Surūsh (1999a:91) certainly suggests that traditional jurisprudence lacks relevance to the condition of modern man, not least because the primitive seventh century nomad society, in which Islamic law has its origin and formative context, differed in its social composition and formation from a modern industrial and technological society. Relating *fiqh* intrinsically to pre-modern nomadic society rather than emphasising its later development in urban milieu, he claims that traditional Islamic jurisprudence has no natural function in modern society, where nation states have emerged on a global level of interaction as redefined actors governing much more of differentiated public space than the pre-modern political order or ruler. As a result, he believes that the very nature of Islamic law, including its language, its priorities and its logic, makes it irrelevant in modernity. While Surūsh's (1999f:36) legal analysis for the most part is designed to be hypothetical rather than an act of *fides quaerens intellectum* (faith seeking to understand itself), his prescriptive style and the contents of his rhetorical argumentation clearly define the potentials of *fiqh* in unconstructive terms:

The capacity and potential of every science such as jurisprudence depend on two kinds of sources: its formation of ideas and its corroborations. In other words, its strength and weakness depend on its inherent conceptual apparatus and theories of which some are *darūnī* (internal) and others are *birūnī* (external). The external theories are tantamount to the specific presuppositions of that science. My conviction is that our *fiqh* is precisely equivalent to the natural sources of the past that have been emptied of their reserves. There are, in other words, no more conceptions and potentials to be drawn out of them the way it used to be. *Fiqh* has no potentiality of new expansion. There is not much to disclose from its framework, since it lacks any instructive or suggestive meanings.

Surūsh (1999a:91) gives therefore a positive answer to the question as to whether *fiqh* is superfluous in the present state of modernity, since he believes that modern man is in the process of becoming 'mature' in terms of being emancipated from his traditional obligations and maintaining socio-ethical justice without recourse to sacred law:

The this-worldly science of *fiqh* is minimalistic since *masāʾil-i ḥuqūqī* (legal issues) only constitute a small part of human life. It corresponds to primitive nomad society and is essentially concerned with solving issues. This is the meaning of Ghazālī's saying that *wilāyat-i faqīh* does not reach the hearts of men but only the bodies. If people act with justice in this world, the disputes will cease to exist and jurisprudence as well as jurists will go bankrupt.

But Surūsh believes that an eventual end of *fiqh* does not influence religion itself, since the esoteric dimension of religion is not contingent on legal change or its *status quo* for its survival but rather on the *dard* (devotion) of the believers. Referring to the trans-historical Qur'anic perspective on the condition of man, he argues that history progresses in a direction that is compatible with the essence of religion apart from jurisprudence. Since change is an inherent ingredient of religious thought *per se*, the eternal religion of Islam is no less in harmony with contemporary modernity than with the medieval world:

Religion does not change because a set of legal norms changes. Non-religion appears when there is no devotion for religion and when there is not a single soul who considers faith as a source of theory and practice. Those who believe that *sharīʿat* disappears with the amendment of a set of legal norms are on a dangerous path, since change is one of the characteristics of *sharīʿat*. In the past, we regarded a certain act as contrary to the Divine Will and, nowadays, we don't, but all at once both claims equally preserve the spirit of religion (Surūsh 1996a:68).

Against the backdrop of this epistemological differentiation of religion and jurisprudence, Surūsh's approach to law constitutes a further break from previous Shi'i reflection on revealed law, in the sense that he dissolves the traditional synthesis of ethics and jurisprudence. By considering Qur'anic revelation as essentially ethical rather than legal in content, his point of departure is that ethics is universal in all religions in contrast to jurisprudence, which always is what is partial and contextual.[70] In his *Taffaruj-i sunʾ*, Surūsh criticises the modern Western distinction of morality and religion by reference to a number of dominant trends in legal philosophy, such as the naturalist philosophy of Hegel, the intuitionism of D. Ross, the pre-utilitarianism of Bentham and Mill and the positivism of J. Austin and A.J. Ayer. He is in particular critical to the positivist implications of Austin's notion of 'performative acts' and John Searl's concepts of 'institutional facts', which he believes do not give accurate credit to and neglect the essential philosophical distinction between value and fact by emphasising the conventional nature of law:

What in Searl's terminology is 'institutional facts' corresponds to what the late *ʿallāmah* Muḥammad Ḥusain Ṭabāṭabāʾī calls *iʿtibār baʿd al-ijtimāʿ* (value beyond the social sphere), which is nothing else than a set of performative norms. But it is important to note that Searl regards these facts as factual reality and infers the 'ought' from these facts in contrast to the late Ṭabāṭabāʾī, who estimates these facts as value rather than fact. In truth, to estimate something such as a piece of paper is distinctive from value, even if there exists such a common judgment among people. To disseminate values on the basis of fact is incorrect. There are many who therefore have criticised Searl by arguing that a person cannot be convinced of a certain performance, such as to pledge one's words, as long as he or she is not convinced of

[70] Cf. Surūsh 1999a:36.

(the good of) performing that act, i.e. to pledge one's words. In other words, it is the acceptance of a basic ethical principle that gives birth to promises (Surūsh 1996b:363).

Reinterpreting the ideas of Ṭabāṭabāʾī on the question of *ḥusn wa qubḥ* (ethics), Surūsh sets out in polemics with the traditional organical mingling of ethics and law which is so characteristic of Islamic law. He approves of the modern separation of scientific disciplines according to modern categories. In his *Taffaruj-i sunʿ* as well as to a larger extent in his previous book *Īdiʾūlūzhī-yi shaiṭānī* (Satanic ideology), Surūsh's normative conception of ethics is grounded in a transcendent standard and remains to some extent immutable, in contrast to the discoveries in science that are supposed to be subject to change. He laments the absence of the emergence of a self-conscious and independent ethics in Islam and believes that Muslim philosophers reduced its importance to a branch of practical philosophy.[71] In *Ḥikmat wa maʿīshat* (Wisdom and sustenance), his effort is also to give ethics and aesthetics a transcendent metaphysical aspect, even if he is no longer convinced of its absolute character and argues that morality is relative to reality and that theosophy transcends any philosophy of ethics (Surūsh 1997c:163 and 151). Against the overwhelming prestige of Islamic law and the traditional conception of ethics as a science of divine origin and purpose, Surūsh asserts in an essay in 1994 that there is no higher ethics than the existing historical morality. In order to free ethics from the clutches of law, he asserts, similar to the champions of legal positivism, that absolute ethics only belongs to gods, and not to humans and denies that laws are grounded upon a higher morality. Instead of developing an exact and systematic theory of ethical behaviour on the Qur'anic ethical contents, he refers instead to ethics in terms of human conventions and constructions and seems to call for a realistic socio-legal theory:

There is no higher morality than the existing morality. By 'existing morality', I mean our familiar exception-bound moral rules. Following these moral values is the best guarantee of justice and desired moderation in society. The history of human vice is replete with moral violations and deceptions perpetrated in the name of a higher morality and justice... The most important thing is to acknowledge that both natural (subordinate) morality and the eternal (detached) morality are incapable of judging a political regime. The former permissively blends morality and society and the latter, with its metaphysical moral universalism, adjusts to all social and moral realities, for it endorses any possible social morality and rejects none. It presents such an angelic, abstract, and featureless image of justice, moderation and wisdom that it seems capable of being incarnated in the body of any beast (Surūsh 1994c:29).

In Surūsh's view, ethics can be made possible only when man is put at the centre of interest, since morals exist for the sake of man. Ethics is, in other

[71] Cf. Surūsh 1994a:185 and 1994b:5–189.

words, not a precise and axiomatic science and its enigma of the enigmas is the simple fact that it has its own 'indeterminacy' theorem. While Surūsh approves of Kant's categorial imperative (i.e. a supermoral principle) as binding and views man as a goal, and not as a means, he departs from Kant's conviction that there is no morality without religion. At first glance, Surūsh's view that men are capable, for instance, of learning the true nature of right and wrong, elaborating their knowledge rationally and applying it to concrete situations seems akin to the traditional notions of ethics represented by the *muʿtazilah* school. He advances beyond the association of ethics with jurisprudence and theology, however, by arguing that there are no absolute ethics in the human sphere:

> Ethics seems to entail its own indeterminacy theorem since as the accuracy of one side of the equation increases, the generality of the other decreases. This lack of determinacy is the enigma of enigmas. It reveals not only that ethics is not a precise and axiomatic science, but also that it will never be. Even if we follow the lead of the *muʿtazilah* school of thought in designing good and evil as natural and objective categories, deriving *ought* from *is*, and establishing commonsensical moral maxims as self-evident, a priori precepts devoid of cultural relativity and contingency, we still have failed to shed even a sliver of light on the problem of the 'indeterminacy' of morality or the nature of rights, justice, fairness, power, and freedom (ibid.:23).

What is essential in Surūsh's concept of ethics is the acknowledgement that an eternal (detached) morality is incapable of judging human conditions, since it in reality adjusts to all social and moral realities. In his view, it endorses any possible social morality and rejects none. "There is no morality higher and more accurate than the existing morality. There is no higher altar of ideal morality in which to sacrifice the actual morality" (ibid.:30). Morality is therefore morality in the humanistic meaning. This can be termed anthropocentric personal ethics, a normative order created by the individual which of course could contradict the notion of God as the absolute value, since the very core of traditional Islamic law is that the norms of human conduct are not a matter of relative convenience for the individual but derive from an eternally valid standard. The major result of his neglect to comprehend Islamic law in ethical as well as in theological terms is consequently that it entails the potential of the secularising *fiqh*. As Farzin Vahdat (1998:400) elucidates, Surūsh's argument that Islamic jurisprudence and ethics are contingent on other scientific knowledge, available in a given context, implies the recognition of the modern secular world-view, that is, "a secular cosmology embodied in modern philosophical anthopology, and sociology" as the standard "to validate religious cosmologies and the search for a religiosity which is 'attentive' to human needs". While Surūsh's implicit religious discourse prevents him from constructing an overall systematic theory of ethics in correlation with the Western humanistic notions of the individual having the status of the measure of everything, there is no doubt that his conception of ethics is highly individual-oriented. Similar to faith, ethics is the domain of the individual, where law has no say since jurisprudence is primarily concerned with the external appearance of actions rather than individual consciousness. *Fiqh* does not concern itself with the inner life of the heart of man, but with the overt acts of man:

Let us learn from Ghazālī. He considered the jurists as this-worldy scholars and jurisprudence as a this-worldy science. He never mentioned *fiqh* among the religious sciences nor believed that *wilāyat-i faqīh* reaches the hearts of men. To begin with, jurisprudence considers only the external, exoteric validity and invalidity of human action, not the inner intention or purpose. *Fiqh* even approves of a conversion to Islam by means of sword (even if this type of Islam is valueless in the hereafter). It values a prayer that lacks the presence of the heart and regards fasting, corrupted by slander, lies and viciousness as accepted, enforceable, obligatory and fulfilled... *Fiqh* is a *qānūn* (law) for the solving of disputes and the implementation of order in society. There is truly no necessity of *fiqh* if people act in accordance with equity and justice and commit no violations or disobediences (Surūsh 1999a:71).

In contrast to al-Ghazālī, who argued that *fiqh* must be related to the inner spiritual life in order to be meaningful for true religion, Surūsh seems to believe that it is condemned to deal with the externals of life alone since it cannot reach the heart of the individual believer. His viewpoint is problematical since it neglects the symbiotic relationship of the religious-ethical and the legal in the traditional structure of *fiqh*. While Islamic law clearly distinguishes between two types of norms, *legal* (which concerns the external and formal and is subject to the judiciary) and *religio-ethical* (which concerns the *forum internum* of the individual and God), Surūsh seems only to consider the former type of norm. In the sense that jurisprudence only considers the *forum externum* of the religious believer or community and never the *forum internum*, he claims that *fiqh* is subjected to the trial of history as much as any other human knowledge but argues that the result of the critical examination of religion never implies that the validity of that religion is equal to the result of the test. Religion is, so to say, not tarnished by scientific examination but scientific scrutiny is rather beneficial to religion as such. Since there are good grounds for supposing that this criterion of seeing whether a theory 'works' in practice applies to religious knowledge, religious thought is, similar to scientific knowledge, a place for experiment, even if scientific falsification usually is concerned with only one single proposition, in contrast to religion, which is part of a whole symbolic system. In this respect, he believes that modernity constitutes an epistemological, and hence methodological, trial for the Islamic jurists, who must prove and display their capability to understand the normative characteristics and the complex structural transformation of modernity:

The element of *zamān wa makān* (time and place) in *ijtihād* demands from us that we acknowledge social transformations. The question is whether we have allowed for rational management, scientific method and planning or not and whether we have understood the relationships in society accurately or not. All structures are not open to *ijtihād*. [...] This means that all structures are not receptive to change in order to produce development. Some structures are deficient on certain points, are subjected to disintegration and cannot progress or expand further. On the scene of historical trial, the science of *fiqh* is also going to appear with all its strength and weakness in terms of indicating the state of human knowledge. In reality, the jurists are compelled to learn to what extent they have acquainted themselves with the essence of modernity and what understanding they have achieved from this encounter (Surūsh 1996a:64).

G. *Ijtihād*

Since contemporary complexities no longer justify traditional marginalisation of the epistemological identity of jurisprudence, Surūsh asserts that no legal reform can take place without re-shuffling the traditional suppositions, and no re-shuffling will be forthcoming unless the jurists are well acquainted with both revelation and modern ideas developed outside the sphere of religion. By juxtaposing Rūmī's distinction between *taḥqīqī* (realised) knowledge and *taqlīdī* knowledge on jurisprudence, he claims that the investigation of new principles is necessary for the scientific study of religion. He asserts that the *mauḍūʿāt-i aḥkām* (the subjects of legal norms) as well as the relevant norms themselves have a *taḥqīqī* character, in contrast to the dominant traditional view, which he believes classifed both categories as *taqlīdī* (Surūsh 1999n:6).[72] For Surūsh, the details as well as the general outlines of traditional legal theory and its conceptual categories have to be set aside in favour of a variety of new hermeneutical and deconstructionist methods which evaluate Islam in consonance with the contemporary meaning and essence of modernity. In this respect, the contemporary interpretation of Islamic law, and religion in general, has three key denotations:

Firstly, the interpretation must be compatible and harmonious with the modern sciences. Secondly, the interpretation must be shaped and predisposed by the central parts and essences of the modern sciences. Thirdly, the interpretation must answer the theoretical questions of modernity (Surūsh 1996c:247).

Rejecting the viewpoint that the traditional philosophy of *ijtihād* has the ability to get to the bottom of the current intellectual spectrum of modernity, Surūsh (1999c:318) clarifies that the aim of contemporary religious

[72] Surūsh departs, however, from Rūmī's (1996:I 3449, II 2427–29) definition of the categories in the latter's *Maṯnawī-yi maʿnawī*, where the distinction is used to distinguish realised knowledge of certainty and immediate vision from discursive and acquired knowledge.

intellectualism should be to *bāz-sāzī* (recreate) and *bāz-fahmī* (reinterpret) the traditional concept of *sharīʿat* in wide-ranging and universal terms. As the traditional Islamic legal theory is unable to re-establish and restore the dynamics of Islamic law, he believes that the *uṣūlī-akhbārī* division and the alleged rational outlook of the former should not be over-emphasised. By asserting that the over-arching purpose of the legal theory of both currents was to restrict the boundaries of reason and independent *ijtihād* in every way, he suggests that the overwhelming part of traditional jurisprudence was *akhbārī* in substance and disposition:

In my view, the growth of the *akhbārī* (trend) in the history of Shi'i jurisprudence is not an exceptional case, but rather a consequence of the very spirit of Shi'i jurisprudence. While the emphasis on literal form was characteristic of the *akhbārī*, the spirit of conservatism has sustained in our jurisprudence as well as in that of Sunni law. Still today, there are jurists who take refuge in *akhbārī* thought from the dissemination of modernity and believe that it is possible to implement *fiqh* unanimously in all societies and contexts without performing *ijtihād* in the *uṣūl* and transforming the theological presuppositions (of the law) (Surūsh 1999f:36).

As Surūsh (1996d:440) argues at first in his book *Qiṣṣah-yi arbāb-i maʿrifat*, no authentic transformation of Shi'i law can be materialised unless what is commonly understood as legal *ijtihād* also covers the *uṣūl* beforehand. In his view, the modern jurists are not challenged by two equivalent religious philosophies, but rather by two secular philosophies, i.e. that of ancient Greece and that of modern philosophy. Since the latter transcends the former in terms of superseding it, Surūsh (1999i:17) believes that *ʿaqlānīyat-i jadīd* (modern rationality) must investigate the philosophical foundation and worldview of traditional legal theory and methodology in order to expand beyond *ʿilm-i uṣūl-i sunnatī* (science of traditional *uṣūl*). In his view, the fundamental criterion of legal change is that legal reform must be accompanied by an alteration of the fundamental epistemological and ontological presuppositions of traditional legal philosophy, theory and methodology:

Ijtihād in the *furūʿ* of jurisprudence is of no benefit as long as no infiltrating *ijtihād* is attempted concerning the *uṣūl* of jurisprudence. If we consider the conflict between *fiqh-i pūyā* and *fiqh-i sunnatī*, we become aware of the fact that this imploration demands *ijtihād* in the *uṣūl*. No matter whether we advocate *fiqh-i sunnatī* or *fiqh-i pūyā*, we have voted for the *uṣūlī* viewpoint. *Ijtihād* in the *uṣūl* means reconstruction, recomprehension and new conceptualisation. There are many factors that have an effect on reconstruction. On the one hand, the neglected aspects of tradition are rediscovered and on the other hand some parts of the geometry of this collection (of thought) is transformed, as new interpretations are made available from old data (Surūsh 1996d:440).[73]

[73] In this respect, Surūsh (1996c:49, 50) also argues that *ijtihād* itself is dependent on *ijtihād*, i.e. that the act of *ijtihād* nowadays demands a greater effort than in premodern times in the

In Surūsh's view, isolated patterns of philosophical modernity in the form of literary themes can be traced in the writings of traditionalist *ʿulamā*, such as Ḥusain ʿAlī Muntaẓirī, whose arguments against, for instance, *irtidād* (apostasy) differ from those of a premodern scholar such as Murtaḍā al-Anṣārī. But as Surūsh argues, the traditionalist position remains incoherent in the sense that it adopts modern terminology without acknowledging or being receptive to the philosophical foundations of modern anthropology. In his view, the traditional Islamic jurisprudence is based on a particular philosophical position as regards ontology, epistemology, anthropology and the boundaries of human reason, which is incompatible with the cognitive premises of the modern philosophy of science. He believes that the legal norms inferred by the jurists, consciously or unconsciously, are affected by a premodern worldview that contradicts the implications of the ontology of modernity:

The [premodern] anthropology and epistemology have not been the object of an adequate and penetrating inspection on behalf of the jurists (which is evident in their works). The legal verdicts they deduce regarding human life, dignity, belief, freedom and social issue, are always unconvincing, dubious and ambiguous. As I mentioned, the axioms of the premodern world are inoperative nowadays due to the development of modern rationality. The jurists must scrutinise their premodern axioms and remove the dustiness of their prerequisites. This is the meaning of *ijtihād*, which is incumbent upon the jurist and which covers not only the *furūʿ* but also the *uṣūl* of the law (Surūsh 1999i:17).

Surūsh's radically new comprehension of *ijtihād* is motivated by his judgment that traditional theoretical assumptions no longer correspond to the overall ontological condition of modern man. Consequently, he criticises, for instance, Murtaḍā Muṭahharī in his discussion on rights in Islam for only paying lip-service to women's rights (being more concerned with the rights of men than 'the rights of women' which is the actual title of his book) and for neglecting to discuss gender issues separately from legal discourse (Surūsh 1999f:36). The core idea of Surūsh's position on *ijtihād* is that legal theory concerns the whole body of religion rather than only jurisprudence and that *fiqh* is not only contingent on the religious sciences such as theology in the formulation of its methodological principles but also on the constant development of science in the general sense. By defining *ijtihād* as a general scientific and intellectual endeavor that constantly deciphers new horizons for the solution of various issues in order to also counter-act the alleged stagnation of *fiqh*, he argues that *ijtihād* concerns not only the realm of law, but all spheres of human life:

---

sense that the absolute categories and standards of traditional *ijtihād* must be amended. "The proclamation of *fiqh-i pūyā* and *fiqh-i sunnatī* in our society, and more importantly, the call for political accomodation and the proclamation by *imām* Khumainī, the messenger of the dignity of Muslims in our century, that the current use of *ijtihād* in the *ḥauzah* is not enough, illustrate that *ijtihād* itself is dependent on *ijtihād*".

Ijtihād applies not only to *fiqh* but to all scientific and intellectual disciplines. A philosopher and a scholar of ethics are also among the *ahl-i ijtihād* (people performing *ijtihād*). *Ijtihād* is an intellectual endeavor and effort which, by acknowledging some specific objectives, opens new horizons and solves modern problems. It applies to religious issues as well as non-religious ones. In my opinion, *ijtihād* does not change the essence of a thing and one cannot, so to say, transform jurisprudence into ethics or vice versa by means of *ijtihād*. *Ijtihād* is, rather, an expansion occuring in science itself that appears with the maintenance of the framework of a particular science, and that's it (Surūsh 1999a:109).[74]

By initiating a process of transforming the heritage of traditional *fiqh* through an amalgamating selection of traditional doctrines to engender *ijtihād*, if it indeed can be called so, without recourse to the traditional methodological and philosophical foundations, Surūsh's aim is evidently to keep to what he believes is the spirit of Islam, but to get rid of those characteristics which he believes are alien to or nonessential to Islam. In this respect, he considers the fundamental distinction between the substances and the accidentals of religion as one relevant framework among others that can be adopted to investigate a transformation of traditional *fiqh* and define in what sense *ijtihād* should be faithful to the religious spirit:

My concern is not what kind of jurisprudence is created from this legal philosophy. The majority of legal norms and even their necessity were and still are categorically accidental (to Islam)... *Ijtihād* based on this thinking is not emptied in the course of *barā'at* (exemption), *istiṣḥāb* (presumption of continuity) and *furū'-i fiqh-i ijmālī* (branches of abridged jurisprudence), but rather implies a cultural transformation that affects all accidentals (of religion). *Ijtihād* transforms the body (of the law) but at the same time maintains the spirit. It pays, in other words, respect to the customs, traditions and inventions of various cultures and maintains the objectives of *sharī'at*, not literally, but in spirit and meaning (Surūsh 1999a:78).

By announcing the decline of the legitimacy of the traditional foundational theory (or, in Lyotard's words, the meta-narrative) of traditional Islamic law,

[74] Inspired by the modernist rejection of the traditional understanding of *fiqh*, where *ijtihād* is the exclusive privilege of the *'ulamā* who are the sole guardians of the interpretative process, Surūsh's purpose is evidently to generate an atmosphere where *ijtihād* may rid itself of much of the opprobrium formerly attached to it. While he (in an interview with the author) insists that *ijtihād* can only be performed by a qualified *mujtahid* educated at the *ḥauzah*, his re-definitions of terms, such as *'ilm* and *'ālim*, beyond doubt break with the traditional Islamic legal discourse. As Wael B. Hallaq (1997:260) highlights, the recent emergence of a new class of lay religious intellectuals, which generated an increased understanding of Islam in congruence with modernity, is one of the most important developments of modern Islam. Their efforts of interpreting Islamic legal tradition is very much based on the element of socio-economical exigency and the fact that the traditional *'ulamā* no longer are in a superior position to the lay intellectuals in the arena of contemporary scientific debates as far as argumentative skills are concerned. "With the virtual disappearance of the traditional class of legists, and with the emergence of codification as an answer to the new social realities imposed by western cultural and technological domination, there emerged a new legal Weltanshhaung that entirely rejected some of the elements of traditional theory, and which demanded that whatever was retained had to be drastically modified".

Surūsh abandons the absolute standards and universal categories of the traditional epistemic schemes in favour of locally, historically contextualised types of scientific inquiries. In an essay in *Kiyān* in 1998, he advocates a deconstructionist method in the endeavour of separating the substances of religion from the accidentals, which in actual fact is the foremost requisite of his definition of *ijtihād*.[75] He believes deconstruction to be the most conclusive method for dismantling the skeleton structure of religion and interpreting the objectives of Islamic law in the present-day, increasingly unstable and unpredictable world:

We have a number of necessary initial and judgemental instruments for entering the setting of religion and contemplating on the exterior of religion: To consider the gradual and historical development of religion and religious texts, to destroy and to split apart its skeleton structure (deconstruction), to determine quasi-preliminary conditions and counter factuals, to infer the *maqāṣid-i sharʿī* (objectives of religious law), to deduce the motives of law, to discover the means and the channels of the periodical development of religion and the junctures interfering therein, to expurgate and to determine our expectations of religion and to test the refutability or irrefutability of theoretical and practical elements of *sharīʿat* (Surūsh 1999a:54).

In this respect, Surūsh's position is characterised by a loss of certainty and a 'God's eye point of view' which also decentralises the traditional unitarian standard of culture, art, ethics and belief. But still, he never embarks on the methodological exercise of exposing and dismantling the various aspects of religious tradition by reference to the Derridean deconstructionist method, but rather refers to the established *sharīʿat* in order to expand beyond it by reference to *ijtihād*, even if it is not clear to what extent he makes a distinction between *ijtihād* and interpretation in the more general sense. In this respect, the fragmentary appeal in his writings to deconstructionism is deficient in providing a hardy arsenal of deconstructive tools. While he aims to open up a critical debate on epistemology, interpretation, and historicity, predisposed by deconstructionism, he still prefers to situate himself within the Islamic tradition and not break with it. But the fact remains that Surūsh's effort is to largely replace the traditional epistemic schemes and the traditional ethico-juristic synthesis with a post-positivistic differentiation and a poststructuralist extension of the various scientific disciplines. By employing a similar second-order epistemology in the analysis of theology and law as well as mysticism and philosophy, his purpose is also to

[75] Deconstruction was initiated by Jacques Derrida who launched a major critique of traditional Western metaphysics in a series of books published in French beginning in the late 1960s. He introduced the words *déconstruire* ('to deconstruct') and *déconstruction* ('deconstruction') in *De la grammatologie* (1967). Amongst other his ideas are powerful critiques of phenomenology (Husserl), linguistics (Saussure), Lacanian psychoanalysis and structuralism (Lévi-Strauss). Like Freud's psychological theories and Marx's political theories, Derrida's deconstructive strategies, which take off from de Saussure's insistence on the arbitrariness of the verbal sign, have established themselves as an important part of postmodernism, especially in poststructural literary theory and text analysis.

'humanise' and 'historicise' these religious discourses all at once. Instead of establishing Islamic self-referentiality to respond to what he identifies as the normative closure of traditional legal methodology, he employs the evolutionary dynamics of cognitive openness in order to propose a theoretically alienating exercise in which Islam is ultimately reduced to the confines of Western cognitive matrices. As Afshin Matin-asgari (1998:295) elucidates, commenting upon Surūsh's rejection of Western-Islamic dichotomies. "This is a commendable sentiment, as long as we acknowledge the problem that Sorush has no independent method for such evaluation and choice outside the critical traditions of Western civilisation itself". The question is hence very much to what extent he is willing to discard the structural disposition of traditional *fiqh* as it has developed historically in his deconstruction of *ijtihād*, since it is precisely the historical expositions of the divine law that allow modern Muslims their spiritual and intellectual continuity in the modern world. No religious community can, so to say, set aside its past and expect to create a future for *itself* as that community. His distinction between the substances and accidentals of religion is a case in this respect.

H. *Ḥauzah*

The main argument in Surūsh's writings on the traditional Shi'i education system is, similar to his account on jurisprudence, that Muslim contemplation on philosophy and the history of science is far behind the contemporary intellectual developments in these fields at large. He argues that the philosophical underpinnings of modern science are systematically neglected at the *ḥauzah*s even if several *ʿulamā* are involved in the so-called 'islamisation' of modern science. In this respect, he believes that the Shi'i intellectual attempts of accommodation to modernity remain largely inconsistent and superficial, since the acceptance of modern science and modern epistemology is not unconditional. While the *ḥauzah*, for instance, has abandoned the traditional *ṭabiʿīyāt* (natural philosophy) in silence, he argues that the position of modern natural science as well as the attitude toward the subject of history in post-Khaldūnian times are far from clear.[76] Notwithstanding the developments within science and philosophy at large, he believes that the *ḥauzah* is still occupied with approaching and explaining *ʿilm-i kalām*, *fiqh* and the traditional sciences according to the criteria of traditional epistemology and protecting traditional cosmological principles:

At the religious seminaries, they keep to the traditional worldview and anthropology to the extent that it sometimes seems as if religion only grows and survives in that geographical place. History has no high position or rank at the *ḥauzah* and there is

[76] Cf. Surūsh 1996c:172 and 1994b:255.

no notice of natural science, anthropology, sociology and modern epistemology there. Still at the time being, ethics is instructed according to the basis of the 'psychology' of the ancients and mastery of theology, theosophy and exegesis is not related to hermeneutics and modern religious science (Surūsh 1996c:191).

In Surūsh's view, the modern scientific research of Islam, as distinguished from the traditional learning in the study halls of the *ḥauzah*, has only occured very recently in Iran. ʿAbd al-Karīm Hāʾirī, who followed the lead of Muḥammad Ḥusain Kāshif al-Ghitā in Najaf, was the first to reorganise the *ḥauzah-yi ʿilmīyah* in Qum. In the 1920s, Hāʾirī transformed Qum into a flourishing educational centre and set up a general curriculum for all courses and books required for each subject and level. Unlike al-Ghitā, he attempted to rationalise rather than modernise the curriculum and did not include modern subjects such as psychology or sociology.[77] Actually, it was first in the 1960s that the *ḥauzah* in Iran attempted to meet the needs of a changing society when the Dār al-tablīgh (House of propagation) and Madrasah-yi Ḥaqqānī (Ḥaqqānī school) were founded with a slightly different conception than the traditional Faiḍīyah, Khān and Raḍawīyah schools.[78] But as Michael Fischer (1980b:83) elucidates, it is first after the 1979 revolution and only by state intervention that Qum's reputation as a centre of traditional Islamic learning in Iran has been challenged. This occured at the same time as the prerogatives of the *ʿulamā* themselves in general increased. Since the revolution, at least two new *madrasahs* have been founded in Qum, the Maʿsūmīyah (The Impeccable) and Maktab-i Zahrā (Zahrā school) schools, which admit more females and also increasingly include modern social sciences and humanities in the curricula. Computers have also been introduced in the *ḥauzah* and public and private funding has increased the number of religious students (Zaryab 1997). Due to the political developments, the *ʿulamā* themselves have been compelled to gain deeper insights into the modern social sciences and natural science that have affected a whole range of modern Shi'i scholarship, such as *tafsīr*, where the present occupation involves the socio-political and scientific realities of the twenty-first century rather than the previous pursuit of hagiography, eschatology and esoteric matters (Ayoub 1988:197).

The increasing enrolment in the *ḥauzah* and the significance of the religious seminaries after the revolution has furthermore persuaded the religious authorities to contemplate a unified and centralised system of

[77] Cf. Akhavi 1980:40–55 and Turki Abbas 1997:176–183.

[78] Madrasah-yi Ḥaqqānī provides a sixteen-year course, the first ten of which are formal classes, the rest guided research and reading. It has, at least until very recently, been very much of a complete cell set apart from the rest of the *ḥauzah* structure, as is evident in its stress on modern languages, English and spoken Arabic as well as certain subjects within modern humanities, such as Islamic psychology, sociology and economics. The school, which at present is directed by Muḥammad Taqī Misbāḥ-Yazdī, publishes a whole range of books on these subjects.

management. In his essay on the possibility of uniting *ḥauzah* and university, Surūsh alludes to the development in the nineteenth century when the *ḥauzah* was gradually pushed aside from mainstream intellectual life as modern national universities were established in Iran. While refraining from tracing various factors behind the decline of *ḥauzah* education in modern times (such as the 'nationalisation' of learning, the continuing discovery of more and more classical texts and the rigidifying of scholastic methods), Surūsh sets out to discuss the issue of its natural function.[79] Referring to the emergence of modern universities in Iran that created a clear-cut dichotomy between the changing mundane *fann* (professional knowledge) of the university and the eternal otherworldly *ʿilm* (religious knowledge) of the *ḥauzah*, he believes that the two, despite the existence of an intellectual dualism, have an educational aim in common (Surūsh 1996a:22).[80]

Despite their shared educational aspiration, Surūsh asserts that the *ḥauzah* differs from the university as far as its philosophical frame-work is concerned. Whereas the *ḥauzah* teaches subjects predicated on belief impervious to criticism, the university embodies a secular philosophical foundation where all intellectual discourses are open to questioning since the empirical sciences (natural as well as human disciplines) have no theory that is considered sacred and no texts that are immune to or above criticism. In contrast, the conception of study as a sacred act prevails at the Shi'i seats of learning, where critical assessment is only allowed when it is based on the unambiguous purport of a *riwāyat* established in the revealed sources. He acknowledges, however, that vigorous debate and critical analysis is not alien to the *ḥauzah* system, which is built on the concept of learned men teaching circles of students through textual exegesis. He also claims that the current intellectual tenor at Iranian universities, characterised by their confidence in self-explanatory texts, structured curriculum, lecture halls, mass instruction and examination does not live up to the condition of a

[79] Cf. Fischer 1980b:55. As a matter of fact, the secular Iranian state authorities have never dictated the subject matter of the curriculum of the Shi'i *ḥauzah*, in contrast to the major Sunni seats of traditional learning, which were rigorously modernised by secular national governments in the first half of the twentieth century. Modern sciences were, for instance, introduced at al-Azhar as early as in the 1890s. In the sense that every education system has an impact on philosophical outlook and that the Iranian *ḥauzah* inculcates a mentality that for the modern world is overly closed, the Iranian *ʿulamā* have kept it hermetically sealed against modernity. This is the reason why a modernist theorist until recently was exceptional among the *ʿulamā* ranks.

[80] In Iran, the Dār al-funūn (Polytechnic school), which was created to train army and civil officers, was the first academic unit not administered by *ʿulamā* and constituted a prelude to the establishment of national universities in the 1920s. Later, in 1934, the ministry of education incorporated the existing institutions at the university as independent faculties (i.e. law, political science, economics, letters, sciences and medicine) and introduced its own curriculum for theological schools, which included courses in *uṣūl-i fiqh* as well as *tafsīr*. The purpose behind the establishment of the Faculty of Theology at Tehran University was to have a state-operated institution, separate from the *ḥauzah*, so that religious teaching would be supervised under the auspices of the government. Cf. Sassani 1948:86–88.

model university either:

The seminarians, schooled in a dialectical tradition, are likely to enter into serious and lenghty debate with their teachers, whereas our university students, especially nowadays, are trained in the passive routine of taking notes, passing exams, making grades and going home. Since these are not the real-world virtues of the university, that is not what is at issue here. The critical point is that the *iltizām-i awwalīyah* (a priori commitment) of the seminary students and the teachers to the religious texts and sacred sources excludes criticism and doubt... The interpretation of sacred texts is based on the important presupposition that the texts are not read to be undermined, replaced nor criticised. We do not read them to discover their faults and flaws, but rather strive to understand them in a sense that entertains no possibility that they might have faults and flaws. We assume these texts as perfect, hallowed and sacred; they are beyond the reach of controversy and scientific inquiry, which thrives on discussion and criticism (ibid.:23–24)

In Surūsh's view, the contemporary Iranian *ḥauzah* as well as universities are characterised by an authoritarian or overprotective atmosphere, which he believes is connected to a phenomenon he terms *shubhah* ('suspicion'). Among the recent examples of *shubhah*, he mentions the controversy that aroused as a consequence of the publishing of *Shahīd-i jāwīd* (The Eternal martyr), a book that cast doubts on the predestined character of Husain b. ʿAlī's martyrdom and the strict prevention of Muḥammad Ḥusain Ṭabāṭabāʾī from writing an explanation of the respected *ḥadīṯ* collection *Biḥār al-anwār* of Muḥammad Bāqir Majlisī, as well as the dominant tendendecy among the *ʿulamā* to neglect the imperative of female emancipation.[81] By refuting the recent trend of integrating the traditional Islamic disciplines of the *ḥauzah* into the modern university, Surūsh asserts that the concrete solution to the question of uniting *ḥauzah* and university as well as sorting out the problem of *shubhah*, is not merely a question of management but, more importantly, a question of methodology. He maintains that the fundamental criteria of any succesful prospect of these kinds is that the *ḥauzah* acknowledges that science is a human endeavor and that religious as well as secular texts must be subjected to revision and critique. He believes that religion might otherwise easily become a historical relic or a curiosity at a museum:

In my view, the unity between *ḥauzah* and university cannot become a reality unless the *ḥauzah* recognises that the knowledge of its scholarship is human and mundane and refrains from treating, in theory as well as practice, merely human opinions as

[81] In Surūsh's (1996a:39–41) view, there is a lack of vigorous debate at the *ḥauzah*, especially on questions related to power and politics, such as the topic of *wilāyat-i faqīh*. He also considers the question of the status of women as being of particular importance and expects more criticism of the traditional view regarding women as articulated in many religious texts that are taught at the *ḥauzah*. While Surūsh (1999o) also questions why no *ʿālim* criticises misogynist *akhbār* that have found their way into several collections of *ḥadīṯ* (which they nevertheless dare not to mention in their preaching), he does not perceive gender difference as a result of socialisation.

beyond questioning. The unity of these two institutions of higher learning will remain shallow and cosmetic as long as their sciences are separated in theory and spirit. The elemental condition for the realisation and the possibility of this unity is their mutual acknowledgement as equally human institutions that are equally susceptible to criticism. Merely human and fallible jurists, clergymen and theologians reside at the *ḥauzah*, not God nor the holy Prophet nor the innocent *imāms*. Whatever they produce is non-sacred human knowledge since the sacredness of the Qur'an and the *sunnat* does not apply to their knowledge and erudition (Surūsh 1996a:31).

Surūsh leaves, in other words, no option for the *ḥauzah* but to adopt the theoretical foundation of modern human science and abandon the methodological premises of Aristotelian logic. As he says, "the unity of the university and the *ḥauzah* is merely guaranteed by their methodological unity" (Surūsh 1996a:43). He endorses the development of a common methodical unity of language and discourse where the two institutions can communicate, agree or disagree. Drawing on the theories of Foucault and Habermas on the relationship between knowledge and power (ultimately derived from the Marxist notion of ideological superstructures of class and economical relationships), Surūsh (1999c:2–6) maintains that the language of instruction, similar to all conceptual orderings prevailing at the *ḥauzah*, is connected to specific human interests of exclusion and is filled with inner contradictions, something that he suggests is increasingly apparent in our age of information-technology. By accentuating the relationship between power and discourse, he asserts that the organic relationship between the Iranian state and the *ḥauzah* in post-revolutionary times is intended to legitimise the *ʿulamā*'s reach for political power, which actually has reduced the autonomy of the *ʿulamā* vs. the state to nothing:

After the revolution, the *rūḥānīyat* (clergy) took over the nation's management and adopted the theory of *wilāyat-i faqīh* as its governing political theory, which requires a *faqīh* trained at a *ḥauzah-yi ʿilmīyah* to be the supreme leader of the country. In other words, someone who is trained at an institution that produces clergymen and *fiqh*. Because the government is religious, the ties of the *ḥauzah-yi ʿilmīyah* to the centres of power are organic and profound, giving it the last word on matters of state. It is self-evident that the religious government entails the empowerment of the religious classes and the representatives of the *ḥauzah*; the religious disciplines actually empower those who possess them. [...] The clergy has always been a corporeal party and when this party reaches power, it puts aside every other oppositional party (Surūsh 1996a:26–28).

Inspired by the anti-clerical viewpoint of ʿAli Sharīʿatī, Surūsh criticises the fact that many religious scholars make their livelihood from religion and have created a social hierarchy of inner checks and balances in an attempt to guard their own interests. In Surūsh's definition, the clergy should, in ideal terms, have no economic income from their religious activities and instead make a living from regular professional work, such as teaching. He believes that the clergy has become corrupted because of their current socio-political power and argues that the modest example of Rūḥullāh Khumainī has ironically not been abided by in the Islamic republic, which was founded on that precise ethical standard of humility.[82]

But while Surūsh considers power as the root of the dilemma of contemporary Islamic discourse, he rejects Foucault's reduction of reason (knowledge) to causes (power) and conceives of knowledge as understanding rather than purely empirical. In his criticism of the *ḥauzah*, he is also reluctant to adopt Habermas' method of psychoanalysis as a model for the social sciences in the ultimate sense that would put the very *raison d'être* of Islamic institutions under serious question.[83] Instead of calling for a wholesome return to the traditional system of learning where all sciences possess a sacred aspect and are never divorced from the total religious life of Islam, Surūsh's proposal of unification in method and its endorsement of a Popperian definition of science as well as philosophy lead undoubtedly to a desacralisation of Islamic learning. In this respect, it might be questioned whether it actually solves the inherent and natural conflict between religious faith and secular knowledge. This is the basis of the conflict between the two institutions of learning as well, which results in the profound disintegration and collapse of independent traditional Islamic scholarship.

[82] Cf. Surūsh 1997a:33, 41 and 1999c:93–95. As Roy Mottahedeh (1987:231) elucidates, while the *ʿulamā* in early times included a wide range of professionals who earned their living from other labour than religious teaching, the founding of the *madrasah* made religious learning into something of a profession and may therefore be said to have provided the *ʿulamā* with their livelihood ever since.

[83] Cf. Surūsh 1999c:4. While Surūsh considers knowledge as an autonomous intellectual structure that happens to be employed as an instrument of power, Foucault (1979:194) argues in his *Discipline and punish: The birth of the prison* that knowledge is intrinsically tied to systems of social control. "[P]ower produces: it produces reality: it produces domains of objects and rituals of truth. The individual and the knowledge that may be gained of him belong to this production".

CHAPTER VII

Surūsh's theory of the contraction and expansion of religious knowledge

A. Its principal objectives

The book *Qabḍ wa basṭ-i tiʾūrīk-i sharīʿat* (The Contraction and expansion of legal theory) is Surūsh's first analysis of epistemology and hermeneutics with reference to the *takāmul* (development) of religious knowledge. His choice of the Arabic terms *qabḍ* and *basṭ* is inspired by traditional Sufi literature where they represent distinct mystical states, the constriction respectively the dilation of the mystic's heart.[1] The book is divided into four parts with an introduction and supplements.[2] In the foreword, Surūsh asserts that the purpose of the book is to provide a philosophical investigation of a specific field of human knowledge, *fiqh*, and at the same time make theoretical reflections on science as such. Another purpose is to create possibilities for the development of a pluralistic *dimūkrāsī-yi dīnī* (religious democracy), which is an outgrowth of the community of believers, by substantiating the concepts of the plurality of reasons and the contingency of religious knowledge with a *mabānī-yi ipīstimūlūzhīk* (epistemological basis).[3] The third purpose of the book is to present what he calls a *dark-i azīzānah-yi dīn* (endearing conception of religion) and to close the possibility of ideological or official interpretations of religion. He argues that the most beneficial advantage of the theory of contraction and expansion is that it makes peace not merely between the eternal and the time-bound and between religion and science, but also between tradition and modernity, by

[1] Cf. chapter twenty-six in ʿAlī b. Uṯmān Hujwirī's *Kitāb-i kashf al-maḥjūb* (The Book of unveiling the hidden). The terms are also mentioned in the Qur'an to denote that God enlarges and straightens the means of spiritual provision for His servants (*Qur.* 28:82).

[2] The first three parts of the book are comprised of a lengthy exposition of the evolution of religious knowledge with specific reference to *fiqh* and *ʿilm al-kalām*. The first chapter may very well be considered a preliminary attempt to sketch an outline of the major features of an Islamic *kalām-i jadīd* (modern theology). Part four includes an article by Aḥmad Naraqī where he elaborates on Surūsh's view of the history of science together with an inquiry posed to Surūsh by some theology students of a *ḥauzah-yi ʿilmīyah* in Qum. The supplementary part covers five articles by Surūsh and other participants, who present their critical contributions to the current epistemological debate.

[3] For Surūsh's writings on the concept of religious democracy and his criticism of the theological doctrine *wilāyat-i faqīh*, cf. 1997a:301–380, 1999a:243–281 and 1999h. Cf. Jahanbakhsh 2001:153–171.

clarifying the relationship between transcendence and immanence as well as revelation and reason (Surūsh 1996c:32, 34, 58).

Surūsh presents no systematic clarification of the terms *qabḍ* and *basṭ* in the sense of a conceptual analysis which would provide his terminology with a theoretical *raison d'etre*. He instead considers the theory of contraction and expansion of religious knowledge as the mechanism behind the alternating moments of epistemic openness and closure of religious knowledge in general terms and claims that it explains how modern science influences and gives rise to change in the traditional Islamic disciplines. He believes that it determines the time-boundness of religious knowledge and understanding and displays the *ramz* (enigma) of divergent opinions in the realm of exegesis and jurisprudence (ibid.:56). Surūsh's overall purpose can hence be said to substantiate the idea of *ʿasrī kardan-i dīn* (temporalising religion), where the age not only adjusts to religion, but religion moreover becomes 'humanised'. By advocating a kind of religious humanism that is fundamentally different from the traditional literary 'humanism' as epitomised in the Islamic *adab* tradition, he suggests, referring to Feuerbach's words that "the root of theology is anthropology", that the transformation of theology should be integrated into a larger 'human' enterprise where human beings are neither manipulated as objects by technology nor by religion.[4] Treating humanism as a feature of religion *per se*, Surūsh (1996f:51) claims that God is dependent on man for His existence as much as man is dependent on God. His affiliation with modern humanism, according to which man is the measure of all things and the centre of the universe, is not a coincidence since Kant, his prototype in philosophy, indeed was deeply influenced by Rousseau's humanistic ideas on nature, culture, education and history in his philosophising about human nature.

In Surūsh's (1996c:79) view, the theory of contraction and expansion is in general terms related to theology, law and mysticism or more specifically to *dīn-shināsī* (science of religion) in the sense that it represents a scientific study of religion from the 'outside' and that it reveals the various presuppositions and expectations of Islamic theological positions from the revealed text. In his definition of *dīn-shināsī*, Surūsh argues that this concept includes the elaboration of philosophy of religion where religion is seen as a definite enough object to become object of a systematic investigation that is not aimed at deciding on the truth of a particular religion (Surūsh 1996a:9). He distinguishes philosophy of religion proper from philosophical theology and seems to suggest that reflection on religion is philosophically respectable only if it confines itself to mere theism and is abstracted from all

[4] For a study of the traditional Islamic *adab* tradition and its role in the emergence of modern humanistic studies in the West through the subject of *studia humanitas* of the Italian Renaissance, cf. Makdisi 1990 and Kramer 1992.

particular religions (anything else is taken to be theology, not philosophy). Influenced by the American scholar Ian G. Barber's work *Religion and science*, he attempts to create a modern and dynamic theology that is contingent on the modern sciences for its articulation and considers the historical development of human thought at large.[5] In contrast to the majority of European as well as Islamic medieval philosophers, whose aim was to develop theology as *scientia* (or *ʿilm*), including sacred theology, Surūsh makes very restricted use of the deliverances of natural human reason and rejects using propositions revealed by God as premises. Besides theology, the theory of contraction and expansion is (as indicated by the title of the book) connected to legal theory in the sense that it aims to illustrate why traditional works of *uṣūl-i fiqh* deal extensively with matters of *ijtihād* as a foundational category and significantly marginalize its cognitive identity. "It demonstrates which other sciences the *faqīh* is dependent on in the process of inferring of rulings and how crucial hidden or pronounced presuppositions are in *iftāʾ* and juristic understanding" (Surūsh 1996c:57). Surūsh similarly argues that the theory presents evidence for the contingency of procedural *ijtihād* in the realm of *furūʿ* to prior structural *ijtihād* in *uṣūl*. He also explains to what extent the theoretical underpinnings of *fiqh* is supplied by theology. In addition, he claims that the theory of contraction and expansion is connected to mysticism in that it renders meaning to the traditional distinction between *sharīʿat*, *ṭarīqat* (the esoteric way) and *ḥaqīqat* (truth), which he believes is grounded in "the eternal differences" of hermeneutical methodology and constitutes "three categories of religious perception, each one of them corresponding to a specific religious faction and heir to a unique philosophical perspective" (ibid.:57).

B. History: The Stage of natural man

Surūsh's philosophy of history wrestles with the idea of progress and supposes that there is a way of rising above the present and viewing it in relation to inquiry in general, where the history of man is essentially considered a mirror of reason, that is, of its contraction and expansion. Influenced by Hegelian purports to have views on progress, synthesis and the self-correcting character of scientific enterprise, he criticises Aristotle and Descartes for their pessimistic comprehension of history that does not consider history to be, strictly speaking, a branch of knowledge at all. Surūsh believes that theology and *fiqh* are in need of history in the sense that no religion may ignore its historical development and every interpretation is

[5] Cf. Surūsh 1996c:87. Ian G. Barbour is most known for his book *Issues in science and religion*, first published in 1966, which was one of the first books to treat these fields as two disciplines that shared a common ground rather than as two completely separate or conflicting spheres of study.

bound to its historical context. The inquiry into our knowledge of religion is part of a larger inquiry into the history of human science and thought. While the historical perspective affects the sacredness of religion from the point of view of the believer, a historical as well as sociological method is indispensable for the study of religion:

> No school of thought can conceal its historical fate and consider it irrelevant or only count its accomplishments and divorce its earnings from its expenditures. Practical successes and defeats are like mirrors of comprehension from which human beings construct opinions in conformity to certain beliefs. Theology and history are hence contrary to the general belief indispensable and necessary for each other (ibid.:33).

Notwithstanding Surūsh's anti-Cartesian view of history, it is not Descartes but Hegel who is the main object of his criticism. While Surūsh in his later works such as *Qabḍ wa basṭ-i tiʾūrīk-i sharīʿat* refutes the Hegelian-style unification of cosmology and theology which is characteristic of his earlier work *Nahād-i nā-ārām-i jahān* (The Restless nature of the universe), describing the unfolding of single events as a divine process (1999b:81–82), he maintains the view that change pertains to existence and not merely to time since both of them are bound to the world. In contrast to the latter work that innovatively links to Ṣadr al-dīn Shīrāzī's concept of *ḥarakat-i jauharī* (essential movement)[6] and considers teleological statements as a condition *sine qua non* of the discovery of meaning in history, Surūsh's definition of progress in *Qabḍ wa basṭ-i tiʾūrīk-i sharīʿat* enfolds progress in history as well as in nature (i.e. evolution in the strict sense) and does not merely view history as process. Inspired by Darwin's concept of evolution which functions as a paradigm in modern science, he argues that the new forms, discoveries and events coming into existence are modifications of the old, which also includes the concept of improvement. Surūsh's view of history is typically modern in the sense that he considers history as liberation from the past through the discovery of new scientific truths and he transcends the traditional view that considers history as the repetitive cycle of birth and decay (containing a transcendent core of eternal truth). Similar to Kant, he believes history to be inherently characterised by progress, necessity and

[6] The theosophical concept *ḥarakat-i jauharī* constitutes Ṣadr al-dīn Shīrāzī's unique contribution to Islamic thought. As Fazlur Rahman (1975:109, 36) argues, its results are that "grades of being are no longer fixed and static but ceaselessly move and achieve higher forms of existence in time" and that this movement from the less perfect to the more perfect is "unidirectional and irreversible, for existence never moves backward". At the bottom of the scale of existence lies primary matter and at the highest point is God, and the movement, as far as the human being is concerned, hence culminates in man becoming the *insān-i kāmil* (perfect human being). Surūsh's (1999b:99) idea of movement in *Nahād-i nā-ārām-i jahān* seems also to be fairly articulated under the influence of the French philosopher Henry Bergson (d. 1941) who established and developed a theory called *evolution créatrice* (creative evolution). Bergson's philosophy also inspired Muḥammad Iqbāl in his poetical formulation of a mystical and self-affirmative evolutionary cosmology as envisioned, for instance, in his Persian poem *Asrār-i khudī* (Secrets of the self).

critical rationality that is ultimately directed to man's attainment of maturity.[7] His notion of history breaks, in other words, with the interest of the traditional view of man's place and involvement in the divine cycle and turns the repetitive and unitary organic cycle into a linear arrow of evolutionary progress, where the transcendent core of human existential reflection dissolves into scientific secularisation.[8]

In contrast to Kant, who uses mythological language to describe the progress of a plan of nature, Surūsh's idea of a 'plan of nature' developing itself in history does not anticipate an actual mind called nature that consciously makes a plan to be carried out in history. The argument is, rather, that history proceeds *as if* there was such a mind in the sense that "the process of enfolding human knowledge lies not in the order of anybody, but is self-governed and results from the free competition of human thought itself" (Surūsh 1999k). Surūsh's concept of history possesses no teleological end towards which it is directed but rather adopts a secularised idea of progress that lacks any original sense of destination and gives ontological weight to history itself and a determining sense to our position within it:

> The historical past is rediscovered by each generation and each time it demands a fresh 'real' *maʿnā* (meaning) and *tafsīr* (interpretation) and not an allegorical one. There is no doubt that Napoleon did not understand the true impact of his campaigns as well as we do today. This is so because the waves of his feats have now expanded and whispered new mysteries into the ears of the historians. The future historians will hence be in a better position to make discoveries about the present. The multitude and variety of human action in history and the gradual and self-unfolding quality of historical knowledge can scarcely be encountered to this degree in any discipline... From now on, we must think of knowledge not as a snapshot of an object that we take once and for all but as a pond that we constantly replenish with new knowledge or a plant that we irrigate and nourish with new data. Even more importantly, we realise that in addition to human action, other things can also become the subject of historical portrayal, the gradual expansion of which invites our gaze and evokes our sense of familiarity. All the moulds and limits must become fluid in the tumultuous flow of history and no science must be branded with the seal of culmination (Surūsh 1994b:259–260).

Whereas Surūsh considers the aspect of evolution as essential to scientific study, he likewise insistently objects to the idealistic historicism that was born of the time of Hegel, characterised by its belief in intractable laws of human history and being as historical *in toto*. He alleges that the most serious mistake of Hegel, who developed his epistemology *pari passu* with ontology, was to make value-judgements on the concept of evolution as well as to make reason, whether true or false, submissive to history and

[7] In 1784, Kant responded to the question posed by a Berlin newspaper, "What is enlightenment?" by equating enlightenment with the attainment of maturity through the use of reason.

[8] Cf. Surūsh 1996c:252.

chronological periods (Surūsh 1996c:179).[9] In the sense that rationality is not the same thing in every age and every place, Surūsh believes that the Hegelian attitude that takes historically and sociologically assumed rationality for granted is nothing but an empty compliment. In fact, he believes that Hegelian historicism denies the possibility of any pluralism of rationalism by adopting an approximately Neo-Platonic notion of human reason as well as throwing doubt on the basic criteria of scientific and critical realism, i.e. the independence of thought from its object:

It must also be mentioned that our argument is not akin to the philosophical belief that *ashiyāʾ fī anfusīkum* (objects in-themselves) have an essence or boundary nor to Hegel's view that history is an independent entity and the stage upon which the Supreme Soul and the Absolute Idea unfold. For one thing, our discourse concerns the discovery of the nature of things (not their objective nature), which as we argued earlier, occurs gradually. The appeal of Hegel's view is due to its affinity with epistemological insight explained in this treatise, not vice versa. Our view does not require imagining history as a singular person with different modes of behaviour. The heart of our case is rather to argue for the existence of knowledge, or in Dilthey's parlance, a reason known as 'historical reason' that could be used to enrich our pure as well as practical philosophy (Surūsh 1994b:260).[10]

Surūsh (1994a:124) considers in fact the holistic and utopian experiments of Hegelianism as well as Marxism as nothing else than ideologies of *shirk* (multitheism) and as substitutes for religion in their worship of history. He argues that these philosophical currents in common with Rousseauesque idealism are based on belief in the innate good of mankind which underestimates the potential power of social evil and produces destructive social utopia (in the form of modern totalitarian states).[11] Whereas the concept of development in the thought of Hegel (as well as Marx) was made possible by Kant's essays on history, which envisioned the possibility of progress in human history, Surūsh endorses the epistemological basis of Kant and is influenced by Kant and Schleiermacher, who of course had their concept of *Entwicklung* not only in common with Hegel, but also with Ritschl, Dilthey and Troeltsch (Murphy 1999:11). By adhering to the position of empirical realism as formulated by Kant, Surūsh (1994b:257) opposes the idealist mingling of phenomena and reason and endorses a diachronical view of science, motivated by his interest in evolution of human thought:

[9] Cf. Surūsh 1994b:269. Surūsh is, however, influenced by Hegel's dialectics. Referring to the Hegelian notion of assimilation, Surūsh stresses the fact of the oppositional structure of existence, where the self is comprehended and becomes itself in and through the *other* discursively. He believes, for instance, that we cannot fully grasp the thought of Murtaḍā Muṭahharī without any acquaintance with Marxist ideology (Surūsh 1996c:139).

[10] Cf. Surūsh 1994b:230.

[11] Cf. Surūsh 1996a:184.

In the same manner, the ancient sages did not propose a historical method for understanding the allegedly unfolding nature of water, man or fire. They did not entrust the definitions of these entities to the vicissitudes of history. Kant, who was awakened from his dogmatic slumber by Hume, recognised the human character of our knowledge, rightly acquiring the title 'Father of modern epistemology'. His main contention was that knowledge always bears the stamp of humanity. For Kant, it is an impossible dream to vanish in the embrace of the naked truth as if there were no knowing subject to capture the truth in the first place. In his view, knowledge is *nasbī* (relative), but only in relation to the world of humanity, not in its relation to this or that specific knowing subject.

While Surūsh's theory of contraction and expansion has some common correspondences with, for instance, Rudolf Otto's (d. 1939) doctrine of *Entwicklungs-lehre geist* (Idea of spiritual development), the correspondence is significantly restricted to the view of evolution as the unfolding of a potential that is essentially qualitative and non-materialist. Surūsh's concept of history exhibits no tendency to teleological thought equivalent to that of the eighteenth century European theology, which teaches that there is a wise and intelligent Creator who ordered the course of things. It does not suppose that the goal of progress is in the future, according to which man has a chief end to which all his other purposes must be subordinated but rather believes that history terminates in the present. Referring to the British philosopher Robin G. Collingwood, Surūsh (1996c:259) argues that the task of the philosopher-historian is to demonstrate how the present with all its problems (in the form of events, opinions, etc) has come into existence and not how the future will be. "Collingwood, the contemporary British historian and philosopher, quoting the nineteenth century historian Lord Acton, advised the historians in the following manner to study problems not periods. That is, study follows from questioning".[12] As Mehrzad Boroujerdi argues, Surūsh adopts the term historicism mainly in a methodological sense rather than epistemological, in the sense that he has an interest in discovering the historical structures, patterns and trends that underlie scientific development. He states that Surūsh's position has some distinct similarities with Hegelian historicism, when defined in its epistemological sense as human knowledge constructed in time and space:

If one were to define 'historicism' in an epistemological sense, however, to denote the view that all human knowledge is essentially relative to time and place, then much of Sorush's own hypothesis can be viewed as 'historicist'. For example, his

[12] Collingwood was one of the first to recognise history as productive of results no less entitled to be called knowledge than those of natural sciences. He made a crucial contribution toward setting the philosophy of history on a new path where historical thought has an object with peculiarities of its own. Collingwood's (1948) attempt was very much to delineate the specific character of historical knowledge and understanding. He developed an account of historical understanding as imaginatively constructing historical events rather than by showing events to be instances of general uniformities that are established by induction.

belief in the idea of the accumulation and successive approximation of knowledge toward truth is itself a shadowy replica of the eighteenth-century enlightenment idea of progress, which fits very well within the confines of Hegel's philosophy of history (Boroujerdi 1996:174).

But it seems that the distinct concept of philosophy of science that emerges from Surūsh's writings, with its stress on falsification, remains very far from an historicist way of thinking. His approach to the philosophy of science is essentially structural. Since no truly 'historical' element is considered relevant in understanding the structure of scientific theories, he is, rather, disposed towards a structuralist interpretation of history than a historicisation of scientific structures. His concept of scientific change is (as will be properly elucidated below), similar to that of Popper (1969:11) in his *The Poverty of historicism*, concerned with historical trends rather than a single law of nature or evolution, and it recognises no religious, scientific or rational laws of historical development that make history predictable. For Surūsh, history is influenced by the growth of knowledge that proceeds from our problems and our independent attempts to formulate theories that go beyond existing knowledge. In contrast to the post-Hegelian epistemological historicists, he clearly differentiates the epistemic value of scientific theories from historical hermeneutics or interpretation and values history as human rather than humanity as historical:

There is an essential difference between our arguments and those of the fatalistic and deterministic school. Our views are in no way based on the assumption that history enfolds according to a predestined plan. Human history is made out of human choice that emanates from human nature. Only in this sense is history natural; it reveals the nature of our understanding of history. My argument is that no external hand can be said to interfer with and alter history or use human beings as instruments for the justification of its own goals and desires. There is no trace of Hegel's 'cunning of reason' in our understanding of history. One hundred percent of what transpires in history is caused by human volition, not a predetermined plan. The free will and action of humanity is the very core and domain of history (Surūsh:269).[13]

Surūsh is nevertheless primarily influenced by writings of Collingwood and Toynbee rather than Kant or Popper in his conceptualisation of history. In contrast to Popper's account on the sociology of knowledge or the public character of science, Surūsh is interested in reconciling philosophy and history in order to present a philosophical reflection upon the enfolding of human knowledge. He is in particular inspired by Collingwood's assertions about the necessity of rational faith and his refusal to ascribe a monopoly of truth to any scientific discipline. He shares Collingwood's ambiguous views on the questioning of any universal characteristic of knowledge and he is not

[13] Aware of the traps of epistemological historicism, Surūsh (1996a:193) also maintains that history cannot be the sole source for religious truth since that would run against Shi'i historical and existential conscience.

wholesomely convinced of finding a truth that is universal and valid for all thought. While Surūsh does not embrace Collingwood's idea of a priori historical imagination, he matches Collingwood's criterion of the ideal historian as being a reflective philosopher whose philosophy in particular includes special attention to the problems of historical thought. But what is most striking in Surūsh's influence from Collingwood is the recognition of historical knowledge as man's knowledge of man rather than man's knowledge of the gods. In his book *Tafarruj-i sun'*, Surūsh makes a conscious break with the traditional Islamic concept of *fiṭrat* (natural disposition). Ultimately inspired in his pessimism by Hobbes, he argues that this term, rather than being a transcendent ethic by content, must be considered anthropologically within the horizons of history. In contrast to the traditional view of *fiṭrat*, which depicts the cosmological state of man as something constant and permanent from which there only are insignificant deviations at certain moments of history, Surūsh (1994b:264–268) claims that *insān-i mustaqīm wa tabīʿī* (immediate and natural man) cannot be found anywhere but in history:

> The rubbish and sewage of the cities inform us of the civilised lifestyle. These pollutions are natural and common; human life itself generates them. Refuse is a problem that must not be wished away but acknowledged and handled. This acknowledgement is necessary for understanding human life on earth. By the same token, medical and biological scientists cannot avoid the study of blood, urine, and the like. Depravities and obscenities can function as a valuable *rāhnamā-yi mitūdīk* (methodical guide). Decadence is necessary for learning about decency, and indecent practise is instructive for method. Jokes, dreams and sexual perversions that for centuries were ignored or merely cursed and damned have provided psychotherapists with insights into the depth of the human psyche. Those who search for the natural dispositions of man have to look into history, which is the place for the most adequate manifestation of immediate and natural man. […] History is the most natural stage on which humankind has expressed itself. It is hence the best means for knowing it. On this stage, human beings have not hidden, altered or exaggerated their true nature. They have not been forced to sway away from their inner nature. They have, in other words, left in their historical wake obvious hints about their nature for the benefit of posterity.[14]

Consequently, Surūsh is highly critical of the a-historic idealism that he believes is characteristic not only of traditional *fiqh*, but also of the writings of several contemporary authors such as Ḥusain ʿAlī Muntaẓirī and ʿAbdullāh Jawādī-Āmulī. In a reply to an article written by Muntaẓirī on the

[14] Cf. Surūsh 1994d:67–73. In his book *Ṣirāṭhā-yi mustaqīm* (Straight paths), Surūsh (1999d:59) draws the radical conclusion that the whole development of the religious phenomenon itself, such as the articulation of specific sectarian positions, has a definite historical mark in terms which come close to reducing the metaphysical to the historical. "There exists no such a thing as genuine Shi'i Islam or genuine Sunni Islam. […] Shi'i Islam is merely the history of Shi'i Islam in the same sense that Sunni Islam is merely the history of Sunni Islam".

nature of Islamic law in the twenty-first century, he rejects in particular the former's supra-historical view of man when it comes to the nature of legal norms that have socio-political implications:

> My impression of the general arguments in the honourable *āyatullāh* Muntaẓirī's article in the journal *Kiyān* is that he considers the addressee of divine legal norms to be *insān-i fiṭrī* (natural man), a supra-historical or non-historical being. He considers generally legal norms in terms of their supra-historical disposition as if topics such as travel, marriage or murder have a one-scale character. This presupposition is not only to be found in his writings but in the writings of most jurists. It seems as if these honourable jurists believe that man on account of being human and possessing a permanent and fixed identity is the addressee of divine norms and not in respect of being a historical being with a social identity subjected to mental, social and political changes (Surūsh 1999i:20).

Surūsh's conception of the historical identity of man runs evidently against the traditional Islamic view of history which includes God among the *dramatis personae*. In fact, he suggests that there no longer can be anything 'mystical' about terrestrial space, since the configuration of history no longer is *payāmbar-parwar* (prophet-nurturing) (Surūsh 2000d:7). By considering history in rational and scientific terms, history is not necessary because revelation is historical (through prophets sent to given peoples at given times) or because life on earth is supposed to culminate in the blissful reappearance of the hidden *imām* (which is the case according to traditional Shi'i milleniarism), but because evolution is inherently self-guiding and governed by an inner dynamic force. By arguing that history cannot be manipulated or distorted by anything external, he releases the subject matter of history from its traditionally determined esoteric and law-based meta-historic vision and makes religious historical conscience amendable to secular and humanistic notions of man's cosmological position (Surūsh 1994b:262). While the historical product of traditional Islamic science and thought may yield insights, it is in Surūsh's view more of an object of judgement for new understanding than an aid to it. The overall results of his exposition on history as well as jurisprudence that considers Islamic law as mutable and subjected to constant flux, makes human knowledge on religion increasingly receptive to external historical circumstances.

C. Critical rationality: Self-determining and liberated

In contrast to the traditional Shi'i belief that certainty is achieved through God's knowledge as revealed to and transmitted through the Prophet and the *imāms*, the point of departure of Surūsh's treatment of rationality is that the believer has the right to employ his or her intellect independently. The human mind is in his view creative, not receptive. Influenced by the enlightenment insistence on the methodical character of reason, he does not accept reason as theologically ordered toward truth but believes that reason invents itself and constructs its truths by way of critical methodologies. Aware of the need to clarify the boundaries of human rationality in order to have a theoretical basis for hermeneutical questions, such as the question of difference of knowledge, experience and form, he considers in general reason as complementary to revelation.[15] In a 1991 essay on the nature of reason, Surūsh (1991:9) acknowledges that the term has multiple meanings and he characterises the human faculty of reasoning as well as reasoning itself. He maintains that reason is adopted in a variety of contexts as an activity and discipline and divided into categories such as *naẓarī* ('visionary'), *ʿamalī* (practical), *kasbī* (acquired), *fiṭrī* (innate), *juzʾī* (particular) and *kullī* (universal). Referring to a number of *akhbār* from ʿAlī b. Abī Ṭālib and Jaʿfar al-Ṣādiq that praise wisdom and intellection, he concludes that reason is the lens man needs for comprehending revelation:

> God has given humankind two proofs: The exoteric proof and the esoteric proof. The exoteric proof is the Prophet and the esoteric is reason. This means that reason and the Prophet are of the same kind, since both have a common source and function as eyes. Reason serves as a lens to see revelation while revelation makes reason catch sight of higher points. The relationship between revelation and reason is similar to the relationship between the eye and a lens, not that of two opposites. It is also similar to the relationship between a lamp that gives little light and a lamp that gives abundant light in the sense that the second makes the former of little value or even ineffective. In our time, the light of revelation has been wiped out and we are in need of reason more than ever before (ibid.:12).

While Surūsh in his early writing *Nahād-i nā-ārām-i jahān* considers reason as an instrument of faith, where science accordingly is defined in mystical terms as a hierarchical light consisting of various inner levels that man discovers with his rational faculty, he seems more aware of the contradiction between critical reason and the transcendent mystical grounding of knowledge in a 1984 essay on the causalistic cosmologies of Muḥammad al-Ghazālī and Jalāl al-dīn Rūmī. He criticises these two followers of *ashaʿrī* theology for placing God above human notions of causality and justice and claims that their God "is an illogical and self-centred God that has no rational and ethical justification for His action" and concludes that "there is

[15] Cf. Surūsh 1999d:73 and 85.

hence no way to have faith in Him" (1996d:192–193).[16] In *Farbihtar az īdiʾūlūzhī* (Loftier than ideology), Surūsh calls furthermore for a transformation of hierarchical relationships between reason and revelation that separates critical philosophical rationalism from mystical metaphysics. He despises the traditional view of reason as depository of truths that allows for its separation from freedom and considers the enterprise of rationality as an all-or-nothing project, or more correctly procedure, since the justification of religion cannot be complete without critique and analysis:

My discussion is about the kind of reason that serves as a dynamic faculty for thinking and seeking the truth. It is about the kind of freedom that is required by reason *qua* reason... There are two categories of reason: reason as destination and reason as path. The first sees reason as the source and repository of truths. The second sees it as a critical, dynamic and forbearing force that meticulously seeks the truth by negotiating tortuous paths of trial and error, for instance, through philosophy. [...] The dynamic view of reason prefers *khaṭā-yi rawishmand* (methodologically acquired error), since it contains the kind of movement that is the only guarantor of life and longevity of reason. The advocates of administered truth need no room for questioning and doubt; dynamic reason sees such an environment as stifling and stupefying (Surūsh 1996a:236–239).

Inspired by enlightenment thinkers, Surūsh adopts the second definition of reason as a dynamic and critical activity and argues that reason must be liberated, unbound and free to function in accordance with its own rules. In *Qabḍ wa basṭ-i tiʾūrīk-i sharīʿat*, he claims that while reason is granted a highly esteemed position in Shi'i law despite the dogmatic effort of the *akhbārī* school to reject it, this high status was never actually concretised, since the ambiguous nature of human rationality was never systematically theorised by traditional Islamic scholars. As he argues, the function of rationality in Islamic law has hitherto been that of a servant of a sacred and polemical notion of religion:

This principle is particularly pertinent and true in the case of Islamic law, since *sharīʿat* invites and persuades people to investigate history, explore the world and examine nature. The kind of *sharīʿat* that has this attribute cannot disavow the products of rational research and analysis or consider them as offensive or improper. It is not possible to invite a person to rational thinking from one angle and reject and degrade the results of rational thinking from the other (Surūsh 1996c:388).

The role of rationality in the arena of religion has hitherto been that of a timid and discreet servant of understanding and defence of religion. Defence and affirmation cannot however be complete without critique and analysis. The enterprise of

[16] This line of argument is also developed in Surūsh's (1996a:285–291) article on the concept of causality and justice in Rūmī's poetry where he asserts that the *ashaʿrī* view, which states that evil as well as good comes from God, believes that God can impose on men obligations that they are incapable of carrying out. He can punish a creature who has not sinned and without owing him any compensation. In Surūsh's view, this God owes man no justice and goodness and is hence an immoral God.

rationality is an all-or-nothing project. One cannot employ reason to attest to the truth of one's opinions without leaving the door open to its fault-finding. The attempt to enjoy the sweet affirmation of reason without tasting its bitter reproach is pure self-delusion. Writing books in defence of women's rights, human rights, and the system of government in Islam, summoning reason to affirm and defend the truth of one's arguments while turning a deaf ear to rational critique of the rest of one's beliefs exemplifies a half-finished enterprise that falls short of the requirements of reasoned discourse and the standard of rationality (Surūsh 1997a:333).

In his criticism of traditional metaphysics, Surūsh (1996c:253) claims that all conscious cognition involves selection, organisation and interpretation, including mystical experience, which is different in the sense that it involves interpreting at another level of meaning. Since the communication of mystical experience has no choice but to use representation it becomes knowledge by correspondence. While metaphysics and the higher levels of consciousness are accepted as a method of understanding metaphysical reality, it is only a method and not necessarily the most elevated method, since the transcendental desire is unsatisfying with respect to the historicality and social heterogeneity of understanding. It is, in his view, a desire that always seems to end in contempt for interpretation and a suspicion concerning the whole idea of interpretative dialogue. Limiting reason to discursive cunning in the modern world, i.e. an analytical function, he believes that the cognitive categories of philosophy and theosophy, however, can help us to acquire a better comprehension of human existence:

This delivery is not merely fostered by science, but also by philosophy and theosophy. The judgements of the philosophers and the experiences of the mystics also assist the understanding of revelation and the comprehension of the world. When we approach the external world, we are forced to give meaning to every object and this meaning is contingent on scientific, philosophical and theosophical theories. Even the sentence 'God has created the world' does not have one single possible meaning (ibid.:138).[17]

Surūsh ultimately leaves religious belief at the mercy of ever-changing scientific theories caught in the process of constant transformation. In the recognition of the limits of dogmatic reason, he argues that reason cannot be supposed to provide truths about transcendent reality, since it rarely figures as the harbinger of righteousness, bliss and common good of mankind. Referring to Rūmī's concept of *ʿaql-i dīw* (demon's reason), he asserts that even the advocates of transcendent reason accept that human beings can be misled by their own reason (Surūsh 1994b:247–257). But while Surūsh's reason, contrary to the pure and untainted intellect of theosophy, has a distinct human character, he is not prepared to sacrifice reason, similar to the sophists, because of its occasional faults and afflictions. Similar to Dilthey, the primary figure in the movement called 'historicism', who wrote his

[17] Cf. Surūsh 1999d:146.

Critique of the historical reason as a prolongation of Kant's *Kritik der reinen vernunft* in order to provide historical sciences with the same character of real science that natural science already had, Surūsh (ibid.:260) considers knowledge as 'historical reason'. But while Surūsh emphasises the importance of historical development in our understanding, he does not place the problem of hermeneutics to the first level of a priori epistemological preoccupations, where it is concerned with questions of ontology. In this sense, he disagrees with Dilthey, who perceives existence as having a radically hermeneutic character, where understanding is the fundamental ontological structure of existence.

Asserting that the majority of human convictions are conjectural, Surūsh suggests that rational belief requires a critical attitude in which we do not simply believe whatever seems to be so but test and probe and insist upon taking account of all relevant considerations. The outcome of his epistemology is the so-called *ʿaqlānīyat-i intiqādī* (critical rationality), where reason is used in an independent and more unrestricted manner to constantly threaten our most cherished and comforting assumptions. His discourse ultimately connects to enlightenment, where reason denotes logical analysis and thinking and the certainty of absolute knowledge is relativised. But while Surūsh, similar to the enlightenment thinkers, attempts to free reason from the clutches of history as well as culture, the theory of contraction and expansion subjects reason to constant change and makes the acquiring of objective culture-transcending knowledge difficult. While reason is indispensable as the major source of scientific theories, together with observation and intellectual intuition, it is no firm authority of knowledge since it is uncertain and unreliable. To be a rationalist is, in his view, hence to deny the omnipotence of pure reason:

> My position is in actual fact that of critical or sophisticated rationality in the sense that I believe that the world of reality, whether religion, philosophy or nature, has become too complex for us to describe with a number of pure rational principles or via the manifestation of our [inner] hearts. The most salient result of critical rationality is that the majority of human convictions are nothing but conjectures. This does not mean that we do not have the capacity to get hold of reality but rather that the grasping of reality has no clear sign and that the indications employed by traditional philosophy, such as *bidāhat* ('invention'), *yaqīn*, and the like, are flawed and insufficient. We cannot therefore simply claim that this is truth or that truth is erroneous. [...] We comprehend conjectures in common experience, in the interpretation of text or in religious experience, *fiqh* and science. As Kant says, these conjectures appear very natural to us and it lies in the nature of reason to arrive at a cul-de-sac from time to time, since multiple rationales disclose a variety of interpretations of one single observable fact and no interpretation is capable of refuting the others (Surūsh 1999d:144–146).

D. Science: Falsification and corroboration

Surūsh's general scientific exposition in *Qabḍ wa basṭ-i tiʾūrīk-i sharīʿat* connects mostly to the modern subject of the history of science, which substantiates the theory of contraction and expansion using a theoretical basis. He draws on the ideas of a broad spectrum of Western philosophers such as Karl R. Popper, Alfred N. Whitehead, Immanuel Kant, Wilfred van Orman Quine, Imre Lakatos and Rene Descartes. His point of departure is that science essentially is different from philosophy, although not its replacement. He defines science as a branch of human learning with a collective and flowing identity, a mirror of all aspects of human existence, composed of subjects, motives and methods:

> Our object with the concept 'science' in this discussion is a branch of subjects that is composed of *guzārahā* (theorems), i.e. a collection of theorems that is unified by a common subject, motive or method, and this we comprehend as a branch of science. It becomes hence obvious that our discussion is not concerned with the conjecture or certainty of theorems, which belongs to the state of the individual scholar, but rather with the relationship between the theorems and reality as well as the relationship between the theorems themselves (Surūsh 1996c:93).

While Surūsh adheres to the Cartesian conviction of the possibility of dividing culture into areas in which we have 'objectivity' and 'rationality', the hard and the mature sciences, he opposes the notion that softer areas of discourse, such as religion, morals and art, do not count as 'knowledge'. He acknowledges that the natural sciences have a mark of objectivity that the human sciences do not have but rejects the strict positivist division of sciences into human science, governed by philosophical and ideological values on the one hand, and non-speculative and objective natural science that operates with mathematical and experimental methods on the other. While claiming that the method of reasoning adopted by modern science is the method of reasoning that philosophy should also adopt in dealing with at least some of its problems, he disagrees with August Comte's notion that philosophical theory must assign a dominant intellectual role to empirical science. Metaphysical thinking should, in Surūsh's view, not be replaced by scientific thinking. He believes, rather, that metaphysical thinking should consist of a kind of scientific thinking. He criticises the stance of positivists who make a very strict distinction between the natural sciences and philosophical speculation and confine science and philosophy to the facts presented by experience. In his view, positivists from David Hume and John Locke to Rudolf Carnap and Carl Gustav Hempel frequently become engaged in the problem of the function of hypotheses in science since not every hypothesis has an empirical basis:

> For this very reason, some distinguished scholars have even made mistakes concerning the nature of natural science. Several positivists are afflicted with the

problem of the position of hypotheses in science, since a scientific hypothesis has non-sensible probability and is not a premise that has been realized through the senses. All hypotheses that possess theoretical concepts cannot be produced solely through the senses (Surūsh 1996c:95).[18]

While Surūsh does not refer to Dilthey's proposition which identifies *comprehension* as the specific cognitive operation of hermeneutic human science and *explanation* as the characteristic cognitive operation of the natural sciences, he seems to be aware of the serious problem involved in the above separation, since it proves impossible to base scientific historical knowledge on simple comprehension. The relationship between human sciences and *sharī'at* is a question that Surūsh is concerned with in his book *Tafarruj-i sun'*. He argues that modern Muslims' ambiguous and sometimes resistant attitude towards the humanities (in contrast to natural sciences) can largely be explained by the fact that the traditional Islamic theocentric concept of man is diametrically opposed to the intricate critical scrutiny of human existence that dominates modern humanities. He also claims that the humanities are not a product of divine law and by no means can be extracted from the revealed sources (Surūsh 1994b:9 and 195). In his attempt to acclimatise a wider acceptance of the human sciences in Iran, Surūsh refers to the writings of the British philosopher Gilbert Ryle (d. 1976) and explains that the human sciences, similar to natural science, have an empirical basis and are scientific and analytical. The human sciences are, in other words, not pure philosophy, which would be a tautology:

The second matter is that the humanities are equal to natural science in the sense that they are empirical science and not ethics or philosophy... It is correct that we need philosophy, ethics as well as theosophy and also other subjects that have not yet been discovered by man in order to know human society but none of these learnings replace empirical human science. An attribute of human science is that it is empirical in an anthropological sense but not *insān-shināsī* (anthropology) in the common sense (ibid.:18).

In his concern to raise the human sciences, including philosophy, to the level of science in some sense similar to mathematics and physics, Surūsh's position has affinities with the Kantian movement. The most fundamental terminological distinction of the theory of contraction and expansion is in fact the originally Kantian division between 'is' and 'ought', which in Surūsh's terminology corresponds to the levels of *taḥaqquq* (fulfilment) and *ta'rif* (description). In his early book *Dānish wa arzish* (Science and value), he examines the relations between these categories as well as other terminologies of modern science such as fact and value, end and means, and so on. He refutes the modern self-confidence that science supplies with a comprehensive alternative worldview to that of religion and argues that the

[18] Cf. Surūsh 1999a:303.

'deadly plague' of modern ethics is "the severe erroneous belief of deducing 'ought' from 'is', 'values' from 'realities' and 'ethics' from 'sciences'" (Surūsh 1983:8).[19] But in *Qabḍ wa basṭ-i tiʾūrīk-i sharīʿat*, Surūsh (1996c:99) argues oppositely that all sciences are characterised by a number of a-historical and abstract descriptions that depict what science ought to be, as well as a historical dimension that explains its gradual development and adopts the modern idea of ordering science as well as society according to 'is'. While all sciences are perfect and complete at the level of 'description', he claims that they engage in a constant and mutual dialogue at the level of 'fulfilment':

It is therefore evident that our object with knowledge, in particular religious knowledge, is a collection of theorems that is produced from a specific form of *dāwarī* (justification). The production of knowledge occurs after justification. We must hence distinguish the two levels of science, the level of 'ought' and the level of 'is'. The level of 'ought' corresponds to the level of description and the level of 'is' corresponds to the level of fulfilment (Surūsh 1996c:96).

It becomes in particular evident that religious knowledge on the level of fulfilment is related and interconnected in a dialogue with other sciences at the level of fulfilment, where they mutually influence each other. Their relation at the level of description is another topic, which is beyond the framework of the present discussion (ibid.:113).

Since Surūsh's theory of contraction and expansion relates to science according to the category of *taḥaqquq*, it does not involve 'first philosophy' as grounding, and sitting in judgement of, science and the rest of the epistemic culture on account of philosophy providing us with apodictic knowledge on the foundations of knowledge. He claims that his analysis is restricted to *tauṣīf* (report) and does not indulge in questions related to *taklīf* (prescription) (ibid.:170). Surūsh refrains, therefore, from rendering a criterion to separate true opinions from false opinions since all interpretations are subjected to flow and variation. His attempt is rather one of giving an empirical and historical account of divine guidance and human rationality (Surūsh 1999d:95–97). He rejects any normative function of epistemology and claims that we can only describe how we arrive at knowledge. In fact, he accentuates that the study of the linear development of religious knowledge is not equal to extracting new philosophical and scientific information and data from the revealed sources:

The purpose of a linear development of legal understanding and religious knowledge is not to bring forth new philosophical and scientific explorations from the Qur'an and *riwāyat* and to demonstrate their compulsory and legally binding character. The

[19] In Neo-Kantian philosophy, a sharp separation is generally made between the existential and normative grounds of the 'is' (*Sein*) and the 'ought' (*Sollen*). Kant himself showed the impossibility of deducing from what 'is' that which is valuable, that which is right and that which 'ought' to be. Cf. Friedrich 1958:166.

argument is rather that a deeper human exploration of reality lends a hand to a deeper exploration of the content of revelation according to the mechanism of falsification, i.e. that meanings are contingent on theories (Surūsh 1996c:303).

Surūsh (ibid.:170) specifies that what distinguishes the modern *raushanfikr-i dīnī* (religious intellectual) from the *ʿālim-i dīnī* (religious scholar), who considers religion only in an a priori way, is his or her understanding of religion from the 'outside'. He argues that since not every religious scholar is a traditionally trained *ʿālim*, new concepts of *ʿilm* and *ʿālim* are necessary in line with the criterion that whoever is "competent to interpret" and shed light on the revealed text is an *ʿālim* (Bodi 1996:20). As opposed to the Iranian climate of a generation ago, when the notion of an Islamic intellectual was almost a contradiction in terms due to the denotation of this term as the enlightened liberation of reason, Surūsh attempts to make religious thinking intellectually respectable.[20] His definition of the term *raushanfikr* (intellectual) is not restricted to religious believers. The intellectual is, rather, the child of modernity and the intelligentsia is comprised of thinkers from the university as well as the *ḥauzah*, who have in common their efforts to create a *guftamān* (discourse) between tradition and modernity in common in terms of criticising tradition in the light of modern knowledge (Surūsh 1997a:188).[21] As far as Islamic law is concerned, Surūsh claims that the whole discourse on *fiqh-i pūyā* and *fiqh-i sunnatī* therefore only states two interpretative possibilities, the one concerned with capacity of law and the other with pureness of law. Indifferent to the specific philosophy of future Islamic jurisprudences, he argues that whether the new methodology of law is called *fiqh-i puyā* or anything else, similar to the story of *ghaimah wa qaimah* (two different ways to spell a Persian meal), is of secondary importance and that "what is of importance is the split peas and the meat, the spelling does not matter":

> Does not all the talk, also in our country, about *pūyā* and *sunnatī* and the emphasis that one group lays on tradition and the love they exhibit for the pureness of religion and the rush another group has in the renovation of thought and reunderstanding of principles, demonstrate that both of the two groups react on the inroad of external knowledge and opinions? Both have found that a flood has arrived that will not leave the house in its prior position and place (Surūsh 1996c:175).[22]

In a recent interview, Surūsh (1999k) refutes the contemporary Shi'i discourse on *fiqh-i pūyā* as "empty talk" and argues that this legal faction establishes all its reasoning on the revealed texts and actually restricts the use of reason in every way. He also claims that most of the advocates of

[20] Cf. Richard 1995:194.
[21] Cf. Surūsh 1999c:22, 35, 47 and 246.
[22] Cf. Surūsh 1999c:318–319, 1999f:37 and 1999a:78. Surūsh's position differs in this respect from the general academic view that portrays him as an advocate of *fiqh-i pūyā*. Cf. Vahdat 1998:394.

fiqh-i pūyā have not articulated any systematic theoretical outlook. They instead focus on minor issues such as the *khulūṣ* of Islamic law instead of producing a critical analysis of the subject matter of the so-called 'dynamic' attribute of Islamic law. Nevertheless, he believes that the effort of dynamising jurisprudence by contemporary jurists "demonstrates that the notion of contingency has penetrated (Islamic) thought" (Surūsh 1996c:176). While the theory of contraction and expansion explains the existence of divergent interpretation, it does not, in other words, attempt to solve the contractions or conflicts at hand:

> The original purpose of the theory of contraction and expansion is not to solve the conflict between traditional jurisprudence and dynamic jurisprudence, to modernise religion, to decipher or complete Islamic law or to relativise and deny truth but to highlight the meaning of how religion is comprehended and in what sense this understanding accepts evolution. As long as the enigma of religious understanding and evolution of religious knowledge is not comprehended, the effort to revive religion remains incomplete (ibid.:57).

Instead of making a systematic study of the historical development of the traditional Islamic disciplines, Surūsh adopts the conceptual framework and terminology of analytical philosophy and divides the sciences into two categories: *taulīd-kunandah* (producing) and *maṣraf-kunandah* (consuming). While he underlines that all sciences are active on a common level since human knowledge in its totality is subjected to mutual transaction, he explains that there is a logical relation between the sciences that motivates a differentiation. As he argues, the producing sciences have "an intrinsic theoretical aspect and are law-making" (ibid.:88). Among the producing sciences, he mentions physics, psychology, mathematics, sociology, chemistry and philosophy in contrast to sciences, such as jurisprudence, theology, medicine and administration, which are consuming sciences. As the classification is basically related to the question of theories, he asserts that scientific theories formed by the producing sciences are adopted by the consuming sciences. Medicine or administration have, for instance, no theories of their own, but adopt the theories used by biochemistry, histology and anatomy respectively psychology and sociology. Acknowledging the existence of exceptions to the above scheme, Surūsh defines the modern discipline of history as a producing science despite the fact that history is contingent on other disciplines, such as economy, psychology and sociology for its growth.[23] The increasing autonomy of certain consuming sciences is therefore explained by their expansion in the realm of theory and methodology that is due to the collecting of ingredients and data from the

[23] In this respect, Surūsh (1996c:89) refers to the scientific classifications of Ibn Khaldūn whom, similar to the British historian Arnold Toynbee, he considers the founder of historical analysis, "even if the extent of his success to implement a sociological study of historical growth can be disputed". Cf. Toynbee 1935:322.

producing sciences:

Science can be divided into two categories: producing and consuming sciences. The producing sciences have an intrinsic theoretical character and are law-making. The consuming sciences are sciences that consume and make use of the theories that are produced by the producing sciences. *ʿIlm-i ṭabb* (medicine) is a delicate example of a consuming science. The consuming sciences are a mixture of knowledge and skill in the sense that the scientist must be knowledgeable about certain theories and also have some skill in their practical use and benefit. Medicine is such as science. There is a group of sciences called 'basic medical sciences', which include biochemistry, histology, anatomy, physiology, and the like. These are producing sciences that in a direct manner give a picture of external reality and describe it in order to articulate laws. The medical doctor studies this group of sciences and learns about their theories in order to implement them in their daily work. In this respect, we characterise medicine as a consuming science (ibid.:88).

In *Qabḍ wa basṭ-i tiʾūrīk-i sharīʿat* (ibid.:151), Surūsh argues that the pure distinction producing/consuming sciences is not exhaustive for elucidating the relationship between the scientific disciplines, but that this does not imply that no relations exist or that all relations pertain to production of theories in science. He claims that many relations are not connected to logic by referring to the use of mathematical methods in many disciplines, such as physics, chemistry and sociology or the relationship between philosophy and natural science. Alluding to Kant's argument of a priori concepts or categories of the pure understanding, he argues that the logical principles themselves rather are based on a priori philosophical premises. He believes that science would prove impossible without a number of a priori ('from what is before– experience') propositions such as the premise that the world of phenomena exists since observations always are interpreted in the context of a priori knowledge.[24] Knowledge of the external world rests not merely on sense experience but requires nonempirical or a priori principles to validate it and human sensory representations are not self-validating:

Another example is the contingency of natural science to philosophy. When human beings initiate scientific research, they take advantage of much preliminary data without which natural science would prove impossible. These preliminary data have

[24] In philosophy, a priori knowledge is frequently equivalent to innate ideas and necessary truths. In Kant's view, a priori knowledge concerns only necessary synthetic judgements that cannot be proved analytically in contrast to a posteriori knowledge that concerns only contingent truths. Kant divided all sentences according to their logical form into analytic and synthetic ones, the analytic being those that are decidable as true or false using logic alone. The synthetic a priori are contributions of our minds to knowledge, prior to experience because they are brought to experience by the mind. A priori concepts and intuitions are hence in a way necessary and universal in their application (Parson 1992). As will be properly elucidated below, Surūsh suggests that whether knowledge is a priori is quite a different question from whether it is innate. As he argues, mathematics provides the most often cited examples of a priori knowledge but is no doubt acquired through experience even though it is justifiable independently of experience.

a perceptual and corroborative basis. In order to pursue natural science, we must, for instance, presuppose that external reality does exist. This is a philosophical preliminary that the whole scientific study rests on. In similar terms, we must acknowledge that our sense organs and intelligence are capable of comprehending reality and that our intellect is reliable, and so on. Therefore, we say that natural science is based on philosophy and without recourse to these philosophical premises all natural science are without meaning (ibid.:151).

Surūsh's reliance on intuitive knowledge independent of experience, as distinguished from deduction, the second source of knowledge, arrived at by unmediated reflecting upon the content of our concepts, fulfills the minimum claim of rationalism, i.e. that some of our a priori beliefs seem to be true. In contrast to several recognised empiricists, who not only deny a priori propositions but also a priori concepts, Surūsh's theory of meaning (inspired by Kant's subsuming of Descartes rationalism and Bacon's empiricism) asserts that there are necessary concepts that are not derived from or correlated with experimental features of the world.[25] While Surūsh does not consider epistemology as Descartian 'first philosophy', where the theory of knowledge is prior to any empirical knowledge, his position is very much foundationalist in the sense that he supposes the existence of non-inferential, nonsensory knowledge acquired by a kind of basic intellectual insight. Needless to say, his position has its dilemmas when combined with Popper's falsification principle which runs against foundationalist claims (as well as commonsensic and reductionistic induction). He is therefore a rationalist in the sense that he supposes that the conditions for science cannot be discovered but only be reasoned to through experience. While he does not yield to the enthusiasms of rationalism as he rejects the dogmatism of reason by affirming a self-critical rationalism, the question remains as to what extent the demonstrative element in his epistemological thought transcends the purely empirical.

Affirming the insistence of epistemological coherentism that the justifiability of belief is determined jointly by all of one's beliefs taken together, Surūsh explains that the principle of coherence elucidates why Islamic philosophers have a dominantly Aristotelian or Platonic interpretation of Islam and why the philosophical perspectives of religion is governed by specific philosophies themselves. In his terminology, the coherence theory is called *intiẓār-i mā az dīn* (our expectation of religion) and states that the validity of any proposition consists in its coherence with some specified set of propositions.[26] In contrast to the correspondence

[25] Kant believed that the principle of universal causality is a priori and Descartes thought there was an a priori argument for God's existence.

[26] Cf. Surūsh 1997a:135. Surūsh seems in this respect to be influenced by Popper's (1972:344) idea that observation always presupposes the existence of some 'system of expectations', i.e. that the process of knowing begins when observations clash with existing theories or preconceptions.

theory, which states that the truth conditions of propositions are not (in general) propositions, but rather objective features of the world, the valid conditions of propositions consist, in his view, of other propositions. Surūsh (ibid.:409–410) refers, for instance, to the dispute between Hādī Sabziwārī and ʿAbd al-Razzāq Lāhijī on the question of the Prophet's *miʿrāj* (body-ascension to Heaven) and argues that Sabziwārī's Greek philosophy legitimised his belief in body-ascension, in contrast to Lāhijī, whose rejection of Hellenistic influences on Qur'anic teachings made him preserve the *ẓawāhir-i sharīʿat* (literal words of *sharīʿat*) and defend a purely spiritual interpretation.

But while Islamic thinkers such as Sabziwārī, Faiḍ al-Kāshānī and Ṣadr al-dīn Shīrāzī attempted to integrate *fiqh* into philosophy with the aim of reaching peace between *sharīʿat* and philosophy, Surūsh (1999a:307) refutes their attempt as a frail and inauspicious compromise in the sense that their positions presuppose a specific traditional philosophical view of Islamic law. He argues, however, that the coherence principle clarifies that the contemporary dilemma of Islamic thought primarily involve a conflict between premodern philosophies and modern ones rather than a disagreement between religion and philosophy. Rejecting contemporary traditionalist interpretations of Islam as epistemologically incompatible, Surūsh believes that the contradictory character of traditionalist interpretations of Islamic law is due to the inconsistency of their philosophical and anthropological viewpoints:

> If the traditionalists' interpretations of jurisprudence are traditional, the secret is that their anthropology, i.e. their conception of man, society and the relationship between God and man, and so on, is traditional. Therefore, their expectation of religion and *fiqh* is traditional. They honestly make an effort to infer legal norms but their presuppositions, i.e. anthropological and sociological data, are bound to interfere with their inference. Their conclusions therefore always become so strange and *traditional* (Surūsh 1996c:189). [27]

But in contrast to modern epistemological coherence theories, Surūsh's analysis supposes the existence of epistemologically basic beliefs (i.e. beliefs that must be justified independent of reason), which distinguishes his position from that of the coherentists. As will be properly elucidated below, he accords this special epistemic status to *tawātur* ("succesive hearsay")[28] which emerges as a privileged subset of his entire doxastic corpus. Surūsh's purpose with the classification producing/consuming sciences is not to

[27] For Surūsh's criticism of Muḥammad Ḥusain Ṭabāṭabāʾī, ʿAbdullāh Jawādī-Āmulī, Ṣādiq Lārījānī and Seyyed Hossein Nasr, cf. Surūsh 1996c:37–41, 222–241, 528–564 and 1999c:87.

[28] In modern Persian, the term *tawātur* denotes a recurrent mode of transmission and is used synonymously with the Qur'an and *ḥadīṯ*. In this respect, it is significant that Surūsh is unconcerned with the possibility of error or forgery of the latter textual material and its channels of transmission despite his view that these sources yield some kind of basic and hence necessary knowledge.

articulate a set of rational arguments for the validation of religious truths but rather to point to the close relationship between modern philosophical anthropology and our understanding of nature, epistemology and religion as if they constitute "part of a circle" (ibid.:91). Reflecting on the constituency of traditional Islamic science, he argues that the religious sciences such as *ʿilm al-kalām* have become consuming sciences:

During one period theology was a producing science in the sense that it formed its own philosophy. Theologians were also philosophers and even opposed the *falsafah* of the philosophers whose philosophical principles were considered distorted. They established hence their own principles in order to clarify and confirm the tenets of *sharīʿat* and to repel doubt. But from the time of Naṣir al-dīn Ṭūsī and onwards theology has truly become a consuming science. Ṭūsī did not believe it necessary for theology and philosophy to work out separate philosophies. Instead, he argued that theology could benefit from the philosophy of the philosophers, which he considered more grounded than the philosophy of the theologians. Theology became contingent on philosophy and lost its previous autonomy, at least among Shi'i thinkers (ibid.:90).

Naṣir al-dīn Ṭūsī's rapprochement of Hellenistic philosophy and Islamic theology was, in Surūsh's view, a determining factor in the decay of Shi'i theology. But what he seems to neglect is that the contingency of theology to philosophical theories and arguments did not result in any particular concession on behalf of theology to the philosophical dogmas.[29] Surūsh argues, however, that the result of the 'contraction' of Islamic theology is that this discipline, in its capacity as a consuming science, has become increasingly receptive to the developments of modern science. He actually claims that theology borrows its theories, methods and terminology from the modern sciences to the extent that "every change in these sciences categorically influences theology" (ibid.:90). As regards *fiqh*, he suggests that jurisprudence is a consuming science "in the complete sense" and is contingent on the methodological principles of theology for its expansion. In the sense that *fiqh* presupposes certain propositions about God, prophethood and man which form the subject matter of theology, he believes that a prior transformation of the theological foundations of *fiqh* is necessary in order to dynamise Islamic law (ibid.:387).[30]

[29] It should be noted that Surūsh's view of Naṣīr al-dīn Ṭūsī is contested. As Wilfred Madelung (1968:27) argues, Ṭūsī's theological thought remained within the context of former Shi'i theological expositions. "His interest in philosophy, however, did not affect the orthodoxy of his position of Imāmite theology. His theological thought is to be viewed as part of that late phase of kalām which adopted some of the terminology, the methods of arguing and the logic of philosophy while rejecting any concession to it in dogma".

[30] Cf. Surūsh 1999i:21. Surūsh neglects to remark that *fiqh* and *ʿilm al-kalām* from their beginnings developed separately and that their relationship first became established when a system of religious sciences was developed. This system required that the *ʿulūm naqlīyah* be distinguished from the *ʿulūm ʿaqlīyah*, the former being set up on a higher pedestal than the latter and that a hierarchical system of religious sciences be elaborated.

For Surūsh, epistemology and hermeneutics (frequently intermingled in *Qabḍ wa basṭ*) stand in close relationship to all scientific disciplines and while the various divisions of philosophy differ in their subject and often in the approaches taken by philosophers to their characteristic questions, they have a common desire of arriving at the truth about reality. Besides the relationship of dialogue between the various sciences that takes place in logical (producing/consuming sciences) and non-logical relationships, he believes that the evolution of human knowledge and understanding is visible in the realm of hermeneutics-epistemology and methodology and in general approaches to specific problems.[31] In principle, hermeneutics is no different from any other branch of science in the sense that each scientific discipline attempts to arrive at a systematic understanding of issues that arise in its particular domain. The conception of knowledge attains, in other words, constantly new consciousness and identity that is collective and flowing in the sense that it occurs *ham-saṭḥī* (on a common level):

In short, the collective character of human learning is a rule that is corroborated deductively as well as inductively and can be observed in the continuous dialogue between the various human sciences (such as religious knowledge) in their response to the developments produced in various fields, in their participation in the reroute and demise of knowledge and in the continuous coordination and harmonization of knowledge (ibid.:212).[32]

Surūsh believes that the fundamental aspect which differentiates knowledge from understanding, which is individual, is that knowledge is *jamʿī wa jārī* (collective and flowing) in its social dimension. Inspired by Popper's evolutionary epistemology, he asserts that the collective character of knowledge is suggested by the fact that even if an *untrue* idea is refuted by a distinguished scientific scholar or even by the scientific community at large, that idea will still continue to exist in the collective knowledge. Collective knowledge implies, in his view, a historical identity as well, in the sense that contemporary scholars continuously partake of the knowledge of several generations of human learning. Referring to Michael Ruse's essay *Darwin's debt to philosophy*, Surūsh argues that Darwin's contribution to science was achieved due to previous scientific discoveries and knowledge and that the

[31] Referring to the ideas of Edwin Burtt and Arthur Koestler, Surūsh (1996c:152) argues that while the new philosophical basis of renaissance science provided modern science with a new epistemological structure, the new scientific discoveries and conclusions never influenced philosophy directly in order to confirm or falsify its conclusions. The new scientific renaissance instead had its roots in changes in *tafakkurāt-i falsafah-yi maʿrifat-shinākhtī* (hermeneutical philosophical thought). Surūsh (1996c:218) argues, for instance, that without the new emphasis of Galileo and Kepler on the quantity of forms, as illustrated in the latter's distinction primary qualities (quantity, shape and motion) and secondary qualities (odour, taste, sound etc), there could be no revival in mathematics. He considers the importance given to quantity of forms, as opposed to quality, to be the mark of modern science, where existence is quantified, mechanised and explained in mathematical terms (Surūsh 1999c:73).
[32] Cf. Surūsh 1996c:101 and 187.

reason why embryology was of chief concern to the theory of the mechanism of natural selection (modelled on Newtonian astronomy) stems directly from Darwin's acceptance of the Herschel-Whewell philosophy of theory-confirmation:

From Newton to Malthus, Herschell and Whewell, everyone played a part in the making of Darwin, and it was by relying on them and their inspiration and by measuring and balancing his own opinions against their opinions that Darwin presented and defended his own hypothesis. This is the meaning of the social identity of science (ibid.:229).[33]

In his assessment of the contraction and expansion of religious knowledge, Surūsh criticises the view of, for instance, Muḥammad Bāqir Ṣadr and others that interprets inductive inquiry in absolute terms as the principal catalyst behind scientific growth.[34] Whereas Surūsh (1994b:419) acknowledges that human understanding overall is based on inductive premises, he refers to the Kuhnian correspondence principle that the main reason behind scientific evolution is due to the fact that earlier theories are amalgamated and fused into the new ones. Suggesting that the Darwinian revolution of the nineteenth century supposes that human beings as the products of evolutionary development are natural beings, Surūsh argues that the human capacities for knowledge and belief are also the products of a natural evolutionary development. Closely resembling the process Darwin called natural selection, he argues, similar to Popper's evolutionary epistemology, that the growth of knowledge advances by means of conjecture and refutations.[35] In his view, there is no sharp division of labor between science and epistemology, and he therefore resorts to pure examples of deduction in the exposition of the theory of contraction and expansion:

[33] Cf. Ruse 1975. Surūsh (1996c:56, 101) also describes the collective nature of knowledge by reference to scientific positivism and Wittgenstein's philosophy, inherited from Kant.

[34] Cf. Surūsh 1994b:462–467. Surūsh (1994b:426) views the philosophical ideas of the Iraqi Shi'i jurist Muḥammad Bāqir Ṣadr (d. 1980) as the first Islamic critique of Western scientific method. Bāqir Ṣadr drew a new synthesis for economics by adapting new notions, such as banking and insurance, to Islamic norms. He also reconceptualised parts of Islamic legal methodology and the notion of *ijtihād* according to a diachronic approach that had no precedent in Shi'i writings. He adhered to *fiqh-i sunnatī* and maintained that reason can discover legal norms and that all legal norms are discovered through categorical judgments derived from the revealed texts based on abstract thought. He developed distinct notions of a popular Islamic political theory that have been influential in the Iranian intellectual context. His major works *Falsafatūna* (Our Philosophy) and *Iqtiṣādūna* (Our Economy) were mainly a response to the growing influence of secular intellectual discourses in Iraq in the 1960s.

[35] Cf. Popper 1972:17. Surūsh (1996c:423) claims that Darwin's theory of evolution altered the scientific as well as theological conception of man's place in the cosmos and also ultimately inspired recent post-positivist philosophers to formulate a modern evolutionary epistemology. He does not mention the arguments presented by European biologists against Darwinism, but rather is primarily interested in the incompatibility of Darwinism with traditional Islamic metaphysics. As far as the philosophical foundations are concerned, Surūsh seems to consider the groundwork of Darwin's theory of evolution as dogma and not as a scientific theory.

The examples that we refer to are not at all inductive examples but pure (or individual) examples that demonstrate the pure influence of external data on knowledge of the Qur'an and *sunnat*. This is so since even one analogical example confirms some premises. Our reservation towards induction is that it does not give us any pure cases, but cases corroborated by hundreds of generalisations (a pure example is a case of one generalisation). We cannot therefore judge which generalisation a certain induction depends on in order to draw a conclusion. In epistemology, mathematics, and logic (at least in a few cases), we give pure examples, not induction, in the sense that our norms are not derived inductively by analysing several deductions. A correct and concrete deduction derives from a deductive example in the general sense (Surūsh 1996c:516).[36]

The most salient feature of Surūsh's concept of science is that theories essentially are bold provisional conjectures that must be subjected to the most severe and searching criticism and experimental scrutiny of their truth claims. Inspired by Popper's idea of theoretical preference, he explains that scientific growth is related to the permanent contradictions that occur while new data and discoveries are introduced that either *iṯbāt* (confirm) or *ibṭāl* (refute, falsify) previous scientific assumptions by relying on other branches of science. The question of preference arises with respect to a set of competing theories. The falsification principle, the major meta-methodology or meta-instrument in the process of contraction and expansion of knowledge, concerns the *naqlī* (empirical-narrative), *ʿaqlī* (rational) as well as *tajrubī* (natural-empirical) sciences and opens two key possibilities to scientific hypotheses: it either falsifies or confirms them. Surūsh argues that whether a hypothesis is confirmed or falsified, allowing for the possibility of neither of these, the internal structure of previous knowledge is changed in the course of which "the circle of meaning" is expanded or contracted:

The way we inevitably settle on the occurrence of falsification and contradiction in science in order to remove contradiction is reliance on the other 'provinces' of science in order to acquire factual capability. In this respect, there is no difference between empirical-narrative, rational and natural-empirical science since each of them are occupied with describing reality (ibid.:401).[37]

[36] Despite its formal adherence to the falsification principle, Surūsh's theory of contraction and expansion derives largely from inductive reasoning since his historical examples in *Qabḍ wa basṭ-i tiʾūrīk-i sharīʿat*, taken together, form the structure of several inductive corroborations. Surūsh (1996c:212) is knowledgeable of this fact but seems to consider the historical examples as a sort of *tazkīr* (notification) in the general sense rather than *iṯbāt-i istiqrāʾī* (inductive corroboration). His theory is also, strictly speaking, arrived at inductively in terms that it initially is bound to exclude some views as false, or at least unworthy of consideration. Cf. 1996c:516.

[37] Cf. Surūsh 1996c:91 and 164. Popper's views on science are almost identical to those of Kuhn, although he considers scientific revolutions as permanent rather than exceptional. As Kuhn (1970:1–2) elucidates, they are both concerned with the dynamic process by which scientific knowledge is acquired rather than with the logical structure of the products of scientific research. "Given that concern, both of us emphasize, as legitimate data, the facts and the spirit of actual scientific life, and both of us turn often to history to find them. From

The adoption and influence of a posteriori knowledge in a priori knowledge includes three categories: 1. Corroboration and confirmation, 2. Refutation and falsification, 3. Contraction and expansion or transformation of the circle of meaning and denotation (Surūsh 1996c:210).

In short, science does not merely evolve in the sense that a theory accepted at one time is frequently rejected in whole or in part at a later time. Theories themselves evolve as they are modified to take into account new data and new calculations. A certain instability characterises the ontological commitments of science, where the entities to which a science is committed at one time may fall out of favour or be replaced by different entities postulated by new theories at a later time. Due to Surūsh's weak philosophical realism, it is not coincidental that his primary interest is philosophical theorising about the scientific enterprise in its historical sweep, where his own philosophical claims are not overtly committed to the content of science at any specific time. For Surūsh (ibid.:211–212), the theoretician who is interested in truth must, in other words, be interested in falsity since finding that a statement is false is the same as finding that its negation is true:

Confirmation and falsification are obviously two logical avenues that signify positive and negative cases in the sense that they have a logical correspondence to what is correct or false. The constant trimming or expansion of prior data by means of discovery of contradictions by later confirmations is a scientific and incontestable rule.

Popper claimed that science is 'to learn from the faults', and I would like to add that a false theory sometimes influences science and is sometimes useful to other disciplines in the sense that the discovery of a false scientific theory may end up in the discovery of a false philosophical, theological or historical theory which also provides evidence of their interrelationships (ibid.:404).

The primary role of the scientist of any discipline is therefore very much that of posing new hypotheses to new problems and discovering and refuting false propositions buried in existing scientific theories and data:

It [the appearance of contradiction in science] either enters deeply into understanding by developing original comprehensive knowledge or overthrows earlier theories, presents new hypotheses or expounds the hidden assumptions of the *baḥṯ* (discourse) by bringing them forward, questioning their validity and altering their incontrovertible character. The scientists rediscover, in other words, the hidden

---

this pool of shared data, we draw many of the same conclusions. Both of us reject the view that science progresses by accretion; both emphasize instead the revolutionary process by which an older theory is rejected and replaced by an incompatible new one; and both deeply underscore the role played in this process by the older theory's occasional failure to meet challenges posed by logic, experiment, or observation. Finally, Sir Karl and I are united in opposition to a number of classical positivism's most characteristic theses".

aspects of data that they supposed they were familiar with and therefore are required to come to know better (ibid.:217).[38]

Knowledge is hence rendered a constantly new identity through the constant interaction between different spheres of science and the development of human knowledge which falsifies and removes false assumptions of earlier scientific theories. Surūsh suggests that scientific theories are not the sort of things that can be known in any philosophically robust sense of the term and claims that the belief in the absolute character of knowledge is erroneous since *khulūṣ* (genuineness) is not an absolute rule. In his view, the evolution of knowledge is a *taḥawwul-i jauharī* (qualititative process), which, similar to the transformation of molecules, is related to substance. "Every new chemical molecule is a new existent that is transformed through the extermination of earlier molecules" (ibid.:164). Referring to Ṣadr al-dīn Shīrāzī's ontological principle *ḥarakat-i jauharī*, he explains that the 'genuineness' of human knowledge, similar to the *t̠abāt-i huwwīyat-i mutaḥarrik* (constants of moving identity) in Shīrāzī's system, is flowing and time-bound:

Some erroneously believe that genuineness is an absolute rule. They have not excavated their minds and hearts in order to see that their religious beliefs in reality belong to a specific 'geography' and are based on external knowledge and data which are related to an ancient view of nature, man and reality. These beliefs are unjustifiable in our day. Genuineness is, indeed, a rule that is time-bound and fluid. Those who are acquainted with *ḥarakat-i jauharī* know that the brilliant innovation of that sage of Shiraz was to describe and establish the constants of moving identity in the substance of movement (ibid.:171).[39]

In contrast to a number of Islamic philosophers, such as Ibn Sīnā and Suhrawardī, who asserted the precedence of essence over existence, Shīrāzī formulated, almost at the same time as the breakthrough in Western science, his doctrine of the priority of *iṣālat-i wujūd* (principality of existence) over *iṣālat-i māhīyat* (principality of quiddity), where existence itself is the nucleus around which all principles of metaphysics revolve. Being, while spiritual, is not an attribute to essence in Shīrāzī's system, but transcends all logical categories. Existence has an element of systematic *tashkīk* (ambiguity) in that its grades are not static but move substantially and

[38] According to Surūsh (1996c:231), this is the major point that distinguishes a modern scientist and philosopher, such as Darwin, from a traditional scholar such as Muḥammad Ḥusain Ṭabāṭabā'ī. While the former works with a number of hypotheses that must be verified by empirical material, the latter accepts a definitive and closed scientific hermeneutics and method.

[39] In this respect, Surūsh (1996c:248) claims that any attempt to restrict the evolution of human knowledge by resorting to the idea that *fiqh* is eternal and immutable is deemed to fail since the dynamics of the evolutionary process are too powerful. He argues that since the belief in the *khulūṣ* of religion is subjected to evolutionary flow, the effort of Islamic scholars should be "to make peace between genuineness of knowledge and its simultaneous evolution". Cf. 1996c:184.

qualitatively towards higher forms. But in contrast to the adoption of the word existence in the writings of modern philosophy (Søren Kirkegaard, Jean-Paul Sartre, etc), where essence denotes the essence of particular individuals, essence is an abstract concept for Shīrāzī, without any concrete reality on its own. Despite Surūsh's references to Shīrāzī's terminology, it seems, however, that Popper's evolutionary epistemology, with its emerging representationalism and critical realism aimed at clarifying and investigating the process by which knowledge grows, rather than the principle *ḥarakat-i jauharī*, is the primary inspiration for Surūsh's account of the historical growth of human knowledge.[40]

Since what distinguishes the whole dialectical thought process in its development (from the nineteenth century onwards) from *ḥarakat-i jauharī* is not its concern with becoming or change, but the reduction of reality to ever-changing and temporal thought processes. In Surūsh's positivistic and diachronic interpretation of reality, science is de-ontologised and denied any ontological significance. With the destruction of the notion of hierarchy in reality, the rapport between degrees of knowledge and the correspondence between various levels of reality upon which traditional Islamic science were based disappears. Metaphysics is abandoned in favour of rationalistic philosophy. Surūsh's approach is marked by an abandonment of the quest after an ontological vision of the whole in the sense that no standpoint exists outside the flow of historically situated experience and that all knowledge is the explanation of previous knowledge. Knowledge becomes externalised, desacralised and separated from Being. Influenced by positivist notions of science where physical science ultimately is the epitome of critical rationality, religion appears to constitute a non-rational set of experiences, since it purports to deal with realities beyond the reach of empirical science.

While this noncognitivist approach to religion is a familiar move in the philosophy of religion, Surūsh is not interested in the religious experience as such in *Qabḍ wa basṭ-i tiʾūrīk-i sharīʿat*, but rather focuses on the nature of religious knowledge in its sequential historical advance. His task is not to vindicate revelation as divine law and by subscribing to an evolutionary view of existence devoid of the sacred. His definition of epistemology comes to represent a loss of all permanence and fixity of human spirituality. Referring to the conflict between science and religion in post-medieval Europe, he claims that science has the last say over religion:

[40] In his description of evolutionary epistemology, W.W. Bartley (1988:21) writes, "Evolutionary epistemology results from pursuing the ramifications of Popper's understanding of the fundamental task of epistemology. This task is, as Popper and his associates conceive it, to clarify and investigate the processes by which knowledge grows. In this context, 'knowledge' refers to the objective products of certain evolutionary processes, ranging from the endosomatic cognitive structures of men and animals to the most abstract scientific theories. The resulting epistemology–drawing from logic, methodology and physics, from psychology, and from physiology–amounts to a systematic development of, vindication of, representationalism".

But what did the Christian theologians do in case contradiction occurred between science and religion? Either they repressed science, or if they were able, they developed a distinct philosophy of science and provided a particular judgment of epistemology. In the end, they acknowledged that when definite (scientific) proof is located in conflict to revelation, we must change our previous judgment and recognize that we have not understood the latter correctly. Coordinating the sciences with each other is consequently reason for leaving off the literal word of Islamic law in case definite scientific proof exists (Surūsh 1996c:231).

Surūsh's view of the growth of knowledge as proceeding through the elimination of error, i.e. through the refutation of hypotheses that are either logically inconsistent or entail empirically refuted consequences, is unmistakably inspired by Popper's evolutionary epistemology and his theory of falsification as a critique of 'verification'. Surūsh also seems to be inspired by the Hungarian post-positivist philosopher Imre Lakatos (d. 1974), who was more concerned with theoretically progressive families or series of theories, so-called 'research programmes', rather than isolated theories. In contrast to Popper's view of falsification as a relation between a theory and an empirical basis, Lakatos' notion of multiple relations between competing theories renders falsification an explicit historical character.[41] While Surūsh (ibid.:212) certainly adheres to Popper's falsification principle in the general sense, Lakatos concept of 'research programmes', referred to three times in *Qabḍ wa basṭ-i tiʾūrīk-i sharīʿat*, concerned a whole family of theories, not merely individual ones appearing one by one. This concept governs his study of Islamic law and theology:

It is this relationship that gives rise to most of the development in religious thought, and our noble claim is precisely that the secret of transformations in religious thought (transformation is a reality that demands interpretation) is nothing but a new consciousness consisting of positive, negative and neutral results, which are formed and does not leave the a priori beliefs in their former condition. Even if the a priori beliefs are not extinguished and replaced, their geometry is given a new character, class, substance and colour. The structure of new data produces hence a new structure from previous data that is not an individual confirmation.[42]

All sciences are, in other words, interconnected and must be analysed as a whole rather than as a collection of individual discrete theories. As far as Surūsh's concept of science considers empiricalness (or scientific character) and theoretical progress as inseparably connected, he remains a Popperian, since although Popper is broadly sympathetic to positivism he voices some reservations about its more specific empiricist elements. Similar to Popper, Surūsh also subscribes to antideterministic metaphysics and believes that

[41] According to Lakatos (1970:120), research programmes (for instance, Marxism, Freudism, Cartesian metaphysics, etc) are characterised by a certain methodological continuity that connects their members.
[42] Cf. Surūsh 1996c:220, 534, 540.

knowledge evolves from experience of the mind. He shares the postpositivist and hermeneutic viewpoint and criticises the epistemic 'foundationalist' certainty in inductive reasoning, believing that there is no guarantee that inductive method is reliable. The human subject does not enjoy any neutral position in the production of knowledge but is contextually conditioned and inescapably includes evaluative elements.

In order to demonstrate how correct and false hypotheses are separated methodologically, Surūsh explains that science functions on two levels in the process of falsification, *maqām-i gird-āwarī* (context of discovery) and *maqām-i dāwarī* (context of justification). He argues that this distinction can be equated to the traditional Islamic distinction between the *naqlī* and *ʿaqlī* sciences in the sense that the first level consists of the collection of pure ingredients that are objects of justification on the second level. He claims that his study, together with his definition of scientific method, takes place on the level of justification, where the scientific character of the relevant hypotheses are subjected to the falsification principle. While the production of knowledge takes place on the level of justification, it remains at all times contingent on the discoveries made prior to the level of discovery:

> The context of discovery is the level of collecting pure data and the context of justification is the level of justifying these pure data. The pure data are collected or discovered in the context of discovery. Discovery does not immediately imply that correct data are exposed, since it is possible to discover correct as well as false data. Discovery is composed of correct and false information. The context of justification or, so to speak the context of confirmation, corresponds to the distinguish of correct data from false data. Since the two levels are repeatedly mixed up, it is the duty of the scientists to differ them from each other. To sum up, all scientific branches are determined on account of the concept of these two categories (ibid.:94).

Since all observation is potentially contaminated, whether by our theories or our worldview or past experiences, Surūsh rejects the traditional conclusion that science can objectively discern and choose from among rival theories in any absolute certain sense. While an hypothesis is correct if it corresponds to the facts, no claim can be made for absolute certainty, i.e. no possibility of error. In contrast to absolutist ideas of truth, all knowledge claims are tentative and subject to revision on the basis of new evidence. No belief is epistemologically warranted merely because it is produced by a method that produces truth more often than not. With the emphasis upon falsification in science, Surūsh rejects an idealist neglect of objectivity in science and adopts his own distinct notion of inter-subjective corroboration, according to which it is possible for other investigators to ascertain the truth content of scientific explanations. While science cannot provide one with certainty, it is the only objective mode of pursuing valid knowledge in the sense that it rests on the bedrock of empirical testability:

A phenomenon that is subjected to *kāwish-i tajrubī* (empirical scrutiny) must be capable of going through an examination by someone. Everyone who has the specific required skills must be able to put the relevant proposition to the test. Matters that only occur once or are unqualified for being subjected to open scrutiny are external to the scientific procedure. The meaning of objectivity in science has no other meaning than inter-subjective testability. Everyone can carry out objective and scientific research and test the result produced from that research. Revelations of holy men and prophets cannot be subjected to scrutiny, since the means of direct revelation is closed to everyone but themselves. Revelations cannot therefore be the object of empirical and scientific investigation (Surūsh 1996b:18).

In this respect, Surūsh's notion of science, inspired by Popper's notion of "the third world of objective knowledge" with its strong confidence in natural science, approaches the question of the contingency of human knowledge as a product of public critique and understanding. Valid knowledge, whether scientific or religious, depends on its being public:

What exists only in the mind of an isolated thinker is not science. Science must lift the veil from its face and expose itself to the judgement and critique of others. What constitutes science is the product of public critique and understanding as well as meanings given to terms by the scientific community (Surūsh 1994b:177).[43]

Surūsh's (1996c:96) purpose with his discussion on objectivity in science is not a pursuit of discovering truth, but an evaluation of the relationship between religious knowledge and modern science and how it is possible to renew the traditional sciences as well as to acquire a more correct understanding of religion from the process of justification. In his view, truth seems to be an imaginative grasp that takes place in the mind of the individual scientist but never crosses the threshold to the continuous flow of knowledge at the level of fulfilment. Referring to the studies of Carl Hempel (d. 1997) and Nelson Goodman (d. 1998) on the logic of confirmation or paradox of confirmation, i.e. how empirical evidence confirms or disconfirms general hypotheses, Surūsh (ibid.:213) argues that scientific explanation occurs continuously and we might very well expect that contemporary 'facts' and discoveries will be falsified in the future:

The contradictions that occur in science are not always direct or apparent. In some cases, it takes years or centuries for abandoned facts to inform a spot that for several reasons make us comprehend falsified contentions in other sciences. If we leave the topic of contradiction in science and consider the confirmed and objective findings, logic alone demonstrates that our falsified hypotheses are never objective. A contemporary understanding of affairs must always wait to see what the future has to say.[44]

[43] Cf. Surūsh 1996a:91.

[44] As a leader of the logical empiricist movement in the philosophy of science, Hempel argues that Popper's proposal of the character of falsification, while correct at its foundations, limits scientific hypotheses to the form of relatively falsifiable sentences and involves a very severe

Following Hempel's criticism of Popper, Surūsh argues that what is wrong is not in the customary way of construing and representing general hypotheses, but rather our reliance on misleading intuition in the matter. The impression of a paradoxical situation is, so to say, not objectively founded but a psychological illusion. Our factual knowledge tends to create an impression of paradoxicality that is not justified on logical grounds but due to misguided intuition in the matter. Surūsh asserts that this largely depends on the nature of inductive basic statements and argues that it is perfectly valid and sound to make the observation 'this leaf is green' and to verbalise the claim, 'there is a green leaf on the ground'. But he claims that no matter how many observations of green one makes, one can never justify the universal claim that 'all leaves are green' based on multiple singular basic statements. 'All leaves are green' has the form of a conditional, that is, a statement of the form 'if *A* then *B*', which means that *if* a given object is a leaf, *then* that object is green. According to the laws of logic, a conditional is equivalent to its contrapositive. The hypothesis 'all leaves are green' has therefore the equivalent form 'all non-green things are non-leaves', or more precisely, 'if an object is not green then it is not a leaf'. If every sighting of a green leaves confirms our hypothesis, then every sighting of a non-green non-leaves equally confirms our hypothesis. Due to Surūsh's (1996c:213–214) criticism of inductive method it seems quite unexpected that he makes much of this form of reasoning that accepts inductive hypotheses and confirmation by experiment by asserting that every observation *except* one that refutes the hypothesis confirms it, even if it is irrelevant:

> The equivalence of two premises implies that the rejection of one of them leads to the rejection of the other. The confirmation of one premise similarly means that the other is confirmed. Two matters that are outwardly isolated are, so to say, interrelated. The statement 'all leaves are green' is equivalent to 'everything that is not green is not a leaf'. The more we see green leaves, our imagination leads us to think that the validity of the hypothesis is correct. Since green leaves confirms the first hypothesis, it also confirms the second hypothesis that 'everything that is not green is not a leaf'. Therefore, green leaves confirm that 'cows are yellow', 'flowers are red', 'pigeons are white' and that 'ravens are black' (yellow cows and red flowers are neither leaves nor green according to 'everything that is not green is not a leaf'). In this respect, red flowers also confirms that leaves are green. In short, we could say that the hypotheses that are confirmed or falsified in the various sciences

restriction of the possible forms of scientific hypotheses. Hempel (1965:45) asserts that "it rules out all purely existential hypotheses as well as hypotheses whose formulation requires both universal and existential quantification". In his view, falsification (verification) has two meanings, the relative verification which belongs to formal logic and absolute falsification, which belongs to pragmatics and is capable of being established definitely. Lakatos (1999:91–92) has criticised Popper for his view on conjecture and anomaly and argues that Popper's definition of scientific method does not discern between what a refutation is and what it is not, if we do not know right from the beginning which anomalies it cannot account for.

are interrelated in a hidden manner and influence each other. A hypothesis that is confirmed in a specific science has automatic effects on the other sciences.

Since human knowledge can never attain a perfect state concerning the forms and the scope of the laws that hold in our universe, human justifications are, in Surūsh's view, always made on the basis of incomplete information, a state that enables us to anticipate the consequences of alternative choices with only probability at best. Hempel's concept of confirmation provides him with a general and formal criterion of confirmation in addition to the criteria of valid deduction/induction (which is supplied by logic). But while Hempel's specific proposal for a systematic and comprehensive logical reconstruction of the concept of confirmation considers confirmation as the base of the methodology of empirical science as well as of epistemology, Surūsh's (ibid.:219) purpose is not final in this case, but rather tries to substantiate his belief that science because of the paradox of confirmation must turn to the field of hermeneutics. Preliminarily, he seems to suggest that no clear-cut method exists for interpreting the revealed sources, since science has no final answer to offer, in the sense that all features of the structure that models theories are not available for observation. The hypothetical character of science may therefore suggest that the positivist contrast between the rationally grounded certainty of science and the literally 'false' character of religious dogmatism can no longer be maintained and that there consequently can be no a priori reason for imagining that science must always be the dominant partner and that theology cannot feel as confident as science in its claims to truth.[45]

[45] Surūsh neglects the criticism that has been presented against the falsificationist approach during the last century. Pierre Duhem, who maintained that the role of theory in science is to systematize relationships rather than to interpret new phenomena, claims that it is impossible to conclusively refute a theory because realistic test situations depend on much more than just the theory that is under investigation. T.S. Kuhn as well as Paul Feyerabend demonstrates the difficulties that falsificationists face in proving their claim and provide a host of examples to undermine the falsificationist thesis. As they argue, there is nothing in their enterprise that proves that they do it in an objective, neutral way. Kuhn (1962) has also noted that Popper neglects the fact that scientific practice is often governed by a conceptual framework (or paradigm) which is highly resistant to change. Surūsh also neglects to consider the major input of values when it comes to the selection process inherent in science, since even at the heart of the positivistic method itself the selection is made on the basis of values and values are brought to the framing of the problems.

E. Religious epistemology: Divine absolute or provisional conjecture?

Surūsh's analysis of science has fundamental importance for his discussion on the central problems of religious epistemology. He draws some major conclusions from his account of falsification in science that are relevant to religion. He claims that all religious knowledge is contingent on external non-religious knowledge for its development and growth and likewise is subjected to flow in the sense that the context of its presuppositions is unfixed and caused by totalities (1996c:157). In his view, the contextual and external factors are responsible not only for change but also for the continuity of religious interpretation throughout the ages:

> Religious knowledge, the learning produced from the understanding of revelation, the *sunnat* and the history of the lives of religious predecessors, is a consuming knowledge that is directly under the influence of producing sciences. My claim in this respect is that there is no knowledge of religion that is not contingent on non-religious external knowledge and understanding. If external knowledge develops, the religious knowledge develops as a result. If external knowledge is stable, the religious knowledge is stable as a result. External knowledge is *taḥawwul-yābandah* ('evolution-seeking') and is always caused by totalities. These rules are, indeed, pertinent to religious knowledge at the level of fulfilment.

Religious knowledge is, in other words, a mirror of scientific and philosophical knowledge. By suggesting that the external non-religious data of the producing sciences, i.e. anthropology, natural science, sociology and psychology, are necessary to inform the foundational assumptions in religious knowledge, Surūsh (ibid.:158, 192) argues that these sciences are "the first ingredients of understanding". He claims that the nature of the systematic questions posed by modern science to religious thought radically differ from those of Aristotelian logic, since they have the shape of systematic questions that are not logically born out of answers or stem from predefined premises or conclusions (ibid.:272). The Islamic jurists and theologians have, in Surūsh's view, therefore to become fully conversant with modern sciences and philosophical approaches, since practical political development in the contemporary Islamic world is dependent on the acceptance of the scientific and philosophical underpinnings of modernity:

> The *modus operandi* or technology of modern life does not epitomise modernity but is rather the fruit of modernity. Modern world and modern life are incarnate in modern knowledge. One of the most essential components of modern knowledge is empirical natural science... If science develops, politics develops and is modernized. Modernization gives meaning to freedom and justice. It gives the intelligentsia its proper place in society and establishes the rights of human beings. We must never forget that politics and governance signify scientific politics and governance in the modern world nor should we forget that modern science transforms philosophy.

While Islamic philosophy may be dear to us, it is not the only possible philosophy neither the most reasonable (Surūsh 2000b:38).

Whoever accepts the basic norms of modernity enjoys, in other words, the benefits of modern rationality and autonomy. In hermeneutical terms, Surūsh (1996c:208) believes that this formation rests in the nature of things, since the Islamic scholars activate their whole personality in the act of interpretation so that "when some parts of reality are analysed, the others' parts (of the worldview) are not abandoned". The subject's initial contribution to the process of understanding occurs, in other words, when external data, stemming from our contextual hermeneutical situation in the world, takes the shape of pre-understandings. The human subject is no *tabula rasa* nor is the object of interpretation considered to be some neutral, non-conceptualised 'thing-in-itself':

Non-religious human knowledge, by pursuing the two-fold role of discovering and justifying religious knowledge, gradually performs its third function, to render religious understanding a 'frame-work', and to improve its understanding. The scientific and philosophical data render religious understanding a specific form and character in interaction with the essential matters of religion, presuppositions about religion and a particular view of God, reality, man, history, language and knowledge (ibid.:281).[46]

As far as Islamic law is concerned, Surūsh argues that since the anthropological basis envisioned in producing sciences such as physics, mathematics, anthropology and sociology has changed and since the new laws and regulations of international economical relations have produced new hermeneutic environments, the contemporary understanding of *fiqh* is bound to change. Since *fiqh* is a human activity that concerns human contexts, he claims that the humanities should guide the comprehension of Islamic law in order to focus more attention on the humane aspects of religion (ibid.:190).[47] He suggests in fact that only the conception of religious knowledge as consuming knowledge in continuous exchange and dialogue with modern science is capable of bestowing dynamism on the interpretation and function of Islamic law:

[46] Surūsh mentions the case of Darwin, who changed his conception of religion according to his scientific view when his religious beliefs turned out to be incompatible with his discoveries in natural science. He also refers to the French Zoologist, George Cuvier, who refuted Darwin's theory of evolution since it was considered to conflict with the literal word of the Bible. Cuvier made use of the Bible to confirm some specific hypotheses in zoology and geology. In line with Cuvier's correlation principle, the physical constitution of the species has a spiritual and non-evolutionary ground, in contrast to Darwin's theory, where evolution is governed by material mechanisms. Needless to say, Cuvier's conclusions are, in Surūsh's view, indifferent to the evolutionary process of scientific knowledge itself and therefore ambiguous and incomplete.

[47] Cf. Surūsh 1999a:23 and 318.

All different branches of knowledge (human science, natural science, philosophy, religious science) are interconnected and separated. They act on a common level in the sense that every expansion or change in one science affects the others. *Sharīʿat* is an eternal, heavenly and divine commandment, but our knowledge of *sharīʿat* is a human, earthly and changeable rule in the sense that it is interrelated with theories of other human knowledge and involves constant evolution and development (ibid.:187).[48]

What has become subjugated and neglected in the quarrel between tradition and dynamism is the point that it is impossible to dynamise a person's *fiqh* as long as his understanding of *sharīʿat* (that is theology, exegesis, ethics and theosophy) remains stagnant and static, and it is impossible for a person to acquire a dynamic understanding of *sharīʿat*, if the contingency of jurisprudence to modern science and learning is unacknowledged. Without mastery of the modern human disciplines, no revival (of Islamic law) will be successful (ibid.:188).

Inspired by Arthur Koestler's major work on the history of science, *The Sleepwalkers: A History of man's changing vision of the universe*, which is among the major works influencing the formulation of the theory of the contraction and expansion in an indirect way, Surūsh (1996d:392) asserts that the renaissance divorce between religion and reason was not the result of a contest for power or intellectual monopoly, even if the Church persisted in a direction that was in conflict with science and humanity. While Western society was forced to chose between the Church or man, as illustrated in the almost mystical confessions of Galileo, Leibniz, Descartes or John Locke, he argues that the overwhelming part of European scientists incorporated substantial religious elements into their work and were genuinely religious thinkers to whom religion transcended the rigid scholastic frame, reaching the mystical Pythagorean inspiration of God as the chief mathematician. Surūsh (1996c:221) also mentions the contrary position of the French physicist Pierre Duhem, who is alleged to have developed a new history of modern science in an 'instrumentalistic' critique against Galileo based on evolutionary metaphysical concepts. Inspired by the enlightenment thinkers, above all those in France, Surūsh looks for a 'religion of reason', which in the enlightenment context was vaguely deist in character with sentimentalist overtones, a religion at one with human nature.[49]

Koestler's work provides Surūsh with evidence of the changing concept of

[48] Cf. Surūsh 1996c:52 and 1999a:158.

[49] In spite of the fact that enlightenment thinkers took reason to be the natural ability of any human being, most of them assumed that the average person's reason has been corrupted by the cultural environment and especially by the influence of the Church. The Church was considered the most corrupting of influences since it put revelation above reason and hold that there is something that transcends reason. While many enlightenment thinkers believed in God, they were deists: God created the universe, but he no longer bothers with it. Using an old metaphor, David Hume argued that God is at least as good a creator as a human clock-maker, and we would respect no clock maker who had to intervene in the workings of a clock once it had been made.

religious as well as scientific knowledge, where all understanding constitutes *yak bāzī-yi ʿaqlānī-yi muḥtaram* (a play for honourable rationality).[50] Koestler's personal and speculative account was met with much controversy when first published in 1959 as a major work within the recently established discipline history of science. While Koestler (1959:14) is particularly interested in the psychological process of discovery, which he considers to be "the most concise manifestation of man's creative faculty", it is rather his comprehension of scientific progress as a zig-zag course of collective obsessions and controlled schizophrenias, rather than as organic, clean or rational advance along a straight ascending line, which appeals to Surūsh. Similar to Koestler, Surūsh (1996c:167) also focuses attention on Copernicus, Galileo, Kepler and Newton, who represent the pioneering break of the modern scientific paradigm. Surūsh asserts that European theologians were forced to attain a renewed understanding of religion due to the effects of the mechanisation and dynamisation that occurred in science with Darwin's theory of evolution, Newton's theory of movement and Einstein's theory of relativity.[51] The Ptolemaic picture of the universe with our earth as its centre, which Islamic astronomy after Rabbān al-Ṭabarī (d. 870) was also built upon, as well as the analogous Christian concept of Christ as the centre of the religious universe, were gradually reversed since they contradicted the modern Copernican system. Traditional religious metaphysics was, so to say, transformed by the new scientific discoveries and data (ibid.:167).

Significantly, Surūsh believes that modern revisions of Christian theology, rather than being mere translation adjustments, were made in light of extra-religious shifts such as the pioneering Kantian theory on the possibilities of knowledge and Foucault's concept of the notions of knowledge, method and theory as anathema.[52] These shifts put new 'thicker' questions to the scientific study of religion and he claims that this process of adjustment applies to religion in the same manner as it does to the Newtonian theory of gravitation, which was discovered by reference to mathematics or the Descartian definition of the soul-body relationship, directly influenced by the new 'mechanicism' in science. From the modern development of the history of science, Surūsh (ibid.:52) imagines that all human knowledge, whether scientific or religious, is unfixed, conjectural and contradictory.

[50] Cf. Surūsh 1996c:35, 85, 87, 207.

[51] Aside from the influence of Darwin's work *Origin of the Species* on Christian and Jewish theology, it was connected to dialectical materialism. It is well known that Marx wrote to Darwin and asked the latter's permission to dedicate *Das Kapital* to him.

[52] Cf. Surūsh 1999a:49. Surūsh (1996c:167–168) suggests that the influence of Kant's theory of the limits of knowledge and Wittgenstein's theory of the limits of speech on modern theological discourse represent the first considerations of the scientific provability of religion. Referring to contemporary theological thinkers, such as Barth, Hick, Smart, Küng, Alston and Platinga, he argues that the majority of theologians today accept that the rationality of religious belief also implies systematic error. Cf. Surūsh 1996a:172 and 184.

Influenced by Kantian cognitive concepts, he asserts that divine religion, similar to the philosophical foundation of empirical science or the fixed formulas of mathematics, depends on certain a priori presuppositions or beliefs that cannot be proved by a posteriori ('from what is after–experience') experience as they are beyond analytical logical truths. He considers in fact a priori principles as a necessary condition of any empirical experience of reality. But while the so-called *qawānīn-i tabī*ʿ*at* (laws of nature) and *qaṭʿiyāt-i ʿilm* (definite postulates of science) count as *badīhiyāt-i maʿrifat* (a priori propositions), they are subjected to the flow of human understanding:

Our understanding of principles is, indeed, flowing. We should not assume that a scholar who believes in the principle of contradiction, the principle of causality or parts of the hypothesis and principles dominant in mathematics, forever, has a static comprehension of these principles and hypotheses or that change never occurs in his understanding of them (ibid.:135).[53]

In other words, while there are facts that can be said to be know a priori intuitively, these intuitions can only be fallible. Surūsh seems hence to anticipate the fact that his definition of constant and non-constant is inconsistent, in the sense that the non-falsified hypotheses that underlie the theory of contraction and expansion are equally subject to the scientific process. As he argues, it would not be 'paradoxical' or 'contradictory' if the theory of contraction and expansion was falsifiable in the future.[54] In contrast to hermeneutical philosophers, such as Gadamer, who claim an ontological perspective according to a phenomenologist conception of truth and method, where truth disseminates through its interpretations, Surūsh (ibid.:157) asserts that the falsification principle as well as the theory of contraction and expansion is open to falsification since there is no fixed laws of hermeneutics:

The principle that all religious knowledge is based on external understanding is open to falsification, since it says that there is no example of understanding of revelation and *sunnat* independent of external thought. To find such a thing results, indeed, in the falsification of this principle.

Surūsh's position on scientific truth-claims (as well as his rejection of inductive reasoning altogether), according to which theories are accepted not because they are true but useful, corresponds very well to the pragmatist view that a particular theory is selected due to the fact that one is warranted in thinking it true. There is, according to this view, nothing to guarantee that science progresses toward anything, least of all toward 'the truth'. In contrast to the conceptual realism of the philosophical realists and scientific positivists, he is not concerned with any ontological commitment to 'the real

[53] Cf. Surūsh 1996c:278–279.
[54] Cf. Surūsh 1996c:332.

existence' of universals and argues that nominalism, for instance, highlights "to what extent the meaning of every particular reference in the Qur'an is open to change" (ibid.:302). To pragmatists such as Rorty or Quine, a theory is not accepted as a truth but as something possessing warranted assertiability. They believe that the universals of science, similar to ontological commitments, are only 'occult entities', that is; they are a logical consequence of the conceptual scheme we adopt to understand the world as we know it through experience.[55]

While Surūsh does not rule out the possibility that certain parts of our belief system will be revised by subsequent experience, his position on the relationship between constants and non-constants (i.e. his idea of ultimately unchanging truths) contradicts contemporary Western philosophy, which is his major intellectual resource. The main problem with his epistemology, as far as his terminology is concerned, is that it is not consistent with Popper's notion of falsification, the nominalist pragmatism of Quine and others or with Kant's doctrine of the synthetic a priori, which was decisively undercut by Einstein's theory of relativity. In contemporary epistemology, the Kantian synthetic a priori has been relativised, whereby no mathematical-physical framework is uniquely possible and fixed for all time. Surūsh's disinclination to reject synthetic a priori judgements all together seems, however, to be due to his will to allow the option of some mode of ontological knowledge (where the Divine Being is known):

> In reality, if there is no a priori religious category and understanding in this world and if what we perceive and know, in other words, is not religion itself, but only the 'guest' of religion, then how are we to trust in the existence and continuance of religion at all? Will not all our investments be worthless if all goods are bought on credit without any ready money? (Surūsh 1999a:165)[56]

Surūsh's purpose with his general account on science, however, substantiates his epistemological discussion on Islamic law with a theoretical basis. Analogous to the universal laws of science, he argues that religion by definition belongs to a priori synthetic judgements or presuppositions. Referring to a Qur'anic metaphor (*Qur*. 3:103) describing religion in terms of a silent rope of salvation, he asserts that religion is a 'silent' rope of guidance and remedy in the sense that it lacks a specific orientation or course.[57] While *sharīʿat* is essentially divine and complete, its boundaries cannot be defined in any systematic way since the hermeneutical results of jurisprudence are formulated gradually in the midst of the expansion and contraction of religious knowledge. In order to illustrate the dual epistemological character of religious knowledge within Islamic tradition,

[55] Cf. Quine 1960:17, 28 and 1963:16–17.
[56] Cf. Surūsh 1996b:18 and 1999d:27–28.
[57] Surūsh (1997a:100–106) argues that the divine rope of salvation is the first tenet of his concept of *dark-i azīzānah-yi dīn* (endearing conception of religion).

Surūsh (1996c:271) refers to a saying attributed to ʿAlī b. Abī Ṭālib depicting the Qur'an as 'silent' in the sense that the believer makes the Qur'an speak through the act of interpretation. ʿAlī's account reads:

Request this Qur'an to speak to you, but it will not speak to you unless I enlighten you about it. It contains the science of the future and events of the past, the cure for aches, and lets you know the order of your matters.

From 'Ali's words, Surūsh asserts that the Qur'an is hungry *for* rather than impregnated *with* meaning. He then transfers this saying to the sphere of law where it is used to legitimise a general epistemological redefinition of Islamic law. In an almost agnostic mode, Surūsh asserts that "if *sharīʿat-i ṣāmit* (silent *sharīʿat*) exists, it exists with the Law-giver". He argues that the attribute silent does not mean that Islamic law is like 'a closed mouth' or 'formless' but rather that it is *khāmūsh* (silent) in the hermeneutical sense.[58] In its heavenly form, *sharīʿat-i ṣāmit* is divine and independent of human reform, but when it enters the threshold of human interpretation it becomes transformed into imperfect *sharīʿat-i nāṭiq* (speaking *sharīʿat*). While the texts of Islamic law and theology are considered to be silent, it is not, however, evident in what way the silence of the text actually leads to the agent and subject of interpretation:

Human understanding of *sharīʿat* is, similar to the human understanding of nature, subjected to a flow. While silent *sharīʿat* and silent nature are constant and free of contradictions, speaking *sharīʿat* and speaking nature are born out of human understanding, flowing and contradictory. This paradox informs us furthermore of another two-fold fact: Science of religion is born and develops out of contradiction and non-religious learning certainly influences religious knowledge (ibid.:167).[59]

Surūsh (ibid.:392) claims that the epistemic distinction above elucidates the reason behind the variety and plurality of legal opinions and clarifies the existence of the three major traditional interpretations of Islamic law; the juristic, the philosophical-theosophical and the mystical. He believes that Muslims ought to constantly make an effort to acquire a new understanding of the revealed texts, even if *sharīʿat* according to the principle of *ʿaqidat* (belief) is beyond interpretation from the perspective of the believers. In fact, he argues that religious beliefs should not be mixed with knowledge and distinguishes *īmān* (faith) and *sharīʿat-i nāzil bar nabī* (*sharīʿat* revealed to the Prophet) from *maʿrifat* (knowledge) as well as *fahm* (understanding).[60]

[58] *Khāmūsh* is one of the poetic persona of Jalāl al-dīn Rūmī in his *Diwān-i Shams-i Tabrīzī*. The term is adopted by Rūmī to point out the paradox of being unable to express in words the mysterium tremendum experienced in the presence of the Divine since true transcendent love is silent.

[59] Surūsh (1996c:305) also describes 'silent' *sharīʿat* as *sharīʿat -i ʿuryān* (naked *sharīʿat*).

[60] As Surūsh (1999a:319) argues in his *Basṭ-i tajrubah-yi nabawī*, there is "an apparent difference between faith and knowledge in that faith is always personal, individual and has a fluctuating degree of vigour while knowledge is always what is collective, general and *khaṭā-pazīr* (conjectural)".

While faith is a universal and ecumenical *ḥāl-i rūḥī* (spiritual state) and revealed *sharīʿat* constitutes the divine and permanent "pillars, principles and branches of religion" intended for the guidance of mankind, he asserts that the realisation of these sources is constructed and generated by human beings themselves (ibid.:206). The most central aspect of the theory of contraction and expansion is consequently that religious knowledge is considered not only time-bound, collective and conjectural, but also is given the attribute *sākhtah-shudah* (constructed). He argues that since human beings, prophets as well as common men, are no divine beings but *ḥaiwān-i ʿāqil* (rational animals) and defective terrestrial individuals, human knowledge is thus relative and socially determined:

> Religious knowledge in terms of a posteriori knowledge from the perspective of second-order epistemology is human in the sense that it is subjected to human norms. This is our particular definition of human knowledge. Human knowledge has, indeed, an observable and completely reasonable meaning, namely that knowledge is constructed in the hands of human beings and generated by human beings. We also believe that the human attribute of knowledge does not only imply that knowledge is always rational. [...] If we are social beings who are confined by language and human qualities such as desire, envy, reflection and sociability, and who are involved in multiple and complex social relationships, these attributes have an impact on our knowledge (ibid.:107).[61]

The more concrete meaning of the idea that knowledge is socially determined is hence that human qualities other than reason, such as social setting, language and interests, are included in and influence the acquisition of knowledge. Besides, Surūsh (1999i:21) argues that the social contingency of religious knowledge, concerning itself with the emergents of history, involves the notion that knowledge is materialised and formed by a particular *sākhtār-i ʿijtimāʿ* (social environment). "The science of *fiqh* is formed by the social environment and is contingent on society and politics in its capacity as a social and political science that is flowing". Surūsh (1996c:246) argues, in fact, that human knowledge is socially determined and constructed to the extent that the only specifically 'religious' aspect of religious knowledge is that it is characterised by "the scholar's constant reference to revelation and *sunnat*" and his religious discourse seems to give very little credibility to any strict knowledge in metaphysical terms. He seems hence inclined to vindicate a religious resurgence solely grounded in contemporary profane thought and learning by permitting the secular age to speak in isolation, in the sense that all knowledge has an explicit social identity confined by time and space and is contextually determined. He acknowledges, however, that contemporary hermeneutics cannot forsake religion but rather should function as a tool or instrument for a better understanding of religion. The key word in his hermeneutics is *listening*:

---

[61] Cf. Surūsh 1994d:62 and 1996f:51.

The claim that the discourse of the age is the same as that of religion and that religion itself has nothing to say is a correct conviction. Our argument is entirely that the contemporary sciences are a listening ear with which to hear the clamour of religion. We are not concerned with making alterations in religion but with the understanding of *sharīʿat* (ibid.:346).[62]

Evidently, Surūsh's thought hence also includes the eradication of the view of rationalism as an attribute of elitism. While his exposition on the history of religious thought by and large is not influenced by any sociologically inspired account of science which looks to the social causes of a person's scientific beliefs in order to deconstruct and undercut any role of a belief in science, his idea that *sharīʿat* is silent involves the negation of any monopolisation of hermeneutical discourse or any attempt to possess religion in any intra-religious polemical way. In fact, the theory of contraction and expansion creates obstacles for the existence of any specific guardian of *sharīʿat*. Since knowledge has a communal identity we all partake of, comprised of both what is false and correct, no interpretation can be absolutely correct and certain. Since no understanding is *muṭlaq* (absolute), *qaṭʿī* (definitive) and *rasmī* (official), Surūsh (ibid.:35) argues that no religious person has the right "to put his or her religion on the market for gaining the status of others" or "to impose his or her understanding of religion on others or enforce it in government and politics". While all Muslims have an historical responsibility of seeking truth and there are no excuses for neglecting this duty, no particular group or faction possesses religion in the absolute sense. "Religion is the property of all the believers and the general blessing of the Divine" (ibid.:34).[63] Since man made a *mīṯāq* (promise) with God in pre-eternal times and will return to God in his capacity of an individual human being on doomsday, he concludes that it is the blessing and duty of all Muslims to pose questions to silent *sharīʿat* and cause it to speak. This is, in his view, the true meaning of Galileo's statement that "every experience is a question":

Speaking and concealment, that is to verbalise and to incite, is the duty of all true believers and is not possible without having some preunderstandings and precommitments. There are springs of water in the depth of the earth. But only those for whom the pain of the thirst prevails dig out of desire and anxiety to find a drop of water. By way of breaking up earth many blessings will be granted them (Surūsh 1996c:271).[64]

---

[62] Cf. Surūsh 1994b:183–184.
[63] Cf. Surūsh 1997a:42.
[64] Cf. Surūsh 1996c:264.

F. Epistemological ambiguities: A priori and a posteriori

In his critical eschewing of traditional metaphysics, Surūsh connects ultimately to the critical philosophy of Kant, which he believes was made possible by way of Newton's theory of movement. For Surūsh, Kant's thought represents "the watershed of modern philosophy" and he considers the birth of a posteriori thought together with the ushering of a whole range of '–logies' and 'isms', where knowledge is relative to man as the essence of modernity.[65] Similar to Kant, Surūsh claims that epistemology is what defines the essential boundaries and competence of science. Epistemology constitutes a branch of philosophy that "turns to knowledge from a scientific point of view and determines its precincts and boundaries as well as its capacities and incapacities" (Surūsh 1996b:97). The impression of Surūsh's (1996c:154) treatment of the subject is that epistemology constitutes the most central area of philosophy since it is the cognitive foundation that substantiates scientific methodology with a theoretical foundation:

> In the Western world, the emergence of modern epistemology influenced science as well as philosophy. It incited the development of science to its present status and its most important impact on philosophy was to make the philosophers sceptical towards traditional metaphysical philosophy. Modern epistemology is a posteriori, not a priori, and came into being as a result of the development of empirical and rational science. Epistemology involves, for instance, the justification of whether science, natural science as well as metaphysics or rational philosophy, is truth-worthy or not. Questions such as whether analogy is permissible according to the philosophical and metaphysical premises or not, are all contingent on epistemology.

But while Kant originally turned from physical and metaphysical science to ethics to find the ground of faith by reconciling the claims of morality and religion with scientific knowledge, Surūsh's interest is rather to defer the traditional principle of epistemic warrant, *yaqīn* (certainty), in order to destabilise the religious discourse.[66] Surūsh does not interpret Kant's writings in an attempt, similar to Heidegger, to lay the ground for metaphysics or to place the problem of metaphysics before us as a fundamental ontology. The particular choice of Kant as principal model of his exposition on epistemology is largely due to Kant's analysis of finiteness

[65] Cf. Surūsh 1994b:259, 1996a:352, 1996c:101–102. While Surūsh (1996b:98) in his early works considers Descartes, and his maxim *cogito ergo sum* (I think therefore I am), as "the founder of modern epistemology", it is Kant who emerges as the great intellectual example in *Qabḍ wa basṭ-i tiʾūrīk-i sharīʿat*. According to Paul Guyer (1992:11), it was through Kant that the fundamental principles of science and morality, such as the form of space and time, came to be viewed as products of human thought alone. Kant was one of the earliest philosophers to make explicit the human foundation of knowledge and being. In his epistemology as well as his ontology the human is prior to all forms of knowledge and existence and it is the pivot around which everything revolves. Cf. Surūsh 1994b:257.

[66] Kant appeals to the immortality of the soul and the postulation of the existence of God to take care of reconciling virtue and happiness.

that contributed to the age of anthropological thought and humanities. Kant's belief in immortality and the existence of God as articulated in his fullest expositions in the second book of his *Kritik der praktischen vernunft* probably also contributes to mould Surūsh's affection to the German philosopher.

The core of Kant's epistemological writings is the thesis that all conscious cognition involves selection, organisation and interpretation, including religious experience, which is different only in the sense that it involves interpreting another level of meaning as mediating the Divine. But in this respect, Surūsh goes further than Kant who himself would not have sanctioned the idea that we in any way experience God, even if divine noumenon is distinguished from divine phenomenon. For Kant, God is not a reality encountered in religious experience, but an object postulated by reason on the basis of its own practical functioning in man's moral agency.[67] Instead of penetrating these aspects of practical epistemology, Surūsh points to the fact that Kant's critical theory of knowledge essentially differs from the traditional Islamic notions of epistemology. In his view, traditional Islamic epistemology represents an idealistic *idrāk-shināsī* (science of perception) which considers the possibility of knowing the external world as absolute. He argues that the traditional epistemology does not attempt to establish any comprehensive system of cognitive categories or any discursive analysis of things nor to account for a historical or contextual view which determines the evolutionary character and interaction of the various sciences:

> It should be emphasised that this view of science is not comparable to epistemology. The science of the ancients was a science of perception that primarily considered the existence of the external world and the possibility to know it as definite and above questioning (and the least quibble in this respect was associated with scepticism or sophistry). It employed furthermore a spiritual attribute or description of knowledge and perception (Surūsh 1996c:323).[68]

As Surūsh argues, the mark of modern epistemology after Hume and Kant has to a large extent been the acceptance of the attribute of systematic conjecture and error of all human knowledge:

> In essential terms, traditional man believed that the human mind has been created properly in the sense that if error occurred it was considered to be a form of *khaṭā-yi taṣādufī* (random error). But from the birth of modern epistemology, some philosophers came to the conclusion that the activity of the human mind perhaps necessitates *khaṭā-yi sistimātīk* (systematic error). These philosophers assumed, in

[67] In the preface to the second edition of *Kritik der reinen vernunft*, Kant (1996:Bxxxvi) argues that his criticism is the necessary preparation for a thoroughly scientific system of metaphysics that must perform its task entirely a priori, to the complete satisfaction of speculative reason and therefore must be treated scholastically.

[68] Surūsh (1999d:5) also argues that the traditional science of perception never reflected upon the question of divergent interpretation and understanding as a matter of theory or principle.

other words, that the human mind originally was created imperfectly and always comprehended everything in an accidental and defective manner. The major problem of Hume, Kant and Descartes was to find a solution to the notion that the activity of the human mind involves systematic error (Surūsh 1996a:90).

The distinction of random and systematic error suggests that knowledge is one thing and reality another and that there is no guarantee that knowledge truthfully represents reality. Following the complex philosophical architectonic made by Kant in the field of epistemology and referring to his discussion on 'is' and 'ought', Surūsh divides human knowledge into two broad categories, *ipīstimūlūzhī-yi pīshīnī* (a priori) and *ipīstimūlūzhī-yi pasīnī* (a posteriori).[69] While a priori knowledge, in Surūsh's (1996c:103) view, consists of natural judgements that take place before the context of justification and involve *idrāk-i ḏihnī* (mental perception), he explains that a posteriori knowledge takes place after the context of discovery and corresponds to the context of justification:

From now on, we can acknowledge a general epistemological division into a priori and a posteriori or *ipīstimūlūzhī-yi sābiqī* (ex-epistemology) which occurs before experience and before the level of fulfilment vs. *ipīstimūlūzhī-yi masbūqī* (post-epistemology) which occurs after experience and at the level of fulfilment. Epistemology before the level of experience or fulfilment represents philosophical epistemology. It involves our mental existence, perception and faculties.

Surūsh's division of a priori and a posteriori is therefore not according to logical form but according to their warrant, that is, if the truth claim of a certain sentence is in need of empirical backing or not. In this respect, he asserts that empirical knowledge has experience as its source in the sense of a posteriori in contrast to his definition of the sacred that represents a priori knowledge. Contrary to Kant, who uses these distinctions in his *Kritik der reinen vernunft* to explain the special case of mathematical knowledge which he regarded as the fundamental example of a priori knowledge, Surūsh is primarily concerned with the nature of religious knowledge. The theory of contraction and expansion makes use of the second epistemological category and its method is a cognitive-historical one. While Kant wanted to find invariable and unalterable truths that could not be affected by time and change, Surūsh claims that it is impossible to identify fundamental principles in valid knowledge. Whereas Kant wanted to secure fixed, uniform, permanent, absolute and universal truths in his static vision of the world, Surūsh's (ibid.:136) notion of epistemology depicts an ever changing, dynamic, pulsating, chaotic world that is always in a state of flux.

Despite the fact that Surūsh's definition of a priori is not primarily made up of the knowledge of mathematical and logical truths, his definition of a

[69] The first recorded occurrence of the terms a priori and a posteriori is in the writings of the fouteenth century logician Albert of Saxony, but the distinction became drawn widely first in the seventeenth century.

priori suggests that there is a knowledge before experience that is not determined by a factual or empirical inquiry but merely on the basis of reflection prior to any investigation of the facts. In contrast, a posteriori knowledge can only be determined after some kind of empirical investigation. But still his definition of synthetic a priori judgements has its ambiguities, since it is not clear whether he defines a priori as transcendental principles, i.e. judgements that give verdict on the conditions of every experience *or* as speculative principles, i.e. judgements that concern what is *beyond* every possible experience. In other words: is the content of the a priori element, i.e. that which cannot be deduced from experience, the same for the individual as for the human race at large? In this respect, Kant himself claimed Newton's dynamics (arithmetic, geometry, the principle of causality, etc) as synthetic and a priori valid. While Kant asserted that we do know the truth of a priori statements intuitively (that is, without proof) but acknowledged that we do not have the knowledge that we think we have, Surūsh's evolutionary perspective, with the falsification principle as its core is at odds with his view of an *ipso facto* necessarily valid synthetic a priori.[70] Similar to Popper, Surūsh rejects the claim of a necessary a priori validity for Kantian categories of thought and intuition and rather provides a perspective under which these categories can be seen as highly edited, much tested presumptions, validated only as provisional scientific truth is validated.[71]

In the sense that Kant attempted to preserve the normative role of reason in the face of the collapse of metaphysics, Surūsh has some reservations to his critical philosophy. Probably inspired by Popper, he asserts that the most fatal mistake of Kant was to accept Newton's dynamics as absolute, making cosmology a branch of physics, and wholesomely rejecting Leibnizian metaphysics. "Kant accepted the absolute basis and validity of Newton's physics and this was the biggest error of his philosophy" (Surūsh 1996c:168). In Surūsh's view, it is consequently possible to believe an a

[70] The distinction phenomenon-noumenon plays a major part in Kant's (1996:B69, B295–315) distinction of the a priori and a posteriori. He points out that since the properties of something as experienced "depend upon the mode of intuition of the subject, this object as appearance is to be distinguished from itself as object in itself". As Paul Guyer (1987:333) argues, Kant's epistemological modesty requires that a theory or conceptual framework is no more demonstrably false than demonstrably true. "What Kant sets out to demonstrate under the name of transcendental idealism is that a spatial and temporal view of things as they really are in themselves, independent of our perceptions of them, would be demonstrable false. Transcendent idealism is not a sceptical reminder that we *cannot be sure* that things as they are in themselves *are* also as we represent them to be; it is a harshly dogmatic insistence that we *can be quite sure* that things as they are in themselves cannot be as we represent them to be". In the view of Patricia Kitcher (1999:415), Kant's thought has also its dilemmas since the first *Kritik* contains several different strands of thought whose mutual consistency can be questioned and whose relative importance has been variously estimated.

[71] Kant's a priori is interpreted in Popper's (1963:47–48) thought so as not to mean 'objectively valid' but only "prior to sense experience".

priori statement to be true, as in Kant's case, when it is not. But while Surūsh as a philosopher looks to a priori statements for security by assuming that inasmuch as these statements may themselves be certain (and necessary) they can certainly be known, he seems to create a contradiction in terms since contemporary epistemology accepts no special set of a priori statements of which it can be said that just these are beyond the reach of doubt.[72] He also professes certain ambivalences towards Kantian notions of rationality that presume the possibility of metaphysics to extend our knowledge of reality as if its propositions are a priori synthetic. By adhering to a kind of postpositivist-postmodernist simulacra, Surūsh's hermeneutical discourse makes it clear that it is not non-problematical to cling to the Cartesian ideal of precision and certitude in thinking, which also includes Kant (1996, B419–420) to whom the subject is always enmeshed in an anthropocentric mode of knowledge but also inseparable from the universal.

While Surūsh leaves questions related to the boundary between the two levels of cognition largely undetermined, such as whether a priori knowledge occurs within or before the context of discovery and exactly which cognitive categories that are included in the term a priori, he uses the general Kantian distinction to combine the views of empiricism and rationalism in an innovative dialectic and synthesis to counter the challenges of metaphysical idealism as well as radical scepticism. While his theory is an empirical one in its denigration of any significance of a priori knowledge by focusing on matters of fact derived from experience, his view of human reason as the ultimate source of knowledge nonetheless affirms that if isomorphism (a mirroring correspondence) between reason and reality were lacking, the effort of human knowledge to understand the world would be impossible. In this respect, it is adequate to stress that Kant in many respects remains one of the most central figures of the whole modern age. By interpreting the limits of our finite apparatus of cognition into a transcendental condition for infinitely progressing knowledge and allowing for the possibility of the self-referential character of the cognitive subject, Kant's epistemology is still the point of departure for the bulk of contemporary Western philosophy from the logical positivism of A.J. Ayer (d. 1989) to the deconstructionism of

[72] This ambiguity in Surūsh's thought is due to the fact that the Kantian realisation that the world as we consciously perceive it (phenomenon) is differentiated from the world and unperceived by anyone (noumenon), results in the notion that it is largely constructed. Kant's epistemological theory leaves the question of how it is certain that reason connects man to noumenon unanswered. If reason connects us directly to noumenon, Kant, then, does not allow for speculative metaphysics as practiced by the rationalists, since reason alone does not determine the positive content of knowledge. For this reason, much criticism has been has been directed towards Kantianism during the two recent centuries, which considers the search for correspondence as logically absurd since every search ends with some belief about whether correspondence holds or not (i.e. it has not advanced beyond belief). To make the distinction noumenon and phenomenon is, in other words, to have noumenon as an ontological object in consciousness and not in itself.

Foucault.[73]

Surprisingly, however, it is not Kant's *Kritik der reinen vernunft* but Jalāl al-dīn Rūmī's *Maṯnawī-yi maʿnawī* which is the most frequently and approvingly cited reference in Surūsh's chapters on epistemology in *Qabḍ wa basṭ-i tiʾūrīk-i sharīʿat* and *Ṣirāṭhā-yi mustaqīm*.[74] Surūsh is in particular influenced by Rūmī's cosmological explanations of concepts such as *manẓar* ('inner sight') and *ḍidd* ('opposition') and his differentiation of *ṣūrat* (form) and *maʿnā* (meaning). The Sufi poet adopts these terms, for instance, to communicate the idea of the transcendent unity of religions, which teaches that religious truth is esoterically one but has different outward manifestations in terms of being channels of divine grace.[75] The famous story of the Indian elephant in the dark house is among the many passages from the *Maṯnawī* that Surūsh consults so as to demonstrate that religious knowledge is formed by external non-religious presuppositions:

We are all familiar with the story of the Indian elephant that was placed for performance in a dark house. We have taken lessons from this story but it seems however as if we only are ready to contemplate on this story in relation to non-religious knowledge. We never even consider that *sharīʿat*, similar to the elephant, cannot without difficulty be enclosed in as much as a hand-clutch human understanding. Besides, we never imagine that other components of *sharīʿat* communicate meanings that are interpreted differently. The significance of the story of the elephant is exactly that unknown learning affects known learning and that non-arrived knowledge influences arrived knowledge. Human error is not an incognito that conceals its knowledge even to itself. Prejudices and contradictions are transmitted over its image. In this way, a posteriori knowledge influences a priori knowledge (Surūsh 1996c:250).[76]

A monistic understanding is neither possible nor desirable. Someone who charges the other's view with error must also scrutinise his or her own *manẓar* and consider it as one among others. "O learned one! The difference among Muslims, Zoroastrians and Jews emanates from their various *manẓar*" (*Maṯnawī-yi maʿnawī* III:3788) (ibid.:305).[77]

---

[73] Cf. Ayer 1956, Heidegger 1997, Habermas 1987, Foucault 1970, etc. Logical positivism adopts Kantian terminology when describing logic and mathematics as a priori sciences since statements within their disciplines are expressed in what Kant called analytic propositions.

[74] To make a comparison, the four chapters of the second part of *Qabḍ wa basṭ-i tiʾūrīk-i sharīʿat*, which constitutes the core of Surūsh's epistemological writings, contain the following quantity of references: Jalāl al-dīn Rūmī (29), modern Western philosophers (26), modern Islamic thinkers (25), the Qur'an (12), premodern Persian poets (6) and a premodern Islamic historian (1). The references to Rūmī as well as to Western philosophers are as a rule of affirmative character, while the references to Islamic thinkers on the whole have the purpose of raising objections against the source. It is also significant that there is no reference at all to the prophetic *ḥadīṯ*.

[75] For the concept *ḍidd*, cf. Surūsh 1996c:140 and 307. Cf. Surūsh 2000a.

[76] This story is also referred to on p. 182 in the same book.

[77] The above verse is also quoted on pp. 57 and 183 in the same book as well as in a number of other contexts (Surūsh 1999d:13, 1996f:47). In his *Ṣirāṭhā-yi mustaqīm*, Surūsh

In his book *Ṣirāṭhā-yi mustaqīm*, Surūsh adopts the second-order epistemology for his comparative study of religion to substantiate his theory of *kaṯrat-girā'ī-yi dīnī* (religious pluralism) and his method is not normative but empirical and descriptive. Making use of the Kantian distinction between noumenon and phenomenon, he advocates, similar to the contemporary British theologian John Hick, a new *mafhūm-sāzī* (conceptualisation) of religious concepts to explain the perceptible multiplicity of religious experiences. He formulates, for instance, a dual classification of God according to which the Divine is understood on the *maqām-i lā ism* (level of namelessness) vs. the *maqām-i nisbat* (level of relation).[78] As it is beyond the purpose of reason to touch upon metaphysical questions, Surūsh refers to the Kantian principle of 'equality of proofs' in the sphere of metaphysics in order to claim that the supremacy of a certain religion over others (or any other metaphysical question for that matter) is not provable a priori. He also compares religions to *ishārī* (indexical) systems, consisting of a number of individual interpretations that are true in the sense that they are bound to individual persons. "Truth and honesty is relative in these indexical interpretations in the sense that they consist of an aspect of 'for me' and 'for you'" (Surūsh 1999d:87 and 160).

While Surūsh supposes the possibility to some extent grade religious phenomena, he claims that there is no means to realistically access religions as totalities or systems of salvation. He considers religions as embodiments of different conceptions of the Divine from within different cultural contexts of being human.[79] The fact that Surūsh is both a realist and a pluralist about

(1999d:13–15) underlines that the concept *manẓar* is an analytical term that is most adequately translated as empirical 'point of view'. Referring to the modern Iranian poet Suhrāb Sipihrī, he argues that "*manẓar* is nothing and no-one except man himself".

[78] Cf. Surūsh 1999d:22. Surūsh adopts Hick's (1984) three labels of religious understanding (exclusivist, inclusivist and pluralist) to explain various possible human answers to the question of multiple religious phenomena. Religious pluralism is diametrically opposed to the theory of *ḥaṣr-girā'ī-yi dīnī* (religious exclusivism) that relates salvation and guidance exclusively to one particular religious tradition. While exclusivism takes many forms, such as in the Catholic dogma of *Extra ecclesiam nulla salus* (outside the Church, no salvation), the thought of Alvin Platinga or the neo-orthodoxy of Karl Barth, Surūsh claims that it is characterised by the belief that the tenets (or some of the tenets) of one religion are in fact true and that any proposition (other religious beliefs) that is incompatible with those tenets are false. Aware of the fact that religious pluralism has difficulties in combining the conflicting truth-claims of various religions and sects, he suggests that religious disagreement "eventually is attributable to the two fundamental differentiations of *truth* and *understanding of truth*" (Surūsh 1999d:foreword).

[79] Surūsh's (1999d:21, 23, 61–66) assertion that followers of other religions might be closer to the divine reality than one is oneself, as well as his tolerance concerning theological disagreements, is very close to the ideas of Hick on religious pluralism. Surūsh argues that the boundary between true and false no longer runs simply between Islam and other religions, but within each of the religions. He distinguishes the higher aspects within every religious tradition from the lower aspects and asserts that while Islam granted humanity cultural richness (i.e. its higher aspect), it also came to establish 'barbarous' penal laws (i.e. its lower aspect).

religions exposes him as a descriptive polytheist (as opposed to a cultic polytheist) as he recognises the reality of several gods but makes clear that he intends his own religious commitments to find their place within the Islamic tradition. This is, of course, not Kant's own account of religious experience or Divine Being, but he takes Kant's terminology of our sensory experience of the world and adapts it to serve as a way of understanding religious experience and its objects. Surūsh also defines pluralism as a mode of 'humanising' religion where spiritual realisation also becomes an individual affair. While he accentuates that the Qur'an (*Qur.* 16:121 and 48:2) uses the word *ṣirāṭ al-mustaqīm* in indefinite form (which indicates the existence of many 'straight paths'), he rejects the view of the mystics that different images of the Divine are esoterically the same and argues that the discourse on pluralism is a discourse on factual pluralism on the level of empirical *tadlīl* (reasoning) and *taʿlīl* (explanation of causes):

> Those who see unity everywhere behind pluralism consistent with their own views (i.e. the mystical view on pluralism), have not at all posed any question or grasped the real nature of the issue. The debate on pluralism is a discourse on empirical pluralism at the level of rational reasoning and explaining of causes, not exoteric pluralism and esoteric unity or reduction of imaginative pluralism to true unity (Surūsh 1999d:63).[80]

But Surūsh's theory of religious pluralism has its dilemmas. It is, for instance, unclear whether many of his statements belong to the a priori level or the a posteriori level of discourse. He does not counter the substantial critique of religious pluralism levelled by Alvin Platinga (1995) and others that proposes that exclusivism is neither irrational or unjustified but instead has epistemic warrant for its beliefs. Platinga refers to the ideas of Roderick Chisholm, coherentism and reliabilism in order to demonstrate that exclusivism is not 'morally suspect', since it reserves to the Christian the right to believe in propositions that are not believed, for instance, by Muslims and leaves it to the Muslims to decide which propositions are and which are not essential to Islam.[81]

The fact that Surūsh largely justifies the epistemological foundation of his theory of contraction and expansion as well as his theory of religious pluralism by reference to the epistemic scheme of traditional mysticism has its dilemmas. While Rūmī is of comparable interest to Surūsh because of the

[80] Cf. Surūsh 1999d:27. As a matter of fact, the Qur'an also adopts the term *ṣirāṭ* (path) in definite form as *al-ṣirāṭ al-mustaqīm* denoting 'the straight path' (*Qur.* 1:5).

[81] Surūsh seems furthermore to account for merely two binary positions on the question of religious pluralism and to ignore other perspectives that are not a posteriori based such as, for instance, the esoteric pluralism of Muḥammad Ḥusain Ṭabāṭabāʾī (1984:64) or the Swiss philosopher Frithjof Schuon (1968) which teaches that esoterical truth is one but has various outward manifestations or the inclusivism advocated by Karl Rahner in his teachings about the 'anonymous Christian' that largely was adopted by Vatican II. For a critique of Surūsh's from the perspective of esoteric pluralism, cf. Ḥusainī-Ṭabāṭabāʾī 1998.

oriented distinction between conditioned reality and unconditioned realities, his doctrine that teaches experience of God through the spiritual heart that guides man from multiplicity to Unity is not a marked critical and rational assessment comparable to that of Kant's. In Rūmī's theosophy, both the *juz'* (partial thing) and the *kull* (universal thing) are distinguished from a third entity, *lā-makān* ('Nowhere place'), the specific and generic nature taken absolutely in itself. Accordingly, every form possesses an inner meaning due to its inner reality and symbolic nature that comes from its character of being transparent, reflecting the *ṣifāt* (attributes) or archetypes that belong to the Divine. In Rūmī's terminology, the *'aql-i juz'ī* (discursive or 'partial' reason) is nothing but the 'illusory' self that places its experience of thinking as the foundation of all epistemology and divorces epistemology from religious ontology.[82] What Surūsh does, however, is similar to Kant. He transforms transparency into opacity by appealing not to pure intuitive intellection as it functions in the heart of man or to revelation but to the individual consciousness of the thinking subject. As knowledge comes depleted of its sacred content, Surūsh indisputably makes a conscious break with the traditional Islamic conceptions of science by imposing the same epistemological principles on legal texts as theological and mystical ones and by also giving primacy to the subject over the object. He neglects, in other words, the theoretical obstacles of applying Rūmī's cognitive monism in legitimising his own brand of second order epistemology. More importantly, he does not seem aware of the danger of anachronism in explaining traditional concepts by using modern standards without differentiating the synchronic parts in a diachronic manner when he projects contemporary meaning into traditional texts and eventually attempts to synchronise all diachrony by emphasising the collective identity of written texts.[83]

In general, many of Surūsh's references to Rūmī must be considered as a departure from the time-honoured Islamic mystical tradition. In Rūmī's view, knowledge is intuitive inspiration (rather than discursive) where the Knower, the known and the process of knowing, i.e. human knowledge, ultimately are identical. He maintains a distinction between the oneness of

[82] Rūmī (1996:VI 2878–2880) says, "The unbeliever's argument is this: 'I see nothing but appearance'. He never considers that appearance gives news of hidden wisdom. The worth of appearance is, indeed, concealed similar to the benefits of medicine". As Annmarie Schimmel (1993:297) elucidates, Rūmī bases his notion of certain knowledge and disdain for empirical knowledge on the Qur'anic term *'ilm ladunnā* that literally means "the wisdom that is with Him" (*Qur.* 18:65). In Rūmī's (1996:II 72–73) view, only the *chashm-i dil* (eye of the heart) is capable of penetrating the *pardah* (veil) of phenomena and distinguishing the permanent light of the Absolute from the transient shadows of imagination. "Once the mirror of your heart becomes pure and clear, you will see pictures from beyond the domain of water and clay. Not only pictures, but also the Painter. Not only the carpet of good fortune, but also the Carpet-spreader".

[83] Cf. Surūsh 1994b:210.

Being and the manyness of knowledge, but the second category of level is only illusory since it borrows its existence from Being.[84] In contrast to Rūmī's idea that knowledge is direct and infallible acquaintance with 'reality', that is, 'truth' drawn from our dominant a priori sense, Surūsh distinguishes in explicit terms between the thing-in-itself and as it appears in perception. The realisation that the world as we consciously perceive it is differentiated from the world in-itself, unperceived by anyone, results in his notion that it is contextually constructed, which is the very anti-thesis of Rūmī's epistemology. Surūsh perceives hence knowledge not as a metaphor of intellectual vision, where knowledge is self-authenticating and infallible, but as conjectural, provisional and probable:

The branch of epistemology that the theory of evolution of religious knowledge is grounded in is not concerned with the *wujūd-i ḏihn* (existence of the mind) or the spiritual origin or qualities of knowledge, but its subject and concern is rather the branches that religious knowledge constitutes a part of. It is not concerned with a priori imagination and concepts, but with corroborations and formations of ideas that construct a specific portion of knowledge among others (Surūsh 1996c:325).[85]

In *Qabḍ wa basṭ-i tiʾūrīk-i sharīʿat*, Surūsh suggests, therefore, that man should be more concerned with the human aspects of his earthly existence than with his own passion for truth. While the ultimate goal of religion is the mystical unity with the Divine, he claims that no human being can foretell when or where "the Sun will rise" (ibid.:196). He dismisses the epistemic standards of traditional mysticism as metaphysical hubris, in the sense that it is elitist and undemocratic and argues that transcendent reason tends to be 'reflexive' since it is hierarchical, relative and closed to inter-subjective corroboration. He defines it as a "strategic theory" and asserts that "in the words of the Westerners; it is reflexive and points back to itself" (Surūsh 1999d:91).[86] He does not, however, mention that modernity from its inception has tended to be reflexive in so far as it constitutes a form of life for which questioning reason is central. Even Kant regards the vindication of reason as a reflexive task, which must assemble certain 'materials' before it can begin. The modern reflexivity differs only in the sense that it is of a qualitatively different order, formed through endless processes of reflexive structuring, de-structuring and restructuring in which new forms of knowledge are generated, adopted or applied (O'Neill 1992).

[84] Rūmī (1996:I 30) says, "Everything is the Beloved and the lover is a veil. The living is the Beloved, and the lover is dead". From this perspective, human perfection culminates in the full activity of the Intellect through knowledge of God. "A knowledge not immediately from Him will soon vanish like paint on a woman's face" (ibid.:I 3449). But the intellective aspect of Rūmī's (1992:2989) poetry must not be overemphasised, since ultimately love is the foundation and source of reality. "The intellect runs crazy in the hope for unity. In love, it moves forward in desire of pilgrimage".
[85] Cf. Surūsh 1996c:519–520.
[86] Surūsh (1999c:63) argues that *ʿirfān* is "a theory not for the majority, but for the minority" and that it results in autocratic totalitarianism when integrated with political governance.

Surūsh's mysticism, or what he calls *īmān-i ʿāshiqānah* (amorous faith), has affinities with premodern forms of mysticism in the sense of facing the suspicion of heresy (which makes it incumbent for him to write in a special code and to maintain plausible deniability). His insistence, however, upon the mystery of God's existence manifested through a sharp division between faith and science, depicting God as purely transcendent, is quite different from traditional mystical notions of the boundaries of God's presence in the world (Surūsh 1999a:202).[87] Inspired ultimately by the deism of nineteenth century Europe and the Darwinian categories of the natural world that consider nature as cut off from the hands of God, Surūsh ontologically separates the Creator from our spatio-temporal framework by suggesting that no certain knowledge of Him is possible. Surūsh's God is utterly detached from the world and seems remarkably similar to no God at all. In this respect, his mysticism has more affinities with the epistemic conditions set by high modernity in the sense that metaphysical realism has come to an end and that our worldview has become very much more pluralized, pragmatic and free-floating. It is not an accident that many today speak of the Death of God as a postmodern type of religious experience, breaking down premodern two-world cosmology, immutable philosophical rationalism and ontological assumptions of enlightenment modernism (i.e. foundationalism) (Taylor 1984).

As divine mystery is entirely beyond human knowledge, Surūsh's invocation of the concept of mysticism as the intrinsic validity of any religious experience differentiates epistemology from metaphysics in due course. The role of religion becomes an 'interiorised' individual and private mode of experience where the concept of reality as the category of God is confined to the noumenal world of in-itself, transcending not only human language but also human knowledge. Surūsh's reductionist elaboration on human cognitive efforts turns God into a subjective privatisation, in the sense that his Kantian views of reality easily appear to make noumenal reality seem redundant. His divorce of reason from the world of faith, or secularisation of reason, connects, in other words, to the secularisation of the cosmos (which has affected a large part of religious mysticism in our modern age) and inevitably results in a downgrading of the role of noumenon in human thinking. If all we can have are concepts of reality, what, then, is the sense of trying to envisage the nature of reality as it is-in-itself? If religion in terms of noumenon is beyond our comprehension, how can we go on being committed to the truth of any religion at all? By

[87] Considering the Persian poet Shams al-dīn Ḥāfiẓ the exemplar of the religious intellectual, Surūsh makes known that it is theosophical love that guides him as an intellectual. As he describes the concept *īmān-i ʿāshiqānah* in chapters 4–8 in his book *Basṭ-i tajrubah-yi nabawī*, this form of personal mysticism is always connected to the guidance of the Prophet of Islam. For Surūsh's writings on mysticism, cf. Surūsh 1996a:157–170, 1996g, 1997b, 1997c:136–170, 1999a:113–281, 321–355 and 2000a.

considering all a priori propositions as *literally* false and by de-emphasising Islamic religious truth-claims, Surūsh asserts that the traditional idealisation of knowledge is not merely tentative but also self-defeating, in the sense that it elevates knowledge to a metaphysical peerage in which it loses all contact with common human experience. He argues that no such epistemic ideal or utopia is possible since all sources of cognition are fallible and lead to error:

In the contemporary period (similar to every period), our knowledge of Islamic law as well as nature is comprised of modest and incomplete components. It relies on and is captive to many other components that have not yet appeared to us in order to be explored. Our contemporary knowledge of the explored components is hence conjectural in the sense that it awaits the arrival of future knowledge to construct a new formation (of ideas) and a new understanding (of knowledge) (Surūsh 1996c:251).

While religion differs from science in the sense that religiosity and personal beliefs are not concerned with objectivity in the true sense of the word, Surūsh believes that religious knowledge is exposed to the same criterion of corroboration as science and that the repudiation of the quest for certainty does not necessarily undermine the quest for the foundations of knowledge. Instead of claiming that basic propositions are certain and that they lend their certainty to propositions derived from them, he supposes that they possess a degree of probability. The most distinctive feature of Surūsh's epistemology is therefore his effort to overcome with unwonted clarity and simplicity the difficulty of how *subjective* conditions of thinking can have objective validity, that is, yield conditions for the possibility of all cognition of objects without grounding the objectivity of eternal truths in a divine and infallible intellect. In his early book *Īdi'ūlūzhī-yi shaiṭānī* (Satanic ideology), he alludes to the Islamic conception of man as God's vicegerent on earth in order to posit a human subjectivity grounded in and mediated by God's subjectivity.[88] He refers innovatively to the theosophical concept *ḥarakat-i jauharī* in order to conceptualise the theological notions of *tauḥīd* that emerge as the centre of his cosmology or *jahānbīnī-yi khudā-markazī* (God-centred worldview):

The *tauḥīdī* view of the world does not deny existential and natural differences. It suggests rather that we are capable of observing the world with the eyes of God and comprehend everything as relying on Him, settled by Him and living in one spirit and moving in one movement... God-centredness means first of all that God is the source of all creation and existence and that no interpretation of the phenomenon of

[88] The term 'mediated subjectivity' is borrowed from Vahdat Farzin (1998:414) who characterises it as "a constant vacillation between affirmation and negation of human subjectivity".

existence is possible or convincing without the belief that all existents perishes in Him (Surūsh 1994a:173).[89]

But while Surūsh is knowledgeable that the discourse of modernity is located within a specific historicity, he presents no Islamic counterforce to nominally Western universal cognitive concepts, presuppositions and terminology. The effort is rather the opposite, to delimit and decentre Western modes of knowledge, since the traditional Islamic civilisation, as he understand it, was not an intended consequence of a systematic methodology nor premised on a given Islamic science or Islamic epistemology. The account of Ghamari-Tabrizi (1999:72) and others that Surūsh "remains critical of modernist claims to universality" seems questionable. In fact, Surūsh rejects any attempts to 'islamise' modernity since there exists no alternative Islamic epistemology upon which a new a priori cognitive theory may be formulated. For Surūsh, religion is not an ideological standpoint through which natural and historical realities are constructed. He does not refer to the concept of man as God's vicegerent on earth in his post-1988 writings such as *Qabḍ wa basṭ-i tiʾūrīk-i sharīʿat*, but rather grounds this status in knowledge as such. He argues that knowledge originates in the faculties of the subject, since the key features of empirical cognition, including the spatial form of intuition and other features of our representations, must be traced to our cognitive constitution. His view of knowledge is hence largely 'subjectivist':

In my view, we cannot acquire a proper analysis of the modern history of man without a proper analysis of the emerging modern knowledge. Man is knowledge as such (Surūsh 1997a:424).

The sacred, complete and unified character of *sharīʿat* does not mean that human understanding of *sharīʿat* is sacred, complete or unified. Religion is aimed at humans and is, therefore, human and natural. Man's cognitive faculties conceptualise religion as it approaches human beings. The standards of human knowledge prevail over religion and transform it into an individual knowledge among others (Surūsh 1996c:207).

Surūsh's position is best described as an expansion of subjectivity that develops into a form of unmediated or 'inter-subjective' subjectivity, beyond the confines of divinely mediated subjectivity where it originates. In contrast to the traditional ideal of the subject's transparency to itself as a total meditation where it transpires to itself the absolute subject, Surūsh's notion of subjectivity is mediated by its social and historical accidentals. The reflecting human subject is, in his view, a non-divine historical, linguistic and social subject that is in search of meaning. It has a transient unmediated

[89] Cf. Surūsh 1994a:185. In general, Surūsh's book *Īdiʾūlūzhī-yi shaiṭānī* contains a larger amount of references to the Qur'an than his other works and embodies an effort to refute Marxist ideology from the perspective of the revealed texts as well as from the perspective of Popperian science.

nature where self-understanding is basically a social and historical becoming or growth rather than a state of contemplation. While his interest is the historical evolution of knowledge rather than the empirical psychological enquiry into how we get our beliefs, his view that knowledge depends on the structure of the mind and not the world results however easily, in knowledge having no connection to the world and hence being no true representation.

G. Epistemic relativism or epistemological relativism?

Surūsh's position on epistemic warrant as well as ontology is clearly identifiable in his discussion on the problem of relativity. The *relativisation* of epistemology is one of the hallmarks of the contemporary Western philosophical commitment and its idea that the 'ontology' of a theory only becomes meaningful relative to the interpretative subject makes every metaphysical or universal predication of ontology ambiguous. While the phenomenological perspective on religious science, where divinity appears in its continuous myriad of manifestations limited by particular social, cultural and historical conditions does not rule out the presupposition of a divine origin of Islamic law, Surūsh favours an inter-subjectivist approach to knowledge, which has some features in common with the philosophical concept of relativism in terms of disentangling epistemology from metaphysics. He seems aware of the fact that if our relativised framework principles are not synthetic a priori but empirical and changeable and revisable under pressure of empirical findings, it becomes uncertain how exactly these framework principles really differ from more straightforward empirical generalisations. In other words, if both framework principles and more straightforward empirical laws are revisable in light of empirical evidence, then what is there to protect religion from the trap of relativism? Surūsh's notion of objectivity is the idea that the third world of objective knowledge cannot be objectively understood but only explained by reference to our knowledge and therefore to something subjective. The rejection of foundationalism does not, for Surūsh, imply relativism in his epistemological position, since the specific aim of the theory of contraction and expansion is not to 'periodise' truth, but to describe the evolution of religious knowledge:

> My object is not, for instance, to demonstrate how relativism functions in mechanics and to draw the conclusion that everything, such as ethics and truth, is relative. My discourse is to describe how concepts of nature and man are given new meaning, whether in mechanics, natural science or anthropology and to depict how the previous meanings and connotations in, for instance, natural science, adjust to these new meanings and how everything will be sorted through once again (Surūsh 1996c:194).

Religious science and the focus on the growth of knowledge do not invite the religious believers to forsake their viewpoints and beliefs, to give up their efforts (of acquiring truth), to intermingle truth and false nor to negate truth or regard it as relative. Religion and religious beliefs are necessary in order to pursue religious science. The religious scientists do not try to demonstrate that religious believers have divergent interpretations regarding, for instance, the Darwinian theory but they consider rather the divergent interpretations of the religious scholars as an observable fact and try to analyse the meaning of the character of religious and human knowledge and in what way it is disposed to evolution. Whether evolution and development is relativistic, static or absolute, all pertains to understanding of *sharīʿat* and religious knowledge and not to faith, *sharīʿat* itself or the challenge of religious scientists (Surūsh 1996c:208).[90]

In Surūsh's terminology, relativism is a form of philosophical scepticism where the a priori and a posteriori levels of epistemology intermingles and therefore it fails to grasp the essential difference between noumenon and phenomenon:

To intermingle the two levels of epistemology, i.e. the a priori and the a posteriori, is to vindicate scepticism and to misunderstand the meaning of evolution of knowledge and to reduce it to quantitative evolution. The sceptic considers truth as relative. If his opinion has a scholarly content it involves a priori and philosophical epistemology and not a posteriori epistemology. Someone who claims that truth is relative and that we have no means of (intelligible) correspondence with reality makes claims about the nature of human perception and not about the branches of a specific knowledge. In contrast, the second-order epistemology only describes the attributes of a priori concepts of change, relativism and contextuality (Surūsh 1996c:331).

But since scepticism is far from identical to relativism in contemporary epistemology, it is useful to differentiate the two terms as well as to distinguish the narrower form of scepticism from the broader. In the broad sense, a sceptic is someone who casts doubts on the availability, at least to us humans, of objective knowledge, i.e. the idea of correspondence between a proposition and the thing(s) to which it refers. In contrast, scepticism in the narrower sense is close to other –isms, such as relativism and nihilism, which wholesomely reject the possibility of certain objective knowledge. But in contrast to these forms of scepticism, relativism also denies the existence of any objective order to have knowledge of at all by reducing all knowledge claims to immanent relations. It is hence a much more complicated phenomenon than the sheer claim that there is no unique truth and no unique objective reality. In this respect, D. E. Cooper (1999:5) argues that "relativists of different shapes and sizes have offered various answers: truth is relative to cultures, or to conceptual schemes, or to individual perspectives, or to 'forms of life', and so on". While the theory of

[90] Cf. Surūsh 1996c:133, 275, and 1997a:219.

contraction and expansion is not based on scepticism in the narrower sense in that it rejects all scepticism towards the objective existence of reality, Surūsh is in fact proudly ambivalent on the question that objects must conform to our knowledge. While part of him inclines to the realistic assumption that we succeed in knowing objects that really conform to our conditions for representing them, another part of him inclines to the view that things as they are in themselves cannot possibly have those very properties that they must appear to have, since truth has no clear sign (Surūsh 1999d:145). Similar to Kant (1996:B 43), who states that "space encompasses all things that appear to us externally, but not that it encompasses all things in themselves", Surūsh denies that we can have any objective knowledge of noumenon or things-in-themselves:

Even if our perception of *sharīʿat* is correct and non-contradictory it is still something else than *sharīʿat* in-itself. The meaning of 'correct perception' is merely that perception corresponds to the phenomenon. Correct perception is, in other words, a perception that corresponds to reality in the sense that the world of phenomenon and the human capacity to know it are necessary facts. The inevitability of differentiating *sharīʿat* from the understanding of *sharīʿat* hence does not mean that all understanding is correct or that correct understanding is impossible but that correct understanding of *sharīʿat* is necessarily different from *sharīʿat* in-itself (Surūsh 1996c:341).

While the pragmatists basically reject Kantian notions, such as a priori-a posteriori or analytic-synthetic judgements, it is possible as, for instance, D.E. Cooper (1999:4) argues, to be a philosophical realist and to confirm that there is an objective order knowable, for instance, by pure reason but also to believe that man does not have the capacity to establish with certainty what that order is. Cooper also believes that it is fully possible for someone to be sceptical towards knowledge-claims in certain areas– such as ethics or religion, but to think that knowledge is perfectly possible in other areas, such as science or mathematics. While philosophical nominalism and its belief that no unshakable foundations exist for human knowledge (which makes the quest for them fruitless) is not characteristic of all modern science, Surūsh's adherence to the nominalist rejection of universal meaning is problematical as regards his belief in constants. His evolutionary epistemology, no matter how minimal his commitment to realism may be, is not oriented towards a phenomenalist ontology that transforms epistemology into a branch of cognitive psychology, but is instead methodological. It does not primarily deal with ontological emergence, but with logical theses about novelties and unpredictable elements of knowledge that have been investigated within the analytical tradition. The ambiguities inherent in his definition of these terms are in fact largely limited to his discussion in *Qabḍ wa basṭ-i tiʾūrīk-i sharīʿat* which vindicates the existence of synthetic a priori principles and tenets of science and religion and at the same time 'denies' them by reducing these constants to the internal and subjective cognitive matrix of human understanding. In the sense that he rejects the claim that we can know an objectively existing world outside of us, his position is very akin to that of the fallibilistic realism of the American philosopher Hilary Putnam, who defines the purpose of science as the development of genuine knowledge about the world even though such knowledge is never known with certainty. As Surūsh argues, science can never reveal the true nature of things or describe the reality in-itself but only how it appears, since we cannot expect our description to correspond to reality in any coherent sense:

> Those who attempt to distinguish the constant part of religion from the non-constant must keep in mind that this distinction is related to religious knowledge and is contingent on a specific comprehension of religion. The constant and non-constant do not occur before religious understanding but are born out of it. We are always confronted with religious knowledge that depicts and describes, but never with religion itself. This rule applies to all human knowledge (Surūsh 1996c:53).[91]

Similar to Kant, who did not think he was a sceptic himself (since his work developed as a critique of the radical scepticism of Hume), Surūsh's central view that the subjective mind determines the structures of human knowledge is definitely a kind of scepticism. Surūsh has accepted much of the sceptical point of view by rejecting the idea of the thing in itself, i.e. the idea that there is no pure given, without realising it. He is, so to say, a sceptic in the sense that he denies not merely the possibility of a general criterion of non-tautological truth, but also man's capacity to establish what the objective order is with certainty (while he does not deny its existence). As A. Tolland (1991:25) argues in his study of relativism in knowledge, there are many sorts of relativism, on a continuum from the stronger *epistemic* relativism to the weaker *epistemological* relativism. While the stronger epistemic relativism takes the extreme position that all truth is relative to particular contexts and that discussions of truth have meaning only in reference to the truth of their context, weak relativism agrees that there is a contextual aspect

[91] Cf. Surūsh 1996c:283 and 288. In the view of Putnam (1987), epistemology should not reject traditional philosophical questions altogether, although it does not have any final correct answers. The struggle with realism and its problems can lead to refinements of the formulations and to cognitive developments. Similarly, Surūsh's realism seems to differ from the kind of critical realism which considers that the purpose of science to be the generation of the most accurately possible description and understanding of the world as noumenon. While he acknowledges that the contradiction between the phenomenon and our perception of it does not involve the dispute between realism and idealism but rather is a semantic question that concerns various forms of realism, he is not concerned with differentiating *ri'ālīsm-i pīchīdah* (sophisticated realism) from fallibistic realism but from *ri'ālīsm-i khām* (direct realism) of empiricism. Surūsh's scepticism to the form of knowledge that states that the thing-in-itself is knowable but only in the knower's categories, not in the thing-in-itself, has also affinities with the Austrian philosopher and ethnologist Konrad Lorenz's (d. 1989) idea that the objective reflection of *das Ding an sich* never achieves expression on the thing-in-itself's own terms. Surūsh shares Lorenz' (1977) concept of the evolutionary character of epistemology as well as his anti-holism that considers all description to be necessarily selective.

to truth but believes that truth must be meaningfully discussed beyond context. Because the most extreme form of relativism involves the contradiction of holding that all truths except the truth of relativism are relative, Surūsh (1996c:178 and 286) advocates a sort of epistemological relativism in the sense that he acknowledges that "everyone's religion is his or her understanding of religion" and that "the world of the individual corresponds to his or her comprehension of the world".[92] He rejects the conception of science as representing the standpoint dictated to us by objective standards of rationality or as offering a 'God's eye point of view', and claims that the whole scientific enterprise is *nasbī* (relative) in the sense that it is "contingent on a selection of presuppositions" (Surūsh 1999a:304). While he claims that the theory of contraction and expansion is a demonstrative one, he makes in fact no notable use of deductive logic but rather presents his case as *a* theory based on a number of inductive examples.[93]

Surūsh's doubt in epistemology is hence not coherent with various types of 'rationalist foundationalism' in the sense that he accepts no class of a priori propositions that register genuine knowledge and that all other propositions are inferred from those basic ones. But while he rejects the notion of warranted basic beliefs, he claims at the same time that the theory of contraction and expansion protects understanding from falling into relativism since it is limited by *tawātur*, which signifies the religious tradition in the general sense, a certain sort of non-inferential known proposition that cannot plausibly be construed as empirical. While Surūsh cannot give a full rational justification for *tawātur*, it is a necessary presupposition of faith rather than non-necessary truth whose necessity transcends the deliverance of sense awareness and averts the generation of solipsism. Even if Surūsh does not divide the human epistemic beliefs into basic and non-basic, he supposes that we have an epistemic right to believe in the self-evidently true notion of *tawātur*. While our understanding is flowing, it does not indicate that everything is in a flow, since *tawātur* can be 'known' by some sort of doxastic a priori intuition which he does not elaborate on further:

[92] Tolland writes, "Epistemological relativism derives its name from the fact that the mere possibility of relativism is only of interest to the epistemologist; it has no practical bearing. Even if all our knowledge is relative to, in some sense arbitrary, presuppositions, this may not matter as long as we all agree in what we presuppose. Consensus could work just as well as absolute foundations... Epistemic relativism claims that radical, rationally insolvable, conflicts between parties with vastly different presuppositions *actually exist*, or are real possibilities, because there really are, or have been, such parties. Epistemic relativism claims that there is no fundamental agreement in presuppositions" (Tolland 1991:25). Cf. Surūsh 1996c:361.

[93] While Surūsh's epistemology is not relativistic as far as it believes that the epistemic norms employed by modern science enjoys a special status, he disregards that modern science itself has evolved through some major shifts during the last two centuries which some observers claim is inconsistent with any objective, universally valid, criteria of truth and rationality.

There are a number of presuppositions for the existence of God and the Prophet that one must take into consideration, such as the validity of *tawātur*, which is the only proof for the existence of a Prophet fourteen centuries ago. If someone rejects the validity of *tawātur* and puts the existence of the Prophet into doubt, i.e. not only his historical existence but also the question of prophet-hood, prophecy, super-naturality, and so on, he or she becomes an apostate. If someone rejects that a Qur'anic verse stems from the Prophet [sic!] the contradiction between that verse and the other verses will not be eliminated (Surūsh 1996c:159).

While Surūsh's epistemology does not propose a seemingly natural knowledge, it suggests a strategy for responding to scepticism in the narrower sense. While truth is not in flow, the theory of contraction and expansion is certainly a relativistic enterprise in the sense that epistemic warrant is only possible relative to things taken for granted. Knowledge is not automatic and normally implies understanding and understanding is only possible in relation to some kind of arbitrary interpretative background. In this respect, Surūsh even goes as far as claiming that ʿAlī b. Abī Ṭālib's understanding of the Divine Essence can be different from contemporary understandings and descriptions of the Divine Essence, which amounts to saying that the word we hear from ʿAlī is not a timeless one:

My claim is that our understanding of everything is flowing. Someone who says that everything is flowing, includes the constant matters in this 'everything'. The question is whether God, who is equivalent to constant is also in flow? Are the hidden worlds, the constant laws of the natural world and the constant laws of mathematics also in flow and change? This is not our claim… It is not possible in any absolute sense to say that God changes but I think that everyone understands that it is possible to change our knowledge of God's constant essence. The God that *amīr al-muʾminīn* (peace be upon him) knew is not the same God as the One we know in the sense that our understanding truly differs (ibid.:116-117).[94]

In the sense that the identity of the Divine Essence in concrete terms is a product and construct of human classification, Surūsh acknowledges that epistemology is relativistic as it is largely based on *muʿallal* ('caused') knowledge. In contrast to deconstructionism that indicates the uncertainty of all prior foundations of epistemology, he claims that the relativistic character of the theory of contraction and expansion is not absolute in the sense that it replaces proofs entirely by causes. Defining pure relativism as *ʿillat-girāʾī* (cause-ism), Surūsh's effort is rather to strike a balance between rationalistic foundationalism and deconstructionism by preserving the function of proofs as long as they have a relevant role in the attainment of knowledge and refuting epistemic relativism because of its incoherent and unscientific character:

To my belief, the emergence of the notion of relativism in modern epistemology is due to the dominant trend to look for the 'cause' behind the production of

[94] Cf. Surūsh 1996c:248–249, 298, 305 and 2000c:49.

knowledge as well as to the weakening of the position of proofs. Relativism is characterised by the tendency to sacrifice proofs for causes in explanation. It is commonly said that relativism means that everything is relatively true, but it is more appropriate to describe relativism in another way according to the current trend in modern epistemology. Modern epistemology, which relies on relativism, proceeds from the idea that the function of proof has been weakened in the sphere of knowledge or even reduced to zero... This is the position of pure relativism. Opposite to this view is the position of philosophers and thinkers before Kant and also Islamic philosophers, who degrade the function of causes in the acquisition of knowledge to the irrelevant, exceptional, accidental or ephemeral. They believed that the function of proof is essential and principal and that the comprehension of reality represents absolute, complete and proved knowledge. It is therefore more appropriate that we make our categorisation in the following and argue that relativism or relativistic epistemology supposes *muʿallal* (caused) knowledge, while non-relativistic epistemology supposes *mudallal* (proved) knowledge [...] With the description I have made, postmodernism constitutes a periodical production or event in the world of knowledge and culture that sacrifices the proofs in the place of causes and does not have any appreciation for proofs. My epistemological position in this context is briefly that proofs plays a role in the production and life of knowledge but that the proofs are replaced by causes when they have fulfilled their function and have reached a cul-de-sac (Surūsh 1999d:147–150).

In Surūsh's view, postmodern theory is equal to deconstructionism.[95] He believes that deconstructionism produces a fundamental paradox that was avoided by Kant by considering knowledge not as representation but pure causes. Surūsh's epistemological affinities are closer to Kantian than deconstructionist thought, since he shares with the enlightenment philosophical tradition a number of convictions such as: the world of phenomena is intelligible; truth is fixed, uniform, permanent, absolute and universal and religion is a *sui generis* reality that is unique and irreducible. While Surūsh's thought partly is a product of the enlightenment representational mode of thinking, his aim is not at all to construct an abstract order proceeding from Kant's epistemology in search of the universal conditions by which propositions can be really true or false. His epistemological relativism rather doubts the correspondence between appearance and reality by suggesting that human reason lacks firm foundations connecting it to the realities that it asserts to exist, which easily makes the representation of these realities become unwarranted.

[95] Cf. Surūsh 1996a:359.

H. Hermeneutics: There is nothing beyond the text

Similar to Richard Rorty, who announces the end of epistemology by turning to hermeneutics, Surūsh identifies epistemology with the broad, generic task of reflecting on the nature and limits of human knowledge. Since all knowledge entails understanding and its presuppositions always postulate other explanations, he believes that all cognitive ambiguities must be assessed in the light of hermeneutics. Epistemology gives way, in other words, to hermeneutics, since the scientific endeavour constantly preys on other readings or interpretations in an endless process and since human understanding always is blocked and empowered by the concrete and changing context of a specific hermeneutical situation. He seems in fact to suggest that the primary task of contemporary Islamic scholars is to understand science and then to understand hermeneutics and to simply relate the two. The situation is nevertheless much more complex in that the two do not stand in isolation and that hermeneutics must be understood not only in relation to science but in relation to the philosophies of science. In contrast to Rorty, who discards Kantian philosophy altogether, Surūsh's (1996c:57) hermeneutics is not the replacement of epistemology as such but the replacement of one epistemology with another.[96] While Surūsh does not attempts to establish a modern Qur'anic discipline of hermeneutics, he suggests that the theory of contraction and expansion accesses the limitations and possibilities of the human world of every individual so as to see what new ways of understanding can arise in the arena of hermeneutical discourse between the individual subject and religion:

The essential objective of the theory of contraction and expansion is not to solve the dispute over *fiqh-i sunnatī* and *fiqh-i pūyā*, to modernise, expound or complete religion nor to relativise or reject truth, but to shed light on religious understanding and the evolution of religious knowledge. As long as the secret of understanding is not revealed, the endeavour to revive religion will remain incomplete. The theory of contraction and expansion is in its essence therefore a *naẓarīyah-yi tafsīrī-maʿrifatshinākhtī* (theory of interpretation-hermeneutics) that is relevant to theology, theosophy and *uṣūl* (sources and theory of religious science).

In *Qabḍ wa basṭ-i tiʾūrīk-i sharīʿat*, Surūsh (ibid.:204) distinguishes the term *maʿrifatshinakhtī* from *maʿrifatshināsī* (epistemology) and translates it as

[96] Cf. Rorty 1979:10, 180, 210 and 315. As Rorty (1986:172) argues, the history of philosophy shows that there are no final answers to the traditional questions about knowledge, truth, and representation. He thinks such questions should be eliminated from philosophy since there is no possibility to get outside of our mind and language. In the view of Rorty, the whole project of analytical philosophy fails after Sellars and Quine's criticism of the distinction between the logically/conceptually necessary and the contingent, between being true by virtue of meaning and being true by virtue of experience. "If there are no intuitions into which to resolve concepts (in the manner of the *Aufbau*) nor any internal relations among concepts to make possible 'grammatical discoveries' (in the manner of 'Oxford philosophy'), then indeed it is hard to imagine what an 'analysis' might be".

hermeneutics. But his definitions are far from clear since he also characterises Kant's theory of knowledge or Muḥammad Bāqir Ṣadr's theory of induction as theories of hermeneutics and not as epistemological respectively methodological theories, which they more correctly are. Surūsh (1999d:192) has retrospectively become very much aware of this fact. In his later works, he instead uses the word *hirminūtīk* to denote hermeneutics, which is strictly defined as a separate human scientific method for the interpretation of texts and other empirical material. His incoherence in the use of the terms epistemology and hermeneutics may very well depend on the fact that Surūsh (1999k) at the time of writing *Qabḍ wa basṭ-i tiʾūrīk-i sharīʿat* was not acquainted with the Western tradition of modern hermeneutics but merely had become familiar with the subject by way of the history of science. While the theory of contraction and expansion is formulated within the theoretical framework of the philosophy of science, it seems that he views hermeneutics as a kind of a meta-science, since he believes that the essential questions of science are hermeneutical in the sense that the emergence of modern epistemology has transformed the concepts of scientific discourse, such as objectivity, certainty and meaning:

> In the course of the past centuries, colossal contractions and expansions have affected human knowledge and beliefs so that even a simple understanding of the term 'eternity' has become difficult. Understanding and preserving the eternal message of religion in the course of such an invasive torrent of change and renewal constitutes the core of the efforts and sacrifices of the religious reformers of our time (Surūsh 1996c:48).

In contrast to the traditional Shi'i belief that knowledge in its entirety is at the disposal of the Prophet and the *imāms* and therefore cannot be separated from the interpretations of it that are given by them, Surūsh claims that a moment of uncertainty clings to all knowledge claims. He suggests that the question of the sources of knowledge should be replaced by completely different questions relating to hermeneutics and acknowledges that there are no ultimate sources of knowledge that are beyond critical examination. As far as his primary epistemological interest rests within hermeneutics rather than physics and biology, Surūsh sets forth on a new path separate from his Popperian exposition of science and neo-Kantian epistemology. In the same manner as he criticises the traditional Islamic sciences for their lack of theories on the pursuit of knowledge, he asserts that the absence of coherent hermeneutical theories in premodern times explains why the problem of solving the distinction between *muḥkam* and *mutashābih* or *taʾwīl* and *tafsīr* was never solved and why *tafsīr bi-raʾy* was vaguely defined and difficult to accept. He argues in fact that the topic of *ikhtilāf* of interpretation should instead be concerned with categories of *tafsīr bi-raʾy* since all interpretations are contingent, provisional and contextual:

In light of this hermeneutical theory it is possible to understand the inevitable entry of the categories of *muḥkam* and *mutashābih* not only in the Qur'an but also in *ḥadīṯ*, *fiqh* and even in the interpretation of history. It becomes also evident that the categories of *aḥkām* (certainty) and *tashābih* (ambivalence) themselves are subject to change. It is not as though a verse would remain certain or ambivalent forever. Hermeneutical theory makes available a lucid definition of *tafsīr bi-ra'y* and the more this issue is scrutinised in the absence of such a theory, the murkier it becomes. A qualified justification of having a *tafsīr bi-ra'y* goes a long way toward the solution of the problem. Hermeneutics explains that interpretation without *tafsīr bi-ra'y* is utterly impossible. My argument here is not over the presence or absence of *tafsīr bi-ra'y* but over its quality and qualifications that also shed light on other questions concerning the legitimacy of *tafsīr* and *ta'wīl* as well (ibid.:58).

By adopting a modern and contemporary view of hermeneutics to solve interpretative contradictions, Surūsh asserts that the traditional terminology of Islamic exegesis is characterised by an overt unpredictability. He points to the fact that Muḥammad Ḥusain Ṭabāṭabā'ī, who himself warned in the introduction of his *tafsīr* against mixing up *taṭbīq* (conforming) and *tafsīr* suffered from the charge of *tafsīr bi-ra'y*. Claiming that all interpretations must be considered in the context of preunderstanding, Surūsh (ibid.:130) also suggests, contrary to the traditional terminological distinction of *ikhtilāf*, that there are a variety of human readings even of basic Qur'anic formulas and that the traditional method of *nāsikh wa mansūkh* is insufficient for textual understanding and explanation. While his discredit of traditional metaphysical hermeneutics provides a general strategy for interpretation, it makes no decision between different interpretations and can from this perspective first of all be considered as a critique. In *Qabḍ wa basṭ-i ti'ūrīk-i sharī'at*, he is concerned with hermeneutics secondary to epistemology and the primary hermeneutical question is whether meaning is historically and sociologically situated or anchored in metaphysics. Suggesting that meaning is constructed by the human mind, he compares religious texts to the world of phenomenon, which also is represented in a variety of ways through human language. In this respect, the text has no well-defined features in terms of unity, totality, authorship or self-referentiality, and meaning is never equivalent to the author's intention. He categorically rejects the notion of *ma'nī-yi wāqi'ī* (true meaning) in the realm of human understanding:

The allegory of the external world is the only accessible allegory for the written text. No written text says its meaning twice. It is rather the human linguistic mind that reads meaning into the text. Phrases are hungry for meaning rather than impregnated with meaning even if they are not satisfied with all kind of food either. The meaning of worldly phenomena is not inscribed on them and neither is it easy to grasp (ibid.:287–288).

In the textual world, we do not have anything such as truth in the meaning of conformity with or intention of the author. The author selects a language for his exposition of meaning and takes into account a specific meaning but there are, indeed, other meanings of that text. If the author is conscious of the fact that a text communicates meaning disengaged from the intention or objective of its author, he or she cannot blame others for misinterpretation (Surūsh 1999d:192).[97]

While intention lends existence to a text, it is hence not the basis of valid interpretation or an ultimate means for attaining an objective interpretation. The inference to the best explanation of a text is not related to the supposed intention of the author, since language by nature does not search for a unified meaning but essentially possesses a number of non-fixed possibilities as far as meaning is concerned. In contrast to the enlightenment notion that language must be rational and transparent and functions only to represent the real world that the rational mind observes, Surūsh suggests that there is no firm or objective connection between the objects of perception and the words used to name them (between signified and signifier). As Derrida would say, language itself effects its own deconstruction since texts are open to multiple interpretations. This undermines attempts to retrieve or repeat the truth of texts since multiple interpretations tend to mean not plentitude but a paralogy that involves conflict and disruption, as well as the ruptures and gaps in understanding. This is, according to Surūsh, the cold hermeneutic truth: The truth is that there is no truth, no master name or as Lyotard would say 'no metanarrative' that holds things captive.[98] His hermeneutics involves hence in some sense a critique of hermeneutics itself and specifically a critique of any attempt to find *the* truth of a particular text:

Language itself never points towards one single specific meaning. Philosophically speaking, the text is a *fiʿlīyat-i nā-yāftah* (not yet actualised) and a potentiality. The text accepts many formal meanings as a potentiality. [...] At the level of justification, we must infer the best explanation that acknowledges pluralism. We are confronted with a lot of cases and meanings that the texts (whether profane or sacred) have in option together with many denotations and probabilities. The best guess or explanation for clarifying meaning is probably the rule that the text possesses an ambiguous and non-fixed essence of meaning (ibid.:195).

By acknowledging that the inferred meaning of a concept or sentence might very well differ from the author's intention, Surūsh (1996c:296) also questions whether we may understand the meaning of a theological concept better than the author himself:

Is it possible to understand the meaning of a concept better than the author? Again, does the meaning of a word change while the author's intention remains permanent? The descriptions we have made earlier seem to give positive answers to these questions. Yes, if meaning is informed by theories and if theories gradually become

[97] Cf. Surūsh 1994a:52.

[98] Lyotard's (1999) argument is that the epoch of postmodernity witnesses the collapse of all grand 'metanarrative' schemas (Kantian, Hegelian, Marxist, etc) that once promised truth or justice at the end of inquiry. A metanarrative is, in his terminology, a 'grand theory', a narrative about narratives.

better, deeper and *wāqaʿ-namātar* (more descriptive of reality), our perception of this single sentence also becomes deeper and better.

In mystical terms, Surūsh (ibid.:299) describes the hermeneutical act as an inner process of *pardah bar dāshtan* (removal of veils) where phenomenona is penetrated. But in contrast to the mystics, he limits hermeneutics, the primary philosophical question, to the horizontal and historical by arguing that "science never takes a halt". While from Plato to Hegel, truth consisted in the complete revelation and presence of the things by a purely intellectual inspection to the infinite mind, Surūsh's hermeneutics takes not place in the wordless realm of the Logos but in finite language. For premodern philosophers, such as Plato and Ibn Sīnā, thinking seemed more like a state of rest or a halting than a movement. From Surūsh's hermeneutical exposition in *Qabḍ wa basṭ-i tiʾūrīk-i sharīʿat*, it seems that reason is only another term for understanding but it emerges that he has in mind a higher role for reason by insisting that we not only make a lot of judgements about the world but also try to integrate all these bits of knowledge into an coherent scheme with general principles. While intention is not considered to be a valid ground of interpretation, that is, finished decidable meaning, he does not rule out the existence of an exit from the labyrinth of a text. Similar to Gadamer, Surūsh is not interested in reconstructing a text to find *the* meaning of a text. Since the meaning of a text is provisional and temporal and changes with the historical context, the fixation of meaning becomes difficult:

> We cannot say that the text exists deposed and disengaged from a context, since it does not bear the meaning on its shoulders but must be placed in a context. The text is theory-impregnated and theory-laden and its interpretation is flowing. Preunderstanding influences textual understanding to the same extent as in other areas of understanding and religious texts are not exempted from this ruling. The interpretation of texts is contingent on the arrived external data and subjected to contraction and expansion on account of questions that are posed to them. These data exhibit a manifest and profuse discrepancy. They may be of philosophical, historical or theological character or of a more specific character, such as linguistic or sociological (Surūsh 1999a:303–304).

Surūsh considers pre-understanding, or more correctly presuppositions, as the starting-point of textual understanding, even if he is not clear on the point of how the prejudices can be transcended aside from Popper's theory of falsification. In contrast to Gadamer, he does not believe that 'tradition' is the only ground for the validity of prejudices since it fails to provide a critical norm as to the requirement of evaluating tradition.[99] Surūsh also

[99] Gadamer (1989) speaks of tradition and historicality in terms of prejudices and what he has in mind is not just the subjective attitude of expectation and prejudgement but also the cultural formation, the social, political and intellectual constructions within which our encounter with the text occurs and which the text always unsettles.

believes that the possibility of dialogue between present and past cannot be taken for granted since the horizon of the original discourse disappears in interpretation. In his discussion on the poetry of Saʿdī, Surūsh (1996c:297), presumably influenced by Kuhn's ideas on scientific revolutions, considers meaning to be a paradigmatic phenomenon limited to clearly separated historical periods where the author's intention is not embedded in meaning:

In this respect, we differentiate the meanings of a phrase from the intention of the author. While the former are related to the discovery of the world of the author, the latter is related to the discovery the world of phenomena. An author employs phrases to communicate an intention but these tend to fall short in this respect. This rule applies to vernacular as well as scholarly language such as in Saʿdī's verse, 'The green leaves of the trees are all notes of knowledge before the intelligent Creator'. The intention of Saʿdī's verses cannot be grasped without reference to his world-view and theories contemporary to him and his theology, botany, and the like. But this verse-couplet might also be explained in the light of new theories and give a deeper meaning that was not in Saʿdī's mind.

Surūsh's (1997a:242) argument is, in other words, that while every interpretation follows a certain paradigm, there are no brute facts in contemporary hermeneutics (similar to contemporary philosophy of science) since what is fixed in writing always frees itself for a new relationship.[100] In his book *Ṣirāṭhā-yi mustaqīm*, Surūsh (1999d:169) calls to attention the contextual nature of interpretation that renders meaning relative due to its entanglement in formative contexts that are relational. He also asserts that, while language functions to reflect a representation of reality, it does not have a clearly demarcated structure containing symmetrical units and that metaphorical language opens new worlds, worlds of possible levels of meaning. Language at its highest level is open. Even the simplest sentence conveyed by the means of natural language must be interpreted, since words take their actual meaning from the connection with a given context and a given audience against the background of a given situation. He argues that the existence of multiple contextually situated interpretations maintains the sparkle of the originally revealed Qur'anic text. While this does not amount to saying that the Qur'an reveals its own being when it is presented in different interpretations, he acknowledges that these interpretations disseminate its multiple meaning, where the inexhaustible character of revelation finds its verification in textual ramifications. Referring to Muḥammad Ḥusain Ṭabāṭabāʾī's view that the Qur'anic verse 2:201 has one million two-hundred-sixty thousand meanings and quoting *akhbār* concerning the existence of seventy or eighty inner levels of the Qur'anic text, he asserts that different understandings of the same text have an elementary relation to each other, their textuality:

[100] For Surūsh reference to Kuhn's ideas, cf. Surūsh 1994b:226.

At the level of interpretation, the arena of the relationship between text and understanding, we are confronted with multiple meanings. The extraordinary variation and quantity of meaning informs us about the structure (of a text), which essentially is non-fixed and leads us to the affirmation of different meanings. In the world of text and symbolism, we are in truth essentially confronted with such a lack of fixed meaning. Even if we consent to the erudition that the *ḥakīmān* (sages) claim that they possess of the external world (i.e. "if something exists, it can be known"), their claim is objectionable in the realm of textual analysis, since the inroad of metaphors and allegory into language is beyond the authority or decision of anyone. Language is in its essence metaphorical and it is impossible to communicate meaning without metaphors (ibid.:191).

Since the text itself, as far as the Qur'an is concerned, never gives any clues to a correct reading or where language is intended to be metaphorical and where not, Surūsh (1999a:314–315) asserts that metaphors as well as meaning stem from the nature of interpretation and the interpreter's presuppositions embedded in the process of understanding:

The presence of metaphors in the Qur'an is expedient on natural understanding of the text and consists of context and location of interpretation. The non-interpreted text has no *muḥkam* and *mutashābih* meanings but the inroad of these two concepts are in-bedded in interpretation… The existence of *mutashābihāt* is hence not restricted to the Qur'an but *muḥkam* as well as *mutashābih* exist in all texts, in particular in revealed texts. The existence of *mutashābih* is also the root and the cause of the contraction and expansion of religious knowledge. When we consider the *farāyand* (justification) for religious textual understanding (the aim of which always is contingent on one supposition among others), we come across the meaning and the rationale of the existence of *mutashābihāt* in the Qur'an. It is interesting that the Qur'an itself gives no clue of how to determine the *mutashābihāt* or how to differentiate them from the other verses.

Allegory is, in other words, inherent in the text and emerges in the context of interpretation, where the exercise of language is considered to be an internal semantic process in which new meanings can be created, and at the same time an outwardly directed referential process in which our linguistically mediated experience of reality can be changed. Interpretation in this broad sense is a process by which we use all the available contextual determinants to grasp the actual meaning of a given message in a given situation. But Surūsh restrains significantly from explaining what differentiates reading from interpretation and also from establishing a criterion to distinguish between those texts whose meaning is completely transparent and those whose meaning lies deeper than the surface meaning. While he suggests that language does not only refer to itself, he neglects to explain when interpretation is complete by acknowledging various modalities of meaning.

Whereas a large part of modern hermeneutics (from Heidegger to Gadamer and Ricoeur) develops hermeneutics to the range of ontology and maintains that a text only is understood by sharing a common linguistic horizon grounded in the ontological features of the subject matter of the text, Surūsh's interpretative endeavour never enters the sphere of modern psychology or finite transhistorical consciousness or indulges in any lengthy discussions on objectivity or intentionality.[101] For Surūsh, the anticipation of meaning that governs our understanding of the text is an act of subjectivity, which does not proceed from the communality that binds us to the 'tradition' or participates in the decentred space covering the intention of the author. While the interpreter in a sense is decentred in the act of textual analysis, Surūsh does not adopt Heidegger's idea of the 'circle of understanding', according to which interpretation is neither subjective nor objective but instead the interplay of the movement of the tradition and the movement of the interpreter. In contrast to Gadamer's (1989:245) notion of the finite effective history consciousness that predetermines individual self-awareness as a flickering in the closed circuits of historical life, he never rules out the pursuit of objective knowledge and is indifferent to the historical horizons of the text and reader. Surūsh has more in common with Ricoeur's (1976:2) idea that the author's intention cannot stand outside the text as the criterion for interpreting the text. A text remains the construct of the human mind, since the author's intention and the meaning of the text ceases to coincide in written discourse.

As the major differences between Gadamer and Surūsh can be found in their conceptions of the text, Surūsh's position has more affinities with the fundamental Kantian principle of the subjective basis of understanding, which has no emphasis on the role of the past, i.e. affections, concepts and practices of a cultural heritage, in constituting present and future understanding. In the light of Popperian scientific method, Surūsh would also rather consider subjectivity as a process of becoming that never fully is. His subject is, in other words, a modern alienated subject, estranged from the objective and from his or her own divine nature. While Kant (1959) presented a model of the subject that reflects itself out of its own historicality, Surūsh's notion of subject remains chained in the structural abyss of historical and horizontal contexts. While Surūsh's reference to the Kantian distinction between noumenon and phenomenon suggests a representational mode of thinking (where meaning in some way corresponds to external reality), his view of human language demonstrates a critical attitude towards meaning and metaphysics as well as towards a structural function of the sacred. Language exposes a far-reaching ambivalence, not merely in symbolic usage, since linguistic description is complicated and

[101] In this respect, Gadamer's (1989:432) position is essentially that what is produced by understanding is new and original, but the interpreter must not think that she or he is writing a new text but be open to the voice of tradition which reveals Being. He remains faithful to Heidegger's idea that the intelligible Being is what is disclosed in an authentic act of understanding. What accedes to language in the play of text and interpreter is truth as the disclosure of Being. "Being that can be understood is language".

multiple. While textual understanding in a sense is limited by the composition and structure of the text, this does not imply that textual meaning is uniform:

The world of meaning is by definition pluralistic. It is only rarely that one single meaning appears in interpretation. The most important norm of textuality is plurality. As regards 'correct meaning', this type of meaning is produced when we use our full methodological comprehension of texts (i.e. methodological and rational capacity). 'Correct meaning' differs from 'true meaning' since texts do not possess any 'true meaning'. A text can have various correct meanings. Indeed, there are alien meanings and these are the meanings which are not presupposed by you and which are not necessarily wrong, either. The structural boundaries of the text do not provide all kinds of meaning but still the text does not have necessarily one single meaning. In the textual world, there is no 'correct' meaning in the sense of conformity with the author's intention (Surūsh 1999d:192).

From a linguistic point of view, the clue to the variety of readings within the structural unity of the text is contingent on the existence of incoherence and contradiction within the text itself, "which is not the design or arrangement of anyone but belongs to the necessity of language itself" (ibid.:191). As far as Surūsh's hermeneutics is disinterested in deciphering any presumable original intentionality of authors, it represents an anti-Kantian perspective that is, nonconceptual and non-representational. In the quest for new paradigms, he actually attempts to extricate himself from the mode of representational thinking so characteristic for enlightenment thought and rather seems to believe in historical condition as a constitutive element of meaning where past meaning only can be reconstructed in regard to historical conditions. In this case, he has also more similarities with the position of the contemporary Pakistani scholar Fazlur Rahman, who has denied the potential benefits of Gadamer's phenomenological hermeneutics and perceives interpretation merely as methodologically guided understanding and not as a consciousness of historical finitude that endeavours to fuse the horizons of the interpreter and his text. Surūsh (2001:5) shares Rahman's conviction that the crucial point of interpretation is to let a past text speak to the present situation from a universal perspective in order to emancipate human rationality from the authority of tradition as well as his belief that the universal meaning by content is ethical in nature:

In the contemporary world, religion fulfills two important functions: On the one hand, it makes possible an inner experience (of the sacred) and on the other hand, it facilitates ethical knowledge. If religion accomplishes these two functions, i.e. to support ethics and religious, spiritual, theosophical and divine experiences, it performs its delicate function and conquers the hearts [of men and women]. To proceed from the perspective of jurisprudence, social norms and strict legal enforcement has the opposite effect and this is exactly what has happened in our society.[102]

While Surūsh does not explicitly discuss the question of language as a tool for human subjectivity, he rules out any transcendental ground for linguistic phenomena where past (tradition) and present (modernity) can have a dialogue on equal terms. He rather argues that the historical situation of modernity necessitates a new understanding of theological concepts, such as the virginity of Mary, and so on (Surūsh 1996c:199). While Surūsh's assertion that the text is 'silent' has some affinities with Gadamer's model of the dialogical nature of language, inspired by Platonic dialogue, where interpretation accordingly moves from what is said to what is unsaid within the text, he rejects the transcendental basis of infinite potentiality of meaning as the criterion for historical continuity of the text. In contrast to Gadamer's notion of ontological 'effective history consciousness', which argues for a transcendent and ontological feature of the subject matter within the text that sheds light on the meaning of every textual understanding, Surūsh speaks of an ordinary historical consciousness of preconditioning that we can overcome by becoming aware of the presuppositions that govern our point of departure. In contrast to Gadamer, Surūsh tends to reduce the text to its interpretation by taking the particular context of the interpreter as the sole criterion for the appearance of textual meaning. Yet, the issue remains for Surūsh as to how subjective presuppositions are to be transcended after they have been put into play in the act of interpretation. While his logocentrism and belief in scientific objectivity, as well as his method of second-order epistemology, cannot easily be reconciled with the deconstructionist denial of any patterns of rational necessity (since the supplementary nature of reason suggests a non-rational origin of reason), his discourse is, however, not captive to an analysis of truth. In fact, he shares Derrida's view that the difference between situations is the one and only starting-point for understanding, since the essence of meaning is not separate from the infinitely different possible situations in which it is understood:

Indeed, our imagination and interpretations are conjectural, miscalculated, adaptable, relative, faulty, one-sided, misleading, partial, cultural-contingent and contradictory. This is precisely what the *ṣāḥib-i waḥy* ('possessor of revelation', i.e.

102 Cf. Surūsh 1996c:190 and 549. While Rahman (1982:9) acknowledges that the basic questions of method and hermeneutics never were squarely addressed by Muslims in pre-modern times, he argues that modern Western hermeneutics either sacrifices objectivity at the altar of the subject (i.e. Heidegger, Gadamer, Ricoeur) or neglects the historical contextual factor (i.e. the objectivity school). He argues that Gadamer's assertion that all understanding is predetermined by presupposition or something else makes any objectivity of anything whatsoever impossible. In this respect, he proposes a process of interpretation that consists of a double movement, from the present situation back to Qur'anic historical times, then back to the present. The past text can hence be objectively known and the tradition can be objectively brought under the judgement of the normative meaning of the context of revelation under whose impact this tradition arose.

God) intended. We are imperfect human beings and our portion of truth is such. No human knowledge is sacred and religious knowledge is no exception to this rule (Surūsh 1999a:319)

Although Derrida as well as Gadamer insists that the text has no fixed meaning in rejecting any notion of a transcendental signified, Surūsh follows Derrida's more radical step with respect to the problem of textual meaning. For Surūsh, it is not the linguistic community (via the reader) that determines the meaning of a text by means of 'the fusion of horizons', but is rather the temporality of language that makes any *authentic* understanding impossible. But while Surūsh, similar to Derrida, can find no determined meanings in texts (for it makes no sense to speak about the meaning of a text apart from our reading of it), he takes into account in his theorising that texts have readers to a greater extent than Derrida, by arguing that no reading is context-free. Surūsh, whose thinking is fully part of the humanist tradition, shares neither Derrida's (1978:292) idea of 'play' as a form of anti-humanism nor his venture "to pass beyond man and humanism", even if Derrida (1988:125–127, 143–144) becomes more disposed to hermeneutical methods in his later works, such as *Limited Inc.*

In his book *Farbihtar az īdi'ūlūzhī*, Surūsh emphatically rejects non-realist approaches to knowledge which he believes signals the death of epistemology with their radical doubt and are no longer doing proper epistemology. He rejects postmodernist (*read* deconstructionist) thought where "God has no successor and the scene has been emptied from every kind of autonomous and divine source" and supposes that the postmodernist critique of reason must be considered in the historical context of anti-scientism, which springs from "the arrogant and extravagant claims of positivism" (Surūsh 1995a:9 and 1996a:256). He laments that the pragmatist and postmodernist philosophical critique of scientific objectivity "has conquered the last trench of rationality held by the neo-Kantian philosophy of Karl Popper" (Surūsh 1996a:359) and also argues that postmodernism has reached a point where it must decide whether to espouse relativism or to appeal to some other method of immediate realisation of truth:

Postmodernism has issued that the verdict of relativity of truth (which is tantamount to denying it) is now, according to its own verdict, either devoid of the truth or else invites the charge of self-contradiction. In either case, it lacks the decisiveness and the power to function as a weapon against science. It is true that science is no longer the only possible form of knowledge and the sole valid method for the discovery of truth but this refutes only a positivistic notion of science. Refutation of positivism is not the same thing as refutation of science (Surūsh 1995a:9).

Even if Surūsh (1996a:361) acknowledges that the paradox of modernism is that "it knows that certainty is unattainable but still wants to have it", neither foundationalism nor deconstructionism seem to be genuine options for him. His epistemological rejection of any foundational pieces of knowledge and the belief that reality is only accessible to us in terms of how we interpret it (which supposes that there is no reality to be independently compared to our understanding) does in fact not necessarily imply deconstruction, since Popper's principle of falsification also rejects foundationalism.[103] If the post-positivism of Popper can be defeated, it should not happen, according to Surūsh, at the expense of reason and science, even if science is nothing but a tool in comprehending reality:

> Philosophers such as Kuhn, Feyerabend (and Richard Rorty from another direction) sacrificed the scientific methods and the logic of discovery at the foot of relativism for the sake of history and decapitated modern sciences, the purest signifier of rationality. They argued that science is an ideological construct and although they are horrified by the consequences of their own deposition, the bridges to the lost heaven have all collapsed... Postmodernism was born out of the belief that no secure (cognitive) foundation exists and the lost hope for any quest for truth. Postmodernism thinks of the world as a text that may have a meaning even if this meaning is entirely mythological and allegorical. The method and object of postmodernism as regards textual analysis is deconstruction, i.e. to find contradictions and hidden assumptions, rather than understanding the intention of the author (ibid.:359).

Referring to Rorty's saying that "While Reason replaced God, today we have no God, no Reason and nothing else", Surūsh (ibid.:359) concludes that postmodernist philosophy, in its attempts to deconstruct reality has been forced to bring back the pre-modern modes of expression. As late as 1992, Surūsh (ibid.:363) actually considered mysticism the only secure escape out of the traps of deconstructionist relativism by claiming that "only one way remains and that is to seek shelter among the theosophers". However much Surūsh departs from the traditional metaphysical foundation of philosophical speculation, he revisits the Persian theosophical tradition to interpret its teachings in a non-cognitive sense to signify the mysteriousness of God. In his ambiguity towards the deconstructionist enterprise and his desire to keep up with a somewhat religiously situated discourse, he claims that "the legacy of Islamic theosophy may be able to face up to the complications arising from the uncertainty and scepticism of contemporary humanity because it has been sceptical towards rationality from its very beginning" (ibid.:363).

Surūsh's viewpoint on deconstructionism gives the impression that if all knowledge, as Foucault (1977:163) suggests, lacks a "right, even in the act of knowing, to truth or foundation for truth", then there is no longer any

[103] Surūsh's turn to hermeneutics from Popper's principle of falsification seems to be due to the fact that hermeneutics avoids any confusion of meaning with truth and understanding with knowledge (in contrast to foundationalism as well as deconstructionism) in terms that it essentially concerns interpretation, which is about meaning, that is, about what is understood. Foundationalism in the form of logical positivism denies that statements can be meaningful if they cannot be (empirically) verified and, at the other end of the spectrum, deconstruction holds that any interpretation of meaning is already true, to the extent that 'truth' means anything, just by being produced.

meaning of the revealed texts as sources of knowledge. Surūsh disapproves of Foucault's *Nietzschean* attitude to epistemology which has nothing optimistic to say, if it does not (as Richard Rorty seems to suggests) avoid epistemology altogether in a mistaken attempt to make archaeology the successor subject to epistemology.[104] Whereas Nietzsche and his successors abandoned the striving for objectivity or any of its substitutes and the intuition of one truth, Surūsh attempts to defend objectivity by re-describing and grounding a plurality of probable truths. In contrast to Foucault, who is interested in how power produces the subject, Surūsh (1996a:91) considers the aspiration to bring about inter-subjective scientific objectivity a noble one, which implies that all knowledge claims also are caught up by accidental error at the level of construction:

The question of objectivity in science concerns whether our human mental faculty generates systematic error or not. It does not concern whether man makes errors at all. The meaning of objective knowledge is not that knowledge corresponds to the external phenomenon nor the presence or the absence of error in knowledge. Objectivity in knowledge means that we are not caught by systematic error at the level of construction of knowledge. Objectivity is comprised therefore of truth as well as falsehood. It is possible that our perception is objective without being true.

In his book *Rāzdānī wa raushanfikrī*, Surūsh is occupied with the question of the distribution of knowledge and information as a major component of power. Discussing the ideas of Foucault and Habermas, he argues that modern life corresponds to the nature of the information at disposal in modernity and suggests that this information undoubtedly affects the realm of, for instance, politics and government. In this respect, he refers, for instance, to the fact that the French revolution was expedited by means of clandestine leaflets, the Iranian constitutional revolution by telegraph wires and the most recent Iranian revolution by audiocassettes. While he does not adopt Foucault's concept of power, he seems prepared to go along with the French philosopher insofar as the social and historical dimensions of knowledge are concerned:

Although science and power have always gone hand in hand, the relationship between the two has now become much stronger and more extensive. This is why people speak of *sākhtan-i ḥaqīqat* (truth as construction) and *ʿitibārī budan-i ḥaqīqat* (truth as convention). The conventionality of truth means that we define truth and influence people's consciousness in such a way as to make them see something as true and something else as false. It is in this context that Foucault's theory about truth-power comes to light and takes meaning. He claims that truth is inextricably intertwined with power. Habermas put forward a similar position in one of his major works, *Knowledge and human interest*, where he argues that knowledge is underpinned by human interests and that the nature of knowledge or scientific investigation varies depending on whether the underlying interest is understanding,

[104] Cf. Rorty 1998:41–49.

control or emancipation. Knowledge bent on understanding is interpretative; knowledge bent on control is empirical and knowledge bent on emancipation is critical. It is this sense that Habermas speaks of knowledge-constitutive human interests. Values are, in other words, deeply ingrained in modern knowledge. Values are tied up with power (Surūsh 1999c:3–4).

As opposed to his strong criticism of deconstructionism (which is not the only represented version of postmodernism), Surūsh is more affirmative to the phenomenon of postmodernism in a 1999 interview with *Kiyān* on the question of "Religion, tolerance and civilisation". He is positive to the postmodernist critic of modern rationality that places universal reason under dispute and similarly evinces all signs of having been chastened by the tyranny of the arrogant knight of modern rationality. Surūsh (1999f:28) suggests that "the boundaries of reason are more accurately understood in the postmodern condition" in the sense that "postmodernism represents a revolt against the narcissism of rationality". While acknowledging that universalism is necessary in the construction of universal ethics and laws such as the Declaration of human rights, he asserts that the contribution of postmodernism to pluralism and tolerance as well as its criticism of the superiority of Reason, is beneficial. "All the stress that postmodernism lays on pluralism and reason's servitude to interests is found among the remaining favours of postmodernism" (ibid.:28–29). He does not, however, reflect upon Derrida's assertion that the enlightenment conception of reason tends to be self-legitimising because it takes one historically and culturally specific notion of reason as its universal standard for all forms of reason. This is a common target of contemporary Islamic criticism concerning the enlightenment project. Many Islamic intellectuals consider the identification of universal structures of human existence as revealed solely in Western philosophy as a major obstacle to inter-cultural dialogue on equal terms.[105] Surūsh acknowledges, nevertheless, that philosophical universality is no longer essentialist and thus no more 'Islamic' than 'eurocentric' in the sense that scientific knowledge (i.e. truth-claims) are not merely 'local' but genuinely universal.

The fact that Surūsh (1999f:28–29) in the same article considers Habermas' work *Knowledge and human interest* as a work that can be related to postmodernism suggests that his definition of postmodernism in this context is very much connected to the recognition of pluralism as a natural part of human rationality and thought. In contrast to the fundamental uncertainties of the deconstructionism of Foucault (1972:229) concerning human knowledge, whose aim is to "question our will to truth, to restore to

[105] Cf. Ahmed 1992, Manzoor 2000, al-Attas 1985, Qadir 1988, etc. In this respect, Derrida (1998a:12) argues that Judaism and Islam, by recalling monotheism at all costs are "still alien enough at the heart of Graeco-Christian, Pagano-Christian Europe" to alienate themselves from a Western modernity that "signifies the death of God" or "the Christianisation of the world".

discourse its character as an event, and to abolish sovereignty of the signifier", Surūsh does not agree that all foundations of epistemology have been shown to be unreliable. While Surūsh in his lectures on *ijtihād* advocates deconstruction at the level of methodology, writers like Derrida (1987:390) deny that deconstruction is a method since it is not reductive like an ordinary method, whether it is primary or derived. Deconstructionism cannot, however, be a complete non-method as it is not singular and homogenous nor does it advocate uncontrollable free-play.

Similar to Surūsh's epistemology, deconstruction turns to hermeneutics, albeit poststructuralist, in the sense of disarranging the construction of terms in a sentence and disassembling the parts of the whole. Its purpose is to locate an instance of otherness within a text, an otherness that reflects logocentric conceptuality, and then to deconstruct this conceptuality from the standpoint of alterity (Derrida 1987:387–388). Surūsh's affinities with postmodern thought are in fact closest in the realm of hermeneutics, where the meanings and significance of texts are not limited to those meanings that conventional historical criticism is designed to recover. Similar to Derrida's deconstructionism, he believes that language refers only to itself rather than to a transparent extratextual reality and asserts multiple conflicting interpretations of a text. He bases such interpretations on the philosophical, political or social implications of the use of the language in the text rather than on the author's intention. What creates problems for hermeneutics is language itself, which is not, as the later Heidegger claimed, the 'house of being', but humanly constructed. The text is therefore not simply a historical source that reduces meaning to the nexus of historical relationships but rather results from the creative interaction of the reading subject with the text. Textual meaning is the result of interpretation that is generated in the space where the text is put to play so that when "a component of this collection (i.e. mental and scientific capital of the interpreter) changes, the result of this formation and relation of components (i.e. meaning and sense) will also change (Surūsh 1996c:182).

In his *Ṣirāṭhā-yi mustaqīm*, Surūsh argues that semantic meaning is relative in relation to the knowledge and comprehension of the interpreter, as there is no original and hidden meaning present in the text. He also argues that hermeneutical divergence is not due to the structure of the text but rather is contingent on the interpreting subject in an absolute sense. By claiming that uncertainty and ambiguity is an attribute of all human language and linguistic communication, including revealed texts, he downgrades textual meaning to subjective understanding:

> Meaning is identical to meaning of understanding. The variety of human minds is identical to the diversity of acquired data. The acquired data comprise the preconditions and presuppositions of meaning. The diversity of meanings of a text, which are located in the human mind, depend therefore in the end on the diversity of

human minds. The essence of the fact that the range of human minds construct different meanings of a single text is basically that the text is not the measure of multiplicity of meanings but rather gives the option of all possible meanings (Surūsh 1999d:195).[106]

Similar to contemporary postmodernism, Surūsh also seeks to move beyond the conventional historical paradigm of tradition, whether this tradition is enlightenment modernity or premodernity. He is essentially sceptical about the recovery of meaning, since the acquisition of valid knowledge is more complex than the ordinary inductive reasoning of common man. In this respect, he takes the non-realist approach to interpretation and denies the existence of an objective, external world outside the text. While the objects are not as privileged as in premodernity, the subject is not as privileged as in enlightenment modernism either. Surūsh claims that the text itself cannot communicate any intention but is contingent upon external commodities in the sense that what matters are relations and contexts which constantly shift. In this respect, he wishes, similar to Derrida (1998:158b) to empty the 'presence' out of the text, approving the latter's maxim *Il n'y a pas de hors-text* ('there is nothing beyond the text'). As Surūsh (1999k) argues, there is no exit from the labyrinth of a text, no finished or decidable meaning:

> My writings are *ṣāmit* and remain insignificant until someone reads them. The readers are the subjects, the individual *nāṭiqīn* (speakers) of my ideas and thought. There is nothing stable outside the text. Any attempt to recover the intention of the author is in vain. Interpretation is endless.

Textuality is not only true of the 'object' of study but also true of the 'subject' which studies. As the text possesses a horizon of indefinite meanings, the neat distinction between subject and object is obliterated, something which also erases the aim of providing objective descriptions. But it seems difficult to see how the inaugurating of an open-ended indefiniteness of textuality, fraught with ambiguities, would provide a way out of the closure of knowledge. The death of the author in Surūsh's thought is not merely the concluding recognition of the physical absence of the author in the process of interpretation but rather the affirmation of the ultimate metaphysical separation between the text and its author. That is to say, while the text is the product of the author, the interpretation is that of the reader. Even a signature or a declaration left by the author in the text has no authority for its interpretation, since these are elements of the text that are subject to further interpretation. The author is hence not only rendered superfluous but the text is considered open and incomplete. An interpretation of a text is considered to be the creation of a new 'text' through which the reader expresses herself (i.e. there is no meaning in speaking of any authorised or authentic versions of a text).

[106] Cf. Surūsh 1999a:315.

In the sense that meaning is solely a function of the reader and interpretation a reflection of the interpreter's response, Surūsh is critical to the intentionality so characteristic of enlightenment thought that would support the original intentionality of the sacred as it is revealed in the world. The initial hermeneutical task of the interpreter is, in his view, not to grasp the intentional structure of the sacred by imaginatively recreating the conditions of a sacred manifestation but rather to make it applicable to new endless contexts where the non-religious external data is projected on the text. By distinguishing faith from reason, his epistemological confessions, while not sceptical in the religious sense, suggest no metaphysical position or any structural position for consciousness that would give certainty and hermeneutical plausibility to the interpretation of the religious phenomenon. In Surūsh's view, there can be no theology of the text since the text is the trace that escapes onto-theological closure even as it inscribes it. By emphasising the non-identity or non-presence that lies at the heart of the Qur'an or any other scriptural identity, his hermeneutics is not exegesis proper, aimed at drawing (or leading) the truth out of the text but a form of *eisegesis* that imposes the reader's beliefs upon or reads them into the text.

Surūsh's recent 'turn to the reader' is, indeed, the application of Kant's 'turn to the subject', where there is, epistemologically speaking, no human escape from her/his own subjectivity and consciousness. In contrast to premodern philosophy, which always maintained that the notions of meaning and truth are intimately related, his relativistic notion of truth includes a metaphysical dichotomy between text and meaning that denies the possibility of true knowledge by rejecting certain meaning, as there are only infinitely possible versions of truth which are also separable from the 'meta-narrative' of Islamic tradition. His thought has not merely an inherent pluralistic and subjectivist character but also invokes a decentralisation that denies any position of the symbolism of the centre in the philosophical mode of thinking as, for instance, was the case with the traditional Islamic philosophical, theological and mystical epistemic schemes, which considered metaphysics as a natural disposition of the philosophical thinker because of the very nature of the intellect. By rejecting that the transcendent and universal referent of the enlightenment philosophy of Descartes and Kant would provide guidance regarding the ultimate meaning of human existence and the goal of human history, it is furthermore not an accident that his epistemological discourse gives way to a hermeneutic plurality of immanent, historically contingent and ultimately normless reasons and actualities which are intimately bound up with specific human contexts. The crisis of meaning, which is one of the predominant themes in Surūsh's thought, is hence nothing but an inevitable consequence of the impoverishment of reason, the denial of its transcendence, which is an outcome of the historicisation of the scientific discourse.

But there is still a vast distance between Surūsh and the deconstructionism of Derrida, who is more concerned with using the tools of metaphysics against itself. Derrida is a post-metaphysical thinker for whom the reality-appearance distinction has *entirely* lost its hegemony over human thought. By pushing philosophy to its limits, he writes about transcendence and metaphysics on the margins of the Western philosophical tradition. While Surūsh rejects Husserl's (as well as Kant's) notion of transcendence, which only grasps the realm of the possible and claims that the grasp is total, he acknowledges Popper's conviction that science and epistemology is a noble quest and that the effort to acquire inter-subjective objectivity in the domain of human knowledge must not be given up. In contrast to deconstructionism, which originally is a definite, negative and critical reaction to the intellectual projects of romantic idealistic and enlightenment representational modes of thinking, Surūsh is not primarily reacting against the background of enlightenment modernism but against the normative wisdom and paradigm of traditional Islam in its entirety. In contrast to deconstructionism, Surūsh's religious intellectual background, similar to that of Kant, also makes him hopeful about the fate of humankind. He has faith in the gradual development towards a future characterised by more human ideals and, more importantly, he is deeply concerned about the relation between virtue and happiness (Surūsh 1995a:2).

I. Divergent interpretations: The problem of truth and probability

From Surūsh's exposition on hermeneutics, it emerges that no interpretation of the revealed sources is absolute and that the task of the believers is to constantly renew and adjust their understanding of these texts to the contemporary context. As he argues repetitively, human knowledge is conjecture and pure guess-work since "whereas the last religion has been revealed to mankind, the final religious interpretation has yet not arrived" (Surūsh 1996c:60).[107] As far as the existence of divergent interpretations are concerned, he suggests that *fiqh*, in contrast to *ʿilm al-kalām* (which does not validate diverse views on the nature of God, revelation and man) is innately disposed to *ikhtilāf*. Islamic jurisprudence is etymologically related to *tafaqquh* (understanding) and allows for a larger degree of interpretative pluralism since the legal discourse is never afflicted by conflict and contradictions:

The difference between theological and legal debate is evident in the fact that refutation or acceptance of legal opinions does not damage the source of *dīn-dārī*

[107] Cf. Surūsh 1996c:110.

(religiosity) since these *ikhtilāfāt* (divergences) are identical to *tafaqquh*. The discussion of theological opinion is, however, concerned with the source of religiosity or cognition of religion itself. Theological discourses on questions such as God's existence, the truth of revelation, predestination, free will, justice or evil, sometimes expel someone from a religion or render new meaning and spirit to someone's religion. Theology concerns the affirmation of a kind of religion while jurisprudence already has accepted a specific type of religion (Surūsh 1996a:49).

In this respect, Surūsh (1994d:360–363) argues in his *Ḥikmat wa maʿīshat* (Wisdom and sustenance) that the word *tafaqquh* was used in early Islam to denote religious understanding in the general sense and was not restricted to jurisprudence. Therefore, he suggests that *tafaqquh* is essentially not an *amr-i dīnī* (religious rule) but rather is connected to understanding in the general hermeneutical sense: it is time-bound and flowing. While he believes that traditional legal theory in every way restricts the interpretative space of the jurist in the inference of norms from the revealed sources, he argues that all attempts to suppress legal discourse are impossible since the hermeneutical methods and tools themselves are human and subjected to flow. In his view, all juristic opinions are provisional and in need of rectification:

The methodological tools that are under the jurist's authority are human. They have a limited capacity and cannot be expected to distinguish the good from bad and the incorrect from the correct in an absolute sense. In the end, the jurist therefore arrives at *ẓann* (conjecture) (Surūsh 1996c:110).[108]

Inspired by Murtaḍā Muṭahharī's discussion on the forgery of legal decrees in early Islam, Surūsh (ibid.:55) argues that the theory of contraction and expansion of knowledge explains why the jurists diverge in their individual viewpoints on law, "why an Arabic *fatwā* gives an Arabic smell and why an Iranian *fatwā* gives an Iranian smell". But while Surūsh considers pluralism "the essence of the theory of expansion and contraction of Islamic law", he departs from traditional notions of *ikhtilāf* in the sense that he believes that divergent interpretation is undesirable in *fiqh*. In this respect, he also transfers the question of legal disagreements from the level of methodology to the level of hermeneutics by arguing that traditional *fiqh* was only concerned with refuting rival legal opinions and inferences:

The texts of Islamic law are from the believer's point of view free of contradictions and error. Since religion has been revealed to work out differences, we must consider how all these genuine and substantial disputes, contradictions and differences among the religious scholars appear. Is religion or the understanding of religion the catalyst behind these disputes? What kind of *ikhtilāf* is this that religion cannot solve and is even afflicted by? (ibid.:246)[109]

Contrary to the traditional epistemic standards of Islamic law, Surūsh

[108] Cf. Surūsh 1996c:541.
[109] Cf. Surūsh 1996c:8 and 1999d:98.

(1996a:6–8) claims that *taqlīd* ought not to be incumbent in matters where *ikhtilāf* exists and he also criticises the advocates of *taqlīd* by arguing that this principle never was implemented in the *mauḍūʿāt* (subjects) or *uṣūl* of jurisprudence:

The Islam of philosophy, theosophy and anthropology accepts questioning, since it operates at the level of *taḥqīq* (research). By approving inquiry, these sciences do not force *taqlīd* upon the individual. The Islam of *fiqh* takes no account of questioning, since it works at the level of *taqlīd*. Indeed, it accepts no function whatsoever for rational inspection and, irrespective of the current theory of *ijtihād* and *taqlīd*, it insists on the fact that the duty of the individual layman is to conduct *taqlīd* and to regard the word of the jurist as *ḥujjat-i taʿabuddī* (unquestionable proof). While *taqlīd* is acceptable in the realm of *furūʿ*, which is also far from recognised, it is entirely objectionable in the realm of *uṣūl*. In the case of deep divergence of the jurists' opinions, one cannot be confident which opinion is true. It is therefore not compulsory to perform *taqlīd* to a jurist. [...] In general terms, there are three branches of matters pertaining to belief: *furūʿ-i dīn* and *aḥkām-i fiqhī* (legal norms), *mauḍūʿāt* of legal norms and principles of belief and knowledge. Only legal norms are actually relevant to *taqlīd*, since it is not optional to carry out *taqlīd* in the *mauḍūʿāt* or *uṣūl*. Only one-third of these branches are, so to say, *taqlīdī*.

While Surūsh (1996c:247) considers science as an objective and universal enterprise and his exposition on hermeneutics suggests that the aim of science is to free itself from metaphysical or other ideological presuppositions, his exposition on epistemology is aimed at being purely descriptive. In his view, the theory of contraction and expansion of religious knowledge takes into account questions such as the relationship between data, belief and judgement and how a judgement turns out to be false from the 'outside', but never makes any theoretical justifications about which suppositions that are true and false. His purpose is rather to describe certain human features of science, history and philosophy and to determine to what extent these descriptions should count as specimens of knowledge.[110] Perhaps due to their problematical ontological status, questions such as how we manage to know the truth or to distinguish what is false from what is true are largely considered irrelevant in his epistemological discourse. In this respect, Surūsh's position on divergent interpretations gives rise to a number of question-marks concerning his definition of conjecture and probability; If we cannot solve the question of divergent interpretation by reconstructing the author's original intention, if words have more than a single meaning and if there are multiple conflicting interpretations, how are we to choose among the various interpretations that can be made from a single text? If religious knowledge is a collection of all interpretations of religion, correct as well as false, then what is the criterion to judge the validity of a certain opinion? Do

110 Surūsh's discourse on Islamic law is actually the first in the Iranian context to be concerned with pluralism from an empirical point of view rather than from a normative one (if we set aside the normative aspects of his descriptive epistemology).

we have anything resembling a deeper understanding if all understanding is flowing? While Surūsh does not present a systematic hermeneutics to answer these questions, his argument is simply that deeper understanding, whether correct or not, is dependent on *dānish* (learning) and *diqqat* (precision), what he also calls *fahm-i rawishmand* (methodological understanding).[111] In his view, the ability to comprehend *bihtar* (better) is contingent on preunderstanding, since interpretation is always an individual validation that corresponds to the knowledge of the interpreter:

Those who are inaccurately familiar with Islamic history, who neither are well read in exegesis nor have examined the theosophy, philosophy or anthropological and cosmological foundation of their own ideas, cannot take hold of more than a limited number of features and ingredients of the natural world and *sharīʿat*. They will also come up with an unpleasant, intransigent and disproportionate knowledge of *sharīʿat*. In order to harmonise and increase their knowledge of *sharīʿat*, they must search for more components and select more ingredients (of Islamic history, exegesis and legal norms). From these ingredients the effort of better understanding progresses. My claim is that this chase and selection does not emerge without beginning or origin and that the human sciences and non-religious data constantly grant the religious scholars increasing ability in their selection and discernment (ibid.:250).

In contrast to Popper's (1972:15–18) so-called 'critical method' and notion of 'best explanation' that suppose the emergence of the 'best' theory, i.e. that which has 'the greatest explanatory power', Surūsh (2000c:58) does not believe in hitting upon *one* true theory since no method can establish its sole truth and the number of possible interpretations remains infinite and inconclusive: a theory may only be better, but not the best. For Surūsh, the game of testing never comes to an end since it is only possible to falsify instrumental theories but not to establish their truth. While no higher standard of rationality than the assent of the relevant community exists, his position presupposes that there is at least an intrinsic possibility of arriving at correct scientific theories. Due to the processes of testing, scientific inquiry is a self-correcting activity that is progressive: it gradually provides better accounts of the ways the world is and eliminates theories that are epistemically defective. In this respect, the idea of progress in science also means some kind of accumulation of 'truth' (which for this reason is relative to the objects investigated). By referring to the relation between Popper and Wittgenstein, Surūsh (1996c:307) explains that the critical philosophical perspective is not so much characterised by the attempt to differentiate false statements from truth as it is to serve the *takmīl-i fahm* (completion of understanding), whereby new epistemic 'truths' modify earlier ones:

It is generally assumed that criticism and rectification are aimed to reveal truth and error. This is correct but criticism accomplishes a greater service and that is the

[111] Cf. Surūsh 1994d:361 and 1996c:282.

fortification and completion of understanding. The opinions are not merely subjected to scrutiny in order to differentiate the correct ones from the erroneous ones but also to assist the acquisition of better understanding. Criticism establishes first of all the channels through which falsification emerges. To know the defects of a theory is a great blessing that elucidates the width of the circle of meaning and proof of the relevant theory. Wittgenstein used the falsification principle of Popper (which claims to discern empirical observations from non-empirical ones) in the realm of interpretation and argued that as long as the circumstances through which an interpretation is falsified remain unknown, one cannot grasp its meaning. While Wittgenstein later on distanced himself from this exaggerated view, his previous view is not altogether pointless. To know how error emerges in theories makes at least better understanding possible.

While the mode of knowing produced by the empirical self is 'science,' regardless of the individual status of the knower, Surūsh believes that the knowledge produced by science only leads toward progress in the sense that knowledge is a succession of theories, where the new are different from the old. While he rejects the enlightenment idea of true and eternal rational knowledge, since there is no stable and coherent knowing self, his concept of *taḥawwul* (progress) does anticipate a value-judgement of some sort that enables us to claim that the new situation is 'better' than the previous one. While he argues that to know things 'better' is not an approximation of objective truth since all interpretations are weaker or stronger, the acceptance of interpretative pluralism does not, in his view, involve the kind of 'epistemological anarchism' that Paul Feyerabend allows for, which claims that "every sect is right or that whatever anyone says is correct" (Surūsh 1999d:56). By considering all probability as conditional, his argument is rather that no monistic interpretation exists and that a theory is *ṣaḥīḥ* (correct) just in the case where all its empirical consequences are true:

Every text is a potentiality and is actualised by the interpreter himself. My method of interpretation, while historical, is not a monistic one, since science never has been or is characterised by a single, universally applicable method, invariant through the history of science and the various fields of scientific study (Surūsh 1999k).[112]

In *Qabḍ wa basṭ-i tiʾūrīk-i sharīʿat*, Surūsh asserts that the key to deeper understanding is to measure various conflicting interpretations against each other and not against the divine law itself. Knowledge is therefore established not by comparing beliefs with anything outside of them, but with each other. While correct interpretations exist, these must be placed and evaluated a posteriori against other interpretations and not a priori against divine law itself:

The epistemic a posteriori predicates are separate from the epistemic a priori predicates. Only epistemological views can be compared with each other or demonstrate each other's deficiencies and evidences. An opinion at the level of a

[112] Cf. Surūsh 2000c:54.

priori must never be compared with an opinion on the level of a posteriori. No obligatory and recommended rule (of *fiqh*), necessary or non-necessary, can be compared with the view that the science of *fiqh* is flowing (which is the genuine nature of the science of *fiqh*) and confirm or falsify it (Surūsh 1996c:328).[113]

When Surūsh (1996c:81–86), for instance, refutes the philosophical and juristic views of Ḥādī Sabziwārī as regards the innate nature of women, his critique takes therefore place on the second level of knowing, i.e. context of justification. He also argues that the plurality of interpretations of revelation must be compared with each other internally rather than against the Qur'anic text itself (Surūsh 1999l:4). In this respect, Surūsh's position corresponds in many respects with the epistemological fallibism of the American scientist and philosopher Charles Sanders Pierce (d. 1914), who rejects the proposal of a new non-foundationalist route to knowledge that would discover the foundations of human knowledge once and for all by identifying basic beliefs or beliefs that can be justified in other terms. Peirce's claim that there are no unshakable foundations for human knowledge and that the quest for them is fruitless corresponds very well to Surūsh's view that no interpretations are absolutely certain or immune to revision.[114] While it is generally believed that fallibism is incompatible with foundationalism (that is if nothing is immune to revision there are no foundations for human knowledge), Charles Landesman (1997:88) argues that this claim is only correct for certain versions of foundationalism and not for the general idea of it:

A basic belief need not to be known with absolute certainty; it need not even be known at all; further, it could very well be false and still be basic. That we have a right to believe something is compatible with our later discovering that we were mistaken, that what we believe probably isn't true, and that we need to revise our belief system accordingly.

Surūsh's epistemology hence occupies the middle ground between foundationalist and deconstructionist assertions on the human cognitive dilemma, since while he presupposes some self-justifying beliefs (such as *tawātur*), it is also the case that he believes that he is not always justified in holding them. But the problem remains for him of moving from these basic beliefs to other justified beliefs that are justified by reasoning from the former. While realism suggests a correspondence theory of truth according to which an interpretation only is true if it corresponds to reality or to fact, that is, truth depends upon the way the world is and not upon what we happen to believe, he reduces revelation emanating from the Divine by

[113] Surūsh (1996c:116) also writes, "To differ the true from the false pertains to the first level of knowing (*that is* a priori), while looking from above and witnessing the human disputes on true and false from the outside is related to the second level, i.e. that of epistemology".
[114] Pierce is noted for his work on the logic of relations and on 'pragmaticism' as a method of research.

setting the standards of truth and error to a cognitive and neutral realm, where it is historisised and de-ontologised. Since scientific theories are representational vehicles that are capable of being true and false, their likelihood of providing knowledge of phenomena is *a matter of degree*. An interpretation may only be probable but it can also be more probable than another. The validation procedure based on Popper's criterion of falsifiability is hence complimented by the conflict between divergent interpretations:

> One of the most fundamental claims of the theory of contraction and expansion is that the various understandings influence each other in the sense that when a new understanding emerges, it invites other understandings to follow it. While no one denies the fact that human understanding possibly develops and is flowing, some do not come to terms with the precise meaning of the idea of better understanding or its mechanism, which is the subject of this study. All hermeneutical theories must, indeed, describe the meaning and mechanism of better understanding (Surūsh 1996c:278).

Surūsh adopts the criteria of relative superiority that can be derived from the subjective probability logic, where the pertinence of a correct opinion of interpretation is related to its methodological and systematic character. But it seems that the inner contradiction between the tendency of realism to represent the external world as it really is and Kant's idea that we can only know the world as it appears to us, not as it is in itself, is essentially overlooked by Surūsh. He does not clarify the distinction between knowledge and probability since the uncertain and fallible character of the principles as well the methods of science indicate that humans are prone to error. In contrast to probabilism, which supposes that opinions are only selected by considering different degrees of probability relative to the available empirical evidence, Surūsh, similar to Popper's notion of degree of corroboration, does not deny the existence of objective (but essentially conjectural) knowledge.[115] While he is indisposed to replace proof by probability, his position is ambiguous since he does not explicitly use the terminology of Popper (corroboration, improbability, etc). The terms preferability and probability can also be used synonymously. While he endorses Kant's critical epistemology according to which our knowledge springs from two fundamental sources of the mind, the capacity for receiving representations and the power of knowing an object through these observations, he denies that knowing includes value judgements, since the purpose of the second level of knowing is not to make value statements about what 'ought' to be, such as the necessity of religion, but rather to

[115] Popper (1972:17) writes, "My theory of preference has nothing to do with a preference for the 'more probable" hypothesis. On the contrary, I have shown that the testability of a theory increases and decreases with its *informative content* and therefore with its *improbability* (in the sense of the calculus of probability).

elucidate the existing variation of values on the level of 'is':

> 'Don't lie' is a prohibition that is present in the science of ethics. The philosophy of ethics never prohibits anyone from lying but rather declares. 'Ethics stipulates that we shall not lie', whereby a value statement is transformed into a description. In similar terms, a Muslim testifies that Muḥammad is the Prophet of Allāh, while a non-Muslim historian never gives a testimony but only describes that Muslims give testimony that Muḥammad is the Prophet of Allāh. It is evident that to inform about a value is not a value itself and that to notify a command or prohibition is not itself a kind of command or prohibition. The meaning of what is being said here, i.e. that the views that are related to a priori knowledge are not confronted with views related to a posteriori knowledge, becomes clear. A descriptive norm cannot contradict or confirm a value, credential or epistolary rule. It is hence impossible for religious epistemology to collide and disagree with the epistolary norms of religion (Surūsh 1996c:335).

But if all interpretations are considered on the second level, even the principle *ḍarūrat-i dīn* (necessity of religion) becomes, as Surūsh (ibid.:336) argues, "an epistemological norm and not a juristic norm", which seems to be a contradiction in terms, since it runs against his previous view that a posteriori knowledge only is related to the level of 'is' and never to the level of 'ought' (ibid.:94–100). The idea that all knowledge must be considered as a posteriori results, so to say, in the fact that nothing has absolute a priori validity in the true sense of the word but only is a construction of the epistemological subject.[116] The inconsistency of his argument arises in fact when Surūsh restricts the right to differentiate correct from incorrect interpretations to the level of a priori knowledge. It seems that Surūsh mixes the meaning of justification in Popperian science with that in contemporary epistemology and he also seems to relate epistemic justification to hermeneutical understanding rather than epistemology. Epistemic justification is more correctly a normative notion, a 'doxastology', i.e. a study of beliefs, in contrast to Popper's argument that knowledge cannot be justified but falsified and as long as it is not falsified we are entitled to regard it as provisionally true. In contemporary epistemology, as John L. Pollock and Joseph Cruz (1999:12) argue, a justified belief is one that is 'epistemically permissible' to hold. "Epistemic justification governs what you should believe or should not believe. Rules describing the circumstance under which it is epistemically permissible to hold beliefs are called *epistemic norms*".

[116] In this respect, Surūsh surely accepts the argument of the philosophical pragmatists that human concepts and beliefs are the joint outcome of experience, even if he is not inclined, similar to Rorty, to reject that there is an intrinsic nature of the world waiting to be discovered by science. In the view of Rorty (1986:6), the idea of the world's intrinsic nature takes for granted an outmoded conception of the world as God's artifact, "the work of someone who has something in mind, who Himself spoke some language in which He described His Project".

In a later essay in *Qabḍ wa basṭ-i tiʾūrīk-i sharīʿat*, Surūsh (1996c:331) acknowledges, however, that the role of the theoretician of knowledge is also to justify and that the justificatory function always is a normative one in the sense that it "both explains and justifies, both informs about the evolution of knowledge as well as about the enigma of this evolution itself". While the question remains as to how he is to estimate the existence of divergent opinions, consisting of false and true, that pertains to a priori knowing without any criteria to discern true statements from false ones, his focus is rather on condemning what he calls the menace of "legal positivism" and "general idealism", which equate interpretation of *sharīʿat* with the divine law itself and results in pure utopian thought (ibid.:342). Despite Surūsh's (ibid.:260) claim that correct theories are only descriptive and not prescriptive, i.e. they are *ghair-i arzishī* (non-valuable), his definition of better understanding requires the acceptance of modern epistemology as its basic value. In this respect, the propositions of the theories of scientific method are comprised of methodological rules as well as values (or ends). Despite his purely explanatory and descriptive intention, the fact remains, in other words, that his exposition at large is both prescriptive and normative in style as it envisions the possibility and occurrence of a certain interpretation of religion that corresponds to certain postulates, such as a secular and pluralistic view of the religious phenomena. On the whole his work must be considered as a critique of traditional speculative metaphysics, even if his primary interest is in the scientific enterprise in its historical sweep and does not accept the ontological commitment of any particular theories, but rather a general and probable belief about the nature of the world.[117]

While epistemology, during its long history, has been engaged in two different tasks, one being descriptive and the other prescriptive, the philosophical study of human knowledge has in general (at least as far as realism is concerned) definite philosophical implications, since it does not merely describe the human cognitive predicament but also claims to improve our cognitive situation. While Surūsh's (1996c:200) account does not indulge in showing which of our beliefs are correct and which are erroneous, his epistemology is unquestionably an instrument for intellectual reform. His work is therefore a provision of epistemic advice that offers guidance towards improving the cognitive situation of the contemporary Islamic community. By making religious propositions subordinate to reason in several dimensions in terms of being probable truths (where reason dictates what the possible content of a proposition allegedly revealed by God might be), he erodes the intellectual status of religious beliefs where no proposition of faith can contradict scientific reason. While Surūsh is not primarily

[117] Besides, Surūsh (1994b:294) also makes several controversial statements on Islamic law and theology regarding the crucifixion of Jesus and the reason behind man's fall from paradise which should be counted as a priori beliefs.

concerned with which beliefs about reality are erroneous and which are not, his inquiry has a normative import since it asks, in effect, what we ideally ought to believe. As Charles Landesman (1997:148) elucidates, the theories created by science as well by the various religions about the external world imply ontological commitments to a variety of unobservable entities:

> Anyone who accepts such a theory, who believes that what is true or likely to be true or the best candidate for the truth, also commits himself to one degree or another to the existence of these entities. And because he accepts these entities as real and the theories as true, he also accepts the transcendent inferences that generated them as being trustworthy, as being such as to generate true theories.

Conclusions

In the foregoing chapters, I have initially described and analysed the theoretical foundations of traditional Islamic epistemology along with its methodological and hermeneutical features in the realm of law and jurisprudence. Secondly, I have presented an analytical account of the contemporary paradigmatic field of Iranian Shi'i positions on Islamic law and epistemology and highlighted the main intellectual representatives of the shifting discourses. The Islamic traditionalism of ʿAbdullāh Jawādī-Āmulī, the Islamic modernism of Muḥammad Mujtahid-Shabistarī and the Islamic postmodernism of ʿAbd al-Karīm Surūsh embody distinct products of the dynamic interaction between Islam and modernity, which have revealed complex relationships between the two entities. In Islamic thought, the problem of change versus tradition is largely apprehended in terms of a dialogue with modernity and of its impact on philosophy and culture. Since any normative question that is asked by contemporary Muslims must be seen in the context of Islamic modernity, the positions that are objects of the present study can successfully be situated in relationship to modernity. To various degrees, they accommodate religion to modernity by absorbing or refuting its normative cognitive and ontological characteristics. As far as Islamic modernism and postmodernism are concerned, these positions cannot be understood without realizing their deep roots in modern post-renaissance conceptions of being, knowledge and human agency, which are based on the different forms of 'subjectivist' epistemology.

In the following, I'll make a very short résumé of the general arguments presented in the chapters above and also attempt to substantiate my thesis that the thought of ʿAbd al-Karīm Surūsh represents an innovative but still indigenous philosophical and legal paradigm in the modern history of Shi'i Islam. As noticed, Islam, similar to all other traditional religions, has witnessed a quite new epistemic and interpretative situation during the recent century, which is generally felt as something of an emergency. This emergency in epistemology and hermeneutics is the result of a radical shift of categories of modern philosophy, science, culture and geography, the consequences of which Muslims in general have been unaware. The epistemological element of modernity undoubtedly involves a revolution in the very concept of knowledge itself. It has far-reaching implications for contemporary Islamic cognitive considerations and it poses a challenge to traditional theological wisdom.

Traditional Islamic notions of epistemology presupposed the existence of a religious and holistic notion of 'subjectivity', in the sense that Islamic theologians and philosophers as well as mystics and jurists considered the Divine as the fountainhead of all knowledge in the universe. According to their conception, knowledge is revealed to man through revelation and through a divine active intellect (*ʿaql*), which has cosmogonic, ethical-epistemological and spiritual dimensions denoting the innate faculty of transcendent knowledge. Intelligence was considered as a part of the soul but at the same time separate from it in the sense of being an incorporeal and incorruptible substance. As far as jurisprudence is concerned, the term *ʿilm* was equated with certainty and it was regarded as the duty of the jurist to seek absolute truth in his legal reasoning. The notion of the existence of a category of knowledge which is necessary (*ʿilm ḍarūrī*) and obtained through the senses, intuition or from revelation was fundamental, but the majority of jurists also considered that knowledge was acquired (*ʿilm muktasab*) through consensus and logical proofs based on premises derived from the revealed sources. From this perspective, every human being was considered to share different kinds of knowledge. Even if the context of knowledge comprised not only theosophical notions, every system of knowledge that cannot reach certain conclusions was regarded as false. The idea of alternative routes to knowledge is an important one in traditional Islamic epistemology, and many jurists combined various cognitive approaches. In this respect, various *epistemic schemes* developed distinct methodologies within the Islamic universe, where sciences such as law and theology were not only considered to belong to different spheres but their methods and principles were also believed to be as diverse as their contents.

The typical Islamic philosophical mode of dealing with the structure of reality was to divide it into hierarchical levels of qualitative vertical, but also horizontal, relationships, where the sciences were perceived to be related to the sacred, extending in a hierarchy from an empirical and rational mode of knowing to the highest form of intuitive intellection. An ontological and cosmic hierarchy was considered to lie at the root of all things, against which the particular always was deduced from the universal, the relative from the absolute and the concrete from the abstract. The major traditional epistemic schemes espoused the idea of the hierarchy and unity of the modes of knowing, where all knowledge is rooted in the divine Knower. As far as the divine law is concerned, it was considered to be connected to our terrestrial existence on the basis that reality is comprised of multiple states of existence of which the physical world is the lowest and furthest removed from the Divine. Knowledge of law meant in general a knowledge of the conduct that would please God and bring humans closer to him. In this respect, the revealed texts were supposed to define the frame of reference in the exercise of the intellect.

The major argument of the adherents to the 'juristic-rational' epistemic scheme was that legal norms could be logically extrapolated from truths that are found in these texts. The domain of epistemic intellectual exercise was accordingly limited to the revealed texts not by way of direct and comprehensive acquaintance with it, but by way of developing the necessary skill to extrapolate from it. The jurists in general defined their deductive method as acquired knowledge, which unlike necessary knowledge does not grip the mind. The fact that it is not immediate, and is obtained only by inferential operations of the mind, renders it subject to error. While the formalisation of Shi'i legal theory to a large extent was the acclimatisation of logic, where the position of faith *in* reason, rather than the polarisation of faith *and* reason came to triumph, the legal subject matter was at the very outset disposed against any 'worldview' that contravened the premise of law squarely grounded in divine deontology. On the one hand, reason was distinctly acquired but on the other hand it was never divorced from *badīhī* (intuitive) and necessary knowledge, nor from revelation. While Shi'i legal theory came to terms with scientific method and modes of thought, it is essential to stress that *ʿaql* as an abstract substance (unlike the other concrete sources of law) was used to arrive at a *qaṭīʿ* (decisive) judgement through Aristotelian syllogism rather than deductive analogy, and denoted an *a fortiori* mediate argument. The Shi'i syllogism was hence not concerned with real analogical deduction *from* the text, but rather with a simple declaration of what was found *in* the text.

While inference ultimately was deduced from reason in the elaborated hierarchy of knowledge, contradictions in terms of *raʾy* (opinion) and *ẓann* (conjecture) was a regrettable practical necessity, since probability, not certainty, was a matter of degree. The majority of traditional jurists argued that the sources and legal decisions had to be based on certainty and that the use of *ijtihād* (independent judgement) was limited to questions left open by the revealed sources, since the Prophet and the *imāms* were considered the chief commentators and expositors of the revealed sources. In other words, the jurists could merely exert lawfinding and not derive any new legal norms. The fourteenth century jurist *ʿallāmah* al-Ḥasan al-Hillī substantiated and defined *ijtihād* in such a way that by making a distinction between *ẓann* and *raʾy*, *ijtihād* was legitimised on the basis of *ẓann*. By referring to *ʿilm* as presumptive knowledge derived from the revealed sources, his follower, the nineteenth century jurist Murtaḍā al-Anṣārī, divided legal decisions into four categories by distinguishing valid and non-valid conjecture by specific terms: *qaṭʿ* (certainty), *ẓann muʿtabar* (valid conjecture), *shakk* (doubt) and *wahm* (erroneous conjecture). While the question whether it is possible to establish an authentic proof by means of evidence derived through *ẓann* was under dispute, the latter was part of an epistemological ranking from *yaqīn* (certainty) to *ghalābah al-ẓann* (likelihood) to *shakk* (uncertainty) to *shubhah* (suspicion). Since there was no attempt of a hypothetical destruction of and universal doubt in the surrounding world of religious tradition comparable to that of the modern Western philosopher Descartes, *ẓann* was not equal to the vernacular English sense of 'presumptive' or 'dubious'. While Islamic jurists had no illusions concerning the 'probabilistic' nature of the practical norms, they acknowledged that their epistemological and ontological status allowed for a limited and valid probability, which depended on the basic epistemic belief that the revealed texts yield necessary knowledge. Since jurisprudence also builds on the structure of theology that establishes the rational proof of religious truths, the valid conjecture of jurisprudence instead meant hesitation towards correctness. The majority of Shi'i jurists were hence against the reliance on probability at large (*ẓann muṭlaq*) in the philosophical sense of the word but rather acknowledged it as a realistic necessity in the realm of legal practice. While jurisprudence approved of the difference between the absolute truth of revelation and the fallibility of human interpretation, the epistemological scepticism of the jurists did not include the conviction that human reasoning is incapable of reaching a knowledge beyond doubt in any systematic manner. On the one hand cognitive certainty was never excluded methodologically and on the other hand no interpretation was considered contingent on historical and social circumstances in any absolute way. While human reason was estimated as a separate source of law, the principle of *muqaddamah-yi wajīb* (obligatoriness of prerequisites) formulated the standard of the interpretative boundaries, and the conjectural nature of particular legal norms did not affect the basic structure of the law.

Similar to the discussions in traditional legal theory, what is under debate in contemporary Islamic thought is, generally speaking, also the question of to what degree religion can accommodate change and be compatible with contemporary facts. In the discussions on revelation, reason and accommodation, the question of *ijtihād* occupies a prominent place among Islamic scholars. The challenge for Islamic thought is essentially the question of the viability of this religion on its own terms, which concerns a genuinely religious problem and is not merely a matter of interrelationship between religion and the other dimensions of social life, economics, polity and culture. The dilemma of religious reform is particularly pressing in relation to *sharīʿat*, since Islam in the sense of being a revelation from God rather than of God in many ways can be said to present more obstacles to religious modernism than, for instance, Christianity. Taking into consideration the existence of non-uniform *varieties* of modernity, where the term modernity itself refers to those features that allow us to speak of a modern age in the first place, we are here concerned with the characteristics of Islamic modernity, which includes Islamic adoptions as well as refutations of (post)modern notions of reason, subject, history, man, God, etc. In this respect, I define modernity as the result of a dialogue between reason and subject rather than something based upon one single principle. In my view, the universality of reason as well as the autonomy of the subject (notions rooted in the enlightenment thought of Descartes and Kant) equally serve as constitutive components of the philosophical vision of modernity.

The question of the relationship between entities such as religion and modernity is a delicate one. While religion in general, and Islam in particular, is above all concerned with God, revelation and the measure that He is believed to have set for mankind, modernity incessantly revises human measures in the light of accomplishment and failure and envisages adjustment to a world that is subjected to ever more thorough transformations. While the transcendent has become insignificant or even removed in philosophy with the process of secularisation, Islam's dialogue with modernity has always required a complete awareness of Qur'anic metaphysics, ethics and teleology. Due to the postmodernist criticism of universal reason, modernism is not any longer able to function as *the* doctrine, since the recognition of a host of local, historical and contingent reasons renders its discourse pluralistic. By asserting the intractable and arbitrary nature of all truth-claims, postmodernism reduces, so to say, all normative claims of enlightenment modernism to the status of cultural and historical prejudices. In contrast to religion, high modernity can hence no longer lay claim of possessing any meaningful cosmology.

Paradoxically, the conditions set by postmodernism in terms of changing the categorisation of the universal and particular, may very well be more favourable to a theoretician of Islamic law, since in principle, *sharīʿat* tolerates social diversity and leaves the mechanism of institutionalisation in the community relatively vague. This is, for instance, the argument of Akbar Ahmed (1992:10) who conceives postmodernism as a positive phenomenon, essentially characterised by "a spirit of pluralism; a heightened scepticism of traditional orthodoxies; and finally a rejection of the world as a universal totality, of the expectation of final solutions and complete answers". But Ahmed's attempt to situate Islam as a 'postmodern' critique of modernity is not without its contradictions since it does not fully account for the critical implications of postmodernism for traditional Islam (Turner 1994:12).

While religion is a much more complex phenomenon than can be approached by simple definitions, both Islam and modernity make claims of universality from different angles. In this respect, any dialogue between Islam and *deconstructive* postmodernism, between a doctrine of truth and transcendence and an anti-doctrine of which is 'fundamentalist' in its rejection of truth, universality and transcendence is a contradiction in terms. The de-legitimation of modernism at the level of doctrine has undoubtedly opened a new intellectual space and created a different agenda for pluralism and dialogue between modernity and tradition, but besides the plane of expediency and practicality, the inherent epistemic relativism of postmodernism acts as a troublemaker within Islamic tradition by rejecting the twin sources of traditional religious metaphysics (i.e. revelation and intellection).[1] By foreclosing the possibility of revelation, high modernity promises no revealed or ulterior standard for human thought and action and proclaims the truth of a closed immanent universe. As far as postmodernism involves the subversive reordering of elements of the religious counterparts (self-referential discourse, heterodoxy, eclecticism, marginality, death of the author, death of utopia, deconstruction, disintegration, discontinuity, fragmentation, de-centering of the subject, pluralism, critique of universal reason, a new epistemic system, dissolution of legitimising narratives, etc), its challenge to Islam goes far beyond the ideological to the higher plane of doctrine and essence. By distorting the ultimate transcendent Truth of Being, cosmos and man, the 'doctrinaire form' of postmodernism cannot hence without difficulty be reconciled with the Islamic faith and conscience. But the fact remains to be seen whether any conversation between these two irreconcilable entities, where postmodernism is recognised and afforded an emancipating account of the modern condition, is intellectually counterproductive for Islamic thought. This is in particular the obvious dilemma for ʿAbd al-Karīm Surūsh.

While Surūsh's ideas are symptomatic of a complex set of developments within Shi'i legal and theological thought, his epistemological project is one in which he, as an isolated individual, constructs inventive hypotheses for the whole edifice of human knowledge. His intellectual endeavour is essentially a personal effort in the sense that the aim is not to present an a priori creedal system consisting of certain formal principles that he claims to have drawn from the revealed sources, and on the basis of which he develops a full-fledged theological system. Surūsh does not offer a comprehensive and systematic methodology for understanding revelation and the Islamic legal tradition, since he believes that there are no uniquely Islamic principles that are specifically designed to produce a inherently Islamic *Weltanschauung*. He rather suggests that the traditional sciences were established on an *ad hoc* basis, dealing with issues in a hazardous manner, producing a kind of pastiche of Islamic principles. Surūsh's ideas are also significant in that he effects a transition from a tradition of religious philosophy preoccupied with the doctrine of our knowledge of God to a modern outlook that offers a philosophical interpretation of the nature of religion and of man's religiousness, cognitive capacities and historical religious development. His view that the problem of religion is distinct from the problem of God as well

[1] As Derrida (1997:11) suggests, deconstructionism is the removal of logocentrism from rationality by means of destructing all the significations that have their source in that of the logos: "The rationality– but perhaps that word should be abandoned for reasons that will appear at the end of this sentence–which governs a writing thus enlarged and radicalised, no longer issues from a logos. Further, it inaugurates the destruction, not the demolition but the de-sedimentation, the de-construction, of all the significations that have their source in that of the logos. Particularly the signification of truth".

as his commitment to de-objectifying traditional concepts of Islamic theology and law nonetheless raises philosophical problems.

Surūsh's works reflects a number of relatively undeveloped ontological assumptions concerning scientific method, epistemic warrant and critical realism. In fact, his realism simply consists in the fallibistic conviction that while there are an external world independent of our knowledge of it, we cannot expect our description of reality to correspond with it in any coherent sense. There exist a number of contradictions and ambiguities in Surūsh's thought, many of them instructive, since it is characteristic that only complex thinking produces instructive contradictions. These contradictions are partly due to his allegiance to and intermingling of three different modes of thinking: philosophy, jurisprudence and theosophy. For instance, his defence of critical rationality, which is considered as the source for reviving Islam, is not consistent with his idea of theosophy as the true method of deciphering religion. While he acknowledges the abstract existence of timeless objective truths (i.e. silent *sharīʿat*), independent of particular perspectives and methods, his hermeneutics seems to argue that there are only a variety of incommensurable truths that change through history and from culture to culture.[2] These inherent paradoxes make his thought a potential risk in a confrontation with traditionalist discourses, which point out that the imperatives of submission to alien cognitive categories ultimately lead to the dissolution of the Islamic religio-cultural matrix.

Balancing on the one side the allegiance of Islamic tradition to divine transcendence and on the other the emerging sense of human autonomy, including an increasingly self-conscious sense of intellectual autonomy that rejects most of the terms in which sacred law has traditionally been understood, Surūsh's thinking goes beyond arguing for the compatibility of the natural scientific outlook and religious faith. The very idea of transcending the earlier attempts of discovering points of compatibility between faith and common human understanding suggests the troubling possibility that emerging scientific discoveries and ideas requiring our respect might also put in question the ontological claims of Islamic philosophy. Surūsh is very much a methodological pluralist and the discourse he presents is eclectic. He is a mediator between opposing scientific and philosophical systems, such as the empiricist and rationalist tradition from the seventeenth century as well as sceptical and dogmatic positions. In his willingness to combine symbols from disparate codes or frameworks of meaning, even at the cost of disjunctions and eclecticism, he abandons the search for all-encompassing or triumphalist myths, narratives or frameworks of knowledge, which can be seen in his detraditionalisation of

[2] It goes without saying that the highly idealistic conception of silent *sharīʿat* as an idea unaffected by variation or permutation makes it increasingly complicated to locate religion in any human context.

the Islamic legal tradition. While detraditionalisation is nothing new (grand religious narratives have for a century been under threat), his call for the death of the author (i.e. God as far as revelation is concerned) is rather novel.

Surūsh's pluralism with respect to scientific method is obvious. It develops from falsifiability into a more comprehensive epistemology founded upon the idea of problem-solving and error criticism, even if it remains largely descriptive. By directing epistemology towards problems and problem-solving, his theory of knowledge takes a hermeneutic and deconstructionist turn, which contains some historical and interpretative dimensions of the intellectual context in which the problems are located. By shifting the emphasis from a formal and problem-solving inquiry based upon theories of evolutionary biology to poststructuralist hermeneutics that raise proposals for interpretation, he seems to argue against the idea of a fixed method in favour of a plurality of methodological rules governing theory evaluation (falsification, deduction, deconstructionism, paradox of confirmation, etc). His position on falsification is ambiguous, since he vindicates deconstruction as a superior model for presenting the distinctive characteristics of religion in the context of our historical situation, i.e. postmodernity, and also acknowledges that methodological rules may vary from time to time, as well as from field to field, within science. New rules may be introduced and old ones modified or discarded. Methodological rules may be further applied in different ways in different fields of science, and different scientists may interpret the same rules in different ways. His pluralism in scientific method hence entails a certain relativism, since the existence of a plurality of methods would provide scientists with rational justification for the acceptance of opposing theories on the basis of alternative sets of rules. While he as a Popperian acknowledges that the purpose of method is to test the refutability of theories, the last word is not spoken on this matter, as he indicates that a deductive model provides the most accurate rational justification in contrast to inductive and pragmatist models.

As far as Surūsh's theory of contraction and expansion is concerned, it derives largely from inductive reasoning despite its formal adherence to deductive reasoning. His historical examples in the book *Qabḍ wa basṭ-i tiʾūrīk-i sharīʿat* together form the structure of several inductive corroborations. His theory is also, strictly speaking, arrived at inductively in the sense that it initially is bound to exclude some views as false, or at least unworthy of consideration. Similar to Descartes who intended his logic to supplant the syllogistic reasoning of the scholastic dialectic in which he had been trained, Surūsh believes that syllogisms are trivial in that they merely enable the mind to deduce the truths it already beholds. But in contrast to Descartes, Surūsh does not conceive the new logic as building upon the immediate experience of truth (which syllogisms can at best only describe but not extend), and articulates a theory of probability that he believes is able to formulate a logic with an innovative conclusion. Inductive reasoning can be most clearly expressed in terms of probability, since it occurs when the logical premises are considered sufficient to justify a conclusion, without being conclusive in the sense of deductive reasoning or when there are some but not yet sufficient reasons for the conclusion and further reasons may be found, so that the sum total of reasons will be sufficient. A successful inductive argument is one that makes its conclusion probable, or more probable than any equally detailed alternative. The logical entailment in inductive reasoning is a matter of degree and does not fit into the neat paradigms of formal validity but has rather to be referred to in terms of a nondemonstrative logic, which is the case with Surūsh's theory of contraction and expansion. By considering inter-subjectivity as the exclusive criteria of worthwhile knowledge, he also rejects any higher standard of rationality than the assent of the relevant community (i.e. consensus), which denotes a theory that is proceduralist, a product of discourse and argumentative reasoning.

As far as Surūsh's methodology on jurisprudence is concerned, he is far from locating himself in the tradition of the Islamic philosophy of law. In fact, he believes that philosophy as a pursuit of eternal truth must be abandoned in a temporalised world, where all boundaries are under siege from within as well as without. In his view, the present cognitive geography has deep implications for traditional tensions between reason and revelation, and demands the adoption of modern scientific methodologies. Surūsh distances himself from traditional Islamic concerns of issues of truth versus error, belief versus disbelief and a single and unique divine mission to the rest of humanity. In contrast to the Islamic traditionalism of Jawādī-Āmulī, he hence rejects that *sharīʿat* may possibly possess a self-referential structure and he seeks rather to establish its mode of operation in the environmental conditions to which it is required to adapt. By adhering to the paradigm of pre-modern Islamic tradition by identifying legal methodology with Aristotelian syllogism, Jawādī-Āmulī posits reason as a cognitive dimension of revelation and argues that legal reasoning by nature must embark on the eternal journey toward certainty. Moving in the opposite direction constitutes, in his view, the essence of the secular passion of modernity. For Islamic traditionalists, jurisprudence is a certain science that provides a certain model of religious conduct by means of *istinbāṭ* (inference) from the revealed sources, that is, by obtaining a legal norm from the revealed sources through syllogical arguments (i.e. *ijtihād* is restricted to the realm of *furūʿ*). By endorsing an ontological hierarchical classification of knowledge, which as mentioned extends from the empirical to the rational and the intuitive modes of knowing, Jawādī-Āmulī claims that no contradiction is possible between *ʿaql-i qaṭʿī* (definite reason) and revelation, but only between defect reason (i.e. wrong inference, false analogues, etc) and revealed texts that are apocryphal and *ẓannī*. In case a contradiction occurs, definite rational proof is superior to conjectural revealed proof. Since juristic knowledge cannot be *iḥtimāl* (probable) but only *mumkin* (possible), *sharīʿat* is not considered to be legislated or produced but discovered, understood and formulated.

Contrary to Islamic traditionalism, Surūsh interprets Islamic law in terms of the normative principles of modernity, where the legal tradition is subjected to critical epistemological and hermeneutical analysis. His point of departure is that the conception of *fiqh* as an all-encompassing system is incorrect and that jurisprudence is complete only in the *ḥadd-i aqallī* (minimalist) sense. In his view, the new theoretical as well as methodological foundations which are available for a transformed Islamic law are not within *sharīʿat* itself, since *fiqh* is characterised by a normative theoretical closure. Similar to Surūsh, the Islamic modernism of Mujtahid-Shabistarī also claims that methodological innovation is a requirement to reinstate the dynamics of *ijtihād*. Both positions depart from the traditional view that restricts *ijtihād* to the *furūʿ* of jurisprudence and assert that legal reasoning always must be grounded in the prevailing rationality of the age. But while they equally suggest that the questions facing modern man are not restricted to a limited number of legal norms but instead extend to the realm of philosophy, Mujtahid-Shabistarī stresses the rational character of *fiqh* and believes that the revealed texts cannot be valuated solely on the basis of modern rationality but must be considered in the light of Qur'anic teachings and *ʿaql-i dīnī* (religious reason). By involving other disciplines, mainly theology or ethics, which traditionally followed distinct methodologies, he insists, however, on disclosing a methodology, not mere juristic devices, which can create a dialectical relationship between the imperatives of the revealed texts and the realities of the modern world.

In contrast to Mujtahid-Shabistarī, Surūsh considers traditional jurisprudence an irrational science in the sense that it is based on *taqlīd* (emulation) and discourages the free inspection of reason. By comparing it with a modern secular legal system and asserting that legal philosophy must be contingent on modern scientific theories and subjects, his discourse on Islamic law, which subjects *fiqh* to the position of a consuming science, is normatively open and adapts constantly to external non-religious settings. On the basis of his methodological distinction between the *ḏātiyāt* (substances) and the *ʿaraḍiyāt* (accidentals) of religion, Surūsh considers *ijtihād*, which is interpreted in its widest and most universal sense, as the *tarjumah-yi farhangī* (cultural translation) of the religious accidentals. His idea of a process of translation of the religious phenomena (where the legal principles and norms are considered as the sixth category of accidentals), is to facilitate a radical transformation of Islam. In this respect, he imposes similar epistemological principles on legal texts as well as theological and mystical ones in an attempt to ascertain and deconstruct some neglected but relevant aspects of the religious spirit. Similar to jurisprudence, he considers ethics as a normative anthropocentric order directed at the fulfilment of human interests that transcends religion. In his view, contemporary man must do without evident truths in ethics in the same sense as he does without evident truths in the knowledge of the world. Legal norms as well as ethical values are, in other words, considered to be constructed, historically variable and inherently revisable (i.e. no longer universal but local, no longer absolute but contingent). In this respect, Surūsh adopts the distinction between value and fact to distinguish the realm of norms and values from the sphere of nature, and considers the Aristotelian notion that the latter might guide the former as offensive, since reality lacks any significant hierarchies and objective values. To describe his notion of law and ethics as a secularisation of knowledge would seem appropriate.

In Surūsh's view, the traditional notions of legal theory consequently has no natural function in modern society, where nation states have emerged on a global level of interaction as redefined actors governing much more of differentiated public space than the pre-modern political ruler. In his criticism of the traditional organic mingling of ethics and law, which is so characteristic of *fiqh*, he suggests that the very nature of Islamic law (its language, its priorities, its logic, etc) makes it increasingly irrelevant in modernity. By emphasising that *fiqh* originally was formulated to respond to issues originating in a primitive nomad society, his effort is not to revive *fiqh* by requesting a more dynamic and practical function, but to plead for its overall closure in terms of an appropriation to the modern conception of law. In his deconstruction of traditional metaphysics, Surūsh's strategy to make Islamic jurisprudence impossible may very well be characterised (to use the expression of Marc C. Taylor) as an a/jurisprudence or a/theology.[3] From this reasoning, Islamic law is obliged to adjust itself to a modern philosophy of law, if it is going to generate any effective force and positive practicability in the contemporary world. While *fiqh* differs from secular legal systems in its religious content, it needs to acquire the same function and coordination as that of any other modern legal system and be considered as the enforcement of a body of rules through a controlling human authority. Surūsh's pragmatic conception of Islamic law as made by the society comes very close to the key ideas of legal positivism in that laws are laws by virtue of their form rather than by their religious or moral content and that legal systems are sets of rules (interpreted in a broad sense) applied by the judiciary as part of societal regulation by states. In fact, he insists that what matters is merely the systematic and empirically reliable analysis of the positive legal materials as they are presented in statutes, ordinances and administrative practice.

In many respects, the positivistic conception of Islamic law is, however, problematical, as far as *sharīʿat* recognises no term *strictissimi juris* for positive law dissociated from the ethical and the religious sense. Islamic law does not have the usual imprint of case law, since it is not judicially created

[3] Cf. Taylor 1984.

in the positivistic sense and permits no independent process of man-made law alongside the divine ordinances. The traditional casuistic method of inferential reasoning in which general principles are adapted to particular circumstances through analogical extension came in fact first under dispute among Islamic scholars in their encounter with modern Western concepts of legality which emphasise abstract analytical thought. While Islamic law possesses a normative and established structure, it also resists codification of any kind as a potential reading of the revealed sources. But since the most striking element of continuity in twentieth century Iran has been the continuing growth of the state, Surūsh's major concern with legislation and codification is only natural. In post-revolutionary Iran, the trend of 'islamising' the modern state has, for instance, been precisely aimed at transforming traditional divine law into state law.

Since Islamic law essentially is transcendent and its boundaries cannot be defined in any systematic way, as it is subjected to interpretative necessity, Surūsh is increasingly concerned with questions of an epistemological and hermeneutical nature. He rejects the ability of the traditional philosophy of *ijtihād* to get to the bottom of the current intellectual spectrum of modernity by arguing that the fundamental criterion of legal change is that any legal reform must be accompanied by an alteration of the fundamental ontological presuppositions of traditional legal philosophy, theory and methodology. By initiating a process of transforming the heritage of traditional *fiqh* through an amalgamating selection of traditional doctrines to engender *ijtihād*, if it indeed can be called so, without recourse to the traditional methodological and philosophical foundations, his aim is evidently to keep to what he believes is the spirit of Islam, but get rid of those characteristics which he believes are accidental to Islam. Surūsh's legal modernism constitutes the penetration of secular science into the very realm of the sacred, into the domain of divine law, which was considered the queen of the sciences in the traditional Islamic scientific endeavour.

Surūsh's definition of religion de-objectifies traditional Islamic law and makes it vulnerable to the modern epistemologies that specify the notion and structure of knowledge for the secular era of modernity. By reason of his positivistic and diachronic construction of human knowledge, science is de-ontologised and denied any metaphysical significance. With the destruction of the notion of hierarchy in reality, the rapport between degrees of knowledge and the correspondence between the various levels of reality upon which traditional Islamic science were based, disappear and metaphysics is abandoned in favour of empirical science. Surūsh's approach is marked by an abandonment of the quest after an ontological vision of the whole, in the sense that no standpoint exists outside the flow of historically situated experience and that all knowledge is the explanation of previous knowledge. In this respect, epistemic matters become externalised, desacralised and separated from Being. The major shift in his thought is hence in the direction of inquiry. While Islamic traditionalism and Islamic modernism in various ways seek to inquire and reason about God, humanity and the world, Surūsh asks what could be known about the very processes of knowing, inquiring, and reasoning. Following Kant's lead, he turns inward, taking the investigation of the interior of the knower as a problem prior to the knower's investigation of the exterior. As the reference point of knowledge is transferred to the knower, all knowledge and experience come to require a kind of self-consciousness. His divorce of reason from the world of faith, where the authority of revelation also ceases to be of philosophical significance, connects, in other words, to the secularisation of the cosmos and results in a downgrading of the role of noumenon in human thinking.

The turning away from things, the object of thinking, to the subject, having thoughts, is in fact the mark of Surūsh's thought. He indisputably makes a conscious break with traditional Islamic conceptions of science by giving primacy to the subject over the object, identifying reason with the thinking ego and considering knowledge as empirical rather than symbolic. For Surūsh, scientific claims are open to falsification or refutation only on empirical grounds and by emphasising the 'subject' pole of cognition to the detriment of the 'object' pole, i.e. reality, his 'subjectivism' also reduces objective reality to accidents in nature lacking in symbolic quality. In my view, his epistemology is relativistic as he acknowledges that the relativity of truth arises from a conception of knowledge and reality as 'formed'– and hence relative to – a contingent subjective cognitive background. While he does not always forsake and deny universals, such as God, his analysis is relativist as far as the phenomenon is not considered to contain any definite symbolic or universal features. While his notion of science posits an intersubjective theory of truth as the criterion of valid knowledge, his hermeneutics accepts no truth that is shared.

For this reason, it is not an accident that the relativistic character of Surūsh's epistemology is a common object of traditionalist critiques. In contrast to Surūsh's claim that knowledge is mediated by mental and linguistic representations, Jawādī-Āmulī argues that the criterion of knowledge is conditioned by its correspondence to the ontological levels of reality and its capacity to bring forth certain knowledge. As a contemporary proponent of Ṣadrāian philosophy, Jawādī-Āmulī gives primacy to ontology and metaphysics over epistemology and methodology, and considers cognitive matters in the light of a basically sacred cosmology. For him, knowledge and reality are not two things, but identical, and questions about criteria of knowledge depend upon questions of reality. His epistemology is clearly 'objectivist' in the sense that knowledge is determined by 'objects', by objects on the plane of ideas as well as objects of the senses, and he also considers the highest reality to be spiritual and independent of man. Implied in the hierarchy of knowing is an ontological analysis of the knowing process in order to get an acquaintance with the things-in-themselves. As a form of transcendent realism, his epistemology suggests that the intrinsic qualities of reality are portrayed in human consciousness as they are. Veiled in the language of Islamic theosophy, Jawādī-Āmulī's mystical theology of unity views the intellect, the subject, as the object, 'Being', and the object as the subject, as a result of which knowing embodies absolute certitude. Ontology grounds, in other words, a world-view and provides an imagery that calls us to change, to transformation. Assuming the possibility of transcendence, it calls us to spiritual realisation.

Contrary to Jawādī-Āmulī's conception of knowledge as something permanent that exists within Divine Being, Surūsh locates the beginning of science in the advent of a critical attitude, and he argues that the epistemologist has to address the question in terms of what knowers produce. In his view, the conditioning factors of person, time, place, and history does not limit the acquisition of knowledge, but quite the contrary. They supply the epistemological tools that make knowing possible. He does not refer to the concept of man as God's vicegerent on earth (in his post-1988 writings), but rather grounds this status in knowledge as such. He argues that knowledge originates in the faculties of the subject since the key features of cognition, including the spatial form of intuition and other features of our representations, must be traced to our cognitive constitution. In Surūsh's view, the reflecting human subject is a non-divine historical, linguistic and social subject, which is in search of meaning. It has a transient nature where self-understanding is basically a social and historical becoming or growth rather than a state of contemplation. His notion of subjectivity is hence explicitly mediated by its social and historical accidentals.

Surūsh's empiricist aim, as distinguished from the pragmatist emphasis on prediction and control of environment, is restricted to producing predictive accurate theories which are empirically well-supported by the observable phenomena. He does not reject science but only scienticism in which the data of modern natural science alone is allowed to contribute to the construction of our worldview. Surūsh demarcates science from non-science and calls his criterion of demarcation falsifiability and isolates science as the only discourse that can say anything about the world. In contrast to philosophical pragmatism, he maintains that philosophy must be concerned with the centrality of basic foundational questions in epistemology. Whatever else a critique of reason attempts, it must, in his view, criticise reason, and since it cannot have only a negative or destructive outcome, the critique of reason has to support at least some standards on which thinking may rely. The outcome of his so-called *ʿaqlānīyat-i intiqādī* (critical rationality) is hence an epistemology, where reason is used in an independent and more unrestricted manner which constantly threatens our most cherished and comforting assumptions.

Surūsh's early specialisation in the disciplines of chemistry, pharmacology and history has a mark on his ideas, in particular his cardinal assertion that scientific discoveries have an impact on epistemology, which causes a new philosophical understanding that affects religious understanding. His argument that there is no longer a world-view to which one can comfortably relate suggests that his notions of knowledge only amount to a knowledge for the sake of knowledge alone and his intellectual enterprise remains in this respect a knowledge of the physical world only. Surūsh's thought is largely concerned with examining the methods, the results and the statements of results of the labours of natural scientists. While his evolutionary epistemology, which builds on the theory of natural selection, marks a major achievement, one single coherent process of knowledge, a problem-solving process, it is not without its ramifications. Surūsh would not agree, for instance, with the basic premise that evolutionary epistemology is an epistemology which is cognisant of and compatible with man's status as a product of biological and social evolution alone. In his view, scientific knowledge is still produced by the same mechanism that governs biological emergence: the highest creative thought is the product of a largely active process of blind variation and selective retention – trial and error. But the question remains as to what extent human creative thought is conscious of this evolutionary process in contrast to the organisms that according to Darwin are passive throughout their adaptation to the environment.[4]

In this respect, the differences of reality as seen in science and faith ultimately reveal that the two sources are unequal in magnitude and in the ultimate significance of their content, since religion has a far more limited rational content (i.e. it has no right to claim objective truth in the scientific sense). While science cannot provide one with certainty, Surūsh asserts that is the only objective mode of pursuing valid knowledge, as it rests on the bedrock of empirical testability. But despite the fact that he claims that a theory is true if it corresponds to empirical reality, he acknowledges that we may only speak of degrees of certainty (i.e. more or less probability). Since a moment of philosophical doubt clings to all human knowledge claims, religious knowledge is overall tentative, hypothetical and conjectural as well: it is ultimately bold guesswork. In his view, the question of the sources of knowledge should therefore be replaced by completely different questions relating to hermeneutics, as every source of knowledge is constantly open to critical examination.

Surūsh's thought signifies more of a 'scientification' of Islam rather than an 'islamisation' of science. By arguing that the case of religion is similar to that of modern science (i.e. there is nothing constant about it except that it is in constant flux), his aim is evidently to strengthen a modern scientific

[4] Surūsh's view of science and philosophy as a process of continual, incremental understanding moving from the known into the unknown, resulting in the unknown becoming known is, of course, a relic of the enlightenment optimism that looked forward to the victory of mind over matter and reason over nature in the inevitable evolution of reason.

comprehension of religion and combat dogmatic thinking. Since modern science very much possesses a specific philosophy that clothes itself in scientific terminology (that is, it is not science proper but rather a secular paradigm that sets the parameters of contemporary epistemology), his exposition is at large both prescriptive and normative by envisioning the possibility of a certain interpretation of religion that corresponds to certain postulates, such as a secular and pluralistic view of the religious phenomena. Despite its purely explanatory and descriptive intention, his thinking embodies a provision of epistemic advice that offers guidance towards improving the cognitive situation of the contemporary Islamic community.

However, the main dilemma of Surūsh's epistemology concerns, however, not its normative aspects but the level of terminology, in particular his definition of a priori. While he does not rule out the possibility that certain parts of our belief system will be revised by subsequent experience, his idea of ultimately unchanging truths (i.e. constants) disagrees with (post)modern philosophy. It is not consistent with Popper's notion of falsification, the nominalist pragmatism of Quine and others, nor with Kant's doctrine of the synthetic a priori, which was decisively undercut by Einstein's theory of relativity. As far as the notion of constants is concerned, Surūsh supposes that we have an epistemic right to believe in the self-evidently true notion of *tawātur*, which can be 'known' by some sort of doxastic a priori intuition that he does not elaborate on further. In this respect, he has the dilemma of solving the question of rationalism, since epistemic basic beliefs must be self-justifying, if they are to provide a foundation for the justification of other beliefs. He must either deny the possibility of basic beliefs or assert the possibility that all justified belief ultimately derives from empirical evidence or rational perception.

In line with Kant's view, Surūsh believes that all knowledge of warrant either is a priori or a posteriori. It cannot be both. A belief either has some perceptual elements in its warranting history (a posteriori) or it has none (a priori), which according to many contemporary philosophers is an exaggeration, since a significant number of beliefs exist with a warranting history that includes both perceptual and ratiocinative processes (Goldman 1999:22). For Surūsh, all a posteriori beliefs are contingent and provisional. The same seems to apply for a priori beliefs, since he believes that it is possible to take such kind of statements to be true (as in the case of Kant's notion of synthetic a priori), when they are not. While Surūsh as a philosopher looks to a priori statements for security by assuming that, inasmuch as these statements may themselves be certain (and necessary), and that they can certainly be known, he seems to make a contradiction in terms since contemporary epistemology accepts no special set of a priori statements of which it can be said that just these are beyond the reach of doubt. In the end, he therefore rejects the claim of a necessary a priori validity for Kantian categories of thought and intuition and rather provides a perspective under which these categories can be seen as highly edited, much tested presumptions, validated only as provisional scientific truth is validated. His theory is an empirical one in its denigration of any significance of a priori knowledge, and his idea that all knowledge must be considered as a posteriori results in the fact that nothing has absolute a priori validity but are rather only constructions of the epistemological subject. The inconsistency of this argument becomes perceptible when he restricts the right to differentiate correct from incorrect interpretations to the level of a priori knowledge. Besides, it is unclear whether many of his statements concerning Islamic law, theology and religious pluralism belong to the a priori level or the a posteriori level of discourse.

In contrast to Kant, who believed that universal truth is a form of synthetic a priori knowledge, Surūsh seems to admit that all scientific and religious truths are contingent and cannot therefore be known a priori. A contingent truth is one that might be or might have been false and might be or might have been true, since it can only be known and tested empirically. His discussion in *Qabḍ wa basṭ-i tiʾūrīk-i sharīʿat* claims the existence of synthetic a priori principles and axioms, but at the same time rejects them by reducing these constants to the internal and subjective cognitive matrix of human understanding. While all a priori knowledge, in Surūsh's view, is necessary, some necessities can hence only be known empirically by inference from the contingent via a conditional known a priori. From this reasoning, his idea of reality emerges as being constructed by human beings through the interaction of their subjective consciousness and scientific problems, theories and institutions.

Surūsh's ambiguous position as regards the a priori is largely due to the interpretation and identification of modernity not merely with science and technology but with the recognition of man as the sole measure and source of values. For him, modernity is characterised as the postulate of human autonomy linked to the categorical separation of subject and object that after Descartes becomes logically prior to all others. In Surūsh's view, humanism with its anthropomorphic foundations coincides with metaphysics and represents the ultimate reduction of everything to the measure of the human subject itself. By employing a similar second-order epistemology in the analysis of the Islamic sciences, his purpose is essentially to 'humanise' and 'historicise' these religious discourses all at once. Instead of establishing Islamic self-referentiality to respond to what he identifies as the normative closure of traditional legal methodology, he employs the evolutionary dynamics of cognitive openness in order to propose a theoretically alienating exercise in which Islam is ultimately reduced to the confines of Western cognitive matrices. His vindication of an Islamic adjustment to secular science remains an adaptive process, largely determined by environmental imperatives, and reflects, in the view of Jawādī-Āmulī, a tragic contradiction as it forgets the ontological difference in the hierarchal relationship between revelation, reason and empirical fact.

In his attempt to transcend established barriers of traditional epistemology, Surūsh is an original thinker by any standard. He argues that the debate in contemporary Islamic thought must shift to a clearer understanding of mediating cultures that inform it rather than being confined to conflicting epistemologies, which he believes is the sole consequence of competing religious claims. He calls for an Islamic revival through which creativity is a product of differences, contradictions. He also calls for a free and open dialogue that conjures up a relationship that guides a liberated normativity, which constantly adapts to secular environmental inputs. In this respect, the relevance of Surūsh's epistemology to the development of an Islamic conceptual frame is, however, questionable, since he makes the substance of traditional thought insignificant and rejects the idea of an authentic Islamic episteme undaunted by external impositions. Instead, he embarks on a counter-experimental exercise of deconstructing religion by historising and de-ontologising its theological beliefs and epistemic hierarchies. Rather than attempting to establish Islamic self-referentiality, he offers a theoretically and methodologically alienating exercise in which Islam ultimately is reduced to the confines of the cognitive matrices of modernity. By rejecting the existence of any Islamic self or essence, he lays, in other words, the ground for a final unequivocal secularisation of the entire field of knowledge.

Surūsh's affinities with postmodern thought are closest in the sphere of hermeneutics, where he initiates a systematic critique of meaning. He is genuinely occupied with the primary interpretative questions of contemporary poststructuralism and hermeneutics in order to better understand the revealed texts. If we cannot reconstruct the author's original intention, if words have more than a single meaning, and if there are multiple and conflicting interpretations, how are we to use discernment between the various interpretations that can be made from a single text? By giving prominence to human contingency and human contexts in the recovery of textual meaning, his hermeneutics is essentially characterised by three qualities: it is *contextual*, *local* and *pluralistic*. In this respect, Surūsh transcends not only the traditionalist hermeneutics of Jawādī-Āmulī but also the phenomenological hermeneutics of Mujtahid-Shabistarī, which follows Husserl's motto 'To the things themselves' and seeks to clarify through reflective analysis that which is immediately given to consciousness. By offering a method for carrying out reflection on experience and understanding, Mujtahid-Shabistarī's reflective analysis is, however, not descriptive in an intuitive or introspective manner but is a distinct interpretative procedure drawn from the basic concepts of the transcendental unity of perception and intentionality. Proposing a weak form of 'objectivist' epistemology, he also contrasts his phenomenological methodology with the

Kantian one and attempts to avoid the hidden relativism of this latter by emphasising that truth is universal but at the same time keeps its limits clearly in view. By turning to Gadamer's philosophical hermeneutics, the question of textual communication as well as the original intention of the author that is supposed to be imbedded within the historical horizon becomes important for Mujtahid-Shabistarī's theory of interpretation. He emphasises the historical situatedness of being and argues that textual understanding can only be considered by acknowledging the existence of a set of historical horizons which, however, are transcended through the so-called 'fusion of horizons'. While he acknowledges that the act or process of understanding contains a subjective element that is bound up with the accidents of history, he also distinguishes this act from its objective outcome, what he calls the *manṭiq-i darūnī-yi payām-i qur'ān* (inner logic of the Qur'anic message).

In contrast to Mujtahid-Shabistarī's Gadamerian hermeneutics, which considers language not as a tool for human subjectivity but as a transcendental ground within which past and present can have a dialogue, Surūsh's theory of interpretation is disinterested in deciphering any presumable original intentionality of authors and signifies an anti-Kantian perspective that is nonconceptual and non-representational. In the quest for new paradigms, he actually attempts to extricate himself from the mode of representational thinking so characteristic for enlightenment thought and denies that historical conditions are a constitutive element of meaning, according to which past meaning can be reconstructed with regard to historical conditions. Surūsh is not interested in reconstructing the text to find *the* meaning of the text. The text has no well-defined features in terms of unity, totality, authorship or self-referentiality, and its meanings are always provisional and temporal. By categorically rejecting the notion of *maʿnī-yi wāqiʿī* (true meaning) in the realm of human understanding, he believes that the possibility of dialogue between present and past cannot be taken for granted, as the horizon of the original discourse disappears in interpretation. Since the essence of meaning is not separate from the infinitely different possible situations in which it is understood, he also tends to reduce the text to its interpretation by taking the particular context of the interpreter as the sole criterion for the appearance of textual meaning.

In Surūsh's view, the function of hermeneutics should hence be reconceived. No longer should one be driven to search for eternal truths or even temporal truths. He believes that the methodological imperative for hermeneutics is that the judgment about what is real and true is not conditioned by some objective exterior referent but by the scientific discourse itself. Truth, reality and all such predicates have meaning by virtue of the current consensus of the users of those terms. In fact, what constitutes a 'thing' of which something may be predicated – an object, a particular – is a product of historical and inter-subjective processes. By reducing discourse to interpretation, including that claim itself, his idea of interpretation cancels itself all the way through and leaves everything (almost) exactly the way it was. For while Surūsh's epistemology denies the possibility of describing the world in itself, it consistently finds itself interpreting the world the way it appears. The issue remains hence for him to answer how subjective presuppositions are to be transcended after they have been put into play in the act of interpretation, since the deconstructionist denial of any patterns of rational necessity cannot be easily reconciled with his logocentrism nor his belief in intersubjective objectivity.

Following Derrida, Surūsh makes the point that language is ineradicably temporal and metaphorical, working through tropes and figures. But in contrast to traditional metaphysics, that considers reality symbolic and transparent, his study of metaphor suggests that language does not simply reflect reality but constitutes it. He believes in a system of floating signifiers pure and simple with no determinable relation to any extra-linguistic referents at all. Meaning is, in his view, not immediately present in one sign alone but scattered or dispersed along the whole chain of signifiers, which have the status of a kind of constant flickering of presence and absence together. Language is considered as a temporal process, where earlier meanings are modified by later ones. From this reasoning, the text is seen to fail by its own criteria; the standards or definitions that the text sets up are used reflexively to unsettle and shatter original distinctions. For instance, it is not clear in what way Surūsh's notion of the 'silence' of the revealed texts actually leads to the agent and subject of interpretation or how it is possible to specify the logic of a 'better' understanding that is independent of the historically conditioned community of interpreters (taking into account his view that the likelihood of scientific theories to provide knowledge of phenomena is a matter of degree). Surūsh's emphasis on human agency in meaning-making enterprises stands in contradiction to traditional Islamic essentialist concepts of rationality. His emphasis that human constructions and contexts make God's presence in the world possible subjects the Divine to a certain historicity, where human contingency empowers God so that His presence has no meaning outside human existence. The concluding outcome of his hermeneutics is therefore a series of open questions, such as what relevance a reappreciation of the 'substances' of Islam by means of deconstruction has in our postmodern condition.

As far as I understand, the heart of Surūsh's argument sets out to defend the unrealised potential of modernity. For him, modernity is intimately linked with the central aspirations of enlightenment: the aspirations of cognitive rationality, moral autonomy and social-political self-determination. He thinks that the rational potential of enlightenment modernism should not be abandoned and that the exemplary originality of the subject lies in the free employment of the human cognitive faculties. As a defender of critical reason, Surūsh stands in the tradition of Kantian philosophy, but of course he cannot be modern in the same sense that Kant is. While his position has affinities with the fundamental Kantian principle of the subjective basis of understanding, he would, in contrast to Kant, consider subjectivity as a process of becoming that never fully is other rather than in terms of maturity. Surūsh acknowledges that modern philosophy has reached a state of exhaustion and that the task now is to find ways around this exhaustion. By identifying postmodernism with deconstructionism, he believes that deconstructionism produces a fundamental irrational paradox by considering knowledge as pure causes.[5] His epistemological affinities are closer to Popper than deconstructionist thought, but he is not a foundationalist as the modern philosophers were. Instead, he thinks that philosophy must recognise that all its claims are fallible instead of absolute. In the realm of hermeneutics, his ideas represent a systematic mistrust of metaphysics and a suspicion of the values of 'truth' and 'meaning'.

So it is tempting to think of Surūsh as a *constructive* or *revisionary* postmodernist who seeks to overcome the modern worldview as such, yet by means of constructing a new worldview through a revision of modern premises and traditional concepts. Unlike deconstructionism, which overcomes modernism through an anti-worldview, he has not abandoned modern philosophy's goal of formulating and defending rationality and universality, and he does not altogether reject or eliminate the ingredients necessary for a worldview (God, self, purpose, meaning, real world, truth as correspondence, etc). While I would prefer to characterise him as *late* modern, by stressing that both 'late' and 'post' suggest 'after', I refer to him as a postmodernist in the sense that he is involved with the question of what to do next, given that in central ways modern philosophy has reached a state of exhaustion. Besides, he is utterly positive to the postmodernist critique of modern rationality that puts universal reason under dispute and he suggests that the boundaries of reason are more accurately understood after the postmodern revolt against the narcissism of rationality. In his view, the contribution of postmodernism to pluralism, tolerance, as well as its criticism of the superiority of reason is beneficial. By also adopting deconstruction at the level of methodology in his lectures on *ijtihād*, it is evident that his reformism comprises a revision of the epistemic premises of enlightenment modernism.

Surūsh's contructive postmodernism is a form of *high modernity* in the sense that it constitutes the flowering of the deepest impulse in the modern project. In many respects, it represents a loss of faith in enlightenment modernism, a spirit of subjectivism, a pluralism, a scepticism and a relativist rejection of final answers. His religious discourse is undoubtedly situated in opposition to the 'settled hegemony' and 'objective certitude' of the

[5] It should be mentioned that Derrida (1983:17), as far as I know, does not see himself as postmodern. In his view, the task of criticism essentially involves a double gesture of formulating, rational questions, about the limits of rational endeavours. In explicit terms, the label 'postmodern' is mainly adopted rather by Lyotard.

metanarrative of Islamic tradition. Similar to contemporary postmodernism, Surūsh seeks to move beyond the conventional historical paradigm of tradition, whether this tradition is enlightenment modernity or premodernity. He is suspicious of traditional notions of truth, reason and objectivity, of single frameworks and ultimate grounds of explanation, and considers the world as contingent, decentred, unstable, diverse and indeterminate. While his thought embodies the persistence of a commitment to the Popperian version of scientific rationality, which demonstrates that the aims and objectives of modernism continue, these features are being called into question and rendered problematic. By considering knowledge to be inherently contextual and determined by the other domains of human knowledge and socio-economic reality, it follows that contexts are local, which means that it is problematic if not impossible to articulate large truths. In contrast to the typical modernists' submission to rational criticism in the name of truth, Surūsh's postmodernism accepts no unshakable foundations on which to adjudicate claims of justified true knowledge and hence also meaning. As noticed, he suggests that the temporality of understanding, which merges with its contextuality, points out both the finitude and reflexivity of human understanding. The result of this contextualism and localism is that knowledge is considered inherently pluralistic and constituted by various claims, each of which rings true to its own advocates. By asserting that modernity creates its own normativity out of itself, he presents no method which escapes the problem of reflexivity.[6]

Surūsh's intellectual and philosophical enterprise involves a creative synthesis of traditional concepts (*sharīʿat*) and the premises of modernism (autonomy of reason) in order to construct a genuinely postmodern worldview. The structure of his worldview is not that of a hierarchy but rather one of competition grounded in the community. By contesting epistemic certainty, cultural essentialism, metanarratives, universal reason and non-pluralist cultures, his approach responds to postmodern thought and sensibilities more directly than any other contemporary Shi'i intellectual figure. Surūsh's Islamic postmodernism has hence paradigmatic relevance and reflects a thoroughly transitional phenomenon within contemporary Shi'i Islam, which has come to influence the whole spectrum of Islamic thought in Iran. In this respect, the traditionalist and modernist positions are continuously occupied with refining and modifying their own original arguments. While there are numerous refutations of Surūsh's ideas, those who have come to his defence rarely share the full implications of his arguments. Most discourses have, however, adopted his terminology (*intiẓār-i mā az dīn*, *fahm-i dīn*, *sharīʿat-i ṣāmit*, etc.) regardless of the

[6] In Bauman's (1992:28) words, it is precisely this sense of uncertainty and fallibility that is the constitutive element of the 'postmodern' habitat, a habitat in which there is "an incessant flow of reflexivity".

content of their critiques. His emphasis on tolerance, pluralism and democracy also has an impact on the articulation of the current socio-political reformism in Iran, which is centred on concepts such as rule of law, divergence and public participation.

Even if there thus is a huge gap between Surūsh and deconstructionism at the level of epistemology (primarily concerning the role of a priori), on the empirical level, the two currents join on many topics connected to text and interpretation. While 'postmodern' interpretations of Islam should not be confused with contemporary postmodern philosophy, there hence are some notable correspondences between the two, such as the emphasis on hermeneutical pluralism, epistemological relativism and scepticism. Since Islamic postmodernism, similar to deconstructionism, promises no alternative orthodoxy, it does not lend itself easily to political action.

Finally, Surūsh's definition of epistemology presupposes a 'subjectivisation' of the subject matter of religious belief, where theology no longer is aimed at providing law with rational principles and faith is a matter of the individual. It is obvious that herein lies the seeds of a form of 'interiorisation' of religion, which breaks with the ethical-legal and theological ideal of traditional Islam but has affinities with *ʿirfān* (gnosticism) in its reliance on the intuitive perception of the self. In his criticism of the increasing tendency in post-revolutionary Iran towards a nomocentric understanding of Islam, Surūsh expresses in fact his concern that religion should not be reduced to jurisprudence, as the depth of human existence cannot be penetrated by recourse to law. By confining transcendence to the noumenal world of the in-itself, he prohibits any confident perception of the transcendent, and his conception of religion represents the flight of faith from cognition in order to make room for faith.

Relegating religion to the domain of the individual consciousness without relevance to public policy, Surūsh's postmodernism attempts to erase all boundaries of divine law and undermine legitimacy in the sphere of metaphysics. By arguing that modernity provides the opportunity for cultivating the higher and more spiritual needs, he claims to offer a new unity of ethical, aesthetic and religious intuitions. In this respect, Surūsh's thought is genuinely concerned with a global postmodern worldview, which involves postmodern persons with a postmodern spirituality. As Lyotard argues in his *Postmodern condition*, the leading sciences and technologies have become increasingly concerned with language during the last thirty years (i.e. problems of communication and cybernetics) and it is also widely accepted that computerised knowledge has become the principle force of production over the last decades. Lyotard believes that the nature of knowledge cannot survive unchanged within this context of technological transformation. To make a comparison, out of the factors that contributed to the growing sense of relativity in the sixteenth century, the spread of printing was the most insidious.

Surūsh's idea of modernity, which makes the concept of the subject's autonomy central to philosophy, signifies the disintegration of sacred symbolism and the divorce between the world created by man and the world of divine creation. By replacing divine subject with man-as-subject, where God is identified and defined in terms of His absence and distance, Surūsh frees himself from the idea of a divine cosmos. The world is no more than a set of objects available for scientific research. He transforms the Islamic idea of a creature made in the image of its Creator (according to which knowledge is something within God) into a philosophy of the socially mediated subject veiled in the language of a postmodern mysticism. Surūsh's vindication of mysticism is interesting from the point of view that the tradition influencing Derrida's thought is sometimes said to be Jewish mysticism. Among others, Habermas (1987:144) explains Derrida's intellectual motivation by suggesting that the postmodern effort to overcome modern enlightenment disguises a desire to return to a premodern anti-enlightenment tradition. He writes that Derrida's stance "may have something to do with the fact that Derrida, all denials notwithstanding, remains close to Jewish mysticism".

While postmodernism signifies the return of the religious in the sense of a breakdown of the philosophical prohibition of religion, the 'return' of the religious is not a simple return, for its globality and its figures (tele-techno-media-scientific, capitalistic, and politico-economic) remain original and unprecedented. As far as postmodernism also involves a further anthropological re-immanentisation (the rights of man and of human life above all obligation towards absolute truth), it is not a simple return of the religious for it comports a radical destruction of the religious itself. But the question remains open as to whether Surūsh's recovery of truths and values from premodern gnostic thought carries the premises of modernity to its logical conclusions in his own Islamic and Iranian context, which is very different from the intellectual milieu where modernity originated. While his mysticism has more affinities with the epistemic conditions set by high modernity, where metaphysical realism has come to an end and epistemology has become very much more pluralised, pragmatic and free-floating, the dilemma before Surūsh remains to either persist within the boundaries of reason and to learn to coexist with the uncertainty of all truth and the partiality of knowledge, or to step outside the borders of reason and create some sense of meaning by conceiving and imagining the whole that always is arbitrary. This conflict involves the difference in outlook between the method of modern science, which by its empirical nature always is necessarily reductionist and man's search for meaning, which is unable to shun the questions of totality and ultimacy.

In the last analysis, Surūsh would have to confess that we have no epistemological or metaphysical grounds for knowing that existence is meaningful; there is no possible way in which the postulate of meaningfulness could be verified. He would also emphasise that the desire for meaning, the hope for the ultimate triumph of sense over nonsense, is not delusory. The phenomenon of postmodernism is after all a transition stage in human thought and speculation. It represents a creative conflict where the voices of the other and the different that were rendered minor by traditional and modern culture are being heard in all their particularity and uniqueness. But it is after all also a time of deep uncertainty, where the 'objectivist' epistemic structures of tradition and the rational foundation of modernity itself are called into question and is giving way to a culture of continuing scepticism and nihilistic doubt.

Surūsh's conviction that Islamic culture has to regain its mastery of the present and its vision for the future in order to renew its insights into the past is well-worth contemplation. From his perspective, Islamic thought does not make sense today without coming to terms with modernity; its contradictions, tensions, paradoxes and anomalies. The very effort of Surūsh and his colleagues is also itself an indication that Islam will not remain only a transitory phenomenon on Iran's road to modernity but rather will continue to use an alien stimulus as a lever for its own creative revitalisation, whereby modern Western intellectualism is becoming a genuinely Islamic legacy. The question mark for contemporary Islam is largely formulated in terms of how to reinstate Islam's historical continuity into the modern age; a continuity that has been temporarily disrupted by modernity. While Islamic philosophy and law is not historically speaking alien to Western philosophy and legal thinking, modernity is originally a European intervention, which was forced on Muslims. In contrast to the West, where modernity is identified with a specific development peculiar to this geographical part of the world (the discovery of the New World, the reformation, the renaissance, the scientific revolution, the enlightenment, the political revolutions, industrialisation, urbanisation, etc.), contemporary Islamic thought is not strictly post-traditional in the Western sense, since modernity did not occur via a critique of religion in the context of Islam but through the *adaptation* of tradition to modernity. In this respect, Islamic modernity will probably continue to develop philosophical discourses that are able to manage the intellectual challenges of modernity as well as its own philosophical tradition, or else it has to accept the secular ontology of modernity in Shilsean terms as an empty Islamic self (Shils 1981:288).[7]

From a philosophical perspective, modernity is in many respects facing a crisis of meaning and a dilemma over its contemporary objectives as a result of the deconstructionist removal of reason from its throne of universality. In the view of deconstructionism, the scientific worldview cultivated by

[7] An exchange program that has developed whereby several Shi'i scholars trained at the theological seminary in Qum undertook a doctoral program at McGill University is a positive indication in this respect.

scientists through centuries lacks the one thing that modern science always proclaimed to be the measure of objectivity, namely, empirical proof that its theories and conceptions are true. Since no universal schemes or metanarratives have any legitimacy, the main achievement of high modernity is to have advanced a set of claims about reason, man and history which it was able to dispose of as false. The most prominent development within the field of scientific methodology during the last two decades has been the emergence of probabilistic and pragmatist accounts of scientific method, which in many respects are different from classical inductivism but are anyhow its heir. By far the majority of contemporary methodologists are influenced by sociological and postmodern theories of science which declare the end of methodology as we have known it from Aristotle to Popper, Kuhn and Feyerabend. As for the justification of epistemology, the case is even more critical. For instance, Laudan (2000:172) and Rorty holds epistemology to be inadequate to the task of rationally reconstructing scientific choices since scientific theories can never be shown to be justified by true beliefs. This is also the case with Quine's pragmatism that casts serious doubt on whether there are statements of the kind termed analytical, which are devoid of any factual component.

The beginning of the twenty-first century seems hence marked by a deep intellectual discomfort about the ways in which Western thought has generally framed its ways of understanding the world. Despite the great success of the modern sciences, there is no epistemological theory that has uncontested possession of the field and the heyday of the theories of scientific method seems to be truly over. While nineteenth-century philosophical thought reflected an optimistic view about modernity and until very recently criticism had only been related to crises emerging in the transitions between stages of development that could be resolved as a new and higher stage of development is reached, more voices are growing suspicious of modernity and its prospects for the human future. Some even diagnose that the Western course of modernity has exhausted its dynamics for promoting human welfare (Li 1999). The question of how religion in general and Islam in particular can survive modernity and also, to quote Seyyed Hossein Nasr (1999:148), of "whether the modern world itself can survive for long while clinging those ideas such as secular humanism, rationalism, individualism, materialism and now more and more irrationalism that have defined modernity and laid the basis for postmodernism" is a question for both the East and the West, for both the believer and the disbeliever.

On the pillow of a jurist in despair,	سر بالین فقیهی نومید
I saw a pot brimful of questions	کوزه‌ای دیدم لبریز سؤال

(Suhrāb Sipihrī)

Bibliography

Primary sources in Persian

Banī-Ṣadr, A. (1978) *Iqtiṣād-i tauḥīdī* (Unitarian economy), Paris.

——— (1979) *Bayānīyah-yi jumhūrī-yi islamī* (The Manifesto of the Islamic republic), Tehran.

Bāzargān, M. (1943) *Muṭahharāt dar islām* (Personal cleanliness in Islam), Tehran.

——— (1974) *Bād wa bārān dar qur'ān* (Rain and wind in the Qur'an), Tehran.

——— (1981) *Tauḥīd, ṭabī'at, takāmul* (Monotheism, nature and development), Tehran.

——— (1995) *Āyā islām yak khaṭar-i jahānī ast?* (Is Islam a threat to the world?), Tehran.

——— (1998) *Ba'ṯat* (Prophetic mission), Tehran.

——— (1999a) *Mabāḥiṯ-i 'ilmī, ijtimā'ī, islāmī* (Scientific, social and Islamic discourses), Tehran.

——— (1999b) *Sair-i taḥawwul-i tadrījī dar qur'ān* (Discourse on gradual development in the Qur'an), Tehran.

Biyāzār-Shīrāzī, A. (1984) *Shinākht az dīdgāh-i qur'ān* (Comprehension from the viewpoint of Islam), Tehran.

Ghaffārī, Ḥ. (1990) *Naqd-i naẓarīyah-yi sharī'at-i ṣāmit* (A Critique of the theory of silent *sharī'at*), Tehran.

Hādawī Tihrānī, M. (1999) *Mabānī-yi kalāmī-yi ijtihād* (The Theological foundations of independent reasoning), Qum.

Ḥaqqpanāh, R. (1999) Naqsh-i pīshfahmhā dar fahm-i qur'ān (The Role of preunderstanding in the understanding of the Qur'an), *Andīshah-yi ḥauzah* (Seminary thought), vol. 4:4, Qum, pp. 135–160.

Himmatī, H. (1983) *'Ilm wa idrāk yā ti'ūrī-yi shinākht dar falsafah-yi islāmī* (Knowledge and perception. The Theory of comprehension in Islamic philosophy), Tehran.

Ḥusainī-Ṭabāṭabā'ī, M. (1998) Naqd-i naẓarīyah-yi plūrālīsm-i dīnī az manẓar-i darūn-i dīnī (A Critique of the theory of religious pluralism from the viewpoint of religious esoterism), *Kiyān* (Source), no. 41, pp. 10–13.

Ja'farī, S.'A.R. (1996) Pūyā'ī-yi fiqh wa naqsh-i zamān wa makān az dīdgāh-i imām Khumainī (The dynamism of jurisprudence and the role of time and place from the perspective of Khumainī), *Majmū'ah-yi āṯār-i kungrih-yi barrisī-yi mabānī-yi fiqhī-yi ḥaḍrat-i imām Khumainī. Naqsh-i zamān wa makān dar ijtihād* (Collection of papers from the congress on Khumainī's juristic foundations. The Role of time and place in independent reasoning), vol. 5:1, Tehran, pp. 89–108.

Jannātī, M.I. (1994) Ijtihād-i zan (Women's independent reasoning), *Kaihān-i farhangī* (Cultural world), vol. 10:9, Tehran, pp. 14–15.

Jawādī-Āmulī, 'A. (.n.y.) *Pīrāmūn-i waḥy wa rahbarī* (On revelation and leadership), Qum.

——— (1983) Hidāyat dar qur'ān (Guidance in the Qur'an), *Yādnāmah-yi 'allāmah Ṭabāṭabā'ī* (In commemoration of Ṭabāṭabā'ī), Tehran, pp. 225–340.

——— (1986) Falsafah, akhlāq, 'irfān-i naẓarī wa 'irfān-i 'amalī (Philosophy, morality, theoretical theosophy and practical theosophy), *Ṣaḥīfah* (The Leaf), vol. 30, Qum, pp. 3–9.

——— (1997a) *Zan dar ā'īnah-yi jalāl wa jamāl* (Women in the mirror of Majesty and Beauty), Qum.

——— (1997b) *Bunyān-i marṣūṣ-i imām Khumainī* (The Stable structure of Khumainī), Qum.

——— (1997c) *Falsafah-yi ḥuqūq-i bashar* (The Philosophy of human rights), Qum.

——— (1998a) *Sharī'at dar ā'īnah-yi ma'rifat* (Islamic law in the mirror of knowledge), Qum.

——— (1998b) *Wilāyat dar qur'ān* (Authority in the Qur'an), Tehran, 5th edition.
——— (1998c) Rābiṭah-yi falsafah wa 'irfān bā tafsīr wa ta'wīl-i qur'ān (The Relationship of philosophy and theosophy to Qur'anic exegesis), *Guftugū-yi dīn wa falsafah* (Dialogue on religion and philosophy), ed. M. J. Saḥibī, Tehran, pp. 261–287.
——— (1999a) Interview with the author, Qum, 14 November 1999.
——— (1999b) Rāhhā-yi hidāyat (Channels of guidance), *Pāsdār-i islām* (Guardian of Islam), no. 216, Qum, pp. 6–8.
Kadīwar, M. (1998) *Ḥukūmat-i walā'ī* (Governance of religious authority), Tehran.
Karīmī,'A. (1990) *Faqr-i tārīkhnigārī* (The Poverty of historiography), Qum.
Kasrawī, A. (n.y.) *Dar pīrāmūn-i rawān* (On the spirit), Tehran.
——— (1957) *Dar pīrāmūn-i khirad* (On wisdom), Tehran.
Khāmina'ī, S.'A. (1995) *Ḍāyi'ah-yi darguzasht-i haḍrat āyatullāh al-uẓmā Arākī* (Bereavement over the demise of Arākī), *Mishkāt* (The Nisch), vol. 45, Qum, pp. 199–205.
Khātamī, M. (1994) *Bīm-i mauj* (Fear of the wave), Tehran.
——— (1997a) *Az dunyā-yi shahr ta shahr-i dunyā: sayrī dar andīshah-yi sīyasī-yi gharb* (From the world of the city to the city of the world. An excursion on Western political thought), Tehran, 3rd edition.
——— (1997b) Ufuq-i nigāh-i tafakkur-i dīnī (Horizons of the perspective of religious thought), *Iṭṭilā'āt* (News), London, 16 August.
Khumainī, R. (n.y.) *Risālah-yi tauzīḥ al-masā'il* (Treatise on the explanation of the questions), Tehran.
——— (1982) *Ṣaḥīfah-yi nūr* (Book of light), vol. 1 (12 vols.), Tehran.
——— (1988) Nāmah-yi imām Khumainī dar tarīkh-i siwwum-i isfand 1367 (A Letter of Khumainī on the 22nd of February 1989), *Pāsdār-i islām* (Guardian of Islam), vol. 88, Qum.
——— (1997) *Wilāyat-i faqīh* (The Authority of the jurist), Qum, 6th edition.
Lārījānī, Ṣ. (1988) Naqdī bar maqālah-yi basṭ wa qabḍ-i ti'ūrīk-i sharī'at (A Critique of the article 'The Expansion and contraction of legal theory'), *Kaihān-i farhangī* (Cultural world), vol. 5:7, Tehran, pp. 9–14.
——— (1993) *Qabḍ wa basṭ dar qabḍ wa basṭ-i dīgar* (Contraction and expansion in another contraction and expansion), Tehran.
——— (1995) Ta'ammulātī dar ḥāshīyah-yi iqtirāḥ (Reflection at the edge of improvisation), *Naqd wa naẓar* (Critique and thought), vol. 1:2, Qum, pp. 45–60.
Madadpūr, M. (1998) Zindigī dar barzakh-i tamaddun-i gharbī wa tamaddun-i islāmī (Life in the margin between Western civilisation and Islamic civilisation), *Kitāb-i naqd* (Critique review), Tehran, pp. 139–153.
Mihrpūr, H. (1992) *Majmū'ah-yi naẓariyāt-i shaurāh-yi nigahbān* (A Collection of proposals of the guardian council), vol. 2, Tehran.
Miṣbāḥ-Yazdī, M.T. (1998) Ma'rifat-i dīnī (Religious knowledge), *Kitāb-i naqd* (Critique review), Tehran, pp. 2–29.
Mugāhī, 'A. (1997) *Aḥkām-i taqlīd wa ijtihād mutābiq bā fatāwā wa naẓarīyāt-i imām Khumainī* (Norms of emulation and independent reasoning according to the legal decrees and opinions of Khumainī), Tehran, 2nd edition.
Muḥaqqiq-Dāmād, M. (1998a) *Mabāḥiṯī az uṣūl-i fiqh* (A Discourse on legal theory), vol. 1, Tehran.
Muḥaqqiq-Dāmād, M. (1998b) *Mabāḥiṯī az uṣūl-i fiqh* (A Discourse on legal theory), vol. 3 Tehran.
Muḥaqqiq-Dāmād, M. (1999) *Mabāḥiṯī az uṣūl-i fiqh* (A Discourse on legal theory), vol. 3 Tehran.
Mujtahid-Shabistarī, M. (1985) Aṭrāf wa ab'ād-i gūnāgūn-i mas'alah-yi gharb (Various borders and dimensions of the subject of the West), *Kaihān-i farhangī* (Cultural world), vol. 1:6, Tehran, pp. 17–19.
——— (1986) Dā'irat al-ma'ārif-i islām wa mafāhīm-i asāsi-yi qur'ān (Encyclopaedia of Islam and fundamental understandings of the Qur'an), *Taḥqīqāt-i islāmī* (Islamic research), vol.1:1, Tehran, pp. 5–9.
——— (1992) Naqd-i tafakkur-i sunnatī dar kalām-i islām (Critique of traditional thought in Islamic theology), *Kiyān* (Source), no. 10, Tehran, pp. 8–11.
——— (1994a) Chirā bāyad andīshah-yi dīnī rā naqd kard? (Why must religious thinking be

critisised?), *Kiyān* (Source), no. 18, Tehran, pp. 16–21.
——— (1994b) Iqtirāḥ (Improvisation), *Naqd wa naẓar* (Critique and thought), vol. 1:1, Qum, pp. 15–106.
——— (1994c) Ta'wīl wa tafsīr dar islām (Exegesis in Islam), *Kaihān-i farhangī* (Cultural world), vol. 10:9, Tehran, pp. 12–13.
——— (1995a) Waḥy wa āzādī-yi ʿaqlī-yi insān (Revelation and rational freedom of man), *Kiyān* (Source), no. 25, Tehran, pp. 16–20.
——— (1995b) Farāyand-i fahm-i mutūn (The Procedure of understanding texts), *Naqd wa naẓar* (Critique and thought), vol. 1:3–4, Qum, pp. 42–61.
——— (1995c) Mutūn-i dīnī wa hirminūtīk (Religious texts and hermeneutics), *Naqd wa naẓar* (Critique and thought), vol:2, Qum, pp. 129–136.
——— (1995d) Mutūn-i dinī wa jahānbinī-yi naqd-i tārīkhī (Religious texts and the historical-critical worldview), *Kiyān* (Source), no. 26, Tehran, pp. 22–24.
——— (1997a) *Īmān wa āzādī* (Faith and freedom), Tehran.
——— (1997b) *Hirminūtīk, kitāb wa sunnat* (Hermeneutics, revelation and *sunnat*), Tehran.
——— (1998b) Jāmiʿīyat-i islām (Islamic multitude), *Īrān*, Tehran, 30 september.
——— (1999a) Dīn, mudārā wa khushūnat (Religion, moderateness and violence), *Kiyān* (Source), no. 45, Tehran, pp. 6–19.
——— (1999b) Bastar-i maʿnawī wa ʿaqlā'ī-yi ʿilm-i fiqh (The Spiritual and rational headstock of jurisprudence), *Kiyān* (Source), no. 46, Tehran, pp. 5–13.
——— (1999c) Falsafah-yi fiqh (Philosophy of jurisprudence), *Guftugū-yi falsafah-yi fiqh*, (Dialogue on philosophy of jurisprudence), Qum, pp 53–99.
——— (1999d) Īmān wa zindigī dar dunyā-yi nau (Faith and life in the modern world), *Īrān*, Tehran, 12 October.
——— (1999e) Waḥy ẓarfīyat-i tafsīr-i pāyān-nāpazīr dārad (Revelation has the capacity of infinite interpretation), *Īrān*, Tehran, 13 October.
——— (2000) *Naqdī bar qarā'at-i rasmī az dīn* (Critique of the official reading of religion), Tehran.
——— (2001b) Correspondence with the author, 24 April 2001.
——— (2001a) Guftugū bā Muḥammad Mujtahid-Shabistarī dar bārah-yi naqdī bar qarā'at-i rasmī az dīn (A Conversation with Mujtahid-Shabistarī on the the book 'Critique of the official reading of religion'), *Īrān*, 5, 7–8, 10 and 15 March, Tehran.
Muṭahharī, M. (n.y.) *Nihḍathā-yi islāmī dar ṣad-sālah-yi akhīr* (Islamic movements of the last century), Tehran.
——— (1979) *Bīst guftār* (Twenty speeches), Qum.
——— (1982) *Barrisī-yi fiqhī-yi mas'alah-yi bīmah* (Juristic analysis of the question of insurance), Tehran.
——— (1992) *Mas'alah-yi shinākht* (The Question of conception), Tehran, 6th edition.
——— (1997) *Dah guftār* (Ten speeches), Tehran, 10th edition.
——— (1998) *Āshinā'ī bā qur'ān* (Acquaintance with the Qur'an), vol. 6 vol., Tehran, 13th edition.
——— (1998b) *Jahānbīnī-yi tauḥīd* (The Unitarian worldview), Tehran, 12th edition.
——— (1998c) *Islām wa muqtaḍīyāt-i zamān* (Islam and the exigencies of time), vol. 1, Tehran, 13th edition.
——— (1998d) *Naqdī bar marksīsm* (A Critique of Marxism), Tehran, 1998 (2nd edition).
——— (1998e) *Falsafah-yi tārīkh* (Philosophy of history), 2 vols., Tehran, 9th edition.
——— (1999) *Āshinā'ī bā ʿulūm-i islāmī. Uṣūl-i fiqh wa fiqh* (Acquaintance with the Islamic sciences. Legal theory and jurisprudence), Tehran, 21st edition.
Nasr, S.H. (1980) *Naẓar-i mutafakkirān-i islāmī darbārah-yi tabīʿat* (The Perspective of Islamic thinkers on nature), Tehran, 3rd edition.
——— (1992) *Maʿārif-i islāmī dar jahān-i muʿāṣir* (Islamic science in the contemporary world), Tehran.
Paimān, Ḥ. (1997) *Kilīd-i fahm-i qur'ān* (Key to the understanding of the Qur'an), 4 parts, Tehran, 2nd edition.
——— (1998) *Andīshah-yi siyāsī nazd-i mutafakkirān-i musalmān* (Political thought of Islamic thinkers), Tehran.
——— (1999a) *Barrisī wa naqd-i mabānī-yi andīshah-yi siyāsī-yi shīʿah* (Analysis and

critique of the foundation of Shi'i political thought), 4 parts, Tehran.
——— (1999b) *Farākhān-i jāwīdānih-yi āzādī* (The Endless profusion of freedom), Tehran.
Rīkhtagarī, M.R. (1999) *Hirminūtīk. Uṣūl wa mabānī-yi ʿilm-i tafsīr* (Hermeneutics. The principles and foundations of exegesis), Tehran.
Ṣāliḥpūr, J. (1993) Naqdī bar naẓarīyah-yi farbitar az īdiʾūlūzhī (A Critique of the theory 'Loftier than ideology'), *Kiyān* (Source), no. 15, Tehran, pp. 47–49.
Sharīʿatī, ʿA. (1968) *Ummat wa imāmat* (Community and *imāmat*), Tehran.
——— (1978) *Bā makātibahhā-yi āshinā* (Familiar correspondance), Tehran.
——— (1996a) *Islām-shināsī* (Islamic studies), vol. 1, Tehran, 3rd edition.
——— (1996b) *Islām-shināsī* (Islamic studies), vol. 2, Tehran, 5th edition.
——— (1996c) *Islām-shināsī* (Islamic studies), vol. 3, Tehran, 5th edition.
——— (1998a) *Rawish-i shinākht-i islām* (The Way of comprehending Islam), Tehran, 3rd edition.
——— (1998b) *Bāzgasht* (Return), Tehran, 6th edition.
——— (1998c) *Maḏhab ʿalaih-i maḏhab* (School against school), Tehran.
——— (1998d) *Taḥlīlī az manāsik-i ḥajj* (Analysis of the rites of pilgrimage), Tehran, 10th edition.
——— (1999a) *Tashayyuʿ-i ʿalawī wa tashayyuʿ-i ṣafawī* (ʿAlīd Shi'ism and Ṣafawī Shi'ism), Tehran, 2nd edition.
——— (1999b) *Shīʿah* (Shi'ism), Tehran, 7th edition.
——— (1999c) *Chih bāyad kard?* (What must be done?), Tehran, 4th edition.
Subḥānī, J. (1988) Taḥlīlī az basṭ wa qabḍ-i tiʾūrīk-i sharīʿat yā naẓarīyah-yi takāmul-i maʿrifat-i dīnī (An Analysis of the expansion and contraction of legal theory or the theory of the development of religious thought), *Kaihān-i farhangī* (Cultural world), vol. 5:9, Tehran, pp. 10–15.
Surūsh, ʿA. (1983) *Dānish wa arzish* (Knowledge and value), Tehran, 8th edition.
——— (1991) Dīndārī wa khirad-warzī (Religiosity and discretion), *Kiyān* (Source), no. 12, Tehran, pp. 8–14.
——— (1992) *Auṣāf-i pārsāyān* (Attributes of the pious), Tehran.
——— (1994a) *Īdiʾūlūzhī-yi shaiṭānī* (Satanic ideology), Tehran, 7th edition.
——— (1994b) *Tafarruj-i ṣunʿ. Gūftārhāʾī dar akhlāq wa ṣanʿat wa ʿilm-i insānī* (Excursion of creation. Discourses on morality, technology and humanities), Tehran, 3rd edition.
——— (1994c) Akhlāq-i khudāyān. Akhlāq-i bartar wujūd nadārad (Morality of the gods. There exists no higher morality), *Kiyan* (Source), no. 18, Tehran, pp. 22–32.
——— (1994d) *Ḥikmat wa maʿīshat: sharḥ-nāmah-yi imām ʿAlī bih imām Ḥasan* (Wisdom and sustenance), vol. 1, Tehran.
——— (1995a) Maʿīshat wa faḍliyat (Sustenance and virtue), *Kiyan* (Source), no. 25, Tehran, pp. 2–11.
——— (1996a) *Farbihtar az īdiʾūlūzhī* (Loftier than ideology), Tehran, 4th edition.
——— (1996b) *ʿIlm chī-st? Falsafah chī-st?* (What is science? What is philosophy?), Tehran, 12th edition.
——— (1996c) *Qabḍ wa basṭ-i tiʾūrīk-i sharīʿat. Naẓarīyah-yi takāmul-i dīnī* (The Contraction and expansion of legal theory. Theory of the development of religious thought), Tehran, 5th edition.
——— (1996d) *Qiṣṣah-yi arbāb-i maʿrifat* (Story of wise-men), Tehran, 3rd edition.
——— (1996e) Īdiʾūlūzhī wa dīn-i dunyawī (Ideology and worldly religion), *Kiyān* (Source), no. 31, Tehran.
——— (1996f) Dīn wa āzādī (Religion and freedom), *Kiyān* (Source), no. 33, Tehran, pp. 42–51.
——— (1996g) *Ḥadīṯ-i bandigī wa dilburdagī* (Story of love and piety), Tehran.
——— (1997a) *Mudārā wa mudīrīyat* (Tolerance and governance), Tehran.
——— (1997b) Sabukbārī wa wiṣāl (Disencumbrance and union), *Kiyān* (Source), no. 35, Tehran, pp. 4–10.
——— (1997c) *Ḥikmat wa maʿīshat: sharḥnāmah-yi imām ʿAlī bih imām Ḥasan* (Wisdom and sustenance), vol. 2, Tehran.
——— (1998a) *Islām-i ḥaqīqat wa islām-i huwwīyat* (Islam of truth and Islam of identity), Two volume audio-cassettes taped by Muʿassasah-yi ṣirāṭ (Foundation of the path), Tehran.

——— (1999a) *Basṭ-i tajrubah-yi nabawī* (Expansion of prophetic experience), Tehran, 2nd edition.
——— (1999b) *Nahād-i nā-ārām-i jahān* (The Restless nature of the universe), Tehran, 3rd edition.
——— (1999c) *Rāzdānī wa raushanfikrī wa dīndārī* (Secret-knowing, intellectualism and religious conviction), Tehran, 4th edition.
——— (1999d) *Ṣirāṭhā-yi mustaqīm* (Straight paths), Tehran, 2nd edition.
——— (1999e) Baʿṯat wa buḥrān-i huwwīyat (Prophetic mission and identity crisis), *Kiyān* (Source), no. 49, Tehran, pp. 4–11.
——— (1999f) Diyānat, mudārā wa madanīyat (Piety, moderateness and civilisation), *Kiyān* (Source), no. 45, Tehran, pp. 20–37.
——— (1999g) Rahā'ī az yaqīn wa yaqīn bih rahā'ī (Deliverance from certainty and certainty of deliverance), *Kiyān* (Source), no. 48, Tehran, pp. 2–9.
——— (1999h) Wilāyat-i bāṭinī wa wilāyat-i siyāsī (Private authority and and political authority), *Kiyān* (Source), no. 44, Tehran, pp. 10–20.
——— (1999i) Fiqh dar tarāzū: ṭarḥ-i chand pursish az maḥḍar-i haḍrat-i āyatullāh Muntaẓirī (Jurisprudence on a pair of scales. A sketch of some questions from Muntaẓirī), *Kiyān* (Source), no. 46, Tehran, pp. 14–21.
——— (1999j) Dū dahah-yi talāsh barāh-yi istiqrār-i dīn dar jāmʿah (Two decades of effort to instigate religion in society), *Nishāṭ* (Happiness), no. 46, Tehran, 19 May.
——— (1999k) Interview with the author, Tehran, 26 October.
——— (1999l) Basṭ-i basṭ-i tajrubah-yi nabawī (Expansion of the expansion of prophetic experience), *Kiyān* (Source), no. 47, Tehran, pp. 4–16.
——— (1999m) Khiradwarzī kilīd-i shakhṣiyat-i Muṭahharī (Discretion is the key for understanding the personality of Muṭahharī), *Nishāṭ* (Happiness), Tehran, 3 May.
——— (1999n) Dīn-dārī wa khirad-warzī-yi Muṭahharī (The Religiosity and discretion of Muṭahharī), *Nishāṭ* (Happiness), Tehran, 5 May.
——— (1999o) Qabḍ wa basṭ-i ḥuqūq-i zanān (The Contraction and expansion of women's rights), *Zanān* (Women), no. 59, Tehran, pp. 32–39.
——— (1999p) Mudārā wa muḥabbat-i dīndārī rā bāyad dar bāṭin-i dīn just (Tolerance and love in spiritual matters must be sought in the inner dimension of religion), *Īrān*, Tehran, 24 October.
——— (2000a) *Qumār-i ʿāshiqān. Shams wa Maulānā* (Gambling of lovers. Shams and Rūmī), Teheran.
——— (2000b) Tausʿah-yi ʿilm, tausʿah-yi siyāsī (Scientific development and political development), *Kiyān* (Source), no. 54, Tehran, pp. 32–38.
——— (2000c) Īmān wa umīd (Faith and trust), *Kiyān* (Source), no. 52, Tehran, pp. 48–58.
——— (2000d) Raushanfikrī-yi dīnī dīn-rā dilrubā, khirad-pasand wa girih-gushā mikhāhad (Religious thinking involves heart-ravishing, intellectual and instructive religion), *Īrān*, Tehran, 23 August.
——— (2001) Dīn, andīshah wa iṣlāḥāt (Religion, thought and reforms), *Jāmʿah-yi madanī* (Civil society), Tehran, 11 February, pp. 5–6.
Ṭabāṭabā'ī, M.Ḥ. (n.y.) *Qur'ān dar islām* (Qur'an in Islam), Tehran.
——— (1976) *Barrisīhhā-yi islāmī* (Islamic discourses), Qum.
——— (1984) *Shīʿah dar islām* (Shi'ism in Islam), Tehran.
——— (1990) *Islām wa iḥtiyājāt-i wāqiʿī-yi har ʿasr* (Islam and the exigencies of every age), Tehran.
——— (1992) *Shīʿah. Majmūʿah-yi muẓākirāt bā prufisur Hinrī Kurban* (Shi'ism. A collection of conversations with Henry Corbin), Tehran, 3rd edition.
——— (1999) *Uṣūl-i falsafah wa rawish-i ri'ālīsm* (The Principles of philosophy and the method of realism), vol. 1, Tehran.
Ṭāhirī, S.Ṣ. (1998) Hirminūtīk, kitāb wa sunnat (Hermeneutics, revelation and *sunnat*), *Kitāb-i naqd* (Critique review), Tehran, pp. 162–187.
Ṭāliqānī, M. (1965) *Islām wa mālikīyat* (Islam and ownership), Tehran.
——— (1979) *Partau'ī az qur'ān* (A ray of the Qur'an), vol. 1, Tehran.
Taqī-Faʿʿālī, M. (1999) *Darāmadī bar maʿrifat-shināsī-yi dīnī wa muʿāṣir* (An Introduction to religious and contemporary epistemology), Qum.

——— (1998) Malāk-i maʿnā-dārī (Criterions of meaning), *Kitab-i naqd* (Critique review), Qum, pp. 117–138.
Taqī-Jaʿfarī, M. (1998) *Rasāʾil-i fiqhī* (Juristic treatise), Tehran.
Yaṯribī (1998) Nigāhi bih naẓarīyah-yi tafsīr-i mutūn-i islāmī (A Glance at the theory of interpreting Islamic texts), *Kitāb-i naqd* (Critique review), Tehran, pp. 199–219.
Yazdī, I. (1998) Interview with the author, Uppsala, 14 October.
Yūsufī-Ishkiwarī, Ḥ. (1996) ʿAqlānīyat-i islāmī wa jaʿl-i qudrat (Islamic rationality and forgery of power), *Kiyān* (Source), no. 31, Tehran, pp. 30–33.
——— (1997a) *Bāzkhānī-yi qiṣṣah-yi khilqat* (Retelling the story of creation), Tehran.
——— (1997b) Interview with the author, Stockholm, 2 December.
——— (1998a) *Nau-girāʾī-yi dīnī. Naqd wa barrisī-yi junbishhā-yi islāmī-yi muʿāṣir* (Religious modernism. Critique and analysis of contemporary Islamic movements), Tehran.
——— (1998b) Sharīʿatī wa naqqādī-yi sunnat (Sharīʿatī and the critique of tradition), *Āftāb-i kawīr. Wīzhah-nāmah-yi simīnār-i barrisī-yi andīshahhā wa āṯār-i duktur ʿAlī Sharīʿatī* (Desert's sun. Special edition of the seminar on the the analysis of Sharīʿatī's thoughts and work), Tehran, pp. 10–18.
——— (1999a) Fiqh, mudarnītah wa sikūlarīzasīyūn (Jurisprudence, modernity and secularisation), *Nishāṭ* (Happiness), Tehran, 4 May.
——— (1999b) Marjaʿīyat wa ḥukūmat dar justujū-yi nisbatī-yi nau (Religious authority and governance in search of a new relationship), *Nishāṭ* (Happiness), Tehran, 3rd May.
——— (1999c) Sharīʿatī-Muṭahharī. Dū nigāh bih rūḥānīyat (Sharīʿatī and Muṭahharī. Two views on the religious class), *Nishāṭ* (Happiness), Tehran, 5 May.
——— (2000) *Khirad dar ḍiyāfat-i dīn* (Wisdom at the reception of religion), Tehran.
——— (2001) *Sharīʿatī wa naqd-i sunnat* (Sharīʿatī and the critique of tradition), Tehran.

Secondary sources in Persian

ʿArablū, M.J. (1983) *Farhang-i iṣṭilāḥāt-i fiqh-i islāmī dar bāb-i muʿāmalāt* (Lexicon of terms of Islamic jurisprudence concerning social transactions), Tehran.
Dikhudā, ʿA.A. (1993) Ijtihād (Independent reasoning), *Lughat-nāmah* (Lexicon), eds. M. Muʾīn and J. Shahīdī, Tehran.
Gurjī, A. (1996) *Maqālāt-i ḥuqūqī* (Legal articles), vol. 2, Tehran.
——— (1994) Ijtihād (Independent reasoning), *Dāʾirat al-maʿārif-i buzurg-i islāmī* (Great Islamic encyclopaedia), Tehran, vol. 6, pp. 599–611.
Hujwīrī, ʿA. (1926) *Kitāb-i kashf al-maḥjūb* (The Book of unveiling the hidden), Leningrad.
Jaʿfariyān, R. (1997) *Tarīkh-i tashayyuʿ dar īrān* (History of Shi'ism in Iran), vol. 2, Qum.
Jāmī, ʿA. (1958) *Nafaḥāt al-uns* (Fragrances of friendliness), ed. Tauḥīdīpūr, Tehran.
Kāẓimī-Mūsāwī, A. (1990) Daurahhā-yi tarīkhī-yi tadwīn wa taḥawwul-i fiqh-i shīʿah (The Historical periods of the compilation and development of Shi'i jurisprudence), *Taḥqīqāt-i islāmī* (Islamic research), vol. 5:1–2, Tehran, pp. 5–36.
Kirmānī, M. (1979) *Tārīkh-i bīdārī-yi īrāniyān* (History of the awakening of Iranians), Tehran.
Rūmī, J. (1992) *Dīwān-i shams* (Collection of lyrics), ed. B. Furūzanfarr, Tehran.
——— (1996) *Maṯnawī-yi maʿnawī* (Spiritual couplet poem), ed. ʿA. Surūsh, Tehran.
Shahīdī, J. (1983) *Az dīrūz tā imrūz. Majmūʿah-yi maqālihhā wa safarnāmahhā* (From yesterday until today. A Collection of articles and travel books), Tehran.
Yaʿqūbī, A. (1997) Nau-āwārī-yi Nāʾinī dar fiqh (Nāʾinī's innovation in jurisprudence), *Ḥauzah* (Seminary), vol. 76–77, Qum.

Primary sources in European languages

al-Farabi, A. (1949) *Idées des habitants de la cité vertueuse*, trans. R.P. Janssen, Cairo.
Farabi, A. (1981) *Al-Farabi's commentary and short treatise on Aristotle's 'De Interpretatione'*, trans. F. W. Zimmerman, Oxford.

Khomeini, R. (1981) Lectures on surat al-fatiha, *Islam and revolution*, trans. H. Algar, Berkeley, pp. 365–436.
Musaddiq, M. (1914) *Le Testament en droit musulman (Secte Chyite). Preécédé d'une introduction sur les sources du droite musulman*, Paris.
Naraqi, E. (1976) Iran's culture and the present-day world, *Sophia perennis*, vol. 2:2, Tehran, pp. 90–104.
Nasr, S.H. (1966) The Immutable principles of Islam and Western education, *The Muslim world*, vol. 56:1, Hartford, pp. 4–9.
——— (1981) *Islamic life and thought*, London.
——— (1988) *Ideals and realities of Islam*, London.
——— (1999) Islam at the dawn of the new Christian millennium, *Encounters*, 5:2, London, pp. 129–154.
Soroush, A. (1998) The Evolution and devolution of religious knowledge, *Liberal Islam. A Sourcebook*, ed. C. Kurzman, New York, pp. 244–251.
——— (2000) *Reason, Freedom, and Democracy in Islam. Essential Writings of Abdolkarim Soroush*, eds. M. Sadri and A. Sadri, Oxford.

Secondary sources in European languages

Abrahamian, E. (1983) *Iran between two revolutions*, Princeton.
Abrahamov, B. (1996) *Antropomorhism and interpretation of the Qur'ān in the theology of al-Qāsim ibn Ibrahīm. Kītāb al-mustarshīd*, Leiden.
Ahmed, A. (1992) *Postmodernism and Islam*, London.
Akhavi, S. (1980) *Religion and politics in contemporary Iran*, New York.
——— (1983a) The Ideology and praxis of Shi'ism in the Iranian revolution, *Comparative studies in society and history*, vol. 25:1, pp. 195–221.
——— (1983b) Shari'ati's social thought, *Religion and politics in Iran: Shi'ism from quietism to revolution*, ed. N. Keddie, New Haven, pp. 125–144.
Akhtar, W. (1987) Introduction to imāmiyyah scholars: shaykh al-ṭā'ifah al-Ṭūsī: life and works, *al-Tawḥīd*, vol. 4:2, Tehran, pp. 126–167.
Algar, H. (1990) Imam Musa al-Kazim and Sufi tradition, *Islamic culture*, Hyderabad, vol. 64, pp. 1–14.
——— (1991) Religious forces in eighteenth- and nineteenth-century Iran, *Cambridge history* of Iran, vol. 7, Cambridge, pp. 705–731.
Amanat, A. (1988) In between the madrasa and the marketplace: the designation of clerical leadership in modern Shi'ism, *Authority and political culture in Shi'ism*, ed. S.A. Arjomand, New York, pp. 98 –132.
Amir-Moezzi, M.A. (1994) *The Divine guide in early Shi'ism. The Sources of esotericism in Islam*, trans. D. Streight, New York.
Amirpur, K. (1996) Ein iranischer Luther? –'Abdolkarîm Sorûsh's Kritik an der schiitischen Geistlichkeit, *Orient*, vol. 37:3–4, Opladen, pp. 465–481.
Arberry, A.J. (1957) *Revelation and reason in Islam*, London.
Ariew, R. (1999) *Descartes and the last scholastics*, Ithaca.
Aristotle (1949) *Aristotle's Prior and Posterior analytics*, ed. W.D. Ross, London.
Arjomand, K.A. (1996) Die Schia-bibliothek des Orientalischen seminars der Universität zu Köln, *Zeitschrift der Deutschen morgenländischen gesellschaft*, vol. 146:1, pp. 173–174.
Arjomand, K.A. and Falaturi, A. (1996) *Katalog der bibliothek des schiitischen schrifttums im orientalischen seminar der universität zu Köln*, München.
Arjomand, S.A. (1981) The Shi'ite hierocracy and the state in pre-modern Iran: 1785–1890, *Archives Européenes de sociologie*, vol. 22, Paris, pp. 40–78.
——— (1981b) The 'Ulama's traditionalist opposition to parliamentarism: 1907–1909, *Middle Eastern studies*, vol. 17:2. pp. 174–190.
——— (1984) Traditionalism in twentieth-century Iran, *From Nationalism to revolutionary Islam*, ed. S.A. Arjomand, London, pp. 195–232.
——— (1988) *The turban for the crown. The Islamic revolution in Iran*, New York.

——— (1997) Imam absconditus and the beginnings of a theology of occultation: Imami Shi'ism circa 280–90 A.H./900 A.D., *Journal of the American Oriental society*, vol. 117:1, pp. 1–12.
Arnaldez, R. (1991) Mantik, *Encyclopaedia of Islam*, Leiden, pp. 442–452.
Attas, M.N. (1985) Islam, secularism and the philosophy of the future, London.
Ayer, A.J. (1956) The Problem of knowledge, London.
Ayoub, M. (1988) The Speaking Qur'ān and the silent Qur'ān: a study of the principles and development of Imāmī Shī'ī tafsīr, *Approaches to the history of the interpretations of the Qur'ān*, ed. A. Rippin, Oxford.
——— (1990) Law and grace in Islam: Sufi attitudes toward the sharī'a, *Religion and law*, eds. E.B. Firmage and J.W. Welch, Winona Lake, pp. 221–229.
Bakar, O. (1997) Science, *History of Islamic philosophy*, vol. 2, eds. S.H. Nasr and O. Leaman, Tehran, pp. 926–946.
Bartley, W.W. (1988) Philosophy of biology versus philosophy of physics, *Evolutionary epistemology, rationality, and the sociology of knowledge*, ed. G. Radnitzky and A. Musgrave, Cambridge, pp. 7–45.
Bar-Asher, M.M. (1999) *Scripture and exegesis in early Imami Shiism*, Leiden.
Bauman, Z. 1992. *Intimations of postmodernity*, London.
Bayat, M. (1982) *Mysticism and dissent: socioreligious thought in Qajar Iran*, Syracuse.
Bello, I.A. (1989) *The Medieval Islamic controversy between philosophy and orthodoxy*, Leiden.
Berman, M. (1988) *All that is solid melts into air: the experience of modernity*, New York.
Binder, L. (1965) Proofs of Islam: religion and politics in Iran, *Arabic and Islamic studies in honour of H.A.R. Gibb*, ed. G. Makdisi, Leiden, pp. 118–140.
Bird, G. (1982) Kant's transcendent idealism, *Idealism– Past and present*, ed. G. Vesey, Cambridge, pp. 71–92.
Blancy, A. (1973) Structuralisme et hermeneutique, *Etudes théologiques et religieues*, vol. 48, Paris, pp. 49–57.
Boroujerdi, M. (1996) *Iranian intellectuals and the West. The Tormented triumph of nativism*, New York.
——— (1997) Iranian Islam and the Faustian bargain of Western modernity, *Journal of peace research*, vol. 34:1, London, pp. 1–6.
Brockelmann, C. (1949) *Geschichte der arabischen litteratur*, Suppl. I, Leiden.
Brown, N.J. (1997) Shari'a and state in the modern Muslim Middle East, *International journal of Middle East studies*, vol. 29, Cambridge, pp. 359–376.
Bruce, S. (1996) *Religion in the modern world: from cathedrals to cults*, Oxford.
Brueggemann, W. (1993) *Texts under negotiation. The Bible and postmodern imagination*, Minneapolis.
Brunschvig, R. (1955) Perspectives, *Unity and variety in Muslim civilization*, ed. G. von Grunebaum, Chicago, pp. 47–62.
——— (1968) Les Uṣūl al-fiqh imāmites a leur stade ancien (Xe et Xie siècles), *Le Shi'isme imamite*, Paris, pp. 201–213.
——— (1976) *Études islamologie*, Paris.
Burton, J. (1977) *The Collection of the Quran*, Cambridge.
Böwering, G. (1980) *The Mystical Vision of existence in classical Islam. The Qur'ānic hermeneutics of the Ṣūfī Sahl al-Tustarī (d. 283/896)*, Berlin.
——— (1998) 'Erfān, *Encyclopaedia Iranica*, vol. 8, Costa Mesa, pp. 551–554.
Calder, N. (1980) *The Structures of authority in Imami Shi'i jurisprudence*, Phd, London.
——— (1982) Accommodation and revolution in Imami Shi'i jurisprudence: Khumayni and the classical tradition, *Middle Eastern Studies*, vol. 18, London, pp. 3–20.
——— (1989) Doubt and pregorative: the emergence of an Imami Shi'i theory of ijtihād, *Studia Islamica*, vol. 70, Paris, pp.57–77.
——— (1993) *Studies in early Muslim jurisprudence*, Oxford.
——— (1996) Law, *Routledge history of world philosophies*, vol. 2, eds. S.H.Nasr and O. Leaman, London, pp. 979–998.
——— (1997) History and nostalgia: reflections on John Wansbrough's The Sectarian milieu, *Method and theory in the study of religion*, vol. 9:1, Berlin, pp. 47–73.

——— (1998) Taklīd, *Encyclopaedia of Islam*, vol. 10, pp. 137–138.
Calmard, J. (1993) Mollā, *Encyclopeadia of Islam*, vol. 7, 1993, Leiden, 221–225.
Carter, M.G. (1997) Analogical and syllogistic reasoning in grammar and law, *Islam. Essays on scripture, thought and society*, Leiden, pp. 104–112.
Charnay, J. (1967) L'Efflorescence théologico-juridique. Fonction de l'ikhtilāf en méthodologie juridique arabe, *L'Ambivalance dans la culture Arabe*, Paris, pp. 191–231.
Chehabi, H.E. (1990) *Iranian politics and religious modernism. The liberation movement of Iran under the shah and Khomeini*, London.
Chittick, W.C. (1987) ʿAql, *Encyclopaedia Iranica*, vol. 2, London, pp. 195–198.
——— (1992) Spectrums of Islamic thought: Saʿīd al-Dīn Farghānī, *The Legacy of medieval Persian Sufism*, ed. L. Lewinsohn, London, pp. 203–218.
Cole, J.R. (1983) Imami jurisprudence and the role of the ulama: Mortaza Ansari on emulating the supreme exemplar, *Religion and politics in Iran: Shi'ism from quietism to revolution*, ed. N.Keddie, New Haven, pp. 33–46.
Coolingwood, R.G. (1948) *The Idea of history*, Oxford.
Cooper, D.E. (1999) *Epistemology. The Classical readings*, Oxford.
Cooper, J. (1988) 'Allama al-Hilli on the imamate and ijtihad, trans. J. Cooper, *Authority and political culture in Shi'ism*, ed. S.A. Arjomand, New York, pp. 240–249.
——— (1989) *The Commentary on the Qur'an by Abu Ja'far Muhammad b. Jari al-Tabari*, Oxford.
Cooper, J. (1998) The Limits of the sacred. The Epistemology of 'Abd al-Karim Soroush, *Islam and modernity*, ed. J. Cooper, London, pp. 38–56.
Corbin, H. (1993) *History of Islamic philosophy*, trans. L. Sherrard, London.
——— (1994) *The Man of light in Iranian Sufism*, New York.
Coulson, N.J. (1969) *Conflict and tensions in Islamic jurisprudence*, Chicago.
——— (1977) Law and religion in contemporary Islam, *Hastings law journal*, vol. 29, pp. 1447–1457.
——— (1997) *A History of Islamic law*, Edinburgh.
Dabashi, H. (1988) Two Clerical tracts on constitutionalism, *Authority and political culture in Shi'ism*, ed. S.A. Arjomand, New York, pp.334–370.
——— (1993) *Theology of discontent: the ideological foundation of the Islamic revolution in Iran*, New York.
Derrida, J. (1978) *Writing and difference*, trans. A. Bass, Chicago.
——— (1983) The Principle of reason: the universality of in the eyes of the pupils, *Diacritics*, vol. 13, pp. 3–27.
——— (1986) But beyond… (Open letter to Anne McCliotock and Rob Nixon), *Critical inquiry*, no. 13, Chicago, pp. 155–170.
——— (1988) *Limited Inc*, Evanston.
——— (1987) *Psyché. Invention de l'autre*, Paris.
——— (1998a) Faith and knowledge, *Religion*, eds. J. Derrida and G. Vattimo, Cambridge, pp. 1–78.
——— (1998b) *Of Grammatology*, trans. G. C. Spivak, Baltimore and London.
Descartes, R. (1996) *Meditations on first philosophy with selections from The Objections and replies*, Cambridge.
Dodd, C.H. (1935) *The Bible and the Greeks*, London.
Donaldson, D.M. (1933) *The Shiite religion*, London.
Eisenstadt, S.N. (1983) *Tradition, change and modernity*, Malabar.
Eliade, M. (1969) *The Quest. History and meaning in religion*, Chicago.
Enayat, H. (1991) *Modern Islamic political thought*, Austin.
Ezzati, A. (1976) *An Introduction to Shi'i law and jurisprudence. With an emphasis on the authority of human reason as a source of law according to Shi'i law*, Lahore.
Feuerbach, L. (1957) *The Essence of Christianity*, trans. M. Evans, New York.
Fischer, M.J. (1980a) Becoming mollah: reflections on Iranian clerics in a revolutionary age, *Iranian Studies*, vol. 13, pp. 83–117.
——— (1980b) *Iran. From dispute to revolution*, Cambridge.
Fischer, M.J. and Abedi, M. (1990) *Debating Muslims*, London.
Floor, W. (1992) Change and development in the judicial system of Qajar Iran (1800–1925),

Qajar Iran, ed. E. Bosworth, Costa Mesa, pp. 113–147.
Foucault, M. (1970) *The Order of things*, London.
——— (1972) *The Archeology of knowledge*, trans. A.M. Sheridan, London.
——— (1977) *Language, counter-memory, practice: selected essays and interviews*, trans. D.F. Bouchard and S. Simon, New York.
——— (1979) *Discipline and punish: the birth of the prison*, trans. A.M. Sheridan, New York.
Friedrich, C.J. (1958) *The Philosophy of law in historical perspective*, Chicago.
Fyzee, A.A.A. (1943) The Creed of Ibn Babawayhi, *Journal of the university of Bombay*, vol. 12:2, Bombay, pp. 70–86.
———Fyzee, A.A.A. (1993) *Outlines of Muhammadan law*, New Dehli.
Gadamer, H. (1976) *Philosophical hermeneutics*, trans. D.E. Linge, Berkeley.
——— (1989) *Truth and method*, trans. J. Weinsheimer and D.G. Marshall, New York.
Garber, G. (1992) *Descartes' metaphysical physics*, Chicago.
Garoussian, V. (1974) *The Ulema and secularisation in contemporary Iran*, Phd, Southern Illinois university.
Genequand, C. (1997) Metaphysics, *History of Islamic philosophy*, vol. 2, eds. S.H. Nasr and O. Leaman, Tehran, 1997, pp. 783–801.
Gibb, H.A.R. (1963) *Mohammadanism. An Historical survey*, London.
——— (1975) *Modern trends in Islam*, New York.
Gibb, H.A.R. and Kramers, J.H. (1953) Shari'a, *Shorter encyclopaedia of Islam*, Ithaca, pp. 624–629.
Ghamari-Tabrizi, B. (1998) *Islamism and the quest for alternative modernities*, Phd, St. Cruz.
Gheissary, A. (1998) Iranian intellectuals in the twentieth century, Austin.
Gieling, S. (1997) The Marja'iya in Iran and the nomination of Khamanei in December 1994, *Middle Eastern studies*, vol. 33:4, London, pp. 777–787.
Goldziher, I. (1916) *Stellung der alten islamischen orthodoxie zu den antiken wissenschaften*, Berlin.
——— (1981) *Introduction to Islamic theology and law*, Princeton.
Goldman, A.I. (1999) A Priori warrant and naturalistic epistemology, *Philosophical perspectives*, vol. 13, Cambridge, pp. 1–28.
Goodman, L.E. (1997) Ibn Bajjah, *History of Islamic philosophy*, vol. 2, eds. S.H. Nasr and O. Leaman, Tehran, pp. 294–312.
Griffin, D.R. (1989) *Varieties of postmodern theology*, eds. D.R. Griffin, W.A. Beardslee and J. Holland, New York.
Guerra, F. (1994) The Paradoxes of modernity, trans. M.A. Balinska, *Modernity and religion*, ed. R. McInerny, Notre Dame, pp. 19–29.
Gutas, D. (1988) *Avicenna and the Aristotelian tradition. An Introduction to reading Avicenna's philosophical works*, Leiden.
Guyer, P. (1987) *Kant and the claims of knowledge*, Cambridge.
——— (1992) The Starry heavens and the moral law, *The Cambridge companion to Kant*, ed. P. Guyer, New York, 1–25.
Habermas, J. (1987) *The Philosophical discourse of modernity*, trans. F. G. Lawrence, Cambridge.
Habil, A. (1987) Traditional esoteric commentaries on the Quran, *Islamic spirituality*. vol.1, ed. S.H. Nasr, London, pp. 24–47.
Hairi, A. (1976) Why did the *ʿulamā* participate in the Persian constitutional revolution of 1905–1909?, *Welt des Islams*, vol. 17: 1–4, Leiden, pp. 127–154.
——— (1977) *Shi'ism and constitutionalism in Iran. A Study of the role played by the Persian residents of Iraq in Iranian politics*, Leiden.
Hallaq, W.B. (1992) Uṣūl al-fiqh: beyond tradition, *Journal of Islamic studies*, vol. 3:2, Oxford, pp. 172–202.
——— (1993) *Ibn Taymiyya against the Greek logicians*, Oxford.
——— (1994) Was al-Shafi'i the master architect of Islamic jurisprudence?, *International journal of Middle East studies*, vol. 25, Cambridge, pp. 587–605.
——— (1995) Ijtihād, *The Oxford encyclopaedia of the modern Islamic world*, vol. 2, ed. J. Esposito, Oxford, 1995, pp. 178–181.

——— (1996) *Iftāʾ* and *ijtihād* in Sunni legal theory, *Islamic legal interpretation: muftis and their fatwas*, eds. M.K. Masud, B. Messick and D.S. Powers, Harvard, pp. 33–43.
——— (1997) *A History of Islamic legal theories. An Introduction to Sunni uṣūl al-fiqh*, Cambridge.
Halm, H. (1991) *Shiism*, Edinburgh.
Hasan, A. (1986) *Analogical reasoning in Islamic jurisprudence*, Islamabad.
Heidegger, M. (1997) *Kant and the problem of metaphysics*, Bloomington and Indiana.
Hempel, C. (1965) *Aspects of scientific explanation and other essays in the philosophy of science*, New York.
Hick, J. (1988) *Faith and Knowledge*, London.
——— (1989) On Conflicting truth-claims, *Religious studies*, vol. 19, London, pp. 485–491.
Hodgson, M.G.S. (1965) Ghulāt, *Encyclopaedia of Islam*, vol. 2, pp. 1093–1095.
——— (1977) *The Venture of Islam. Conscience and history in a world civilisation: the classical age of Islam*, Chicago.
——— (1993) *Rethinking history. Essays on Europe, Islam, and world history*, Cambridge.
Hourani, G. F. (1985) *Reason and tradition in Islamic ethics*, Cambridge.
Howard, I.K.A. (1982) The possible origins of Imami-Shi'ite legal teachings, *Union Européens de arabisants et islamisants 10th congress proceedings*, ed. R. Hillenbrand, Edinburgh, pp. 16–21.
Hurgronje, C.S. (1957) *Selected works of C. Snouck Hurgronje*, eds. J. Schacht and G.H. Bousquet, Leiden.
Hye, M.A. (1963) Ash'arism, *A History of Islamic philosophy*, vol. 1, ed. M.M. Sharif, Wiesbaden, pp. 220–243.
Inati, S. (1997) Logic, *History of Islamic philosophy*, vol. 2, eds. S.H. Nasr and O. Leaman, Tehran, pp. 802–823.
Ivry, A.L. (1974) *Al-Kindi's metaphysics: a translation of Ya'qub ibn Ishaq al-Kindi's treatise 'On First philosophy'*, Albany.
Iqbal, M. (1984) *The Reconstruction of religious thought in Islam*, New Dehli.
Jackson, S. (1996) Taqlīd, legal scaffolding, and the scope of legal injunctions in post-formative theory: muṭlaq and ʿamm in the jurisprudence of Shihāb al-dīn al-Qarafī, *Islamic law and society*, vol. 3, 1996, pp. 165–192.
Jahanbakhsh, F. (2001) *Islam, democracy and religious modernism in Iran (1953–2000). From Bāzargān to Soroush*, Leiden.
Jalaeipour, H. R. (1997) *The Iranian Islamic revolution: mass mobilisation and its continuity during 1976–96*, Phd, University of London.
Johansen, B. (1997) Truth and validity of the qadi's Judgement, *Recht von der Islam*, vol. 14, pp.1–26.
——— (1998) *Contingency in sacred law*, Leiden.
Judovitz, D. (1988) *Subjectivity and representation in Descartes. The Origins of modernity*, Cambridge.
Kamali, M.H. (1991) *Principles of Islamic jurisprudence*, Cambridge.
——— (1993) Fundamental rights of the individual: an analysis of ḥaqq (right) in Islamic law, *The American journal of Islamic social sciences*, vol. 10, Herndon, pp. 340–366.
Kant, I. (1959) *Foundations of the metaphysics of morals and What is enlightenment?*, trans. L. White Beck, Indianapolis.
——— (1996) *Critique of pure reason*, trans. W.S. Pluhar, Indianapolis.
——— (1997) *Prolegomena: to any future of metaphysics that will be able to come forward as a science*, Cambridge.
al-Karaki, M. (1985) Ṭarīq istinbāṭ al-aḥkām (The Method of derivation of the rules of sharīʿah), *al-Tawḥīd*, vol. 2:3, Tehran, pp. 42–55.
Kazemi-Moussavi, A. (1996) *Religious authority in Shi'ite Islam. From the office of mufti to the institution of marja'*, Kuala Lampur.
Kerr, M.H. (1966) *Islamic reform. The Political and legal theories of Muhammad 'Abduh and Rashid Rida*, Berkeley.
Kessler, C.S. (1997) Fundamentalism reconsidered: towards the reactualisation of Islam, *Islam: essays on scripture, thought and society*, Leiden.
Khadduri, M. (1953) Nature and sources of Islamic law, *The George Washington law review*,

vol. 22, Washington D.C., pp. 3–23.
——— (1987) *al-Risāla fi uṣūl al-fiqh. al-Shāfiʿī's Treatise on the foundations of Islamic jurisprudence*, Cambridge.
Kitcher, P. (1999) Kant's epistemological problem and its coherent solution, *Philosophical perspectives*, vol. 13, Cambridge, pp. 415–441.
Knysh, A. (1992) Irfan revisited: Khomeini and the legacy of Islamic mystical philosophy, *Middle East journal*, vol. 46:4, pp. 631–653.
Koestler, A. (1959) *The Sleep-walkers. A History of man's changing vision of the universe*, London.
Kohlberg, E. (1979) The Term muḥaddath in Twelver Shi'ism, *Studia Orientalia memoriae D.H. Baneth dedica*, Jerusalem, pp. 39–47.
——— (1985) Akbārīya, *Encyclopaedia Iranica*, vol. 1, London, pp. 716–718.
——— (1986) Barāʿa in Shīʿī doctrine, *Jerusalem studies in Arabic and Islam*, vol. 7, Jerusalem, pp. 1139–1175.
——— (1987a) Astarābādī, Mollā Moḥammad Amīn, *Encyclopaedia Iranica*, vol. 2, London, pp. 845–846.
——— (1987b) al-uṣūl al-arbaʿūmīyah, *Jerusalem studies in Arabic and and Islam*, vol. 10, Jerusalem, 1987, pp. 128–166.
Kramer, J.L. (1992) *Humanism in the renaissance of Islam: the cultural revival of the Buyid age*, Leiden, 2nd edition.
Krämer, G. (1999) Techniques and values: contemporary Muslim debates on Islam and democracy, *Islam, modernism, and the West*, ed. G.M. Muños, London, pp. 174–190.
Kuhn, T.S. (1962) *The Structure of scientific revolutions*, Chicago.
——— (1970) Logic of discovery or psychology of research?, *Criticism and the growth of knowledge*, ed. I. Lakatos and A. Musgrave, Cambridge., pp. 1–23.
——— (1977) *The Essential tension: selected studies in scientific tradition and change*, Chicago.
Lakatos, I. (1970) The Methodology of scientific research programmes, *Criticism and the growth of knowledge*, ed. I Lakatos and A. Musgrave, Cambridge.
Lakatos, I. and Feyerabend, P, *For and against method*, ed. M. Motterli, Chicago and London.
Lambton, A.K.S. (1981) *Continuity and change in medieval Persia. Aspects of administrative, economic and social history*, London.
——— (1987) *Qajar Persia. Eleven studies*, London.
Landesman, C. (1997) *An Introduction to epistemology*, New York.
Lash, S. (1987) *The End of organised capitalism*, Cambridge.
Laudan, L. (2000) Is epistemology adequate to the task of rational theory evaluation?, *After Popper, Kuhn and Feyerabend. Recent issues in theories of scientific method*, eds. R. Nola and H. Sankey, Dordrecht, pp. 165–175.
Lawson, B.T. (1993) Akhbārī Shīʿī approaches to tafsīr, *Approaches to the Qurʾān*, eds. G.R. Hawting and A. Shareef, London, pp. 173–210.
Le Roy Finch, H. (1987) Epistemology, *The Encyclopeadia of religion*, ed. M. Eliade, New York, 1987, pp. 133–135.
Lee L.T. and Lai, W.W. (1978) The Chinese conceptions of law: Confucian, legalist, and Buddhist, *The Hastings law journal*, vol. 29, pp. 1307–1329.
Lewis, B., Menage, V.L., Pellat, C. (1965) ʿIlm, *Encyclopaedia of Islam*, vol. 3, Leiden, pp. 133–1134.
Li, K. 1999. *Western civilization and its problems. A Dialogue between Weber, Elias and Habermas*, Aldershot.
Liebesny, H.J. (1972) Comparative legal history: its role in the analysis of Islamic and modern Near Eastern legal institutions, *The American journal of comparative law*, vol. 20, Berkeley, pp. 38–52.
——— (1975) *The Law of the Near and Middle East. Readings, cases and materials*, New York.
Linant de Bellefonds, Y. (1956) *Traité de droit musulman comparé*, 3 vols., Paris.
——— (1970) Droit imamite, *Le Shi'isme imamite*, Paris, pp. 183–199.
Lindbom, T. (1988) *The Tares and the good grain*, trans. A. Moore Jr., Lahore.

Lorentz, K. (1977) *Behind the mirror: a search for a neutral history of human knowledge*, London.
Luther (1970) *Luther's works*, vol. 39, ed. H. T. Lehman, trans. E.W. Gritsch, Philadelphia.
Lyotard, J. (1999) *The Postmodern condition: a report on knowledge*, trans. G. Bennington and B. Massumi, Manchester.
Madelung, W. (1968) Imamism and muʿtazilite theology, *Le Shi'isme imamite*, ed. J. Aubin, Paris, pp. 13–30.
——— (1971) Imāma. Imāmiyya, *Encyclopaedia of Islam*, vol. 3, 1971, Leiden, pp. 1166–1169.
——— (1979) Shi'i attitudes toward women as reflected in fiqh, *Society and the sexes in medieval Islam*, ed. A.L. al-Sayyid-Marsot, Malibu, pp. 69–79.
——— (1980) Akhbāriyya, *Encyclopaedia of Islam*, Suppl. Facs. 1–2, Leiden, pp. 56–57.
——— (1980b) A Treatise of the Sharīf al-Murtaḍā on the legality of working for the government, *BSOAS*, vol. 43:1, London, pp. 18–31.
——— (1982) Authority in Twelver Shiism in the abscence of the Imam, *Le Notion d'authorité au moyen age: Islam, Byzance, Occident*, eds. G. Makdisi, D. Sourdel and J. Sourdel-Thomine, Paris, pp. 163–173.
——— (1998a) ʿAbd Allāh b. ʿAbbās and the Shi'ite law, *Law, Christianity, and modernism in Islamic society*, eds. U. Verweulen and J.M.F. van Reeth, Leuven, pp. 13–25.
——— (1998b) Ebn al-Jonayd, *Encyclopaedia Iranica*, vol. 8, Costa Mesa, 1998, pp. 31–32.
Makdisi, G. (1970) Madrasa and university in the middle ages, *Studia Islamica*, vol. 31, Paris, 1970, pp. 255–264.
——— (1974) The Scholastic method in medieval education, *Speculum*, vol. 49, Boston, pp. 640–661.
——— (1980) On the origin and development of the college in Islam and the West, *Islam and the medieval West*, ed. K.I. Semaan, New York, pp. 26–49.
——— (1981) *The Rise of colleges. Institutions of learning in Islam and the West*, Edinburgh.
——— (1984) The Juridicial theology of Shāfiʿī. Origins and significance of uṣūl al-fiqh, *Studia Islamica*, vol. 59, pp. 5–47.
——— (1990) *The Rise of humanism in classical Islam and the Christian West*, Edinburgh.
Makdisi, J. (1985a) Formal rationality in Islamic law and the common law, *Cleveland state law review*, vol. 35, Cleveland, pp. 97–112.
——— (1985b) Legal logic and equity in Islamic law, *The American journal of comparative law*, vol. 33, pp. 63–258.
Manzoor, P. (2000) Islam and the crisis of modernity, *islam21*, no. 23, London, pp. 3–10.
Martin, V. (1989) *Islam and modernism. The Iranian revolution of 1906*, London.
——— (1996) A Comparison between Khumaini's Government of the jurist and the commentary on Plato's Republic of Ibn Rushd, *Journal of Islamic studies*, vol. 7:1, pp. 16–31.
Matin-asgari, A. (1997) 'Abdolkarim Soroush and the secularisation of Islamic thought in Iran, *Iranian studies*, vol. 30:1–2, pp. 95–115.
——— (1998) Review, *Iranian studies*, vol. 31:2, Chicago, pp. 294–296.
McDermott, M.J. (1978) *The Theology of al-Shaikh al-Mufid (d. 413/1022)*, Beirut.
Melchert, C. (1997) *The Formation of the Sunni schools of law*, Leiden.
Messick, B. (1992) *The Calligraphic state. Textual domination and history in a Muslim society*, Berkeley.
Michalson. G.E. (1999) *Kant and the problem of God*, Oxford.
Millward, W.G. (1973) Aspects of modernism in Shi'a Islam, *Studia Islamica*, vol. 37, Paris, pp. 112–128.
Mir-Hosseini, Z. (1993) *Marriage on trial*, London.
——— (1999) *Islam and gender: the religious debate in contemporary Iran*, Princeton.
Modarressi (Tabataba'i), H. (1984a) *An Introduction to Shi'i law. A Bibliographical study*, London.
——— (1991) The Just ruler or the guardian jurist: an Attempt to link two different Shi'ite concepts, *Journal of the American Oriental society*, vol. 3:3, New Haven, pp. 549–562.
——— (1993) Early debates on the integrity of the Qur'an. A Brief survey, *Studia Islamica*, vol. 77, Paris, pp. 5–39.

Mohaghegh, M. (1971) The Study of philosophy in contemporary Iran, *La Philosophie contemporaine*, vol. 4, ed. R. Klibansky, Firenze, pp. 584–588.
Momen, M. (1985) *An Introduction to Shi'i Islam. The History and doctrine of Twelver Shi'ism*, Oxford.
Mouzelis, N. (1999) Modernity: a non-European conceptualisation, *British Journal of sociology*, vol. 50:1, pp. 141–159.
Murata, S. (1992) *The Tao of Islam*, New York.
——— (1983) Akhund Korasānī, *Encyclopaedia Iranica*, vol. 1:2, London, pp. 734–35.
Mottahedeh, R. (1985) *The Mantle of the Prophet. Religion and Politics in Iran*, Harmondsworth.
Murphy, T. (1999) The Concept of 'Entwicklung' in German religionswissenschaft: before and after Darwin, *Method and theory in the study of religion*, vol. 2, Leiden, pp. 8–23.
Nettler, R. (1983) A Shi'i-Sunni debate on discursive reasoning, *Annual of the Swedish theological institute*, vol. 12, Leiden, pp.113–126.
Nicholson, R.A. (1922) *Studies in Islamic mysticism*, Cambridge.
Nielsen, K. (1959) An Examination of the Thomistic theory of natural moral law, *Natural law forum*, vol. 4, pp. 44–71.
Nuseibeh, S. (1997) Epistemology, *History of Islamic philosophy*, vol. 2, eds. S.H. Nasr and O. Leaman, Tehran, pp. 824–840.
Nwiya, P. (1962) Le Tafsir mystique attribué à Ga'far Sadiq, *Melànges de l'Université Saint-Joseph*, vol. 43, Paris, pp. 181–230.
Nyberg, H.S. (1953) al-Muʿtazila, *Shorter encyclopaedia of Islam*, ed. H.A.R. Gibb, Leiden, pp. 421–427.
O'Neill, O. (1992), Vindicating reason, *The Cambridge companion to Kant*, ed. P. Guyer, Cambridge, pp. 280–308.
Paret, P. (1978) Istiḥsān and istiṣlāh, *Encyclopaedia of Islam*, vol. 4, Leiden, pp. 255–259.
Parsons, C. (1992), The Transcendental aesthetics, *The Cambridge companion to Kant*, ed. P. Guyer, Cambridge, pp. 62–100.
Plato (1997) *Complete works*, ed. J.M. Cooper, Indianapolis.
Platinga, A. (1995) A Defence of religious exclusivism, *The Rationality of belief and the plurality of faiths*, ed. T.D. Senor, Ithaca and London, pp. 191–215.
Poonawala, I. (1988) Ismāʿīlī taʾwīl of the Qurʾān, *Approaches to the history of the interpretation of the Qurʾān*, ed. A. Rippin, Oxford, pp. 199–222.
Popper, K.R. (1963) *The Poverty of historicism*, London.
——— (1969) *Objective knowledge. An Evolutionary approach*, Oxford.
——— (1972) *Conjectures and refutations*, London.
——— (1992) *The Logic of scientific discovery*, London.
Pourjavady, N. (1999) Opposition to Sufism in Twelver Shi'ism, *Islamic mysticism contested*, ed. F. De Jong and B. Radtke, Leiden, pp. 614–623.
Powers, D.S. (1988) The Exegetical genre nasikh al-Qurʾān, *Approaches to the history of the interpretation of the Qurʾān*, ed. A. Rippin, Oxford, pp. 117–138.
Pullock, J.L. and Cruz, J. (1999) *Contemporary theories of knowledge*, Lanham.
Putnam, H. (1987) *The Many faces of realism*, La Salle.
Quine, W.O. (1960) *Word and object*, Cambridge.
——— (1963) *From a logical point of view*, New York.
Qur., The Meaning of the glorious Koran. An Explanatory translation by Mohammed Marmaduke Picktall, London, 1953.
Rahman, F. (1970) Revival and reform, *The Cambridge history of Islam*, vol. 2, Cambridge, pp. 632–656.
——— (1971) Functional independence of law and theology, *Theology and law in Islam*, ed. E.G. von Grunebaum, Wiesbaden.
——— (1975) *The Philosophy of Mulla Sadra*, New York.
——— (1982) *Islam and modernity. Transformation of an intellectual tradition*, Chicago.
Reinhart, A.K. (1983) Islamic law as Islamic ethics, *Journal of religious ethics*, vol. 11, Notre Dame, pp. 186–203.
——— (1997) Shakk, *Encyclopeadia of Islam*, vol. 9, 250–251.

Richard, Y. (1980) *Le Shi'isme en Iran: Imam et revolution*, Paris.
——— (1981) Contemporary Shi'i thought, *Roots of revolution*, ed. N. Keddie, New Haven, pp. 202–228.
——— (1988) Sharīʿat Sangalajī: A Reformist theologian of the Riḍā Shāh Period, *Authority and political culture in Shi'ism*, ed. S.A. Arjomand, trans. K. Arjomand, New York, pp. 159–177.
——— (1990) Clercs et intellectuels dans la république Islamique d'Iran, *Intellectuels et militants de l'Islam contemporain*, eds. G. Kepel et Y. Richard, Paris, pp. 29–70.
——— (1995) *Shi'ite Islam. Polity, ideology and creed*, trans. A. Nevill, Oxford.
Ricoeur, P. (1974) *The Conflict of interpretations: essays in hermeneutics*, ed. D. Ihde, Evanston.
——— (1976) *Interpretation theory: discourse surplus of meaning?*, Fort Worth.
——— (1977) Toward a hermeneutic of the idea of revelation, *Harvard theological review*, vol. 70:1–2, pp. 1–37.
——— (1981) *Hermeneutics and the human sciences: essays on language, action and interpretation*, trans. J. B. Thompson, New Haven.
Rider, S.P. (1998) *Avoiding the subject. A Critical inquiry into contemporary theories of subjectivity*, Stockholm.
Rocher, L. (1978) Hindu conceptions of law, *The Hastings law journal*, vol. 29, pp. 1283–1305.
Rorty, R. (1979) *Philosophy and the mirror of nature*, Princeton.
——— (1986) The Contingency of language, *London review of books*, vol. 8, London, pp. 3–6.
——— (1998) Foucault and epistemology, *Foucault: a critical reader*, Oxford, pp. 41–49.
Rosenthal, E.I.J. (1958) *Political thought in medieval Islam. An Introductory outline*, Cambridge.
Rosenthal, F. (1970) *Knowledge triumphant. The Concept of knowledge in medieval Islam*, Leiden.
Roy, O. (1996) The Crisis of religious legitimacy in Iran, *The Middle East journal*, vol. 53:2, Washington D.C., pp. 201–216.
Ruse, M. (1975) Darwin's debt to philosophy, *Studies in history and philosophy of science*, vol. 6, London, pp. 159–181.
Sachedina, A. (1988) *The Just ruler (al-sulṭān al-ʿādil) in Shi'ite Islam. The Comprehensive authority of the jurist in Imāmate jurisprudence*, New York.
Sassani, A.H.K. (1948) Higher education in Iran, *College and university*, vol. 24, Menasha, pp. 78–107.
Saussure, F. (1983) *Course in general linguistics*, Oxford.
Scarcia, G. (1968) Intorno alle controversie tra ahbari e usuli presso gli imamiti di Persia, *Rivista degli orientali*, vol. 33:1–2, Rome, pp. 211–250.
Schacht, J. (1950) *The Origins of Muhammadan jurisprudence*, Oxford.
——— (1955) The law, *Unity and variety in Muslim civilization*, ed. G. von Grunebaum, Chicago, pp. 65–86.
——— (1960a) Fikh, *Encyclopaedia of Islam*, vol. 2, pp. 886–891.
——— (1960b) Problems of modern Islamic legislation, *Studia Islamica*, vol. 13, pp. 99–130.
——— (1964) *An Introduction to Islamic law*, Oxford.
——— (1965a) Ikhtilāf, *Encyclopaedia of Islam*, vol. 3, Leiden, pp. 1061–1062.
——— (1965b) Modernism and traditionalism in a history of Islamic law, *Middle Eastern studies*, vol. 1, London, pp. 388–400.
——— (1971a) Idjtihād, *Encyclopaedia Islamica*, Leiden, pp. 1026–1027.
——— (1971b) Theology and law in Islam, *Theology and law in Islam*, ed. E.G. von Grunebaum, Wiesbaden, pp. 3–23.
Schimmel, A. (1993), *The Triumphal sun. A Study of the works of Jalaloddin Rumi*, New York.
Schirazi, A. (1997) *The Constitution of Iran: politics and the state in the Islamic republic*, trans. J. O'Kane, London, 1997.
Schleiermacher, F.E.D. (1959) *Hermeneutik. Nach den handschriften neu herausgegeben und eingeleitet von Heinz Kimmerle*, ed. H. Kimmerle, Heidelberg.

Schmidtke, S. (1994) al-ʿAllāma al-Hillī and Shi'ite muʿtazilite theology, *Spektrum Iran*, vol. 7:3–4, Bonn, 1994, pp. 10–35.
Schulze, R. (1995) Citizens of Islam. The Institutionalization and internalization of Muslim legal debate, *Law and the Islamic world*, ed. C. Toll, Copenhagen, pp. 167–184.
Schuon, F. (1968) *De l'unité transcendente des religions*, Paris.
Seligman, A.B. (1991) Towards a reinterpretation of modernity in an age of postmodernity, *Theories of modernity and postmodernity*, ed. B.S. Turner, London, pp. 117–135.
Shils, E. (1981) *Tradition*, London.
Smart, N. (1998) Tradition, retrospective perception, nationalism and modernism, *Religion, modernity and postmodernity*, ed. P. Heelas, Oxford, pp. 14–29.
Smith, W.C. (1965) The Concept of shari'a among some mutakallimun, *Arabic and Islamic studies in honour of H.A.R. Gibb*, ed. G. Makdisi, Leiden, pp. 581–602.
——— (1980) The True meaning of scripture: an empirical historian's non-reductionist interpretation of the Qur'an, *International journal of Middle Eastern studies*, vol. 11:4, London, pp. 487–505.
Smolinski, H. (1988) The Bible and its exegesis in the controversies about reform and reformation, *Creative Biblical exegesis*, ed. B. Uffenheimer, Sheffeild, pp. 115–130.
Solomon, R.C. (1988) *Continental philosophy since 1750. The Rise and fall of the self*, Oxford.
Sourdel, D. (1969) Les Conceptions imamites au début du XIe siècle d'après le shaykh al-Mufīd, *Religion in the Middle East*, vol. 2, ed. A.J. Arberry, Cambridge, pp. 187–200.
Stanton, C.M. (1990) *Higher learning in Islam: the classical period*, New York.
Stewart, D.J. (1998) *Islamic legal orthodoxy. Twelver Shiite responses to the Sunnite legal system*, Salt Lake City.
Strothmann, R. (1926) *Die Zwölfer-schia*, Leipzig.
Taylor, M.C. (1984) *Erring: a postmodern a/theology*, Chicago.
Taylor, P.J. (1999) *Modernities: a geohistorical interpretation*, Cambridge.
Tibi, B. (1990) *Islam and the cultural accommodation of social change*, trans. C. Krojzl, Boulder.
Therborn, G. (1995) Routes through/to modernity, *Global modernities*, eds. S. Lash and R. Robertson, London.
Tolland, A. (1991) *Epistemological relativism and relativistic epistemology*, Phd, Göteborg.
Toynbee, A. (1935) The Relativity of Ibn Khaldun's classification of the sciences, *The Muslim world*, vol. 81, Hartford, pp. 254–261.
Touraine, A. (1995) *Critique of modernity*, trans. D. Macey, Oxford.
Turki Abbas, H.A. (1997) *Imām Kāshif al-Ghitā. The Reformist marjiʿ in the Shi'ah school of Najaf*, Phd, University of Arizona.
Turner, B. (1994) *Orientalism, postmodernism, and globalisation*, London.
Vahdat, F. (1998) *God and the juggernaut: Iran's intellectual encounter with modernity*, Phd, Brandeis.
Vakili, V. (1996) *Debating religion and politics in Iran: the political thought of Abdolkarim Soroush*, New York.
Vattimo, G. (1988) *The End of modernity. Nihilism and hermeneutics in post-modern culture*, trans. J.R. Snyder, Cambridge.
Vesey-Fitzgerald, S.G. (1955) Nature and sources of the shari'a, *Law in the Middle East*, ed. M. Khadduri, vol. 1, Washington D.C., pp. 85–112.
——— (1979) *Muhammadan law. An Abridgement according to its various schools*, Aalen.
Vikør, K. (1996) Shi'ismen– historias lim, *Tidskrift för Mellanöstern studier*, no. 2, Lund, pp. 9–93.
Watkins, J. (1970) Against normal science, *Criticism and the growth of knowledge*, eds. I. Lakatos and A. Musgrave, Cambridge, pp. 25–37.
Wansbrough, J. (1978) *The Sectarian milieu. Content and composition of Islamic salvation history*, Oxford.
Watson, A. (1984) *Sources of law, legal change, and ambiguity*, Philadelphia.
Watt, M. (1963) *Muslim intellectual. A Study of al-Ghazali*, Edinburgh.
——— (1974) The Closing of the door of igtihad, *Orientalia hispanica*, vol. 1, Leiden, pp. 675–678.

——— (1985) *Islamic philosophy and theology. An Extended survey*, Edinburgh.
Weinsheimer, J.C. (1985) *Gadamer's hermeneutics: a reader of truth and method*, New Haven.
Weiss, B. (1978) Interpretation in Islamic law: the theory of ijtihad, *The American journal of comparative law*, vol. 26:2, Berkeley, 1978, pp. 199–212.
——— (1990) Exoterism and objectivity in Islamic jurisprudence, *Islamic law and jurisprudence*, ed. N. Heer, Seattle, pp. 53–71.
——— (1991) Law in Islam and in the West: some comparative observations, *Islamic studies presented to Charles J. Adams*, Leiden, pp. 239–253.
Wensick, A.J. (1932) *The Muslim creed. Its Genesis and historical development*, Cambridge.
Whelan, E. (1998) Forgotten witnesses: evidence for the early codification of the Qur'an, *Journal of American Oriental society*, vol. 118:1, New Haven, pp. 1–14.
Whitehead, A.N. (1926) *Religion in the making*, Cambridge.
Widengren, G. (1979) The Pure brethren and the philosophical structure of their system, *Islam: past influence and present challenge*, eds. A.T. Welch and P. Cachia, Edingburgh, pp. 57–69.
Wild, S. (1996) 'We have sent down to thee the book with the truth…' Spatial and temporal implications of the Qur'ānic concepts of nuzūl, tanzīl, and 'inzāl, *The Qur'ān as text*, Leiden, pp. 137–153.
Wittrock, B. (2000) Modernity: one, none or many?, *Daedalus. Journal of the American academy of arts and sciences*, vol. 129:1, Cambridge, pp. 31–60.
Zaryab, A. (1997) Education–v. The Madrasa in Shi'ite Iran, *Encyclopaedia Iranica*, vol. 8, pp. 184–187.
Ziyai, H. (1997) Shihab al-din Suhrawardi: founder of the illuminationist school, *History of Islamic philosophy*, vol. 2, eds. S.H. Nasr and O. Leaman, Tehran, pp. 434–464.
Zubaida, S. (1997) Is Iran an Islamic state?, *Essays from the Middle East report. Political Islam*, ed. J. Beinin, Berkeley, pp. 102–119.
Zysow, A. (1997) Ejtehād, *Encyclopaedia Iranica*, vol. 8, pp. 280–286.

Index

a posteriori, 31, 142, 235, 272, 279, 291, 294, 296, 298, 299, 301, 302, 303, 310, 311, 325, 337, 340, 358, 359
a priori, 16, 27, 29, 30, 60, 66, 67, 112, 130, 135, 142, 157, 169, 181, 192, 199, 204, 210, 239, 249, 261, 266, 270, 272, 273, 279, 282, 286, 291, 292, 296, 297, 298, 299, 300, 301, 302, 303, 305, 307, 308, 309, 310, 311, 313, 337, 338, 340, 341, 348, 358, 359, 365
  as provisional, 299
a/jurisprudence, 353
Abadan, 103
ʿAbbāsīd, 49, 66
ʿAbd al-Jabbār, Q., 71, 72
ʿAbduh, M., 220
al-ʿĀbidīn, Z., 53
abrogation, 89, 95, 112, 318
absolute knowledge, 20, 29, 31, 53, 55, 56, 60, 84, 95, 127, 129, 137, 141, 200, 219, 235, 241, 266, 280, 283, 292, 297, 304, 305, 315, 333, 344
acquired knowledge, 31, 59, 66, 70, 84, 344, 345
Acton, L., 259
Adīb-Sulṭānī, M.S., 188
administration, 41, 49, 60, 117, 130, 199, 207, 218, 271, 353
aesthetics, 26, 166
al-Afghānī, J.. *See* Asadābādī, J.
agronomy, 91
ahl al-ʿamāʾim, 20
Ahmad-Abad, 146
Ahmed, A., 35, 347
Aḥsāʾī, A., 64
akhbār, 61, 62, 71, 72, 81, 88, 89, 103, 112, 131, 139, 161, 179, 194, 249, 321
  categories of, 81
  inception of Shi'i, 80
  Shi'i collections of, 60, 62, 80
akhbārī, 60, 61, 62, 63, 81, 99, 103, 114, 165, 228, 242, 264
  compared to empiricism, 114
  notion of law, 62
akhlāq. *See* ethics
Ākhūndzādah, F.ʿA., 104
Āl-i Aḥmad, J., 147, 208
Āl-i Aḥmad, S., 189
ʿAlawī school, 187
alchemy, 52
Algar, H., 215
ʿAlī b. Abī Ṭālib, 80, 126, 155, 171, 263, 293, 314
alienation, 12, 26, 193, 293, 323, 359, 360
Allāh-Karam, Ḥ., 191
allegiance, 224
allegory, 11, 94, 95, 96, 154, 195, 196, 205, 257, 318, 322, 327
alms, 89, 223
Alston, W., 290
ambiguity, ontological, 280
American, 166, 215, 255, 312, 338
Americanisation of the world, 26
al-ʿĀmilī, Ḥ, 64
al-ʿĀmilī, Z., 62
Amīnī, F., 139
amr bi-l-maʿrūf. *See* enjoing the lawful, concept of
Amul, 126
anachronism, 10, 50, 304
analogy, 47, 59, 60, 62, 65, 66, 70, 71, 73, 82, 83, 85, 86, 87, 93, 114, 118, 119, 201, 278, 296, 345, 351, 354
  and analytical thought, 47
  categories of, 86
  distinct from syllogism, 86
  probative value of, 83
  Shi'i notions of, 60, 71, 73, 85, 86, 87
  Sunni notions of, 65
analytical jurisprudence, 46
analytical mathematics, 29
analytical philosophy, 29, 188, 271, 311
anatomy, 271, 272
Anjuman-i guftār-i māh, 148
Anjuman-i shāhanshāhī-yi falsafah, 113
Anṣār-i ḥizbullāh, 191
al-Anṣārī, M., 73, 74, 90, 119, 243, 345
Anṣārī-Zanjānī, I., 145
ante rem, 30
anthropocentrism, 300
anthropology, 34, 162, 173, 182, 212, 216, 223, 224, 228, 233, 239, 243, 246, 254, 261, 268, 274, 275, 287, 288, 297, 309, 335, 336
anti-scientism, 326
anti-worldview, 34

apostasy, 204, 226, 243
appropriation, 8, 23, 31, 115, 140, 141, 210
ʿaql. *See* reason; rational knowledge
ʿaql-i dīnī. *See* reason, religious
Aquinas, T., 49, 152, 210, 211
Arab, 93, 105, 126
Arabia, 225, 226
Arabic, 19, 20, 40, 51, 55, 56, 63, 65, 87, 89, 93, 109, 111, 114, 147, 154, 155, 176, 194, 197, 214, 215, 247, 253, 334
Arabic language, 20, 89, 92, 118, 121, 122, 131, 132, 163, 183, 214, 215
Arak, 114
Arākī, M.ʿA., 119
Ārām, A., 188
arbitration, legal, 47, 60
archaeology, concept of, 35
Ardakan, 117
Aristotelianism, 68
Aristotle, 23, 29, 30, 58, 65, 68, 85, 86, 109, 111, 114, 132, 146, 156, 167, 173, 174, 188, 200, 234, 235, 250, 255, 273, 287, 345, 351, 353, 368
arithmetic, 299
art, 5, 8, 26, 205, 207, 208, 245, 267
  for art's sake, 26
Asadābādī, J., 104, 146
asbāb al-nuzūl. *See* occasions of revelation
ashaʿrī, 58, 66, 183, 231, 235, 263, 264
al-Ashʿarī, A.Ḥ., 67
Ashtiyānī, J., 110, 113
aṣl. *See* Islamic law, sources of
al-asmāʾ al-ḥusnā. *See* God, Attributes of
ʿAṣṣār, M.K., 110
Astarābādī, M.A., 61, 62, 63, 73, 76
astrology, 198
astronomy, 20, 68, 75, 203, 277, 290
atheism, 135, 155, 175
Augustine, St., 12, 211
Austin, J., 45, 46, 237
authenticity, 105, 178, 209, 212, 305, 326
autonomity, 9, 26, 29, 175, 178, 288, 326, 347, 349, 359, 362, 364, 366
ʿAwānī, G., 113
Aʿyān Zarūrah, A., 84
Ayer, A.J., 237, 300, 301
al-Azhar, 90, 248

al-Babūyah, M.ʿA., 62, 71, 81, 94, 141
Bacon, F., 34, 197, 203, 273
badīhī. *See* a priori; intuition
Bāhunar, M.J., 187, 189
Baigūm Amīn, S.N., 139
Banī-Ṣadr, A., 148, 154–155
banking, 108
al-Baqillānī, A., 71
al-Bāqir, M., 53
barāʿah. *See* exemption, juristic
Barbour, I.G., 166, 255
Barth, K., 166, 169, 290, 302
Basra, 66, 71
al-Baṣrī, Ḥ., 66
bayʿat. *See* allegiance
Bāzargān, M., 105, 148, 149, 150–153, 155, 185, 211, 216, 220
bāzgasht bih khīshtan. *See* return to the self, concept of
beauty, 5, 31
being. *See* ontology
Belgian, 51
belles-lettres, 91, 254
Bentham, J., 237
Bergson, H., 256
Berkeley, G., 111, 157, 199
Berlin, 257
Berman, M., 25
Berque, J., 155
best explanation, concept of, 319, 336
Bible, 12, 45, 181, 182, 288
Biblical humanism, 12
bidʿah. *See* innovation
al-Bihbahānī, M.ʿA., 57
al-Bihbahānī, M.B., 61, 73
biochemistry, 271, 272
biology, 111, 233, 317, 350
Biyāzār-Shīrāzī, ʿA., 111
botany, 321
British, 192, 213, 221, 259, 268, 271, 302
Brueggemann, W., 34
Brunner, E., 166, 169
Brussels, 118
Buddhism, 42, 227
burhān. *See* demonstration
Burtt, E.A., 192, 276
Burūjirdī, Ḥ., 74

Cairo, 90
Calvin, J., 12, 181
Canon law, 45, 46, 93, 99
canonisation, 14, 16, 44, 49
cantillation, 13, 91
capitalism, 118, 153
Carnap, R., 267
Carrel, A., 151
Cartesian circle, 29
Castelli, C., 183
Catholicism, 89, 109, 139, 166, 182, 302
causality, 58, 168, 263, 264, 273, 291, 299
CD-rom, 37
centre of meaning, concept of, 181
certainty, epistemic, 30, 34, 118, 120, 128, 134, 137, 138, 167, 170, 178, 197, 204, 224, 241, 245, 263, 266, 267, 283, 286, 295, 296,

300, 307, 311, 312, 317, 318, 326, 332, 338, 344, 345, 346, 351, 356, 357, 364
and religious faith, 133
concept in religion, 5
in traditional Islam, 55–56, 60, 63, 65, 67, 70, 72, 74, 75, 84, 85, 89, 100, 101
rejection of, 23, 29, 283, 296
Champeaux, W., 30
chemistry, 188, 200, 201, 203, 271, 272, 356
Chinese, 86
Chisholm, R., 303
Christian, 12, 25, 30, 36, 49, 89, 99, 108, 130, 131, 151, 164, 165, 169, 200, 211, 212, 282, 290, 303, 329
Christianisation of the world, 329
Christianity, 7, 21, 25, 45, 49, 55, 86, 93, 139, 152, 166, 182, 227, 346
and ecclesiastical authority, 45, 89, 99
and modernity, 33, 290, 346
status of theology in, 39
Church, 36, 46, 55, 93, 164, 182, 289, 302
Cicero, M.T., 152
citizenship, concept of, 48, 205
civilisation, 55, 118, 124, 146, 148, 159, 204, 205, 206, 208, 209, 217, 221, 246, 308, 329
class struggle, 156, 162
clergy, 12, 89–90, 109, 193, 218, 250
codification, 48, 49, 51, 104, 106, 144, 145, 226, 227, 228, 229, 231, 354
and hermeneutical necessity, 49–51
in post-revolutionary Iran, 51
cogito ergo sum, 27, 296
cognitive theory. *See* epistemology
coherentism, 273, 274, 303
collective obligation, 73, 89
Collingwood, R.G., 259, 260, 261
colonialism, 104, 105, 108, 146
Common law, 45
common sense, 59, 63, 120
commonsenseism, 32, 273
communism, 105, 149
community, 15, 35, 48, 49, 71, 75, 82, 101, 103, 106, 139, 196, 204, 222, 240, 246, 253, 276, 284, 326, 336, 341, 347, 351, 358, 362, 364
and conflicting interpretations, 99
and consensus, 70, 81, 82, 97
history, 14, 43
in Canon law, 45
linguistic, 10, 326
comparative law, 15, 41, 50
comparative religion, 191
Comte, A., 197, 212, 267
confirmation. *See* verification
conflicting interpretations, 6, 58, 97–101, 117, 121, 122, 142, 182, 183, 184, 215, 254, 269, 271, 293, 295, 297, 310, 317, 318, 321, 330, 333–342, 339, 359, 360, 365
and normativity, 335, 340–341
Confucian, 42
conjecture, epistemic, 23, 29, 42, 60, 70, 73, 74, 86, 88, 100, 118, 134, 138, 169, 234, 266, 267, 277, 278, 285, 287, 290, 293, 294, 297, 305, 307, 325, 328, 333, 334, 335, 339, 345, 346, 351, 357
and legal norms, 42
as probable belief, 100
valid and non-valid, 74
consciousness, 23, 26, 28, 35, 150, 154, 157, 160, 172, 173, 180, 199, 213, 230, 240, 265, 276, 282, 300, 304, 323, 324, 325, 328, 332, 349, 355, 356, 359, 360, 365
critical, 23
historical, 26, 203, 323, 324, 325
material conditions of, 34, 332
consensus, 57, 65, 70, 71, 79, 81–82, 83, 88, 89, 97, 98, 100, 105, 125, 139, 145, 174, 227, 234, 313, 344, 351, 361
as coincidence, 183
as infallible, 81
as non-verifiable, 234
as oppressive, 174
indefinite nature of, 52
Shi'i notions of, 71, 81–82
Sunni notions of, 52, 81
constitution, 36, 108, 109, 110, 114, 121, 135, 145, 153, 165, 194, 229
constitutional law, 109, 121
constitutional revolution (of 1906), 4, 104, 108, 109, 146, 201
constitutionalism, 104, 105, 108, 145, 229
constructive postmodernism, 34, 363
consultation, 224
consultative assembly, 104, 109, 118, 146, 161, 163
contextuality, 9, 11, 24, 34, 89, 92, 136, 147, 159, 160, 169, 173, 175, 177, 178, 179, 180, 182, 196, 207, 214, 225, 237, 245, 283, 287, 288, 294, 297, 305, 310, 312, 314, 316, 317, 320, 321, 322, 325, 326, 349, 356, 361, 364
continental philosophy, 163
contingency, 28, 34, 124, 131, 173, 190, 198, 200, 201, 214, 224, 225, 228, 229, 237, 239, 243, 253, 255, 265, 270, 271, 272, 275, 283, 284, 287, 289, 294, 296, 312, 313, 316, 317, 320, 322, 324, 325, 330, 331, 332, 336, 346, 347, 352, 353, 355, 358, 359, 360, 362, 364
continuance, juristic, 74, 82, 137, 244
continuity, theological concept of, 114, 117, 137
contraction and expansion, theory of epistemic, 119, 125, 135, 167, 199, 208, 211, 219, 222, 235, 253, 254, 255, 259, 266, 267, 268, 269,

271, 277, 278, 279, 289, 291, 294, 295, 298, 303, 309, 311, 313, 314, 316, 317, 322, 334, 335, 339, 350, 351
as inductive, 278, 313, 350
contradiction, principle of, 291
Copernicus, N., 29, 202, 290
Corbin, H., 8, 12, 68, 96, 111
correlation, principle of, 288
correlation, rules of, 84
correspondence, epistemic, 30–31, 34, 58, 65, 68, 69, 113, 121, 122, 125, 129, 135, 136, 140, 142, 198, 201, 265, 273, 281, 300, 310, 311, 312, 313, 323, 338, 349, 354, 363
cosmology, 23, 25, 30, 32, 42, 49, 52, 57, 58, 107, 126, 127, 153, 193, 203, 239, 246, 254, 256, 261, 262, 263, 277, 286, 289, 290, 299, 301, 306, 307, 336, 344, 347, 348, 355, 366
Qur'anic, 58
court circles, 20
courts, 42, 48, 49, 50, 51, 106, 166
critical epistemology, 23, 28, 29, 30, 126, 136, 197, 203, 235, 245, 257, 264, 266, 296, 297, 299, 323, 336, 339, 349, 356
critical legal hermeneutics, 165
critical realism, 30, 136, 197–202, 258, 281, 312, 349
cult of change and fashion, 26
customary law, 17, 40, 47, 49, 50, 54, 79, 100, 104, 106, 108, 115, 137, 147, 174, 215, 229, 230
Cuvier, G., 288
cybernetics, 37, 365

Daftar-i pazhūhishgāh-i farhangī-yi duktur ʿAlī Sharīʿatī, 161
Dāmād, S.M., 118, 126
Dār al-funūn, 248
dār al-islām, 205
Dār al-tablīgh, 247
Dār al-tablīgh-i islāmī, 147
dark-i azīzānah-yi dīn. *See* endearing conception of religion, notion of
Darwin, C., 256, 276, 277, 280, 288, 290, 306, 310, 357
Darwinism, 130, 153, 277
Dashtī, ʿA., 147
Dāwar, ʿA.A., 147
death of author, concept of, 331, 348, 350
deconstructionism, 29, 34, 214, 241, 245, 246, 300, 314, 315, 319, 325, 326, 327, 329, 330, 333, 338, 348, 350, 352, 353, 360, 362, 363, 365, 367
and mysticism, 327, 366
deduction, 56, 59, 65, 70, 85, 86, 100, 111, 119, 120, 125, 131, 234, 269, 273, 276, 277, 278, 286, 313, 345, 350, 351. *See also* analogy
defensive literature, 112
deism, 289, 306
Deleuze, G., 35
democracy, 104, 105, 108, 118, 138, 148, 164, 192, 193, 224, 227, 253, 305, 365
as incompatible with Islam, 138
instrumentalist concept of, 164
religious, 191, 253
demonstration, 65, 67, 87, 98, 114, 116, 118, 120, 123, 131, 273, 313, 351
de-objectification, 349, 354
Derrida, J., 34, 35, 204, 210, 245, 319, 325, 326, 329, 330, 331, 333, 348, 362, 363, 366
de-sacralisation, 12, 23, 27, 34, 155, 218, 251, 281
Descartes, R., 5, 25, 26, 27, 28, 29, 31, 32, 34, 100, 109, 111, 157, 169, 188, 194, 210, 255, 256, 267, 273, 282, 289, 290, 296, 298, 300, 332, 346, 347, 350, 359
description, level of, 268, 269
descriptive discourse, 3, 92, 175, 228, 269, 302, 335, 341, 358, 360
determinism, 156, 188, 260, 282
de-traditionalisation, 35, 349
development, socio-political, 150, 155, 164, 165, 169, 206, 224, 232, 287
as the fruit of modernity, 287
dharma, 42
diachrony, 10, 113, 258, 277, 281, 304, 354
Dībā, F., 113
differentiation, 20, 21, 26, 33, 34, 36, 217
Dilthey, W., 8, 9, 157, 177, 258, 265, 266, 268
direct realism, 27, 136, 312
discourse, 4, 20, 21, 34, 51, 77, 192, 195, 250, 270, 279, 323, 330, 348, 351, 361
definition of, 21
discovery, context of, 283, 298, 300
discursiveness, 11, 12, 21, 30, 35, 42, 59, 71, 84, 85, 107, 126, 127, 128, 178, 241, 258, 265, 297, 304
divergence. *See* conflicting interpretations
doubt, methodological, 5, 28, 32, 49, 74, 94, 136, 137, 205, 213, 249, 345, 346, 357, 358, 367, 368
universal, 32, 100
doxastology, 340
Duhem, P., 286, 289
Durkheim, E., 157
dynamic jurisprudence, 4, 117, 137, 152, 234, 242, 270, 271, 275, 288, 289, 316
dysisplexia, concept of, 149, 190, 208

eclecticism, 115, 144, 348, 349, 363
economics, 150, 152, 154, 155, 176, 205, 207, 222, 235, 247, 248, 271, 288
education, 51, 57, 75, 110, 116, 117, 143, 185, 187, 189, 190, 205, 229, 246, 248, 251, 254

in Iran, 20, 248
in traditional Islam, 67, 90, 91, 101
Egypt, 25
Egyptian, 117, 183
Einstein, A., 198, 290, 292, 358
Eisenstadt, S.N., 25
Eliade, M., 181
Ellul, J., 206
emanation, 58, 68, 150
empirical knowledge, 29, 31, 35, 56, 57, 59, 61, 62, 67, 76, 103, 111, 121, 125, 126, 128, 130, 133, 134, 135, 136, 142, 170, 182, 197, 198, 199, 201, 202, 206, 207, 229, 248, 251, 258, 267, 268, 269, 272, 273, 278, 280, 281, 282, 283, 284, 286, 287, 291, 296, 298, 299, 300, 302, 303, 304, 308, 309, 313, 317, 329, 335, 337, 339, 344, 351, 353, 354, 355, 356, 357, 358, 359, 360, 365, 366, 368
empirical realism, 30, 199
empiricism, 27, 32, 114, 125, 130, 135, 136, 197, 198, 210, 273, 282, 284, 300, 312, 349, 356
definition of, 27
endearing conception of religion, notion of, 253, 292
England, 114, 188, 189, 190, 194, 206
English, 3, 18, 19, 27, 100, 104, 109, 118, 163, 189, 191, 194, 198, 231, 247, 346
enjoining the lawful, concept of, 149, 174
enlightenment, 5, 12, 26, 32, 35, 104, 130, 143, 147, 180, 197, 231, 257, 260, 263, 264, 266, 289, 315, 319, 324, 329, 331, 332, 333, 337, 347, 357, 361, 362, 363, 366, 367
and pluralism, 33, 329
concept of reason, 26, 27, 31, 32, 180, 197, 263, 264, 266, 289, 329, 337
criticism of, 29, 34, 319, 329, 332, 333
modernism, 4, 26, 33, 34, 148, 203, 306, 326, 331, 333, 346, 347, 362, 363, 364
normative principles of, 26
epistemic belief, 30, 32, 100, 124, 125, 131, 132, 179, 210, 273, 274, 283, 292, 309, 311, 313, 337, 338, 340, 341, 358, 368
basic and non-basic, 32
self-justifying, 274, 313, 338, 358
epistemic coherentism, 273
epistemic probabilism, 339
epistemic schemes, 32, 57, 58, 74, 81, 245, 332, 344
definition of, 57
epistemological fallibism, 338
epistemology, 3, 4, 5, 6, 15, 18, 23, 26, 27, 28, 34, 35, 55–76, 103, 105, 106, 107, 111, 112, 118, 119, 121, 122, 123, 124, 125, 126, 129, 130, 131, 132, 135, 136, 142, 143, 144, 146, 150, 151, 153, 156, 160, 161, 162, 164, 166, 169, 170, 173, 175, 176, 183, 188, 190, 191, 194, 197, 198, 199, 200, 201, 207, 214, 218, 219, 222, 224, 225, 226, 228, 234, 235, 237, 240, 241, 242, 243, 245, 246, 247, 253–255, 257, 258, 259, 260, 265, 266, 269, 273, 274, 275, 276, 278, 281, 282, 286, 287–315, 316, 317, 318, 325, 326, 328, 330, 332, 333, 335, 337, 338, 340, 341, 343, 350, 355, 356, 357, 358, 360, 362, 365, 366, 368
and contingency, 124, 135, 289, 309, 312, 318, 339
and logic, 65, 75, 103, 111, 120, 122, 132, 169, 201, 234, 272, 279, 284–286, 287, 293, 313, 350
and receptivity, 127
and religious faith, 132, 133, 169, 172, 204, 211–213, 293, 306, 332, 357, 365
constants and non-constants in, 280, 291, 292, 300, 311, 312, 358, 359
definition of, 23
division of, 111
end of, 316, 326
foundations of, 23, 126, 135, 146, 173, 198, 269, 273, 314, 330, 338, 344, 364
grading of, 69, 111, 128, 134, 141, 345, 351
in the West, 111, 135, 156, 166, 169, 170, 290, 296, 309
in traditional Islam, 55–76, 75, 81, 297, 304, 344, 345
notion of unity in, 58
of presence, 69, 111, 132
separated from ontology, 169, 210, 304, 306, 309, 354
sources of, 31, 125, 127, 128, 130, 201, 211, 215, 273, 300, 307, 317, 339, 347, 357
esoterism, 5, 13, 20, 31, 51–53, 59, 60, 63, 68, 79, 84, 95, 96, 110, 126, 129, 131, 136, 139, 140, 141, 144, 148, 159, 176, 182, 216, 237, 247, 255, 262, 263, 303
in Shi'i Islam, 51–53, 60, 106
essence, concept of, 14, 19, 113, 157, 207, 208, 280, 281, 348, 360, 364
ethics, 23, 26, 32, 40–42, 43, 45, 46, 47, 48, 64, 66, 80, 84, 91, 118, 128, 133, 134, 142, 143, 148, 153, 157, 166, 188, 202, 204, 205, 207, 214, 216, 218, 219, 220, 223, 227, 230, 231, 236, 237–241, 244, 245, 247, 251, 261, 263, 267, 268, 269, 289, 296, 297, 309, 311, 324, 329, 340, 347, 352, 353, 362
and law, 41–43, 84, 116, 128, 133, 153, 165, 174, 223, 237–241, 353
and religious faith, 296
and theology, 66, 143, 144, 238, 239
as constructed, 26, 238–240, 352–353
as deontology, 81, 231, 239
as natural command, 153
categorical, 26, 239, 329

in the Qur'an, 41
social justice, 144
ethnology, 312
etsi Deus non daretur, 49
eurocentrism, 329
Europe, 4, 7, 12, 15, 16, 18, 19, 21, 25, 26, 33, 36, 48, 50, 51, 103, 104, 108, 109, 110, 143, 145, 146, 148, 168, 176, 188, 194, 219, 224, 255, 259, 277, 281, 289, 290, 306, 329, 367
event, 10, 11, 12, 43, 44
evolution, 151, 154, 256, 257, 258, 259, 277, 280, 281, 288, 289, 290, 299, 357
as a paradigmatic modification, 256
as qualititative, 280
creative, 256
of Islamic law, 3, 11, 15, 16, 44, 45, 47, 71, 78, 96, 99, 103, 167, 226
of knowledge, 119, 120, 124, 125, 130, 135, 136, 176, 197, 211, 243, 245, 246, 253, 255, 256, 257, 258, 259, 260, 262, 269, 271, 275, 276, 277, 279, 280, 281, 287, 288, 289, 290, 292, 297, 305, 309, 310, 312, 316, 341
evolutionary epistemology, 276, 277, 281, 282, 311, 312, 350, 357, 359
exegesis, 3, 12, 13, 14, 15, 43, 44, 62, 63, 64, 78–79, 91, 92, 93–97, 97, 96, 99, 112, 114, 121, 122, 126, 139, 140, 141, 143, 154, 172, 175, 176, 177, 178, 180, 183, 228, 247, 248, 254, 257, 289, 316, 317, 318, 332, 336
and jurisprudence, 43, 92
categories of traditional, 79
esoteric, 13, 53, 79, 96–97, 141, 176, 317, 318
in the West, 8, 12, 181
legal, 78, 121, 122
opinionative, 79, 317, 318
principles of, 95, 139
subject, 139
exemption, juristic, 98, 244
existentialism, 156, 170, 188, 211
exoterism, 51, 52, 95, 96, 111, 131, 139, 140, 141, 157, 159, 216, 263, 303
expedient jurisprudence, 4
experience, 19, 21, 26, 27, 29, 30, 123, 128, 156, 157, 168, 169, 172, 173, 174, 178, 179, 180, 197, 198, 199, 201, 203, 212, 219, 227, 229, 263, 266, 267, 272, 273, 281, 283, 291, 292, 295, 297, 298, 299, 300, 303, 304, 306, 316, 322, 324, 340, 350, 354, 358, 360
and history, 179
and method, 8, 156–157, 166, 168–169, 179, 180, 267, 299
as contingent, 27, 27, 28, 29, 34, 157, 168, 170, 181, 198, 229, 281, 283, 297, 306
as intentional, 180, 214
conjectural, 169
intuitive, 96, 128, 129, 219, 265
Qur'an on, 56
sovereignty of, 26
experiment, 27, 123, 128, 134, 157, 240, 267, 278
extension, 28
external world. *See* phenomenal realm
extra ecclesiam nulla salus, 302

factualism. *See* naive realism; empiricism
Fāḍil-Tūnī, Ḥ., 126
Faiḍīyah school, 247
Falāṭūrī, ʿA., 16, 110
fallibilistic realism, 312
falsafah. *See* philosophy
falsafah ūlā. *See* philosophy, first
falsification, 70, 120, 121, 188, 198, 199, 200, 202, 211, 212, 214, 219, 220, 228, 240, 260, 267, 270, 273, 276, 278, 279, 280, 282, 283, 284, 286, 287, 291, 292, 299, 320, 327, 337, 339, 350, 355, 356, 358
familial affinity, theory of, 213
Fanon, F., 156
al-Fārābī, A.N., 133, 207
Faraghānī, S., 69
farḍ al-kifāyah. *See* collective obligation
Fardīd, A., 208, 209
Fariman, 112
Fārsī, J., 189
fascism, 149, 190, 193
Fāṭimīd, 90
Fès, 204
Feuerbach, L., 212, 254
Feyerabend, P., 286, 327, 337, 368
Fichte, J.G., 157
fideism, 32, 211
fides quaerens intellectum, 236
finitude, 14, 31, 172, 183, 296, 300, 320, 323, 324
fiṭrat. *See* natural disposition
fiqh. *See* jurisprudence
fiqh-i jawāhirī. *See* traditional jurisprudence
fiqh-i maṣlaḥatī. *See* expedient jurisprudence
fiqh-i pūyā. See dynamic jurisprudence
fiqh-i sunnatī. *See* traditional jurisprudence
Flacius, M., 181
forum externum, 42, 232, 240
forum internum, 42
Foucault, M., 34, 35, 194, 204, 250, 251, 290, 301, 327, 328, 329
foundationalism, 32, 199, 273, 283, 306, 309, 313, 314, 326, 327, 338, 356, 363
definition of, 32
France, 36, 146, 151, 289
Frankfurt school, 198
free will, 71, 230, 260, 334

freedom, 42, 97, 106, 151, 165, 181, 184, 210, 231, 232, 239, 243, 264, 287
French, 8, 18, 34, 47, 104, 109, 111, 118, 145, 152, 155, 163, 164, 183, 192, 197, 210, 245, 256, 288, 289, 328
Freud, S., 34, 198, 245, 282
fulfilment, level of, 268, 269, 284, 287, 298
fuqahā. *See* jurists
furūʿ al-fiqh. See jurisprudence, branches of
Furūghī, M.ʿA., 109
fusion of horizons, 12, 179, 180, 181, 326, 361
futurism, 156

Gadamer, H., 8, 9, 14, 156, 160, 166, 168, 173, 178, 179, 180, 182, 291, 320, 322, 323, 324, 325, 326, 361
Galileo, G., 34, 146, 183, 235, 276, 289, 290, 295
Garaudy, R., 155
gender issues, 139, 214, 224, 233, 243, 249, 265, 324, 338
genealogy, 92
genuineness, ontological, 271, 280
geography, 26, 109, 204, 205, 214, 225, 247, 343, 351
geology, 288
geometry, 32, 218, 282, 299
German, 93, 112, 160, 163, 166, 176
Germany, 118, 163, 197, 297
Ghaffārī, Ḥ., 119, 122, 123–124
gharbzadigi. *See* dysisplexia, concept of
al-Ghazālī, M., 57, 58, 67, 75, 168, 174, 193, 194, 211, 214, 233, 234, 235, 236, 240, 263
ghulāt, 52, 60, 84
globalisation, 4, 25, 32, 33, 37, 161, 162, 163, 164, 209, 236, 353, 366
de Gobineau, A.C., 109
God, 11, 13, 28, 31, 34, 37, 40, 42, 44, 46, 49, 51, 52, 55, 56, 58, 60, 62, 66, 67, 68, 69, 70, 73, 75, 83, 84, 85, 90, 93, 94, 95, 97, 99, 112, 113, 115, 116, 124, 127, 128, 129, 132, 135, 138, 139, 140, 141, 145, 147, 148, 149, 150, 153, 155, 159, 160, 164, 166, 169, 173, 175, 183, 191, 199, 200, 210, 212, 214, 216, 228, 229, 230, 231, 232, 239, 240, 245, 250, 253, 254, 255, 256, 262, 263, 264, 265, 273, 274, 275, 288, 289, 295, 296, 297, 302, 304, 305, 306, 307, 308, 313, 314, 326, 327, 329, 333, 334, 340, 341, 344, 346, 347, 348, 350, 355, 356, 362, 363, 366
  as attribute of matter, 28
  as chief mathematician, 289
  as dependent on man, 254
  as human construct, 212, 297, 306, 362, 366
  as individual, 29
  as manifested in revelation, 139
  as object postulated by reason, 297
  as principle of being, 67
  Attributes of, 112, 128, 129, 136, 140, 150, 304
  death of, 306, 329
  Essence of, 112, 140, 150, 314
  immanence of, 58, 306
  immoral, 263–264
  mysteriousness of, 306, 327
  vicegerency of, 30, 129, 145, 150, 307, 308, 356, 366
Goodman, N., 284
goodness, concept of, 238, 239, 258, 264, 265, 289, 334
  objective existence of, 66, 83, 84, 118, 231
  truth as, 5
governance, 33, 36, 45, 108, 109, 115, 116, 137, 145, 150, 152, 161, 164, 166, 183, 189, 194, 203, 205, 207, 217, 218, 219, 221, 223, 224, 227, 229, 233, 249, 250, 262, 265, 277, 287, 294, 295, 305, 328, 330, 353
gradualness, ontological, 57
grammar, 20, 59, 91, 101, 122, 126, 133, 233
grammatica in Spiritus sancti verbis occupata, 182
gravitation, theory of, 290, 296
Greece, 242
Greek, 8, 23, 31, 36, 40, 48, 49, 55, 58, 65, 67, 68, 75, 123, 131, 146, 151, 156, 164, 165, 203, 207, 210, 220, 234, 235
Grotius, H., 49
Guardian council, 120
Gulpāigānī, M.R., 113, 119, 121
Gunabad, 187
Gurvitch, G., 155, 156

Habermas, J., 26, 188, 203, 250, 251, 301, 328, 329, 366
Ḥabībī, Ḥ., 189
ḥadīṯ, 11, 14, 61, 62, 63, 64, 65, 71, 72, 73, 78, 80, 81, 84, 89, 90, 92, 94, 96, 99, 110, 114, 126, 138, 139, 143, 145, 161, 178, 179, 215, 249, 274, 301, 318
  and jurisprudence, 14, 62
  as transmitted knowledge, 59
  fabrication of, 15, 80, 274
  'followers of', 59, 61
  science of the reliability of, 58
  Shi'i collections of, 81, 110
  transmitters of, 78, 81, 89, 122
Ḥāfiẓ, S., 193, 195, 203, 306
hagiography, 247
Hā'irī-Yazdī, ʿA., 74, 110, 114, 153, 247
Hā'irī-Yazdī, M., 110, 113
al-Ḥakam, H., 84
Ḥakamīzādah, ʿA.A., 147
Ḥakīm-Yazdī, M.ʿA.A., 115
halakha, 40

Hamburg, 118, 163
Hanbal, A., 66
al-Hanīfah, A., 40, 53, 73, 81, 99
happiness, 132, 296, 333
ḥarakat-i jauharī. *See* substantial motion
Hart, H.L.A., 227
ḥashwīyah, 165
ḥauzah, 11, 90–91, 105, 113, 116, 117, 118, 119, 120, 126, 134, 135, 142, 143, 147, 153, 161, 163, 167, 182, 184, 187, 189, 193, 196, 207, 214, 215, 228, 243, 244, 246–251, 253, 270
  autonomity of, 99, 250
  for women, 139, 247
  information technology at, 15
  reform of, 105, 247
  text discourse at, 135
heart, spiritual, 13, 51, 59, 68, 127, 139, 141, 195, 232, 240, 253, 266, 304
Hebrew, 36
Hegel, G.W.F., 41, 109, 112, 123, 157, 181, 199, 207, 208, 237, 255, 256, 257, 258, 259, 260, 319, 320
hegemony of companies, 26
Heidegger, M., 12, 30, 156, 160, 169, 176, 177, 188, 296, 322, 323, 325, 330
Hellenism, 66, 75, 274, 275
Hempel, C.G., 120, 267, 284, 285, 286
Heracleit, 26
hereafter, 202, 216, 218, 225, 234, 235, 240, 295
heresy, 16, 20, 22, 73, 99, 306
hermeneutical circle, 15, 122, 160, 177, 178, 323
hermeneutical situation, 15, 177, 181, 183, 316, 343
hermeneutics, 3, 5, 6, 7–13, 14, 15, 23, 77, 92–97, 112, 119, 121, 131, 135, 139–142, 146, 150, 154, 156, 159, 160, 168, 169, 170, 171, 172, 173, 175–182, 184, 185, 190, 201, 223, 226, 227, 228, 231, 233, 234, 241, 247, 253, 255, 260, 263, 266, 276, 280, 283, 286, 288, 291, 292, 293, 294, 295, 300, 316–333, 324, 325, 327, 330, 332, 333, 334, 335, 339, 340, 343, 349, 350, 355, 357, 360, 361, 362, 363
  and alien cultures, 9
  and conformity, 169, 183, 318, 329
  and language, 8, 93, 94, 96, 97, 139, 140, 142, 179, 182, 318, 319–325, 330,
  and legal theory, 77–79, 241
  and paradigm, 321, 331
  as dialogue, 177, 179
  as *eisegesis*, 332
  as innovative creation, 331
  as method, 7, 170, 268, 317, 324
  as participation, 140
  as revelation, 172
  as translation, 179
  definition of, 8
  in the West, 6, 7, 8, 12, 92, 160, 163, 168, 171, 173, 175, 176, 178, 179, 180, 181, 182, 322
  in traditional Islam, 12, 42, 43, 44, 45, 78, 79, 92–97, 98, 99, 101, 317, 346
  of love, 139
  of suspicion, 9
  Qur'anic, 11, 13, 44, 45, 79, 92, 94, 121, 139, 175, 177, 178, 181, 318, 321, 322, 325
  hermeticism, 52
Herschel, W.F., 277
Hick, J., 193, 212, 290, 302
Hidāyat, Ṣ., 189
hierarchy of levels, 30, 36, 56, 57, 58, 70, 99, 107, 121, 126, 127, 128, 134, 136, 141, 144, 159, 263, 264, 275, 281, 305, 344, 345, 351, 353, 354, 355, 360, 364
High council of cultural revolution, 189, 190
ḥikmat al-ishrāq. *See* illumination
ḥikmat-i muta'ālīyah. *See* transcendental wisdom
al-Hillī, Ḥ.Y.'A., 11, 42, 73, 86, 87, 89, 99, 114, 345
al-Hillī, I., 72
al-Hillī, N.M.Q., 86
Himmatī, H., 111
Hinduism, 42, 227
histology, 271, 272
historical criticism, 165, 166, 181
historical determinism, 156, 188
historical objectivism, 177
historical phenomenology, 171
historicism, 112, 119, 157, 257, 258, 259, 260, 265
historicity, 92, 179, 223, 245, 265, 308, 320, 323, 362
history, 3, 9, 10, 13, 14, 15, 16, 25, 30, 42, 43, 44, 65, 75, 78, 88, 92, 107, 109, 129, 132, 142, 144, 149, 151, 153, 154, 155, 156, 165, 166, 171, 172, 173, 179, 181, 182, 184, 188, 193, 198, 202, 206, 208, 213, 217, 219, 221, 222, 226, 227, 235, 237, 238, 240, 242, 246, 254, 255, 256, 257, 258, 259, 260, 261, 262, 264, 266, 271, 278, 287, 288, 289, 294, 295, 301, 308, 318, 323, 325, 327, 332, 335, 336, 337, 340, 341, 343, 346, 349, 356, 358, 361, 368
  and hermeneutics, 3, 9, 92–93, 132, 178, 179, 181, 182, 323, 324, 325, 361
  as divine process, 256, 262
  as mirror of reason, 255
  as nostalgia, 43
  as repetitive cycle of birth and decay, 256
  effect in, 180, 323, 325

of modernity, 25
'questioning' of, 178
history of law, 167
history of philosophy, 30, 157, 255, 259, 316
history of religions, 181
history of science, 156, 188, 246, 253, 267, 290, 317
Hobbes, T., 27, 261
Hodgson, M.G.S., 8, 39, 52
holism, 197, 212, 312, 344
homo homini Deo, 212
homosexuality, 216
horizon, concept of, 12, 136, 173, 178, 180, 181, 321, 322, 323, 324, 331, 361
al-Hudail, A., 174
Ḥujjatī-Kirmānī, ʿA., 110
Hujwīrī, ʿA., 52, 253
Humāʾī, J., 110
human rights, 126, 138, 151, 164, 171, 172, 191, 230, 231, 232, 265, 329
human sciences, 25, 124, 130, 134, 145, 164, 172, 173, 189, 190, 192, 206, 207, 228, 234, 247, 250, 267, 268, 276, 288, 289, 297, 336
humanism, 12, 27, 162, 164, 206, 218, 219, 231, 239, 246, 254, 262, 303, 326, 359, 368
Hume, D., 168, 188, 234, 259, 267, 289, 297, 298, 312
Hungarian, 282
Huntington, S.P., 204
Husain b. ʿAlī, 249
Ḥusainī-Bihishtī, M., 187, 189
Ḥusainī-Sīstānī, S.ʿA., 119
Ḥusainī-Shāhrūdī, S.M., 119
Ḥusainīyah-yi irshād, 148, 155
Husserl, E., 153, 156, 157, 168, 169, 170, 173, 176, 245, 333, 360
hypothesis. *See* scientific theories

ibāḥah. *See* openness, hermeneutical
Ibn al-ʿArabī, M., 141
Ibn Hanzalah, ʿU., 137, 138
Ibn Ḥazm, ʿA., 57, 75
Ibn al-Muqaffā, ʿA., 49
Ibn Rushd, A.M., 67, 68, 116
Ibn Sīnā, A.ʿA.Ḥ., 68, 110, 280, 320
Ibn Taimīyah, A., 57, 67, 75, 76, 105, 148, 168
idealism, 21, 27, 30, 47, 105, 111, 197, 199, 200, 216, 220, 222, 226, 257, 258, 261, 283, 297, 299, 300, 307, 312, 333, 341, 349
identity, 205, 209, 213, 216
ideology, 4, 144, 149, 150, 151, 153, 154, 155, 156, 158, 162, 163, 191, 202, 207, 216, 219, 220, 238, 250, 258, 307, 308
as systematic error of reason, 219
circle of, 202, 220
political, 163
iḥtiyāṭ, *See* prudence, juristic
ijāzah, 89, 91, 118, 153, 163
ijmāʿ. *See* consensus
ijāzah, 89, 91
ijtihād, 14, 15, 59, 71, 72, 77, 82, 87–89, 91, 101, 107, 108, 110, 111, 114, 116, 117, 118, 120, 122, 137, 138, 143, 147, 148, 152, 155, 158, 161, 163, 164, 166, 167, 169, 171, 172, 173, 174, 175, 182, 184, 209, 213, 221, 222, 224, 226, 227, 240, 241, 242, 243, 244, 245, 255, 277, 330, 335, 345, 346, 351, 352, 354, 363
and women, 139
as cultural transformation, 244, 352
as infallible, 59
as permanent revolution, 158, 161
fallible nature of, 25, 71, 73, 88, 100, 169
extra-legal, 142, 158, 161, 171, 173, 182, 184, 242–246
gate to, 88, 118, 166
grades of, 88
legal, 31, 77, 87–89, 114, 116, 122, 124, 137
preliminaries of, 89, 108, 111, 114, 122, 167, 175
Shi'i concept of, 60, 73, 84, 85, 87–89, 100, 105
'spirit' of, 148
Sunni concept of, 85, 88, 105
traditional definition of, 87–89
ikhtilāf. *See* conflicting interpretations
Ilāhī-Qumshaʾī, M.M., 126
ʿillah. *See ratio decidendi*
illumination, 69, 132
ʿilm, 20, 31, 55, 56, 58, 60, 64, 65, 66, 68, 72, 73, 78, 84, 87, 90, 91, 92, 93, 94, 99, 100, 141, 145, 158, 187, 189, 190, 195, 196, 197, 207, 214, 231, 242, 244, 248, 250, 255, 270, 344, 345. *See also* science
and legal reasoning, 31
and religious belief, 56
as esoteric knowledge, 63
as knowledge of law, 40
as presumptive knowledge, 73
distinct from profane knowledge, 147
Qur'anic usage of, 55
religious and mundane, 56
Shi'i notion of, 53
status in Islam, 55
ʿilm al-ḥuḍūrī. *See* epistemology, of presence
ʿilm al-kalām. *See* theology
ʿilm al-lughah. *See* linguistics
ʿilm ḍarūrī. *See* necessary knowledge
ʿilm al-manṭiq. *See* logic
ʿilm muktasab. *See* acquired knowledge
ʿilm al-tafsīr. *See* exegesis

imām, 52, 53, 54, 60, 66, 70, 71, 79, 81, 84, 87, 94, 100, 101, 105, 116, 129, 138, 141, 148, 155, 171, 191, 213, 235, 262, 263, 317, 345
as keeper of Islamic law, 82
as Logos, 52, 96
as revolutionary, 156
as 'speaking' law, 140
as 'speaking' Qur'an, 94
knowledge of the, 53
in re, 30
India, 105, 151
Indian, 58, 86, 203, 210, 301
individuality, 10, 14, 21, 29, 35, 37, 73, 145, 147, 206, 208, 211, 213, 216, 218, 219, 224, 228, 230, 231, 232, 239, 240, 251, 276, 281, 299, 302, 303, 304, 306, 310, 313, 316, 323, 331, 335, 336, 337, 368
of legal norms, 41
Indonesian, 194
induction, 56, 65, 111, 120, 121, 122, 123, 128, 136, 153, 197, 198, 234, 259, 273, 276, 277, 278, 283, 285, 286, 291, 313, 317, 331, 350, 351
Shi'i rejection of, 85
unfinished nature of, 120, 278
industrialisation, 367
inference, juristic, 46, 65, 70, 71, 77, 82, 84–85, 92, 103, 107, 108, 109, 113, 120, 121, 122, 123, 134, 137, 138, 139, 142, 143, 153, 165, 167, 174, 177, 182, 183, 226, 228, 233, 243, 244, 246, 255, 269, 334, 344, 345, 351, 359
and probability, 42, 70, 100, 142, 183, 334
as acquired, 70, 153, 225, 226
as non-acquired, 46, 138
as relative to the principles of law, 158, 167, 174
as relative to the subjects of law, 114
individuality of, 73
Qur'anic concept of, 56
infitāh. *See* openness, juristic
information technology, 11, 37, 250, 328, 365
innovation, juristic, 61, 72, 92, 99, 266
insān-i kāmil. *See* perfect man, concept of
ʿinsidād bāb al-ijtihād. *See ijtihād*, gate to
instant-paradigm, 22
institutional facts, 237
instrumentalism, 157, 162, 164, 289
insurance, 108, 114, 277
intellect. *See* reason
intellection. *See* intuition
intellectual debate, 3, 4, 5, 6, 22, 23
intellectuals, 3, 4, 5, 6, 7, 8, 10, 16, 17, 18, 19, 20, 21, 22, 23, 25, 33, 104, 105, 109, 111, 112, 113, 132, 146, 147, 148, 158, 159, 188, 190, 194, 209, 223, 234, 244, 270, 287
as the child of modernity, 270
religious, 270
in premodern Iran, 20
intellectus, 59, 84
intention of author, 8, 9, 11, 121, 148, 160, 178, 180, 181, 214, 318, 319, 320, 321, 323, 324, 327, 330, 331, 360, 361
intentionality, concept of, 170, 180, 323, 324, 332, 360, 361
Internet, 37
intersubjectivity, 260, 283, 284, 305, 308, 309, 328, 333, 355, 362
intiẓār-i mā az dīn. *See* our expectation of religion, concept of
intuition, 12, 31, 52, 56, 57, 66, 69, 84, 111, 126, 127, 128, 129, 132, 134, 135, 219, 266, 273, 285, 291, 299, 304, 305, 308, 313, 316, 328, 344, 345, 351, 356, 358, 360, 365
as non-acquired knowledge, 84, 128–129, 273, 299
Qur'anic concept of, 56
intuitionism, 237
Iqbāl, M., 161, 173, 174, 221, 226, 227, 235, 256
Iran, 3, 4, 5, 6, 8, 17, 18, 20, 33, 36, 49, 51, 90, 99, 101, 104, 105, 106, 108, 109, 110, 114, 115, 117, 118, 119, 124, 126, 139, 145, 146, 148, 150, 151, 153, 155, 158, 159, 161, 163, 168, 184, 187, 188, 189, 190, 192, 194, 196, 201, 214, 217, 219, 220, 222, 223, 224, 229, 232, 233, 247, 248, 368, 354, 364, 365, 367
Iran Teacher's association, 187
Iranian, 4, 5, 6, 17, 18, 21, 23, 32, 33, 51, 90, 104, 106, 109, 110, 111, 112, 119, 147, 149, 151, 161, 162, 163, 164, 165, 188, 190, 191, 192, 193, 194, 196, 208, 209, 223, 225, 229, 248, 249, 250, 270, 277, 302, 328, 334, 335, 343, 366
Iranian culture, 33, 206, 208, 209, 217
Iranian law, 36, 51, 114, 143, 147
Iranian studies, 155
Iraq, 80, 115, 277
ʿirfān, 20, 39, 57, 63, 91, 113, 115, 126, 132, 133, 167, 176, 214, 215, 219, 305, 365. *See also* theosophy
definition of, 63
Isfahan, 118
Islamic culture, 5, 19, 20, 206, 208, 215, 235, 245, 367
unity and diversity in, 20
Islamic discourses, 3, 4, 6, 7, 8, 20, 21, 22, 25
definition of, 20–22
Islamic law, 3, 4, 5, 6, 11, 14–17, 18, 19, 21, 31, 35, 36, 37, 39–54, 63, 69–76, 79, 82, 83, 88, 89, 90, 91, 93, 97, 103, 104, 105, 107, 108, 109, 110, 113, 115, 116, 117, 120, 121, 123, 124, 129, 131, 133, 136–138, 139, 140, 142, 143, 144, 145, 146, 147, 152, 153, 159,

161, 163, 165, 166–172, 173, 174, 182, 190, 194, 195, 196, 199, 203, 209, 210, 214, 215, 217, 219, 220, 221, 222, 223–246, 255, 262, 264, 268, 270, 271, 274, 275, 278, 282, 288, 289, 292, 293, 294, 295, 296, 301, 307, 308, 309, 310, 311, 334, 335, 336, 341, 343, 344, 346, 347, 349, 351, 352, 353, 354, 359, 364, 365
and ethics, 40–42, 46, 74, 116, 128, 133, 219, 237–241, 353, 365
and individuality, 14, 41, 45, 70, 78, 82, 88, 98, 100, 147, 224, 231–232, 240
and natural science, 134
and philosophy, 43, 67, 113, 167, 168, 272, 274, 282, 292–293
and social practice, 15, 35, 47, 48, 54, 103, 115, 137, 153, 225, 231, 232, 236, 347, 353
and state, 48, 49, 51, 99, 103, 104, 105, 106, 112, 116, 117, 161, 165 , 216–218, 231
as compound system, 40
as human construction, 159, 292–293
as metaphor, 46
as system of duties, 47
embodying the Divine Will, 43, 46, 67, 120, 229, 230, 237
immutability of, 16, 107, 108, 113, 117, 123, 180, 22, 238, 280
non-ecclesiastical character of, 46, 49, 106, 182
objectives of, 146, 168, 174, 214, 244, 245
probability in, 70, 74, 85, 86, 87, 100, 120, 125, 134, 138, 169, 183, 225, 333, 334
'silent' (in-itself), 124, 160, 161, 293, 295, 311, 349, 364
sources of, 3, 31, 63, 72, 77, 78, 79, 82, 83, 87, 115, 121, 122, 123, 137, 147, 152, 173, 17, 345
'speaking', 140, 160, 293
'spirit' of, 242, 244
Islamic modernism, 4, 5, 6, 22, 23, 32, 36, 105, 108, 112, 117, 143–185, 211, 216, 220, 224, 226, 235, 343, 346, 352, 355, 364. *See also* Mujtahid-Shabistarī, M.
and Islamic traditionalism, 108, 168, 112, 115, 117–118, 148–150, 180
criticism of, 138, 211, 224
definition of, 23, 161
inception of, 105
on conflicting interpretations, 182–184
on epistemology, 22, 143, 144, 146, 156, 157, 161, 162
on ethics, 143, 144, 153, 171
on hermeneutics, 143, 146, 154, 158, 160
on hierarchy, 144, 159
on history, 144, 151, 153, 156
on ideology, 149, 151, 152, 155
on *ijtihād*, 143, 147, 152, 158, 161
on inference, 143, 144, 146, 148, 158, 159
on method, 23, 105, 116, 143, 145
on modern law, 144, 145, 146, 159
on modern science,
on modernity, 144, 148, 149, 159, 162
on reason, 144, 147, 152, 157
on science, 115, 144, 145, 146, 148, 150, 155
on subjectivity, 150, 157
on theology, 143, 149, 165, 166
Islamic modernity, 7, 144, 158, 162, 163, 185, 343, 346, 367
Islamic postmodernism, 5, 6, 7, 23–25, 37, 343, 364, 365. *See also* Surūsh, ʿA.
definition of, 23
on epistemology, 22, 23
on hermeneutics, 23
Islamic 'protestantism', 123
Islamic republic of Iran, 17, 114, 115, 118, 153, 161, 189, 229, 233, 251
Islamic studies, 15, 16, 17, 18, 21, 22
Islamic traditionalism, 6, 23, 106–143, 147, 148, 149, 150, 160, 211, 226, 243, 274, 343, 349, 351, 352, 355, 364. *See also* Jawādī-Āmulī, ʿA.
and Islamic modernism, 108, 168, 112, 115, 117–118, 148–150, 180
criticism of, 175, 180, 243, 261, 274
definition of, 23, 106
distinct from traditional Islam, 106
inception of, 109
on conflicting interpretations, 121, 122
on epistemic probability, 120, 125
on epistemology, 22, 23, 106, 111, 113, 114, 117, 123, 124, 125
on ethics, 116, 118, 128, 133, 142
on exegesis, 23, 112
on hierarchy, 107, 121
on history, 107, 114, 132, 141, 142
on *ijtihād*, 113, 114, 122, 124
on inference, 107, 113, 115, 116, 117, 120, 122, 124
on modernity, 106, 107, 113, 115, 117, 118
on ontology, 111, 117, 121, 126, 127, 128, 130, 131, 132, 134, 136
on reason, 117, 111, 113, 118, 125, 127
on science, 107, 120, 122
islamisation, 103, 106, 151, 190, 219, 229, 232, 246, 308, 354, 357
Ismāʾīl, A.S., 60
ismāʿīlī, 90
isomorphism, 300
Istiʿlāmī, M., 189
istiṣḥāb. *See* continuance, juristic
istiṣlāḥ. *See* public interest, juristic

istinbāṭ. *See* inference, juristic
istiḥsān. *See* preference, juristic
Italian, 18, 254
Iʿtimād al-Salṭanah, 109

Jabhah-yi millī, 147
jahānbīnī. *See* worldview
Jāmī, ʿA., 52
Jannatī, A., 191
Jannātī, M.I., 139
Jawādī-Āmulī, ʿA., 6, 18, 126–143, 144, 145, 146, 147, 148, 149, 150, 151, 152, 153, 154, 155, 156, 157, 158, 159, 160, 161, 261, 274, 343, 351, 356, 360
  biography of, 126
  concept of law, 136
  criticism of, 164
  division of philosophy, 132
  on conflicting interpretations, 142
  on epistemic certainty, 128, 131, 133, 134, 137, 138
  on epistemology, 126, 127, 128, 129, 135, 136, 351, 355, 356, 359
  on governance, 137
  on *ḥauzah*, 142–143
  on hermeneutics, 135, 139–142
  on *ijtihād*, 136–138
  on inference, 136, 137, 138, 142, 351
  on method, 127, 128, 133, 351
  on modernity, 129
  on philosophy, 127, 130, 131, 132, 355
  on reason, 127, 128, 131, 132, 133, 134, 135, 137
  on science, 127, 128, 129, 133, 136, 138
  on subjectivity, 129
Jawāhirī, M.Ḥ., 117
Jesus Christ, 181, 290, 341
Jewish, 40, 79, 130, 155, 290, 301, 366
jihād. *See* religious war
Judaism, 152, 329
judicial, 16, 40, 42, 48, 50, 79, 138, 145, 153, 224, 227, 229, 240, 353
al-Junaid, A.ʿA.M., 62
Junbish-i musalmān-i mubāriz, 159
jurisprudence, 4, 5, 6, 14, 16, 17, 18, 20, 39–54, 60, 62, 64, 66, 67, 68, 69–76, 77, 78, 79, 80, 81, 82, 83, 87, 90, 91, 92, 95, 96, 97, 98, 99, 103, 104, 106, 108, 111, 112, 113, 114, 115, 116, 117, 118, 120, 121, 122, 123, 126, 128, 131, 133, 134, 136–138, 139, 142, 143, 144, 147, 148, 149, 152, 153, 158, 161, 163, 165, 166–172, 173, 174, 175, 177, 184, 187, 195, 196, 200, 211, 214, 215, 216, 217, 220, 221, 222, 223–241, 242, 243, 244, 246, 250, 253, 255, 261, 262, 266, 270, 271, 274, 275, 280, 288, 289, 292, 294, 318, 324, 334, 335, 338, 343, 344, 346, 349, 351, 352, 353, 354, 365
  and comparative methods, 93
  and language, 79, 89, 92, 93, 94, 95
  and pluralism, 98, 142, 183, 293, 333, 334
  and spirituality, 51, 46, 68, 120, 128
  and theology, 39, 42, 65, 73, 103, 104, 168, 275, 333, 334
  as hermeneutical, 11, 14, 40, 42, 43–45, 60, 77, 168, 169, 171, 175, 182, 254
  as irrational, 83, 223, 352
  as 'minimalist' science, 233, 236, 352
  as positive law, 45, 48, 50, 51, 77, 146, 153, 215, 217, 229–230
  as rational, 165, 174
  as 'swollen' science, 223
  as this-worldly, 235, 240
  branches of, 62, 71, 72, 77, 81, 98, 117, 121, 137, 143, 158, 171, 173, 225, 242, 243, 244, 255, 335, 351, 352
  inception of, 47, 53, 65
  scale of ethical values in, 41
  subjects of, 105, 108, 109, 114, 117, 123, 137, 241, 335
  traditional definition of, 40
jurists, 4, 16, 20, 31, 35, 37, 39, 40, 43, 46, 47, 48, 49, 51, 55, 57, 60, 61, 62, 63, 64, 67, 69, 70, 71, 72, 74, 75, 78, 79, 81, 83, 84, 85, 86, 87, 88, 89, 90, 91, 92, 93, 94, 95, 98, 99, 101, 103, 105, 108, 109, 110, 115, 121, 122, 123, 136, 148, 161, 168, 169, 174, 182, 183, 184, 185, 195, 209, 215, 222, 225, 228, 229, 234, 240, 241, 242, 243, 249, 250, 255, 277, 334, 335, 344, 345, 368
  as the successors of the *imām*, 90
jus, 50
justice, 31, 41, 47, 66, 71, 85, 110, 118, 144, 145, 147, 162, 171, 236, 238, 239, 240, 263, 264, 265, 287, 319, 334
justice privée, 47
justification, context of, 283, 298, 338
justification, epistemic, 30, 32, 122, 125, 131, 135, 176, 207, 228, 260, 263, 264, 269, 272, 273, 274, 283, 284, 286, 291, 296, 298, 303, 309, 313, 314, 315, 318, 319, 322, 335, 338, 340, 349, 350, 358, 368
Justinianus, 45, 46, 49, 50
al-Juwainī, M., 88

Kadīwar, M., 115, 191
kalām-i jadīd. *See* modern theology
Kant, I., 4, 5, 25, 26, 28, 29, 30, 31, 34, 109, 111, 135, 153, 157, 166, 168, 169, 170, 188, 194, 196, 197, 199, 200, 203, 210, 239, 254, 256, 257, 258, 259, 260, 266, 267, 268, 269, 272, 273, 277, 290, 291, 292, 296–301, 302, 303, 304, 305, 306, 311, 312, 315, 316, 317,

319, 323, 324, 326, 332, 333, 339, 347, 355, 358, 359, 361, 362, 363
Kānūn-i islāmī, 148
Kānūn-i nashr-i ḥaqā'iq-i islāmī, 148
al-Karakī, N.ʿA., 86
Karbala, 53, 90
Karīmī, ʿA., 119
al-Kāshānī, M.F., 63, 78, 193, 195, 274
Kāshānī, S.A., 21, 141
Kāshif al-Ghitā, M.Ḥ., 247
Kasrawī, A., 147, 189, 191
Kelsen, H., 227
Kepler, J., 146, 201, 276, 290
Khaldūn, I., 246, 271
khalīfatullāh. See God, vicegerency of
Khāmina'ī, S.ʿA., 119, 120
Khānsārī, M.T., 153
Khātamī, S.M., 117–118, 192, 194
al-Khū'ī, A., 74, 115, 119
khulūṣ. *See* genuineness, ontological
Khumainī, R., 17, 74, 110, 113–117, 118, 121, 126, 137, 147, 149, 151, 158, 188, 189, 215, 225, 243, 251
khums. *See* alms
Khurasan, 112, 155, 187
al-Khurāsānī, M.K., 74, 100
Khurramshahr, 103
al-Kindī, A.Y., 131
Kirkegaard, S., 281
Kirmānī, M.Ā.K., 104
knowledge. *See* absolute knowledge; acquired knowledge; empirical knowledge; objective knowledge; rational knowledge
Koestler, A., 35, 36, 217, 276, 289, 290
Kuhn, T.S., 21, 22, 30, 202, 277, 278, 286, 321, 327, 368
al-Kulainī, M.Y., 54, 60, 62, 81, 94
kull mā ḥakama bi-l-ʿaql ḥakama bi-l-sharʿ, 84
kull mujtahid musīb, 101
Kunya, 189
Küng, H., 166, 290
Köln, 16

Lacan, J., 35, 245, 368
Lāhijī, ʿA., 274
Lahore, 205
Lakatos, I., 267, 282, 285
Lālihzār, M., 109
language, 3, 8, 10, 34, 68, 70, 78, 93, 94, 95, 96, 97, 139, 173, 179, 194, 196, 202, 205, 208, 209, 215, 233, 236, 250, 257, 288, 294, 306, 316, 318, 319, 320, 321, 322, 323, 324, 325, 326, 330, 340, 361, 362, 365
  and deconstruction, 319
  arbitrary nature of, 10, 245
  as gate to understanding law, 79
  as symbolic, 142, 323
  as 'house of being', 330
  polysemy of, 11, 95, 319, 321, 322, 330
  rationality of, 10, 319, 321
  subjective conditions of, 28, 319, 320, 322, 323, 324, 330
  variations, 3, 10
  veils of, 140–141
langue, 10
Lārījānī, Ṣ., 119–122, 123, 124, 274
Latin, 8, 12, 25, 36, 55, 59, 81, 112
lawfinding, 50, 72, 83, 113, 115, 120, 345
lawmaking, 15, 49, 50, 104, 106, 109, 114, 116, 117, 138, 226, 227, 229, 232, 352, 354
Lebanon, 194
Lecomte de Noüy, P., 151
legal norms, 31, 40, 41, 42, 43, 45, 46, 49, 50, 52, 64, 65, 72, 74, 77, 82, 88, 92, 98, 101, 103, 105, 108, 113, 114, 121, 122, 124, 137, 138, 142, 145, 146, 150, 161, 168, 169, 171, 174, 182, 217, 225, 226, 232, 233, 234, 237, 240, 241, 243, 244, 262, 274, 277, 335, 336, 345, 346, 352, 353
  and ethics, 41, 42
  and spirituality, 52, 128
  epistemic ranking of, 100, 345
  in modern law, 106
legal positivism, 46, 48, 50, 51, 153, 200, 227, 238, 353
legal sociology, 153
legal system, 14, 39, 48, 50–51, 54, 77, 103, 106, 209, 214, 215, 217, 226, 227, 228, 229, 230, 232, 233, 352, 353
  and hermeneutical necessity, 11, 51, 228
legal theory, 6, 14, 17, 18, 35, 45, 46, 48, 53, 62, 63, 66, 70, 71, 72, 74, 76, 77–79, 80, 82, 83, 86, 87, 88, 92, 97, 99, 100, 103, 105, 108, 110, 113, 114, 116, 118, 122, 153, 167, 168, 172, 180, 190, 214, 224, 225, 232, 238, 241, 242, 243, 248, 253, 255, 334, 345, 346, 353
  as product of history, 14, 225–226
  inception of, 62, 70
  levels of discourse, 77
  logic in, 103
  traditional definition of, 77
legalism, 39, 50, 109, 225, 232, 233
legality, concept of, 47, 145, 165, 229
legislation. *See* lawmaking
Leibniz, G.W., 31, 49, 289, 299
Lévi-Strauss, C., 245
lex, 49, 50
li, 42
liberalism, 105, 191, 193, 223, 231
linguistic philosophy, 125
linguistic sign, 10, 11, 245, 319, 362
linguistic structure, 177

linguistics, 8, 9, 10, 78, 79, 92, 93, 95, 122, 141, 245, 308, 318, 320, 322, 323, 324, 325, 326, 330
literal meaning, 12, 59, 67, 78, 92, 95, 96, 101, 140, 150, 182, 242, 244, 274, 288, 317
literary criticism, 92, 182
literary style, 10, 195, 196
Little, D., 192
Locke, J., 27, 32, 76, 168, 188, 267, 289
logic, 7, 9, 27, 37, 48, 52, 60, 63, 64, 65, 69, 71, 72, 75, 76, 78, 82–87, 91, 101, 103, 111, 114, 120, 122, 126, 128, 131, 133, 134, 138, 142, 144, 156, 158, 166, 182, 183, 197, 201, 233, 234, 250, 272, 275, 276, 278, 279, 281, 284, 285, 286, 287, 291, 298, 301, 313, 327, 339, 344, 345, 350, 351, 353, 361, 362
  in traditional Islam, 52, 62, 64–65, 71, 72, 75, 76, 82–87, 83, 103
logic of confirmation, 284
logical empiricism, 284
logical positivism, 125, 188, 197, 198, 199, 207, 300, 301, 327
Logos, 52, 96, 320
logocentrism, 62, 63, 67, 68, 69, 71, 72, 73, 74, 75, 84, 85, 165, 325, 330, 348, 362
London, 155, 188, 192, 205
Lorenz, K., 312
love, 31, 51, 127, 139, 193, 195, 200, 216, 220, 270, 293, 305, 306
Luther, M., 12, 181, 182, 192, 203
Lyotard, J., 34, 245, 319, 363, 365

mā baʿd al-tabīʿah. *See* metaphysics
Machiavelli, N., 203
Madadpūr, M., 124
madhab. *See* schools of law
madrasah. *See* education
Madrasah-yi Ḥaqqānī, 191, 247
Madrasah-yi Marwī, 113, 126
Madrasah-yi Sipahsālār, 153
al-Majlisī, M.B., 63–64, 249
al-Majlisī, M.T., 64
Makārim-Shīrāzī, N., 110, 145
Maktab-i Zahrā, 247
Malaysia, 194
Malik, A., 53, 57, 73
Malikī Darjazīnī, J., 115
Malkam Khān, M., 104, 145
Malthus, T.R., 277
Mamaqānī, A., 105
al-Maʾmūn, A.ʿA., 66
maqāṣid-i sharīʿat. *See* Islamic law, objectives of
Maʿrashī-Najafī, S., 119
marātib al-ʿulūm. *See* science, hierarchy in
marātib al-wujūd. *See* hierarchy of levels
marjaʿ al-taqlīd, 4, 74, 89, 90, 100, 110, 111, 115, 119, 161, 180, 182, 228
  women as, 139
Markaz-i islāmī, 118, 163
Markaz-i isnād-i inqilāb-i islāmī, 158
Mary, Virgin, 325
Marx, K., 109, 112, 156, 157, 202, 220, 245, 258, 290
Marxism, 34, 111, 151, 153, 154, 155, 156, 158, 188, 193, 198, 219, 230, 250, 258, 282, 308, 319
Mashhad, 112, 148, 155, 196
mashrūṭah. See constitutionalism
maṣlaḥah. See public interest, juristic
Massignon, L., 8, 155
Maʿsūmīyah school, 247
mathematics, 27, 49, 75, 123, 126, 133, 142, 150, 151, 197, 267, 268, 271, 272, 276, 278, 288, 290, 291, 292, 298, 301, 311, 314
maturity, concept of, 236, 257, 363
'maximalisation', concept of, 217, 233
Mazinan, 155
Mecca, 204
mechanisation, 164, 290
mediation, 12, 28, 129, 145, 173, 179, 182, 183, 297, 307, 308, 322, 355, 356, 366
medicine, 91, 126, 134, 152, 212, 248, 271, 272, 304
Medina, 80, 226
metanarrative, concept of, 34, 245, 319, 332, 348, 349, 364
metaphysics, 21, 27, 28, 30, 31, 33, 67, 68, 69, 75, 96, 103, 111, 122, 126, 130, 132, 133, 142, 150, 153, 155, 164, 166, 169, 170, 172, 173, 188, 190, 194, 197, 198, 200, 202, 212, 217, 218, 220, 238, 245, 261, 264, 265, 267, 277, 280, 281, 282, 289, 290, 294, 296, 297, 299, 300, 302, 305, 307, 309, 318, 323, 327, 331, 332, 333, 335, 341, 347, 353, 354, 355, 359, 362, 363, 365
  and humanism, 27
  and method, 265
  as experience, 169
  as preceding the sciences, 128
  in the West, 30, 290, 296, 299, 300, 302, 333
  sources of, 31, 347
method, 3, 7, 23, 30, 31, 40, 50, 57, 61, 64, 70, 72, 74, 75, 77, 78, 82, 83, 111, 113, 120, 123, 128, 130, 131, 133, 135, 138, 143, 145, 151, 159, 164, 169, 179, 187, 190, 192, 201, 211, 218, 219, 220, 223, 224, 225, 227, 234, 235, 240, 241, 242, 243, 244, 245, 246, 248, 249, 250, 251, 255, 256, 259, 261, 265, 267, 270, 271, 275, 276, 277, 278, 280, 281, 282, 283, 285, 286, 290, 296, 298, 302, 308, 311, 317, 318, 323, 324, 325, 326, 327, 330, 334,

336, 337, 338, 339, 341, 344, 345, 348, 349, 350, 351, 352, 357, 360, 364, 366, 368
and conflicting interpretations, 97, 334, 336, 339
and cultural borrowing, 168
and pluralism, 9, 34, 300, 317, 349, 350
as anathema, 290
as content-based, 116
casuistic, 47, 83, 165, 183, 354
comparative, 93
empirical, 121, 128, 130, 133, 134, 170, 283, 286, 300, 303, 309
historical-critical, 166
historical-empirical, 58, 72, 75, 76
in enlightenment, 27, 33
normativity of, 7, 170, 302, 335, 341, 342
phenomenological, 168, 170, 171, 309, 324
scholastic, 47, 65, 93, 130, 248, 297, 350
Middle East, 50, 205
Mill, J.S., 197, 237
milleniarism, 262
Mīr Dāmād, M.B., 69
Mīr Findiriskī, A.Q., 69
mi'rāj, 274
Miṣbāḥ-Yazdī, M., 120, 191, 247
modern, concept of, 25, 106
modern law, concept of, 39, 48, 50, 103, 104, 106, 109, 114, 144, 146, 165, 227
modern philosophy, 5, 8, 21, 25, 26, 27, 29, 31, 32, 33, 107, 108, 111, 114, 122, 123, 125, 132, 144, 145, 155, 162, 163, 171, 172, 177, 188, 194, 196, 197–202, 207, 208, 210, 216, 221, 226, 230, 242, 243, 188, 190, 197, 199, 200, 203, 207, 208, 210, 211, 212, 214, 217, 219, 220, 221, 222, 228, 229, 234, 235, 241, 246, 247, 248, 254, 255, 256, 258, 259, 260, 264, 265, 266, 267, 268, 269, 270, 271, 272, 273, 275, 276, 277, 281, 282, 284, 287, 288, 289, 292, 296, 299, 300, 316, 317, 326, 327, 329, 332, 333, 335, 336, 340, 343, 352, 363
and religion, 211, 218, 228, 235, 240, 241, 254, 274, 281
periodisation of, 8
modern science, 21, 33, 104, 105, 107, 112, 115, 119, 121, 123, 124, 127, 128, 130, 144, 146, 148, 165, 167, 172, 185, 254, 255, 256, 267, 268, 275, 276, 284, 287, 288, 289, 311, 313, 327, 343, 350, 351, 352, 354, 355, 356, 357, 358, 359, 366, 368
and jurisprudence, 107, 172
and religion, 145, 146, 147, 151, 154, 167, 183, 253, 254, 255, 267, 275, 284, 286, 289, 290, 349, 357
as reductionistic, 120, 130
as self-correcting, 336
foundations of, 27
introduction in Iran, 27
levels of, 269
modern society, 4, 26, 36, 108, 144, 152, 162, 165, 174, 182, 206, 209, 218, 223, 225, 232, 233, 236, 269, 325, 353
disintegration of, 26
modern state, 4, 21, 36, 48, 51, 99, 103, 104, 105, 106, 108, 115, 116, 117, 119, 153, 161, 190, 216, 218, 221, 226, 229, 231, 236, 248, 250, 353
and religious institutions, 21, 99, 106, 250
as contestant of intellectual autonomity, 161
mythology of, 117
modern theology, 8, 12, 120, 163, 166, 169, 177, 189, 212, 253, 254, 255, 365
as anthropology, 254
modernisation, 21, 26, 32, 34, 51, 105, 119, 145, 146, 159, 229, 287
modernism. *See* enlightenment, modernism
modernity, 5, 6, 7, 12, 17, 19, 21, 22, 23, 25–37, 103, 104, 106, 107, 109, 112, 115, 126, 129, 138, 144, 145, 147, 151, 159, 162, 163, 164, 171, 194, 196, 201, 202–210, 216, 220, 221, 222, 223, 224, 236, 237, 240, 241, 242, 243, 244, 246, 248, 253, 270, 287, 288, 296, 305, 306, 308, 325, 328, 329, 331, 343, 347, 351, 352, 353, 354, 359, 360, 362, 363, 365, 366, 367, 368
and Islam, 5, 7, 13, 18, 20, 21, 22, 23, 33, 35, 103, 105, 343, 347, 348
and subjectivity, 5, 26, 27
as conjunction, 25
as lowering of the systems of values, 206
as mode of thinking, 26
break with Christianity, 33
closure of, 34
constitutive components of, 26, 347
criticism of, 104, 106, 115, 117, 118, 138, 164, 351
equal to development, 206
global relevance of, 25, 164
introduction in Iran, 20, 104, 105, 109
ontological foundations of, 5, 6, 27, 33
Shi'i expressions of, 5, 33, 35, 364
varieties of, 25, 32–34, 35, 118, 346
monarchy, 115, 154, 189, 205
monism, 301, 304, 337
monopoly, 4, 22, 37
monotheism, 33, 44, 154, 157, 329
morality. *See* ethics
Mudarris, Ḥ, 27
mu'āmalāt. *See* social transactions
Mu'assasah-yi dā'irāt al-ma'ārif-i buzurg-i islāmī, 161, 194
Mu'assasah-yi ṣirāt, 190
al-Mufīd, A.'A., 42, 57, 61, 71, 72, 98
Muḥajirānī, 'A., 192

Muḥammad, Prophet, 13, 14, 47, 52, 53, 59, 60, 70, 75, 79, 80, 81, 93, 96, 126, 140, 154, 159, 160, 171, 213, 215, 226, 250, 263, 274, 293, 306, 314, 317, 340, 345
biographies of, 93
family of the, 80, 96, 141
as 'speaking' law, 140
Muḥaqqiq, M., 110, 118
Muḥaqqiq-Dāmād, M., 110, 118–119
muḥkam, 94, 96, 112, 121, 139, 154, 317, 318, 322
Mujāhidīn-i khalq, 154
Mujtabā'ī, F., 111
mujtahid, 77, 87, 89–91, 100, 111, 114, 137, 138, 139, 229, 244
as free struggler, 158
education of, 89–91
female, 91
Mujtahid-Shabistarī, M., 6, 18, 163–185, 343, 352
biography of, 163
criticism of, 112, 122
on conflicting interpretations, 182, 183
on epistemology, 165, 166, 169, 171, 176
on *ḥauzah*, 184, 185
on hermeneutics, 169, 171, 172, 173, 175–182, 183, 184, 360, 361
on *ijtihād*, 167, 171, 172, 173, 174, 175, 182, 352
on inference, 165, 166–169, 171, 172, 173, 174, 177, 182, 183
on method, 164, 166, 167–171, 177, 352
on modernity, 163, 164, 171, 185
on phenomenology, 169, 170–173
on philosophy of law, 166–168
on probability, 170, 178, 181, 183
on rationality, 165, 170, 172, 173, 174, 175
on religious faith, 166
on science, 164, 165, 166, 167, 170, 172
on secularism, 163, 165
on subjectivity, 166, 173
on technology, 164
on theology, 165, 166, 170, 172, 184, 185
multitheism, 155, 156, 258, 303
mundus imaginalis, 35
municipal law, 48
Muntaẓirī, Ḥ.ʿA., 243, 261, 262
muqaddamah-yi wājib. *See* obligatory prerequisite
muqaddamāt. *See ijtihād*, preliminaries of
Muṣaddiq, M., 146–147, 151
Mūsāwī-Shīrāzī, S.ʿA., 119
Muslim, 4, 5, 8, 13, 19, 33, 36, 39, 40, 46, 48, 50, 57, 65, 98, 107, 116, 118, 122, 131, 137, 145, 146, 154, 158, 159, 162, 163, 164, 174, 185, 188, 196, 204, 205, 207, 208, 209, 210, 213, 214, 215, 221, 222, 223, 224, 225, 226, 227, 231, 232, 233, 234, 235, 238, 243, 246, 268, 293, 295, 301, 303, 325, 340, 343, 367
definition of, 19
welfare and security, 108
Muslim lands, 10, 11, 27, 32, 36, 48, 50, 90, 103, 106, 145, 149, 196, 287
mustamarr. *See* continuity
Mustashar al-Daulah, Y.K., 145
Muṭahharī, M., 17, 108, 110, 112, 113–114, 117, 119, 122, 123, 137, 148, 184, 187, 189, 193, 207, 228, 243, 258, 334
mutashābih, 94, 112, 139, 154, 317, 318, 322
muʿtazilah, 32, 56, 60, 61, 66, 71, 72, 73, 81, 83, 84, 95, 113, 118, 174, 183, 231, 235, 239
mysticism, 5, 13, 15, 20, 31, 52, 55,57, 63, 64, 68–69, 75, 78, 81, 92, 96, 111, 115, 123, 141, 164, 165, 176, 246, 253, 254, 256, 262, 263, 264, 265, 289, 293, 303, 304, 305, 306, 320, 327, 332, 344, 366
and law, 39, 52
and modernity, 262, 289, 305, 306, 327, 365, 366
and Qur'an, 58
mythology, 117, 149, 198, 257

Nā'īnī, M.M.Ḥ., 74, 86, 105, 108, 111
naive realism, 59, 67, 76
Najaf, 89, 90, 111, 115, 119, 247
al-Najafī, M.Ḥ., 89
Nakhshab, M., 148
Napoleon, 25, 257
naql. *See* transmitted knowledge
Naqshbandī order, 52
Narāqī, A., 137, 253
Narāqī, I., 192, 209
Nāṣir al-dīn Shāh, 109
Nasr, S.H., 16, 18, 107, 110, 111, 113, 148, 162, 274, 368
al-naṣṣ, theological concept of 53, 60, 66, 85
nationalism, 148
naẓar. *See* pure reason
natural disposition, concept of, 42, 126, 138, 261, 332
Natural law, 45, 49, 113, 144, 152, 153
natural laws, 29, 40, 49, 113, 235, 291
natural right, concept of, 48, 113, 138, 152, 163, 171, 214, 224, 230,
natural science, 31, 120, 122, 123, 130, 133, 134, 135, 142, 144, 151, 164, 170, 177, 183, 199, 206, 207, 211, 228, 246, 247, 248, 259, 266, 267, 268, 272, 273, 284, 287, 288, 289, 296, 309, 349, 356, 357
natural selection, theory of, 277, 357
naturalism, 153, 237
Naubakhtī, A.S., 66

necessary knowledge, 31, 65, 66, 70, 84, 212, 272, 273, 274, 291, 299, 300, 311, 313, 316, 344, 345, 346, 358
neo-Kantianism, 135, 156, 169
neo-Platonism, 58, 68, 164, 207, 234, 258
neo-positivism, 119, 170, 210
neo-traditionalism, 22
Newton, I., 34, 146, 199, 277, 290, 296, 299
Nicholson, R.A., 189
Nietzsche, F., 29, 34, 157, 188, 328
Nihḍat-i khudāparastān-i sūsiyālīst, 148, 159
Nihḍat-i muqāwimat-i millī, 153
Nihḍat-i āzādī-yi Īrān, 151
nihilism, 26, 34, 310, 367
Niʿmatullāhī order, 187
al-Nishāpūrī al-Akhbārī, M., 103
noesis, 175
nomad society, 233, 236, 353
nominalism, 28, 29, 199, 200, 208, 217, 292, 311, 358
nomocentrism, 39, 68, 91, 365
nomos, 40, 49
normal science, 21
normative jurisprudence, 46
normativity, 7, 144, 170, 175, 203, 209, 213, 269, 299, 302, 325, 333, 335, 340, 341, 342
nostalgia, 176
noumenal realm, 30, 31, 112, 136, 156, 161, 169, 170, 178, 258, 288, 297, 299, 300, 302, 305, 306, 310, 311, 312, 323, 333, 339, 355, 362, 365
nous, 65
Nūrī, F., 108, 109

objective knowledge, 30, 31, 33, 49, 58, 68, 84, 126, 128, 134, 136, 169, 170, 176, 180, 197, 200, 206, 211, 266, 274, 283, 284, 299, 309, 310, 311, 313, 323, 328, 337, 339
third world of, 123, 124, 284, 309
objective realism. *See* philosophical realism
objectivist epistemology, 27, 30, 31, 129, 169, 355, 360
objectivity, 13, 26, 31, 35, 120, 123, 178, 181, 211, 230, 258, 260, 267, 283, 284, 285, 307, 309, 310, 312, 317, 319, 323, 325, 326, 328, 333, 357, 362, 364, 368
obligatory prerequisite, 108, 346
occasions of revelation, 93, 95, 112, 214, 215
occultation, theological concept of, 52, 53, 59, 60, 63, 66, 70, 81, 82, 100, 101, 262
Ockham, W., 28, 29, 49, 199
ontology, 5, 6, 8, 9, 27, 28, 29, 30, 31, 32, 58, 63, 68, 70, 105, 107, 111, 113, 116, 117, 121, 124, 127, 128, 129, 130, 131, 132, 133, 134, 135, 136, 138, 139, 141, 149, 150, 157, 169, 173, 176, 177, 178, 190, 196, 197, 199, 200, 202, 207, 208, 210, 212, 213, 218, 231, 242, 243, 254, 256, 257, 258, 266, 279, 280, 281, 291, 292, 296, 300, 303, 304, 305, 306, 309, 311, 323, 325, 335, 339, 341, 342, 343, 344, 346, 349, 351, 354, 355, 360, 361
and science, 27, 31, 131, 132, 134, 135, 212, 279, 280, 281, 309, 311, 335, 342, 343, 349
divorced from religion, 130, 291, 292, 304, 306
hermeneutic, 8, 9, 126, 176, 322, 323, 325
religious, 126, 127, 128, 129, 130, 355, 356
openness, 221, 227, 246
epistemic, 246, 254, 359
hermeneutical, 12, 98, 177, 182, 331
juristic, 86
of historical processes, 32
of language, 11, 173, 321, 331
Orientalism, 7, 8
Orientalists, 8, 14–16
on *ijtihād*, 15, 88
original discourse, 9, 10, 11, 160, 177, 178, 180, 180, 181, 195, 199, 214, 318, 319, 320, 321, 323, 330, 331, 332, 360, 361. *See also* intention of author
orthodoxy, 20, 97, 99, 167, 275, 302, 347, 365
Otto, R., 259
Ottoman, 48
our expectation of religion, concept of, 131, 273, 274, 364

Pahlawī dynasty, 146, 154, 229
Pahlawī, M.R., 189
Pahlawī, R., 151
Paimān, Ḥ., 148, 159–160, 161
Pakistan, 234, 324
pantheism, 46
paradigm, concept of, 19, 21, 22, 23, 25, 35, 286, 290, 321
and competition, 22
as an epistemic type, 21
in modern Islam, 6, 21–22
paradox of confirmation, 127, 284, 285, 286, 350
parerga, 210
Paris, 155
Pascal, B., 188, 211
penal law, 302
perfect man, concept of, 140, 256
peripatetic philosophy, 69, 132, 133, 234, 235
Persian, 6, 7, 8, 18, 19, 20, 58, 63, 74, 104, 109, 110, 112, 146, 147, 175, 176, 188, 189, 191, 194, 195, 196, 209, 211, 214, 215, 256, 270, 274, 301, 306, 327
pharmacology, 356
phenomenal realm, 27, 28, 29, 31, 35, 112, 113, 127, 136, 141, 156, 157, 160, 162, 169, 170, 177, 178, 197, 198, 199, 200, 201, 202,

212, 258, 265, 266, 272, 273, 286, 288, 297, 299, 300, 302, 304, 307, 310, 311, 312, 315, 318, 320, 321, 322, 323, 328, 331, 333, 338, 339, 341, 342, 344, 349, 353, 354, 355, 356, 362
as theophany, 139
as a veil, 304
destruction of, 35
knowledge limited to, 30, 298, 305, 310, 311, 312, 339, 362
phenomenological hermeneutics, 8
phenomenology, 153, 156, 157, 160, 168, 169, 170, 171, 172, 173, 176, 180, 181, 185, 188, 245, 291, 309, 311, 324, 360
definition of, 156
philology, 7, 11, 12, 20, 43, 78, 92, 126, 182
philosophical hermeneutics, 92, 166, 173, 176, 179, 360
philosophical materialism, 111, 113, 119, 129, 130, 133, 135, 154, 156, 184, 290, 368
philosophical realism, 30, 111, 113, 306, 311, 366, 356
philosophy, 5, 8, 12, 15, 20, 21, 25, 26, 27, 29, 30, 31, 32, 34, 39, 41, 42, 43, 55, 57, 58, 63, 65, 67–69, 70, 71, 73, 75, 78, 93, 101, 104, 105, 109, 111, 112, 113, 114, 116, 118, 120, 121, 122, 123, 124, 125, 126, 128, 129, 130, 131, 132, 133, 135, 142, 143, 145, 146, 151, 153, 155, 156, 162, 164, 165, 167, 168, 169, 170, 171, 173, 176, 177, 182, 184, 187, 197–202, 206, 207, 223, 224, 235, 238, 241, 246, 253, 261, 265, 269, 274, 275, 288, 343, 347, 348, 349, 354, 355, 356, 357, 358, 362, 363, 366, 367. *See also* modern philosophy; postmodern philosophy
and the Qur'an, 43, 58, 126, 130, 164, 165
as an integrated part of religion, 43, 58, 67, 68131
division of, 132, 166
first, 122, 126, 132, 166, 269, 273
Greek, 31, 58, 65, 67, 68, 75, 123, 131, 164, 207, 234, 235, 242, 274, 275
in traditional Islam, 20, 30, 143, 207, 255, 264, 273, 274, 275, 315
philosophy of history, 255, 259
philosophy of law, 5, 23, 42, 166, 167, 168, 209, 232, 237, 242, 244, 351, 352, 353, 354
philosophy of religion, 254, 281
philosophy of science, 55, 188, 189, 197, 243, 260, 282, 284, 316, 317, 321
physicalism, 34
physics, 69, 134, 152, 157, 187, 203, 268, 271, 272, 281, 288, 296, 299, 317
physiology, 272, 281
Pierce, C.S., 338
pilgrimage, 50, 116
Platinga, A., 290, 302, 303
Plato, 27, 29, 30, 31, 41, 45, 49, 58, 67, 140, 143, 169, 273, 320, 325
Platonist academy, 49
play, concept of, 130, 202, 218, 290, 326
Plotinus, 68
pluralism, 191, 221, 253, 324, 329, 332, 347, 350, 363, 365
epistemic, 33, 34, 35, 97, 99, 100, 183, 253, 258, 303, 319, 329, 332, 335, 337, 338, 364, 366
poetry, 11, 189, 191, 195, 256, 264, 301, 305, 321
political philosophy, 5, 109
politics. *See* governance
Popper, K.R., 120, 121, 123, 124, 188, 190, 193, 194, 196, 198, 207, 219, 234, 251, 260, 267, 273, 276, 277, 278, 279, 281, 282, 284, 285, 286, 292, 299, 308, 317, 320, 323, 326, 327, 333, 336, 337, 339, 340, 350, 358, 363, 364, 368
positive law, 36, 45, 48, 51, 62, 77, 147, 165, 191, 215, 217, 226, 229, 230, 231
positivism, 27, 46, 48, 111, 120, 125, 128, 129, 130, 146, 153, 165, 170, 177, 188, 193, 197, 198, 200, 206, 223, 226, 237, 238, 245, 267, 277, 279, 281, 282, 286, 291, 300, 301, 326, 327, 341, 353, 354
post-islamism, 192
postmodern hermeneutics, 34, 326, 330, 332, 360
postmodern philosophy, 34, 35, 327, 329, 330, 365, 368
postmodern theology, 34, 327
postmodernism, 34, 35, 197, 204, 206, 218, 245, 300, 315, 326, 327, 329, 331, 343, 347, 348, 363, 364, 365, 366, 367, 368
and governance, 33
and Islam, 5, 6, 35, 329, 347, 360, 363, 364, 365, 366, 367
and modernism, 34, 329, 347, 363
definition of, 33
postmodernity, 203, 214, 319, 350
postpositivism, 283, 300, 327
poststructuralism, 21, 245, 330, 360
power, concept of, 35, 194, 200, 201, 202, 232, 239, 249, 250, 251, 258, 289, 326, 328, 336, 339
practical philosophy, 8
practical reason, 85, 118, 122, 157
pragmaticism, 338
pragmatics, 285
pragmatism, 34, 197, 199, 291, 292, 311, 326, 340, 350, 356, 358, 368
Prague school, 10
prayer, 50, 52, 99, 116
pre-Islamic law, 47, 54, 79
predestination, 249, 334

preferability, epistemic, 339
preference, juristic, 70, 73, 114
preunderstanding, 12, 112, 122, 136, 175, 176, 178, 179, 180, 182, 183, 184, 254, 255, 274, 287, 288, 291, 292, 301, 308, 313, 314, 316, 318, 320, 322, 325, 330, 335, 336
priesthood. *See* clergy
probability, epistemic, 36, 134, 181, 183, 211, 234, 268, 283, 286, 290, 305, 307, 317, 319, 328, 333, 335, 337, 339, 341, 345, 346, 350, 351, 357
probable opinion, 47, 59, 70, 73, 79, 87, 99, 345
'followers of', 59, 61
procedural principles, juristic 74, 119, 137
progress, 26, 129, 169, 206, 232, 255, 256, 257, 258, 259, 260, 282, 290, 336, 337
secular idea of, 26, 257
prophetic light, concept of 53
Protegra, 28
Protestantism, 12, 163, 181, 221
prudence, juristic, 74, 90
psyche, 65
psychoanalysis, 198, 245, 251
psychological hermeneutics, 9
psychology, 111, 157, 176, 233, 247, 271, 281, 285, 287, 290, 309, 311, 323
Ptolemy, 29, 68, 290
public interest, juristic, 41, 73, 114, 115, 116, 117, 137, 217, 224, 225
pure reason, 25, 29, 31, 32, 58, 59, 66, 71, 84, 85, 118, 135, 157, 169, 266, 272, 297, 311
Pūrjawādī, N., 189
purposive system, 151
Putnam, H., 312
Pythagora, 58

qabḍ wa basṭ, tiʾūrīk-i. See contraction and expansion, theory of epistemic
qaʿidāt al-mulāzamah. See correlation, rules of
Qājār, 17, 20, 105
qalb. See heart, spiritual.
qānūn, 48, 104, 108, 115, 116, 121, 137, 138, 151, 240
qaṭʿ. See certainty, epistemic
al-Qazvīnī, ʿA., 60
Qazwīnī, Ḥ., 115
qiṣāṣ. See retaliation
qiyās. See analogy
Quine, W.O., 267, 292, 316, 358, 368
Qum, 11, 111, 112, 114, 118, 120, 121, 126, 135, 153, 161, 163, 175, 187, 189, 191, 192, 196, 204, 247, 253, 367
Qunawī, Ṣ., 141
Qur'an, 3, 13, 13, 40, 41, 43, 44, 45, 47, 53, 55, 56, 58, 60, 62, 63, 67, 70, 78, 79–80, 81, 83, 84, 92, 93, 94, 95, 96, 97, 99, 111, 112, 125, 126, 129, 130, 132, 133, 139, 140, 141, 142, 146, 147, 150, 151, 153, 154, 156, 158, 159, 160, 161, 164, 165, 169, 172, 174, 175, 177, 178, 179, 181, 182, 183, 184, 194, 197, 200, 203, 214, 215, 225, 226, 234, 237, 238, 250, 253, 269, 274, 278, 292, 293, 301, 303, 304, 308, 314, 316, 318, 321, 322, 325, 338, 347, 352, 361
as source of knowledge, 55, 56, 130
as source of law, 40, 44, 79–80
as symbolic, 94
as unified entity, 171, 175
iconic force of, 13, 43
inner levels of, 139, 141, 321
legal matter of, 40, 41, 80, 89
non-identity of, 332
notion of meaning in, 94
on hierarchy, 58
'silent' and 'speaking', 94, 293
uncreated, 13, 43

Rabbinic, 40, 43
Raḍawīyah school, 247
al-Raḍī, S., 80
Rahman, R., 143, 234, 256, 324, 325
Rahnamā, ʿA, 21
Rahner, K., 166, 172, 303
ratio, 59, 84
ratio decidendi, 87, 119
ratio legis, 73, 83
rational knowledge, 30, 32, 42, 52, 57, 59, 60, 61,62, 63, 64, 65, 66, 67, 68, 71, 72, 73, 76, 78, 83, 84, 85, 86, 89, 93, 103, 111, 118, 121, 123, 125, 128, 131, 134, 142, 152, 201, 202, 210, 211, 212, 219, 223, 232, 239, 260, 262, 263, 264, 265, 266, 273, 275, 278, 281, 290, 294, 296, 300, 303, 304, 313, 319, 324, 325, 335, 337, 344, 345, 346, 350, 351, 352, 357, 358, 362, 363, 364, 365
rationalism, 26, 27, 31, 32, 107, 198, 199, 206, 217, 235, 258, 264, 266, 273, 295, 300, 306, 313, 314, 349, 358, 368
definition of, 32
rationality, 10, 29, 32, 37, 92, 165, 172, 174, 175, 203, 211, 232, 242, 243, 257, 258, 263, 264, 266, 267, 269, 281, 288, 290, 300, 313, 324, 326, 327, 329, 336, 348, 349, 351, 352, 356, 362, 363, 364
of jurisprudence, 83, 84, 86
raʾy. See probable opinion
al-Rāzī, F., 57, 207
Razmjū, Ḥ., 158
realism, 30, 47, 111, 122, 129, 135, 136, 172, 187, 197, 198, 199, 200, 212, 258, 279, 291, 302, 311, 312, 326, 331, 338, 339, 341
definition of, 30

reason, 21, 27, 28, 29, 31, 32, 46, 59, 60, 63, 64, 65, 66, 67, 68, 70, 71, 72, 73, 74, 75, 82–87, 103, 107, 111, 113, 114, 118, 119, 125, 127, 128, 131, 132, 134, 135, 137, 138, 139, 144, 145, 147, 152, 165, 169, 170, 172, 174, 175, 180, 182, 197, 202, 203, 204, 205, 219, 223, 227, 231, 235, 242, 243, 248, 251, 255, 257, 258, 260, 263–266, 267, 270, 273, 274, 277, 282, 289, 294, 297, 299, 300, 302, 305, 306, 307, 315, 320, 325, 327, 332, 336, 341, 344, 346, 348, 355, 356, 362
and law, 31, 82–87, 103, 104, 115, 128, 137, 147, 174, 214, 235, 242,
and madness, 204
and power, 251
and religious faith, 32, 56, 63, 83, 123, 127, 132, 133, 165, 211, 260, 263, 293, 306, 332, 341, 345, 351
and revelation, 32, 60, 67, 72, 82, 113, 125, 127, 131, 133, 134, 135, 137, 235, 254, 263, 264, 282, 351
and transcendence, 31, 170, 265, 305, 332, 344
and universalism, 32, 33, 34, 173, 261, 329, 332, 344, 347
as distinct from illusion, 128
as gate to understanding law, 79
as means of divining law, 128
as source of law, 31, 82–87, 103, 137, 174
categories of, 263
free use of, 97, 144, 147, 158, 161, 174, 263, 356
historical, 255, 258, 266
in traditional Islam, 59, 60, 65, 66, 67, 70, 71, 72, 75, 82–87
plurality of, 33, 34, 253, 326, 327, 329, 332, 347, 363, 364, 366
random error of, 297, 298, 328
religious, 172, 175, 211, 352
secular, 32, 132, 175, 263, 306, 332
Shi'i emphasis on, 52, 66, 83, 84
systematic error of, 290, 297, 298, 328
reflexivity, 24, 26, 28, 29, 180, 305, 364
reform, 105, 142, 143, 157, 170, 205, 242
educational, 20, 142, 184
legal, 4, 12, 104, 137, 145, 164, 182, 220, 241, 242, 346, 354
religious, 21, 143, 144, 146, 192, 219–223, 235, 242, 293, 317, 341, 346, 360
reformation, 12, 21, 181, 185, 367
reformism, premodern, 105, 107, 143
refutation. *See* falsification
Reid, T., 32
relativism, 10, 29, 33, 34, 135, 136, 157, 180, 213, 220, 204, 206, 208, 239, 259, 271, 285, 292, 294, 296, 302, 305, 309, 310, 312, 313, 314, 315, 316, 321, 325, 330, 332, 336, 339, 350, 355, 361, 365.
as a form of scepticism, 310
epistemic, 26, 197, 312, 314, 347
epistemological, 26, 118, 124, 157, 309, 312, 313, 365
relativity, theory of, 290, 292, 358
reliabilism, 303
religion, 4, 13, 14, 17, 19, 20, 23, 30, 21, 32, 36, 37, 43, 46, 50, 53, 55, 58, 60, 98, 104, 106, 107, 108, 109, 113, 115, 120, 124, 125, 128, 129, 131, 134, 135, 136, 142, 144, 145, 146, 147, 149, 151, 155, 158, 159, 161, 162, 163, 164, 165, 166, 169, 170, 171, 174, 175, 180, 185, 190, 192, 193, 195, 200, 202, 203, 205, 207, 208, 209, 210–223, 224, 228, 230, 231, 232, 233, 234, 235, 236, 237, 239, 240, 241, 243, 244, 245, 246, 249, 250, 254, 255, 258, 262, 264, 266, 267, 268, 270, 271, 274, 275, 280, 281, 282, 284, 287, 288, 290, 292, 293, 294, 295, 296, 302, 305, 307, 308, 309, 311, 312, 313, 315, 316, 317, 324, 333, 334, 335, 339, 340, 341, 343, 346, 347, 349, 350, 352, 354, 357, 360, 365, 366, 367, 368
'accidentals' of, 213, 214, 215, 232, 244, 245, 246, 352
and decadence, 105, 152, 158, 162
and law, 14, 19, 31, 41, 43, 56, 116, 113, 116, 120, 135, 152, 158, 167, 214, 215, 217, 228, 232–237, 241, 243, 244, 245, 293, 346, 365
and method, 7, 11, 127, 128, 143, 145, 168, 201, 220, 234, 254, 264, 348, 349
and rationality, 32, 37, 165, 290
as distinct from knowledge, 124, 161, 166, 281, 289, 293, 294, 295, 308, 316, 341
as divine ontology, 127
as ideology, 4, 144, 149, 150, 151, 155, 156, 157, 162, 163, 170, 202, 216, 224, 253, 308
as indexical system, 302
as nomothetic, 39, 50, 109, 225, 232, 233
as paradigmatic field, 21, 23
as socially constructed, 124
function of, 159, 174
higher and lower aspects of, 302
'humanisation' of, 219, 254, 303, 359
nature of, 7, 13, 212, 220, 223, 348
official interpretations of, 165, 232, 253, 295
purification of, 108, 148, 220, 270
'spirit' of, 174, 222, 237, 244, 352, 354
'substances' of, 200, 213, 214, 215, 244, 245, 246, 352, 362
religious belief, 21, 44, 52, 64, 75, 144, 154, 156, 157, 158, 161, 166, 172, 190, 195, 197, 204, 211, 212, 213, 214, 227, 229, 230, 243,

245, 248, 256, 257, 258, 260, 263, 265, 269, 274, 277, 280, 288, 290, 293, 297, 300, 302, 307, 308, 310, 311, 314, 317, 324, 325, 327, 335, 341, 351, 365
epistemic status of, 56, 132, 157, 210, 212, 213, 265, 293
principles of, 72, 98, 138, 148, 150, 213
religious exclusivism, 302, 303
religious experience, 166, 167, 168, 169, 170, 171, 181, 212, 266, 281, 297, 302, 303
postmodern, 306
religious faith, 41, 52, 56, 63, 65, 66, 67, 70, 83, 127, 132, 133, 145, 154, 157, 165, 166, 169, 172, 180, 181, 202, 204, 210, 211, 212, 219, 221, 223, 224, 236, 237, 240, 251, 260, 263, 264, 293, 294, 296, 306, 310, 313, 332, 341, 345, 348, 349, 355, 357, 365
and reason, 32, 83, 123, 127, 132, 133, 345
as individual, 213, 293, 303, 306, 365
as objective, 132
religious inclusivism, 302, 303
religious pluralism, 191, 193, 223, 301–303, 341, 358, 359
religious war, 99
renaissance, European, 21, 27, 36, 148, 197, 254, 276, 289, 343
Renan, E., 146
representation, 29, 30, 31, 41, 42, 65, 68, 69, 132, 197, 199, 200, 219, 265, 272, 281, 298, 299, 308, 309, 311, 315, 316, 319, 321, 323, 324, 333, 339, 356, 361
research programmes, 282
retaliation, 230, 233
return to the self, concept of, 149, 208, 209
revelation, 13, 21, 25, 31, 32, 41, 42, 43, 44, 45, 46, 50, 55, 56, 57, 58, 59, 62, 66, 67, 72, 73, 75, 80, 82, 83, 84, 92, 93, 94, 95, 96, 98, 111, 112, 117, 121, 125, 127, 128, 130, 131, 134, 135, 137, 139, 140, 141, 146, 148, 151, 153, 154, 157, 159, 160, 171, 172, 173, 175, 177, 178, 181, 214, 215, 226, 231, 234, 235, 237, 241, 262, 265, 270, 281, 284, 287, 289, 291, 294, 304, 320, 321, 325, 333, 334, 338, 344, 345, 346, 347, 348, 350, 351, 355, 360
as non-metaphysical, 172
as single hermeneutical norm, 181
'continuous', 172
de-ontologised, 338
God as manifested in, 139
'message' of, 127, 141, 147, 154, 159, 160, 161, 170, 171, 172, 175, 180, 361
revolution, 36, 115, 159, 189, 192, 205, 210, 226, 250, 328, 367
of 1979, 4, 5, 17, 51, 121, 142, 151, 155, 183, 188, 189, 190, 222, 223, 247
revolutionary council, 113, 163
rhetoric, 44, 78, 89, 91, 92, 101, 195
rights, legal, 205, 226, 230, 231, 239, 243. *See also* natural right, concept of
Ricoeur, P., 8, 9, 44, 322, 323, 325
Riḍā, R., 220
Ritschl, A., 258
Roman, 25
Roman law, 46, 49, 50, 93, 209
romanticism, 333
Rorty, R., 34, 197, 292, 316, 327, 328, 340, 368
Ross, D., 237
Rousseaux, J., 188, 254, 258
Rudsar, 161
rūḥ. *See* spirit
Rūḥānī, S.Ḥ., 158
Rūḥānī, S.M., 119
rūḥānīyat. *See* clergy
Rukhṣifat, S.M., 190
rule of law, 152, 365
Rūmī, J., 12, 189, 191, 193, 195, 199, 205, 211, 215, 216, 241, 263, 264, 265, 293, 301, 303, 304, 305
Ruse, M., 276, 277
Russell, B., 32, 188
Russia, 36
Rūzbih, R., 187
Ryan, A., 192
Ryle, G., 268

al-Saba'ī, M., 117
Sabziwārī, H., 115, 274, 338
al-Ṣādiq, J., 53, 95, 138, 263
Ṣadr, M.B., 277, 317
Ṣadr al-Ashraf, S.M., 21
Ṣafawīd, 17, 39, 60, 61, 63, 64, 90, 115, 155, 229
salvation, 26, 42, 43, 63, 181, 292, 302
Sangalajī, R.Q., 147–148
sapientia, 55
Sarton, G., 188
Sartre, J., 156, 188, 281
Saussure, F., 9, 10, 11, 245
Saxony, A., 298
Sayyid al-Murtaḍā, ʿA.Ṭ., 72, 78, 86
scepticism, 27, 29, 34, 43, 83, 97, 121, 123, 136, 157, 205, 296, 297, 299, 300, 310, 311, 312, 314, 327, 331, 332, 346, 347, 349, 363, 365, 367
variations of, 310
Schia-Bibliothek des Orientalischen seminars, 16
Schimmel, A., 304
Schleiermacher, F., 9, 12, 177, 178, 258
Schlick, M., 197
scholasticism, 25, 30, 36, 49, 350
school of Isfahan, 63, 68, 69, 91, 141

schools of law, 50, 53, 54, 61, 65, 66, 79, 80, 88, 90, 91, 98, 118, 227, 228
tolerance between, 98
Schopenhauer, A., 199
Schuon, F., 303
science, 4, 21, 23, 27, 30, 31, 32, 34, 36, 111, 113, 119, 121, 122, 123, 125, 126, 127, 128, 129, 130, 132, 133, 134, 135, 136, 137, 138, 142, 145, 148, 150, 152, 157, 158, 159, 164, 165, 166, 167, 168, 170, 172, 173, 176, 177, 178, 182, 188, 189, 192, 194, 198, 201, 202, 203, 206, 207, 209, 210, 211, 212, 218, 219, 228, 233, 236, 238, 243, 244, 248, 249, 253, 258, 262, 267–286, 311, 344, 348, 354
and theoretical preference, 278, 339
as qualitative, 126
as succesion of theories, 337
as universal, 207
collective character of, 120, 122, 123, 138, 167, 267, 272, 276, 277, 279, 280, 282, 284, 287, 288, 289, 290, 293, 294, 295, 304, 337
division of, 57, 58, 115, 120, 128, 132, 133, 267, 271, 274, 344
hierarchy in, 57, 128, 344
in traditional Islam, 55, 57, 58, 59, 75, 78, 144, 145, 281
non-Qur'anic epistemic basis of, 164
'producing' and 'consuming', 271, 272, 274, 275, 276, 287, 288, 352
religious knowledge as contingent on, 287
reduction of, 28, 359, 366
social identity of, 276, 277, 294, 295
scientia, 55
scienticism, 130, 135, 356
scientific ethics, 188
scientific determinism, 179
scientific revolutions, 21, 148, 202, 277, 278, 321
scientific theories, 27, 103, 119, 120, 121, 122, 123, 134, 151, 153, 156, 176, 190, 198, 199, 200, 201, 202, 204, 206, 210, 211, 212, 213, 214, 219, 222, 224, 228, 229, 234, 235, 236, 237, 238, 239, 240, 242, 244, 245, 248, 250, 260, 265, 266, 267, 268, 269, 270, 271, 272, 273, 274, 275, 277, 278, 279, 280, 281, 282, 283, 284, 285, 286, 288, 289, 291, 309, 317, 319, 321, 336, 337, 339, 341, 342, 350, 352, 359, 362, 368
individuality of, 267, 282, 284
Searl, J., 237
second-order epistemology. *See* critical epistemology
sectarianism, 215, 261
secular, 4, 21, 23, 36, 49, 75, 90, 103, 104, 105, 107, 127, 132, 144, 147, 150, 151, 159, 161, 163, 175, 187, 189, 196, 203, 205, 216, 218, 219, 221, 223, 226, 227, 228, 229, 230, 232, 233, 235, 239, 242, 248, 249, 251, 257, 262, 277, 294, 341, 351, 352, 353, 354, 358, 359, 360, 367, 368
secularisation, 18, 26, 35–37, 105, 106, 109, 144, 151, 154, 206, 216–219, 235, 257, 306, 347, 353, 355, 360
as partial process, 37, 217
as non-religion, 218
in postrevolutionary Iran, 36
secularism, 25, 37, 49, 50, 124, 128, 151, 163, 165, 192, 193, 208, 217–218, 219
as theory of truth, 37
self-awareness, 5, 12
self-relatedness, 28, 300
Sellars, W., 316
semantics, 3, 10, 11, 78, 89, 93, 94, 141, 200
semiotics, 10, 95
Semitic, 55
sentimentalism, 289
Shabistar, 163
al-Shāfiʿī, M.I., 53, 70, 71, 81, 83, 85, 88, 97, 101
Shahīdī, J., 40, 99
Shaʿrānī, A., 126
sharīʿat. *See* Islamic law
Sharīʿat-Madārī, ʿA., 189
Sharīʿatī, ʿA., 17, 18, 108, 112, 144, 145, 148, 149, 150, 153, 155–159, 160, 161, 162, 163, 170, 174, 185, 187, 189, 209, 216, 220, 221, 250
Sharīʿatī, M.T., 148
sharīʿat-i ṣāmit. *See* Islamic law, 'silent'
sharīʿat-i nāṭiq. *See* Islamic law, 'speaking'
al-Shāṭibī, I., 174, 214
Shābirī-Zanjānī, S.M., 119
Shabistarī, M., 211, 215
Shāhābādī, M.ʿA., 115
Shākib Niyā, A., 148
Shams al-Wāʾizain, M., 190
Shāyigān, D., 111
Shiraz, 159, 280
Shīrāzī, M.Ḥ., 146
Shīrāzī, M.T., 100
Shīrāzī, Ṣ. (Mullā Ṣadrā), 64, 69, 110, 111, 132, 136, 139, 188, 193, 200, 208, 210, 234, 256, 274, 280, 281, 355
Shīrāzī, S. (Saʿdī), 195, 203, 321
shirk. *See* multitheism
shūrā. *See* consultation
silence, concept of, 293, 325, 331, 362
silsila. *See* transmission chain
simplicissimae Scripturae simplicissimus sensus, 216
Sinakī, M.K., 104, 145
Sipahbudī, ʿI., 111
Sipihrī, S., 302, 368

slavery, 205, 214
Smart, N., 35, 290
social autonomisation, 26
social sciences, 190, 192, 193, 247, 251
social theory, 156, 356
social transactions, 225
socialism, 148, 157, 159, 162
sociology, 111, 144, 149, 150, 153, 156, 157, 159, 170, 176, 221, 228, 231, 235, 239, 247, 256, 258, 260, 271, 272, 274, 287, 288, 295, 318, 320, 368
solipsism, 313
sophia, 68
Sophist school, 28, 49, 265
sophisticated realism, 312
sophistry, 111, 135, 136, 297
speculative ontology, 8
Spengler, O., 206
Spinoza, B., 31, 49, 66, 109, 188
spirit, 51, 59, 69, 126, 133, 138, 150
'spirit' of the author. *See* intention of author
spirituality, 4, 7, 18, 35, 36, 51–53, 68, 84, 96, 97, 124, 127, 128, 129, 130, 136, 140, 162, 171, 178, 182, 187, 193, 197, 203, 206, 208, 210, 213, 218, 220, 228, 240, 246, 253, 259, 274, 280, 281, 288, 294, 297, 303, 304, 305, 324, 355, 365
stagnation, 221, 222, 243
Strasbourg, 17
structuralism, 8, 9, 11, 188, 223, 245, 260
studia humanitas, 254
Subḥānī, J., 119, 121, 122–123
subject, 4, 5, 23, 26, 27, 29, 132, 160, 170, 173, 195, 199, 203, 209, 210, 213, 218, 219, 238, 239, 246, 250, 254, 288, 299, 300, 308, 309, 312, 316, 323, 325, 330, 331, 332, 340, 346, 348, 355, 356, 359, 362, 366
  alienated, 323
  and contingency, 283, 288, 300, 312, 304, 318, 323, 331, 356, 359
  and transcendence, 35, 173, 180, 323
  cognitive, 5, 27, 28, 29, 31, 35, 66, 68, 69, 135, 136, 259, 300, 304, 355, 359
  destruction of, 35
  'illusory', 304
  in computerised societies, 37
  'speaking', 10
subject–object dichotonomy, 5, 23, 26, 27, 28, 31, 69, 129, 140, 160, 304, 355
subjectivism, 5, 11, 27, 34, 132, 170, 178, 180, 308, 332, 355, 363, 365
  definition of, 5
subjectivist epistemology, 5, 28, 30, 308, 343
  definition of, 27
subjectivity, 5, 26, 27, 28, 29, 35, 129, 145, 150, 157, 169, 172, 200, 219, 304, 307, 308, 309, 323, 325, 332, 343, 344, 351, 356, 361, 363, 366
  and power-relations, 35
  mediated, 145, 150, 173, 307
  as process of becoming, 323, 356, 363
  as symbolic, 129
  as theomorphic, 31, 129, 150, 166, 173, 268, 307, 344
  definition of, 5, 27
  denial of, 26
  inter-subjective, 308
substantial law, 4, 166
substantial motion, 136, 256, 280, 281, 307
Sufi, 20, 39, 51, 52, 53, 57, 58, 63, 68, 76, 96, 141, 171, 187, 211, 215, 216, 235, 253, 301
Suhrawardī, S.Y.H., 68, 69, 132, 141, 207, 235, 280
sunnat, 4, 15, 52, 53, 79, 80–81, 83, 112, 116, 117, 125, 136, 165, 169, 172, 175, 177, 179, 203, 214, 242, 250, 270, 278, 287, 291, 294, 316
Sunni, 14, 16, 17, 39, 43, 45, 51, 52, 53, 57, 59, 60, 61, 65, 66, 67, 68, 70, 71, 73, 75, 76, 77, 80, 81, 83, 84, 85, 86, 87, 88, 94, 96, 98, 99, 100, 105, 110, 116, 118, 137, 145, 148, 173, 174, 214, 215, 222, 231, 242, 248, 261
  modernism, 105
Sunni law, 53, 54, 71, 77, 81, 83, 85, 88, 98
Surūsh, ʿA., 3, 4, 6, 17, 18, 24, 119, 120, 121, 122, 123, 124, 135, 136, 142, 152, 160, 162, 167, 170, 187–342, 343, 348, 349, 350, 351, 352, 353, 355, 356, 357, 358, 359, 360, 362, 363, 365, 366, 367
  biography of, 187–194
  criticism of, 119, 120, 121, 123, 124, 135, 136, 160, 161
  on conflicting interpretations, 215, 254, 269, 271, 293, 295, 310, 321, 330, 333–342
  on epistemology, 6, 23, 197–202, 222, 234, 245, 253–255, 258, 259, 265, 266, 269, 273, 276, 277, 286, 287–315, 316, 317, 325, 326, 330, 335, 338, 340, 341, 349, 350, 354, 355, 358, 360, 366
  on ethics, 205, 214, 219, 237–241, 269, 324, 353
  on hermeneutics, 6, 24, 227, 228, 266, 276, 288, 291, 293, 300, 316–333, 334, 335, 336, 340, 360, 361, 362
  on *ijtihād*, 209, 222, 223, 226, 241–246, 255, 330, 334, 354
  on inference, 226, 228, 233, 243, 255, 334
  on Islamic modernism, 224
  on Islamic traditionalism, 243, 261, 274
  on law, 214, 216, 223–246, 255, 261, 264, 270, 274, 288, 292, 293, 295, 308, 352, 353, 354

on method, 120, 201, 219, 224, 225, 234, 241, 242, 245, 249, 250, 255, 263, 264, 265, 267, 276, 278, 283, 285, 286, 298, 300, 302, 317, 318, 326, 330, 336, 339, 341, 349, 352
on modernity, 202–210, 205, 222, 236, 241, 262, 270, 288, 296, 305, 308, 325, 331, 367
on philosophy, 207, 235, 254, 260, 267, 268, 269, 271, 273, 274, 296, 299, 354, 363
on philosophy of religion, 210, 213, 254
on reason, 202, 203, 204, 211, 219, 242, 251, 253, 258, 263–266, 274, 297, 300, 305, 306, 320, 327, 328, 329, 332, 363
on religious faith, 210–223, 260, 293, 306, 313, 332, 365
on religious pluralism, 301–303, 341, 358, 359
on science, 188, 197, 198, 202, 206, 207, 211, 253, 254, 267–286, 287, 290, 306, 307, 317, 327, 328, 335, 336, 337, 349, 356, 357, 359
on secularism, 217–219
on technology, 205, 254, 287
al-Suyūṭī, ʿA., 67
Swiss, 9, 303
Switzerland, 146
syllogism, 23, 63, 65, 70, 83, 85, 86, 109, 111, 113, 116, 122, 134, 226, 345, 350, 351
definitions of, 85
symbolism, 10, 12, 23, 30, 52, 94, 95, 96, 142, 150, 169, 170, 198, 210, 240, 292, 304, 305, 321, 322, 323, 332, 349, 355, 366
and law, 44, 46
synchrony, 3, 10, 304

al-Ṭabarī, A.J.M., 40, 79
al-Ṭabarī, R., 290
Ṭabāṭabāʾī, M.Ḥ., 17, 110, 111–113, 114, 119, 121, 126, 129, 131, 135, 141, 164, 184, 187, 189, 193, 200, 228, 237, 238, 249, 274, 280, 303, 318, 321
Ṭabāṭabāʾī-Burūjirdī, Ḥ., 110, 114, 121, 126
Tabriz, 110, 121
Tabrīzī, Ṭ, 108
Tabrīzī, M.J., 119
Tabrīzī, R.ʿA., 207
tabula rasa, 27
tafsīr. *See* exegesis
tahājum-i farhangī. *See* West, cultural invasion of the
taḥkīm. *See* arbitration, legal
al-Taḥtawī, R.R., 183
tajwīd. *See* cantillation
Ṭālibūf, ʿA., 104
Ṭāliqānī, A., 153
Ṭāliqānī, M., 105, 108, 148, 149, 150, 153–154, 211
Taqī-Āmulī, M., 126
Taqī-Faʿʿālī, M., 119, 124–125
Taqī-Jaʿfarī, M., 110, 148
Taqī-Khānsārī, S.M., 113
Taqīzādah, S.Ḥ., 147
taqlīd, 88–90, 118, 144, 147, 155, 161, 166, 211, 215, 216, 223, 224, 241, 335, 352
taṣawwuf. *See* Sufi
tashkīk. *See* ambiguity
tartīb. *See* hierarchy of levels
tauḍīḥ al-masāʾil, 74
tauḥīd. *See* unity, theological concept of
tawātur. *See* transmitted authority
technology, 34, 37, 117, 164, 190, 193, 205, 206, 208, 236, 250, 254, 287, 359
Tehran, 113, 118, 123, 126, 139, 147, 148, 150, 151, 153, 155, 159, 161, 163, 187, 188, 189, 190, 191, 192, 194, 229, 248
telefinalism, theory of, 151
teleology, 8, 66, 170, 181, 256, 257, 259, 347
temporality, 24, 222, 320, 326, 351, 361, 362, 364
text, 7, 8, 9, 10, 11, 12, 13, 23, 112, 140, 141, 160, 172, 175, 176, 177, 178, 179, 180, 181, 182, 183, 196, 254, 266, 270, 293, 316, 319, 320, 321, 322, 323, 324, 325, 326, 327, 330, 331, 332, 335, 337, 338, 361, 362
and context, 9, 320, 321, 322, 325, 326, 360
and reader, 4, 9, 141, 160, 176, 177, 179, 323, 326, 331, 332, 360
and tradition, 10, 178, 179, 180, 320, 323
as 'hungry' for meaning, 318–319
as spiritual substance, 140
as theory-impregnated, 320
as unity, 178, 181, 324, 361
composition, 10
dependency towards, 140
distrust of, 11
part–whole of, 12, 156, 160, 181
reduced to interpretation, 325, 330, 331
structure, 8, 9, 10, 177, 324, 330
teleology of, 178
theism, 27, 254
theocracy, 4
theodicy, 44
theological positivism, 153
theology, 5, 8, 12, 14, 15, 17, 18, 20, 25, 32, 39, 40, 42, 43, 46, 52, 56, 57, 58, 59, 64–67, 71, 72, 73, 75, 78, 81, 83, 84, 92, 98, 105, 111, 113, 117, 120, 126, 128, 131, 133, 137, 142, 143, 146, 149, 150, 153, 163, 165, 166, 167, 168, 170, 173, 178, 182, 184, 185, 187, 192, 196, 202, 210, 211, 212, 215, 219, 220, 222, 228, 230, 231, 239, 243, 245, 246, 247,

253, 254, 255, 263, 271, 275, 289, 293, 321, 333, 343, 344, 346, 349, 352
and conflicting interpretations, 98, 333–334
and Natural law, 153
as *scientia*, 255
in Christianity, 55, 164, 165, 169, 211, 254–255, 259, 282, 290
theophany, 129, 140
theory of interpretation. *See* hermeneutics
theosophy, 20, 39, 55, 68, 73, 96, 105, 111, 126, 128, 129, 132, 139, 141, 146, 148, 157, 162, 188, 193, 200, 208, 210, 215, 223, 224, 234, 235, 238, 247, 256, 265, 268, 289, 293, 304, 306, 307, 316, 324, 327, 335, 336, 344, 349, 356
criticism of, 154, 159, 176, 182
division of, 132
thermodynamics, 150, 218
thing in-itself. *See* noumenal realm
third world knowledge, concept of, 123, 124, 284, 309
Tillich, P., 166, 172
time and place, concept of, 117, 184, 240
Torah, 43
totalitarism, 149, 190, 258, 305
Toynbee, A., 221, 260, 271
tradition, concept of, 10, 50, 59, 178, 179, 180, 203, 320, 323, 324, 325, 331
traditional jurisprudence, 4, 116, 117, 242, 243, 270, 271, 277, 316, 352
transcendence, 13, 27, 30, 31, 34, 35, 44, 98, 107, 128, 150, 180, 212, 213, 230, 234, 238, 254, 257, 261, 263, 265, 293, 301, 305, 306, 325, 332, 333, 342, 347, 349, 356, 365
and experience, 36, 169, 173, 183, 356, 299
and logic, 31, 34, 128, 183, 265, 305, 332
and method, 5, 30, 36, 128, 139, 170, 234
and subject, 5, 35, 172, 173, 323, 361
and symbol, 30, 129, 212, 304
and truth, 34, 98, 183, 256, 265, 347, 348
and understanding, 44, 139, 170, 180, 325, 326, 360
transcendent knowledge. *See* absolute knowledge
transcendental ego, 176
transcendental idealism, 30, 199, 299
transcendental phenomenology, 169
transcendental theology, 172
transcendental wisdom, 126
translation movement, 131
translation, concept of, 20, 178, 179
transmission chain, 53, 81
transmitted authority, 81, 248, 269, 274, 313, 314, 338, 358
transmitted knowledge, 52, 58, 59, 64, 65, 71, 75, 84, 91, 110, 111, 121, 125, 127, 134, 139, 180, 248, 263, 274, 301
transparency, 30, 169, 173, 176, 177, 178, 181, 304, 308, 319, 322, 330
Troeltsch, E., 258
truth, 5, 23, 29, 31, 32, 34, 52, 56, 63, 67, 69, 75, 76, 101, 112, 115, 127, 131, 132, 135, 138, 162, 165, 166, 169, 170, 176, 183, 198, 202, 204, 210, 211, 212, 215, 216, 218, 232, 234, 237, 251, 254, 256, 259, 260, 264, 265, 266, 271, 276, 278, 279, 283, 284, 286, 291, 295, 296, 298, 299, 301, 302, 303, 305, 306, 309, 310, 313, 314, 315, 316, 318, 319, 320, 322, 323, 325, 326, 327, 328, 329, 332, 333, 334, 335, 336, 337, 338, 342, 346, 347, 348, 349, 350, 351, 355, 357, 359, 361, 363, 364, 366
accumulation of, 336
and method, 8, 13, 33, 60, 97, 127, 141, 177, 263, 283, 291, 326, 336, 263, 283, 291, 326, 336, 344
as absolute, 30, 146
as ambiguous, 311
as certainty, 5, 16, 56
as conditioned, 135, 182
as contingent, 28, 302, 305, 310, 347, 355
as construction, 263
as convention, 328
as correspondence, 30, 34, 113, 129, 274, 338, 363
as 'encounter with God', 169
as experience, 178, 180, 284, 291
as universal, 298
as unintelligible, 157
Turkey, 194
Turkish, 163, 194
al-Ṭūsī, A.J., 72, 78, 79, 81, 82, 94, 95, 98, 172
al-Ṭūsī, N., 12, 73, 109, 275
al-Tustarī, S., 13

ʿulamā, 4, 20, 21, 45, 53, 58, 63, 79, 88, 89, 90, 91, 92, 93, 94, 104, 108, 110, 111, 114, 115, 130, 140, 141, 184, 187, 190, 196, 223, 227, 229, 236, 243, 244, 246, 247, 248, 249, 250, 251, 270
and modernisation, 21, 33, 104, 229
and state, 21, 36, 251
as intermediates of the Prophet, 120
as narrators of *akhbār*, 62
authority of Shi'i, 89, 90
criticism of, 158, 162
educated in the West, 110
intellectual field of traditional, 64
livelihood of, 251
Umayyad, 47, 48, 54, 131
understanding, 9, 12, 23, 27, 28, 30, 39, 43, 59, 60, 69, 78, 79, 92, 93, 94, 95, 120, 122, 124, 127, 131, 135, 136, 140, 141, 145, 147, 150, 155, 156, 158, 159, 161, 167, 169, 170, 171,

176, 177, 178, 179, 180, 181, 182, 197, 199, 201, 202, 205, 218, 227, 228, 230, 241, 251, 254, 255, 259, 262, 265, 266, 275, 277, 281, 287, 288, 289, 290, 291, 292, 293, 294, 295, 297, 301, 302, 303, 308, 309, 310, 311, 312, 313, 314, 316, 317, 319, 320, 322, 323, 324, 325, 326, 327, 330, 333, 334, 336, 337, 339, 340, 341, 348, 349, 359, 360, 361, 363, 364
and method, 7, 111, 127, 128, 168, 170, 176, 177, 259, 265, 324
and translation, 19, 178, 179
as distinct from explanation, 140, 176
as distinct from knowledge, 276
as horizontal, 179, 320, 323
as non-automatic, 8, 176, 201
as subjective, 9, 12, 15, 97, 160, 180, 200, 312, 316, 323, 330, 339
better, 336, 337, 362
completion of, 336
correct, 157, 284, 311, 324, 337
internal–external, 180, 291
ontology of, 12, 135, 169, 177, 266
United Nations, 138, 172, 232, 329
unity, theological concept of, 112, 138, 149, 150, 154, 155, 157, 161, 162, 166, 171
unity of existence, 157
unity of the knower and the known, 31, 69, 129, 136, 200, 304
universal reason, 26, 32, 33, 34, 42, 63, 173, 216, 263, 329, 347, 348, 363, 364
universalism, 10, 26, 211, 238, 260, 298, 300, 308, 313, 315, 329, 347, 361, 363, 367
universals (constants), 30, 31, 200, 217, 245, 280, 291, 292, 300, 311, 312
urbanisation, 367
ʿurf. *See* customary law
uṣūl al-dīn. *See* religious belief, principles of
uṣūl al-fiqh. *See* legal theory
uṣūl ʿamalīyah. *See* procedural principles, juristic
uṣūlī, 60, 61, 66, 86, 99, 108, 110, 114, 119, 137, 228, 242
utilitarianism, 147, 237
utopia, 258, 307, 341, 348

value ('ought') and fact ('is'), 46, 207, 237, 268, 269, 298, 339, 340, 353
Veda scriptures, 42
verification, 27, 120, 121, 123, 130, 131, 134, 136, 138, 151, 170, 197, 198, 202, 207, 211, 212, 213, 218, 232, 234, 267, 273, 277, 278, 279, 282, 283, 284, 285, 286, 305, 307, 339, 350, 355
virtue, 42, 296, 316, 333
vox populi vox Dei, 81
Vienna circle, 197

waḥdat al-wujūd. *See* unity of existence
Walīullāh, S., 226
warrant. *See* justification, epistemic
Wāsil ibn al-ʿAṭā, 66
Weber, M., 46, 83, 188
West, 4, 7, 105, 117, 129, 137, 148, 164, 167, 188, 193, 202, 203, 206–210, 254, 367, 368
and Islam, 149, 246, 359, 367
cultural invasion of the, 123, 137
Western, 5, 6, 7, 16, 18, 21, 25, 29, 32, 35, 36, 47, 48, 51, 55, 59, 78, 86, 100, 106, 107, 109, 110, 111, 112, 114, 118, 122, 123, 124, 129, 132, 143, 148, 149, 151, 153, 155, 159, 162, 163, 165, 168, 171, 188, 194, 196, 197, 204, 205, 207, 208, 209, 210, 217, 229, 230, 231, 237, 239, 245, 246, 267, 277, 280, 289, 292, 296, 300, 301, 305, 308, 309, 317, 325, 329, 333, 346, 354, 359, 367, 368
Westernisation, 33, 209
Whewell, W., 277
Whitehead, A., 193, 213, 267
wilāyat-i faqīh, 115, 116, 137, 149, 215, 236, 253
Wilāyatī, ʿA.A., 191
Wittgenstein, L., 34, 188, 213, 277, 290, 336, 337
workers' rights, 152
worldview, 25, 34, 83, 112, 114, 127, 128, 130, 131, 132, 133, 150, 152, 157, 161, 163, 164, 190, 201, 206, 218, 224, 239, 242, 243, 246, 268, 283, 288, 306, 307, 345, 348, 356, 363, 364, 365, 367
worship, 21, 52, 116, 130, 193, 194, 213, 225

Yazdī, I., 151
Yazdī, S.M.K., 89
Yūsufī-Ishkiwarī, Ḥ., 146, 159, 160–163

ẓāhirī, 63, 99
zakāt. *See* alms
al-Zamakhsharī, M.ʿU., 57
zamān wa makān. *See* time and place, concept of
zoology, 288
Zoroastrians, 301